Drama and Pride in the Gateway City

Memorable Teams in Baseball History

Drama and Pride in the Gateway City

The 1964 St. Louis Cardinals

Edited by **John Harry Stahl and Bill Nowlin**

Associate Editors: **Tom Heinlein, Russell Lake, and Leonard Levin**

Published by the **University of Nebraska Press** Lincoln & London, and the **Society for American Baseball Research**

Library of Congress Cataloging-in-Publication Data
Drama and pride in the gateway city: the 1964 St. Louis Cardinals /
edited by John Harry Stahl and Bill Nowlin; associate editors, Tom
Heinlein, Russell Lake, and Leonard Levin.
pages cm. — (Memorable Teams in Baseball History)
Includes bibliographical references.
ISBN 978-0-8032-4372-9 (pbk.: alk. paper) 1. St. Louis Cardinals
(Baseball team)—History—20th century. I. Stahl, John Harry.
GV875.S3D73 2013
796.357'64097786609046—dc23
2012038299

Set in Sabon by Laura Wellington.

Table of Contents

Introduction

Mark Armour

The 1964 world champion St. Louis Cardinals. Back row (*left to right*): Ray Sadecki, Bob Uecker, Ed Spiezio, Dal Maxvill, Tim McCarver, Mike Shannon, Ron Taylor, Charley Jones, Jerry Buchek. Middle row: Gordon Richardson, Ray Washburn, Curt Simmons, Bob Gibson, Bob Skinner, Mike Cueller, Roger Craig, Lou Brock, Bob Milliken (batting practice pitcher), Carl Warwick, Bob Humphreys. Front row: Curt Flood, Ken Boyer, Dick Groat, Howard Pollet (coach), Joe Schulz (coach), Johnny Keane (manager), Vern Benson (coach), Red Schoendienst (coach), Bill White, Barney Schultz, Julián Javier. Front: Bob Baker (batboy). (Photo by Allied Photocolor Imaging Center)

Although the St. Louis Cardinals have had much success in the past one hundred years, including eleven World Series titles, by 1964 they had gone seventeen years without a pennant and had rarely contended in the interval. Three-time champions in the 1940s, the Cards had slowly faded from relevance in the early 1950s and largely sat on the sidelines during what would become a fabled era for the National League.

Jackie Robinson joined the Brooklyn Dodgers in 1947, integrating the Major Leagues and dramatically changing what was still the National Pastime. Soon there were five black players, then ten, then twenty, including many of the greatest players ever to play the game, men such as Willie Mays, Henry Aaron, and Roy Campanella. All of them, or nearly so, played in the National League, for teams like the Dodgers, the Giants, and the Braves. During this historic period, the Cardinals and their fans watched their team wither away, while the integrated teams won pennant after pennant.

The story began to change in 1953, when August A. Busch Jr. bought the team and famously asked where all the black players were. Under the leadership of men like Bing Devine and Johnny Keane, the Cardinals began signing and acquiring talented players regardless of color, and slowly, sometimes very slowly, they began their rise.

The team Bing Devine built was a well-integrated team, and its black players were some of its most proud and memorable leaders: Bill White, who would one day run the entire National League; Curt Flood, who would challenge baseball's very structure in 1970; Lou Brock, whose June acquisition sparked the club's turnaround; and, most especially, Bob Gibson, whose demeanor and pride helped define the team right until the final game.

If the 1964 Cardinals were not an all-time great team, they were a fascinating team and a great story. Assumed dead in midseason (forcing Busch to fire Devine and almost fire Keane), the team roared back into the race and won a dramatic pennant race on the final day. All of the men come alive again on these pages—Tim McCarver, Ken Boyer, Mike Shannon, Branch Rickey, Bob Uecker—men whose names are still famous today in St. Louis and everywhere baseball is played.

If you are lucky enough to remember this proud team and its dramatic rush to glory, or if you wish to discover it for the first time, you will enjoy the stories in these pages.

MARK ARMOUR

St. Louis
CARDINALS

50c

1964 Yearbook

Chapter 1. **Dave Bakenhaster**

Joe Schuster

AGE	W	L	PCT.	ERA	G	GS	GF	CG	SHO	SV	IP	H	BB	SO	HBP	WP
19	0	0	.000	6.00	2	0	2	0	0	0	3	9	1	0	0	0

During spring training before the 1964 baseball season, a photographer for the Newspaper Enterprise Association took a picture of St. Louis Cardinals rookie pitcher Dave Bakenhaster side by side with coach Red Schoendienst. The light-hearted photo shows the two laughing, Schoendienst pointing to Bakenhaster's name on the back of the rookie's jersey. When the photographer put the picture on the news wires with a caption proclaiming that, despite the eleven letters in the pitcher's name, Schoendienst maintained his record of having the "longest name on a Cardinals' jersey," it appeared in a number of newspapers across the country from early March into early April.[1]

Bakenhaster had every reason to be in good spirits that spring. The previous summer, after a spectacular high school career in which he had thrown nine no-hitters, the Cardinals had given him an estimated $40,000 signing bonus, outbidding most of the other Major League teams for the rights to what one sportswriter called "the much-sought-after . . . whip-armed . . . pitcher."[2] Bakenhaster was one of two first-year "bonus babies" the Cardinals had that year (the other was infielder Ed Spiezio). The rules at the time required that St. Louis keep at least one of them with the big-league club and gave the team the option to designate the other as a member of the twenty-five-man roster but assign him to a Minor League team. The Cardinals elected to take Bakenhaster north with them when they broke camp.

As it would turn out, that photograph was one of the few bright moments in Bakenhaster's Major League career. Between Opening Day that season and late July, he appeared in only two games

In 1964 the nineteen-year-old Dave Bakenhaster pitched three innings in two games, allowing two earned runs. The Cardinals sent him to the Minors in late July. (Collection of Bill Nowlin)

for a total of three innings; his line for his meager appearances showed 9 hits, 6 runs (2 earned), 1 walk, and no strikeouts. On July 23, the day after Bakenhaster's second and last appearance, the Cardinals sent him out, assigning him to Winnipeg in the Class A Northern League. While he persevered in the Minor Leagues until 1970, he never got back to the Major Leagues.[3]

David Lee Bakenhaster was born as the youngest of eight children to Monford and Lara Bakenhaster on March 5, 1945, in Columbus, Ohio.[4] The family worked as crop farmers in the Dublin, Ohio, area, just outside Columbus; the land they worked at one point eventually became Don Scott Airfield, now operated by the Ohio State University.[5] According to a story published at the time of his signing in 1963, his parents died in 1953, and sometime after that his brother Paul became his legal guardian.[6] Bakenhaster began dreaming of playing Major League ball as early as nine, and the first scouts started paying attention to him when he was thirteen.[7]

Bakenhaster was a talented athlete at Dublin High School (later renamed Dublin Coffman), lettering in basketball and baseball in all four years. He twice earned all-county honors in basketball, but it was in baseball that he truly excelled.[8] His catcher in high school, Craig Duffey, recalled Bakenhaster as having a superior fastball that had good movement on it. "I can remember catching games in which he was so fast, the opposing batters' knees would be shaking," Duffey said.[9] He remembered that Bakenhaster once struck out all twenty-one batters he faced in a game against Columbus Academy in his junior year, the almost-perfect game marred by a passed ball on a third strike allowing the batter to reach first.[10] In four seasons as a pitcher at the school, Bakenhaster accumulated a 41-5 record; among his nine no-hitters were two perfect games.[11] During his high school career, he averaged fifteen strikeouts a game.[12] In each of his four seasons, he was named to the all-county baseball team; three times he was all-district and twice all-state.[13]

If scouts were already paying attention, Bakenhaster's senior year cemented his reputation as a legitimate professional prospect. That year, when his team reeled off twenty-one consecutive victories to earn a spot in the Class A state finals, he went 17-0, including a four-hit victory in the regional championship and a no-hitter in the semifinals.[14] Although his coach asked him to start the

state championship game the day after his semifinal gem, Bakenhaster's brother/guardian worried that taxing his arm might hurt his professional chances, so Bakenhaster skipped the game; his team lost.[15] Five days after his graduation, Cardinals scout Mo Mozzali signed him to a contract.[16]

Bakenhaster split his first professional season between Brunswick (Georgia) of the Georgia-Florida League and Winnipeg (Manitoba) of the Northern League, finishing with a combined 6-6 record, striking out 65 and walking 49 with a 4.44 earned run average in seventy-seven innings.[17]

In 1964, though bonus-baby Bakenhaster began the season with the Cardinals, most observers expected that he would not do much. A preseason evaluation by *Baseball Digest* evaluated him this way: "Has good fastball and had a good curve at times, but has a tendency to throw too many curves. Wild at times. May have a chance."[18] And Bakenhaster indeed did little, having to wait more than two months before he saw action in a regular-season game. In that Major League debut, on June 20, 1964, Bakenhaster pitched the last two innings in a home game against the San Francisco Giants. His debut was a portent of the bad luck that followed him for most of his professional career. Entering the game with San Francisco leading 10–1, Bakenhaster allowed a lead-off double to Harvey Kuenn. He retired the next two hitters before Cardinals shortstop Jerry Buchek made an error on a ground ball by Willie Mays. Bakenhaster then allowed three consecutive singles, scoring three unearned runs. In the top of the ninth the Giants scored a fourth unearned run before Bakenhaster closed out the inning.[19]

More than a month later, on July 22, Bakenhaster appeared in his second and last Major League game, pitching the ninth inning of another blowout loss, this one 13–2 to the Pittsburgh Pirates. He allowed a double by Willie Stargell and a two-run home run by Bill Mazeroski to start the inning before retiring the side.[20] The next day the team reassigned him to Winnipeg, recalling Spiezio to the Major League roster to protect both players from the waiver draft.

Back in Class A, Bakenhaster struggled; in his first two weeks after being sent down, he had an 0-2 record with a league-worst ERA of 13.75.[21] He finished the year 1-5, with a 5.36 ERA, 28 strikeouts, and 25 walks in forty-two innings pitched.

Sports columnist Fred Collins of the *Winnipeg Free Press* called Bakenhaster "a symbol, the innocent victim of baseball's biggest headache, the bonus system." Collins went on to defend Bakenhaster, despite his poor showing: "The crime of it is that David Lee is not a bad pitcher. No one will ever know now but it's a good bet that, had he been allowed to develop in the minors, Bakenhaster wouldn't have the headaches he must be having these nights."[22]

After Bakenhaster's season in Winnipeg ended in September, the Cardinals announced they were recalling him again, but it was only a technicality, since he never actually rejoined the team.[23] Instead, he returned home, where he married Kim Ann Hilling on September 16, 1964.[24] (They divorced in 1968.[25])

Bakenhaster earned one more bonus from the Cardinals that season: after the team won the World Series in seven games from the New York Yankees, the players voted Bakenhaster a one-fourth share of the player's pool; it amounted to $2,155.54.[26]

Bakenhaster spent five more seasons in the Minor Leagues, all in the Cardinals organization, although he lost one year to military service, 1968, serving as a member of the military police in Uijongbu, Korea.[27] Any prospects he may have had to advance as a professional were probably hurt that year, as he suffered a rotator cuff injury shortly after his discharge.[28] His best year as a professional was 1966, when he helped lead St. Petersburg to the Florida State League's best record under future Hall of Fame manager Sparky Anderson; he finished the season 16-6 with a 1.90 ERA and 160 strikeouts. One of the highlights of that year was a marathon 170-pitch complete-game 16–9 victory over Tampa in May. In that game—during which Bakenhaster reportedly lost fourteen pounds over the three hours—he struck out thirteen, nailing down the team's twentieth consecutive win at that point.[29] After he stopped playing following the 1970 season, the Cardinals offered to make him their Major League bullpen coach; he accepted, but a week later changed his mind, citing "personal reasons." The team replaced Bakenhaster with Lee Thomas, who subsequently became the Cardinals' director of player development and later the Philadelphia Phillies' general manager.[30]

After leaving baseball, Bakenhaster worked for thirty-four years in a warehouse operated by Exel Logistics, serving the Nabisco Brands Food Company in Columbus, Ohio.[31] In 1975 he married the former Carolyn Harr.[32] In 2002 he was elected to the inaugural class for the Dublin Coffman High School Athletic Hall of Fame.[33]

Some years after leaving the game, Bakenhaster told a writer, "I never achieved what I really set out to do. My abilities were not as good as I thought they were. I felt sorry for myself when I first got out. But when I got my head screwed on right, I was okay."[34]

Chapter 2. **Ken Boyer**

Burton A. Boxerman

AGE	G	AB	R	H	2B	3B	HR	TB	RBI	BB	SO	BAV	OBP	SLG	SB	GDP	HBP
33	163	628	100	185	30	10	24	307	119	70	85	.295	.365	.489	3	22	2

Signed by the St. Louis Cardinals as a pitcher, Ken Boyer became a third baseman in his second Minor League season, then spent eleven years at that position with the Cardinals, becoming what many consider the best third baseman in the team's history. (Indeed, Bill James ranks him as the twelfth-best third sacker of all time.) Boyer was a superb fielder and an excellent hitter, with a .287 career batting average, 282 home runs, 68 triples, 316 doubles, and 1,141 runs batted in. Despite these credentials, some fans criticized Boyer as a casual player who did not hustle. However, he was so skillful that he made the game seem effortless. Aware of this criticism, Boyer shrugged it off, saying, "That's the way I am."

Kenton Lloyd Boyer was born into a baseball-playing family on May 20, 1931, in Liberty, Missouri. He was the third-oldest son in Vern and Mabel Boyer's family of fourteen children. Ken grew up in nearby Alba, Missouri, where his father operated a general store and service station.

After he graduated from high school in 1949, Boyer was invited to a special tryout at Sportsman's Park in St. Louis on the recommendation of Cardinals scout Runt Marr. Though Boyer could play both the infield and the outfield, the Cardinals were more interested in his strong right arm and signed him as a pitcher who might play an occasional third base. The Cardinals signed him to a contract in 1949 for a $6,000 bonus, $1,000 under the limit that would have required him to be on the Major League roster for his first two seasons.

Boyer was originally assigned to the team's Triple-A club, the Rochester Red Wings, until a roster spot became available at a lower level. His older

The 1964 Cardinals' captain, Ken Boyer led the National League with 119 RBIS and was the NL MVP for 1964.

brother, Cloyd, was also with the Red Wings. Ken spent his time at Rochester on the bench until he was sent to the Cardinals' Class D North Atlantic League club, the Lebanon Chix. As a pitcher he compiled a 5-1 record in twelve games with a 3.42 earned run average in his rookie season. He struck out 32 batters but walked 34. At the plate, however, Boyer batted .455 (15 hits in 33 at bats), hitting 3 home runs with 9 runs batted in. Despite his prowess at the plate, the Cardinals still wanted to develop Boyer as a pitcher.

Boyer spent his second Minor League season (1950) with the Hamilton Cardinals in the Class D Pennsylvania-Ontario-New York (PONY) League. His pitching record at Hamilton slipped to 6-8 with an ERA of 4.39. During the season, Hamilton needed a third baseman, and manager Vedie Himsl inserted Boyer into the lineup at third base in what was supposed to be a temporary move. The move became more permanent when Boyer displayed both the ability to hit and remarkable defensive skills at third. Boyer still pitched occasionally, but his batting average of .342 in eighty games, with 9 homers and 61 runs batted in, helped his team to a third-place finish and a playoff berth.

The Cardinals finally realized that Boyer was a better hitter than a pitcher, and in 1951 they promoted him to the Class A Omaha Cardinals in the Western League, where he would be their regular third baseman for the season. He started the season poorly, but with the help of manager George Kissell, Boyer improved both his offense and his defense. He appeared in 151 games at Omaha and hit .306, with 28 doubles, 7 triples, 14 home runs, 90 runs driven in, and a .455 slugging percentage during his first full season as a position player.

At the end of the 1951 season, Boyer was drafted into the army during the Korean War and served two years overseas. He continued playing ball for the army in both Germany and Africa. In April 1952 he married Kathleen Oliver.

Out of the service in 1954, Boyer was assigned to the Houston Buffaloes of the Double-A Texas League. Former National League batting champion Dixie Walker was Boyer's manager there. Walker made great strides with Boyer's hitting technique, getting him out of an early season slump and making him productive. Boyer played in 159 games for Houston and ended the season with a .319 batting average, belting 21 home runs and driving in 116 runs. He helped the Buffaloes win the postseason playoffs against the Fort Worth Cats, 4 games to 1.

Boyer excelled in '64, his seventh season as an All-Star. He scored an even one hundred runs, but naturally there were times he couldn't beat the ball to the bag.

After the 1954 season the Cardinals asked Boyer to play winter ball. He played for Havana, where his manager was former Cardinals coach Mike Gonzalez. Boyer's winter-ball stint ended abruptly when a fastball hit him behind his left ear, resulting in a severe concussion that left him unconscious for three days. He made an unsuccessful attempt to resume play but was forced to return home instead.

In the off-season the Cardinals were so confident that Boyer would be their starting third baseman in 1955 that they traded Ray Jablonski, their incumbent third sacker, to the Cincinnati Redlegs, along with pitcher Gerry Staley, for relief pitcher Frank Smith.

Recovered from his concussion, Boyer debuted with the Cardinals in 1955, joining, among others, teammates Red Schoendienst and Stan Musial.

Boyer had a relatively good rookie year, appearing in 147 games and hitting .264 with 18 home runs and 62 RBIs. The next season he did not suffer the sophomore jinx, as many young players do: Boyer's second year in the Majors was far superior to his rookie season. He appeared in 150 games, improving his batting average to .306, and finished the season with 26 homers and 98 RBIs. He was also selected to participate in his first All-Star Game.

In 1957 Boyer volunteered to play center field to allow an exceptional rookie, Eddie Kasko, to play his natural position, third base. The Cardinals lost no defense in the outfield by this move; Boyer led all National League outfielders in fielding percentage that year. But Kasko was injured in 1958 and the Cardinals acquired Curt Flood from Cincinnati to play center field. Boyer returned to third base, where he won the first of five Gold Glove Awards.

Boyer hit .307 in 1958 and .309 in 1959. He hit 51 home runs those two years and in 1958 drove in 90 runs. That same year Boyer participated in 41 double plays, which equaled the second-highest total in National League history to that point. In 1959 he had a twenty-nine-game hitting streak for the Cardinals, four shy of the team's record held by Rogers Hornsby. Boyer was named to eleven All-Star squads covering seven seasons—1956 and 1959–64.

In 1960 and 1961 Boyer led the Cardinals in batting average (.304 and .329), home runs (32 and 24), and RBIs (97 and 95). His .329 batting average ranked third in the National League in 1961. Boyer also became the team captain during this period.

Although Boyer's statistics dropped in 1962 and 1963, he still had stellar years. He missed only two games during the 1962 season and three in 1963. His average fell below .300 in both years, but he hit a solid .291 in 1962 and .285 the following year. He hit 24 home runs in each year

(in fact, Boyer hit 24 round-trippers in each season from 1961 through 1964). In 1962 and 1963 his runs batted in were among the highest of his career—98 in 1962 and 111 in 1963.

By far Boyer's greatest season in the Major Leagues was 1964, when, playing in every one of the Cardinals' 162 games, he helped lead the team to its first pennant and World Series title in eighteen years. That year he topped the National League in RBIs with 119 (the first National League third baseman to accomplish that feat since Heinie Zimmerman in 1917) and batted .295. He also won his only MVP Award.

Boyer's 1964 season was climaxed by his clutch performance in the World Series against the New York Yankees. In Game Four, he hit a grand slam off Al Downing to give the Cardinals a 4–3 victory. In the decisive Game Seven, Boyer had three hits, including a double and a home run, and scored three runs as the Cardinals won the Series.

Ken's brother Clete, playing in his fifth consecutive World Series in 1964 with the Yankees, later admitted that he was privately thrilled for his brother because it was Ken's first World Series. Clete also homered in that seventh game, the only time in World Series history that brothers have homered in the same game. Clete had a sixteen-year career in the Major Leagues. He debuted with the Kansas City Athletics on June 5, 1955, and made his final Major League appearance with the Atlanta Braves on May 23, 1971. His career figures were .242, 162 home runs, and 654 RBIs. Ken's older brother, Cloyd, also played in the Major Leagues, pitching for the Cardinals from 1949 to 1952, and for the Kansas City Athletics in 1955, the year that brothers Clete and Ken both made their Major League debuts. Over five seasons, Cloyd won twenty games and lost twenty-three with an ERA of 4.78. Four other Boyer brothers had brief experiences in the Minor Leagues but went no further.

In 1965, his eleventh year and final year with

the Cardinals, Ken began to suffer from back problems. His batting average dropped to .260 and his power numbers dipped to 13 home runs and 75 RBIs. After the season the Cardinals traded Boyer to the New York Mets for pitcher Al Jackson and third baseman Charley Smith. Boyer fans criticized the trade, recalling all his accomplishments over the years. Cardinals manager Red Schoendienst defended the trade as necessary, claiming that the Cardinals had received two good players in return for Boyer — a power-hitting third baseman in Smith and an excellent starting pitcher in Jackson.

At the time it was the biggest trade in Mets history. Bing Devine, the Mets' general manager, thought an older Boyer (he was thirty-five) might bring veteran leadership to his young team and perhaps regain his own MVP form as well. Boyer played in 136 games for the Mets in 1966, including 2 at first base. He hit .266 with 14 home runs and 61 RBIs. The Mets finished that year in ninth place, ahead of only the cellar-dwelling Chicago Cubs.

Boyer began the 1967 season with the Mets, appearing in fifty-six games before being traded on July 22 to the pennant-contending Chicago White Sox for Bill Southworth. Each team included a player to be named later in the deal. On August 15 the Mets sent Sandy Alomar to the White Sox; on November 27 the White Sox sent J. C. Martin to officially complete the deal.

Boyer's stint with the White Sox marked the only time he spent in the American League. His manager in Chicago was Eddie Stanky, who had managed him in his rookie season with the Cardinals. The White Sox were in first place until August 13. They regained the lead about a week later but eventually fell to fourth place. Boyer played in fifty-seven games for the 1967 White Sox and hit .261 with 4 home runs and 21 runs batted in.

Boyer began the 1968 season with the White Sox, appearing in ten games before he was

released. On May 10 he signed with the Los Angeles Dodgers with the understanding that he would be a pinch hitter and bench player, not a regular. Under manager Walt Alston, Boyer split his time between third base and first base and appeared in eighty-three games. For the Dodgers he hit a respectable .271 with 6 home runs and 41 runs batted in.

Boyer returned to the Dodgers in 1969 for the final season of his fifteen-year Major League career. The thirty-eight-year-old appeared in only twenty-five games for the Dodgers in 1969 (all but four as a pinch hitter) and batted .206. The Dodgers asked him to return the following year as a coach, but he informed the team that he wished to pursue a possible managerial career in the Minor Leagues. On October 8 the Dodgers gave Boyer his unconditional release.

In the off-season the Cardinals hired Boyer as a coach of their Arkansas affiliate in the Texas League. He then coached with the big-league team for two seasons before returning to Minor League managing. The Cardinals replaced manager Red Schoendienst after the 1976 season with Vernon Rapp, a known taskmaster. Many had felt that Boyer would replace Schoendienst. The disappointed Boyer was hired instead by the Baltimore Orioles to manage their Triple-A farm club, the Rochester Red Wings, in the International League.

Rapp managed the Cardinals to a third-place finish in 1977. The following year Cardinals owner August Busch decided to fire Rapp after he had compiled a record of 6-11. According to catcher Ted Simmons, "Rapp was a disciplinarian, and in a major-league clubhouse it's difficult to be one." On April 29, 1978, Busch named Boyer the new Cardinals manager. The Cardinals finished the 1978 season in fifth place, but in 1979 he guided the team to eighty-six victories and a third-place finish. The team began the 1980 season slowly, and on June 8, between games of a doubleheader in Montreal, with the team's record at 18-33, Cardinals general manager John Claiborne appeared in the clubhouse and informed Boyer that he was fired and that Whitey Herzog was the club's new skipper. Boyer compiled a record of 166-190 in three seasons (1978–80).

Boyer remained in the Cardinals organization as a scout through 1981. He was slated to manage their Triple-A team at Louisville but had to decline when he was diagnosed with lung cancer. Boyer died on September 7, 1982; he was just fifty-two years old. Two sons and two daughters survived him in addition to his brothers and six sisters. In 1984 the Cardinals retired his No. 14, which he wore throughout his career with the team. He is the only player whose number has been retired by the Cardinals who is not in the Baseball Hall of Fame.

Boyer's name was on the Baseball Writers Association of America's Hall of Fame ballot for fifteen years, from 1975 through 1994. His highest vote percentage was 25.5 percent in 1988. (The minimum required for membership is 75 percent.) It will require the vote of the Veterans Committee for Boyer's admission into the Hall of Fame.

Two of Boyer's former teammates were among his most ardent supporters. Stan Musial said, "The ballplayers know he's a good one, but nobody else does." Tim McCarver said, "He was the boss of our field. He was the guy everyone looked up to. He was the guy who really filled that role, if that role needed to be filled." Musial and McCarver summed up the problems with Ken Boyer—a quiet man who just did his job well without any fanfare.

Chapter 3. Lou Brock

Dave Williams

AGE	G	AB	R	H	2B	3B	HR	TB	RBI	BB	SO	BAV	OBP	SLG	SB	GDP	HBP
25	103	419	81	146	21	9	12	221	44	27	87	.348	.387	.527	33	2	2

Some in the press and in the stands considered him too casual about his job, but that was a misperception. In fact, he was driven, not merely by a desire, but by a rage to succeed.

—*David Halberstam,* October 1964

When the June 15 trading deadline rolled around in 1964, Cardinals general manager Bing Devine knew that his job was on the line. The Cardinals had played mostly flat and uninspiring baseball and had hovered around the .500 mark, clearly a disappointment to the St. Louis faithful and, more important, to team owner Gussie Busch.[1] Devine had a gaping hole in left field after the retirement of Stan Musial, and he was ready to trade a valuable commodity, a starting pitcher, to plug that gap.[2] His target was a relative unknown, a man whose career so far could not be called mediocre as much as one of expectations unfulfilled. When he made the trade that day for Lou Brock, there was much happiness, not so much in St. Louis but instead in the home of its league rival three hundred miles north, Chicago. For it was the Chicago Cubs that had moved an obviously talented but raw outfielder in exchange for a pitcher who had won eighteen games in 1963; that was something to celebrate. The celebration, as it turned out, was misplaced, because when Bing Devine made the trade, not only did he get the solution to his left-field problem, but he also acquired the pennant.

Louis Clark Brock was born on June 18, 1939, in El Dorado, Arkansas, the son of Paralee and Maud Brock. For Paralee this was the second of her three marriages, and Louis was one of nine children she bore. Shortly after Louis's arrival,

Lou Brock's .348 average after he came to the Cardinals would have won him the NL crown had he had been able to discount his slow start with the Cubs.

she moved to Collinston, Louisiana, a mixed-race town with a population of three hundred. The area was very poor, and the school Lou attended had only one teacher and no running water.[3]

Brock's childhood memories do not include his father, who left shortly after his birth, but they do include the feeling of insecurity growing up poor and black in the South. It took him several years to overcome the shame of his skin color and having to bus several miles past white schools to the black school. Even at a young age he was very aware of

9

Traded to the moribund Cardinals in June 1964, Brock sparked the club, hitting .348 with a .391 OBA in 103 games. The Hall of Fame inducted him in 1985.

his surroundings, the large number of unemployed people and old, run-down homes, and would lie awake at night wondering how he would avoid a similar fate.[4] The answer, it would turn out, was baseball.

The introduction to baseball came in the form of punishment. Sent to the library in the fourth grade for throwing a spitball, and given the assignment of researching the careers of Joe DiMaggio, Stan Musial, Don Newcombe, and Jackie Robinson, young Brock was enlightened not only by the achievements of these great ballplayers but also by the money they earned.[5] The numbers that followed the dollar signs on the players' salaries were so large that Lou had to ask the teacher what they were, and this became his motivation to become a big-league ballplayer. Despite this inspiration it was still some time before he actually began to play ball. There was softball in gym class, but it wasn't until the summer before high school that he joined a sandlot team. His lack of experience relegated him to being a backup outfielder, but it

was not long before the coach saw the strong left-handed throwing arm of his neophyte outfielder, and he was moved to the pitcher's mound. At first he was limited to throwing batting practice until he became comfortable on the mound, but Brock was soon pitching in real games.[6]

Lou made the high school team the following spring mainly because he could throw the ball farther than anyone else. During his high school career, he did more than just display a strong arm. He batted at least .350 every year, hitting .535 in his senior season and even occasionally turning around to bat from the right side.[7] Despite his success on the diamond, there were no athletic scholarships awaiting him upon graduation. He did, however, receive an academic scholarship from the all-black Southern University, where he studied math.[8] The transition to college was not easy for Lou, though, and he lost the scholarship because he did not keep his grades at an acceptable level. He did like school, and not wanting to go back home, he tried out for the baseball team with the hope of gaining an athletic scholarship.[9] This too proved difficult in the beginning, as he attended practice every day for four weeks and did little more than shag fly balls. Frustrated and determined to get noticed, one day he sprinted after every fly ball until he passed out. When he came to, the coaches let him hit five balls. He clouted every one over the right-field fence and secured his place on the team.[10]

Success was not immediate, as Brock batted just .140 as a freshman. His sophomore season was nothing less than spectacular, though, as he batted a lofty .545 with 80 hits and 13 home runs in only twenty-seven games. Southern became the first black school to win the NAIA championship by defeating Omaha University, 10–2. Brock hit a tiebreaking home run, went 2 for 5 with three RBIs in the championship game, and was named to the all-tournament team. His outstanding season attracted Major League scouts, but he loved school and decided to return for his junior year. He batted .370 and that summer was invited to Chicago for tryouts with both the Cubs and the White Sox. He was offered contracts by both teams but signed with the Cubs because he felt they offered a better path to the big leagues. His contract included a $30,000 bonus. The Cubs sent him to the Instructional League, where he batted .387 but was seen as a raw talent still needing to develop the fundamentals. The Cubs did see enough that they invited him to the Major League spring training camp in 1961, and he did not disappoint, batting .400.

When spring training broke, Brock was sent to the Cubs' Northern League affiliate in St. Cloud, Minnesota. He made an immediate impression when he homered on the very first pitch that he saw and went on to win the batting title with a .361 average. He also led the league in runs scored with 117, doubles with 33, hits with 181, and put-outs with 277. In addition, he stole 38 bases. He earned a September call-up to the Cubs, appearing in four games and managing just one hit in eleven at bats.

Brock had undeniable ability. He showed power, smashing a 480-foot home run in spring training, and he had speed, running from home to first at 3.4 seconds and 3.1 on a drag bunt. But he was still a raw talent. When he made the big-league club in 1962, he did not know how to use sunglasses both because of inexperience and because he had played almost nothing but night games the previous year at St. Cloud.[11] His defense was particularly bad, especially when it came to ground balls. Bob Smith of the *Chicago Daily News* wrote in April 1963, "Lou Brock is the worst outfielder in baseball history. He really isn't but he hasn't done much to prove it."[12] Brock's development at the big-league level was further hampered by his extremely intense attitude; he seemed to press on every play. Teammate Larry Jackson recalled, "He'd break out in a big sweat just putting on his uniform."[13] The Cubs' rotating system of coaches at the time, rather than a single manager, did not help his development. One coach stressed the importance of hitting the ball to the opposite field, while another told him to bunt more to take advantage of his speed, and yet another said to pull the ball more because he had shown power.[14]

That power was on full display on June 17, 1962, in the first game of a doubleheader at the Polo Grounds against the expansion New York Mets. With two outs in the first inning, Brock drove a slider from lefty Al Jackson to deep center. As he headed toward first base he could see center fielder Richie Ashburn racing back and was immediately thinking triple. As he neared second base, he saw umpire Stan Landes giving the home-run sign, but he thought he was signaling to Brock that he could make an inside-the-park home run so he continued to sprint around the bases. It was not until after he crossed home plate and was informed by a teammate that the ball had gone out of the park that he was aware of what he had just done. He had become only the third player to hit a ball out of the Polo Grounds to center field in a Major League game. (Babe Ruth did it in 1921 before the stadium was remodeled and Joe Adcock repeated the feat in 1953, while Luke Easter did so in a Negro League game in 1948; the next game after Brock's homer, Henry Aaron also hit one out to center, becoming the fourth Major Leaguer to do so.)

Brock's 1963 was very similar to his 1962. He played in 148 games and hit .258 with 9 homers and 37 RBIs. In July 1963, during a 16–11 slugfest, he blasted two home runs and a triple to help the Cubs sweep the Cardinals in a doubleheader before a large Wrigley Field crowd. In 1962 Brock had batted .393 against the Cardinals; it is likely that performances like these put him on Devine's radar.

Brock began the 1964 season slowly, hitting .251 a third of the way through it and fielding erratically. Then on June 15 came the trade that turned out to be one of the most famously lopsided ones in history. Brock was sent to St. Louis along with pitchers Jack Spring and Paul Toth for pitchers Ernie Broglio and Bobby Shantz and outfielder Doug Clemens. Essentially, the trade was Brock for Broglio. At the time, the Cubs were desperate for starting pitching, and Broglio, still only twenty-eight years old, had won twenty-one games in 1960 and eighteen in 1963. Broglio was only 3-5 at the time of the trade and was nursing a sore arm, which he assured the Cubs would soon pass. The sore arm did not pass, and he compiled a 7-19 record with a 5.40 ERA during parts of three seasons as a Cub, retiring from professional baseball after spending the 1967 season in the Minor Leagues. Brock, meanwhile, went on to a Hall of Fame career and batted .334 against the Cubs during the next sixteen seasons.

Brock thrived in St. Louis under manager Johnny Keane. Keane told Brock that he had the speed to steal bases and should do so when the time felt right; in Chicago he could run only when given the sign. Brock stole thirty-three bases for the Cardinals in 1964, batting .348 with his new team and helping to overtake Philadelphia and Cincinnati to win the National League pennant. St. Louis trailed Philadelphia by six games on September 15, but starting on September 21 the Phils lost ten in a row, the last three against the Cardinals. With Brock getting two hits and scoring twice, the Cardinals defeated the Mets on the final day of the regular season, claiming the right to face the New York Yankees in the World Series.

In his first World Series at bat, Brock lined a single to right field off Whitey Ford after fouling off five consecutive pitches. The advance scouts had said that the Cardinals should be able to run on Mantle, who was playing right field to protect his aching knees. When Dick Groat singled to right, Brock raced to third without a throw and moments later he scored on Ken Boyer's sacrifice fly to Mantle. That first inning showed that the Cardinals were the quicker and more aggressive of the teams and foreshadowed more of the same to come. In the second inning he threw out Ford at the plate, and St. Louis went on to win 9–5.

Brock went hitless in the next three games, two of which the Cardinals lost, but in Game Five he got two hits and St. Louis took a 3–2 Series lead, with Tim McCarver hitting a three-run homer off Pete Mikkelsen in the tenth inning to give the Cards a 5–2 victory. Despite three hits by Brock in Game Six, the Yankees evened the Series on the strength of back-to-back homers by Roger Maris and Mantle and a grand slam by Joe Pepitone. In Game Seven, with St. Louis leading 3–0, Brock ignited a three-run fifth with a booming home run off Al Downing that cleared the right-field pavilion and landed on Grand Boulevard. The Cardinals went on to win, 7–5. For the Series Brock went 9 for 30 (.300), with 2 doubles, 1 home run, and 5 RBIs. It was quite a year for the young outfielder: he began the season as an underachiever for the Cubs and ended it as the catalyst for the World Series champion.

DAVE WILLIAMS

Besides being an intense competitor, Brock was also very cerebral. When he heard that Maury Wills kept a little black book in which he noted pitcher idiosyncrasies, he asked Wills if he would share some of his notes. Not surprisingly, Wills was not eager to share the information he had painstakingly recorded with a player from an opposing team. So Brock went out and bought an 8 mm camera in late 1964 and began to record the league's pitchers to study their pick-off moves. Dodgers pitcher Don Drysdale asked Brock one day what he was doing with the camera, and he replied that he was taking home movies. "I don't want to be in your goddamn movies, Brock," Drysdale replied, and true to his nature, he threw at Brock the next time up.[15]

The results were immediate. Brock began to pick up pitchers' habits and twitches from watching his movies and improved his technique, becoming the premier base stealer in the league. Beginning in 1966 he led the National League in stolen bases for eight of the next nine years. He got off to a hot start in 1965 and was batting .315 in May before his shoulder blade was broken by a Sandy Koufax pitch. He felt that Koufax was not adept at fielding bunts, so in his first at bat he dropped a bunt that he beat out and then stole two bases before scoring. Koufax drilled him in the back the next time up, causing the shoulder-blade injury. Once Brock recovered from the injury he struggled mightily, and his batting average shrank to .261. A big reason for his struggle was that he was jumping away from inside pitches — out of fear, he admitted years later. He overcame this fear by standing up to it. "I made myself do it. I even closed my eyes and stepped into a few. Then you hit a few and you realize you're over it."[16] He finished the year strong, raising his average to .288. Around midseason, Brock was moved to the lead-off spot, where he remained for most of his career.

Brock had another fine season in 1966. He accumulated 183 hits, including 24 doubles, 12 triples, and 15 home runs, and batted .285. He had 74 stolen bases. This was followed by an even better season in 1967 with career highs in hits (206), home runs (21), and RBIS (76). He made his first All-Star team and started in left field. The season concluded for Brock with another outstanding World Series performance and another Cardinals championship. The Cardinals won 101 games that year and won the pennant easily ahead of the San Francisco Giants. Their opponents in the World Series were the Boston Red Sox, the surprise winner of a wild four-team American League pennant race.

St. Louis won the opener at Fenway Park, 2–1, and Brock scored both runs. He led off the top of the third with a single to center field off Boston starter Jose Santiago and advanced to third on a double by Curt Flood, then scored on a ground out by Roger Maris. In the seventh inning he led off with another single off Santiago and stole second base. He moved to third on a ground ball to first by Flood and scored on a ground ball by Maris. He finished the game with four hits, a walk, two stolen bases, and two runs scored.

Brock went hitless in Game Two as Red Sox ace Jim Lonborg fired a one-hitter to even the Series. In Game Three, in St. Louis, Brock led off the Cardinals' first with a triple to left-center and scored moments later on Flood's single. With St. Louis leading 3–1, he led off the bottom of the sixth by reaching on a bunt single, advanced to third on an errant pickoff throw, and scored when Maris singled to right-center. The game ended in a 5–2 Cardinals victory in which Brock contributed two hits and two runs scored.

Brock sparked a four-run first inning in Game Four as he led off the game with an infield single and scored on a double by Maris. He finished the game with two more hits and a stolen base as St. Louis moved to within one victory of another championship behind the masterful pitching of Bob Gibson, winning 6–0. Lonborg again came to the Red Sox's rescue as he beat the Cardinals for the second time, a three-hitter as Brock went hitless for the second time against the Boston ace. Back home in a delirious Fenway Park, the Red Sox forced the Series to a seventh game as they pounded out twelve hits in an 8–4 win. Brock had another stellar performance with two hits, including a home run, and three RBIs. He tied the game at 1–1 in the third when he singled home Julián Javier, then stole second and scored when Flood singled to left. He came through again in the clutch in the top of the seventh against John Wyatt, belting a two-run home run to right-center that knotted the game at 4–4.

Brock capped his brilliant World Series with two more hits and three stolen bases as the Cardinals won the championship, 7–2, in Game Seven. He broke an 0-for-10 slump against Lonborg when he followed a Gibson home run in the fifth with a single. He stole both second and third and scored on a sacrifice fly by Maris. He added a double in the sixth and a walk and a stolen base in the ninth to finish the Series with a .414 average (12 for 29), 2 doubles, 1 triple, 1 homer, 3 RBIs, 7 stolen bases, and 8 runs scored. Gibson, who won and completed all three of his starts, was named the Most Valuable Player in the World Series, and radio station KMOX gave Brock a Cadillac in recognition of his outstanding performance.

In 1968 Brock led the National League in stolen bases (62), doubles (46), and triples (14) while again playing a leading role in another Cardinal pennant. Gibson dominated the American League champion Detroit Tigers in Game One, striking out a World Series–record seventeen batters en route to a 4–0 victory. Brock contributed a home run off Pat Dobson in the bottom of the seventh that capped off the Cardinal scoring. Mickey Lolich evened the Series the next day with a complete-game, nine-strikeout performance and held Brock to one single. Brock did steal two bases and scored the only St. Louis run.

He was back to his pesky self in Game Three.

In the top of the fifth with Detroit leading 2–0, Brock, who already had a single, a walk, and two stolen bases, singled with one out. He stole second and scored the Cardinals' first run on a Flood double. By the time the inning was over the Cardinals had a 4–2 lead and went on to a 7–3 win. Brock had another big day in Game Four as St. Louis rolled over the Tigers, 10–1, to take a commanding 3 games to 1 lead. Brock hit the second pitch of the game into Tiger Stadium's right-center-field upper deck off thirty-one-game-winner Denny McLain, and added a triple in the fourth and a bases-clearing three-run double in the eighth. It now appeared that a third world championship in five seasons was imminent for St. Louis.

Lolich was back on the hill for Game Five and this time he was on the ropes early. Brock led off the game with a double down the left-field line, igniting a three-run rally. Detroit tallied two runs in the bottom of the fourth to slice the lead to 3–2 as St. Louis came to bat in the most pivotal inning of the 1968 World Series. With one out, Brock doubled again. Javier came to the plate, and most thought the Cardinals were about to deliver the knockout blow of the Series. Instead, what followed proved to be the turning point in a great Tigers comeback. Javier singled sharply to left and Brock wheeled around third heading to the plate. Tigers left fielder Willie Horton, not known for a strong throwing arm, fielded the ball on one bounce and gunned the ball home. Brock could see Detroit catcher Bill Freehan blocking his path, so he felt he would not be able to get to the plate if he slid, and therefore he decided to come in standing up, attempting to catch the plate with his left foot. The ball arrived at the same time and Freehan applied the tag before Brock could touch the plate. Brock said he was safe even though the replay seems to show that he never touched home. No matter, he was called out and the Tigers rallied for three runs in the bottom of the seventh to win the game, 5–3, and send the Series back to St. Louis.

In Game Six the Tigers shocked the Cards with a ten-run third inning en route to a 13–1 rout, and for the third time Brock and his teammates were in a Game Seven. This time Lolich, not Gibson, was the World Series hero as he outdueled the Cardinals ace, 4–1, to complete the comeback. Brock's only hit came leading off the sixth inning in a game that was scoreless at the time, but he was picked off. The Tigers followed that with three runs in the seventh, and Lolich held on to nail down the Series. Despite the pick-off and the nonslide at home in the fifth game, Brock again put up stellar postseason numbers. He banged out 13 hits in 28 at bats for a .464 average, hit 3 doubles, 1 triple, and 2 home runs, drove in 5 runs, scored 6, and stole 7 bases. This would be the last World Series Brock would play in, but his reputation as an outstanding player in the clutch was solidified forever. In twenty-one games in three World Series, he batted .391 with 34 hits. He had 7 doubles, 2 triples, 4 home runs, 13 RBIS, 16 runs scored, and 14 stolen bases—among the best postseason numbers in baseball history.

The next season was disappointing for St. Louis, as the Cardinals slipped to fourth place in the newly formed National League Eastern Division. Of the many reasons that led to the Cardinals' fall, one of them was not their left fielder; Brock had another strong year, batting .298 with 33 doubles, 10 triples, 12 home runs, 97 runs scored, and a league-leading 53 stolen bases. His average climbed over .300 in 1970 at .304. His streak of leading the league in stolen bases ended at four, as his total of 51 was good only for second behind former teammate Bobby Tolan, now with Cincinnati, who topped the circuit with 57. Brock scored 114 runs and had 202 hits.

He began another run of four consecutive seasons of leading the league in stolen bases in 1971 when he tallied 64. He led the Major Leagues with a career-high 126 runs scored and batted .313 with 37 doubles and 7 triples among his 200 hits. It was more of the same in 1972 as he batted .311, led the league with 63 steals, scored 81 runs, had 26 doubles, and knocked 8 triples. There was some talk in 1973 that Brock was losing a step, as he got off to a slow start stealing bases. He picked up the pace as the year went on, though, and finished with 70, his highest total since 1966. His average dipped under .300, to .297, and he scored 110 runs.

Brock was thirty-four years old as the 1974 season got under way, but there were no signs that he was slowing down. He had 56 steals by mid-July and was ahead of Maury Wills's pace when he set the record of 104 steals in 1962. It seemed as if the baseball world was tuned in to see if Brock could break the record. On September 10, in a game against the Phillies, Brock singled in the first inning and stole second to tie Wills's record. He singled again in the seventh inning. With the St. Louis crowd wild with anticipation, Brock stole second to break the record. The game was delayed as players from both teams offered their congratulations. Besides his record-setting 118 stolen bases, he batted .306 on the strength of 194 hits, scored 105 runs, and finished second in the National League MVP voting. When the award went to Steve Garvey of the pennant-winning Dodgers, he could not hide his disappointment. "I'm not bitter," he said, "I just think I deserved it. I earned it."

Brock headed into the twilight of his career still a productive and consistent player. He hit .309 in 1975 but his stolen-base total fell to 56, still pretty good for a player who finished the year at thirty-six years old. He stole another 56 bases in 1976 and batted .301. His average slipped to .272 in 1977 year with 35 stolen bases, his lowest since 1963. However, on August 29, in San Diego, Brock stole his 893rd base, surpassing Ty Cobb as the all-time leader. (Rickey Henderson broke Brock's record in 1991 and finished his career with 1,406 stolen bases.) In 1978 injuries and age limited Brock to ninety-two games, and he batted only .221 with 17 steals.

When the 1979 season got under way, Brock was 100 hits shy of 3,000 for his career. On August 13 he was 2 hits from the historic number. Taking on the Cubs in St. Louis before a crowd of 44,457, he singled to left field off Dennis Lamp in the first inning for hit 2,999. In the fourth, after being low-bridged by a 1-and-2 fastball, he smashed a line drive off Lamp's hand, literally knocking the Cubs hurler out of the game and becoming the fourteenth Major Leaguer to join the 3,000-hit club. On September 9, 1979, the Cardinals honored him with Lou Brock Day at Busch Stadium. A crowd of more than 47,000, including his eighty-year-old mother, saw Brock receive a thirty-three-foot cabin cruiser from August Busch Jr. and a new car from KMOX radio, among many other gifts. In the first inning, Brock reached on a force play and then stole second base. He finished his career with a .293 average, 3,023 hits, 1,610 runs scored, and 938 stolen bases.

Brock's No. 20 was retired by the Cardinals in 1979. He was elected to the Louisiana Sports Hall of Fame in 1983, and he was a first-ballot selection for the Baseball Hall of Fame in 1985. He became involved with several successful business ventures, including the Brockabrella hat, for which he owns the patent. He was a Cardinals broadcaster from 1981 to 1984 and in 1995 became a special instructor in spring training for the team. Brock and his wife, Jacqueline, were ordained as ministers at Abundant Life Fellowship Church and became active in several charitable causes in the St. Louis area.

Chapter 4. **Ernie Broglio**

Russell Lake

AGE	W	L	PCT.	ERA	G	GS	GF	CG	SHO	SV	IP	H	BB	SO	HBP	WP
28	3	5	.375	3.50	11	11	0	3	1	0	69.1	65	26	36	1	4

Some athletes earn disapproval for their failures on the field. Ernie Broglio became the object of scorn of media and fans alike for being the pivotal piece of a one-sided trade during the 1964 season. The six-foot-two right-handed pitcher had been a solid part of a strong starting rotation formed in the early 1960s under the direction of St. Louis Cardinals general manager Bing Devine, but was traded to the Chicago Cubs for a then unknown outfielder, Lou Brock. Brock went on to be instrumental in two Cardinals World Series championships and eventually was elected to the Baseball Hall of Fame, but the unfortunate Broglio won only seven more games in his career.

Ernest "Ernie" Gilbert Broglio was born in Berkeley, California, on August 27, 1935, the second child of Anna and Joseph Broglio, and in 1945 moved with his family five miles north to El Cerrito. "I had played a lot of 'street ball' while growing up in Berkeley," he recalled.[1] "I never had anybody influential push me. My dad carried two jobs seven days a week. He was a painter [sprayer] for American Standard [bathroom fixtures], and he did gardening work, so he did not have much time to see me play." As a middle-school eighth grader, Broglio played on the varsity high school teams, mainly baseball and basketball. He also played one season of football.

"When I was thirteen, I played American Legion baseball," Broglio said. "Besides pitching, I played first base, shortstop, and the outfield. In high school, my catcher was Elijah 'Pumpsie' Green, who later played in the Majors."

During the spring of 1953, Broglio recalled, "all sixteen Major League teams and three Pacific

An eighteen-game winner in 1963, Ernie Broglio had a 3–5 record with a 3.50 ERA in mid-June 1964. Needing more offense, the fast-fading Cardinals traded him for Brock.

Coast League teams were interested in me. I signed right out of high school with the Oakland Oaks." He won two games and lost four for the Pacific Coast League team. The next season the Oaks farmed him to Modesto of the California League, where he won nine games in a month and a half before being recalled by the Oaks and going 5-8.

Broglio also enrolled at West Contra Costa Junior College, where he met Barbara Ann Bertellotti of Oakland. They were married on November 20, 1954.

In 1955 Broglio was assigned to Stockton (California League) and won twenty games. He started twenty-nine games with twenty-five complete games in a 20-10 season. He had 230 strikeouts and 137 walks.

Team locations changed dramatically for Broglio after the 1955 season, when his contract was bought by the New York Giants organization. In 1956 he had a 6-12 record in thirty-one games at Johnstown, Pennsylvania, of the Class A Eastern League. Broglio was with the Dallas Eagles (Texas League) in 1957 and was 17-6 in thirty-four games with a 2.51 ERA. He had twenty-nine starts and fourteen complete games in 222 innings. He was voted to the Texas League all-star team, the third time he had earned that distinction. (The others were in 1954 and 1955 in the California League.) Broglio started the 1958 season with the Phoenix Giants (Pacific Coast League) before he was transferred to the Toronto Maple Leafs (International League). He was 8-1 for Phoenix and 9-4 for Toronto in 212 innings.

On October 8, 1958, Broglio was part of a five-player swap between the Giants (by then relocated to San Francisco) and the St. Louis Cardinals. He and pitcher Marv Grissom went to the Cardinals for reliever Billy Muffett, catcher Hobie Landrith, and infielder Benny Valenzuela. Broglio said the Giants told him there had been a "paperwork problem, and they had to trade me or lose me to another organization." *St. Louis Post-Dispatch* sports editor Bob Broeg was not very complimentary with his initial assessment of the trade. Broeg wrote, "The general feeling was that the Giants got the edge." However, Broeg included an observation from a reporter who watched Ernie pitch in Toronto. "Broglio should be of great help to the Cardinals," said Neil MacCarl of the *Toronto Star*. "He's quite a workhorse with a good curve and fastball which he throws with the same overhand motion. He won five games down the stretch with just two days' rest, never allowing more than

two runs a game. He also broke the Toronto club strikeout record the first night with the team, fanning 15 in 11⅓ innings."

After the trade, Broglio joined the Cardinals for an exhibition tour of the Orient. "The Japan trip was a lot of fun and good baseball," he recalled. "It gave me a chance to pitch in front of large crowds, and I was not used to that. We also made stops in Hawaii, the Philippines, and Korea to play all-star teams."

Broglio made his Major League debut on April 11, 1959, against his former organization, the Giants. He struggled through a four-walk first inning and took the loss, but he stayed in until the sixth. Broglio's next start, on April 16, in Los Angeles, was eventful. The Cardinals used a then record twenty-five players in a 7–6 loss to the Dodgers. Broglio lasted an inning and gave up two homers that just got over the 42-foot screen at the 251-foot mark in left field of the Coliseum. In his *St. Louis Post-Dispatch* column, Neal Russo dubbed the round-trippers "Chinese," but he also labeled Broglio "one inning Ernie."

After four appearances, Broglio was 0-2 with an ERA of 9.00 when he got a call from Bing Devine to come talk with him and manager Solly Hemus. He recalled, "I knew I was supposed to start again, but after they contacted me I started packing my stuff because I thought I was being sent to Rochester [International League]. When I got to the meeting, though, they both said that I was pressing too much and to get more relaxed. That worked because I pitched into the seventh inning with nine strikeouts the next game."

However, Broglio was 0-5 by the middle of June. His first win came in St. Louis against Philadelphia on June 16. He scattered ten hits through seven innings and won a 5–2 decision. On June 27 he had his best Major League game so far. At Crosley Field in Cincinnati he pitched a complete-game, two-hit shutout, winning 5–0. He had six strikeouts and walked no one. (He had come into

RUSSELL LAKE

the game having walked thirty-three batters in fifty-four innings.) Broglio appeared in thirty-five games and started twenty-five during the 1959 season and ended with a 7-12 record in 181 innings. His ERA was 4.72 with six complete games and three shutouts (which tied for the team lead). He was second on the team with 133 strikeouts.

Broglio was not projected as a part of the regular rotation in 1960. He came into the second game of the season on April 13 in relief and pitched six strong innings against the Giants in San Francisco. His first start came four days later in Los Angeles. He did not get through the fourth inning, walking six and giving up five runs. Broglio's next start came on May 30, when he was matched against the Dodgers' Don Drysdale at the Coliseum. The Cardinals jumped on Drysdale for five runs in less than two innings. Broglio struck out eight, scattering four hits and three walks in his first complete game of the season as the Redbirds romped to a 15–3 victory. He even chipped in with two hits, three runs batted in, and two runs scored. Manager Hemus said he was thinking of putting Broglio into the regular rotation.

After a bad start and a loss to the Giants, however, Broglio was back in relief for two games. Two starts and a relief appearance netted him three victories between June 12 and 19. At the halfway mark of the season, Broglio was 9-4 with an ERA of 2.86. He was in the starting rotation for eighteen of his final twenty-one appearances as the Cardinals climbed into the pennant race. In Pittsburgh on August 11, facing the league-leading Pirates, who had won seven in a row, Broglio outdueled Bob Friend in an extra-inning thriller. Both pitchers went twelve innings and each struck out nine, with Friend walking one and Broglio none. Broglio retired twenty consecutive Pirates from the fifth inning through the eleventh. Stan Musial hit a two-run homer in the twelfth to give the Cardinals a 3–1 lead. In the bottom of the inning, the Pirates got a run and had the tying run on second

when Broglio struck out Dick Stuart for his fourteenth win. The victory was the thirteenth out of fifteen for the Cardinals and moved them into second place, four games behind Pittsburgh. Broglio recalled, "After the game, I wanted to take Musial out for a brew, but Stan insisted that he would take me out!"

Broglio won seven of his next nine decisions to move his record to 21-7, with an ERA of 2.52. But the Cardinals faded after mid-August to end the season in third place behind Pittsburgh and Milwaukee. Broglio was 4-0 against the Pirates and 5-2 against the Braves, and he finished the season with a 21-9 mark. His ERA of 2.74 was second in the league. He tied Warren Spahn for the league lead in wins and led the league in winning percentage (.700). After the season, he was offered a $5,000 raise by the Cardinals.

In 1961 Broglio was the Opening Day starter, but he pitched with a sore right shoulder most of the season and received close to twenty cortisone shots. He ended 1961 with a 9-12 mark. He had twenty-six starts, seven complete games, and two shutouts. He hoped the off-season would give his shoulder time to heal.

In 1962 Broglio finished with a 12-9 record and 3.00 ERA. He boasted a career-high eleven complete games in thirty starts. His four shutouts were part of a staff total that led the NL at seventeen.

Broglio was the Cardinals' Opening Day starter on April 9, 1963, against the Mets in the Polo Grounds, when he pitched a two-hit shutout and struck out eight. He two-hit the Mets in New York again on June 8, this time striking out ten.

From August 30 through September 15, the Cardinals won nineteen of twenty games and pulled to within a game of the league-leading Dodgers. Broglio had four quality starts during this streak with two victories, improving his season mark to 16-8. Then on September 16 he started the first game of a big three-game series in St. Louis and went eight strong innings. A stiff right elbow, however, led him to be removed for a pinch hitter with the game tied. The Dodgers scored twice in the ninth against two Cardinal relievers to win, 3–1. Broglio won two more games to finish with an 18-8 record. In a career-high thirty-five starts, he had eleven complete games to go with five shutouts and an ERA of 2.99. He had four two-hit shutouts.

On April 14, 1964, Broglio was again the Opening Day starter, at Los Angeles, and lost to Sandy Koufax. On April 18 he defeated the Giants in San Francisco; on April 28 he shut out the Mets. But Broglio lost three straight starts from May 14 through May 24 to drop to 2-4, and manager Johnny Keane's confidence in him started to fade. Keane kept juggling the rotation and now had six starters. On May 30 in St. Louis, Broglio beat the Reds, 7–1, in a complete-game effort. But from then through June 14, the Cardinals lost eleven of fifteen games and dropped to eighth place. The bats of several Cardinals went silent and the outfield platoon to replace the retired Musial was not working. It was alarm time within the front office with rumors that something would happen before the trade deadline.

Broglio started on June 12 in Los Angeles, but Koufax blanked the Cardinals again. Broglio's record was now 3-5. In eleven starts his strikeouts were noticeably down to three per game. On June 14, after the Dodgers swept the series, the Cardinals boarded their plane for Houston.

General manager Bing Devine had been busy on the phone right up to their departure, and later he sat by Keane during the flight. Devine said, "I can make the deal with Chicago." Keane's response was either "Make it!" or "What are we waiting for?"—depending on what account the St. Louis fans read. As soon as they landed in Houston, Devine called Cubs general manager John Holland. Three other trades in the Major Leagues were announced on June 15, but none proved larger than the one between the Cardinals and the Cubs.

Broglio, pitcher Bobby Shantz, and outfielder Doug Clemens were sent to Chicago for outfielder Lou Brock, pitcher Jack Spring, and pitcher Paul Toth. Keane summoned Ernie to his hotel room to tell him about the trade, and Broglio was shocked. Several veteran Cardinals were very negative about the deal and declared that the Cubs got the better of the trade. Keane called a team meeting before their game to tell the players to cease their grumbling. Meanwhile, *Chicago Daily News* columnist Bob Smith was jubilant as he wrote about acquiring Ernie, "Thank you, thank you, oh, you lovely St. Louis Cardinals. Nice doing business with you. Please call again anytime."

Broglio reflected, "I do not know what caused the disagreement I had with Johnny Keane. I had just won eighteen games and thought I was pretty stable with the ball club. The trade was a big surprise and I guess I never really got over it. I was hoping to finish my career with the Cardinals."

Broglio joined a Cubs team that included eight of his former St. Louis teammates. Most notable was Larry Jackson, who was on his way to a twenty-four-win season. The Cubs got the better of that deal before the 1963 season, so they figured they would try again. Chicago had no field manager, as they were in the third season of the College of Coaches instituted by owner Philip K. Wrigley. Broglio commented, "Bob Kennedy was the best one, but playing for several head coaches was a joke. One problem was that each coach had a different set of signs that you had to learn."

Broglio added, "When I was traded, my right arm was not in fine tune. My elbow was really bothering me, and pitching in so many day games was not my piece of cake. In my opinion, the hitters see the pitches better than they do at night." For the Cubs, Broglio started 0-4 with an 8.22 ERA before he won against the Mets on July 16. He started against the Cardinals and Bob Gibson on July 28 in Chicago. He held his own for three innings before being touched for six earned runs and was lifted in the seventh ending with a no-decision. Broglio rebounded to win his next three starts, improving his combined record to 7-9 and lowering his ERA to 4.42.

On August 23 Ernie woke up in his New York hotel room with a problem. His right elbow had swelled to the size of a cantaloupe and was in a locked position. Broglio was to start one of the games of a doubleheader that day at Shea Stadium. He knew that was not going to happen, so he called Bob Kennedy to tell him about the issue. Kennedy had Broglio return to Chicago to get treatment.

After two more losses, Broglio took the mound on September 6 to start the series finale against the Cardinals in St. Louis. While the Cubs had dropped to eighth, the Cardinals were now in third place. Broglio allowed six hits, but St. Louis could not break through against him. In the bottom of the seventh, he held a 3–1 lead and was lifted in favor of Lindy McDaniel. Chicago was still leading 4–2 in the bottom of the ninth. A run scored when Brock grounded out as Flood took second. One more out and Broglio would have a satisfying victory over his former team. But Bill White singled to tie the game, and in the eleventh Brock's bad-hop single drove in the winning run.

Broglio started again against St. Louis on September 11 at Wrigley Field before a small afternoon crowd and lost, 5–0. He was now a combined 7-12 and was shut down for the rest of the season due to his elbow problem. His record with the Cubs ended at 4-7.

"It hurt when the Cardinals won the World Series," Broglio said. "A lot of the players called me from their party at Stan Musial's restaurant after the last game. They passed the phone around and I really appreciated it. I popped open my own bottle of champagne and drank along with them. I looked at it like they won the pennant by one game and I won three games for the Cardinals before I was traded, so I thought I had helped them win it."[2] Broglio received neither a championship ring nor a share of the postseason money as the eligibility was different then. "It would have been nice to have a ring," Broglio said, "but I didn't get one, so I didn't worry about it."[3]

In November, Broglio had surgery on his right elbow to remove bone chips and a damaged ulnar nerve. He recalled, "I was back for spring training in February, which gave me a total of three months' rest. Nowadays, for the same operation, they give you a year or more. That [decision by the Cubs] made my career shorter than I wanted it to be."

Broglio made his first 1965 appearance on April 27 at Cincinnati, a one-third-inning relief stint. He appeared in twenty-six games and had six starts during the season. On June 27 in St Louis, he lasted one and two-thirds innings and left trailing 4–0. It was apparent that he had not been given the time needed to recuperate. His season record ended at 1-6 with a 6.93 ERA, with his last appearance on September 19.

Leo Durocher was named the Cubs' manager for 1966. Broglio had several outstanding spring-training performances at Long Beach, California. Durocher noted that Ernie had become a pitcher again by mixing a slider and a fast curve before using his fastball. Broglio was put into the rotation, but things did not go well. He started the second game of the season, on April 13 at San Francisco. He was wild but went seven innings. He gave up four runs and took the loss as the Cubs were shut out. Broglio made his last start for the Cubs on June 22 in Chicago in the second game of a doubleheader with the Giants. It was dismal as he allowed seven runs and was booed by the Wrigley Field fans. After two relief appearances, on July 5 he was sent to Tacoma of the Pacific Coast League. Broglio started thirteen games for Tacoma and had a 5-4 record with a 2.86 ERA.

Broglio gave pitching one more shot in 1967 with the Buffalo Bisons, the Triple-A affiliate of Cincinnati. He was 12-13 in twenty-eight starts with a 3.69 ERA, but no call came from the Reds.

During this season, one of his catchers was nineteen-year-old Johnny Bench, who was five years old in 1953 when Broglio started playing baseball for a living.

At age thirty-two, Broglio went home to San Jose, California, and took a full-time position with the liquor warehouse where he had worked in the off-seasons.

Ernie and Barbara Broglio raised four children—Stephen, Nancy, Donna, and Vince—and had three grandchildren and one great-grandchild. (Their son Stephen died in October 2007 at the age of fifty-two.) As of 2011 the Broglios still lived in the San Jose home they bought in 1959. Broglio invested in an award-winning winery run by his son-in-law Jack Salerno in Healdsburg, California. In April 2009 Broglio was inducted into the El Cerrito High School Athletics Hall of Fame.

Broglio kept active with his family and still took time for sports, especially golf, about which he said, "I'm not all that good, but it gives me exercise." He said he was also busy providing instruction as a high school pitching coach, and he gave private lessons too. "I enjoy working with the kids to prevent arm trouble," Broglio said. "I work on pitching mechanics for all ages. But for the older ones, I try to get into their heads about what pitches to throw at what time of the game."

Broglio's eight-year Major League career showed a 77-74 mark in 259 games. In 184 starts, he had 52 complete games, 18 shutouts, and an ERA of 3.74. Broglio chuckled about a 1990s appearance with Lou Brock at an old-timers game at Wrigley Field: "They introduced me next-to-last, and Lou was last. The Cub fans sure didn't forget Brock for Broglio. As I came out, everybody stood up and gave me a great ovation of boos. I started laughing, removed my cap, and took a bow. Then they introduced Lou, and my God, I thought Wrigley Field was going to collapse the way they cheered him."[4]

Broglio said that in his house he proudly displayed an autographed picture of Brock. He told one sportswriter that he often advised Brock not to die first: "As long as people remember him, I know they also are going to remember me!"[5]

Chapter 5. Jerry Buchek

Mark Simon

AGE	G	AB	R	H	2B	3B	HR	TB	RBI	BB	SO	BAV	OBP	SLG	SB	GDP	HBP
25	35	30	7	6	0	2	0	10	1	3	11	.200	.273	.333	0	0	0

When Jerry Buchek was growing up on the south side of St. Louis, he and his father, John, made the trip to Sportsman's Park a few times a year. They would usually sit in the outfield bleachers, and one day a couple of balls came their way. "Do you think you can hit a ball this far?" John Buchek asked his son. "Not now," Jerry replied. "But one day I might." One day, many years later, Buchek again answered that question, on the same field.

Born on May 9, 1942, Buchek (pronounced BOO-check) grew up in a middle-class St. Louis neighborhood, playing baseball daily against older, bigger kids until he started to grow in his teen years. Buchek idolized his father, an electrician, who played third base for the local team in the semipro Central Illinois League. John Buchek led the league in home runs in 1936, and his son aspired to a future with similar power skills.

Jerry was good enough to make his McKinley High School varsity team as a freshman and became a starter as a sophomore, playing third base until his senior year, when he moved to shortstop.

In the summer between his junior and senior years, playing for the Aubuchon Dennison Post 186 American Legion team, he was the Player of the Year and began to attract the attention of Major League scouts.

In 1959 the Cardinals offered Buchek, then eighteen, a $65,000 signing bonus, which he accepted, passing up scholarship offers to play football or basketball at the University of Missouri and Bradley University, in Peoria, Illinois.

That fall Buchek played in the Florida Instructional League. He earned an all-star selection and

In 1964 Jerry Buchek played in thirty-five games and hit .200. As a backup infielder, he played at shortstop, second base, and third base.

a ticket to start his pro career as a shortstop at Double-A Tulsa. After thirty-six games, in which he hit .333, he was sent up to Triple-A Rochester to replace an injured player. There, he struggled to hit breaking pitches and hit just .226 for the Red Wings.

The next year the five-foot-eleven, 185-pound Buchek hit .277 for Triple-A Portland and earned a brief recall to the Major Leagues, where he was overmatched, hitting a dismal .133, with 12 hits in 90 at bats. He set what was then a Major League record for most strikeouts (28) in a season by a position player without drawing a walk. The mark has been broken twice since and as of 2011 stood at 33 (Jerry Gil, 2004 Diamondbacks). "That shows you how anxious I was," Buchek said. "When I came up, I really wanted to do well. They never threw it around the plate. They'd be wasting pitches and I would commit myself."

"I needed more seasoning and I think the Cardinals knew that," Buchek said. "I got a little nervous playing in my hometown. I'd have to leave tickets for a bunch of guys. My buddies would get on me for my bad games. That made it a little stressful. I didn't have that same kind of pressure when I played on the road."

Buchek spent all of 1962 and almost all of 1963 in the Minor Leagues, as the Cardinals were set in the middle infield spots with Julio Gotay, Julián Javier, Dal Maxvill, and Dick Groat among those in front of him. Buchek had a poor season in 1962, hitting just .183 at Double-A Tulsa and Triple-A Atlanta. He blamed it on a lack of confidence. Team consultant Branch Rickey suggested that he switch to pitching because of his strong arm, but the Cardinals decided against it. "At one point, I called my father and said I didn't know if I could play anymore," Buchek said. "He told me that I couldn't give up."

Buchek worked with Atlanta Crackers manager Harry Walker, tweaking the uppercut in his swing, which helped his hitting greatly. In 1963 he batted .287 with a team-high ninety-two runs batted in and worked his way back to the Major Leagues. He earned a spot as a backup infielder for the 1964 Cardinals. He filled in at shortstop, second base, and third base, playing in thirty-five games.

In thirty-five games he went 6 for 30 (.200) with one RBI—but he considers his contribution to the team significant. In his four starts that season, the Cardinals won three. His most noteworthy contribution was a triple off Art Mahaffey in a 4–1 St. Louis win over the Philadelphia Phillies in the second game of a doubleheader sweep. The Cardinals were in sixth place at the time, seven games out of first place.

"We won [the pennant] by one game, and I helped us win *a* game," Buchek said. "So I helped [win the pennant]."

Buchek played in four of the seven World Series games as a defensive replacement at second base. He got a hit in his only at bat, a single off Jim Bouton in the ninth inning of an 8–3 loss to the New York Yankees in Game Six. As of 2011 he is one of thirty-eight players who have a World Series batting average of 1.000.

Buchek was in the bullpen when Bob Gibson got the final out of Game Seven and ran onto the field with teammates Bob Uecker and Roger Craig to celebrate. He took his winner's share and put a down payment on a two-family home. Years later, he said he still had his World Series ring and a ticket stub from one of the games as mementos. "When I see Tim McCarver, I kid with him that I was the leading hitter in the World Series, and he wasn't," Buchek said with a laugh.

Over the next two seasons, Buchek remained in a utility role, starting eighty games in 1966. His primary claim to fame was being the last base runner at Sportsman's Park in its final game on May 8, 1966, and scoring the first run at the new Busch Stadium in the first game there four days later on May 12.

On September 22, 1965, he hit a home run against the New York Mets, playing in the park where he'd watched many games as a fan. "My dad was at the game," Buchek said. "After the game, my dad told me what I had said about hitting a home run into the bleachers [as a kid]. My dad said to me that you only had to wait fifteen years do it. We laughed."

Just before the 1967 season, Buchek was traded to the Mets in a five-player deal orchestrated by Mets general manager Bing Devine, who had formerly worked in the same role for the Cardinals.

The deal gave Buchek the chance to become an everyday player. A month into the season, on May 14, he hit a go-ahead home run off Gibson in a 3–1 Mets win. That snapped Gibson's nine-game winning streak against the Mets. "I didn't know how I was going to hit Gibson, but he hung a slider," Buchek said. "I can still remember Tim McCarver saying, 'Oh ——.'"

Buchek had a few other highlights in his Mets career, the first coming on July 9, 1967, when he hit a game-tying home run with two outs in the ninth inning against the Braves, pinch-hitting for Bud Harrelson, who was 4 for 4 in the game to that point. The Mets won the game later in the inning on a bases-loaded walk to Ron Swoboda.

Buchek's best game in the Major Leagues came against the Astros on September 22, 1967. With the Mets down two runs in the bottom of the eighth inning, he hit a three-run home run to give New York the lead. The Astros tied the game in the ninth on a base hit off Buchek's glove, but in the eleventh inning, he redeemed himself with a walk-off home run. "The thing I remember about that game is that I didn't particularly feel good [at the plate] that day," Buchek said.

Buchek's six RBIs in that game tied a team record for RBIs in a game by a shortstop that still stood as of 2011. He primarily played second base that season, and his fourteen home runs were the most by a Mets second baseman until the record was surpassed by Jeff Kent's twenty-one in 1993.

The Hall of Famer Buchek hit best was former San Francisco Giant Juan Marichal. Buchek hit .364 with eight hits (all singles) against him. "Juan once said to me, 'How can a .230 hitter hit me like you do?' I said, 'You give me good balls to hit and I don't foul them off. I hit them.'"

Buchek wasn't as fortunate against Los Angeles Dodgers stars Sandy Koufax and Don Drysdale. He went 2 for 11 with seven strikeouts against Koufax and 0 for 17 with eight strikeouts against Drysdale. "One of my teammates, Carl War-wick, said I wasn't going to be able to hit Koufax," Buchek said. "I went 1 for 3 against him. The next time I went 1 for 4. I told Carl I was starting to get some confidence, but the next time around, Koufax struck me out all four times." Buchek hit only one ball to the outfield off Drysdale. "I couldn't pick up his ball," he said. "I remember one night Ken Boyer and I went to a lounge and Drysdale was there. I told him how nasty he was against me. A few weeks later, I hit a shot to right center, and their right fielder goes three feet off the ground to make a great catch. Drysdale was laughing so hard, probably thinking, 'You'll never get a hit off me.' He was right."

In December 1968 Buchek was traded back to the Cardinals, but was sent to the Minor Leagues. He did not reach the big leagues again in his career. The Cardinals traded him to the Phillies before Opening Day 1969, and he wound up with the Eugene (Oregon) Emeralds of the Pacific Coast League, where he teamed with future Phillies shortstop Larry Bowa on the club that won the PCL championship. He did get to meet up with his former Mets teammates in Chicago, when they invited him to a team party after the Mets clinched the National League East championship.

After the season Buchek asked to be released so he could sign with the Atlanta Braves organization. The Phillies refused to release him, and he had no interest in spending another season in the Minor Leagues, so he walked away from the game on his terms. He finished his Major League career with a .220 batting average in 421 games.

After baseball Buchek went to work as a meat cutter, a job he held for twenty-five years. After that, he was a car salesman for ten years until he retired in 2004. As of early 2011, he lived with his second wife, Jan, about 250 miles from his native St. Louis, on a lake in Branson, Missouri, where he enjoyed bass fishing.

One of Buchek's four sons, David, signed with the Cardinals but was released. He worked for two years as a strength and conditioning coach in the Minor Leagues and then turned to hitting instruction at baseball camps.

Buchek said he still watched baseball avidly as a fan of the Cardinals and took part in their winter fan festivals. He said he appreciated that he got to live out a childhood dream.

"I want to be remembered as someone who tried hard and did his best," Buchek said. "The game was hard for me and I struggled with it. I was in and out of the lineup and could never really get into a routine. I admire the guys who are geared for that now."

Chapter 6. **Lew Burdette**

Alex Kupfer

AGE	W	L	PCT.	ERA	G	GS	GF	CG	SHO	SV	IP	H	BB	SO	HBP	WP
37	1	0	1.000	1.80	8	0	2	0	0	0	10	10	3	3	0	1

Throughout his eighteen-year Major League career, Lew Burdette was known for his antics as much as for his success on the mound. One of the best control pitchers of the 1950s, the right-hander paired with his roommate and best friend Warren Spahn to form one of the greatest and most durable pitching combinations in baseball history.

Typically in collaboration with Spahn, Burdette was a notorious prankster who did everything from slipping snakes into umpires' pockets to intentionally posing as a lefty for his 1959 Topps baseball card. On the mound his nervous mannerisms such as fixing his jersey and hat, wiping his forehead, touching his lips, and talking to himself could, in the words of one of his managers, Fred Haney, "make coffee nervous."[1] Burdette's behavior undoubtedly helped to distract batters, but it also led to frequent accusations that he threw a spitball. While the pitcher, supported by his teammates and umpires, always denied that he threw the spitter, he saw the benefit of cultivating the reputation that he did; as he famously stated, "My best pitch is one I do not throw." He relied on a sinking fastball, slider, and change-up to reach the two-hundred-win mark on the way to helping to lead his team to two World Series appearances. Above all, though, Burdette is best remembered for turning in one of the most dominant performances in postseason history when his three complete-game victories over the New York Yankees helped lead the Milwaukee Braves to the 1957 World Series title.

Selva Lewis Burdette Jr. was born on November 22, 1926, in Nitro, West Virginia, to Agnes Burnett and Selva Lewis Burdette Sr., a plant fore-

Lew Burdette pitched in eight games, posting a 1–0 record with a 1.80 ERA. On June 2 the Cardinals traded him to the Cubs for Glen Hobbie. (Collection of Bill Nowlin)

man at an American Viscose Rayon plant in Nitro. Generally known by his middle name, throughout his life he spelled it "Lou." While he played a lot of sandlot baseball as a child, his first athletic success came with the Nitro High School football team, because the school didn't have a baseball team. He failed to make the local American Legion team, but after graduating from high school in 1944, he used his father's connections to get a job at the Viscose plant (his sister and younger brother also

27

worked there) as a message boy on the condition that he pitch for the company's baseball team. At seventeen years old, playing in the Industrial League of the Viscose Athletic Association, Burdette went 12-2 against teams from companies including DuPont, Monsanto, and Carbide.

Burdette's fledgling baseball career was put on hold when he entered the Air Corps Reserve in April 1945. Because the ranks were full, he was never given the opportunity to fly and instead was placed with a welding outfit. Released from active duty after six months, he enrolled at the University of Richmond and joined the baseball team. Burdette quickly drew the attention of scouts from a number of Major League teams, including one from the Boston Braves who told him, "I don't like the way you pitch. You may as well forget about baseball."[2] Signed by the Yankees in 1947 for $200 a month, Burdette was assigned to Norfolk, Virginia, in the Class B Piedmont League to begin his professional career.

Burdette pitched in only six games in Norfolk, then was sent to Amsterdam, New York, of the Class C Canadian-American League. In 150 innings he showed a great deal of promise, posting nine wins against ten losses and a stellar 2.82 earned run average. He continued to improve the following season with Quincy, Illinois, in the Class B Three-I League, finishing the season at 16-11, with an ERA of 2.02 and a league-record 187 strikeouts. He moved up the organizational ladder once again, spending 1948 and 1949 with the Yankees' Triple-A affiliate in Kansas City, where he roomed with Whitey Ford. Facing tougher competition, for the first time, Burdette struggled and was relegated to the bullpen.

During his time in the Yankees system, Burdette occasionally worked with roving pitching coach Burleigh Grimes. Though known as one of the great spitball pitchers, Grimes refused to teach Burdette how to throw the spitter out of a concern that if caught Burdette would be banned from professional baseball. However, Grimes suggested that because of his behavior on the mound and the movement on his breaking pitches, particularly his sinking slider, Burdette could use the spitball as a psychological weapon, so that even though he didn't throw it, batters would convince themselves that he was and would come to the plate looking for it.

While with Kansas City, Lew married his fiancée, Mary Ann Shelton. They had met in a bowling alley in Charleston, West Virginia, in October 1948, and they decided to get engaged as Lew was leaving for spring training the following March. Upon hearing that the wedding was scheduled for the fall of 1949, the Kansas City front office wanted to stage the wedding at home plate. Mary nixed the idea and the couple married quietly in Charleston in June 1949. Their first son, Lewis Kent, was born in July 1951.

Despite his pitching struggles in Triple-A, Burdette was called up to the Yankees when the rosters expanded in September 1950. He made his Major League debut for the defending World Series champions on September 26 against the Washington Senators, getting Gil Coan to ground out to end the fifth inning. The next spring he was invited to spring training, then was optioned to San Francisco in the Pacific Coast League. Playing for manager Lefty O'Doul, Burdette started twenty-six games and did his best to show that he belonged back in the Majors, striking out 118 while walking 78 in 210 innings. And although his record stood at 14-12, half of the losses were by one run. Then, on August 29, 1951, Burdette's career radically changed when he was traded to the Boston Braves as a throw-in when the Yankees sent $50,000 for pitcher Johnny Sain to help them with their push for the postseason.

Burdette spent the final month of the season with the Braves, making three short relief appearances. In 1952 he worked mostly out of the bullpen and demonstrated that he could ably shoulder a heavy workload, leading the team with forty-five appearances, foreshadowing the durability that highlighted his career. (During his career Burdette was consistently among the league leaders in innings pitched, games started, and complete games.)

Before the 1953 season, frustrated by his team's second-tier status in Boston, owner Lou Perini moved the club to Milwaukee. The Braves were immediately embraced by the fans, as the players were showered with everything from cars to free dry cleaning. While the Braves had drawn only 281,278 fans in their final year in Boston, they surpassed the mark after only thirteen home games in Milwaukee. That first year, they set a National League attendance record, as 1,826,397 saw the Braves play at the new County Stadium.

The Braves' popularity coincided with their emergence as one of the dominant teams in the National League. Adding Hank Aaron and a number of other key players to the roster, the Braves became perennial pennant contenders, finishing no lower than third in the standings from 1953 to 1960. Beginning the 1953 season in the bullpen, Burdette moved into the starting rotation when Johnny Antonelli and Vern Bickford were injured. Despite making only thirteen starts, Burdette finished the season with six complete games, a record of 15-5, and a 3.24 ERA; he was clearly ready to move into the team's rotation as soon as a spot opened up.

The Brooklyn Dodgers became the Braves' biggest rivals during this period, finishing one spot ahead of the Braves in the final standings in each of the Braves' first four years in Milwaukee in races that often went down to the final week. Twice Burdette found himself at the center of run-ins with one of the Dodgers' African American stars and was accused of being racially prejudiced—charges that he and his teammates vehemently denied. In August 1953 the Dodgers' Roy Campanella charged Burdette on the mound with

his bat in hand after he struck out, and the two men exchanged angry words. Both benches emptied, but no punches were thrown and play quickly resumed. After the game Jackie Robinson told the press that Campanella only charged the mound after Burdette had addressed him with a racial slur. A similar incident occurred three years later when, during pregame warm-ups, Jackie Robinson threw a baseball at Burdette's head (he missed) in response to being called a "watermelon." Burdette emphatically denied that his comment was racially motivated, claiming that he was joking about Robinson's "spare tire, not his race." The two spoke after the game, and Robinson was placated by Burdette's apology and explanation, and put the matter behind him.

Based on Burdette's stellar 1953 season as both a starter and a reliever, expectations were high for Burdette and the team coming into 1954. Burdette moved into the starting rotation when Antonelli and Bickford were traded. Throughout the season the Braves were plagued by injuries to position players and inconsistent pitching—at the All-Star break, the Braves' trio of Spahn, Burdette, and Bob Buhl were a combined 15-26 and the Braves sat fifteen games out of first place. Burdette had a strong second half, however, going 8-5 to end with a 15-14 record, with an impressive 2.76 ERA, second best in the National League. Despite Burdette's performance, the Braves were never able to seriously contend for the pennant. In 1955 Burdette finished with a 13-8 record and a 4.03 ERA. But once again, the team was never in contention, as the Dodgers simply ran away from the rest of the National League en route to their first World Series title.

During his time in the Minor Leagues and his first few years in the Majors, Burdette returned to Nitro each off-season. Lew and Mary's second child, Madge Rhea, was born on Christmas Day 1954. Her birth was particularly newsworthy because Lew helped deliver the baby in a police ambulance on the way to the hospital. Then the growing Burdette family began to split their time between Milwaukee and Sarasota, Florida, where Lew spent his off-seasons as a vice president in a local real-estate firm. The couple's third child, Mary Lou, was born only days before Burdette's masterful performance in the 1957 World Series. A third daughter, Elaina, was born in May 1960.

As his career was taking off, accusations that Burdette threw a spitball became increasingly common from opposing managers and players. Cincinnati manager Birdie Tebbetts (who became Burdette's manager on the Braves in 1961 and 1962) and National League president Warren Giles even went as far as separately commissioning motion pictures of Burdette pitching—though the films never showed that he was using the illegal pitch. Braves manager Fred Haney countered that his pitcher was not doing anything wrong, saying, "He's just a fidgety guy on the mound." Every time the charges arose, Burdette, along with his teammates and even the umpires, would deny them and emphasize the psychological advantage his nervous actions on the mound provided.

Burdette started on Opening Day in 1956 and cruised to a 6–0 win over the Chicago Cubs, allowing only five hits and one walk. The Braves battled Brooklyn and Cincinnati for the pennant until the final game of the season. With the Braves one game behind the Dodgers on the last day, Haney started Burdette against the St. Louis Cardinals needing a win plus a Pittsburgh win over Brooklyn to take the pennant. While Burdette led his team to a 4–2 victory, the Dodgers also won, and the Braves finished one game back. Although the season ended disappointingly, it was another successful season for Burdette. He led the league in ERA at 2.70 (Spahn finished second at 2.78) and in shutouts with six. His nineteen wins, against ten losses, were the fourth highest in the league, and he received a handful of votes for the Most Valuable Player Award.

Expectations were extremely high for the Braves going into the 1957 season. Burdette performed to his now-usual standards and was named to his first All-Star team. The Braves finally won the pennant, in large part by relying on their top three starters; Spahn, Burdette, and Buhl combined to finish with a record of 56-27. Burdette was 17-9 with a 3.72 ERA.

Spahn lost the World Series opener at Yankee Stadium to Whitey Ford; then Burdette pitched a complete game to defeat Bobby Shantz, 4–2. Taking the mound four days later with the Series knotted at two games apiece, Burdette shut out the powerful Yankees to lead the Braves to a 1–0 victory over his former Kansas City roommate Whitey Ford. When the Yankees won Game Six, it was assumed that Spahn would take the hill for the Braves in the finale. However, with Spahn unable to recover from a bout of Asian flu, Burdette, with only two days of rest, started against Don Larsen. Burdette pitched another complete-game shutout, holding the Yankees to seven hits and allowing only one walk as the Braves won, 5–0. Posting an ERA of 0.67, Burdette matched the greatest World Series pitching performances by being the first pitcher since Stan Coveleski in 1920 with three complete-game victories, and the first since Christy Mathewson in 1905 to have two shutouts. As the World Series MVP, Burdette was showered with awards and honors. He gave talks on the lecture circuit, made numerous appearances on television (including *The Steve Allen Show* and Camel cigarette ads), and even cut a novelty record, "Three Strikes and You're Out."

Burdette turned in another great season in 1958 as the Braves repeated as National League champions. At 20-10 he reached the twenty-win mark for the first time, and he tied with Spahn for the best winning percentage in the National League. His batting even improved significantly, as he finished the season with a .242 batting average and fifteen runs batted in. On July 10 against the Los Ange-

ALEX KUPFER

les Dodgers at their temporary home in Memorial Coliseum, Burdette smashed two home runs, one a grand slam off Johnny Podres. This was the second time in two seasons that Burdette had hit two home runs in a game—he had also done so against Joe Nuxhall in Cincinnati on August 13, 1957.

Facing the Yankees once again in the World Series, after a Spahn victory in the opener, Burdette cruised to a 13–5 victory in Game Two in which he hit a three-run home run in the first inning. But although Milwaukee jumped to a 3–1 Series lead, Burdette lost Games Five and Seven, giving up a combined ten earned runs and allowing the Yankees to battle back and win the title.

Vying for their third consecutive pennant in 1959, the Braves relied heavily on their core veterans. Eddie Mathews and Hank Aaron responded with stellar offensive seasons and were among four Braves, along with Burdette and Del Crandall, to finish in the top 12 of the MVP voting that season. Although Burdette had a career-high twenty-one wins, tying him with Spahn for the league lead, and appeared in both 1959 All-Star Games, he lost fifteen games, and the heavy workload took its toll as he gave up career highs in home runs (38) and hits allowed (312)—both the highest in the league.

Burdette was a central player in one of the most memorable games in history when he took the mound against Harvey Haddix and the Pirates on May 26, 1959, in Milwaukee. Haddix pitched twelve perfect innings, retiring thirty-six Braves in order, only to lose in the thirteenth inning when Joe Adcock drove in Felix Mantilla (who had reached on an error). While not as perfect as Haddix had been, Burdette turned in an excellent performance, giving up twelve hits and no runs. After the game a sympathetic Burdette phoned Haddix to tell him, "You deserved to win, but I scattered all my hits, and you bunched your one." Not sharing Burdette's sense of humor (or at least his timing), the taciturn Haddix hung up on him.

Tied with the Dodgers at the end of the season,

the Braves and Dodgers had a best-of-three playoff for the pennant. Down one game after Carl Willey lost the playoff opener, Burdette took a 5–2 lead into the bottom of the ninth inning of Game Two and seemed well on his way to tying the series. However, after giving up three straight singles to Wally Moon, Duke Snider, and Gil Hodges with no outs, Burdette was pulled and could only watch helplessly as the Dodgers drove in all three to send the game to extra innings. In the twelfth inning, facing reliever Bob Rush, the Dodgers' Carl Furillo drove in Gil Hodges to end the Braves' season.

After four seasons in which Milwaukee either reached the World Series or came up just short, it was becoming increasingly evident that the Braves dynasty was coming to an end, in large part due to the advancing age of many key players. Burdette performed as consistently as ever, though, going 19-13 with a 3.36 ERA in 275⅔ innings. On August 18, 1960, facing Philadelphia and former teammate Gene Conley, he pitched a no-hitter, defeating the Phillies, 1–0. Allowing no walks, Burdette faced the minimum twenty-seven batters. The only thing that kept him from a perfect game was hitting the Phillies' Tony Gonzalez with a pitch in the fifth inning. Gonzalez was subsequently erased by a double play.

After dropping to fourth place in 1961 (Burdette was 18-11), the Braves made a concerted effort to bring in younger players in 1962. Birdie Tebbetts, Burdette's former nemesis from Cincinnati, replaced Chuck Dressen as manager late in the 1961 season. Inconsistent all season long in 1962, Burdette was one of the victims of the youth movement, starting only nineteen games, about half his usual number. Then his thirteen years with the Braves came on June 15, 1963, when he was traded to the St. Louis Cardinals for Minor League pitcher Bob Sadowski and utility man Gene Oliver.

Although Burdette preferred to start, the Cardinals traded for him because they thought he could be used as both a starter and a reliever. His first game with the Cardinals, a complete-game victory over the New York Mets on June 18, seemed to suggest a return to form as a front-line starter. Burdette faced his former roommate Spahn when he faced off against the Braves on July 25. Once again going the distance, Burdette won, 3–1. But he struggled most of the season, posted only a 3-8 mark with the Cardinals, and against his wishes, he was increasingly relegated to long relief appearances.

Despite again being on a contending team, Burdette was unhappy with his role on the Cardinals and pushed for a trade. He was traded early the next season to the Cubs for pitcher Glen Hobbie, missing out on the Cardinals' 1964 World Series title. Reunited with Bob Buhl, Burdette was again given the chance to start. His struggles continued, though, and he finished the 1964 season with a 10-9 record and an ERA near 5.00. On May 30, 1965, Burdette was sold to the Phillies. Two starts he made in September represented his continuing struggles and inability to pitch for extended stretches. Against Cincinnati on September 5, he gave up six earned runs in one and two-thirds innings, and in his next start, the Braves scored five earned runs off him in two innings.

Released by the Phillies at the end of the season, Burdette spent his final two seasons in the Majors with the California Angels. Adding a knuckleball, Burdette had an excellent season in 1966 when he made fifty-four appearances out of the bullpen as a key middle reliever. He won his two hundredth game on July 22 when he entered a game against the Yankees with the score tied 4–4 and the Angels scored two runs to win, 6–4. But the resurgence was short-lived, and Burdette pitched in only nineteen games in 1967. His final Major League pitching appearance came on July 16, when he threw a scoreless eighth inning in a loss to the Minnesota Twins. In August the Angels sent him to their Pacific Coast League affiliate in Seattle, his first trip to the Minors since 1951. Burdette appeared in thirteen games in Seattle before being recalled in September; however, now forty years old and recognizing that he was not going to be used in any significant capacity, he retired.

After retiring, Burdette took a job scouting pitchers for the Central Scouting System. In 1969 and 1970 he split time between coaching pitchers in the Gulf Coast League and his hometown of Sarasota, where he tried his hand at various businesses, including a gas station and a nightclub. In 1972 he became the Atlanta Braves' pitching coach, and he was reunited with longtime teammate Eddie Mathews when Mathews was named manager halfway through the season. Burdette was excited about rejoining the Braves organization, saying, "They've always been my club. Everything good happened when I was with the Braves. They've been my life."[3] But he left the Braves after the 1973 season, going on to work in public relations for a Milwaukee brewery and then in cable television in Florida for twenty years until he retired.

Embracing his connections to the Braves, Burdette was a regular at old-timers' games and baseball functions over the years. He appeared on the Baseball Hall of Fame ballot for the first time in 1973, the year Spahn was elected. Burdette received votes in each of the fifteen years he was eligible, peaking in 1984 at 24.1 percent. In 1998 he was inducted into the Florida Sports Hall of Fame and in 2001 was elected to the Braves Hall of Fame.

Burdette died on February 6, 2007, in Winter Garden, Florida, after battling lung cancer. One of the most fitting tributes came from a longtime teammate, shortstop Johnny Logan, who summed up Burdette's career and personality by remarking, "I don't know if he threw a spitter or not. His ball would really sink. He was a hell of a battler. Whatever Spahnie did, Lew wanted to do better. They had that competition between them. Lew was a big star but he always gave Spahnie the credit."[4]

ALEX KUPFER

Chapter 7. **Timeline, April 14–April 30**

John Harry Stahl

April 14 — DODGERS 4, CARDINALS 0 — The Cardinals opened the season in Los Angeles against the 1963 world champion Dodgers. In front of a crowd of 50,451, Ernie Broglio faced Sandy Koufax, the 1963 National League Most Valuable Player. Koufax began the game by striking out two of the first three hitters he faced. The Dodgers scored one run in both the sixth and the seventh inning. They added two more in the eighth on Frank Howard's home run. Koufax pitched a complete game, striking out five with no walks.

The starting Cardinals lineup on Opening Day of the 1964 season:

Julián Javier, 2B
Dick Groat, SS
Bill White, 1B
Charlie James, LF
Ken Boyer, 3B
Carl Warwick, RF
Curt Flood, CF
Bob Uecker, C
Ernie Broglio, P

April 15 — CARDINALS 6, DODGERS 2 — Bob Gibson and Don Drysdale were the starting pitchers. Tied 1–1 after seven innings, the Cardinals broke the game open with five runs in the top of the eighth after two outs with consecutive singles by Ken Boyer, Johnny Lewis, Curt Flood, and Tim McCarver. Although Howard hit a solo home run in the ninth, Gibson pitched a complete game.

April 16 — CARDINALS 2, GIANTS 0 — Curt Simmons pitched a three-hit complete-game shutout and beat Bob Hendley. The Cardinals scored their two runs in the third inning on a single, an error, a run-scoring single, and a sacrifice fly.

April 17 — GIANTS 5, CARDINALS 4 (ten innings) — Acquired by the Cardinals in an off-season trade with the Mets, Roger Craig started the game. Before the game, Craig received special permission from the umpires to use a $3.95 hand warmer while on the mound because of the bitter cold. He helped his own cause with a double that drove in two runs in the second inning. Willie Mays hit a three-run home run in the bottom of the sixth. Entering the tied game (4–4) with the bases loaded and one out in the bottom of the tenth, Ron Taylor relieved Bobby Shantz. He struck out Jesus Alou for the second out. Taylor then walked Chuck Hiller to force in the winning run and end the game.

April 18 — CARDINALS 3, GIANTS 2 — With Flood moving to the lead-off spot in the batting order for the first time in 1964, Broglio pitched a complete game. The Cardinals' Boyer, Lewis, and Flood all hit home runs. Broglio worked out of potential trouble in both the eighth and the ninth inning.

April 19 — CARDINALS 6, COLT .45s 1 — With a 20 mph wind blowing from right to left, Gibson started and pitched a complete-game victory as he struck out eight hitters but walked seven. After Houston scored on a James error in the first, McCarver's single sparked a two-run Cardinal second inning. In the fifth, the Cardinals scored two more runs paced by a Flood double and a Dick

Groat single. Javier also hit a two-run home run in the seventh. A double play in the sixth with two on ended a Houston threat. Houston reliever Bob Bruce struck out the Cardinals in order on nine pitches in the eighth inning.

April 20 — COLT .45S 7, CARDINALS 1 — Ray Sadecki started his first game in 1964 against Turk Farrell. Scoring four runs on five hits in the second inning, Houston knocked out Sadecki. In the fourth, Houston scored three more runs on three hits. Boyer hit a solo home run in the ninth for the Cardinals' only score.

April 21 — No game scheduled.

April 22 — CARDINALS 7, DODGERS 6 — Simmons and Koufax started the Cardinals' home opener in front of a record 31,410 fans at Busch Stadium I. In the bottom of the first, after James hit a three-run home run, an arm injury forced Koufax to immediately leave the game. Craig relieved Simmons in the seventh with the score 6–5. Although the Dodgers scored a run in the eighth, Bill White's home run in the seventh provided the winning margin.

April 23 — DODGERS 7, CARDINALS 5 — Broglio and Drysdale started the game, but neither finished. For the Cardinals, Flood hit a double and a home run and drove in four runs. With the game tied 5–5 in the eighth, Cardinals reliever Taylor walked the Dodgers' first two hitters. Both runners scored on a Johnny Werhas single off Bobby Shantz. Ron Perranoski was the winner and Taylor took the loss.

April 24 — CARDINALS 3, COLT .45S 2 (11 innings) — Gibson and Don Nottebart started the game. Charlie James's single tied the score in the ninth inning. In the bottom of the eleventh, pinch hitter Phil Gagliano singled home Groat with the

winning run. In relief, veteran Lew Burdette was the winner. It would be Burdette's only win for the 1964 Cardinals.

April 25 — COLT .45S 4, CARDINALS 2 — Houston scored four runs in the ninth inning to beat the Cardinals. Craig and Farrell started the game. McCarver hit a two-run home run for the Cardinals in the seventh inning. In the ninth, Houston pinch hitter Mike White hit a two-run triple, driving in both the tying and go-ahead runs.

April 26 — COLT .45S 6, CARDINALS 4 — Simmons and Bill Owens started the game. Jim Wynn hit a two-run home run in Houston's first inning. In the bottom of the sixth, White hit a solo home run to give the Cardinals a 3–2 lead. With two runners on and Houston ahead (6–4) in the ninth inning, Hal Woodeshick got pinch hitter Jeoff Long to hit into a game-ending double play.

April 27 — No game scheduled.

April 28 — CARDINALS 8, METS 0 — Broglio pitched a complete-game shutout, allowing five hits and walking two. Al Jackson lasted only one and two-thirds innings and took the loss. Boyer went 3 for 4 (including a home run), scored two runs, and had two RBIS. Gagliano also drove in two runs.

April 29 — CARDINALS 4, METS 3 (11 innings) — Gibson started against Jack Fisher. Tim Harkness hit a three-run home run off Gibson in the first inning. After the first, Gibson allowed two hits and no runs until he was replaced in the eighth inning. Larry Bearnarth walked Long with the bases loaded to give the Cardinals the win. Shantz pitched shutout ball for the last two innings to get the victory.

Standings, April 30, 1964

	W	L	PCT	GB
Philadelphia Phillies	9	2	.818	—
San Francisco Giants	8	3	.727	1
Milwaukee Braves	8	5	.615	2
St. Louis Cardinals	8	6	.571	2½
Pittsburgh Pirates	7	6	.538	3
Cincinnati Reds	6	7	.462	4
Houston Colt .45s	7	9	.438	4½
Los Angeles Dodgers	6	10	.375	5½
Chicago Cubs	4	7	.364	5
New York Mets	2	10	.167	7

April 30 — No game scheduled. During the off day, Johnny Keane ordered extra hitting drills for everyone.

Cardinals April win-loss record: 8-6.
Cardinals year-to-date win-loss record: 8-6.

Chapter 8. **Doug Clemens**

John Harry Stahl

AGE	G	AB	R	H	2B	3B	HR	TB	RBI	BB	SO	BAV	OBP	SLG	SB	GDP	HBP
25	33	78	8	16	4	3	1	29	9	6	16	.205	.271	.372	0	1	1

Personable, intelligent, and soft-spoken, the athletic Doug Clemens also brought a key intangible to his professional baseball career: a dedication to improving his skills. He played parts of nine seasons in the Major Leagues with three teams: the St. Louis Cardinals, the Chicago Cubs, and the Philadelphia Phillies. Emerging from the Cardinals' farm system, Clemens started the 1964 season with the Major League club. In thirty-three games, he hit .205 with 6 walks and 16 strikeouts. On June 15 the Cardinals traded Clemens, Bobby Shantz, and Ernie Broglio to the Cubs for Jack Spring, Paul Toth, and future Hall of Famer Lou Brock.

Douglas Horace Clemens was born on June 9, 1939, in Leesport, Pennsylvania, about fifty miles northeast of Harrisburg, the state capital. He played a lot of football and baseball as a teenager, and played both sports at Muhlenberg High School, where his coach in both sports was his father, Lloyd "Scoop" Clemens.[1]

"He coached everything," Doug Clemens remembered. "He had the record for the most victories of all the coaches in the state of Pennsylvania."[2] Doug starred as a first baseman in baseball and a halfback in football. His father also scouted for the Phillies. In 1997 the Muhlenberg School District Hall of Fame inducted both father and son.

As an outstanding halfback, Clemens received a full football scholarship to Syracuse University. In his freshman year he suffered a serious injury to his right knee that required two operations.[3] Fortunately for Clemens, Syracuse switched his scholarship to baseball. He played first base and lettered in baseball in both 1959 and 1960.

Doug Clemens played thirty-three games for the 1964 Cardinals. On June 15 the Cardinals traded him and two other players to Chicago for Lou Brock.

During summer break, Clemens played baseball in the Basin League, a premier summer college baseball league, with teams in towns located along the Missouri River basin in the upper Midwest. Clemens played for the Mitchell (South Dakota) Kernels. Several Basin League alumni played in the Major Leagues, including Clemens's good friend pitcher Dave Giusti,[4] who pitched in the Majors for fifteen years.[5]

On July 21, 1960, after Clemens's junior year at Syracuse, Cardinals scout Benny Bergmann signed him to a contract.[6] He received $40,000 in bonuses and salary spread over four years.[7] The Cardinals sent the six-foot, 180-pound Clemens to their Minor League team in Billings, Montana, in the Pioneer League (Class C). He immediately tore up the league, hitting .389 in thirty-nine games,[8] and in October the Cardinals brought him up to the Major Leagues. On October 2, the last day of the regular season, the twenty-one-year-old Clemens made his first Major League appearance when he was sent in to play right field in the sixth inning against the San Francisco Giants in Candlestick Park. "I was very, very nervous," Clemens remembered. "A screaming line drive came at me and I made a diving catch. Not only were the 28,000 fans clapping from the catch, but my knees were clapping from being so nervous!"[9] The season over, he returned to Syracuse University. Several years later, he achieved both bachelor's and master's degrees in physical education.

In 1961 the Cardinals initially sent Clemens to their Tulsa team in the Double-A Texas League. In ninety-seven games, Clemens hit .342. In July the Texas League managers selected him to play in the league all-star game.[10] Anxious to see how he would fare against better competition, the Cardinals then promoted Clemens to their Charleston team in the Triple-A International League, where he hit .310 in fifty-two games. Again the Cardinals called him up toward the end of the season. He played in six games, and in twelve at bats he got two hits. His first Major League hit, a pinch-hit single, came off the Dodgers' Ed Roebuck on September 23.

Clemens started the 1962 season with the Cardinals. Although he had less than two years of professional experience, manager Johnny Keane considered him ready for immediate duty.[11] Before the season The Sporting News's baseball writers picked him as the "likeliest player to improve" on the Cardinals.[12]

St. Louis began the 1962 season with seven outfielders, including future Hall of Famer Stan Musial. Of the seven, Clemens had the least Major League experience. Within this crowded environment, he played in parts of forty-eight games, starting fifteen and batting .237. In mid-July, the Cardinals sent him to the Atlanta Crackers in the International League, where he stayed for the remainder of the season.

Shortly before he was sent to Atlanta, Clemens and his wife, Ginny (they were married in 1961), became parents of a son, Theodore Williams Clemens—named after Ted Williams. Not only did he and his wife like the name Ted, but Williams had always been his boyhood baseball idol.[13] (As of November 2008, Doug and Ginny had three children and seven grandchildren.[14])

At Atlanta, Clemens helped the Crackers on the team's march to victory in the Junior World Series. After languishing in sixth place for most of the season, the Crackers gained a playoff spot by finishing in third place, won the league championship by defeating Toronto and Jacksonville, then won the Junior World Series against Louisville of the American Association in seven games, with Clemens driving in the decisive run in two of the games. The 1962 Atlanta team included Ray Sadecki, Tim McCarver, and Phil Gagliano, all teammates on the 1964 Cardinals.[15]

As the 1963 season began, Clemens again faced stiff competition for an outfield spot with the Cardinals. Over the winter the team had acquired slugging outfielder George Altman from the Chicago Cubs. In late March, Clemens was sent to Atlanta. Playing mostly in the outfield but also appearing in thirty-four games at first base, he hit .278 and matched his career high in home runs (13). He made an unassisted double play when he made a difficult catch of a liner in left-center and ran to second base to double off a base runner who had left the base thinking the ball would fall in.[16] When the Crackers' season ended, Clemens returned to the Cardinals and played in five games at the end of the season.

Clemens started the 1964 season with the Cardinals, sharing time in left field and right field with Charlie James, Johnny Lewis, Carl Warwick, and Mike Shannon. Before being traded to the Chicago Cubs in the Lou Brock deal on June 15, he played in thirty-three of the Cardinals' first fifty-eight games. He hit .205 with 1 home run and 9 RBIs.

The trade to Chicago upset Clemens, particularly when he saw several of his former teammates in the Cardinals' Minor League system (McCarver, Sadecki, and Shannon) play in the 1964 World Series. In his five years, he played in ninety-three games for St. Louis and batted .217.

With the Cubs, Clemens appeared to be moving into a regular spot in right field, but his progress was abruptly interrupted when he broke the little finger on his left hand when he was hit by a throw while trying to break up a double play. He went on the disabled list on August 27 and did not return until September 27. In fifty-four games for the Cubs, he batted .279, for an overall .252 batting average.

Clemens won the Cubs' starting right-field job in spring training of 1965 by hitting .406. But when the season began, he started slowly. His batting average stood at .234 by the end of May. From the beginning of June to the end of August, it ranged between .228 and .266. He tailed off in September and October and finished the year at .221 for the 72-90 eighth-place Cubs. But he reached personal highs in games played (128) and hits (75). He had two four-hit games, one against the Cardinals.

"To be honest," he recalled in 2004, "the Cubs gave me a great opportunity in 1965. It was my best opportunity to play on a regular basis. I wish the results were better. I just did not produce. The pitchers at the major-league level have better control, regardless of what the count is. They nibble and get pitches that may be a little off the plate. They get to know you and determine what your weaknesses might be. I just wasn't getting the hits. But I did the best I could."[17]

In January 1966 Clemens was traded to the Philadelphia Phillies for outfielder Wes Covington. For Clemens it was a homecoming. His family lived within driving distance of Philadelphia. They could watch him play. He always loved the Philadelphia area and followed the Phillies as a youngster.

During his three seasons with the Phillies (1966–68), Clemens was primarily a pinch-hitting specialist. In 1966 he pinch-hit a Major League–leading fifty times in his seventy-nine game appearances and had a .256 batting average.[18]

"As everyone knows," he reflected in 2004, "pinch hitting is one of the toughest jobs in the business. You either do or you don't. You get up to the plate once every three days and that's it."[19]

For the Phillies, Clemens was a tireless off-season speaker at fan-related gatherings promoting both the team and baseball in general. On the field in 1967, he was unable to duplicate his 1966 hitting performance, and his batting average dropped to .178. He pinch-hit in fifty-nine of his sixty-nine games played. His bench role wore him down both physically and mentally. "Being a fringe player," he commented, "sitting on the bench . . . that's the hardest job in baseball. It gets a person down mentally . . . not to mention how it physically affects your timing."[20]

At the beginning of 1968, the Phillies sent Clemens to San Diego in the Pacific Coast League, where he played in 104 games and hit .248. In mid-August the Phillies recalled him, and he played in enough games to qualify for a Major League pension.

Clemens thought about playing in 1969 but decided against it. A friend had offered him a job that allowed him to stay close to his family. He thrived in the business world and became the vice president of sales and marketing for General Machine Products. He retired in 2004.

JOHN HARRY STAHL

Clemens spent parts of nine years in the Major Leagues. He played in 452 games and batted .229. He appeared as a pinch hitter 185 times.

Reflecting on his baseball career, Clemens told a baseball biographer, "I'd like to be remembered as someone who gave it his best shot, who tried to excel for the benefit of the team and himself."[21]

Chapter 9. **Roger Craig**

Richard L. Shook

AGE	W	L	PCT.	ERA	G	GS	GF	CG	SHO	SV	IP	H	BB	SO	HBP	WP
34	7	9	.438	3.25	39	19	12	3	0	5	166	180	35	84	4	2

Roger Craig and "split-finger fastball" will forever be linked in baseball history. It was Craig's work teaching first Jack Morris and then Mike Scott how to throw the pitch that gave the former right-handed pitcher lasting fame. "People think I invented that," Craig said. "I did not. Bruce Sutter did. I just found a way to teach it and it worked out."

A split-finger fastball is cousin to the forkball, the difference being that the latter is set way back in the hands near the webbing while the former is closer to the fingertips. "The forkball is deeper and you can't throw it as hard," Craig said. "The key to it is you throw it like a fastball. You don't try to turn it over or cut it." The pitcher uses the same motion, arm slot, and arm speed as he does for his fastball, but the ball dips as it nears the plate. The pitcher has to figure out what release point works for him, but its effectiveness comes because the batter's brain says a fastball is coming and by the time he figures out that it isn't, it's too late. The ball dives under the bat.

"The first guy I really worked on was Milt Wilcox," Craig said. "He was a gutty pitcher." Wilcox came to the Majors with an overpowering fastball, but a sore shoulder prompted him to go into the trickery business. He got by with a sharp slider, but Craig wanted to tinker. "Let's try something else," he told Wilcox. "You have to have pretty good hands, and he did not, but it became a good pitch for him.

"But with Jack [Morris], it became a great pitch. Any pitching coach would be glad to have him. He was kind of tough to handle at times," Craig said. "Jack used a blooper pitch, but he telegraphed it.

Starting and relieving for the 1964 Cardinals, Roger Craig appeared in thirty-nine games and posted a 7–9 record with a 3.25 ERA. He won Game Four of the 1964 World Series in relief.

He had big fingers so we worked on it between starts. He had a good one but he didn't want to throw it during a game. He said, 'Naw, I like my change-up.' But I asked him, 'For one game, let's just try it.' So the first six innings he had about eight strikeouts and he ended up having one of the best around."

Craig said Randy O'Neal, who pitched in the Majors from 1984 to 1990, "had one of the best I ever saw. It was so good he could hardly get it over the plate. Juan Berenguer [whose big-league career stretched from 1978 to 1992] had a good one, so did Aurelio Lopez [1974–87]. I taught Mike Scott [of Houston], and a lot of my pitchers for San Francisco threw it."

That secured Craig's reputation as a pitching guru. He went on to manage the San Francisco Giants for seven seasons, taking over in September 1985.

Craig enjoyed a successful career as a pitcher, helping the Brooklyn Dodgers to their first World Series win, in 1955, and also pitching for the 1959 World Series champion Dodgers—the franchise having relocated to Los Angeles—and being traded to St. Louis in time to help the Cardinals win the World Series in 1964.

Oh, and along the way Craig also gained a measure of notoriety for losing twenty games in consecutive seasons for the 1962–63 New York Mets.

"I played and coached and managed in the World Series. That's quite a feat. Not many guys have done that," Craig said.

He came to the Tigers after two years of managing the San Diego Padres, 1978–79. "Sparky [Anderson, Detroit manager] called me. He wanted me to come up and be his coach. So I did," Craig recalled.

After the Tigers fell just short in 1983, when most of the team felt it was a better outfit than the league champion Baltimore Orioles, general manager Bill Lajoie made a late spring-training trade that solidified the Tigers, acquiring left-handed reliever Willie Hernandez from the Philadelphia Phillies to take over from Aurelio Lopez as Detroit's closer.

"I had a really good feeling in spring training. I started doing a diary. I did notes every day. Vern [Plagenhoef, who covered the Tigers for Booth Newspapers at the time] saw me doing it and said, 'You ought to write a book.' So I did." The book, *Inside Pitch: Roger Craig's '84 Tiger Journal*, was snapped up by Detroit fans hungry for anything that celebrated their world championship team.

"We got off to such a great start," Craig said of the Tigers' renowned 35-5 record out of the gate in '84. "We had a balanced team. At every position we had maybe not a superstar, but a good ballplayer. Lance [Parrish] was a great catcher and leader. We had a pretty good pitching staff. Berenguer and Rozey [Dave Rozema] could start and relieve. But Willie was the key. And Sparky did a great job. I've been around a lot of them and he probably was one of the greatest. But it wasn't an easy year for him. He worried. Every time we lost a couple of games he'd say, 'Toronto is going to catch us.' But he was right on top of everything. He was married to baseball, 24/7. He'd stay up all night watching games. He was easy to work for, though. He'd give you a job to do and let you do it."

The magic ended after the World Series win in 1984, though. Craig asked for a raise, didn't get it, and decided his time in Detroit had come to an end. In his book Craig said he decided to retire. But baseball had other ideas.

"In the middle of the [1985] season, Al Rosen called me," Craig said. "He asked if I was interested in becoming his manager. Bob Lillis was the manager with Houston then and I told Al I wouldn't take his job. Al told me, 'You won't be taking his job, I'm moving to the San Francisco Giants and they're about to lose 100 games.'"

In San Francisco in 1985, Craig made Will Clark his first baseman and Robby Thompson his second baseman, even though neither player had any Triple-A experience. The infusion of young talent and energy bumped San Francisco from one hundred losses to a brief visit to first place before fading to third at the end of the season. Under Craig, who made "humm baby" a baseball catchphrase during this era, San Francisco won its division in 1987, then won the 1989 pennant, getting swept in the so-called Earthquake Series by Oakland. "I spent seven years there," Craig said. "It was a great city and a lot of fun. I enjoyed managing there." Craig retired after the 1992 season, giving his advice when asked.

"I helped Bob Brenly when he managed the Arizona Diamondbacks," Craig said. "I did it for three years and he ended up giving me a World Series ring—paid for it out of his own pocket, I found out later. He said, 'You trained me to become a Major League manager.' It's nice to know people don't forget you. I helped Tram [Alan Trammell, who managed Detroit from 2003 to 2005] a little bit in spring training, too. Since then, I've been retired. I've played a lot of golf."

Craig returned to Detroit on September 27, 2009, to help the Tigers celebrate the twenty-fifth anniversary of the 1984 season despite learning the day before that he had prostate cancer. "I'm 79 and they told me I might die of something else before I die of cancer. If I went today I'm one of the luckiest guys who ever lived. I played, coached, and managed baseball. I'd have done it for nothing, but it kept my family going."

Family was always big for Craig, one of ten children raised by John Thompson and Mamie Irene Craig in Durham, North Carolina. Roger Lee Craig was born on February 17, 1931.

"My dad was a shoe salesman; he was on the road a lot," Craig said. "Raising ten kids, I don't think he made more than $50 a week in his life. I was number eight. My mom worked at Watts Hospital in Durham. She was like the housemother at a nursing home. My parents never really had a lot. It's still amazing they raised ten kids with the little money they made. But we never felt we were poor. We never complained about it."

That's where Craig got his rock-solid roots. He said his parents were the biggest influences on his life.

Craig's road to the mound started at shortstop. Although he was six feet four, big for a shortstop even now and huge by the standards of the 1940s and '50s, Craig was slender and was only the number two pitcher on his high school team.

"We had an outstanding pitcher, Julius Moore. We ended up being the two best in the state [North Carolina]. He signed with the Yankees but broke his wrist in a car accident and never pitched much higher than B ball [there was Class A, B, C, and D in those days, as well as Double-A and Triple-A]. But he had a major-league arm in high school. He'd strike out 17, 18 a game. He had better control than I did."

Craig was followed in high school by what is still known as a bird dog, a person who gets paid sort of on a freelance basis to scout amateur prospects. His bird dog reported to Frank Rickey, the brother of the boss of the Brooklyn Dodgers, Branch Rickey. It was Frank Rickey who signed Craig for the Dodgers out of high school.

In 1950 Craig was sent to Class D Valdosta of the Georgia-Florida League. He pitched twenty-three games for Valdosta, turning in a 14-7 slate and a 3.13 earned run average, which got him promoted to Newport News of the Class B Piedmont League, where he pitched six more games, losing once and being tattooed for a 7.11 ERA.

Craig spent all of the 1951 season with Newport News. He went 14-11 with a 3.67 ERA in thirty-eight games, twenty-eight of them starts. Then he was drafted, serving his obligatory two years in the army.

"I was lucky," he said. "I was pretty good in basketball and I played both baseball and basketball at the Fort Jackson [South Carolina] post. I was a little disappointed. All my buddies went to Korea, but in those days you did what they told you. I wanted to go." He married Carolyn Anderson in November 1951. The couple had four children.

Future Major Leaguers Ed Bailey (Cincinnati), Frank House (Detroit), and Haywood Sullivan (Boston) caught Craig in those years and kept telling him his stuff was good enough to get him to the Majors.

"Then in 1954 I broke my left elbow. I tripped,"

RICHARD L. SHOOK

Craig said. "I talked the doctor into not putting a cast on it and went to spring training the next day."

Al Campanis, the Dodgers' scouting director, saw Craig doing one-handed push-ups and came over to yank on his left arm. Nice move, Al; it put Craig out of action until midseason.

Even with his truncated season, he wound up splitting time with three teams in 1954, working twenty games back at Newport News (8-3, 2.50) before moving up to Class A Pueblo of the Western League, where he pitched in six games (1-1, 9.64), and then working two innings in three games for Elmira of the Class A Eastern League, giving up six runs, two of them earned.

Craig opened 1955 with Triple-A Montreal of the International League and was 10-2 with a 3.54 ERA before being summoned to help the Brooklyn Dodgers win the pennant and then their first World Series.

"I was 10-2 in July when they called me up," he said. "I beat the Yankees in the fifth game of the World Series that year."

Craig pitched twenty-one times in 1955, starting ten games and going 5-3 with a 2.77 ERA, and the following season he was a regular member of the rotation.

"I hurt my arm in the last game the Brooklyn Dodgers ever played. It was raining and sleeting in Philadelphia when I pitched. Today I know it was a rotator cuff, but this was 1957. I had to learn how to pitch all over again.

"One of best things that ever happened to me came in 1958," Craig said, although the good fortune came in a most roundabout way.

"My arm was hurting so bad in spring training they sent me to St. Paul," he said. "The manager, Max Macon, pitched me every fourth day to see if I could build up arm strength." Craig struggled through twenty-eight games for St. Paul of the Triple-A American Association in 1958, going through a 5-17 season with a 3.91 ERA. On top

of that, he was still having arm problems, so near the end of the season Macon gave Craig shock treatment.

"He told me, 'We got a chance to win this thing so you'd be better off to go back home to get your education. You're never going to pitch in the big leagues again.'" Craig said. That lit a fire under Craig, who tossed a couple of complete games down the stretch.

Craig pitched in fourteen games (6-7, 3.19 ERA, six complete games, and a shutout) for Spokane of the Pacific Coast League in 1959 but was brought up to what had become the Los Angeles Dodgers, where he posted a 2.06 ERA, missing the ERA title because he was 1⅓ innings short of the 154 needed to qualify for the title (one inning pitched per game the team played); the Giants' Sam Jones led with a 2.83 mark. Craig showed his effectiveness by winding up in a seven-player tie (Johnny Antonelli, Bob Buhl, Lew Burdette, teammate Don Drysdale, Sam Jones, and Warren Spahn) for the league lead with four shutouts. He clearly held his own in excellent company.

"They had all those great players," Craig said. "I saw Jackie Robinson, Duke Snider, Pee Wee Reese, Roy Campanella, Don Newcombe, Jim Gilliam. . . . It was like an All-Star team and I said, 'I don't really belong here.'

"It was very special, a great experience. I was just fortunate enough to be on the only world championship they won [in Brooklyn]. The Los Angeles Dodgers, that was a different club," he said. "We still had Gil Hodges and Snider, but Pee Wee was a coach. Maury Wills came up and was an outstanding player. We had Gilliam and Wally Moon, who was famous for what they called 'moon shots,' home runs over the left-field fence in the Los Angeles Coliseum. We had Don Drysdale and Sandy Koufax, Stan Williams, and Clem Labine. We beat the Chicago White Sox in the World Series [in 1959]."

Craig was used more and more out of the bullpen in 1960 and '61, then was allowed to be taken by the New York Mets in the 1962 expansion draft. He gained a certain amount of fame for going 10-24 and 5-22, losing eighteen straight decisions over the 1962 and '63 seasons.

"I lost a lot of ballgames," he said, "but I had twenty-seven complete games in those two years. I started the first game the New York Mets ever played."

The St. Louis Cardinals traded for Craig after the 1963 season. Although he was only 7-9 in thirty-nine games, nineteen of them starts, he posted a 3.25 ERA and helped the team come from seventh place in late July to gain a berth in the World Series, where the team defeated the last great New York Yankees team of that era; Craig won Game Four in a relief effort.

Craig worked long relief for Cincinnati in 1965 and pitched a handful of games for Philadelphia the following season before his arm gave out. He also returned to the Minors, working six games for Seattle of the Pacific Coast League in 1966.

The Dodgers hired Craig to scout in 1967 and in 1968 made him the manager of their Albuquerque farm club in the Double-A Texas League, where he also pitched his last pro game.

After terms as a Major League pitching coach for San Diego and Houston, Craig was hired by the Padres to manage their team in 1978. He guided San Diego to its first over-.500 finish in the franchise's history, at 84-78, but a slip back in 1979 to 68-93 cost him his job.

That was when Anderson rescued him to teach Detroit's young pitchers.

Chapter 10. **Mike Cuellar**

Adam J. Ulrey

AGE	W	L	PCT.	ERA	G	GS	GF	CG	SHO	SV	IP	H	BB	SO	HBP	WP
27	5	5	.500	4.50	32	7	6	1	0	4	72	80	33	56	1	1

Mike Cuellar was a four-time 20-game winner for the Baltimore Orioles, and the winner of 185 Major League games. He could also lay claim to being one of the most superstitious players in base-ball. "He had a routine and please don't inter-fere with it," remembered a teammate, Paul Blair. "He would walk to the mound the same way, same steps. Step on the mound. Go to the front of the mound, and the rosin bag couldn't be on there. Somebody had to come and kick the rosin to the back of the mound or he wouldn't get on the mound. Then he'd walk off the mound the same way. He would come in the dugout the same way; make the same number of steps to the water cooler. Everything had to be the same every time he went out there."[1] Before taking the field, Cuellar sat on the "lucky end" of the training table, wearing a gold-chain medallion, while the trainer massaged his arm. He took batting practice on the day he pitched even after the designated hitter rule was in place. When the team traveled, he wore a blue suit. Whether his superstitions helped his pitching can be debated. But there is no doubt that for most of his eight years with the Orioles, Cuellar was one of the most effective pitchers in the Major Leagues. A nasty screwball, developed mostly in winter base-ball in the Caribbean, saw to that.

Miguel Angel Cuellar Santana was born on May 8, 1937, in Santa Clara, Las Villas prov-ince, Cuba. His family, which included four boys, worked in the sugar mills. Cuellar did not want to follow in his family's footsteps, so he enlisted in the Cuban army for seventy pesos a month because he knew he could play baseball on Saturdays and Sundays. He pitched for Cuban dictator Fulgencio

Promoted in June from the Minors, Mike Cuellar posted a 5–5 record with a 4.50 ERA in thirty-two games. His pitches included a nasty screwball.

Batista's army team in the winter of 1954–55. He hurled a no-hitter that season and was heavily fol-lowed by Cuban and American scouts.

After his discharge, the thin (six feet, 165 pounds) left-hander pitched in the summer of 1956 with a Nicaragua Independent League team, fin-ishing 10-3 with a 2.95 earned run average. His manager, Emilio Cabrera, immediately brought him to his Almendares team in Cuba for the 1956–57 winter league season. He pitched in relief (1-1, 0.61 ERA). Before the 1957 season, he was signed

45

by the Cincinnati Redlegs, who optioned him to their Cuban Sugar Kings (often called the Havana Sugar Kings) affiliate in the International League. He impressed Sugar Kings manager Nap Reyes, who said, "I have coached a lot of pitchers, here in Cuba and in the U.S., but none so quick to learn as this boy. I have put him in the toughest spots in relief to test him out. He has a good curve but he doesn't have to vary much. He makes the left-handed batters look pretty bad when he does."[2]

Cuellar made a sensational pro debut with Havana in 1957 against Montreal, striking out seven men in a row in 2⅔ innings of no-hit relief. He led the league with a 2.44 ERA and posted an 8-7 record in forty-four games, sixteen of them starts. After another winter with Almendares (4-5 with a 3.03 ERA), he returned to Havana in 1958 and pitched 220 innings, with a 13-12 record and a fine 2.77 ERA. That winter he pitched again for Almendares, which won the Caribbean Series title. Cuellar was 5-7 with a 3.79 ERA.

In 1959 Cuellar began the season with the Redlegs but was ineffective in two relief appearances: four innings, seven earned runs on seven hits, for a 15.75 ERA. He was returned to Havana and did not see the big leagues again for five years.

He found the International League much more to his liking, and he hurled 212 innings, finishing with a 10-11 record but a 2.80 ERA. The Sugar Kings wound up the regular season in third place but upset Columbus and Richmond to win the International League championship, and then captured the Junior World Series title by defeating the Minneapolis Millers of the American Association in seven games. (The decisive seventh game was decided in the bottom of the ninth inning.)

The Junior World Series was notable for more than baseball. In Cuba, Batista had just been overthrown by Fidel Castro's forces, and the games in Havana were played in a fortress-like atmosphere. Because of winter-like weather in Minneapolis, the last five games were all played at Havana's Gran Stadium. Nearly three thousand soldiers were at the stadium for the seventh and deciding game, many lining the field and others stationing themselves in the dugouts, their rifles and bayonets clearly evident. "Young people not more than 14 or 15 years old were in the dugout with us, waving their guns around like toys," recalled Millers pitcher Ted Bowsfield. "Every once in a while, we could hear shots being fired outside the stadium, and we never knew what was going on."[3] Millers manager Gene Mauch reported that the soldiers were not above trying to intimidate the Minneapolis players. "Our players were truly fearful of what might happen if we won," said Mauch. "But we still tried our hardest, figuring we'd take our chances."[4] Cuellar started Game Two and pitched seven and one-third innings, giving up four earned runs in a no-decision. He pitched in relief in the next two games, picking up a win in Game Four, before getting knocked out early in a Game Six loss. He did not pitch in the final, won 3–2 by the Sugar Kings.

From 1960 through 1963, Cuellar bounced around the Minor Leagues and the Mexican League, playing for six different teams with not a lot of success. After Castro began tightening travel into and out of Cuba, Cuellar chose to play winter ball in Venezuela or Nicaragua rather than return to his native land. By 1964 his contract had been passed from Cincinnati to Detroit to Cleveland to St. Louis, but the twenty-seven-year-old seemed no closer to a return to the Major Leagues.

After five consecutive seasons with under-.500 win-loss records in the high Minors, Cuellar turned things around in 1964. Ruben Gomez, a winter league teammate, persuaded him to start throwing a screwball, the pitch that changed Cuellar's life. He practiced the pitch all winter and spring, and during the 1964 season he threw it 30 percent of the time. For Triple-A Jacksonville, Cuellar logged a 6-1 record and a 1.78 ERA into mid-June. The St. Louis Cardinals called him up to the Majors on June 15, and he got into thirty-two games the rest of the season, starting seven. The August 26 game was special for Mike. When hitless Gene Freese popped weakly to shortstop for the last out, Cuellar finally had his revenge after five and a half seasons. "I hit a pinch-hit home run with the bases loaded off Cuellar in 1959 and that blow sent him back to the minors for five years," Freese said. "He's a lot faster and has come with quite a scroogie."[5] Cuellar finished 5-5 but did not see action in the 1964 World Series, in which the Cardinals defeated the New York Yankees.

Cuellar went to Puerto Rico to pitch that winter, and he finished 12-4 with a 2.06 ERA for Arecibo. At one point he had a stretch of twenty-seven scoreless innings and threw four shutouts. He went to spring training hoping to land in the Cardinals' rotation but instead was optioned back to Jacksonville after Opening Day. After dominating the International League for ten weeks (9-1 with a 2.51 ERA), he was traded in an all-pitchers deal on June 15 to the Houston Astros with Ron Taylor for Hal Woodeshick and Chuck Taylor. He spent the rest of 1965 with the Astros, finishing 1-4 with a 3.54 ERA in twenty-five appearances.

At nearly twenty-nine years old, Mike had finally reached the Major Leagues to stay. By 1966 he was using his screwball between 50 and 60 percent of the time, and he had added a curve ball that made his fastball appear even sharper. Astros pitching coach Gordon Jones taught Cuellar the curve. Cuellar had been releasing his curve with almost a slider motion but without the good slider break. Jones showed him how to get rotation on the ball by bending the wrist in toward himself and popping the ball loose with the overhand motion.

On June 25, 1966, Cuellar beat the Cardinals and recorded a team-record fifteen strikeouts, running his record to 6-0 with a 1.73 ERA. He ended the season by throwing six complete games in a row, including his first Major League shutout, a 2–0 victory over the Pirates on August 29. He fin-ished 12-10 with a 2.22 ERA that was second best in the National League behind Sandy Koufax.

The next season, 1967, Cuellar did it all again, this time with a bit better luck in run support. His ERA rose to 3.03, but he finished 16-11 in 246 innings, including sixteen complete games. He pitched two shutout innings in the All-Star Game in Anaheim. After the season the Astros told Cuellar he couldn't pitch winter ball, which did not sit well with the star. At the time many Major League players played in the winter, and to the Latin players in particular it was an important part of their culture. Cuellar blamed his arm trouble the following season to his not playing in the winter. In 1968 he was just 8-11 (for a last-place team), though with a fine 2.74 ERA in 170 innings.

Apparently overreacting to his win-loss record, the Astros traded Cuellar and Minor Leaguers Elijah Johnson and Enzo Hernandez after the season to the Orioles for infielder-outfielder Curt Blefary and Minor Leaguer John Mason. Cuellar was having some off-field difficulties, mainly a struggling marriage and related financial problems. Baltimore General Manager Harry Dalton's scouts told him that his off-field issues could be rectified. Scout Jim Russo raved about Cuellar and recommended his acquisition. When Cuellar came to Baltimore, the Orioles helped him get rid of his debt, and Cuellar was soon divorced and remarried. He became immensely popular with his Baltimore teammates. "Cuellar was a wonderful person," remembered manager Earl Weaver.[6]

With the Orioles, the combination of his great left arm and the tremendous Orioles team made Cuellar one of baseball's biggest pitching stars. In his first year with Baltimore, 1969, he put up a 23-11 record with a 2.38 ERA, and he shared the Cy Young Award with Denny McLain of the Tigers. Cuellar set Orioles pitching records for wins and innings pitched (291) and tied the club mark with eighteen complete games. He threw five shutouts. In the first game of the American League Championship Series against the Minnesota Twins, Cuellar allowed two earned runs in eight innings in a game the Orioles won in the twelfth. In the World Series, he outdueled the New York Mets' Tom Seaver to win the first game, 4–1, but his seven-inning, one-run performance was not enough in Game Four, which the Mets won in the tenth. The Mets won the Series in five games, but Cuellar had a stellar 1.13 ERA in sixteen innings.

Cuellar's Baltimore teammates called him Crazy Horse for his weird sense of humor and especially his strange superstitions. Since he had pitched well in 1969 spring training with coach Jim Frey warming him up, only Frey was permitted to catch the Cuban southpaw's pregame tosses the rest of the year. Only Elrod Hendricks—nobody else—could stand at the plate for part of that period, simulating a batter. Cuellar would not finish warming up until the opposing starter had finished. He never stepped on the foul line when he took the field; he always picked the ball up from the ground near the mound himself. He would not warm up before an inning with a reserve while his catcher got his gear on—Cuellar waited for the catcher to get behind the plate. As he kept winning, the importance of ritual only grew.

Cuellar's ERA rose to 3.48 in 1970, but his run support and his remarkable durability allowed him to finish 24-8, with 297⅔ innings pitched and 21 complete games. He typically started slowly, posting a record of 8-5 with a 4.34 ERA through the end of June. As the weather heated up, Cuellar caught fire; in the final three months he went 16-3 with a 2.78 ERA, completing 14 of his 21 starts. Cuellar was joined in a great rotation by Dave McNally (24-9) and Jim Palmer (20-10). The trio made 119 starts and pitched 899 innings. Their 68 victories are the most by three teammates since the 1944 Tigers (also 68).

Paul Blair later said, "With Cuellar, McNally, and Palmer, you could almost ring up 60 wins for us when the season started because each of them was going to win 20. And with Cuellar and McNally, you never knew they were winning 10–0 or losing 0–10. They were the same guys. They were two really great left-handers, and the reason they were so great was they didn't have the talent Palmer had. They didn't have the 95-mile-per-hour fastball Palmer had. They had to learn to pitch, know the hitters, hit corners, and they did it. And they never complained. Those kind of guys, you just die for. You break your neck to go out there and win for them."[7]

In the first game of the 1970 ALCS against the Minnesota Twins, the Orioles gave Cuellar a 9–1 lead (in part, based on a grand slam he himself hit off Jim Perry in the fourth) but he failed to finished the fifth, though he left the game with a 9–6 lead. Reliever Dick Hall shut down the Twins the rest of the way, beginning an Orioles sweep. Cuellar next got the ball in Game Two of the World Series but could not survive the third inning in a game the Orioles pulled out with a five-run fifth inning over Cincinnati. In Game Five he allowed three hits and three runs in the first before shutting the door, going all the way in a 9–3 victory for his only World Series title, the second for Baltimore.

Cuellar again won twenty games in 1971, finishing 20-9 with a 3.08 ERA. This time he, McNally, and Palmer were joined by a fourth twenty-game-winner, Pat Dobson. The Orioles thus became the second team to have four twenty-game winners, joining the 1920 Chicago White Sox. Cuellar was 13-1 with a 2.88 ERA at the All-Star break, and pitched two shutout innings for the American League in the All-Star Game. It was the third of his four All-Star selections. Cuellar cooled off in the second half of the season, but the Orioles easily won their third consecutive division title. He defeated Oakland's Catfish Hunter with a 5–1 six-hitter as the Orioles swept the ALCS. He lost his two World Series starts, against the Pirates, allowing all five runs in a 5–1 loss in Game Three and then falling short in a tough 2–1 loss to Steve Blass in Game Seven. For his career, Cuellar was 2-2 with a 2.61 ERA in five World Series starts.

In 1972 the Orioles' run of championships ended, though it was mostly the offense that fell off. Cuellar pitched 257 innings with a 2.57 ERA, but slipped to 18-12. After a slow start, he finished 16-8 after June 1, with fifteen complete games, including six straight at one point. The Orioles finished third in a tight American League East.

During a May 26 game with the Indians, Cuellar's superstitious behavior was on full display. After Cleveland left fielder Alex Johnson caught Boog Powell's fly ball to end the third inning, he slowly jogged the ball back to the infield. Timing his pace with Cuellar's approach to the mound, Johnson tossed the ball to the pitcher, but Cuellar ducked just in time, and the ball rolled free. Helpfully, the batboy retrieved the ball and threw it to Cuellar. Once more he dodged the ball, which dribbled toward first baseman Boog Powell. Momentarily forgetting his teammate's habits, Powell threw it squarely at Cuellar, who had no choice but to catch the ball in self-defense. Disgusted but undeterred, Cuellar tossed it to the umpire and asked for a new ball. The umpire obliged, and Cuellar again sidestepped the ball, which trickled past him and stopped right at the feet of his second baseman, Bobby Grich. At long last Grich rolled the ball to the mound, and Cuellar picked it up, satisfied now that no evil spirits had invaded his place of business.

Cuellar started slowly again in 1973 (4-9 with a 4.00 ERA through July 7) before again turning it on in the second half of the season (14-4, 2.64 the rest of the way). He was now thirty-six years old and there were concerns that perhaps his days as an elite pitcher were behind him. Not yet, as manager Earl Weaver again got 267 innings out of Cuellar, including seventeen complete games, en route to his 18-13 final record as the Orioles returned to the postseason. In Game Three of the ALCS against the Oakland A's, Cuellar hooked up with Ken Holtzman in a great pitching duel. Through ten innings, Cuellar allowed just three hits and one run, but he gave up a game-winning home run to Bert Campaneris in the bottom of the eleventh inning to lose 2–1. Holtzman pitched all eleven innings for Oakland and tossed a three-hitter. The Athletics prevailed in the series, 3 games to 2, and went on to win the World Series over the Mets.

Cuellar returned to the twenty-game circle in 1974, finishing 22-10 with a 3.11 ERA, twenty complete games, and five shutouts. He was now thirty-seven but showed no signs of aging. His performance earned him the Game One assignment against the A's in the ALCS, and he pitched eight strong innings to earn the 6–3 victory. His next start, in the fourth game, was not nearly as successful—he had to be relieved in the fifth after allowing just one hit but walking nine. After walking in a run, the first run of the game, he was relieved, and the Athletics won the game, 2–1, to capture the series. It was Cuellar's twelfth and final postseason start, finishing his log at 4-4 with a 2.85 ERA.

Cuellar finally began showing his age in 1975, dropping to 14-12 with a 3.66 ERA, his highest since 1964. He still threw seventeen complete games and had five shutouts, but he did not have the consistency that had been his hallmark during his Oriole years. After seven years with the Orioles, he had 139 victories, just shy of a twenty-win average. The following season, the thirty-nine-year-old finally imploded, finishing just 4-13 with an ERA of 4.96. Earl Weaver was used to Cuellar's slow starts, in a season and also in a game, and he was patient with the pitcher long after others thought he needed to make a change. He finally pulled his beloved left-hander at the beginning of August and put him in the bullpen.[8]

Cuellar was released in December 1976 and was picked up a month later by the Angels, whose general manager was old friend Harry Dalton.

But after a terrible spring training and two forgettable regular-season appearances (three and one-third innings, seven runs), he was released by the Angels. Cuellar's Major League career had come to an end, just shy of his fortieth birthday. He continued to pitch in the Mexican League and in winter ball, before finally calling it quits after the 1982–83 winter league season. He was a few months short of his forty-fifth birthday.

Cuellar remained occasionally active in baseball, serving as a pitching coach in the independent leagues and for many years in Puerto Rico. He was an instructor with the Orioles during the last years of his life, and showed up often for team functions and reunions.

Cuellar was a healthy man for many years when he was suddenly diagnosed with stomach cancer in early 2010. He died on April 2 in Orlando, Florida, where he had lived for several years. He was survived by his wife, Myriam; his daughter, Lydia; and his son, Mike Jr. The latter pitched for five years in the Toronto Blue Jays farm system but did not rise past Double-A ball.

"He was like an artist," Palmer said after Cuellar died. "He could paint a different picture every time he went out there. He could finesse you. He could curveball you to death or screwball you to death. From 1969 to '74, he was probably the best left-hander in the American League."

Chapter 11. **Dave Dowling**

Rory Costello

AGE	W	L	PCT.	ERA	G	GS	GF	CG	SHO	SV	IP	H	BB	SO	HBP	WP
21	0	0	.000	0.00	1	0	1	0	0	0	1	2	0	0	0	0

Caught up in the numbers and derailed by injuries, this promising southpaw appeared in just two games in the Majors. "I didn't get a cup of coffee," he joked in 2010. "I got a demitasse!" Yet the bright and scholarly man had mapped out his direction. After his final pro season in 1968, he turned his hand to dentistry, which he had begun to study in 1967. Dave Dowling, DDS, became a practicing orthodontist in 1973.

David Barclay Dowling was born on August 23, 1942, in Baton Rouge, Louisiana. When he was very small, his mother, Regina Moffett, divorced Dave's father (a man named Gill, the boy's surname at birth). She remarried a man named Clarence "Tad" Dowling, a salesman whose family came from Washington State. The Dowlings moved northwest when Dave was about two years old. There were two other children in the family, an older brother named Robert and a sister named Molly. Their new home was Chehalis, about eighty miles southwest of Seattle.

Tad Dowling (who also owned and flew several small planes) had been a catcher in high school. He played catch with young Dave every day. "From when I was a little kid," said Dowling in 2010, "his big thing was control. He started me off throwing from thirty feet and got me to hit the mitt, then he moved me back to forty-five feet." The lad displayed great ability in Little League, Babe Ruth, and American Legion ball.

At Chehalis High School, Dave was a three-sport star. In basketball the sharpshooting forward led the Bearcats to the 1960 Class A state championship and was a unanimous choice for the state all-star team. In football he was the quarter-

In mid-September 1964 the Cardinals called up Dave Dowling from the Minor Leagues. The promising southpaw pitched one shutout inning in the second to last game of the season.

back and punter. "I enjoyed all the sports," said Dowling, "but I was better at baseball." Dave was also the student body president and an academic standout. In May 1960 the *Centralia Chronicle* wrote that he and two other young men had "already laid a foundation for success in future life . . . [with] almost identical scholastic and athletic records." Reading and chess remained his hobbies off the field as a pro.

The New York Yankees had hoped to sign

Dowling out of high school, as had the Red Sox, but he decided on college instead. Several schools recruited him, and he chose the University of California over Stanford, in part because Cal had won the NCAA basketball title in 1959. Dave played baseball and basketball for the freshman teams in 1961. That summer, he played for Lethbridge, Alberta, in the independent Western Canada League. Several other future big-leaguers were there, including Tim Cullen and John Boccabella. Dowling recorded eighteen strikeouts twice and seventeen in another game.[1]

Dowling had a strong first season on the varsity with the University of California Golden Bears in 1962. He struck out ninety-two men in fifty-seven innings. By that time he had focused on his primary sport. "Baseball season started in February and basketball didn't end until mid-March. I stuck with baseball. The basketball players were also too good."

One of his classmates and fellow hurlers at Berkeley, Larry Colton, described Dave in his 1993 book Goat Brothers as "a wacky lefthander . . . whose curveball fell off the earth." Colton (who pitched one game for the 1968 Phillies) added that Dowling had already turned down a $25,000 bonus offer from St. Louis.[2] The San Francisco Giants also made Dave an offer in September 1961, but he stayed in school. "I threw BP for the Tacoma Giants, and they offered X, but my dad said no—if we don't get this amount, close to six figures, we won't sign." Indeed, newspaper accounts show that by 1962, his value was reportedly $100,000.

The Western Canada League was no more in 1962, so instead Dowling played summer ball with a local semipro team in Washington, the Lewis County Pavers. He struck out twenty in one game against the Santa Maria Indians, a strong semipro squad from California. As a junior for the Golden Bears in 1963, though, "it was not a not a very good year. I spent a lot of time in different labs [his major was chemical engineering]. I was concerned about my grades."

In the summer of 1963, Dave acted on a tip from a high school friend who lived in Fairbanks. He went to play baseball with the Alaska Goldpanners.[3] Since it began play in 1960 the team has sent two hundred men to the Majors—including such notables as Tom Seaver, Dave Winfield, and Barry Bonds. Dowling became the first alumnus on this long list—and it wasn't surprising, based on his performance (11-3, 217 strikeouts in 116 innings, and an ERA of 0.85). "It was a real good summer up there. Everything fell into place, I felt like I was in a groove."

Although he'd already received much attention, Dowling got a bigger showcase when the Goldpanners went to Wichita, Kansas, to play in the 1963 National Baseball Congress (NBC) World Series. Dave won his first three games, and though he lost in the semifinals, he struck out fifty-five in thirty-two innings while allowing just ten hits and two earned runs. The NBC honored him as "Sandlotter of the Year."[4]

A little over a week later, Cardinals scout Bill Sayles, a former Boston Red Sox pitcher, signed Dowling and Nelson Briles of Santa Clara University "for what a club spokesman termed a sizable bonus."[5] "I was offered some pretty good money, and this time I decided to take it. St. Louis also offered to help pay my tuition. I wanted to continue with school because I'd left after my junior year."

When Dowling and the other Minor Leaguers reported to camp in the spring of 1964, they found that Eddie Stanky, the director of player development, also sought to build their character. "Everybody had to go to church with Eddie Stanky!" Dave recalled.

Dowling started the 1964 season with the Cards' Double-A club, Tulsa. He was 7-1, with a 2.59 ERA in fourteen games for the Oilers, starting thirteen times and displaying "unusual poise

RORY COSTELLO

and polish as well as good stuff." Clyde King, then a pitching coach in the St. Louis farm system, called him "the finest prospect I've seen in 21 years of baseball." King was impressed with the young pitcher's use of a change-up to complement his fastball and curve.[6] Dowling said of King in 2010, "He could really build you up, give you confidence. I really liked him."

Dave himself offered various insights in the same *Sporting News* feature that quoted King. He reaffirmed his decision to get higher education, saying that he didn't think he'd have been any further along if he had signed out of high school. He found the difference between semipro and Organized Baseball to be "the business-like attitude . . . there just isn't any margin for error." He also described retiring the great Al Kaline on a 3-1 curve ball in an exhibition game between the Cardinals and Tigers at Detroit on June 1.[7]

Dowling won promotion to Triple-A Jacksonville on June 24. At the higher level of play, he was 3-3, with a 4.69 ERA in fifteen games (twelve starts). "Harry Walker was the manager. He wasn't a big person for rookies, and I was one of the youngest guys there. One time I made a mistake and gave up a homer to Jake Gibbs, a lefty batter, and you should have heard the expletives coming out of the dugout!" Dave also remembered veteran Joe Morgan, the future Red Sox manager, swearing a blue streak. "He was getting dunning letters meant for the other Joe Morgan, the one who's a broadcaster now."

On August 10, with the Cardinals in fifth place, seven and a half games out, Branch Rickey issued his "Memo of Surrender." If it had carried any weight, Dave might have been called up as part of a sweeping change.[8] Instead, the Cards stood pat and went 34-17 the rest of the way. Dowling pitched the game that clinched the International League pennant for the Jacksonville Suns.

On September 19 the Cardinals brought up Dave along with another lefty who became a three-hundred-game winner in the Majors: Steve Carlton. Carlton would not make his big-league debut until the following April — but Dave did appear in the second-to-last game of the season on October 3. The Mets were ahead 15–5 when the rookie replaced Ray Washburn for the top of the ninth inning. He got the first two outs and retired the side after Joe Christopher and Jim Hickman singled.

Dave recalled, "I was throwing batting practice every day. I looked at Steve Carlton and said, 'Who's it going to be?' Howie Pollet, the pitching coach, said, 'Dowling, get loose.' It was a Saturday Game of the Week, so my folks were watching back in Washington." If Dave hadn't been able to finish the mop-up job, Carlton was next. In 1968 (he was still talking to the media then), Steve recalled, "I was the last man left in the bullpen and I couldn't even see Dave Ricketts, who was warming me up, because I was so nervous."[9]

Dowling added his recollection of Carlton. "He was a really introspective guy. He was ambidextrous and could throw nearly as well right-handed. He was also one whale of a pool player. Be careful of guys who have their own cue!"

Shortly after the Cards won the '64 World Series, Dave came in for praise from Sheldon "Chief" Bender, director of player development. "For a first-year pitcher, Dowling showed extreme poise and pitching know-how. He could help the Cardinals next year. He has a good curve, which he can get over the plate when he is behind. His fast ball is good enough. If his control continues to get better, he's got a good chance."[10]

Dowling started the 1965 season with the Cardinals but did not get into a game. On May 11, facing the requirement to cut the big-league roster down from twenty-eight men to twenty-five, St. Louis waived him. The Cubs claimed him for $8,000. Under a rule then in effect, "Dowling was a first-year player who could not be farmed out without asking waivers which, in this case, were irrevocable."[11] The Cardinals had to choose among Carlton, Briles, and Dowling—and Dave was the odd man out. In 1968 Cardinals manager Red Schoendienst said, "Dowling actually was further ahead at the time because he knew more about pitching and his control was better than Carlton's. But we felt that Carlton could throw harder and could become consistent with his fast ball."[12]

Dowling played in the Texas League in 1965, going 14-7 with a 2.77 ERA for the Dallas–Fort Worth Spurs. He went to the Triple-A Tacoma Cubs in the Pacific Coast League in 1966. His record (10-8 with a 3.42 ERA) was deceptive; Dave said, "That was a last-place club, and there were at least three blown saves. I was a second-team All-Star."

Dowling pitched just one more game in the Majors, a complete game for the Cubs on September 22, 1966, a little short of two years after his debut. He pitched well, beating Cincinnati 7–2 at Wrigley Field. His lifetime marks remained at 1-0 with a 1.80 ERA, though. Earlier that summer, while serving two weeks in the Army Reserves, he had hurt his shoulder in a freak accident while moving wall lockers upstairs. Dave's torn rotator cuff led him to retire a couple of years later, after he had been traded back to the Cardinals organization. In 2010 he joked, "I threw my hardest, and the umpire called me for delay of game."

Inspired and encouraged by NFL quarterback Gary Cuozzo, who also went to dental school during his playing career, Dave had already begun his transition. After earning his doctor of dental surgery degree from the University of Tennessee in 1971, he then got his master's in orthodontics from Northwestern University in 1973. For more than twenty years, he practiced in Longview, Washington, on the border with Oregon between Chehalis and Portland.

Dowling and his wife, Linda (née Summers), were married on December 12, 1970. They raised three daughters: Jennifer, Rebecca, and Mollie. All became successful professionals, but Rebecca inherited the family's aeronautic gene, becoming the navy's first female Top Gun pilot.

In 1996 Dave and Linda moved to Arizona. Over the next decade, he established and sold group practices in the Tucson and Phoenix areas. The Dowlings then moved again, to Manteca, California. "I took about two years off, but I got really bored. I went back to work. I enjoy working with kids, watching them flower."

For a while during the '70s, Dave gave a hand to the pitching coach at Lower Columbia College (located in Longview). "Bud Black went to school there for a couple of years." He also coached some girls' fast-pitch softball as his daughters were growing up. Dowling remains a baseball fan today; his background in chess and on the mound show through. "The mental aspect, trying to outguess the managers—that's the part of the game I really enjoy."

Chapter 12. **Harry Fanok**

Rory Costello

AGE	W	L	PCT.	ERA	G	GS	GF	CG	SHO	SV	IP	H	BB	SO	HBP	WP
27	0	0	.000	5.87	4	0	1	0	0	0	7.2	5	3	10	0	2

One of baseball's eternal debates is naming the hardest-throwing pitcher of all time. A dark horse in the field is Harry "The Flame Thrower" Fanok. The righty appeared in just sixteen big-league games for St. Louis in 1963–64—but his fastball branded the memories of those who saw him.

Just ask Joe Morgan. The former Red Sox manager was Fanok's roommate with the Atlanta Crackers in 1962 and '63. Back then he was a veteran in the Cardinals chain as the prospect was poised to break through. In his flavorful Boston accent, "Walpole Joe" said in 2007, "He threw the ball as hahd as anybody I ever saw. There's no one today throwing the ball as hahd, even [Joel] Zumaya with the Tigers. You heard me—no one."

Signed as a third baseman in late 1958, Fanok was converted to the mound, where he had also starred as a youth. He proceeded to lead his league in strikeouts for three straight years (1960–62) as he rose through C, Double-A, and Triple-A ball. And while he wasn't as scary-wild as Steve Dalkowski, he piled up the walks too. In the Minors, the righty averaged 8.8 ks and 4.8 bbs per nine innings during his first four years after he was converted. (A switch hitter, he still always loved swinging the bat.)

In his two brief stints with the Cards, Fanok struck out thirty-five and walked twenty-four in thirty-three and one-third innings. He picked up wins in his very first two outings, and it seemed as if great things lay ahead. Canny observers such as Branch Rickey, Preston Gómez, and Eddie Sawyer certainly said so that year. But manager Johnny Keane meddled with the hurler's motion. Keane

Nicknamed "The Flame Thrower," Harry Fanok pitched seven innings for the 1964 Cardinals. Sent to the Minors to improve his curve, he injured his arm.

had compared Harry to Sandy Koufax and tried to remold him with a similar over-the-top style.

Unsettled, Fanok was sent back to Atlanta, where he learned a curve ball from veteran master Sam Jones. He was dominating the International League and dazzled the Yankees in an exhibition game on August 19 as the IL All-Stars shut out the World Series champs in Buffalo. Of the six men he faced, he struck out Yogi Berra, Héctor López, and

Joe Pepitone. What's more, he was really becoming a pitcher, not a thrower.

Then came August 26. On a steamy southern night, with a no-hitter and nine strikeouts through five innings, arm problems struck suddenly after a rain delay. Harry didn't appear again that season, and he was never the same.

As the 1964 season started, Fanok—still highly touted—made the big club again. Though he appeared in just four games in April and early May, the Cardinals still awarded him a one-eighth World Series share (without a ring). But nursing the sore shoulder caused a mental block and a critical hitch in his delivery. His control gave out entirely, with over seven walks per nine innings during the rest of '64 as he went from Triple-A to Single-A to "find himself" (he was recalled to St. Louis in September but did not get into a game). His BB/9 ratio ballooned to more than ten the next season. Harry gave up pro ball after sitting out the year in 1966 and a comeback attempt with the Cincinnati Reds chain in '67.

Harry Fanok lives by himself today in Chardon, Ohio, a pleasant town in the northeast corner of the state. He retired from his longtime job as a tool and die maker in 2005. He was divorced twice, with one daughter. He enjoys hobbies he has pursued for decades, duck hunting and photography, along with Cleveland Cavaliers basketball. After his second divorce, in the mid-1970s, he performed with a local band at local bars, clubs, and county fairs. Recently he has taken up his guitar again. He remains fit and vigorous—by any standards, not just those of a man who turned seventy in 2010. In addition to tending his yard and gardens, Fanok collects and splits all his own firewood.

Harry tells his own story with verve. When he first expressed interest in helping with his bio, he seized on the idea of describing his youth and playing ball with his neighborhood friends. Whippany, New Jersey (where Harry Michael Fanok III was born on May 11, 1940), has been a Ukrai-

nian cultural center since 1908. In 1922 Maxim Fanok—Harry's great-uncle—helped obtain land for the community's Ukrainian Catholic church. Harry vividly remembers a bygone rural patch of the Garden State. The village where he grew up, Malapardis, has been consumed by development and now lives on in just a few place names.

After just a few e-mails, an autobiography (originally published in full on the SABR BioProject in 2007) emerged. The course was plain to see: step back and just weave the installments together as Harry delivered them. Like the logs he uses to heat his home, his words still have the bark on. And they retain the rock 'n' roll pep of the young Elvis fan who played guitar and drums and sang.

Below are the pitcher's reminiscences about the championship season.

"I don't recall pitching too much after the injury. I know they sent me back down to the Instructional League after the '63 season ended. I threw in games down there, but I know I didn't have it. John Keane came down there to watch me on the sidelines, I recall. I could still throw hard, but with pain and much less control. They asked me how the arm was, and I would say it's okay. There would be no pain in the beginning of a warm-up, then something strange would take place. I developed a HITCH! Either my brain would not let me throw free and easy, or the injury was actually the physical culprit. At any rate, I had to get from mild throwing to some serious heat. That was the problem. That was a bridge that I was unable to cross. When I did, occasionally, the ball flew hard, but with pain. Now I had to get used to throwing with pain. It got worse the longer I threw.

"In 1964, I recall spending many hours in the training room during spring training down in St. Pete. The pain was still there, but I figured I could get through it. I can't recall any games that I pitched in the '64 spring training. That is weird because I made the team that year. So I must have impressed someone. Or maybe the Cards figured

RORY COSTELLO

they owed me for having a good year in '63, then getting injured. Who knows? I'm thinking that I must have had something left in the tank.

"I do recall a few games in which I pitched, though. One game in particular comes to mind. We were playing the Colt .45s [his first appearance, on April 20]. I don't remember the circumstances in how I came into the game, but, the longer I pitched, the numbness in my arm would bring out the hitch that I developed. Now I was becoming very conscious of this hitch. And, instead of just throwing the ball naturally without thinking, I had to think my delivery out each time I threw the ball. Bad news!

"These were bad times for me. Now, even during batting practice, I would be tossing the ball in the outfield with someone, and they would mention to me that I was hitching. I was really becoming aware of it more and more. When I would get into a game, I'd have to grit and bear it. As I have said previously, I could throw the ball mildly in the beginning, but to get to full bore, that was the problem. Another way to explain it would be where a pitcher warms up in three stages: soft tossing till he gets to midrange, throwing to where he reaches full throttle. I could not do the midrange throwing. That really brang out this hitch that I developed.

"An example of this was evident in a day game against the Pirates, I think [his last Major League appearance, on May 3]. A ball was squibbled back to me. All I had to do is throw the ball to first base. I had plenty of time. I've done it a thousand times before. But with my arm and the way it was, I threw the bitch away. Can you imagine that?? This was the way it was in '64. I always thought to myself as to why I even made the club that year. I could not use what I had learned the year before when I really learned how to pitch. As far as I was concerned, I would continue to fight through this, hoping the arm would return.

"I'm sure the Cards were disappointed. When I got the word that I was being sent down, I recall asking the clubhouse guy as to where my long sleeved sweatshirts were. Butch told me that Bing Devine told him to remove them as they were club's property. I confronted Devine about the situation, and he promptly jumped all over my ass. So, that was that. I moved on to Jacksonville, I think [and from there to Raleigh]. But, wherever I played, the bad arm was always there.

"But I guess it's like the old saying goes—the Lord giveth, and the Lord taketh away. Baseball was my life growing up. It was all our lives—the kids from Malapardis and Whippany, NJ! I'll never forget those days. Nor will I forget all my teammates and the guys I got to know playing against them. So, in closing, I would have to say that I was blessed. And, although it was a short amount of time, I played major league ball!!!!"

Chapter 13. Curt Flood

Terry W. Sloope

AGE	G	AB	R	H	2B	3B	HR	TB	RBI	BB	SO	BAV	OBP	SLG	SB	GDP	HBP
26	162	679	81	211	25	3	5	257	46	43	53	.311	.356	.378	11	9	5

Playing center field and leading off for most of the season, Curt Flood batted .311 and led the NL with 211 hits. He later pioneered in baseball's labor matters by challenging baseball's reserve clause.

Curt Flood was a vital cog in the 1964 Cardinals' world championship run, but that achievement may have been all but forgotten in light of Flood's subsequent role in the arrival of free agency for baseball players.

Curtis Charles Flood was born in Houston, Texas, on January 18, 1938. His parents, Herman and Laura Flood, moved the family to Oakland, California, when Curt was a toddler. He was the youngest of six children, two of whom, sister Rickie and a brother, Alvin, were the product of his mother's first marriage. Curt's other siblings were Barbara, Herman Jr., and Carl. Curt's relationship with Carl would prove to be particularly complex over the course of their lives. As children

they were both athletic and artistic. In addition, Carl was incredibly intelligent and charismatic, but as Curt later said, his brother "treated his gifts as if they were a curse. He took awful chances and paid awful prices."[1] Carl's behavior caused problems for Curt years later.

Flood said of his childhood, "We were not poor, but we had nothing. That is, we ate at regular intervals, but not much."[2] Initially settling in a middle-class, mostly white neighborhood in East Oakland, they later moved into a less affluent neighborhood in West Oakland in order to get away from the growing hostility of local whites after World War II. Herman found steady work during the war in various defense-related industries around Oakland, and Laura ran a small café and mended parachutes to make ends meet. After the war they both worked in menial jobs at Fairmont Hospital.

When he was nine years old, Curt joined the Juniors Sweet Shop team in a local midget league. The team was managed by George Powles, a white man who coached baseball in local amateur leagues as well as at Hoover Junior High School and, later, McClymonds High. Over the years Powles developed a significant cadre of talented baseball players who went on to play Major League baseball.[3] He also treated his players with great kindness. Flood's interactions with Powles began to change the way he viewed the relationship between whites and blacks: "If I now see whites as human beings of variable worth rather than as stereotypes, it is because of a process that began with George Powles."[4]

Jim Chambers, Flood's art teacher in junior high school, was impressed with his skills with a brush and pencil and attempted to develop in him a broader appreciation for his talents. "Before I met him, I sketched and painted but had not the slightest sense of the larger significance of art," Flood said. "He taught me art not as technique alone but as one of the great resources of the human spirit."[5] As a teen, Curt created the artistic backgrounds for school proms and plays. He also earned extra money designing storefront window displays and advertising signs for a furniture store owned by Sam Bercovich. Later on in St. Louis, Flood received recognition for oil portraits of Cardinals owner August A. Busch Jr. and Martin Luther King; the King portrait was presented to King's widow, Coretta Scott King, who years later gave it to President George W. Bush to hang in the White House.[6] Teammates and other players around the league also commissioned family portraits from Flood and called him "Rembrandt." Flood later explained, "Baseball and painting make a good balance. Baseball is virile. It's rough and tough. Painting is sensitive; quiet. It's an outlet to overcome tension."[7]

Flood played for Powles on the Bill Erwin American Legion team while he was still in junior high. He attended McClymonds High School in West Oakland for a year before transferring to Oakland Technical High School. A biographer, Brad Snyder, asserts that the move was engineered by George Powles and Sam Bercovich so that Flood could continue to play for the American Legion team. Curt played third base and hit .440 for the team in 1954; in 1955 he was named captain, moved to center field, hit .620 in twenty-seven games, and helped lead the team to the state championship. In addition to his American Legion play, Curt played for semipro teams coached by Powles in the Alameda winter league.[8]

Powles was a bird-dog scout for the Cincinnati Redlegs (as they were called then). After Flood graduated from high school in 1956, he signed a contract with the Redlegs for $4,000 (no bonus) and an invitation to spring training camp in Tampa, Florida. If Curt had been shielded to some extent from the ugliness of racial hatred while growing up in California, his bubble burst when he was ushered out of a side door of the Redlegs' training camp hotel and hustled across town to Ma Felder's boarding house, where the black players were housed.

"Until it happens you literally cannot believe it. After it happens, you need time to absorb it. . . . Rules had been invoked and enforced. I was at Ma Felder's because white law, white custom and white sensibilities required me to remain offstage until needed. I was a good athlete . . . but this incidental skill did not redeem me socially. Officially and for the duration, I was a nigger."[9]

Flood was assigned to Cincinnati's team in High Point–Thomasville of the Class B Carolina League for 1956. He played well despite the subjugation of his humanity to the social mores of the times. He could not have the same accommodations as his white teammates; he could not eat in restaurants with his teammates but was forced instead to go to the back door for "service" or to wait on the team bus until a teammate brought him food. He could not use the restroom in the gas stations where the team bus stopped; instead, the bus would stop on some deserted stretch of highway where Curt could disembark and "wet the rear wheel." Fans around the league expressed their displeasure at the appearance of a black man on the diamond as well: "One of my first and most enduring memories is of a large, loud cracker who installed himself and his four little boys in a front-row box and started yelling 'black bastard' at me. I noticed that he eyed the boys narrowly, as if to make sure that they were learning the correct intonation."[10]

His teammates and manager weren't any more supportive. "Most of the players on my team were offended by my presence and would not even talk to me when we were off the field. The few who were more enlightened were afraid to antagonize the others. The manager, whose name mercifully escapes me, made clear his life was already sufficiently difficult without contributions from me. I was completely on my own."[11]

Flood's acclimatization to his situation was difficult at first. It was not uncommon for him to return to his room late at night after a game and cry at the treatment he received. Thoughts of quitting entered his mind, but as he said later, "What had started as a chance to test my baseball ability in a professional setting had become an obligation to measure myself as a man. These brutes were trying to destroy me. If they could make me collapse and quit, it would verify their preconceptions. And it would wreck my life. . . . Pride was my resource. I solved my problem by playing my guts out. . . . I completely wiped out that peckerwood league."[12]

Flood led the league with a batting average of .340. He set a team record with 29 home runs and a league record with 133 runs scored. He finished second in runs batted in with 128. He also covered a lot of ground in the outfield, leading the league with 388 putouts. He was named the league's Player of the Year and earned a late-season call-up to the Redlegs. He made his Major League debut as a pinch runner on September 9, 1956, in St. Louis. Three days later, in his only official at bat of the season, he was struck out by Johnny Antonelli of the New York Giants. The highlight of his stint with the big club was the opportunity to be on the same field as one of his heroes, Jackie Robinson. After the season, Flood briefly played winter ball in the Dominican Republic.

Flood started the 1957 season with Cincinnati but soon was sent to the Savannah team of the Class A South Atlantic League. The Redlegs moved him to third base at Savannah, believing it might speed his development. Flood hit .299 in Savannah and led the league in runs scored with ninety-eight. He was named to two league all-star teams. He also committed forty-one errors at third base. He endured many of the same indignities he had suffered at High Point–Thomasville, if not more.

Called up to Cincinnati again at the end of the 1957, Flood went to bat just three times, but he got his first Major League hit, a home run off the Chicago Cubs' Moe Drabowsky. He played winter ball after the season in Maracaibo, Venezuela, with instructions to learn how to play second base. Then in December he received a telegram from Cincinnati telling him he had been traded to the St. Louis Cardinals. (He was part of a five-player deal.) If Flood had any trepidation about the trade, it was swept away when he received a contract for $5,000 for the 1958 season.

Flood began the 1958 season with the Cardinals' Double-A team in Omaha. After hitting .340 in thirteen games, he was called up. He took over as the starting center fielder under manager Fred Hutchinson and hit well for the first couple of months. A thirteen-game hitting streak between June 22 and July 3 raised his batting average to

TERRY W. SLOOPE

.331. As the season wore on, however, Flood's productivity dropped and he finished the year with an average of .261 and 50 runs scored in 121 games. It was a good, but not a great, rookie season. Defensively, he was already receiving accolades for his prowess in center field.

Flood married Beverly Collins in February 1959. She already had two small children, Debbie and Gary. Curt adopted her two children, and although he and Beverly had three children of their own (Curtis Jr., Shelley, and Scott), the marriage was not a happy one. The disharmony in his marriage, along with the financial pressures of providing for a family of seven, became a constant source of stress for Flood that became worse after they divorced in 1966.

The Cardinals fired Fred Hutchinson before the end of the 1958 season. According to Flood, the new manager for 1959, Solly Hemus, was a racist who "did not share the rather widely held belief that I played center field approximately as well as Willie Mays. He sat me on the bench . . . [and] acted as if I smelled bad. He avoided my presence and when he could not do that he avoided my eye."[13] In 1959 Flood again played in 121 games for the Cardinals but had less than half as many at bats (208) as he had in 1958 under Hutchinson. He batted just .255 and fell to .237 in 1960.[14] Hemus was fired in July 1961 and was replaced by third base coach Johnny Keane.

As much as Flood suffered under Hemus, he blossomed under Keane. In early August, Keane installed him as the full-time center fielder, and he and the Cardinals played well for the rest of the season. Flood finished the season with a .322 average in 335 at bats. His offensive performance became more consistent as he recognized the need to cut down on his swing and learn to hit to all fields.

From 1962 through 1968, Flood enjoyed seven seasons of offensive excellence. He batted .302 during that time, including five seasons over .300

with a career high of .335 in 1967. He had 200 hits in 1963, and in 1964 he tied Roberto Clemente for the National League lead in hits with 211. He was an important cog in the Cardinals' world championship teams in 1964 and 1967, as well as their National League championship in 1968. He was named to three All-Star teams. His defensive play was remarkable as well. In 1966 he handled 396 chances without an error. At one point he played 226 consecutive games without an error. He won the Gold Glove Award six times during this period. The August 19, 1968, cover of *Sports Illustrated* pictured Flood making a leaping catch at Wrigley Field, with the caption "Baseball's Best Center Fielder." In 1965 he and Tim McCarver were named team cocaptains, a title Flood held until 1969.

Flood's personal life during this period had its ups and downs. In 1962 he met Johnny and Marian Jorgensen, an older white couple from Oakland's Montclair district with whom he bonded closely. Johnny Jorgensen owned an industrial engraving plant and gave Curt an opportunity to learn the trade. Flood excelled at it; he and Johnny made plans for Curt to join the company as a partner when his playing days were over. The Jorgensens also opened their house to him, shared their extensive library with him, and even allowed him to live with them for a time. They spent many nights talking about politics and social issues. About first meeting the Jorgensens, Flood said, "I have relived that evening many times. . . . It was . . . an emotional discovery bordering on the spiritual. . . . What it boiled down to was that the Jorgensens and Flood loved each other on sight. . . . The Jorgensens' wide interests aroused an intellectual hunger in me."[15]

His family life was more unsettled. Beverly sued for divorce after the 1963 season and was granted an initial decree in March 1964.[16] Later that spring, they began a process of reconciliation; Beverly became pregnant with their last child in

May and they were remarried that fall after the 1964 World Series. The reconciliation did not last, however. Beverly sued for divorce again after the 1966 season and was awarded custody of the children and $1,400 a month in alimony and child support, in addition to one-half of their community property.[17]

To make matters worse, Johnny Jorgensen was killed in late 1966 by a mentally unstable intruder. Curt was so concerned about Marian that he asked her to move to St. Louis to live with him and take care of his affairs. Marian moved to St. Louis after the 1967 season.[18]

After his divorce Flood moved back to St. Louis and took up residence in a fashionable area. As one publication noted, "Off the field, he was the darling of the St. Louis fans. They marveled at his ability as a fine painter; admired his expensive clothes, and gossiped about his jet-setting exploits. Curt Flood was a man with the world in his hands."[19] He became involved in a number of personal relationships, some more serious than others; among those relationships was one with actress Judy Pace.[20]

Flood's increasing popularity led to the creation in 1967 of Curt Flood Associates, Inc. It was run by Bill Jones, a business promoter and an acquaintance of Flood's. A Curt Flood Photography studio opened with the goal of getting a significant piece of the school picture business in the St. Louis area, selling photography studio franchises, and obtaining portrait commissions for Flood. He was not involved in the day-to-day business of CFA; he was the celebrity "face" of the company.

In 1968 Flood hit .301 as St. Louis won the National League pennant and faced the Detroit Tigers in the World Series. The Cardinals took a 3 games to 1 lead, but Detroit won Games Five and Six to even the Series. Game Seven was a pitcher's duel between Bob Gibson and the Tigers' Mickey Lolich. With the game scoreless and with two outs in the top of the seventh, the Tigers had two runners on base when Flood misjudged a liner off the bat of Jim Northrup and slipped trying to reverse his direction. Northrup ended up with a triple and the Tigers won the game, 4–1. Flood was branded the "goat" of the Series.

The next year, 1969, was a disaster for the relationship between Flood and the Cardinals. The club offered him a nominal raise for the season. Flood rejected the offer and pointedly told the Cardinals' front office that he would not play for less than $90,000 in 1969. (The Cardinals had offered "just" $77,500 for the year. He made $72,500 in 1968.) His demand, and the way it was expressed, became public knowledge and did not sit well with team officials. Then, in the middle of spring training, Carl Flood's problems came back to haunt his brother. Carl, who had been imprisoned for bank robbery, was living in Curt's apartment in St. Louis after being released on parole. In March 1969 he and an acquaintance tried to rob a jewelry store. They took hostages and a police car and proceeded to lead the police on a chase through the streets of downtown St. Louis before finally being caught. All of this was televised by KMOX-TV in St. Louis, and Carl was identified prominently as Curt's brother. The St. Louis brass did not appreciate the negative publicity.

A couple of days later, August Busch delivered a now-famous lecture to his players at a spring training meeting to which front-office personnel, Anheuser-Busch directors, and the press were invited. Busch admonished his players not to be so greedy, to devote themselves singularly to their performance on the field, and to be more aware of the need to foster positive relationships with the fans and press. Flood, among others, viewed the speech as a direct threat to his long-term position with the team.

"In 1969, we lost the championship of the National League on March 22, before the season started. I feared that if I so much as hinted at the truth about that meeting I would be gone from the team in a week. I was sick with shame and so was everyone else on the Cardinals. . . . The speech demoralized the 1969 Cardinals. . . . We became a morose and touchy team."[21]

Embarrassing Flood even further, at some point before the season he was removed as cocaptain of the team.

Flood's relationship with the front office became even more strained as the season wore on. He missed an important public function in May, drawing the wrath of the front office and a $250 fine. Flood was incensed that the front office failed to take into account the fact that he had been severely spiked during the previous night's game and had spent a restless night dealing with the pain and the effects of the painkillers he had been given. As August turned into September, the local press reported on comments from Cardinals veterans criticizing the front office for giving up on the team's chances to make the postseason by making manager Red Schoendienst play several rookies late in the season. Flood was the source of much of that criticism, and although his name was never mentioned, the Cardinals' front office, including general manager Bing Devine, suspected that he was responsible for those comments. The Cardinals finished in fourth place in the National League's new East Division with a record of 87-75, thirteen games behind the division champion New York Mets. Flood finished with a .285 average, eighty runs scored (his highest total since 1965), and another Gold Glove Award.

On October 8, 1969, Flood received a call from Jim Toomey, an assistant to Devine, informing him that he had been traded to the Phillies. He did not react well to the news of the trade. In addition to the realization that he was leaving his St. Louis family, he was resentful that he had received the news from a "mid-level front office coffee drinker" instead of Devine. Contemplating his apparent destination, Flood thought, "Philadelphia. The nation's northernmost southern city.

Scene of Richie Allen's ordeals. Home of a ball-club rivaled only by the Pirates as the least cheerful organization in the league. When the proud Cardinals were riding a chartered jet, the Phils were still lumbering through the air in propeller jobs, arriving on the Coast too late to get proper rest before submitting to murder by the Giants and Dodgers. I did not want to succeed Richie Allen in the affections of that organization, its press and its catcalling, missile-hurling audience."[22]

Flood talked to Phillies general manager Bob Quinn, who offered him a salary package of $100,000 for 1970. Flood had few options. He did not want to go to Philadelphia and did not want to retire. He could not sell his services to another team because of the reserve clause. The reserve clause (paragraph 10 in the Uniform Player Contract) gave a club the right to renew a player's contract for a period of one year in perpetuity. Flood consulted a local attorney, Allan H. Zerman, who discussed with him the possibility of suing Major League Baseball. In 1890 Congress had passed the Sherman Anti-Trust Act. The legislation was intended to prevent collusion and monopolistic business practices designed to restrain trade and/or commerce among the various states (i.e., "interstate" commerce). The reserve clause prevented players from selling their talents to the highest bidder. Such a system certainly worked to the owners' advantage by keeping their labor costs artificially low and their profits artificially inflated. Flood noted at the time, "Unless I have misread history, we have passed the stage where indentured servitude was justifiable on the grounds that the employer could not afford the cost of normal labor."[23]

Baseball had been sued before for alleged violations of the Sherman Act. In 1922 the U.S. Supreme Court, in *Federal Baseball Club of Baltimore, Inc. v. National League of Professional Baseball Clubs*, ruled that baseball was exempt from the Sherman Act because it was *not* engaged in interstate commerce. The act of playing base-ball, the court said, was a *local* activity insufficiently connected to the concept of interstate commerce to bring it under the umbrella of the law.[24] Thirty years later, in *Toolson v. New York Yankees* (1953), the court upheld its 1922 decision. The decision in *Toolson* seemed to suggest, however, that the logic behind the decision in *Federal Baseball* was no longer valid. Since *Federal Baseball*, the court had significantly expanded its definition of interstate commerce (thereby expanding the range of activities within Congress's power to regulate), but the justices at the time of *Toolson* were not inclined to examine the evolution of precedent in regard to that concept. Since Congress in the intervening years had not attempted to explicitly bypass the court's earlier opinion, the *Toolson* court declined to overturn its own precedent. Ironically, the Supreme Court never applied the logic of *Federal Baseball* to other sports. Football, basketball, hockey, and the like did not enjoy the same protection from antitrust laws that professional baseball then enjoyed.

Flood turned to Marvin Miller, the executive director of the players union (the Major League Baseball Players Association). Miller took Flood through the existing legal precedent. He told Flood the odds were very much against him. A legal challenge would be very expensive and might take two years or more; even if he won, it was unlikely Flood was going to benefit directly from his victory. If he sat out two years, he would be thirty-four or thirty-five before the lawsuit was over. Owners were not likely to want him on their club if the lawsuit was decided in his favor, if at all, and he was not likely to receive any type of large financial windfall if he won. In the meantime Flood would be forfeiting significant compensation he would have received had he played instead of suing. Finally, he could forget any ideas about becoming a coach or manager at some point in the future.

Once Miller was convinced that Flood was committed to the cause, he invited him to the Players Association's executive committee meeting in San Juan, Puerto Rico, in early December to plead his case to the union and seek their financial support. Flood received their unanimous blessing and commitment to finance the lawsuit.[25] In return he agreed to let the union choose his legal counsel. Miller already had someone in mind: Arthur Goldberg, his former colleague in the United Steelworkers union, a former secretary of labor under President Kennedy, and a former associate justice of the U.S. Supreme Court. Goldberg seemed like an obvious choice.[26]

Thus, the wheels were set in motion, starting with Flood's letter to Baseball Commissioner Bowie Kuhn on December 24, 1969: "After twelve years in the Major Leagues, I do not feel that I am a piece of property to be bought and sold irrespective of my wishes. . . . I believe I have the right to consider offers from other clubs before making any decisions. I, therefore, request that you make known to all Major League clubs my feelings in this matter, and advise them of my availability for the 1970 season."

As expected, Flood's request was summarily rejected by the commissioner. His letter was made public, as was his intention to sue. A large segment of the national press and most fans could not understand how someone who made $90,000 playing baseball could be unhappy or view himself as a "slave." Flood's claim on a nationally televised show that "a well-paid slave is, nonetheless, a slave" did not help his cause.[27] He came off as a whining ingrate who threatened to destroy the national pastime. Baseball reacted by noting that the reserve clause was the linchpin of professional baseball and had served it well for many years. Its abolition would destabilize the game by allowing the rich teams to sign the best free agents, thus destroying competitiveness. It would encourage corruption among the players; players might throw games in favor of opposing teams with whom they might later sign huge contracts for the following season.

The trial in *Flood v. Kuhn* began on May 19, 1970, in federal court in New York City and lasted three weeks. On August 12 the court issued its ruling in favor of the owners. Flood's legal team appealed the ruling to the U.S. Court of Appeals. That court also ruled against Flood, in April 1971. The Supreme Court accepted the case for review, and oral arguments were heard on March 20, 1972. On June 19 the court ruled against Flood by a vote of 5–3.[28] Justice Harry Blackmun's majority opinion acknowledged that the logic behind baseball's antitrust exemption as laid down in *Federal Baseball* and affirmed in *Toolson* was an "aberration," but that it was up to Congress to remedy the situation.[29]

Why, then, has Flood come to be viewed as the father of free agency? The 1968 Basic Agreement between the owners and players expired after the 1969 season. With negotiations on a new agreement taking place and the cloud of Flood's lawsuit hanging over their heads, the owners and players agreed on a new Basic Agreement for 1970 that allowed the players to take grievances to independent arbitration, a huge concession on the part of management. Flood's challenge to the reserve clause raised public awareness of the one-sided nature of the system. It raised awareness among the players as well, many of whom had blindly bought into management's arguments without really thinking about the inherent inequities in the system. Baseball had argued in court that the reserve clause was a subject that should be dealt with through negotiation (despite their unwillingness to do so over the course of the previous two years) and not in the courts. Now the pressure was on the owners to engage in meaningful negotiations. Changes to the reserve system were most likely to occur through negotiation, as Miller had always expected.[30] Over the years

the players would chip away at the reserve clause piece by piece. The arbitration component of the 1970 Basic Agreement was the key that opened the door. In 1974 Catfish Hunter won his freedom from the Oakland Athletics when an arbitrator ruled that Athletics owner Charles Finley had violated the terms of Hunter's contract. The following year, Miller used the arbitration process to win free agency for Andy Messersmith and Dave McNally, who had played the 1975 season without contracts. They argued that the owners' right to renew a player's contract was good for only one year if a player had refused to sign a new contract. To the shock and dismay of the owners, the arbitrator, Peter Seitz, agreed, changing the owner-player relationship forever. After that decision the players were able to win significant modifications to the reserve clause through the negotiation process, although those negotiations were not always easy. In 1973 the Players Association was able to negotiate a new agreement that included the "10/5 Rule" (also known as the "Curt Flood Rule"), which gave players with ten years of Major League experience, including five years with their current club, the right to veto a trade. Other concessions from the owners would follow in later years.

While the lawsuit progressed, personal problems were mounting for Flood. He quit paying child support a few weeks after the 1968 World Series and was in serious arrears to his ex-wife.[31] His business interests in St. Louis were failing; bills were not being paid, resulting in several lawsuits against CFA, Inc., and Flood himself. Worse still, payroll taxes were not being paid to the Internal Revenue Service. The IRS went after the assets of the photography business and threatened to take an apartment building in Oakland that Flood had purchased for his mother. Curt, by his own admission, spent most of 1970 "bedding and boozing" instead of taking care of business. With little or no income being generated, he was facing serious financial problems. A few weeks after the district court trial was over, with his business interests in St. Louis in tatters, Flood flew to Copenhagen to get away from the stress and media frenzy. It was there that he learned he had lost his case in the district court.

Then, in October of 1970, Flood received a phone call from Washington Senators owner Bob Short. Short had reached a deal with the Phillies that allowed him to negotiate with Flood to bring him to the Senators for the 1971 season. After determining that returning to active status would not threaten his legal standing to pursue his case in the appellate courts, Flood and Short agreed on a contract worth $110,000 for the 1971 season. There also was a verbal agreement that Short would grant Flood his release after the season if Flood so desired.[32]

In retrospect, the move seemed destined to failure. During his hiatus from baseball, Flood had done nothing to stay in shape. To the contrary, as one biographer noted, "without baseball, drinking had come to dominate Flood's life. He no longer had an incentive to remain sober each day."[33] In November, Flood reported to the Senators' facility in the Florida Instructional League at St. Petersburg to begin light workouts. He had difficulty completing even the most basic drills. He was clearly out of shape.

The Senators' spring training camp in Pompano Beach, Florida, opened in February 1971, at about the same time Flood's book, *The Way It Is*, was published.[34] While everyone smiled for the cameras and said all the right things to the reporters gathered there, it became very apparent that his skills had declined significantly. Many felt Flood did not have his heart in the comeback; he had, after all, returned primarily for financial reasons. He stayed to himself and drank heavily in his hotel room at night. As Brad Snyder noted, "Flood read books on the bus during spring training road trips. He kept his distance from most teammates. They liked him and admired him, but also pitied him.

They knew he was not the player he had once been."[35] Senators manager Ted Williams publicly supported Flood but told people privately that Flood was finished. Nevertheless, Flood was the Opening Day center fielder. He batted second in the game against Oakland, getting a bunt single, walking twice, and scoring two runs. After that, things on the field quickly deteriorated for Flood. He failed to hit with any consistency or power. He had lost the gracefulness that previously characterized his outfield play, and he could not throw with any strength. Williams benched him after just five games, relegating him to pinch-hitting duties and occasional late-inning defensive substitutions. Flood's financial difficulties, in addition to his alcoholism, had taken a severe physical and psychological toll on him. His inability to perform on the field in the glare of the public spotlight pushed him over the edge. On April 26 he left the team without warning, deciding instead to flee the country to escape the mounting pressures. From the airport in New York, he sent Bob Short an apology in the form of a telegram, saying only that he had been away from the game too long and that he had serious financial troubles. Flood went 7 for 35 (.200) in his comeback with no extra-base hits in thirteen games.

Flood eventually settled on the Spanish island of Majorca. He was in dire straits financially. Beverly had sued him again to try to recover a significant sum in back alimony and child support, and he was still responsible for judgments arising out of his failed businesses in St. Louis. He invested in a bar, the Rustic Inn, in the town of Palma with a newfound girlfriend. The island was a popular resort, and American tourists, including vacationing Hollywood crowds, and military personnel stationed in the Mediterranean frequented the bar. Howard Cosell, the broadcaster, went so far as to send videotapes of boxing matches to Flood to show at the bar.

In 1975 Flood was forced to give up the Rustic

Inn and leave Majorca. He later claimed that the Spanish police suspected illegal activities because of the heavy traffic at the bar. Flood went to the tiny principality of Andorra, located between Spain and France, where he continued to drink heavily and lived out of a duffle bag with whoever was kind enough to offer him a place to stay. Hitting rock bottom on October 1, Flood tried to rob a department store while in a drunken stupor. The charges were dropped because he had been drunk and had not taken anything. He was immediately deported to Barcelona, Spain, where he was hospitalized for alcoholism. Spanish authorities, working through the U.S. State Department, released Flood a few weeks later when someone in his family provided a plane ticket for him to return to Oakland.

Flood was destitute. His childhood benefactors in Oakland tried to help him. In 1978 Sam Bercovich purchased the radio broadcast rights for the Oakland games and persuaded the A's to give Flood a job as color commentator. He struggled in that job, in part because of his alcoholism, failing to engage the audience with the kind of insight expected of a color commentator. Bercovich did not renew the rights after the season and Flood was out of a job. He also coached the American Legion team he had played for years earlier.

Another former mentor, Bill Patterson, got Flood a job with the Oakland Parks Department as commissioner of its youth baseball program. His primary duty was fund-raising; the parks department paid for only 60 percent of the program's cost. Curt enjoyed some success in this position; he arranged coaching clinics with a number of current and former Major League players and by all accounts was quite successful at raising money and obtaining donations of equipment.

In 1980 Flood entered a rehabilitation center and, for a while at least, found sobriety.[36] He also attempted to reestablish his reputation as a portrait painter, although it is not clear to what extent this effort was successful. In 1985, after fifteen years apart, Flood rekindled his friendship with Judy Pace and moved to Los Angeles; they were married in December 1986. Judy was able to get him more help with his drinking; by the early 1990s, he had achieved, and was able to maintain, his sobriety.

In 1989 Flood was named commissioner of the Senior Professional Baseball Association, a Florida-based league of retired players. The job paid $65,000 a year, but financial difficulties forced the league to fold after its second season. Flood later created the Curt Flood Youth Foundation, to help youngsters in foster care and those who suffered from HIV/AIDS.[37] In 1994 he was featured in Ken Burns's PBS documentary *Baseball*, discussing the difficulties he encountered as a black player coming of age in the 1950s and '60s and his efforts to overturn the reserve clause. He was inducted into the Bay Area Hall of Fame in 1995. That same year, he was diagnosed with throat cancer. He died in Los Angeles from the effects of that disease on January 20, 1997. No then-current players attended the services.

In 1998 Congress passed the Curt Flood Act, which eliminated baseball's antitrust exemption in regard to labor issues. Flood received one final posthumous accolade in 1999, when *Time* magazine named him one of the ten most influential athletes of the past century.

Curt Flood's life came crashing down around him when he decided to sue baseball. There is no doubt many of his wounds were self-inflicted. But was it worth it? Did he have any regrets? Publicly, he never complained about the fact that he did not benefit from the changes that took place after his lawsuit. He told *Ebony* magazine in 1981, "I certainly don't begrudge the players getting that money. They're finally getting a fair share of the incredible amount of money they're making for the baseball teams." Several years later he privately admitted to some people that he might have paid too high a price. What seemed to bother him the most about his lawsuit was the lack of support he received from his peers during the district court trial. "I spent six weeks in New York during the trial . . . and not one player who was playing at the time came just to see what was going on because it involved them so dramatically. . . . No one came to just sit and say, 'Hey, this is pretty important.'"[38] Even his best friend in baseball, Bob Gibson, told Curt, "You're crazy," and stayed away from the trial itself.[39]

Flood's legacy continues to benefit players more than ever, even if his name has been lost to history. Brad Snyder summarized Flood's place in most contemporary players' lives: "Today's athlete have some control over where they play in part because in 1969 Flood refused to continue being treated like hired help. But while [Jackie] Robinson's jersey has been retired in every major league park, few current players today know the name Curt Flood, and even fewer know about the sacrifices he made for them."[40]

A couple of years before Flood died, George Will wrote, "He lost the 1970 season and lost in the Supreme Court, but he had lit a fuse. . . . Six years later—too late to benefit him—his cause prevailed. The national pastime is clearly better because of that. But more important, so is the nation, because it has learned one more lesson about the foolishness of fearing freedom."[41]

Chapter 14. **Phil Gagliano**

Bill Nowlin

AGE	G	AB	R	H	2B	3B	HR	TB	RBI	BB	SO	BAV	OBP	SLG	SB	GDP	HBP
22	40	58	5	15	4	0	1	22	9	3	10	.259	.290	.379	0	1	0

Phil Gagliano grew up in a baseball-oriented family. Though his grandparents on his father's side of the family hailed from southern Italy (Sicily and Calabria), and on his mother's side from the Tuscany region, the second-generation Americans took to baseball whole-heartedly. Phil's father, Ralph, who was a director of purchasing at a wholesale food business in Memphis, Tennessee, played second base for a local semipro baseball team. Phil's uncle Tony Gagliano, who coached Phil through high school and American Legion baseball, signed with the New York Giants as a pitcher and spent time in Class D for Portageville, Missouri, in 1935, before injuring his arm. Phil had three younger siblings, each spaced five years apart: Ralph, Elizabeth, and Paul; the two brothers also starred at baseball. Ralph signed with the Cleveland Indians, which outbid sixteen other Major League clubs for his services, though Ralph appeared in only one Major League game, playing two more years in the Minors after returning from the Vietnam War. Paul, meanwhile, earned a full scholarship to play baseball at Vanderbilt University. Phil reminisced, "My whole family — my uncles, my cousins — we were all baseball players." Through it all, Phil's mother, a "stay-at-home mom," "kept the food on the table."[1]

Philip Joseph Gagliano was born on December 27, 1941, in Memphis. His first competitive baseball was in Catholic Youth Organization baseball, when he was in the fifth grade. "That's when I saw I had a little talent," he said. "I was a pretty good hitter and I pitched, just like most of your better athletes. They'd hit and pitch." Phil continued to play as he grew up, both for Christian Broth-

A high school teammate of Tim McCarver, Phil Gagliano was in the second of eight seasons for St. Louis in 1964. He played the first half of the season and was back at the end, but he was not on the World Series roster.

ers High School and American Legion baseball. "My junior year is when scouts started hanging around. That was when I really started thinking I might have a chance at this game." He was good at basketball as well, being named his high school's MVP in 1959. That summer, the high school baseball team coached by his uncle Tony won the state championship.

Gagliano's high school team featured another future Major Leaguer and member of the 1964

Cardinals, Tim McCarver. Phil and Tim graduated together in 1959. Whereas McCarver signed immediately, Gagliano, still seventeen years old, waited a few months, when he, like McCarver, then signed with the St. Louis Cardinals. After signing he was scheduled to play for Class D Billings in 1960. The signing scout was Buddy Lewis, who signed both Christian Brothers graduates. It was a dream signing for young Phil, who, like most of the kids in Memphis, was a Cardinals fan growing up. "St. Louis was only a few hundred miles away. We'd get them on the radio every night."

There was no draft at the time. The best bidder prevailed. McCarver had signed for a $75,000 bonus in the spring of 1959. Phil said his own bonus was $10,000, and later quipped, "We were the gold dust twins. Tim got the gold, I got the dust." It was no small sum at the time, though dwarfed by McCarver's bonus.[2] Phil's bonus may have been smaller than otherwise because he'd waited until September, and some of the big-league budgets may have been tapped out. When asked, he allowed that he might have received a little more money if he'd not stuck with his uncle's Legion team through the summer.

Phil signed a Billings contract but never played there. That was Class C ball, and soon after he reported for spring training, he was shifted downward to Class D, where he played eighty-nine games in 1960 as shortstop for the Dothan Cardinals in the Alabama-Florida League. There he hit .280 — but leapt over several classifications and hit even higher (.315) when he finished the season in Double-A playing both shortstop and second base back in his own hometown with the Memphis Chickasaws (Southern Association).

That success in the latter part of the 1960 season led to Gagliano's being placed with the Portland Beavers in December. In 1961 with the Triple-A Pacific Coast League club, Phil hit .260 but boosted his power numbers, hitting 11 homers and 29 doubles and playing exclusively at second base.

The Beavers performed above expectations, and as sportswriter Lee Irwin said, "The work of a pair of 19-year-olds at short — Jerry Buchek and Phil Gagliano — was a good part of the reason."[3] The two infielders later roomed together as Cardinals.

In 1962 Gagliano played for the Atlanta Crackers in the International League, another Triple-A ball club. He hit .284 and slugged the same .381 as he had with Portland. Even more noteworthy, he had made league all-star teams for three years in a row: 1960, 1961, and 1962. Late in 1962 Phil married Mary Palmer Ashford. At the time of his December 2009 interview, the couple had just celebrated forty-seven years of marriage. They raised three daughters and one son.

Gagliano's first year training with the Cardinals was 1963. It was particularly special because of the overlap with one of his childhood heroes, Stan Musial, who was entering his final year in baseball. Phil made the team out of spring training that year. "That's back when they would take 27 north. Twenty-seven players would break camp, and then they had to cut back to 25 after the first month. So I got a month in and they sent me back to Atlanta. I was number 26 or number 27. But I got to see Musial for a month. As a kid, listening to him play . . . I was in another world, man."

Phil had his Major League debut on April 16, 1963, an uneventful one. He had both his first Major League hit and his first run batted in on April 23 in Houston, playing the Colt .45s. His old Christian Brothers teammate Tim McCarver had tripled to lead off the ninth, and Gagliano, who had come in to play second base for Julián Javier in the bottom of the eighth (the Cards were winning 11–0), singled in McCarver for the twelfth St. Louis run. It was the only run he drove in during the ten games (six plate appearances) he appeared in in 1963. With two hits and a walk, his Major League line saw him batting .400 with an on-base percentage of .500, but Jack Damaska got the playing time as backup infielder. It wasn't the easiest infield to break into, by any means: Bill White, Ken Boyer, Dick Groat, and Julián Javier. Among the four of them, the Cardinals claimed every infield position in the starting nine at the 1963 All-Star Game. After the roster was trimmed to twenty-five, Gagliano spent most of the year back with Atlanta. In his second season with the Crackers, his average dipped considerably, to .242.

For his time with the Cardinals, Phil received a quarter share of the team's second-place earnings. Phil played in the Dominican Republic in the winter of 1963–64, and the Cardinals' brain trust had already perceived his true potential as a utility man. Cardinals veteran Red Schoendienst declared, "He's got guts and he looks to me as if he could play any of three infield positions at least adequately," and manager Johnny Keane chimed in, "He was the best hitter I saw in the Dominican League last winter. He'd make a good pinch-hitter as well as handyman, because he seldom strikes out, and he runs well."[4]

In 1964 Phil opened the year with St. Louis. *The Sporting News* selected him as the hardest worker in the spring training camp, and his thirteen exhibition-game RBIs led the team. Gagliano had his first key hit for the Cardinals on April 24—his first hit of the season, a pinch-hit single in the bottom of the eleventh inning that drove in the winning run to beat the Houston Colt .45s, 3–2. On May 5 he drove in the first of two runs and scored the second as St. Louis beat Jim Bunning and the Phillies, 2–1. On June 20 Phil hit the first of his fourteen Major League home runs, in the bottom of the eighth inning at Busch Stadium against right-hander Jim Duffalo of the San Francisco Giants. It came in a game the Cards lost 14–3. Phil was playing first base for the first time at any level of play, because regular first baseman Bill White had been ejected from the game. His parents were visiting from Memphis, so it was a happy day all around. Phil had one of the more dramatic splits that season—he hit .342 at Busch but only .100

in road games. He also often tended to hit right-handed pitchers better. Over his career, however, he hit both about equally well, and there was only a slightly higher average at home.

He stayed with the team through July 19, when the Cardinals brought up pitcher Gordon Richardson and infielder Ed Spiezio. Gagliano was batting .259 in fifty-eight at bats and was sent down to Jacksonville, the new St. Louis Triple-A affiliate in the International League. With the same All-Star infield intact, there still wasn't much playing time with the Cardinals. They began to think of converting him to an outfielder, and he played twenty-seven games in the outfield the following season, but more of his outfield work was later in his career. He hit .262 in the forty-eight games he played with Jacksonville (which won the league championship). These were his final 183 at bats in Minor League baseball. Phil was recalled on September 5, but with the Phillies collapsing and the Cardinals contending for the pennant, he saw no further action. Still, for the remainder of his playing career, he was in the Major Leagues.[5]

The Cardinals won the 1964 pennant under manager Johnny Keane and beat the Yankees in seven games in the World Series. Gagliano was not on the World Series roster; he followed the Series from his home in Memphis. He'd appeared in forty games, however, and he was awarded a three-quarters share of the World Series payout. Phil worked hard in the Instructional League in Florida after the 1964 season. "That's where I learned to hit. I learned to handle the bat. I learned how to handle the outside pitch, and I learned the strike zone there."[6]

Phil played regularly for St. Louis in 1965, getting into 122 games, batting .240 with 8 homers and 53 RBIs, and playing second and third base and the outfield. Early in the '65 season, with new manager Red Schoendienst on board, the Cardinals benched Javier, the second baseman, and inserted Gagliano there. The move paid off quickly, as Phil contributed to three consecutive wins: a game-winning single on April 30, another game-winning single on May 1, and a pinch-hit double to kick off a three-run rally that helped win the second game of a May 2 doubleheader. The three wins helped lift the Cardinals out of the cellar.

One event that stood out in 1965 came during a game on May 11. Phil collided on the base paths with Ron Hunt of the New York Mets, fracturing his shoulder as Hunt tried to make a play at second base. Ron's shoulder was first held with pins, and in mid-June, Hunt underwent surgery and was out until August 5. After the collision, Phil said it was "an unfortunate accident . . . nobody's fault." Hunt wasn't entirely sure how Phil could have failed to see him right there in the base paths making the play, but he allowed, perhaps with a touch of skepticism, "I guess it was unintentional."[7] Gagliano was far from a popular man in New York after the accident; he even received some threatening letters in the mail. He also proved a nemesis to the Mets that year. On July 3 Phil's two-run sixth-inning homer gave the Cardinals the only runs of a shutout of the Mets, and on July 16 in St. Louis, he was 3 for 4 with a triple and two RBIs, sparking another victory. Phil got some infield play at this time, because Schoendienst wanted to keep his often-hot bat in the lineup. In mid-June, Javier broke his hand and was out for a month and a half. This provided Phil more playing time.

Sportswriter Neal Russo characterized Gagliano as "an adequate outfielder" but wrote that he "doesn't possess enough glove magic at second."[8] A few years later Russo more fully appreciated Gagliano's role as the "dean of the bench."[9] As for Gagliano himself, he said the right things: "I'll play anywhere, just to play. I'd even catch."[10]

In the second half of 1964, Bob Howsam joined the team as general manager; following the Cardinals' seventh-place finish in 1965, they decided to go younger and look for more power. Phil was young enough but didn't have a lot of power. There were postseason rumors that the Mets were interested in him. Gagliano had played primarily at third base and pinch-hit a lot in 1966, getting into ninety games but with only 213 at bats. He had one prolonged 2-for-41 slump, but still hit .254 and drove in fifteen runs.

When the Cardinals traded Charley Smith to the Yankees that December, to acquire Roger Maris, Gagliano hoped he might have a chance to break into the starting lineup at third base, but it wasn't to be. Mike Shannon, heretofore an outfielder who had no experience with infield play, became the regular Cardinals third baseman. Gagliano was a utility man once again. In 1967, "I was told that I was going to get a shot in spring training, which I never did," he recalled. "They gave it to Shannon. I think it was preplanned and that their telling me that was to get me to sign my contract. That's the way they negotiated back then. I just never got the opportunity. He was a more powerful hitter than I was. He was going to hit more home runs. He did a commendable job, I'll say that." Gagliano played when he could and did a decent job, filling in nicely when Julián Javier pulled a thigh muscle on August 2.

Even though star pitcher Bob Gibson broke his leg in mid-July, the 1967 Cardinals were not to be denied. Lou Brock, Curt Flood, Orlando Cepeda, and Tim McCarver were all strong on offense, and the team won 101 games even with Gibson at 13-7 and without anyone winning more games than the 16 Dick Hughes won. Gibson made up for it all in the World Series, though, winning three of St. Louis's four victories over the Boston Red Sox, with a sterling 1.00 earned run average. Gagliano—who had hit only .221 in the regular season—appeared in just one game; with Javier on second and St. Louis losing 1–0, he popped up to shortstop to end the eighth inning in Game Five. Boston won the game, 3–1.

In 1968 Phil was back but got only about half

as much work as the season before. He had 105 at bats, hitting .229, and drove in 13 runs. One of the RBIS came on his game-winning triple on August 23 in the eleventh inning against the Pittsburgh Pirates. It was one of three game-winners for him that year. It wasn't the first time he wished he'd had a chance to play more. "Everybody wants to be a regular, because that's where the good money is. You like to get a chance to satisfy your personal goals. . . . It's a matter of pride. Something even when you win, you feel down when you know you're not contributing."[11] St. Louis made the World Series again, and Gagliano got three pinch-hit at bats, in Games Two, Five, and Seven—with a fly out sandwiched between two ground outs. There was one postseason game he won with a home run, but it didn't come until November 10, in Tokyo. After losing the World Series to the Tigers in seven games, the Cardinals went to play in Japan, and Gagliano beat the Yomiuri Giants with a ninth-inning homer in the twelfth game of the scheduled eighteen-game series.

It was clear that the Cardinals highly prized Gagliano's utility role. They broke up the 1968 team, for reasons that mystified Gagliano, but he was brought back for a seventh season in 1969 and contributed in the usual fashion, helping out when he could. He got a few more at bats, hitting .227, but his RBIS were down to just ten. One of them, though, was a pinch-hit game-winner that made August 5 another happy day for Bob Gibson, who banked a 2–1 victory.

When Mike Shannon went down with a serious kidney condition in 1970 spring training, the Cardinals might have been expected to give Gagliano more work, and he did appear regularly in May; but they still didn't view him as a regular—and proved it by trading him to the Cubs on May 29 for right-handed reliever Ted Abernathy. Cubs GM John Holland said the team had been looking for an extra infielder, at least to fill in for a couple of weeks when Don Kessinger had military service commitments. As early as spring training 1964, Holland had coveted Gagliano.[12] Phil had been struggling with St. Louis, hitting only .188, and didn't even do that well for the Cubs, batting .150 for the rest of the season in very limited use. Cubs skipper Leo Durocher didn't seem to see fit to use him much.

A change of league led to a remarkable rebound in 1971. At the winter meetings on December 2, 1970, Gagliano was sold to the Red Sox for cash. Some later sources suggested that it was actually a trade for Carmen Fanzone, and that it didn't occur until the day after it was first reported among the transactions of the day. It was kind of a mystery, as the *Chicago Tribune* mused on September 10, 1971. Fanzone himself told the press that he'd been sent to the Cubs as part of the deal. Regardless of what and wherefore, Phil Gagliano became a member of the Boston Red Sox. Manager Eddie Kasko was looking to strengthen the Boston bench at the middle infield positions. The Red Sox didn't seem to have the strongest bench going into the season, but Phil had a terrific start, hitting well over .500 through June and only dipping to .500 on July 5.

By the time he got to Boston, Phil said, he had reconciled himself to being known as a bench player, a utility player. And resigning himself to that made him better at it. Both Phil and "Super Sub" John Kennedy did excellent work for the Red Sox in 1971. Kennedy was acquired first, but as Phil said, "I never knew of a club that went with only one spare infielder." He complimented Carl Yastrzemski soon after the All-Star break, "He gets a good piece of the ball every time he goes up there."[13] Gagliano's average by the end of the year was .324 and he had played four defensive positions without making an error: left field, right field, second base, and third base. Primarily, though, he pinch-hit. Taking eleven bases on balls helped pump his on-base percentage up to .413.

All manager Eddie Kasko looked forward to for

1972 was more of the same, from both Kennedy and Gagliano. Kasko said, "The secret to the success of a utilityman is realizing the importance of being a utilityman. These players have the proper attitude and realize a major part of their job is to be ready at all times."[14] There was some talk of Gagliano trying out for the first base job. He said he had enjoyed it briefly with the Cardinals and admitted once more that he'd like to play more regularly: "I'm not complaining, mind you, but I'd like to play regularly over a long stretch to see how well I could do."[15] He played only two innings at first base, yet when Yaz went down with torn knee ligaments, Gagliano filled in for twelve games in left field. His stats dipped in 1972, but he still managed a .333 on-base percentage. Along with everyone else on the 1972 Red Sox, Phil wished he could have helped win just one more game. This was the strike-shortened season when the Red Sox missed out on a playoff berth by half a game to the Detroit Tigers.

Phil had been active in the labor talks. He had taken over from Gary Peters as the main contact between the Red Sox players and the union. "I was the player rep during those negotiations. After those negotiations were firmed up and we got back to playing ball, I nominated Carlton Fisk for the job. That wasn't too secure a job for a guy like me." Had his work as player rep led to him being traded away by Boston? "I don't know. I don't think so. Who knows? It was something else, really. What Marvin Miller did for us is what these guys are reaping today."

At the time, Gagliano had been working as an off-season printing salesman in the St. Louis area (he'd earlier worked doing public relations work for a packing company in Memphis) and had just opened a sporting-goods store in partnership with three others.

Near the end of spring training, at the end of March 1973, the Red Sox decided that Mario Guerrero gave them more upside in the infield and traded **both Gagliano and** Andy Kosco to the Cincinnati Reds for pitcher Mel Behney. The Sox got very little out of the deal; Behney pitched that year at Pawtucket but never made it back to the big leagues.

"I figure Gag is really going to help us," said Cincinnati manager Sparky Anderson.[16] That he did. Gagliano had another very good year, hitting .290 (with 15 walks taking his OBP to .402) and went to his third postseason. "The job the bench has done had been remarkable," said Sparky on the eve of the first round of playoffs. "This year's bench is the best I've seen the Reds have since that 1956 club. . . . There's a terrific amount of pride among those fellows who don't play regularly. There're all eager to make a contribution toward the success of the club." Gagliano had fourteen hits in forty-one pinch-hitting at bats during the season.[17]

The Reds fell to the New York Mets in the National League Championship Series. Phil was 0 for 3 at the plate. The Mets won the pennant but the Shea Stadium crowd became a little unruly, and at least one Cincinnati official's wife was knocked to the ground, while another had her hair pulled. Phil punched the guy who pulled her hair.[18]

Gagliano's last year in baseball was 1974, and he approached setting a Major League record when he walked fifteen times as a pinch hitter. The National League record was eleven, but the Major League mark was eighteen, set by Elmer Valo of the 1960 Senators. Phil had only two base hits in forty-six plate appearances—but because of the walks he had an on-base percentage of .370 to go with his .065 batting average. Near the end of October the Reds released Phil. He had booked twelve seasons as a Major League utility player, hitting .238 overall, scoring 150 runs and driving in 159. It had been a good, long career and now it was time to do something else. He and Mary had bought a house in St. Louis in 1969.

"I was 32 years old with four kids, and I had to

get a job. I had to make the adjustment, like everybody. The biggest adjustment was financial. I went from making $40,000 to $16,000 a year. I was starting all over again, and I was 10 years behind. . . . It took me a good five years of adjustment to get baseball out of my blood." For two years, he worked as a salesman for Paramount Liquors and then went to work for Durbin Durco, Inc., an industrial hardware manufacturer. He started out as a salesman, then moved into operations, and finished his seventeen years with the company as its operations manager.[19]

After leaving Durbin Durco, Phil worked a number of odds and ends of jobs until his children all completed school, and then he fully retired in 2002. He and Mary moved to the small southwestern Missouri town of Hollister, not far from Branson, after living in St. Louis since 1969. "It's really country living," he told Rob Rains. "In the summer I play a lot of golf and the kids all come and visit. I don't do much of anything in the winter."

Looking back on his career, Gagliano agreed that perhaps his versatility might have hurt him a bit. "I played six positions. When I was younger, I was kind of, I guess, disappointed that I never got an opportunity [to play regularly]. I think I got myself labeled as a guy that could come off the bench and play. Not everybody can do that. By me playing so many different positions, they could carry another pitcher. That was another advantage of keeping me on the bench.

"I was fortunate because I played on winning ballclubs. I didn't play on too many losing ballclubs. In my early days with the Cardinals, yeah, but after that I was always on a contender. I have no regrets. It was a great life. The only thing you do regret is that you become friends with a lot of guys and then everybody goes their own ways and you never see them again. That's pretty disappointing, but that's the way it is."

There is already some more baseball in the family. Phil and Mary have ten grandchildren, and Phil has his baseball eyes on a couple of them. Grandson Kyle Mach signed out of the University of Missouri with the San Francisco Giants, a third baseman who was a twenty-seventh-round pick in the 2009 June draft. He played in the Arizona Rookie League and hit .216 in ninety-seven at bats, and by 2010 had progressed to Class A. "And I have another grandson, Conner Mach, at Missouri University that's going to be a dandy."

Chapter 15. Timeline, May 1–May 31

John Harry Stahl

May 1 — CARDINALS 6, PIRATES 2 — Craig pitched a complete game, allowing seven hits and striking out six. Opposing starter Vern Law lasted three and one-third innings before Tom Butters relieved him. The Pirates scored one run in the top of the fourth, but the Cardinals responded with six hits and four runs in the bottom of the inning. Key Cardinals hits included a double (James) and four singles (Groat, White, Boyer, and Lewis).

May 2 — PIRATES 5, CARDINALS 4 — The Cardinals started the ninth inning leading 4–3 with starter Simmons still pitching and facing the bottom of the Pirates' batting order. After getting the first out, Curt walked Julio Gotay (former Cardinal) and gave up a double to Dick Schofield (former Cardinal). Shantz relieved, retired the next hitter, and intentionally walked Roberto Clemente. With the bases loaded, Gene Freese (former Cardinal) hit a two-run single, giving the Pirates the lead. In the bottom of the ninth, the Cardinals loaded the bases with one out. McCarver then hit into the game-ending double play.

Pitcher Ray Washburn rejoined the Cardinals after a rehabilitation stint at Jacksonville (Triple-A).

May 3 — PIRATES 12, CARDINALS 8 — The teams combined for twenty-nine hits in this wide-open slugfest. The Pirates began the scoring in the first inning as Willie Stargell hit a three-run home run off starter Broglio. Trailing 3–1 in the second, the Cardinals scored five runs off Pirates starter Bob Veale. Flood's bases-loaded triple was the key hit in the inning. With the Cardinals leading, 7–3, the

Pirates scored five runs in the top of the fifth. Bill Mazeroski drove in two runs with a key single. After the Cardinals tied the score in the bottom of the fifth, the Pirates scored two runs in the sixth off Sadecki to take the lead for good.

May 4 — CARDINALS 9, PHILLIES 2 — The Cardinals easily won the game. However, a "duster parade" erupted in the second, third, and fourth innings. After Flood's home run in the second, Phillies starter Dennis Bennett fired a pitch inches from Javier's head, as he believed the Cardinals were starting to "dig in" on him. When Bennett batted in the third, Gibson threw consecutive pitches over Bennett's head. Gibson received an umpire warning. When Gibson batted in the fourth, Phillies reliever Jack Baldschun hit Gibson on the ankle. On his way to first base, Gibson "flipped" his bat at Baldschun, who caught it with his glove. The umpires intervened, threw out Gibson, and warned Baldschun. Both subsequently paid $50 fines and the ejection cost Gibson a victory. Warwick, the Cardinals' next hitter after Gibson, hit a two-run home run.

May 5 — CARDINALS 2, PHILLIES 1 — Philadelphia ace Jim Bunning started and pitched five innings, but lost to Washburn with relief help from Taylor. In the ninth after a lead-off single and a successful sacrifice, Taylor retired both Tony Taylor and Richie "Dick" Allen to preserve the victory.

May 6 — PIRATES 1, CARDINALS 0 — In Pittsburgh, Bob Friend pitched a complete-game shutout, scattering six hits. Sadecki was also working on a shutout of the Pirates going into the ninth inning. After Clemente led off with a double, Gibson relieved Sadecki and intentionally walked Donn Clendenon. Attempting to move the runners, Bob Bailey bunted. Gibson fielded the bunt but threw wildly to first, and Clemente scored the winning run.

May 7 — CARDINALS 4, PIRATES 2 — Recovering from a shaky first inning, Simmons pitched eight innings and won with ninth-inning help from Craig. The Pirates scored in the first as Clemente hit a two-run home run. The Cardinals scored all of their runs in the fourth inning on four singles and a Pirates error. After a lead-off single in the ninth by Freese, Craig relieved and got the final three outs.

May 8 — METS 5, CARDINALS 4 — In the Cardinals' first-ever game at Shea Stadium, the Mets jumped to an early lead off Broglio with two runs in the first inning on three hits, including a triple by Jesse Gonder. Behind 4–1 in the eighth, Warwick hit a three-run home run to tie the score. In the bottom of the ninth, reliever Shantz gave up a single to George Altman and then a successful sacrifice. After issuing an intentional walk, Shantz allowed the game-winning single to pinch hitter Joe Christopher.

May 9 — CARDINALS 5, METS 1 — Gibson pitched a complete-game victory, scattering eight hits and striking out seven. Leading 1–0 on Boyer's fourth-inning homer, the Cardinals put together three walks and three hits to score four runs in the seventh inning. Gonder hit a solo home run in the bottom of the seventh for the Mets' only run.

May 10 — METS 4, CARDINALS 1 (game one) — Mets pitcher Tracy Stallard pitched a complete game, allowing one run on five hits and striking out nine. Tied 1–1 into the bottom of the eighth, St. Louis starter Craig allowed a tie-break-

ing home run to Rod Kanehl. A double and a single led to another run. Frank Thomas homered off reliever Burdette to end the scoring.

May 10 — CARDINALS 10, METS 1 (game two) — The Cardinals produced fourteen hits, including five doubles and two triples. Every Cardinal in the starting lineup had at least one hit. Javier led the Cardinals' attack with three hits, two runs scored, and two RBIs. Cardinals starter Washburn pitched six and two-thirds innings for the win and Taylor pitched the last two and one-third innings.

May 11 — CARDINALS 3, PHILLIES 2 — Sadecki pitched his first complete game in 1964 as the Cardinals came from behind to beat Ray Culp. Javier hit a two-out three-run home run in the seventh to give the Cardinals the lead.

May 12 — CARDINALS 4, PHILLIES 2 — With Simmons on the mound, the Cardinals jumped out to a 4–0 lead. In the sixth with the score 4–1 and two runners on, Bobby Wine smashed a long fly to right-center field. Flood made a spectacular catch. "I was lucky," Simmons said after the game. "Flood made a great catch. That was the ballgame." Clemens, Groat, and Javier each had two hits.

May 13 — Game rained out.

May 14 — PHILLIES 3, CARDINALS 2 — Bunning won his fourth game of the season as Philadelphia came from behind to win. Clemens had two hits and one RBI to lead the Cardinal hitters. Allen, Johnny Callison, and John Herrnstein each had two hits for the Phillies.

May 15 — CARDINALS 10, BRAVES 6 — The teams combined for twenty-nine hits. Javier, James, Long, and Groat were the Cardinals' hitting stars: Javier hit a grand slam; James hit two home runs;

Long had a home run that hit high off the score-board and two RBIs; and Groat had two hits and two RBIs. However, Gibson lasted only three innings. After Taylor replaced Gibson and pitched one and one-third innings, Craig pitched the last four and two-thirds innings for the win.

May 16 — CARDINALS 6, BRAVES 5 — Sadecki went seven and two-thirds innings and won his second game. Boyer had four singles and a walk, scoring two runs and driving in two more. Javier added a two-out two-run single in the fifth. Taylor pitched the final one and one-third innings, allowing two runs on three hits.

May 17 — CARDINALS 7, BRAVES 3 (game one) — Simmons pitched a complete game for his fifth win. Groat had three hits and two RBIs. Both White and McCarver hit solo home runs. Flood also had four hits.

May 17 — BRAVES 4, CARDINALS 2 (game two) — Braves pitcher Tony Cloninger pitched a complete game for his third victory. He allowed six hits and struck out nine. The Cardinals scored their two runs in the sixth inning on a home run by Clemens. The Braves had home runs from Denis Menke, Ed Bailey, and Felipe Alou. Washburn lost his first game.

May 18 — No game scheduled.

May 19 — CUBS 7, CARDINALS 4 — Chicago's Dick Ellsworth allowed eleven hits but pitched a complete game. The Cardinal battery of Broglio-Uecker had a miserable game. Uecker made two errors and Broglio uncorked a record-tying three wild pitches in one inning. All three pitches were curves that bounced in front of the plate. "I should have blocked all of them," a frustrated Uecker said after the game. Billy Williams and Ron Santo homered for the Cubs, and Boyer homered for the Cardinals.

May 20 — CARDINALS 1, CUBS 0 — Gibson struck out twelve in a complete-game victory. Chicago's Larry Jackson also pitched a complete game and suffered his third loss. The Cardinals scored the only run in the eighth inning on consecutive singles by Groat, Boyer, and White.

May 21 — CARDINALS 10, CUBS 3 — Sadecki pitched a complete game, allowing twelve hits for his third victory. White and McCarver both hit two-run home runs. Clemens drove in three runs with a bases-loaded triple in the second inning. Chicago's Glen Hobbie went six innings and lost for the second time.

May 22 — CARDINALS 6, BRAVES 1 — Simmons won his sixth game with a three-hit complete game. Boyer and Javier hit home runs. The Braves committed three errors overall, including a key one in the second inning that gave the Cardinals two unearned runs.

May 23 — BRAVES 8, CARDINALS 4 — Craig gave up ten hits and five earned runs in four innings to lose his second game. The Braves added three more runs off reliever Taylor. Hank Aaron, Rico Carty (two), and Felipe Alou hit home runs for Milwaukee. Billy Hoeft won his first game with three and two-thirds innings of scoreless relief.

May 24 — BRAVES 7, CARDINALS 4 (game one) — Warren Spahn went five and one-third innings, giving up eleven hits but winning his fourth game. Bob Sadowski also pitched three and two-thirds innings of scoreless relief. In relief of Washburn, Sadecki worked one and one-third innings, allowing four hits and four earned runs to take the loss. Boyer had two hits and two RBIs for the Cardinals. Flood also had four hits and one RBI.

May 24 — BRAVES 10, CARDINALS 0 (game two) — Denny Lemaster dominated the Cardinals, allowing three hits and striking out ten en route to a complete-game shutout. Aaron, Menke, and Joe Torre (two) hit home runs for the Braves. Cardinal starter Broglio pitched one and one-third innings and received the loss.

May 25 — No game scheduled. Ground is broken for a new stadium in downtown St. Louis.

May 26 — No game scheduled.

May 27 — GIANTS 2, CARDINALS 1 — Juan Marichal struck out eleven and defeated the Cardinals for a complete-game victory. Gibson went eight innings in the loss. The Giants scored all their runs in the first inning on back-to-back home runs by their first two hitters: Chuck Hiller and Duke Snider. Boyer homered in the bottom of the second for the Cardinals' only score.

May 28 — GIANTS 2, CARDINALS 1 — Although Simmons shut out the Giants for seven innings, Mays hit a two-run home run with two outs in the eighth that led to a Giants victory. With relief help from Bobby Bolin, Hendley went seven innings while allowing only one run.

May 29 — CARDINALS 4, REDS 3 — Sadecki pitched a complete game for his fourth win. The Reds received home runs from Frank Robinson and Tommy Harper. Boyer, McCarver, and Sadecki drove in the Cardinals runs. Jim O'Toole took the loss. The Cardinals' victory ended a five-game losing streak (May 23–28), which would tie for their longest of the season.

May 30 — CARDINALS 7, REDS 1 — Broglio pitched a complete game, struck out six, and allowed only one run on a home run by Gordy Coleman. Boyer belted a home run and a triple, driving in three runs. Groat had a double and triple with two runs scored.

Standings, May 31, 1964

	W	L	T	PCT	GB
Philadelphia Phillies	25	15	0	.625	—
San Francisco Giants	26	17	0	.605	½
St. Louis Cardinals	25	20	0	.556	2½
Milwaukee Braves	23	21	0	.523	4
Pittsburgh Pirates	23	21	0	.523	4
Cincinnati Reds	21	21	1	.500	5
Los Angeles Dodgers	21	23	1	.477	6
Chicago Cubs	19	22	0	.463	6½
Houston Colt .45s	21	26	0	.447	7½
New York Mets	14	32	0	.304	14

May 31 — REDS 6, CARDINALS 0 (game one) — The Reds scored four runs in the first inning as Cardinals starter Washburn walked three and allowed two singles before Craig relieved him. The Reds' Bob Purkey pitched a complete-game shutout.

May 31 — CARDINALS 2, REDS 1 (game two) — Gibson pitched a complete game, allowing one run and six hits and striking out seven. The Cardinals scored their two runs in the eighth inning on a sacrifice fly by Groat and an RBI single by Boyer. Gibson faced a serious ninth-inning challenge. With the Cardinals leading 2–1 and runners on first and second with one out, Gibson retired the final two hitters without additional runs scoring.

Cardinals May win-loss record: 17-14.
Cardinals year-to-date win-loss record: 25-20.

Chapter 16. **Bob Gibson**

Terry W. Sloope

AGE	W	L	PCT.	ERA	G	GS	GF	CG	SHO	SV	IP	H	BB	SO	HBP	WP
28	19	12	.613	3.01	40	36	3	17	2	1	287.1	250	86	245	9	6

Hoot, you're on your way. Nothing can stop you now.

—*From Ghetto to Glory*

Prophetic words indeed. The 1964 World Series was a coming-out party for Bob "Hoot" Gibson. Pitching complete-game victories in Games Five and Seven, Gibson and his teammates on the 1964 St. Louis Cardinals had just disposed of the vaunted New York Yankees, bringing St. Louis its first world championship since 1946. The words were spoken to him privately by his manager, Johnny Keane, during the clubhouse celebration. Keane had been Gibson's first manager in professional baseball and, later, his savior. There were few men who could have spoken more meaningful words to Gibson at that moment. Gibson was named the Series MVP, and his performance put the rest of the baseball world on notice that he was a force to be reckoned with. When Keane was asked during the postgame press conference why he had stuck with Gibson in the finale even though he was obviously spent, Keane replied gently, "I was committed to this fellow's heart."[1]

Over the next ten years, Gibson would carve out a reputation as one of the toughest competitors to ever play the game. His longtime catcher, Tim McCarver, once reflected on Gibson's approach to pitching: "For my money, the most intimidating, arrogant pitcher ever to kick up dirt on a mound is Bob Gibson. . . . If you ever saw Gibson work, you'd never forget his style: his cap pulled down low over his eyes, the ball gripped—almost mashed—behind his right hip, the eyes smoldering at each batter almost accusingly. . . . [He] didn't

Bob Gibson posted a 19–12 record and pitched 287 innings with a 3.01 ERA. He was the MVP of the 1964 World Series. He was inducted into the Hall of Fame in 1981.

like to lose to anyone in anything. . . . Bob was a man of mulish competitive instinct."[2]

Gibson worked quickly, relying on pinpoint control of a vicious slider and two different fastballs for his success. His delivery, in which the right side of his body hurtled violently toward the first base line after he released the ball, gave hitters the impression that he was exploding toward the plate. He also took full advantage of his reputation as a pitcher who would not hesitate to hit a batter for the smallest of transgressions. That reputation was undeserved, at least in Gibson's mind.

80

He rarely hit batters deliberately. Any batter who got too comfortable in the batter's box, any hitter determined to reach across the plate to drive an outside pitch, could count on getting shaved by an inside pitch. If the batter's body happened to get in the way of the ball, if he had to go down on his backside to avoid getting hit, so be it. Gibson made no apologies.

He would not fraternize with opposing players, even when he played with them in All-Star Games. Joe Torre told a tale of catching Gibson in the 1965 All-Star Game. After the game, as they were showering, Torre complimented Gibson on his performance. Gibson didn't say a word. He showered, got dressed, and left. His aloof demeanor carried over to the press as well. The press respected him, but few understood or knew him well.

Gibson was the first to admit that he was competitive; everything he did was geared toward winning. Winning was his raison d'être. He was going to use every tool, physical and mental, to achieve that goal. He balked at some of the harsher descriptions of his attitude and pitching style.

"I'd like to think that the term 'intensity' comes much closer to summarizing my pitching style than do qualities like meanness and anger, which were merely devices. . . . My pitching career, I believe, offers a lot of evidence to the theory that baseball is a mental discipline as much as a physical one. . . . The part of pitching that separates the stars from everyone else is about 90 percent mental. That's why I considered it so important to mess with a batter's head without letting him inside mine."[3]

Born in Omaha, Nebraska, on November 9, 1935, Pack Robert Gibson was the youngest of seven children.[4] He was named after his father, who died shortly before Bob's birth. His mother, Victoria, worked in a laundry and cleaned houses to make ends meet. Bob spent most of his childhood living in the Logan-Fontenelle housing project on Omaha's north side.

Bob's oldest brother, Josh, became his surro-

Fireballing Bob Gibson seemed to put everything he had into each pitch he threw.

gate father and mentor. Josh was educated, earning degrees in history from Creighton University, near their home in Omaha. He became the program director at a recreation center near the projects and spent much of his life mentoring young boys in the local community. As Bob later recalled, "He had always been the central figure in my life—father, coach, teacher, and role model. . . . Josh led by example. He required no more from any of us than he gave himself. . . . He would have loved to have the opportunity . . . to pursue a career in professional sports. . . . But since that avenue was closed for him—the color barriers were not broken in time to help Josh—he did as he told me I would otherwise have to do: He got an education. And don't think the boys on the team didn't notice. . . . We were all, one way or another, a reflection of Josh."[5]

Josh organized youth sports teams—primarily basketball and baseball—at the recreation center, and Bob spent much of his early childhood there watching and, eventually, playing ball with his brother. On the Y Monarchs baseball team, Bob was a catcher and shortstop while pitching only occasionally. He was lean, strong, and quick; he became a switch hitter who could hit for high average with some power. In 1951 the Monarchs became the first black team ever to win the American Legion city championship. Bob was selected to the all-city team as a utility player.

Bob's favorite sport, however, was basketball. In addition to playing on the recreation center teams, he played on the Omaha Technical High School team for two seasons and was a unanimous choice for the all-city team in his senior season.

Gibson was not allowed to try out for the baseball team during his junior year, ostensibly on the grounds that he had reported a day late for tryouts. Several years later he discovered he had been excluded because the coach at that time did not allow blacks on the team. Instead, he ran track that year, setting an Omaha indoor record in the high jump and also participating in the broad jump and sprint relays. By Gibson's senior season, a new baseball coach was in place at Tech and Bob joined the team, playing the outfield and pitching. He finished second in batting average among city players at .368. Tech won the intercity tournament and Gibson was selected to the all-city team as a utility player.

After high school, Cardinals scout Runt Marr offered him a very modest contract, but his brother Josh insisted he should go to college. Bob tried to get a basketball scholarship to Indiana University but was denied entry because the school "already had its quota of Negroes." Thanks to Josh's connections at Creighton University, Bob became the first African American to receive a basketball scholarship from the Blue Jays. By the time his career at Creighton was over, Gibson was the university's all-time leader in points per game (20.2) and third in total points (1,272). Gibson's basketball jersey number (No. 45) is one of three that have been retired by Creighton (as of 2011), along with Paul Silas's and Bob Portman's.[6]

Gibson also played baseball at Creighton, although baseball was treated as a minor sport at the time. His first baseball coach was Bill Fitch, an aspiring basketball coach who had been hired to coach baseball. (Fitch went on to have a successful coaching career in the NBA.) Bob was a superb utility player at Creighton, where he caught, pitched, and played third base and the outfield. In his senior year he led the Nebraska College Conference with a .333 batting average and went 6-2 as a pitcher. The Dodgers, Yankees, White Sox, Phillies, and Athletics all contacted him about playing professional baseball, but none offered a substantial bonus. He seemed to have flown below the radar of most NBA scouts as well. The Minneapolis Lakers were the only NBA team to talk to him, but they never made an offer.

Opportunities to play both sports eventually developed, however. The Harlem Globetrotters were barnstorming the country exhibiting their brand of highly entertaining basketball against a group of college all-stars that accompanied them on their tours. For publicity, the Globetrotters typically asked a local college player in each city in which they played to join the all-star team. When the Globetrotters played in Omaha in the spring of 1957, Gibson was asked to join the collegians for that game. When given the chance to play late in the third quarter, Gibson made such an impression that he was recruited to join the Globetrotters. Gibson, who had married Charline Johnson the previous day, told the Globetrotters he could not consider their offer until the baseball season and school were over. The Cardinals were still interested in him as well. Gibson finally negotiated a deal that allowed him to play the rest of the baseball season in the Cardinals' Minor League system, after which he would join the Globetrotters for four months. At the end of his four months with the Globetrotters, Gibson and the Cardinals agreed on a deal that allowed Bob to focus solely on baseball.

Gibson reported to Triple-A Omaha of the American Association in June 1957. Johnny Keane, who was managing Omaha, determined that Gibson should focus on pitching. Gibson was taken by the fact that Keane "had no prejudices concerning my color. . . . He was the closest thing to a saint that I ever came across in baseball."

Gibson appeared in ten games for Omaha. He notched his first win on June 23, defeating Columbus (Ohio), 4–3. He posted a 2-1 record before being sent to the Class A Columbus, Georgia, farm club (South Atlantic League) in July. It was there that Gibson first faced a blatantly hostile environment in which blacks were subjugated to second-class citizenship (at best) every day and in every aspect of life. That's not to say there hadn't been problems while he was growing up in Omaha; certainly he had encountered episodes of racial bigotry when he was younger. In Columbus, Gibson

became aware of the extent to which racial hatred had been institutionalized throughout all aspects of southern society. He was forced to live and eat in the "black" part of town, away from his teammates. Local fans did not hesitate to voice their racial prejudices at the ballpark. Bob was exposed to racial taunts and language he had never heard before. Thankfully for him, his time with Columbus was brief. He appeared in eight games, all as a starter, finishing 4-3 with a 3.77 ERA.

At spring training with the Cardinals in St. Petersburg, Florida, in 1958, Gibson was subjected once again to the humiliation of being forced to live apart from his white teammates. He split the season between the Cardinals' Triple-A clubs in Omaha and Rochester and finished with an overall record of 8-9 and a 2.84 earned-run average in thirty-three games. League managers voted his fastball "best-in-league" after the season.

Gibson was a candidate for the Cardinals' rotation in 1959, but establishing himself in the big leagues would prove difficult: "The bad news was that my performance would be judged by the Cardinals' overmatched new player-manager, a utility infielder named Solly Hemus. . . . [His] treatment of black players was the result of one of the following. . . . Either he disliked us deeply or he genuinely believed that the way to motivate us was with insults. . . . He told me, like he told Curt Flood, that I would never make it in the majors. . . . I made the team in 1959, but Hemus had me convinced that I wasn't any damn good and, consequently, I wasn't."[7]

Gibson made his Major League debut on April 15, 1959, pitching two innings of relief in a 5–0 loss to the Dodgers. He surrendered two runs, including a home run to Jim Baxes, the first batter he faced. For the next two seasons, Gibson shuttled back and forth between St. Louis and the teams in Omaha and Rochester. He finally returned to the Cardinals for good in June 1960. Gibson offered a sarcastic summary of the situation years later: "My best hope lay in the fact that Hemus, as much as he seemed to dislike me, might not really *know* me. He kept calling me Bridges, confusing me with Marshall Bridges, who was several years older than me, skinnier, and pitched left-handed. But he was black. Solly got *that* much right."[8]

Gibson was not alone in his assessment of Hemus's dislike for black players. Curt Flood later said of his former manager, "Hemus did not share the rather widely held belief that I played center field approximately as well as Willie Mays. . . . He acted as if I smelled bad. . . . My roommate, Bob Gibson, was just as badly off. He could throw as hard as any man alive. . . . [Hemus] never used him if someone else was available."[9]

All doubts about the genesis of Hemus's attitude toward his black players vanished one day in Pittsburgh when, after a fight between Hemus and Pirates pitcher Bennie Daniels, Hemus told his club he had called Daniels a "black son-of-a-bitch." Hemus's revelation was not meant as an apology. As Flood noted later, "We had been wondering how the manager really felt about us, and now we knew. Black sons of bitches. . . . Until then, we had detested Hemus for not using his best lineup. Now we hated him for himself."[10]

When the 1961 season began, Hemus used Gibson irregularly out of the bullpen and as a spot starter before giving him a place in the starting rotation. Independence Day came on July 6 that year for Gibson and the other black players on the club when Hemus was fired and replaced by Johnny Keane. "It was a whole new world for the black players," Gibson said later. Flood echoed Gibson's feelings about Keane: "Johnny Keane . . . was a man of great sensibility, with a great sense of leadership. . . . The most important thing, however, was this: Keane didn't give a damn about color. He said 'You're my best nine men.' What a powerful, supportive feeling that was!"[11]

Gibson went 11-6, and the team 47-33, after Keane took over. (They had been 33-41 under Hemus.) For the entire season, Gibson was 13-12 with a 3.24 ERA.

With Hemus gone and people like Gibson, Flood, and Bill White leading the way, the Cardinals established an atmosphere that virtually eliminated racial tensions among the individual players and allowed the team to go on to great success in the coming years. White players who were not inclined to be so open-minded were challenged by the black leaders on the club in a way that forced them to rethink their attitudes about race. Tim McCarver, from Memphis, Tennessee, was hardly a beacon of progressive thinking when he first joined the Cardinals in 1959 at the age of seventeen. One sweltering day in spring training in his early years, McCarver got on the team bus after a game with an ice cream cone. (Flood remembers it as a bottle of orange pop.) Gibson asked McCarver if he could take a lick of his ice cream. McCarver was clearly taken aback by the request and fumbled around for an answer before finally telling Gibson he'd "save him some." Gibson used McCarver's own prejudices to put him in an untenable position. His goal was not to exacerbate racial tensions between the players, however. His ultimate goal was to force his white teammates to confront their own racial bigotries. McCarver did change, and he and Gibson became good friends. As McCarver later recalled, "I believe Bob taught me a good deal about relationships with other human beings. If I came to that first spring training with many of the preoccupations of my birthplace, it was probably Gibson more than any other black man who helped me to overcome whatever latent prejudices I may have had."[12]

Curt Flood also exulted in the cohesiveness of the Cardinals of that era. They were "as close to being free of racist poison as a diverse group of twentieth-century Americans could possibly be. Few of them had been that way when they came to the Cardinals. But they changed. . . . The initiative

TERRY W. SLOOPE

in building that spirit came from black members of the team. Especially Bob Gibson. . . . We blacks wanted life to be more pleasant, championships or not. . . . It began with Gibson and me deliberately kicking over traditional barriers to establish communication with the palefaces. . . . After breaking bread and pouring a few with us, the others felt better about themselves and us. Actual friendships developed. Tim McCarver was a rugged white kid from Tennessee and we were black, black cats. . . . Without imposing blackness on Tim or whiteness on ourselves, we simply insisted on knowing him and on being known in return."[13]

With improved control over his fastball and slider, and the confidence of Johnny Keane, Gibson took his first steps toward star status in 1962. He made the National League All-Star team and finished with a 15-13 record and a 2.85 ERA. His season was cut short in September, however, by a broken ankle suffered during batting practice. Gibson was not very conscientious about rehabbing his ankle in the off-season; as a result, he got off to a slow start in 1963. The Cardinals were in the pennant race by midseason, however, and made a strong run in September before dropping out of the race. Gibson won eighteen games that year, and the nucleus of the club that would win the pennant in 1964 had been established.

The Cardinals were far back in the standings in June of 1964 when they acquired an underachieving young outfielder, Lou Brock, from the Chicago Cubs. Paired with Curt Flood at the top of the order and batting in front of either Bill White or Dick Groat and then Ken Boyer, Brock saw his bat come alive, and the Cardinals slowly moved to get back into the race. By late July their prospects were still so remote, however, that owner August Busch openly courted Leo Durocher as a possible replacement for Johnny Keane, and general manager Bing Devine was fired in August. The Cardinals managed to get within six games of the league lead with two weeks left in the season.

An epic collapse by the Phillies, who lost twelve of their last fifteen games, including a streak of ten straight, allowed the Cardinals to win the pennant on the last day of the season. Gibson pitched four innings of relief that day against the Mets to get the win, his nineteenth of the year. Years later, Gibson reflected on that Cardinal team: "The Cardinals were the rare team that not only believed in each other but genuinely liked each other. . . . As a team, we would simply not tolerate any sort of festering rancor between us, personal or racial. . . . We bought our racial feelings out into the open and dealt with them. . . . I'm confident I had a lot to do with it, and so did guys like White and Flood. . . . None of us gave an inch to racism. The white players respected that . . . and in turn we respected them. . . . Of all the teams I was on . . . there was never a better band of men than the '64 Cardinals."[14]

Johnny Keane resigned immediately after the 1964 World Series and was replaced by Red Schoendienst. Team chemistry wasn't enough to carry the Cardinals through the 1965 and 1966 seasons. Although Gibson flourished during those seasons, winning twenty and twenty-one games, respectively, the Cardinals struggled. Production from both White and Boyer slipped precipitously in 1965, and after the season they, along with Dick Groat, were traded. After finishing seventh in 1965, the Cardinals only managed to improve to sixth place in 1966.

An improved offense led by Orlando Cepeda and the development of a number of young pitchers, including Steve Carlton, Ray Washburn, Dick Hughes, and Nelson Briles, allowed the Cardinals to make a shambles of the 1967 pennant race. They won 101 games and took the pennant by 10½ games over the San Francisco Giants. The development of the young pitchers was critical to the Cardinals' drive to the pennant when Gibson was forced onto the disabled list on July 15 after suffering a broken leg. In that day's game against the Pirates, a liner off the bat of Roberto Clemente caromed off Gibson's right shin. Gibson pitched to three more batters before his leg finally snapped just above the ankle. The episode cemented Gibson's reputation as a competitive, gutsy player. He returned to the rotation in September and finished the regular season with a 13-7 record. He won all three of his starts in the 1967 World Series as the Cardinals defeated the Boston Red Sox in seven games. All three of his starts were complete games, giving him five consecutive World Series–game victories and adding to his reputation as a big-game pitcher. He also homered in Game Seven. He was named the World Series MVP for the second time. His first autobiography, *From Ghetto to Glory*, written with assistance from Phil Pepe, was published between the 1967 and 1968 seasons.

In what became known as the "year of the pitcher," Major League Baseball witnessed a number of amazing pitching feats in 1968. In the American League, the Tigers' Denny McLain won thirty-one games, the first pitcher to win thirty games since Dizzy Dean in 1934. In the National League, Don Drysdale set a record of fifty-eight and two-thirds consecutive scoreless innings pitched. Gibson's performance in 1968 outshone them all, however. He finished with a record of 22-9 and a 1.12 ERA, the lowest earned run average of any pitcher since the Deadball Era. He had his own streak of forty-seven and two-thirds scoreless innings. He threw twenty-eight complete games, including thirteen shutouts. He was voted league MVP and was a unanimous selection for the National League Cy Young Award, while the Cardinals again outdistanced their closest rival, the Giants, by nine games for their second consecutive pennant. Gibson's dominance in 1968, along with the performances of Drysdale and McLain, was the driving force behind Major League Baseball's decision to narrow the strike zone and lower the mound from fifteen to ten inches for the 1969 season to invigorate the offensive side of the game.

Gibson defeated the Tigers and Denny McLain in the first game of the 1968 World Series, striking out seventeen batters in a record-setting performance that most view as one of the most dominating performances in World Series history. He had another complete-game victory and hit his second World Series home run in Game Four, giving the Cardinals a 3–1 lead in the Series and giving Bob a record seven consecutive complete-game victories in World Series play. The Tigers won Games Five and Six, however, setting up a showdown between Gibson and Tigers lefty Mickey Lolich. Game Seven was scoreless in the seventh inning when Detroit, capitalizing on a misplay by Curt Flood in center field, scored three runs. Detroit won the game, 4–1.

Things went downhill for the Cardinals after 1968, although Gibson still had some productive seasons ahead of him. Cepeda, their clubhouse cheerleader, was traded to the Atlanta Braves for Joe Torre before the 1969 season. As the players union threatened to delay the start of the 1969 season with a strike, owner Busch publicly blasted his team in spring training for being complacent and too concerned with monetary matters, further lowering club morale. Although Gibson went 20-13 with a 2.18 ERA, the Cardinals dropped to fourth place in the National League's new Eastern Division.

Gibson won twenty-three games and picked up his second Cy Young Award in 1970, although the Cardinals struggled. It was the last time he would win twenty games in a season. His record slipped to 16-13 in 1971, although he pitched his only no-hitter, on August 14 against the Pittsburgh Pirates in Three Rivers Stadium.

Gibson rebounded to win nineteen games in 1972 and made his last appearance in an All-Star Game. In 1973 the Cardinals were in pennant contention in August when he tore knee cartilage while running the bases. The Cardinals didn't play well while Gibson was out and lost the division

TERRY W. SLOOPE

flag to the Mets by one and a half games. Gibson's season record was just 12-10.

By 1974 Gibson no longer had the stamina and strength to pitch with the overpowering style he had become accustomed to. His personal life also weighed heavily on him as he and his wife, Charline, divorced. He reached the three-thousand-strikeout mark in July, the first pitcher in National League history to do so. The Cardinals were in contention right down to the final day of the season, however. In what must have been a bitter denouement, they lost a chance to win the division when Gibson gave up an eighth-inning home run to the Montreal Expos' Mike Jorgensen and lost the game, 3–2. Gibson finished with a record of 11-13, his first losing season since 1960.

The 1975 season was Gibson's last. He didn't pitch well and was eventually sent to the bullpen. Gibson picked up his last win in the Major Leagues on July 27 in a relief appearance against the Philadelphia Phillies. Bob left the team prior to the last road trip of the season and called it a career. He finished with a career record of 251-174 and an ERA of 2.91. When he retired, his 3,117 strikeouts were a National League record and second overall only to Walter Johnson. He tossed 255 complete games, including 56 shutouts. He was 7-2 in World Series play and was selected to the All-Star team eight times. During his playing career, he was widely regarded as one of the best fielding pitchers of his generation, winning the National League Gold Glove Award at his position each year from 1965 to 1973.[15]

Gibson got involved in a number of other activities after his playing days were over. In the early 1970s, before he retired, he did some postseason broadcasting work for ABC. He parlayed that experience into a stint on ABC's Monday Night Baseball broadcasts for a couple of seasons after his retirement, and contributed to an HBO baseball series in 1978. He also did basketball commentary for a New York radio station and later for WTBS in Atlanta. He hosted a Cardinal pregame and postgame radio show for KMOX in the mid-1980s. In 1990 he joined the ESPN baseball broadcast team but quit after one season for family reasons. (He remarried in 1979, to Wendy Nelson. They had one son, Christopher, together. Gibson had two daughters, Renee and Annette, by his first marriage.)

Gibson was also involved in several commercial ventures in the Omaha area. He was the chairman of the board of directors of Community National Bank, which catered primarily to Omaha's black community. He was the primary financial backer of a radio station in Omaha for several years before selling his stake. He was involved in a print advertising venture that had promise, but he had to abandon that effort when, he asserted, many commercial establishments declined to do business with the firm after learning it was owned by blacks.

In the late 1970s, Gibson opened a restaurant near the Creighton University campus. He was heavily involved in the day-to-day operations of the restaurant. It was quite successful as long as Gibson was around to keep tabs on things; when other opportunities arose a few years later that pulled him away from Omaha, he found it difficult to find reliable people who would maintain his standards of service, and he closed the restaurant after ten years in business.

Jobs in baseball were harder to come by. On his last day with the Cardinals in 1975, general manager Bing Devine (who had been rehired by Busch in December 1967) had spoken to him about an unspecified position in the organization. Gibson begged off, telling Devine he wanted to rest and clear his head before making any decisions about his future. The subject was never raised with him again. "I've often thought how different my life would have been if I had said 'yes' that day," he said later.

In 1981 his friend and former teammate Joe Torre hired him as an "attitude coach" for the

New York Mets. Torre and his coaches were fired after the 1981 season. Gibson had some conversations with the owners of the Louisville Cardinals about managing that team in 1982. He said that opportunity was blocked by the St. Louis front office, although he never knew why.

Torre was hired to manage the Atlanta Braves in 1982, and Gibson joined him as pitching coach. After winning the National League West in 1982, the Braves began to decline and Torre and his staff were fired after the 1984 season. Gibson contacted a number of organizations about coaching vacancies in the years that followed, to no avail. Several years later, he had discussions with his friend Bill White, the National League president, about a job as supervisor of umpires; that job never materialized either. At the time his second autobiography, *Stranger to the Game*, was published in 1994, Gibson was convinced his reputation for being outspoken and difficult to get along with was being held against him. He also believed some people in the Cardinals organization may had been quietly working behind the scenes to keep him out of the game. One contributing factor may have been an incident at the Baseball Hall of Fame. Gibson, elected to the Hall in 1981 in his first year of eligibility, gave a nonscripted acceptance speech and inadvertently forgot to thank Busch, Devine, and others in the Cardinals organization. Gibson was horrified when informed later about the oversight and, although he immediately contacted Busch to explain and apologize, he wondered if his breach of etiquette wasn't partly responsible for the difficulties he had finding a job in baseball. A disillusioned Gibson noted in his autobiography, "It baffles me . . . that baseball would feel so antagonistic toward me as to keep me out of its ranks when all I ever did was try to play it to the best of my ability."

In 1990 Gibson had a brief flirtation with a group of investors, including Donald Trump, who were interested in forming a rival baseball league, but the endeavor folded when the investors realized they could never compete with the newly found riches Major League teams enjoyed as a result of Major League Baseball's new broadcasting contract with ESPN.

Gibson had one last fling as an on-field coach. Joe Torre was hired to manage the Cardinals in 1990, and in 1995 Gibson came aboard as pitching coach. Torre was fired in mid-June, however, and Gibson was out at the end of the season. He later served as a special instructor for the Cardinals for several years.

As of 2011 Gibson continued to live in suburban Omaha. He was on the board of directors of the Baseball Assistance Team (BAT), an organization that provides aid to old ballplayers who are down on their luck. In addition to his other honors, he was named to MLB's All-Century Team. He was the first inductee into the Creighton University Athletics Hall of Fame (1968), and the university created the Robert Gibson Scholarship in 2005 in honor of his career achievements. He was inducted into the Missouri Valley Conference Hall of Fame in 2005 and the Omaha Sports Hall of Fame in 2007. In 2009 he and fellow Hall of Famer Reggie Jackson teamed with Gibson biographer Lonnie Wheeler to offer their perspectives on the battle between pitchers and batters in *Sixty Feet, Six Inches: A Hall of Fame Pitcher and a Hall of Fame Hitter Talk about How the Game Is Played* (Doubleday).

TERRY W. SLOOPE

Chapter 17. **Dick Groat**

Joseph Wancho

AGE	G	AB	R	H	2B	3B	HR	TB	RBI	BB	SO	BAV	OBP	SLG	SB	GDP	HBP
33	161	636	70	186	35	6	1	236	70	44	42	.292	.335	.371	2	15	0

Before Bo Jackson and Deion Sanders made "two-sport athletes" a vogue term in the 1980s and '90s, there was Dick Groat. Groat lacked the power of Jackson or the speed of Sanders, but what he lacked in physical gifts he more than made up in guile and spirit. His collegiate career at Duke University earned him All-American honors in basketball and election to the College Basketball Hall of Fame. His baseball career saw him rise from the college ranks directly to the Major League level. He did not play an inning of a Minor League game.

At five feet eleven with a modest build, Groat may not have looked the part of a professional athlete. But he excelled under the guidance of two giants of their profession. At Duke, Groat was coached briefly by Red Auerbach, who went on to a career as coach and then general manager of the Boston Celtics that earned him election to the Basketball Hall of Fame. Later he was signed by Branch Rickey, a Hall of Famer as a baseball executive, to join the Pittsburgh Pirates. These two larger-than-life personalities helped shape Groat into the athlete and person he became: Auerbach taught Groat how to attain a competitive edge in competition, and Rickey instilled a mental discipline and fortitude in him.

Richard Morrow Groat was born on November 4, 1930, in Wilkinsburg, Pennsylvania, which is adjacent to Pittsburgh. He was the fifth and youngest child (after Martin, Charles, Elsie, and Margaret) of Martin and Gracie Groat. Martin Groat worked in the real-estate investment business.

At Swissvale High School, Groat earned letters in basketball, baseball, and volleyball. He attended Duke University on a basketball scholar-

A former MVP with prior World Series experience, Dick Groat hit .292 for the 1964 Cardinals. One of his specialties was the hit-and-run play.

ship. He became a two-time All-American in both basketball and baseball. On the hardwood, Groat was named the National Player of the Year after his senior season (1951–52), when he averaged 26 points and 7.6 assists per game. He is the only player in NCAA history to lead the nation in both scoring and assists in a season. On May 1, 1952, he was the first player at Duke to have his uniform number (10) retired.

In baseball Groat played shortstop and helped

Groat takes a throw from Roger Craig and picks off Mickey Mantle in Game Four of the World Series.

to lead the Blue Devils to a 31-7 record and their first College World Series appearance in his senior year, 1952. He hit .370 and led the team in doubles, hits, runs batted in, and stolen bases. He was a two-time winner of the McKelvin Award, given to the Athlete of the Year in the Southern Conference.

In the summer of 1951, between Groat's junior and senior years, Branch Rickey, general manager of the Pirates, invited Groat and his father to stop in his office. "We got there in the afternoon and Mr. Rickey pulled out a document and said: 'If you sign this contract, you can play shortstop against the Phillies tonight,'" Groat recalled. After Groat pointed out that he still had another year of college, Rickey suggested that he could complete his education during the off-season. "Mr. Rickey, I'm down at Duke on a basketball scholarship," Groat said. "I feel obligated to play the full four years. But I will tell you this much — if you make the same offer to me next June, I'll sign."[1] (That was in the days before the free-agent draft.)

True to his word, Groat signed with the Pirates the next year, in June 1952, after Duke had been eliminated from the College World Series. His contract included a bonus said to be in the $35,000 to $40,000 range. Bypassing the Minor Leagues, he joined the Pirates in New York, where they were

playing the Giants. His first day in uniform, June 17, Groat observed the action from the visiting team dugout at the Polo Grounds. The next day he made his Major League debut, pinch-hitting and grounding out to Giants hurler Jim Hearn. Groat got his first two hits the next day, stayed in the lineup for the rest of the season, and led the team in hitting with a .284 batting average. Only two other regulars ended the season with a batting average above .270: catcher Joe Garagiola (.273) and first baseman–outfielder George Metkovich (.271). Under manager Billy Meyer, Pittsburgh finished the 1952 campaign in last place with a 42-112 record, fifty-four and a half games behind first-place Brooklyn.

Groat was helped during his rookie season by Pirate Hall of Famer Paul Waner, who operated some batting cages in nearby Harmarville. Groat would visit the batting cages before heading to Forbes Field each morning for practice. "He was fun to be with, I really liked Paul Waner," Groat said. "He couldn't have been nicer to me in every way. He helped me build confidence. . . . He was very patient, very understanding, and had a great hitting philosophy. Even at that age (49), he could still hit that machine and hit that ball hard."[2]

After the season Groat returned to Duke to fin-

JOSEPH WANCHO

ish his degree. He was drafted by the Fort Wayne Pistons in the first round (third pick overall) of the NBA's college draft. (Groat always favored basketball, feeling that was the sport he excelled at the most.) "I never practiced with them," Groat said of the Pistons. "I was still trying to get those credits from Duke, and the Pistons would fly me from school to games in a private plane. I loved pro basketball. Basketball was always my first love, mainly because I played it best and it came easiest to me."[3] In twenty-six games with the Pistons, he averaged 11.9 points per game.

His basketball season was cut short when he was drafted again, this time by the U.S. Army. For the next two years he fulfilled his military commitment at Fort Belvoir in Virginia. While serving in the military, he kept in shape playing basketball and baseball on the Belvoir Engineer teams.

Although the Pirates floundered during the Rickey era, the general manager was laying the groundwork for future success. In addition to signing Groat, Rickey also selected Roberto Clemente from Brooklyn via the Rule 5 Draft in 1954 and signed Bill Mazeroski the same year. Clemente and Mazeroski were key ingredients in bringing two world championships to Pittsburgh, and both are in the Baseball Hall of Fame.

A move Rickey made before Groat got to Pittsburgh benefited the player. He brought George Sisler to Pittsburgh in 1951. Sisler, who had worked for Rickey in Brooklyn, was the Pirates' scouting supervisor and unofficial hitting coach. "Sisler teaches us to be ready for the fastball and adjust our swing for the curve," Groat said at the time. "If you're looking for a curve and get a fastball, you never hit it. But you can cut down on the speed of your swing to hit the curve."[4]

When Groat returned from military duty in 1955, he wanted to play both baseball and basketball. "Basketball was fun to me, and baseball was work," he said. The Pistons offered a higher salary and would allow him to leave the team early for spring training. Groat cited the example of Gene Conley, who pitched for the Milwaukee Braves and played basketball for the Boston Celtics. "Don't bring up Conley with me," Rickey told Groat. "As a starting pitcher he only works every fourth or fifth day, and he's only a backup center in basketball. You are a regular player in both baseball and basketball. I think you should realize that eventually you won't justify your salary in either sport."[5] Persuaded by Rickey's logic, Groat chose to focus on baseball.

Groat started slowly in 1955, hitting .229 in April and .235 in May. A slow start might have been expected, but Rickey would cut him no slack. Groat recalled talking to himself in the batting cages when he heard Rickey say just loud enough to be heard, "There is no way that the boy can improve. He never was an All-American in baseball and basketball."[6] This may have been Rickey's way of getting him to concentrate more at the plate. Groat ended the year hitting .267 for the last-place Pirates, who finished thirty-eight and a half games out of first place under manager Fred Haney. He capped off the year by marrying Barbara Womble, once a top New York model, on November 11. They eventually had three daughters, Tracey, Carol Ann, and Allison.

Before the 1956 season, Rickey was replaced as general manager by Joe L. Brown. Brown did not share Rickey's high opinion of Sisler, and dropped him as one of his first moves. He brought in Bobby Bragan to replace Haney. The change made little difference: the Pirates rose to seventh place but were still a distant twenty-seven games behind pennant-winner Brooklyn. When Bragan began 1957 with a record of 36-67, he was fired and replaced by third base coach Danny Murtaugh.

Groat began to flourish under Bragan, and then Murtaugh. His batting average leaped from .273 in 1956 to .315 in 1957 and .300 in 1958. The Pirates went from a last-place finish in 1957 to second place in 1958, with a record of 84-70, eight games behind Milwaukee. Both Groat and the Pirates regressed in 1959. He still hit well, batting .275, but he led the league with twenty-nine errors at shortstop as the Pirates ended the season in fourth place. Groat appeared in the 1959 All-Star Game, the first of five appearances in his career.

One knock against Groat was that he could not hit with power. He did not strike out much, fanning more than sixty times in only one season. But as a contact hitter he was adept at hitting the ball through the open hole in the infield. Murtaugh allowed Groat to pick his spots to hit and run, often with Groat flashing a sign to the base runner. Critics also pointed to his lack of range at shortstop and his weak arm. Fellow shortstop Alvin Dark defended him. "They say he doesn't have much range at shortstop. What's range but getting to the ball?" Dark said. "You watch Groat. He's always in front of the ball. He's smart and he knows the hitters and plays position as well as anyone I ever saw. Maybe he doesn't have a great arm, but he makes up for it by getting the ball away quicker than anyone else."[7]

Pittsburgh put it all together in 1960, winning the pennant by seven games over the Milwaukee Braves and then capturing the team's first world championship since 1925 by defeating the New York Yankees on Mazeroski's dramatic walk-off home run. Groat led the league in hitting with a .325 batting average, finished third with 186 hits, and was named the National League's Most Valuable Player by both *The Sporting News* and the Baseball Writers Association of America. He had his best day at the plate on May 13 in Milwaukee when he went 6 for 6 with 3 doubles. He earned MVP honors (though teammate Roberto Clemente felt he should have won the award) even though he was sidelined for most of September with a broken left wrist after being hit by Milwaukee pitcher Lew Burdette. Returning to the lineup just before the end of the season, Groat hit .214 in the World Series with 2 doubles and 2 RBIS.

Over the next two years, the Pirates slipped back to the middle of the pack. In 1962 Groat led the league's shortstops with thirty-eight errors. After the season rumors circulated that Groat, who turned thirty-two in the off-season, would be traded.

Meanwhile, in St. Louis, August Busch Jr. had lured Branch Rickey to work as a senior consultant to the Cardinals' front office. Busch was dismayed at the Cardinals' inability to win a championship since 1946. Cardinals general manager Bing Devine and Rickey clashed immediately. Their relationship was rocky at the beginning and got worse as the months went by. Devine had been working to acquire Groat from the Pirates, but Rickey quashed it. Rickey believed in trading older players, not acquiring them. He looked to dump players a year early, when there was some value, as opposed to a year too late.

Cardinals skipper Johnny Keane also wanted Groat to join the team. "With Groat to assist and guide him, I believe Julian Javier would develop into a truly great second baseman," Keane said. "Our infield also would be improved by the presence of a take-charge guy such as Groat. Our infield as constituted last season was not an aggressive combination."[8] A deal was made on November 19, 1962, and Groat went to St. Louis with relief pitcher Diomedes Olivo in exchange for pitcher Don Cardwell and shortstop Julio Gotay.

After some initial apprehension, Groat was happy to be heading to St. Louis. "I think the Cardinals are a good club that got some tough breaks last season," he said. "I know I am not young, and I'd like to play on a contender a few more years."[9]

The Cardinals started 1963 with a 14-6 record in April. They held a slim one-and-a-half-game lead over the Dodgers and Giants at the end of June. The infield quartet of first baseman Bill White, second baseman Julián Javier, third baseman Ken Boyer, and Groat were having very good years at the plate. At midseason White, Boyer, and

Groat were hitting .300 or better and Javier was holding steady with a .270 batting average. All four infielders started for the National League in the All-Star Game.

Late in the season the Cardinals went on a torrid pace, winning nineteen of twenty games from August 30 to September 15. On September 16 they trailed Los Angeles by one game, with the Dodgers coming to St. Louis for a three-game series. The Dodgers swept the series, including a four-hitter by Sandy Koufax in the second game and a 6–5 Dodgers victory in thirteen innings in the finale. The Cardinals went on the road and dropped five games in the final week of the season, putting an end to their pennant hopes.

Groat ended the 1963 season with career highs in hits (201), doubles (43), triples (11), and RBIS (73). His .319 batting average tied for third and his 43 doubles led both leagues. He finished second to Koufax in voting for the MVP.

During the season, center fielder Curt Flood said he learned a lot about positioning from the veteran shortstop. "I'll play a hitter a certain way, and then I'll notice that Dick is a bit further to the right than I would have thought. His knowledge of the hitters is so good, I figure he must be right, so I move to the right too," Flood said.[10]

The Cardinals finally broke through in 1964, capturing their first world championship since 1946. Groat hit .292, drove in 70 runs, and stroked 35 doubles. In a thrilling race to the finish, St. Louis went 21-8 in September. The Philadelphia Phillies held a six-and-a-half-game lead over St. Louis and Cincinnati on September 20, but then closed out the month on a ten-game losing streak. When the Cardinals sewed up the pennant in the final game of the season, against the New York Mets, Groat hit two doubles and scored twice in the Cardinals' 11–5 victory.

After going down 2 games to 1 in the World Series against the Yankees, the Cardinals won 3 out of 4 and were crowned world champions.

Groat had only 5 hits for a .192 batting average, but also got on base 4 times with walks.

In Game Four, relief pitcher Roger Craig walked Mickey Mantle and Elston Howard with two outs in the third inning. The next batter was Tom Tresh. Groat knew that Craig had an excellent move to second base, and at times they ran what they called "the daylight play." If Groat got inside the runner at second base and there was daylight between them, they would try for the pick-off. There was no signal to the play; Craig and Groat just did it. Groat was able to get between Mantle and the base. Craig turned and threw, and they picked Mantle off. Mantle headed back to the dugout, past Craig. "You son of a bitch," Mantle said. "You show me up in front of forty million people."[11]

Manager Johnny Keane surprised everyone by resigning after the World Series and replacing Yogi Berra as manager of the Yankees. Cardinals coach Red Schoendienst took over for Keane. Groat was happy for the switch. "He understands ballplayers," Groat said of Schoendienst. "Everything he does, he does for the good of the players. He's considerate of their feelings at all times. That's why I think he is going to do a tremendous job for us."[12]

Neither Groat nor the Cardinals enjoyed a successful season in 1965. The team slipped to seventh place in the ten-team league, and the thirty-four-year-old Groat hit .254. After the season the Cardinals traded Groat with first baseman Bill White and reserve catcher Bob Uecker to Philadelphia for pitcher Art Mahaffey, outfielder Alex Johnson, and catcher Pat Corrales. "We got him because I know he can still hit. But, more important, he knows he can still hit," said Phillies manager Gene Mauch. "And a player like Groat always hits better when his ballclub is in the game all the time."[13]

Besides playing shortstop for the Phillies, Groat also played twenty games at third base, a position he disliked but nonetheless was willing to play. The team finished fourth, eight games behind the first-place Dodgers. On May 18, facing the Cardinals, Groat got his two thousandth career hit, a single to center field off Bob Gibson.

Groat was hobbled during the 1967 season by cellulitis, an inflammation of the tissues and veins in his right ankle. The ankle swelled to three times its normal size and Groat's temperature rose to 104 degrees. He was hospitalized for two weeks and missed two months of the season. He played in only ten games for the Phillies before being sold to San Francisco on June 22. After batting a puny .156 for both teams, he retired after the season. Groat ended his playing career with a batting average of .286 in fourteen Major League seasons.

For many years Groat had worked during the off-season as a salesman for Jessup Steel in Washington, Pennsylvania. In 1965 he took a new direction. Groat and former Pirates teammate Jerry Lynch built a public golf course, called Champion Lakes, in Laurel Valley, fifty miles east of Pittsburgh. As of 2011, Groat was still spending half his time living at Champion Lakes and keeping active in the day-to-day operations of the course. He also spent thirty-three years (as of the 2011–12 basketball season) as a color analyst on radio broadcasts of University of Pittsburgh basketball games.

In 1990 Barbara Groat died of lung cancer. She and Dick had been married for thirty-five years.

In November 2007 Groat was inducted into the National Collegiate Basketball Hall of Fame in Kansas City, Missouri. He has also received the Arnold Palmer Spirit of Hope Award, given annually to people who serve as an inspiration to children all over the world. He has remained active with charity events involving the Pittsburgh Pirates Alumni Association.

Chapter 18. **Glen Hobbie**

Jim Leefers

AGE	W	L	PCT.	ERA	G	GS	GF	CG	SHO	SV	IP	H	BB	SO	HBP	WP
28	1	2	.333	4.26	13	5	4	1	0	1	44.1	41	15	18	1	0

Signed to a Triple-A contract at the age of nineteen, Illinois-born Glen Hobbie quickly discovered that he was overmatched at that level. He fared little better in Class C, then was sidelined by a muscle spasm in his back, which he cured by swimming in the Mississippi River. Two seasons later, he was in the Major Leagues. The swan song to his eight-year big-league career was about two months with the 1964 world champion Cardinals.

Glen Frederick Hobbie was born on April 24, 1936, in Witt, a farming town with a population of less than a thousand in south-central Illinois. He was the ninth of ten children (seven boys, three girls) born to Herman Hobbie, a salesman of home and farm goods, and his wife, Anna.[1]

After graduating from high school in 1955, Hobbie pitched in a local amateur league. A part-time scout, Leonard Scheibal, saw him pitch and signed him for general manager Danny Menendez of the Charleston Senators in the Triple-A American Association. But after he quickly went 0-4, Menendez shipped him to Superior of the Class C Northern League, where he fared a little better with a 2-4 record, then developed the muscle spasm and was sidelined. Hobbie's self-prescribed rehab program was to swim in the Mississippi River for almost two months, and the injury never recurred. In 1956, still the property of Charleston, Hobbie was 8-2 with Class D Dubuque (Midwest League) and 0-2 with Duluth/Superior.

Charleston went bankrupt and Menendez resurfaced in 1957 as the general manager of Memphis in the Southern Association, taking Hobbie along with him. On August 14 Hobbie was 14-11 and the Chicago Cubs purchased his contract from

Traded to the Cardinals on June 2, Glen Hobbie appeared in thirteen games and compiled a 1–2 record with 4.26 ERA. At the end of July, the Cardinals optioned him to the Minors. (Photo by Allied Photocolor Imaging Center)

Menendez for $50,000. Hobbie finished the season with Memphis, winding up with a 15-15 record in nineteen starts and thirty-four relief appearances. His manager, Lou Klein, said, "He's a throwback to the days when a pitcher wanted to pitch every chance he could get."[2]

Hobbie finished the season with the Cubs. His first Major League appearance came at Wrigley Field against first-place Milwaukee on September 20, and he gave up two runs in two innings as the Braves won, 9–3. Four days later, against the Cincinnati Reds, he gave up three runs in two and one-third innings on two hits and five walks.

In 1958 during spring training, Cubs manager Bob Scheffing called Hobbie one of his top candidates for the number five starting position. Hobbie made his first Major League start on April 17 at Busch Stadium against his childhood favorites, the St. Louis Cardinals. He left in the sixth inning with a 3–2 lead, and the Cubs won, 4–3, giving him his first Major League victory. On May 6 he shut out Cincinnati, 4–0, on four hits. A controversial decision by first base umpire Frank Secory helped preserve the shutout. With runners on first and second and one out in the eighth inning, the Reds' Steve Bilko drove a ball to deep right field. Secory had called time, however, when a ball rolled onto the playing field from the Cubs bullpen, and the at bat was negated. Hobbie walked Bilko to load the bases but retired the side without a run.

After making twelve starts (3-5, 4.71 ERA), Hobbie was moved to the bullpen on June 5. He relieved in thirty-nine games and made four starts the rest of the year. He had a 6-1 record with two saves working out of the bullpen and picked up one more victory as a starter. For the season he was 10-6 with a 3.74 ERA as the Cubs finished in fifth place.

After the season Hobbie and fellow Cubs pitcher Dick Drott did six-month army hitches. Back with the Cubs, he pitched the finest game of his Major League career on April 21, shutting out the Cardinals on one hit. Hobbie had a perfect game until Stan Musial lined a double to left with two outs in the seventh inning. He ended the 1–0 game by getting Musial on a comebacker. Hobbie told reporters, "The first thing I said to myself when Stan got the hit was, 'I'm glad he didn't hit a lollipop; he hit my best pitch.'"[3]

After being sidelined for eight days with tonsillitis, Hobbie defeated Milwaukee 5–4 on July 28 to put the Cubs only four and a half games back of the Giants. But Chicago went into a seven-game tailspin and never recovered, sinking to fifth. (Manager Bob Scheffing was succeeded after the season by Charlie Grimm.) Hobbie was again the workhorse of the young staff, starting thirty-three games and making thirteen relief appearances. On September 13 he pitched another gem against the Cardinals, shutting them out on three hits. Hobbie recorded a 4-1 mark against the second-place Braves during the year, making his career record against Milwaukee 7-1 in his first two seasons. Seventeen of his twenty-six victories in his first two seasons came against first-division clubs.

After the season Hobbie married a high school classmate, Sharon Lee. Then he began the 1960 season on a bright note by shutting out the world champion Dodgers on five hits.

But on May 4 the Cubs were 6-11, and Grimm was replaced as manager by Lou Boudreau, whom the Cubs grabbed from behind the microphone at WGN radio and placed in the dugout. Hobbie was 6-10 through June, though one of his victories was a two-hit victory over Milwaukee. On July 20 he improved his record to 9-11 by pitching a two-hit shutout over Cincinnati.

The most memorable game in Hobbie's career came against the Pittsburgh Pirates on July 30. Glen's wife, Sharon, was about seven and a half months pregnant and woke up that morning with some discomfort. She requested that Glen take her to the hospital prior to the game. Since the baby wasn't due until early September, Glen just assumed he would go back to the hospital after the game and take her back home. Glen left for the game around noon.

The Pirates were enjoying a three-game lead in the National League while the Cubs had lost eight in a row and were twenty-three and a half games out of first and wallowing in the cellar. As the Pirates were taking a 1–0 lead against Glen in the first inning, Sharon was giving birth to a boy,

Glen Jr. The news reached Wrigley Field during the third inning, but the Cubs' officials were reluctant to tell Glen, thinking he might lose his concentration. Manager Boudreau finally decided to tell him when he came in the dugout after the top of the fifth. After a lot of handshakes and congratulations, the Cubs went out and put six runs on the board in the sixth and seventh innings. Earlier, the Wrigley Field public address announcer, Pat Pieper, barked to the crowd of 13,365 that Glen had become a father for the first time.[4] Meanwhile, Glen maintained his focus, went the distance in the 6–1 win, and scattered seven hits to pick up his tenth victory of the season. (Dick Ellsworth's wife also gave birth to a boy on the same day.)

On August 25 Hobbie faced the Pirates again and won it, 2–1, with a walk-off home run, his first homer in the Major Leagues. The Cubs finished the season in seventh place, and for the third year in a row Hobbie led the team in victories, with sixteen, but suffered twenty losses.

Boudreau was fired after the season, and the Cubs' "College of Coaches" was formed. It was an eight-man brain trust with each coach taking a turn as "head coach." Hobbie was not an admirer of the plan. He remembered, "They hired some Olympic track coach to be our trainer. What they didn't understand was that a track coach trains you for one event. But you don't train that way for 154 events. Before the end of spring training, we were all worn out."[5] The real downside was that he injured his lower right back. The pain caused him to alter his follow-through, which in turn injured his shoulder. "I lost quite a bit off my fastball, and everything went downhill from there," he said.[6]

At the start of spring training in 1961, Hobbie had the most career victories, forty-two, of the fifteen pitchers in camp. Chicago would again have one of the youngest pitching staffs in the Majors. Only Hobbie was certain of a starting berth. He got his first Opening Day assignment at Cincinnati and lost, 7–1, allowing all of the Reds' runs in four

and one-third. A 7-18 May put the Cubs in seventh place. On May 23 the Cubs were 12-22 and Hobbie was 2-5; both of his victories were shutouts. Hobbie provided some muscle at the plate on July 2 against the Cardinals at Wrigley Field, hitting two home runs off Al Cicotte. The Cubs won but Hobbie did not get the decision. He went 5-8 for the remainder of the season, finishing with a 7-13 record as the Cubs finished in seventh place in the final year of an eight-team National League.

The Cubs started the 1962 season dropping their first seven games and went 4-16 in April. The first-year Mets were the only reason Chicago stayed out of the National League cellar, though they fell into tenth place on nineteen different dates in May. Hobbie started out poorly, losing six games before he got his first victory, a 2–1 victory over the Braves (Warren Spahn's two hundredth loss). After that Hobbie lost his next three decisions, to fall to 1-9. He made five brief appearances over the next three weeks out of the bullpen, then defeated the Reds, 6–3, on July 14, and topped the Philadelphia Phillies, 5–3, on July 24. Hobbie finished the season 5-14, and the Cubs, with 103 losses, finished ninth, eighteen games ahead of the first-year Mets. The Cubs had finished in the lower division of the National League for sixteen straight years.

After several years of having some of the younger mound staffs in the league, Chicago entered 1963 with a comparatively veteran mound corps with the addition of Larry Jackson and Bob Buhl via trades. After two years of leading the Majors in coaches, Chicago named Bob Kennedy as head coach for the entire season. Early in spring training, Hobbie looked very sharp. Pitching coach Fred Martin had very good success early in the season with the pitching staff. After five weeks of play, Chicago had an earned run average of just over 2.00. Martin worked with Hobbie to fix his awkward delivery, not quite side-arm and not quite three-quarters. Martin's fixes helped Hobbie compile a 0.95 ERA after three starts. Unfortunately for the Cubs' pitchers, the team lacked a sustained offense. In the first sixteen games of the season, Chicago lost seven games in which their opponents were held to three runs or less. Despite Hobbie's 2-5 record in mid-June, he had been looking very sharp. He developed a slider that made him considerably tougher. Still, after a loss to the Cardinals on July 14 that dropped his record to 4-8, he was removed from the starting rotation. He returned to the rotation in September and shut out the Giants on two hits on the 2nd, and got the victory in a shutout of the Houston Colt .45s on the 6th. Kennedy and Martin had done some tinkering with Hobbie's delivery, and it seemed to turn him back into a winner.

Hobbie had been using almost a no-windup type of delivery. He would bring his hands just up around the belt and then, as he pivoted, he would swing the arms straight back away from his body. The Cubs coaches converted his motion into the orthodox windup of bringing his arms over his head. "The batters seemed to time him too easily with that waist-high pivot motion," said Kennedy. "The overhead windup tends to make you follow through better. Glen's follow-through wasn't good at all, probably because the back pain had got him into a straight-up style of delivery. We don't know whether this is going to be the full solution, but we're keeping our fingers crossed."[7]

Hobbie's good run ended on September 10 at St. Louis when he lasted only one and two-thirds innings in an 8–0 loss to the red-hot Cardinals. Hobbie himself seemed baffled about the success of his new pitching style, but happy about it. "After all, I did pretty well with my original delivery when I came up with the Cubs," he said. "I believe the real reason that I slumped so badly in 1961 and 1962 was that I subconsciously was protecting my back. I didn't follow through because I'd get a terrific pain just as I released the ball. The doctors diagnosed it as a pinched nerve in the back. They prescribed certain exercises and finally it slowly corrected itself. When it starts to recur on me, I do those exercises and in three or four days it goes away."[8]

Hobbie ended the year with a 7-10 record. Chicago finished in seventh place with an 82-80 mark, the first time they had finished over .500 since 1946, even though the pitching staff had an ERA of 3.08, second only to that of the world champion Dodgers.

Chicago's quest to build on 1963's improvement was dealt a severe blow on February 13, 1964, when the Cubs' promising young second baseman, Ken Hubbs, died in the crash of his plane during a snowstorm. At his funeral Hobbie served as a pallbearer along with head coach Bob Kennedy, Ron Santo, Ernie Banks, Dick Ellsworth, and Don Elston.

The Cubs were counting heavily on Hobbie being the number four starter in 1964. The improvement he showed late in 1963 and an excellent spring training gave them reasons to be upbeat. In his first three spring appearances, Hobbie didn't permit a run in eight innings of work. His new delivery got the credit. Hobbie said, "What got me off the full windup were those hot, humid days in the Southern Association with Memphis in 1957. In order to keep from perspiring so badly, I tried to cut down on the effort involved in pitching. The only thing I could think of was cutting out the windup. However it was harder on the arm and probably was the cause of the back injury that bothered me back in 1961 and 1962."[9] In an effort to protect his back, he pitched without bending it. "He couldn't possibly get as much on the ball because he was just slinging it," said pitching coach Martin. "In other words, he was merely throwing with his arm. Now he's getting his entire body in the throw. It not only protects his arm, but gives him more stuff."[10]

Unfortunately for Hobbie, the optimism of spring did not transfer into the regular season. At the end of May he had an 0-3 record and a 7.90 ERA. On June 2 Chicago, in an attempt to find a reliable fourth starter, traded the twenty-eight-year-old Hobbie to the Cardinals for thirty-seven-year-old Lew Burdette. Cardinals manager Johnny Keane said he figured on using Hobbie in long relief at first. "When he starts will depend on the progress of [Ray] Washburn," Keane said.[11] Hobbie could not have had a much better debut than he had on June 5 against Cincinnati. In his first at bat he homered off Bob Purkey. He was in front 4–1 when he was relieved in the eighth with one out. The bullpen failed to hold the lead and cost him the Cardinal victory. "I tired fast, but my arm never felt better," said Hobbie. St. Louis pitching coach Howie Pollet said, "Hobbie could turn out to be the steal of the year."[12] Hobbie said, "The Cubs always treated me fine, but after three bad seasons on top of three good ones, it seemed that every time I went out to pitch, I was thinking it was do-or-die." He and Sharon were also pleased with the switch because their new home, in Hillsboro, Illinois, was not far from St. Louis.[13]

His next start, on the 10th, was a two-hit victory over the hard-hitting Giants, 2–1. It turned out to be his final Major League victory. He struggled in his next two starts and found himself relegated to the bullpen. Five appearances out of the bullpen totaling ten innings resulted in only two earned runs and earned Hobbie another start, in which he struggled again. He made three more appearances out of the bullpen; then the Cardinals sent him down to Triple-A Jacksonville and brought up Barney Schultz. For the season he was 1-5 in twenty-one appearances with Chicago and St. Louis.

The Jacksonville Suns were in a battle with Syracuse for the International League crown. Hobbie made his mark on the pennant race early when he one-hit Buffalo. In eight starts for Jacksonville, he went 5-1 to help the Suns win the league championship. The Cardinals were also busy win-ning a championship, overcoming the Phillies and the Reds in the last week for the National League pennant, and defeating the New York Yankees in seven games in the World Series. The Cardinals players voted Hobbie a half share of the winners' pot, $4,311.09, but he was disappointed that he never received a ring.

An off-season Minor League deal sent Hobbie to the Detroit Tigers affiliate at Syracuse. He accepted an invitation from the Tigers to spring training in 1965 and general manager Jim Campbell said he felt Hobbie "could be a sleeper. . . . I like his attitude."[14] Jacksonville owner Bobby Maduro told Campbell, "Hobbie has a chance with Detroit because he is a terrific competitor."[15] But Hobbie did not make the Tigers in spring training and was assigned to Syracuse. He made a determined bid to return to the majors, with a 7-3 record halfway through June, but never received the call. He finished the year with an 8-8 record. Syracuse released Hobbie in April 1966.

Hobbie finished his Major League career with 62 wins, 81 losses, and 6 saves in 284 appearances. He had 45 complete games in his 170 starts, including 11 shutouts.

After leaving baseball, Hobbie worked twenty-five years for the Roller Derby Skate Corporation in Litchfield, Illinois, a maker of roller skates, ice skates, and baseball spikes. He worked his way up to plant manager. His wife, Sharon, was a fourth-grade teacher for many years. Glen Jr. was a stand-out athlete at Hillsboro High School, pitched for Greenville (Illinois) College, and was drafted by the Tigers in the twenty-fourth round of the 1982 amateur draft. He played one season for the Bristol Tigers of the Appalachian League. Glen and Sharon also had a daughter, Linda, two years younger than Glen Jr.

Retired at the time this biography was written in 2011, Hobbie lived on a small farm near Ramsey, Illinois, about twenty miles from his hometown of Witt. He still liked to hunt and fish, but his knee problems curtailed some of his out-door activities. Attending sporting events involving his grandchildren also occupied some of his time. Grandson Bryan played baseball for Greenville College for three years; Eric played basketball for McKendree College in Lebanon, Illinois; and granddaughter Laura played basketball for Greenville College.

Hobbie said he followed baseball just enough to argue with the local guys over coffee, but he kept hoping the Cubs could finally put it all together and win a World Series.

Chapter 19. **Bob Humphreys**

John Harry Stahl

AGE	W	L	PCT.	ERA	G	GS	GF	CG	SHO	SV	IP	H	BB	SO	HBP	WP
28	2	0	1.000	2.53	28	0	10	0	0	2	42.2	32	15	36	1	2

"YOU CAN'T MAKE IT!" Bob Humphreys once wrote that in large letters on the wristband of his baseball glove. The words summarized an early 1963 evaluation of his pitching skills by a Major League team.[1] Although the glove subsequently wore out in 1963 winter ball,[2] Humphreys continued to use those words as a motivator to fashion a nine-year Major League pitching career, including a trip to the World Series with the 1964 St. Louis Cardinals. Humphreys later identified "playing in the '64 World Series with St. Louis" as his outstanding baseball achievement.

Robert William Humphreys was born on August 18, 1935, in Covington, Virginia. His father, Russell, worked as a contract hauler. Bob had three sisters, Sylvia, Betty, and Linda.

In 1954 he graduated from Montvale (Virginia) High School, where he played baseball and basketball. In his junior and senior years his team won its baseball district title. In the fall of 1954 he entered nearby Hampden-Sydney College, where he lettered in both baseball and basketball for the Hampden-Sydney Tigers and, as a pitcher and third baseman, was the team's most valuable baseball player for two of his four seasons. After suffering a serious eye injury in batting practice that could have ended his baseball career, Humphreys concentrated on pitching, and in 1957 and 1958 he made the All Mason-Dixon Conference baseball team. During the summers he played semiprofessional baseball in the Roanoke and New Market (Virginia) areas.

Standing five feet eleven and weighing 165 pounds, Humphreys was not as physically imposing as many pitchers. Instead, he relied on his intel-

Called up at the end of June, Bob Humphreys appeared in twenty-eight games and posted a 2.53 ERA. He also pitched in one World Series game.

ligence and moxie. In his senior year he began using what he called a "weird" pitching windup. Hiding the ball in his glove with his hands together, he pumped pendulum-style in a wide arc to a point behind his right hip, then fired. The unorthodox motion was sometimes characterized as his "rocking chair." His approach emphasized hiding the ball from hitters as long as possible. It was successful enough for him to use throughout his Major League career.[3]

Off the diamond, Humphreys was elected vice president of his senior class. He graduated from Hampden-Sydney with a bachelor's degree in liberal arts. In 1988, during the inaugural year, Hampden-Sydney inducted him into its Athletic Hall of Fame.[4]

After Humphreys graduated, Detroit Tigers scout Frank Skaff signed him to a contract for a $1,000 bonus and a $250-a-month salary, and he broke in with Montgomery of the Alabama-Florida League (Class D), where he pitched 126 innings and posted a 10-5 record with a 2.29 earned run average. After the 1958 season he fulfilled his military obligation, serving with the Marines for six months. Then from 1959 through 1961 he worked his way up through Detroit's Minor League system, pitching for Durham in the Carolina League (Class B), Victoria in the Texas League (Class Double-A), Knoxville in the Sally League (Class A), and Birmingham in the Southern League (Class Double-A), pitching both as a starter and in relief. (At Knoxville, Humphreys pitched what would be a career-high 169 innings.)

Humphreys began the 1962 season with Denver in the Triple-A American Association. Used exclusively in relief, he appeared in a career-high fifty-eight games and posted a 9-7 record with a 2.88 ERA. His solid performance earned him a late season call-up to the Tigers, where he made his Major League debut on September 8, 1962, in Detroit. Entering at the beginning of the eighth inning with the Tigers losing 8–2 to the Minnesota Twins, he gave up a single to Earl Battey, the first hitter he faced, and a subsequent double and an infield single plated another Twins run. Despite giving up a three-run homer in the ninth inning, Humphreys earned his first Major League save the next day.

Two days later, against the New York Yankees, Humphreys entered the game in the ninth inning with the score tied, 9–9, and two Yankees on base. He promptly got Clete Boyer to hit into a double play. In the tenth, though, Yogi Berra hit a home run and Humphreys suffered his first Major League loss.[5]

By the end of the season, he had pitched a total of five innings in four games, posting an 0-1 record with a 7.20 ERA.

After the season, the Tigers embarked on a six-week exhibition tour of Japan. After two Tigers pitchers dropped out, Humphreys was added to the group, and he was able to take his new bride, Tania Lee Taylor, along. They were married on October 6, 1962. "Quite a week for me," he exclaimed. "I never thought I'd be taking a honeymoon trip to Hawaii, Japan, and places like that."[6] (The couple later had two daughters, Kristina and Kari, and a son, Scott.) However, Humphreys pitched only five innings on this trip, signaling the beginning of the end of his time with the Detroit organization. During spring training in 1963, Humphreys saw no action, and eventually the Tigers informed him that he was being returned to the Minors "because we have too many pitchers like you." That led him to write "YOU CAN'T MAKE IT!" on the back of his glove. "Every time that glove goes up before my eyes," he said later, "I seem to pitch just a little bit harder."

Although Humphreys's time with the Tigers ended on a sour note, he received important help from a teammate, pitcher Frank Lary, who taught him how to throw a slider/cutter. When Humphreys subsequently hurt his elbow in 1965, he was forced to rely heavily on the slider/cutter, which became his best pitch.[7] Later, after an arm injury, he came to rely on a knuckle ball.

On March 25, 1963, instead of farming Humphreys out, the Tigers sold him to the St. Louis Cardinals. The Cardinals' Eddie Stanky had scouted Humphreys at Denver and liked him. He was assigned to their Triple-A team in Atlanta where, working in relief, he posted a 5-1 record with a 1.13 ERA before being recalled by the Cardinals in late May. (Before he left Atlanta, Humphreys was taught by teammate Bobby Tiefe-

JOHN HARRY STAHL

nauer how to throw the knuckler, which helped extend his career later when he suffered a shoulder injury.[8])

On June 28 Humphreys suffered a torn lumbar muscle and a tear in the abdominal wall, and was sidelined for nearly a month. He was later optioned back to Atlanta and ended with a 7-2 record and 1.92 ERA for the Crackers. During the International League playoffs, Bob was pitching in relief when him manager, Harry Walker, moved him to left field for one hitter. Humphreys then returned to the mound and struck out two more batters to save the game. Bob was brought back to St. Louis and appeared in one more game before the season ended. In all, for the Cardinals, he pitched in nine games, posting an 0-1 record and a 5.06 ERA.

Like many Major League players at the time, Humphreys played winter ball in the Dominican Republic to supplement his income. In later years he said his success facing Major Leaguers in winter ball boosted his confidence. In 1963 he played for the Licey team managed by Cardinals third base coach Vern Benson.

In 1964 Humphreys was back in Triple-A, with Jacksonville. Once more he began fast, posting a 6-2 record with a 3.07 ERA, and when the Cardinals needed pitching help, they brought him back to the Major Leagues at the end of June. He saw his first action on July 2 against the Braves in Milwaukee, holding them scoreless and hitless for three innings and earning a save. His first victory came over the Chicago Cubs on September 6 in St. Louis. Entering the game in the tenth inning with runners on second and third and no one out, he held the Cubs scoreless. He did the same in the eleventh, and got the win when the Cardinals scored in the bottom of the inning. The win was particularly special for Humphreys because it was the first time his father saw him pitch in the Major Leagues. The elder Humphreys had driven from Virginia to see the game.

Three days later Humphreys won his second game, holding the league-leading Phillies scoreless in the tenth and eleventh innings as the Cardinals rallied for a come-from-behind victory. In the top of the eleventh inning, Humphreys got his first Major League hit and RBI with a solid single to center field, scoring Javier from second base.

Humphreys made one appearance in the World Series, pitching a scoreless ninth inning during the Game Six loss to New York. His teammates voted him a three-quarters share of the players' World Series money. During the regular season, Humphreys appeared in twenty-eight games, going 2-0 with a 2.53 ERA.

Shortly after the World Series, Humphreys went back to the Dominican League. During the sixty-four-game season, he pitched ninety-nine and two-thirds innings in forty-four games, a workload he characterized as "not too smart," because he injured his elbow. Some good came out of his misfortune. Because his curve ball put a lot of stress on his elbow, Humphreys began relying more on the cutter/slider he had learned from Frank Lary while with the Tigers, and it became his best pitch.

On April 7, 1965, the Cardinals traded Humphreys to the Chicago Cubs, who already had a deep bullpen headed by Ted Abernathy and Lindy McDaniel. Pitching mostly in middle relief, Humphreys made forty-one appearances for the Cubs, totaling sixty-five and two-thirds innings. He won two games but had no saves. His ERA was 3.15.

At the end of the season Humphreys asked Cubs general manager John Holland to trade him. He said he did not enjoy pitching in Chicago because of all the day games. Just before the end of spring training on April 2, 1966, the Cubs traded Humphreys to the Washington Senators, where after being on three Major League teams for parts of five seasons, he found some stability. Except for a two-game stay in Buffalo in 1968, Humphreys stayed with the Senators for four full seasons and part of another (1966–70), pitching 396 of his 566 Major League innings. In 1966 he reached highs in appearances (58) and innings pitched (111⅔). He won seven games (three in five days in August) and saved three, a solid record for a club that finished eighth in the American League with a 71-88 record.

During the remainder of his time with the Senators (1967–part of 1970), Humphreys was 14-12 for Senator teams that posted a combined 253-287 record. While in Washington he was the team's player representative, an important but thankless job. During several off-seasons, he also worked in the Capitol Hill office of a Virginia congressman.

Before the 1970 season Humphreys began light training at a University of Maryland indoor facility. One day the Maryland baseball coach asked him to demonstrate his breaking ball for his pitchers. Humphreys promptly reinjured his right elbow. Then he tore a muscle in his right shoulder during spring training, and the Senators sent him to Denver. After he returned, he pitched six and two-thirds innings in five games with a 1.35 ERA before Washington suddenly released him on June 13. Humphreys later described himself as the "most surprised man around" when the team let him go.

Humphreys wasn't jobless for long. On June 15 he signed with the Milwaukee Brewers. Milwaukee manager Dave Bristol liked him. "He's a competitor," Bristol said. "He can pitch his way out of a jam, and that's the kind of performance our club needs." Bristol told Humphreys to use his knuckleball as his primary pitch.[9] Humphreys did, and with good results. In his first seven appearances he notched three saves and one victory. By the end of the season he had appeared in twenty-three games, pitching forty-five and two-thirds innings with a 3.15 ERA and a 2-4 record. Win number two came in his last Major League appearance, and it was in an unaccustomed role. He started the second game of a doubleheader against the White Sox in the last week of the season and pitched five innings, allowing one run in the Brewers' 3–2 victory.

Of the 319 Major League games Humphreys appeared in, all but 4 were in relief. In his Major League starts, including his swan-song appearance with the Brewers in 1970, he was 3-1 with an ERA of 0.95.

The Brewers released Humphreys near the end of spring training in 1971. He caught on with the Brewers' Triple-A affiliate in Evansville (American Association). He pitched in ten games, recording a 1-2 record with a 7.11 ERA. Frustrated with his performance, Bob asked his manager, Del Crandall, for his release, and his request was granted. That was the end of the road for Humphreys as a player. In fifteen seasons in professional baseball, he had appeared in exactly six hundred games and pitched 1,392⅔ innings.

From 1974 to 1978 Humphreys was the baseball coach at Virginia Tech University. During his five-year tenure, his teams won 135 games and lost 60, twice making the NCAA regional playoffs, and winning 31 games in a row in 1977. Humphreys acknowledged that he wanted to get back in the Major Leagues as soon as possible. "The job at Virginia Tech is a great opportunity," he said, "but I'd leave tomorrow for a job in the majors." He got his wish in February 1979 when the Toronto Blue Jays hired him as a Minor League pitching instructor. In 1981 Humphreys managed the Blue Jays Triple-A affiliate in Syracuse. The team finished 60-80, and Humphreys went back to instructing the Jays' Minor League pitching prospects. From 1984 through 2004 he was a Minor League pitching coach for Baltimore, Milwaukee, and St. Louis, with two years out (2000–2001) while he recovered from major knee surgery. He also spent thirteen years as a pitching coach in winter ball in Venezuela.

In 1983 Humphreys married his second wife, Genevieve Stanley Wood of Bedford, Virginia. The couple honeymooned in Medicine Hat, Alberta, one of the places he visited as the Jays' Minor League pitching instructor.

In early 2011 Bob was living in Bedford, in southwestern Virginia, where he was active in several community organizations and enjoyed playing golf.

Asked in a questionnaire during his career whether, if he could do it all over, he would still play professional baseball, Humphreys responded, "Definitely yes."[10]

Chapter 20. **Charlie James**

Russell Lake

AGE	G	AB	R	H	2B	3B	HR	TB	RBI	BB	SO	BAV	OBP	SLG	SB	GDP	HBP
26	88	233	24	52	9	1	5	78	17	11	58	.223	.261	.335	0	6	1

Some former Major League ballplayers are remembered for hitting an unforgettable home run, while others are remembered for a very successful business career after retiring from playing baseball. Charlie James, a St. Louis native who played for the Cardinals from 1960 to 1964, is remembered for both.

Charles Wesley James was born on December 22, 1937, a son of Charles S. and Josephine D. James. Charlie (spelled Charley during his baseball career) spent his Midwest childhood in the St. Louis suburb of Webster Groves. This tree-filled city, just southwest of St. Louis, is on the famous Route 66 and was the setting for the short-lived NBC television series *Lucas Tanner*. Longtime baseball broadcasters Harry Caray and son Skip Caray attended high school in Webster Groves.

James was active in baseball growing up. He was a pitcher until he gave it up after losing a kids' league game, 5–4. He fondly remembered attending Cardinals games with his father at Sportsman's Park before it was renamed Busch Stadium. Surveying the St. Louis ballpark from his seat during one of their outings, Charlie told his dad that it would be nice to be a player down there on the field someday.

Webster Groves High School provided an abundance of sports activities for Charlie. Foremost, it is a football school, and the Statesmen square off on the gridiron to play nearby Kirkwood High School each Thanksgiving Day for the coveted Frisco Bell Award. By his senior year, in 1954, James had matured to a six-foot-one, 195-pound fleet halfback. He accepted a football scholarship to play at the University of Missouri. James also

Playing a reserve role for most of the year, Charlie James hit .223 in eighty-eight games. As a pinch hitter in the 1964 Series, Charlie unfortunately went 0 for 3.

received permission from football coach Don Faurot to play on the Missouri baseball team.

In 1956 James set a University of Missouri football record (since broken) for pass receptions (30) by a halfback, racking up 362 yards receiving and scoring 1 touchdown. While playing the outfield the following spring under the tutelage of John "Hi" Simmons, James caught the eye of the St.

Louis Cardinals. One of their scouts, Joe Monahan, reported to the Cardinals' brass that James had a good arm, better than average speed, and a chance to be a power hitter.

James suffered an injury in the 1957 football season but still led the Tigers with twelve pass receptions in a run-oriented offense under new coach Frank Broyles. Broyles left after one season for Arkansas and James started wondering about his own collegiate sports career. He and Jo Denty had discussed marriage, but they knew it would be tough with finances being so tight while he was in college. Even though his college baseball career covered just forty-one games, he wanted to pursue playing baseball professionally, so he let the Cardinals know that.

Cardinals general manager Bing Devine, fearing that another team would reach out to James, offered him an estimated $15,000 bonus contract on January 6, 1958. After James accepted the offer, meaning he would bypass his senior season in baseball, a firestorm erupted from the Missouri campus. The anger toward the Cardinals organization involved new football coach Dan Devine, Don Faurot, and Hi Simmons, who all sounded off about St. Louis taking James away from them. Simmons charged that the Cardinals and other Major League clubs were becoming greedy and failing to cooperate with colleges that could provide a proving ground for professional baseball. Bob Broeg, the sports editor of the *St. Louis Post Dispatch*, saw a long-range regional sports problem developing, so he decided to write about it.

Broeg interviewed James, then twenty, to get his take on the heated words coming from the Missouri campus. James responded, "I'd like to emphasize two things. First, I let the Cardinals know I wanted to turn professional now. They didn't influence me. Second, I was treated very well at Missouri and have high regard for the university, the coaches, and the fine folks I met in Columbia. It's just that the changed bonus rule has enabled me to do what I've always wanted to do—that is, get a chance at professional baseball with a financial head start and, at the same time, be given the proper training in case I've really got the chance to reach the big leagues. And I've gone far enough in college now to know that I won't quit without getting my degree."[1] James was a junior in electrical engineering, so he enrolled at Washington University in St. Louis to stay on track for his program of study. It was also announced that he and Jo would marry on February 1, 1958.

The Cardinals' initial plan was for James to be assigned to Billings (Pioneer League), but they promised him a chance to make a higher-classification roster. James started the spring of 1958 in Daytona Beach with Houston (Texas League, Double-A) and performed well enough to make the team. He was a fixture in left field for the Buffs and manager Harry Walker. He was named Texas League Rookie of the Year. In 153 games he had 600 at bats, 167 hits (66 for extra bases), and 104 runs batted in. His fielding average was .975 and he provided 17 assists with his outfield prowess and strong right arm.

James was promoted to Rochester (International League, Triple-A) for the 1959 season. He had another noteworthy season with a .300 batting average in 607 at bats. His RBI total (79) was down from the previous year, but he had 182 hits (63 for extra bases). James was chosen for the International League all-star team. During the off-season he was an engineering instructor at Washington University in St. Louis. It seemed that he was assured of making the 1960 Cardinals roster when he was invited to train with the club in St. Petersburg. When camp broke, he was assigned to start another season with Rochester. However, a lengthy batting slump took him out of the regular lineup for the first time in his Minor League career. The Cardinals' front office decided that they had a lot of money ($50,000) invested in James, so he was loaned to Charleston, West Virginia (American Association, Triple-A), instead of continuing to sit on the Red Wings bench.

Charleston was an affiliate of the Washington Senators, and James soon caught fire again at the plate. He realized that he was holding the bat lower than he had in the past, so he raised his arms and started to hit again. The power numbers were down, but his average was .370 after twenty-three games when the Cardinals decided to bring him back to their organization for the purpose of promoting him to the big leagues. Charlie's wife, Jo, had a different perspective on the ups and downs of Minor League life during that era. She felt she worked hard handling the issues that could affect a player's career. She recalled, "Things were very different at that time. Charlie wasn't near as nervous as I was. It's harder on the wives."[2]

James and Tim McCarver were promoted to the Cardinals' roster just before the July 31 trade deadline. James reported to the Cardinals on August 2 in St. Louis and suffered an embarrassing gaffe at the start of the game with the Milwaukee Braves. He looked at the dugout lineup card and saw his name on it, so he grabbed his glove and headed for right field prior to the National Anthem. Ken Boyer looked puzzled and asked James where he thought he was going when Charlie ran just behind third base. James looked up and saw Joe Cunningham standing in right field, so he quickly put on the brakes. Since there was no hole to crawl into, he returned to the dugout. Further analysis of the posted lineup provided him the realization that he had glanced at manager Solly Hemus's scribbling and mistook Javier for James. Later, Charlie made his Major League debut, entering the game in the ninth inning as a defensive replacement for Stan Musial, who was playing left field.

Hemus said James would see a utility role for the remainder of the 1960 season. In his first Major League at bat, on August 3, he grounded out to third in the seventh inning. He got his first Major League hit on August 9 in Philadelphia, a ringing double to center field off the Phillies' Al Neiger. On August 12 in Pittsburgh he scored his first run and later singled to get his first RBI. The next day James got his first start as he patrolled right in Forbes Field and went 1 for 4. In St. Louis on August 20, James hit his first Major League home run, off Danny McDevitt of the Los Angeles Dodgers. It appeared that his line drive solo blast would hold up for the margin of victory, but he made a bad throw from right field after fielding Gil Hodges's double in the top of the ninth to allow the winning run to score from first base.

A month later, on September 20, James's two-out pinch-hit single off Sandy Koufax (in a relief appearance) in the bottom of the ninth inning drove home two runs for a thrilling 3–2 victory. St. Louis was still in the hunt for the pennant, and Hemus said that he played a hunch to send James to the plate with the bases loaded. James had been watching Koufax struggle with his control that inning, so he figured that Sandy would start him out with a fastball. James was ready for it, and although his bat splintered, the ball made it to left-center to drop in for the game-winning safety. This mental note that he made on Koufax would help him later in his career. In forty-three games for the Cardinals in 1960, James batted .180 (9 for 50).

As the 1961 season began, James found himself in tight competition with Don Landrum and Don Taussig for an outfield position. General Manager Devine expressed disappointment that none of the young Cardinals outfielders really took charge of the situation during spring training to allow the team to move away from its current outfield platoon system. Charlie had several notable games during the season, including four three-hit games. On June 20 he had five hits in a doubleheader at Cincinnati. He had four RBIs against the Giants on July 8, and he was able to maintain a .300 average through July 23. He finished with a .255 average in 349 at bats. His 84 starts found him in either right field (50) or left field (32), and he mainly batted from the sixth position in the lineup. The Cardinals chose to protect James in the 1961 expansion draft, and an August 30 article in *The Sporting News* listed him among the top National League rookies in 1961. However, while Charlie went back to his off-season job as a college instructor, local rumors circulated that he was going to be part of a nine-player trade with the Cubs involving outfielder George Altman. It was later reported that the Cardinals' board of directors nixed the transaction at the last minute.

The 1962 season proved memorable for James, but the first part of the campaign did not look promising for his being a regular part of the lineup. Devine and manager Johnny Keane decided to surround center fielder Curt Flood with age and experience. Musial (age forty-one) was shifted to right field and the club acquired former All-Star Minnie Minoso (age thirty-nine) from the Chicago White Sox to play left field. Both moves had James facing another year of spot starts, pinch-running, and use as a late-inning defensive replacement. However, Minoso pulled a muscle in the second game of the season and then was severely hurt on May 11 when he ran into the left-field wall at Busch Stadium. Musial moved back to left, and Charlie got his chance. He had two hits, two RBIs, and three runs scored in a May 18 contest at Dodger Stadium. This raised his average to .351, after which he commented, "Getting into the game more often has been the big difference. You're not as cold as you are coming off the bench now and then, and you don't have to press as much."[3] The media noticed Charlie's resurgence: Neal Russo penned a lengthy piece for *The Sporting News* on July 14 with the headline "James Boy Rides Again—As Cards Headline Bandit."

James had a Friday-night-performance phenomenon that proved quite newsworthy for the 1962 season. On Friday nights he batted .411 with 23 hits and 6 of his 8 home runs (with 23 RBIs). For the season, he batted .276 with 59 RBIs and added 7 assists on the defensive side.

Two Friday performances stood out. On June 29 he hit a long first-inning home run off Harvey Haddix of the Pirates. The two-run shot at Busch Stadium flew down the line high over the left-field bleachers and landed outside the ballpark on Sullivan Avenue. Later he singled and scored, and then made a running grab of a line drive off the bat of Roberto Clemente to preserve a shutout for Curt Simmons. On September 22 against the Dodgers, James had the most memorable at bat of his career. Most of the fans were at Busch Stadium that evening to see if Maury Wills would break Ty Cobb's single-season stolen-base record. Sandy Koufax was back as the Los Angeles starter, as he had been troubled by a circulation problem with the little finger on his left hand. Koufax walked Curt Flood and Julián Javier, then retired Musial and Ken Boyer. Bill White walked on four pitches to load the bases and James came to the plate. Dodgers manager Walter Alston figured that Koufax would be fine if he got out of the first inning. James worked the count to 2-2, and Sandy fired a low fastball toward the outside part of the plate. Charlie shifted slightly and met the pitch on the sweet spot. The sound from the crack of the bat was unmistakable as a line drive soared toward the right-field pavilion roof. Dodgers outfielder Frank Howard had about one second to glance up and see the ball disappear high above him for a grand slam that started the St. Louis scoring in its 11–2 triumph. Almost fifty years later, James still joked to those who ask him about it, "I closed my eyes and swung real hard."[4] But he also offered a serious analysis of the at bat: "That was a big thrill. You couldn't hit Koufax's 100-mph fastball, but if the ball started at the knees, it would rise to belt high by the time it got to the plate. That was the only way you could hit it."[5]

Before the 1963 season, James knew his role would be more firm than in the previous two campaigns. In the off-season, the Cardinals finally acquired Altman from the Cubs and he appeared set for the right-field spot. Musial hit .330 in 1962 and was in left field, but he was forty-two years old and most likely in his last season. The local media had tagged James with the nickname Chop-Down Charley. This label was due to his not walking much (ten BBs in '62) while trying to make contact and not pop the ball up. James was okay with the moniker; as he explained, "You don't make big money waiting for walks, unless you get an awful lot of them." General Manager Devine was pleased with James for acknowledging that each year Charlie had done a bit more than he was expected to. Meanwhile, Charlie had completed his bachelor's degree, continued his part-time teaching, and was finishing up his master's degree at Washington University.

James took aim on Dodgers pitching again during the 1963 season, collecting three hits and three RBIs in a 9–5 win at Los Angeles on April 28. He had four hits and a tie-breaking three-run home run in the eighth inning in a 10–7 victory over the Dodgers in St. Louis on May 9. James hit this home run off Ed Roebuck, whom he admitted having trouble batting against because of his great sinker. James shifted in the outfield between left and right during the season and made several great catches up against the now padded outfield walls of Busch Stadium. A possible trade (with Curt Flood) to Milwaukee was nixed by the Cardinals in mid-May, and Charlie's average hovered around .300 until mid-July. A late-season run at the pennant came up short, but James ended the 1963 season with a career-high ten home runs and a .268 average.

Stan Musial's retirement after 1963 created an outfield opening for the coming season. Manager Keane admitted that James had never been given a full shot at left field and added that he might be the one to fill the gap. For the 1964 season opener in Los Angeles, Keane batted Charlie in the cleanup spot, explaining that James had become consistent getting runners in from third. This move lasted for only five games, as James batted only .158.

He returned to the more familiar fifth position of the batting order and victimized Koufax with another big home run. The April 22 home opener attracted a then record 31,410 excited fans as St. Louis hosted the Dodgers. James brought them all to their feet with a three-run first-inning home run off Sandy on the way to a 7–6 victory. Musial threw out the ceremonial first pitch and was pictured in the clubhouse with James after the win.

James struggled with the bat through the early part of the season, and Keane rotated six outfielders around Curt Flood to try to find a consistent unit. Charlie raised his average to .262 until a 4-for-45 slump as well as the trade for Lou Brock drastically reduced his playing time. James was hitting .229 when Mike Shannon was recalled from the Minors. The local youngster performed well enough in right field to leave Charlie as the odd man out. The Cardinals caught fire over the last half of the season, but James started in only four games from July 18 until October 3. He ended the season with a .223 batting mark, 5 home runs, and 17 RBIs.

Although James sat on the bench during the stretch run, he said that watching and later celebrating the 11–5 pennant-clinching win over the Mets on the final day of the 1964 season was his biggest thrill in professional baseball. He conceded that the Cardinals probably would not have won the flag had they not acquired Brock. James did get three pinch-hit opportunities in the World Series triumph over the Yankees, but he was hitless in those attempts. Almost fifty years later, he still wore his World Series championship ring proudly.

James did not get to savor the championship feeling in St. Louis for long, as he and pitcher Roger Craig were traded to the Cincinnati Reds on December 14, 1964, for starting pitcher Bob Purkey. It was hard to leave his hometown team, but James was glad to be going to a ballpark where he had hit well. Crosley Field had a short left field at 328 feet, and center field was only 387 feet. James was hoping to play more, and he knew that the Reds' left fielder, Tommy Harper, had struggled during the previous season. At spring training in March 1965, Reds manager Dick Sisler stated that he thought James could chase everybody out of left field. With Harper in left field, however, the Reds started out fast, leading the league after seventeen games, so Sisler did not want to make any lineup changes. For James, that meant he was the one chased out, as he started just six games for the Reds. He hit .188 at Crosley Field and .205 for the season. The high point was on June 22, 1965, in the ninth inning when his sharply struck pinch single to right field off Hal Woodeschick defeated the Cardinals, 5–4.

During the off-season the Reds traded Frank Robinson and initially planned to move Harper to right field. That meant the Reds' left-field position was going to be available again during spring training. Cincinnati had hired Don Heffner as its new manager, and he had James, Marty Keough, Art Shamsky, Mel Queen, and Dick Simpson competing for either the starting outfield job or a spot on the season-opening roster. Charlie did not make the cut, as Cincinnati optioned him to Buffalo (Triple-A). He refused the Minor League assignment and retired on April 14, 1966. His final Major League at bat was on September 27, 1965, at Los Angeles. James faced Johnny Podres as he batted for Ted Davidson in the fifth inning and rolled into a third-to-second-to-first double play.

At twenty-eight, Charlie James ended his Major League career with a .255 average in 1,406 at bats. True to his Chop-Down Charley nickname, he managed only 48 walks. He slugged 29 home runs and drove in 172 runs. His fielding average for 411 games in the outfield was .976. James had completed his electrical-engineering degree work at Washington University in St. Louis and was ready to pursue a full-time job other than baseball. The best offer he received was from Bussmann Manu-

facturing. The company made small-voltage electrical fuses and had been part of the St. Louis area since 1914. Charlie was employed at Bussmann for five years when an opportunity arose to purchase a portion of Central Electric Co. in Fulton, Missouri, about ninety miles west of St. Louis. James became the president of Central Electric in 1972. The company manufactured industrial electric power equipment and had annual sales of about $1 million. He said he felt that the competition he had faced in baseball helped him with competition in the business world. It must have helped, because when he retired in 1998, Central Electric Co.'s annual sales had reached $22 million.

Charlie and Jo celebrated their fifty-third wedding anniversary in 2011. They raised two children, Shari and Sammy, and had five grandchildren as of 2011. Fulton remained their home, and they lived in a beautiful brick residence on a golf course. They were active in numerous local events, charities, and their church. Charlie said, "The (Missouri) baseball fellows and I still get together once a year for a golf outing in Fulton."[6] Besides golf, he enjoyed hunting, fishing, and spending time with Jo and his family. He was usually in the stands when one of his grandchildren played in a sporting contest. Asked about some of his special Major League baseball moments, Charlie James summed up one story this way: "It was a nice honor to have a chance to play for my hometown team."[7]

Chapter 21. Julián Javier

Paul Geisler Jr.

AGE	G	AB	R	H	2B	3B	HR	TB	RBI	BB	SO	BAV	OBP	SLG	SB	GDP	HBP
27	155	535	66	129	19	5	12	194	65	30	82	.241	.282	.391	9	9	1

Besides being a superb fielding but often light-hitting second baseman with the St. Louis Cardinals for more than a decade, Julián Javier was a central figure in the history and development of baseball in the Dominican Republic.

Javier completed his playing days with a career .257 batting average. But in nineteen World Series games, he batted .333 and belted a three-run home run in the 1967 Series. The bespectacled Javier also became one of the greatest defensive second basemen ever for the Cardinals, as well as one of the best bunters in baseball.

Manuel Julián Javier Liranzo, better known simply as Julián Javier, was born on August 9, 1936, in San Francisco de Macoris, Dominican Republic, which became his lifelong hometown. From 1960 to 1972, he played twelve seasons with the St. Louis Cardinals and one with the Cincinnati Reds. Tall and lanky at six feet one and 175 pounds, he batted and threw right-handed. A second baseman throughout his career, he won two World Series championships—1964 and 1967 with the Cardinals—and played on two All-Star teams.

The son of a truck driver and the tallest of eight children, Julián developed his speedy running by racing other children to and from school—that is, when he wasn't skipping school to listen to World Series broadcasts. In high school he played shortstop and batted cleanup, hitting .375. He learned to type nearly as fast as he could run, and considered a career in accounting or engineering. But when the Pittsburgh Pirates held a tryout in 1956 with two hundred aspirants, scout Howe Haak persuaded Javier to set aside any other career choices

Julián Javier hit .241 for the 1964 Cardinals and provided range at a key position. His late-season leg injury limited him to one appearance in the World Series.

and sign the only contract the Pirates offered that day, for only $500.[1]

Hampered by injuries, Javier's professional career started slowly. But after three seasons working his way up the Pirates chain, he flourished at their Triple-A affiliate in Columbus in 1959, leading the International League with nineteen sacrifice hits and batting .274. The *Baseball Digest* scouting report on him for 1960 accurately described his coming Major League legacy: "Fastest man in league last year and has good range on grounders. Good arm and excellent hands. Fair hitter, but no power. Has good chance despite lack of power at plate."[2]

Javier wanted to succeed quickly and said, "I want to build a home and need the money,"[3] but the Pirates already had an All-Star, Gold Glove second baseman in their lineup: future Hall of Famer Bill Mazeroski, who was four weeks younger than Javier.

Javier's big break came on May 28, 1960, when the Pirates traded him and pitcher Ed Bauta to the Cardinals for veteran pitcher Wilmer "Vinegar Bend" Mizell and pitcher Dick Gray. The swap helped both sides, as Mizell helped the Pirates become champions in 1960, while the Cardinals had found their starting second sacker for the next twelve seasons.

Javier made his Major League debut the day of the trade, and got two hits against the San Francisco Giants. The Cardinals kept the deal secret until they posted their lineup. Even broadcaster Harry Caray did not hear about it until he reached the ballpark. Cardinals general manager Bing Devine surprised most observers by giving up a veteran starting pitcher for an unproven Minor League prospect; however, Eddie Stanky, the Cardinals' director of player procurement, had insisted that Javier was one of the best he had seen.[4]

Julián, or Hoolie, as many called him by his rookie year, finished the season as the lead-off hitter. He batted only .237 and led the National League in errors with 24, but also led the league with 15 sacrifice hits, and in the field he showed good range and quickness, enough to be named to the Topps All-Rookie team.

A year later Javier continued to impress with his glove and sparked debates as to who was the fastest in the league, he or Vada Pinson. Commentators began to link him to the great Cardinals second basemen Rogers Hornsby, Frank Frisch, and Red Schoendienst, all of whom won championships with the Redbirds.[5]

Javier returned to his home country during off-seasons to hunt, work on his farm, and play winter ball. He got in trouble in early 1963 for participating in exhibition games not authorized by Major League teams and was fined $250 by baseball commissioner Ford Frick. Under their agreement with Frick, winter league teams agreed not to sign any players from the United States without their team's approval, and Latin players would play in their home countries only in regularly organized and preapproved games.

Javier improved his batting average more than 40 points to .279 in 1961, and he hit .263 in both 1962 and 1963. He posted career highs in stolen bases (26) and runs scored (97) in 1962. He led the league in put-outs by a second baseman two years in a row with 377 in 1963 and 360 in 1964.

In 1963, when Bill Mazeroski dropped off the All-Star roster due to an injury, Javier completed an all-Cardinals starting All-Star infield, with Bill White at first base, Dick Groat at shortstop, and Ken Boyer at third base. He also played in the 1968 All-Star Game.

Bothered by a sore back in 1964, Javier nonetheless managed to play in 155 games in the Cardinals' championship season, with 12 home runs and a career-high 65 RBIs. His batting average dropped to .241, and he once again led the league in errors with 27. A sore hip limited his World Series efforts to only the first game, in which he had no plate appearances, pinch-ran and scored a run, and played two innings in the field. Dal Maxvill played second base in place of Javier.

The injuries continued to limit Javier the next two seasons, and his offensive performance diminished to its lowest point with the Cardinals. He batted .227 in only 77 games in 1965, then .228 in 147 games in 1966. He faced losing his starting job to versatile utility fielder Jerry Buchek, who could play second, third, and short.

Javier started 1967 with some major changes. He added ten pounds in weight, employed new wraparound glasses, and picked up a heavier bat, going from a 31- to a 35-ounce one. During spring training, bullpen coach Bob Milliken threw curve after curve to him, working to control Javier's tendency to bail out on tough right-handed pitchers. The changes paid early dividends as he opened the season with a seven-game hitting streak and a .407 average.

Manager Schoendienst noticed the obvious improvement, saying, "Hoolie's been watching the ball a lot better. I think his new glasses might be helping as much as anything. He's been taking the bad pitches he used to swing at, especially those balls outside."[6]

The good returns continued throughout the season, as Javier stayed healthy and produced one of his best offensive seasons, with a .281 average (.325 against left-handers) in 520 at bats, and a career-high 14 homers. He finished ninth in voting for the National League Most Valuable Player Award, as he helped propel the Cardinals into the postseason for the second time in four years.

In July 1967 a double play started by a little tap Javier hit back to the pitcher led to a spontaneous quip by Cardinals broadcaster Jack Buck. The 1–6–3 play went from pitcher John Boozer to shortstop Bobby Wine to first baseman Tony Taylor, but Buck reported, "That double play went from Boozer to Wine to Old Taylor."[7]

The Cardinals followed Bob Gibson's pitching to beat the Boston Red Sox in the first game of the 1967 World Series. In the second game, a 5–0 Cardinals loss, Javier broke up Jim Lonborg's no-hitter in the eighth inning with a double to the left-field corner with two outs. Lonborg went on to surrender only Javier's hit in a complete-game shutout.

After two more wins by each team, the World Series went to a Game Seven. In the sixth inning of that deciding game, Hoolie smashed a three-run home run off Lonborg and ensured Bob Gibson's third Series victory and St. Louis's second cham-

pionship in four years. Javier's renewal from the beginning of the season carried through to the end, as he compiled a .360 batting average in the Series.

Javier returned to his native Dominican Republic a national hero. President Joaquin Balaguer conferred on him the Order of the Fathers of the Country, the country's highest decoration.[8] The Pittsburgh Pirates played an exhibition game against Dominican stars in Santo Domingo about a week after the Series ended, with natives Matty Alou and Manny Mota and Puerto Rico native Roberto Clemente, but the biggest welcome of the day went to the Cardinals' second sacker.[9]

The Cardinals won the pennant again in 1968, but Javier's batting average dropped 21 points, to .260. He played in the All-Star Game that season. Despite his .333 batting average in the 1968 World Series, the Cardinals lost in seven games to the Detroit Tigers.

Javier's average rebounded in 1969 to a personal best of .282, and he continued as a Cardinals starter through 1970. Early in the 1971 season, Javier returned to the Dominican Republic to be with his brother, Luis, who died while he was there. His playing time lessened considerably that season, as he started only sixty-eight games at second base, yielding a major part of the playing time to Ted Sizemore.

Javier's orientation to professional baseball in the United States did not include a full understanding of his obligations to the Internal Revenue Service. In October 1970 the IRS filed tax liens against him for as much as $84,320, covering the tax years of 1961 and 1963 through 1969. His annual salary came to an estimated $50,000 at the time. When he received word of the proceedings, he had already returned home to the Dominican Republic. The unresolved debt jeopardized his return to the United States to play in 1971.[10] Apparently he had received no advice, or perhaps misguided information, as he had filed no tax returns for several years. He thought the withholding from his paycheck satisfied his obligations.[11] He employed a lawyer, settled the debt for considerably less than the original claim, and arrived in Florida in 1971 in time for spring training.[12]

In March 1972 the Cardinals traded the thirty-five-year-old Javier to the Cincinnati Reds for pitcher Tony Cloninger. He became very much a part-time player, starting only seventeen games for the World Series–bound Reds, now playing mostly third base and batting only .209. Still a contributor until the end, Javier started at second base in the final regular-season game of his career, on October 1. In his last regular-season at bat, he bunted to help set up the only run of the game in a Reds 1–0 win over the Los Angeles Dodgers.

Javier played in his fourth World Series with the Reds that season. His sacrifice bunt in his very last plate appearance contributed to a run for the Reds in Game Four, as the Reds fell to the Oakland Athletics in seven games. The Reds released him two days after the Series ended.

Without a job in the big leagues, Javier headed home to the San Francisco de Macoris, where he began to organize a professional franchise to compete in the Dominican winter league. He took a turn at managing in 1974 with the Yucatan Leones of the Mexican League, then returned home to stay with family and to help further develop baseball in his home country. To give youngsters a good start in baseball, he founded the Dominican branch of the Khoury League, later renamed the Roberto Clemente League to honor the Pirates legend.

In 1975 Javier put together a summer league of four teams that competed in his home territory. He and his son Stan teamed to form the Gigantes del Cibao, which became one of the regular contenders in the Dominican winter league. He was chosen the all-time second baseman for the Aguilas Cibaeñas, and his No. 25 was retired by the Dominican Winter Baseball League.

Julián Javier built his Major League career

largely around his speed and slick glove. Multiple sources rated him as the widest-ranging second baseman in the league, largely due to his great speed and quickness. His especially long fingers reminded many of a concert pianist, yet he said, "They help me in typing."[13]

Gene Mauch called Javier "the greatest I ever saw on getting pop flies and as good as anyone on coming in on a ball." His middle-infield partner, Dal Maxvill, considered him one of the best ever, especially at going to his right. "I've never seen that play made by anyone else," Maxvill said. "I'm spoiled if he doesn't make it." On slow grounders, Maxvill said, "He goes in low, doesn't straighten out and fires the ball with something on it. I've seen him throw just this far [six inches] off the ground."[14]

Javier earned another nickname, the Phantom. Orlando Cepeda pointed out his smooth moves around second base: "Hoolie comes out of nowhere like a phantom." Maxvill said, "Hoolie's like a ghost out there. Runners try to nail him, but he gets the throw off so smoothly—and then he disappears."[15]

Javier combined his speed and stick skills to become rated one of the league's best bunters. He ranked first or second in sacrifice hits three out of his first four years with the Cardinals. He also produced the rare combination of a skillful short game and a surprising ability to hit the long ball, especially in clutch situations. His three home runs hit in 1–0 games place him in a tie with many others for sixth all-time, behind Ted Williams, who had five, and four others with four.[16]

Javier often surprised with his sudden displays of oomph, like the grand slam he hit in 1961 on his twenty-fifth birthday to beat the Pirates, 4–0. In May 1964 the Cardinals rode his three-run homer to victory over the Phillies, 3–2. That day he claimed he had stuffed himself with vitamins given to him by his brother, who was a doctor. Four days later he hit a grand slam and ended the week with twelve runs batted in.[17] In July 1969 he launched a ball to the roof of Connie Mack Stadium in Philadelphia, after which he said, "I didn't eat any breakfast, and all I ate before going to the park was a small salad. If I had eaten a big salad, I would have hit the ball over the roof and out of the park."[18]

Javier's batting average fluctuated greatly from year to year, partly due to injury but also because of other factors such as pitch selection. According to batting coach Dick Sisler, the better numbers seemed to come when he refused to swing at bad pitches, especially low and outside sliders and curves from right-handed pitchers.[19]

Sisler saw a major constant in Javier's statistics: he always hit much better against left-handers than against right-handers (.299 lifetime against lefties, .233 when facing righties). In three seasons (1965, 1968, and 1970) the gap amounted to more than 150 points in batting average against left-handers. The old stalwart Branch Rickey suggested once that Javier might become a really great hitter if he learned to switch-hit, but Javier continued to hit from one side of the plate.[20]

An incident in February 1964 in the Dominican winter league involving Javier and umpire Emmett Ashford, then a nine-year veteran of the Pacific Coast League, played a major role in vaulting Ashford through the racial barrier to become the first African American umpire in the Major Leagues. With Javier at bat, Ashford called two strikes on him on low outside pitches, Javier's common nemesis at the plate. He protested the calls, saying, "Why you call the pitch on me? You know I don't like that pitch."

"Why the hell do you think he's throwing it?" answered the ump.

Javier shot back: "Oh, a comedian!" Ashford told Javier to get quiet and bat. As Javier stepped back in, he took a called third strike right down the middle of the plate. He turned in protest and landed a punch on Ashford's jaw.[21] The umpire responded with a couple of his own shots, using his mask and actually drawing blood. The fans "could have strung me up on the spot," remembered Ashford. "But they were with me, and I think that's what put me over the top."[22]

Javier received an indefinite suspension at first, but the penalty was quickly reduced to three days and a $50 fine because of the Dominican's popularity. Ashford's first reaction led him to resign from the Dominican league for the rest of the season. He finally relented when Javier apologized on the radio. Soon afterward, American League president Joe Cronin purchased Ashford's contract, apparently convinced that he knew how to face difficult situations. The popular Ashford then made history in his American League debut on Opening Day 1966 in Washington.

Among his seven children, Javier's son Stan, named for Cardinals great Stan Musial, played Major League baseball for eighteen seasons with eight different teams. Another son, Julián J. Javier, built a successful medical practice as a cardiologist in Naples, Florida. A third son, Manuel Julián Javier, became an engineer in Santiago, Dominican Republic.

Estadia Julián Javier, the stadium in San Francisco de Macoris, was built to honor one of the pioneer Dominican Major Leaguers. It became both the home of the Gigantes del Cibao, the baseball team he formed, and a tribute to the popularity and success of Manuel Julián "Hoolie" Javier Liranzo.

Chapter 22. **Johnny Lewis**

John Harry Stahl

AGE	G	AB	R	H	2B	3B	HR	TB	RBI	BB	SO	BAV	OBP	SLG	SB	GDP	HBP
24	40	94	10	22	2	2	2	34	7	13	23	.234	.324	.362	2	1	0

Standing six feet one and weighing 189 pounds, young Johnny Lewis had all the raw tools necessary to become a baseball star. Lewis could run, throw, field, and hit both for average and power. St. Louis Cardinals manager Johnny Keane once described the left-handed-hitting Lewis as "one of the few five-point players I have ever seen," and compared him to Willie Mays, Hank Aaron, and Roberto Clemente.

Overcoming a 1961 family tragedy, Lewis played in forty games for the 1964 Cardinals and spent three seasons with the New York Mets, completing four years in the Major Leagues. After his playing career he worked as a baseball front-office executive, a Major League hitting coach, a Minor League manager, and a Minor League hitting instructor.

Johnny Joe Lewis was born on August 10, 1939, in Greenville, Alabama. When he was an infant, his family moved to Pensacola, Florida, where Johnny starred in football, baseball, and basketball for Washington High School. He attended Washington Junior College. According to Baseball-Reference.com, he signed with the Detroit Tigers before the 1959 season, then was sent by the Tigers to the Cardinals.

Lewis played for three Cardinals Class D farm teams in his first season: Wytheville (Appalachian League), Keokuk (Midwest League), and Hobbs (Sophomore League). He spent most of the season at Wytheville, where he hit .306 and was named to the league all-star team. The Cardinals promoted him in 1960 to Winnipeg in the Class C Northern League, where he played for former Major Leaguer Whitey Kurowski. Lewis had his best sea-

Johnny Lewis played forty games for the 1964 Cardinals. After his playing career, he held various positions as a Cardinals executive, coach, and manager.

son in professional baseball there. He batted .299, led the league in home runs (23), total bases (247), and RBIS (104), and again made the all-star team. Kurowski and Lewis both moved up to Tulsa in the Double-A Texas League in 1961, where Johnny hit a solid .293, led the league in walks (96), was second in home runs (22), and made the league all-star team for the third season in a row. To earn extra income for his family, Lewis played winter baseball in Venezuela.

During his absence the twenty-two-year-old

Lewis suffered a major family tragedy: his wife was killed in a car accident, leaving him with two infant sons, Jeremiah and Johnny Jr., to raise. Johnny's mother took the two young boys so he could continue his baseball career.[1]

In 1962 Lewis got off to a very slow start with Atlanta in the Triple-A International League. After 41 games his batting average was just .178. The Cardinals sent him back to Tulsa, where he rebounded strongly under Kurowski. He finished at Tulsa with a solid .293 batting average and 18 home runs in 85 games. He returned to Atlanta in 1963 and had a good year, hitting .280 in 136 games.

During the Cardinals' 1964 spring training, Lewis was clearly one of the best young players in camp. He hit .333 and showed tremendous speed and potentially awesome power. The Cardinals took notice. Assessing Lewis's spring performance, team vice president Stan Musial liked what he saw. "Johnny doesn't have to hit a ton to help," said Musial, "because he's fast on the bases, an alert runner, and a good defensive outfielder with a pretty strong throwing arm. I'm sure he'll hit enough and even if he doesn't hit many home runs—few young players do—he'll hit with enough power."[2]

Teammate Ken Boyer hoped the Cardinals would nurture the young player, saying, "The kid should be a good player. I just hope they don't expect him to break down the fences the first few years."[3] First baseman Bill White volunteered to room with Lewis on the road and school him on the opposing pitchers.

After nearly winning the 1963 National League pennant, finishing in second place behind the Los Angeles Dodgers, the Cardinals needed to quickly regain their momentum in 1964. Lewis's strong spring-training performance raised his expectations and those of the Cardinals. His first start came in Los Angeles against Don Drysdale on April 15. In four at bats, he got his first hit and scored his first run. Four days later, against San Francisco, he hit his first Major League home run. Lewis started twenty of the team's first twenty-five games. On May 10 he was batting .275.

On May 27 Lewis was struck out four times in a row by the Giants' Juan Marichal in St. Louis. After that his batting average began a slow but steady decline. His hitting problems were compounded when he suffered a severe ankle injury while playing against San Francisco. On June 11 the Cardinals sent Lewis to Triple-A Jacksonville, where his batting woes continued. In his first 94 at bats, he hit .234 with 22 hits, 2 home runs, 13 walks, and 23 strikeouts. Meanwhile, the Cardinals traded for Lou Brock, who went on to stardom in 1964.

According to *The Sporting News*, in early August the Cardinals discovered that Lewis had actually suffered a hairline fracture of his left ankle in late May.[4] At Jacksonville he wound up hitting .262 in seventy-two games as the team won the International League pennant. In mid-September, Lewis and eleven other Minor Leaguers were called up by the Cardinals, but he didn't get off the bench as the Cardinals fought for the pennant, and after they won it he was ineligible to play in the World Series. When the team divided its winning World Series shares, Lewis was awarded a half share ($4,311.99).

At the start of the Cardinals' fall 1964 East Coast Instructional League, Lewis remained the Cardinals' "best young outfield prospect." They tried to make him a switch hitter but it didn't work out.[5] On December 7 the Cardinals traded Lewis and pitcher Gordon Richardson to the New York Mets for pitcher Tracy Stallard and Minor League infielder Elio Chacon.

Reflecting a year later on his 1964 Cardinals season, Lewis said he believed his performance was directly related to the pennant-race environment. "Playing with the Cardinals, it was a case of making good instantly or you were gone," he said.

"I don't blame them for that. They were pennant contenders and they couldn't afford to wait. But for me it meant that I always was more conscious of making mistakes. I couldn't take chances. I was constantly tight."[6]

Although the 1964 Mets had been one of the worst teams in history, Lewis viewed his trade as a positive career opportunity. "With [the Mets] I can be relaxed," he said. "They can let me develop. I don't have to worry about each and every play. If I make a mistake, I can try to do better the next time."[7]

Unfortunately for Lewis, the 1965 Mets again finished last (50-112), 47 games out of first place. The team tumbled into last place on May 28 and never left, spending its last 122 games of the season in the cellar. Wes Westrum replaced the seventy-four-year-old Casey Stengel as the manager after 96 games.

The Mets as a team may have been atrocious, but Lewis had his best season in the Major Leagues. Playing in 148 games, the most in his Major League career, he hit .245 with 15 home runs and led the Mets in runs, walks, and on-base percentage. He posted a .975 fielding average while playing the most innings of any Mets outfielder (1,127). He led Mets outfielders in assists and putouts, while splitting his playing time between center field (383 innings) and right field (744 innings).

Primarily playing right field and usually hitting near the top of the batting order, Lewis started strong and finished April with a .288 average. He also played exceptional defense. In three consecutive games in the first week of the season, he threw out base runners at second, third, and home. The out at home plate, on April 15, was part of a triple play.[8] With runners on first and third, Jim Wynn hit a fly ball that Lewis grabbed in medium right field. His one-bounce throw nailed Walt Bond at the plate, then catcher Chris Cannizzaro threw to shortstop Roy McMillan, who tagged out Bob Aspromonte at second to complete the triple play.

On June 14 at Cincinnati, Lewis hit a towering home run in the eleventh inning to spoil Jim Maloney's bid for a no-hit game. Overpowering throughout, Maloney struck out eighteen Mets, including Lewis three times. Facing him at the start of the eleventh inning, Maloney attempted to throw a fastball inside but got it a little too far over the plate. Lewis crushed it for a home run to dead center, and the Mets won the game, 1–0.[9]

Asked about his game-winning blast, Johnny redirected the spotlight to Maloney's outstanding performance. "He did get the ball out over the plate on me," Lewis said, "but I want to tell you I'm not sure I saw the pitch. All I know is that it was a fastball. In my entire career, I never saw any fastballs like he threw in this game."[10]

Lewis hit .242 in May and .222 in June. After a strong July (.312), he slumped again in August (.191). Concluding that the reason for his slumps was his inability to see certain pitches clearly, the Mets in early August told him to begin wearing eyeglasses. The glasses helped a little bit, as he hit .242 in September.

Lewis had a busy off-season after the 1965 campaign. Shortly after the season, he married again in Pensacola, Florida, and moved his family to New York.[11] In early 1966 he sought a 100 percent raise from his 1965 salary (estimated at $10,000). In late February he settled with the Mets for a reported $15,000.[12]

During 1966 spring training, the Mets concluded that Lewis's hitting problems might be due not to eyesight but to his batting stance. In 1965 he had unconsciously begun closing his batting stance, allowing his shoulder to effectively block his view of inside breaking pitches. Lewis experimented with new batting stances throughout the spring.[13] He again got off to a good start, hitting .292 in April. He slumped badly in May (.179) and June (.203). On June 30 his batting average was .209. On July 7 the Mets sent Lewis to Jacksonville, by then a New York farm team. At the time, the Mets stood in ninth place (35-44), fourteen and a half games out of first place and well on their way to losing ninety-five games. Lewis reportedly was "bitterly disappointed" and publicly expressed his frustration. "I had more homers and runs batted in than the Mets' four other outfielders," he said. "I only played when someone was hurt but I was always in there against the top pitchers. If [manager Wes Westrum] had something against me, or if I had done something wrong, I'd understand. I must say I didn't get a fair shake by the Mets. But I'll give them 100 percent."[14]

Reporting to Jacksonville, Lewis played in seventy-one games, hitting .284 with thirteen home runs. In September the Mets brought him back to the Major Leagues, where he played in thirteen games and finished the year. For the season he hit .193 in sixty-five games for the Mets.

Lewis started the 1967 season with the Mets but played in only thirteen games before being sent to Jacksonville. Those thirteen games were his last in the Major Leagues. Lewis's four-year Major League career totals were 175 hits in 771 at bats (.227), 74 RBIS, 22 home runs, 95 walks, and 194 strikeouts.

At Jacksonville in 1967 Lewis played in 103 games and hit only .218. A freak accident in early August didn't help. As Lewis sat in the dugout, an opposing first baseman crashed into him when he fell into the dugout while chasing a pop-up. Lewis's face was badly cut and three teeth were knocked out.[15]

The 1968 season was Lewis's last as a player. With a Philadelphia Phillies farm team, the San Diego Padres of the Pacific Coast League, he played in 123 games and hit .270 with 16 home runs. (The Padres became a Major League team the next season.)

After retiring as a player, Lewis had a long career in front-office and coaching positions. In December 1969 the Cardinals appointed him assistant sales and promotions director. In 1971

General Manager Bing Devine made Lewis the Cardinals' administrative coordinator of player development and scouting. In 1971 Johnny and June had their third child, Leslie.[16]

In April 1973 Devine made Lewis the Cardinals' first black coach, noting, "Lewis has always been a good man for the organization and seems to be better oriented to a field position."[17] Lewis was the first-base coach under manager Red Schoendienst through 1976.

From 1985 through 1989, Lewis was the Cardinals' hitting coach under manager Whitey Herzog.[18] He also was a Minor League manager (Calgary and Gastonia) for the Cardinals.[19] From 1999 through 2001, he was the Minor League hitting coordinator for the Houston Astros before being named the team's hitting instructor.

As of August 2011, Lewis lived in retirement in Cantonment, Florida.

Chapter 23. Timeline, June 1–June 30

John Harry Stahl

June 1—No game scheduled.

June 2—CUBS 5, CARDINALS 2—The Cardinals began a sixteen-game road trip. Jackson pitched a complete game for his seventh victory. Cardinals starter Simmons pitched five and one-third innings but ran into trouble in the fourth and sixth innings. In the fourth, Billy Williams, Ron Santo, and Billy Cowan each hit solo home runs. Jimmie Schaffer also hit a two-run home run in the sixth. White had two hits for the Cardinals.

The Cardinals traded pitcher Lew Burdette to the Chicago Cubs for pitcher Glen Hobbie.

June 3—CARDINALS 7, CUBS 5—Cardinals starter Sadecki went seven and two-thirds innings for his fifth victory. The Cubs scored twice in the first inning on a two-out single by Ernie Banks. After the Cardinals scored a run in the second, Boyer hit a three-run home run in the third. White's double in the seventh scored two more. Sadecki went into the bottom of the eighth with a 7–2 lead but Santo hit a three-run home run. In relief, Craig held the Cubs scoreless for the rest of the game.

June 4—CUBS 2, CARDINALS 1—In a game dominated by good pitching, both Dick Ellsworth and Gibson pitched complete games. All of the game's scoring happened in the fourth inning. In the top of the inning, James hit a solo home run for the Cardinals. In the bottom of the inning, Santo hit a two-run home run. The 1-hour-and-42-minute game ended up as the Cardinals' shortest game of the season.

June 5—REDS 5, CARDINALS 4—At Crosley Field, the Reds stunned the Cardinals by scoring four runs in the bottom of the ninth inning to win the game. Newly acquired Glen Hobbie started for the Cardinals, pitching seven and one-third innings and allowing one run and hitting a home run. With Craig and Shantz pitching in the ninth, however, the Cardinals' infield made two errors, allowing two runs to score before Deron Johnson singled home the tying and winning runs.

June 6—REDS 3, CARDINALS 0—John Tsitouris and Sammy Ellis combined to shut out the Cardinals. The Reds scored all of their runs off Washburn in the first inning on two hits and a Cardinal error.

June 7—REDS 11, CARDINALS 6—With the help of a grand slam by Johnny Edwards in the first inning, the Reds beat Simmons and swept the three-game series. The two teams produced twenty-seven hits, including six home runs. Javier hit two home runs and drove in four runs. The Reds' Deron Johnson had five hits, including a double and a home run. The other Cardinal home run was by James, and Frank Robinson also homered for the Reds.

June 8—No game scheduled.

June 9—CARDINALS 1, GIANTS 0—At Candlestick Park, Sadecki pitched his best game of the year, beating Giants ace Juan Marichal. James singled home Flood in the ninth for the only run of the game. Ray's complete-game shutout was his

121

sixth victory. "That was probably the best I've seen of Sadecki," said Keane after the game.

June 10 — GIANTS 3, CARDINALS 0 (game one) — Striking out thirteen hitters, Bob Hendley and Gaylord Perry combined to shut out the Cardinals. Willie McCovey's two-run home run in the sixth and Tom Haller's sacrifice fly in the eighth provided the Giants' runs. Gibson pitched a complete game but suffered his third loss.

June 10 — CARDINALS 2, GIANTS 1 (game two) — Hobbie allowed only two hits and pitched a complete game for his first victory. Flood's two stolen bases followed each time by White singles accounted for the Cardinals' runs. Mays's single scored the Giants' only run in the first inning.

June 11 — DODGERS 5, CARDINALS 0 — Drysdale won his eighth game with a complete-game shutout. The Dodgers had fourteen hits while Drysdale held the Cardinals to four. A key episode in the game came in the fourth inning when McCarver batted with the bases loaded and no score. McCarver hit the ball but grimaced in pain as the ball slowly trickled down to first base for an easy out. McCarver and the Cardinals claimed he hit the ball off his right foot. Tim offered to take his shoe off to show the umpire his black-and-blue toes. Instead, they based their decision on the absence of shoe polish on the ball and declared Tim out. After the game, McCarver sat in the training room showing off his three blue toes.

Because of the team's inability to score (three runs in the last four games), Keane called a special hitting practice for Bill White, Charlie James, and Carl Warwick.

The Cardinals sent outfielder Johnny Lewis to Jacksonville (Triple-A).

June 12 — DODGERS 3, CARDINALS 0 — Koufax pitched a complete-game shutout as he won his eighth game. Javier made a throwing error in the seventh inning that allowed two Dodgers runs to score. Broglio's record fell to 3-5.

June 13 — DODGERS 3, CARDINALS 2 — The Dodgers completed a three-game sweep as Joe Moeller got his fourth victory with relief help from Bob Miller and Ron Perranoski. McCarver hit a two-run home run in the fifth inning. Sadecki lost his fifth game. The loss sent the Cardinals' season record to 28-29.

The Cardinals traded a Minor Leaguer plus $35,000 to the Cincinnati Reds for outfielder Bob Skinner.

June 14 — COLT .45s 4, CARDINALS 1 — In Houston, the slumping Cardinals lost their fourth consecutive game as Gibson lost his fifth game. Gibson ran into trouble in the fifth inning when he gave up three runs on three hits and two walks. Houston pitcher Farrell pitched a complete game with nine strikeouts.

June 15 — COLT .45s 9, CARDINALS 3 — The Cardinals continued their slide as this loss put them in eighth place, seven games behind the Phillies and Giants. Trailing the Cardinals 3–0 in the sixth inning, Houston scored four times, including a two-run home run by Bob Aspromonte. Houston added four additional runs in the seventh inning. Cardinals starter Hobbie lost his fourth game, though just his first for St. Louis. In their Cardinals debuts, Jack Spring gave up three hits and Lou Brock struck out as a pinch hitter.

In a major reshuffling, the Cardinals traded pitchers Ernie Broglio and Bobby Shantz and outfielder Doug Clemens to the Chicago Cubs for outfielder Lou Brock and pitchers Jack Spring and Paul Toth.

The Cardinals assigned Toth to Jacksonville (Triple-A), and they called up Mike Cuellar from Jacksonville.

June 16 — CARDINALS 7, COLT .45s 1 — Boyer hit for the cycle in order with three RBIs, Javier went 3 for 4 with two stolen bases, and Simmons pitched a complete game. In the Cardinals' lineup for the first time, Brock went 2 for 3 with two walks and a stolen base. The Cardinals' victory ended a five-game losing streak (June 11–15). The streak tied with May 23–28 for their longest losing streak of the season.

June 17 — CARDINALS 2, COLT .45s 1 — Taylor struck out Houston pinch hitter Joe Gaines with the tying run on third base and two outs to end the game. Boyer's home run and Brock's run-scoring single provided the runs for Washburn's third victory.

June 18 — CARDINALS 7, GIANTS 6 — Beginning a thirteen-game home stand, the Cardinals banged out fourteen hits led by Javier's three hits (including a home run) and five RBIs. In the ninth inning with one out and the tying run on second and the lead run on first, Taylor entered the game to face Willie Mays. He struck him out and got the next hitter, Orlando Cepeda, to foul out. Sadecki won his seventh game.

June 19 — CARDINALS 3, GIANTS 1 — Gibson struck out eight in eight innings as he won his sixth game. Brock had a run-scoring double in the sixth and Javier hit a two-run home run in the seventh.

June 20 — GIANTS 14, CARDINALS 3 — Harvey Kuenn led off the game with a home run on the way to a 5-for-6 game as the Giants pounded four Cardinals pitchers for twenty hits. Mays and Cepeda hit home runs for the Giants, Cepeda hitting a pair.

June 21 — GIANTS 7, CARDINALS 3 — Rookie Hal Lanier went 4 for 5 with three RBIs as Jack Sanford won his fifth game and Perry pitched four innings

of scoreless relief. The Giants got solo home runs by Lanier and Mays in the top of the ninth. Brock hit his first Cardinal home run in the third inning. Simmons lost his sixth game.

June 22 — No game scheduled.

June 23 — CARDINALS 5, COLT .45s 4 — Boyer hit a two-run home run and Brock had two hits and two stolen bases as Taylor won his first game in relief. After newcomer Brock had stolen four bases in his first eight games with the Cardinals, Keane warned opposing teams, "We may squander a few, but we'll be running the bases."

June 24 — COLT .45s 7, CARDINALS 5 — The Cardinals had ten hits, but Houston had thirteen and won the game. Trailing 3–1 going into the seventh inning, Houston scored six runs to pull ahead, 7–3. Gaines, Walt Bond, and Jerry Grote had key hits to spark the rally.

June 25 — CARDINALS 4, COLT .45s 2 — Doubles by Boyer and Groat highlighted a three-run eighth inning that put the Cardinals ahead. Leading 4–2 with two runners on and one out in the ninth, Hobbie got Bob Lillis to hit into a game-ending double play. Craig won his fourth game.

June 26 — PHILLIES 6, CARDINALS 5 — After the Cardinals took the lead for the first time with three runs in the bottom of the eighth, the Phillies scored two in the top of the ninth on Clay Dalrymple's two-run homer to win the game.

June 27 — CARDINALS 9, PHILLIES 4 — Each Cardinal hitter in the starting lineup had at least one hit as the team pounded out fourteen against three different Philadelphia pitchers. Phillie fielders also contributed five errors. Simmons scattered ten hits and pitched a complete game for his eighth win.

June 28 — PHILLIES 5, CARDINALS 0 (game one) — Chris Short pitched a complete-game shutout, striking out seven. Mike Cuellar started his first game of his career. He went seven innings and allowed three earned runs.

June 28 — CARDINALS 8, PHILLIES 2 (game two) — Sadecki pitched a complete game for his eighth victory. The Cardinals had fourteen hits, led by White going 4 for 5 with three RBIs. The Phillies also committed six errors, leading to four unearned runs.

June 29 — BRAVES 7, CARDINALS 4 — Leading 4–3 in the ninth and with Gibson on the mound in relief, the Cardinals lost the game. The Braves rallied with a home run, a walk, an error by Brock, and three singles to score four runs and win. Braves slugger Eddie Mathews batted in the leadoff spot. He walked four consecutive times and clubbed a home run to start the Braves' ninth-inning comeback.

June 30 — BRAVES 5, CARDINALS 4 — Ty Cline hit a two-run pinch-hit home run in the eighth inning to provide the winning margin. Aaron went 4 for 5 with a home run and a double. Craig allowed twelve hits but pitched a complete game for his fourth loss. The loss ended the Cardinals' thirteen-game home stand at six wins and seven losses. Brock led the Cardinal hitters with a .429 (24 for 56) average for the home stand.

The Cardinals called up pitcher Bob Humphreys from Jacksonville (Triple-A). They also sent pitcher Jack Spring to Jacksonville (Triple-A) and pitcher Harry Fanok to Atlanta (Triple-A).

Cardinals June win-loss record: 11-18.
Cardinals year-to-date win-loss record: 36-38.

Standings, June 30, 1964

	W	L	T	PCT	GB
San Francisco Giants	45	28	0	.616	—
Philadelphia Phillies	43	27	0	.614	½
Pittsburgh Pirates	38	32	0	.543	5½
Cincinnati Reds	38	34	1	.528	6½
Chicago Cubs	35	34	0	.507	8
Milwaukee Braves	36	37	0	.493	9
St. Louis Cardinals	36	38	0	.486	9½
Los Angeles Dodgers	34	38	2	.472	10½
Houston Colt .45s	35	40	0	.467	11
New York Mets	22	54	1	.289	24½

Chapter 24. Jeoff Long

Rory Costello

AGE	G	AB	R	H	2B	3B	HR	TB	RBI	BB	SO	BAV	OBP	SLG	SB	GDP	HBP
22	28	43	5	10	1	0	1	14	4	6	18	.233	.340	.326	0	1	1

Jeoff (which rhymes with "off") Long signed as a pitcher but made it to the Majors with his bat. This burly Kentuckian could hit balls a long way. That got him into fifty-six games in 1963 and 1964 as a first baseman/outfielder, first with the St. Louis Cardinals and then with the Chicago White Sox. A bad knee limited his career, however—he first hurt it playing high school football and reinjured it while with the White Sox.

Jeoffrey Keith Long was born in Covington, Kentucky, on October 9, 1941. Covington lies just across the Ohio River from Cincinnati. His father, Chester Long, and his uncle Oren were entrepreneurs. They founded Long Brothers Bag Company in 1944; two years later they started Cincinnati Drum Service. Over the next several decades, Chester and Oren's hard work built a remarkable little empire. It remains today a classic American success story.

Chester and his wife, Pauline Bramel Long, had four more sons and five daughters after Jeoff, their oldest child. Pauline was a homemaker. When she died in 2002, Jeoff described her as "a quiet Christian who served faithfully. She loved her family dearly and her church." This industrious Baptist family loved sports too. Chester played football and Oren basketball, but as Pauline said when Jeoff turned pro, "There are baseballs flying around here most of the time."[1]

Years after his retirement, his heart remained with the Cardinals, but as one would expect, Long was a Reds fan growing up. He attended many games at old Crosley Field. "I used to go out to the park whenever I had a chance," he said. "This was when I was 12 years old, and like most kids I had

Jeoff Long could blast long home runs, but a bad knee limited his baseball career. In 1964 he hit .233 in twenty-eight games before the Cardinals sold him to the White Sox.

my heroes. Johnny Temple used to be one of my favorites. One particular day I remember, I yelled at Temple every time he came in from the field. I was sitting behind the Redleg dugout. Finally, around the seventh inning, he came over and said: 'What's with you, kid? Why don't you get off my back?' Well that really cut me. I thought the whole world had come to an end."[2]

Long attended Lloyd Memorial High School in Erlanger, Kentucky, eight miles southwest of Covington. In a state mad for basketball, he played on

125

the varsity for three years. He also played football for half of his sophomore year and was named the team's quarterback in his junior year. An idea of Jeoff's strong right arm came from Harry Fanok, who was his roommate with the Tulsa Oilers in 1961 and who also played for the Cardinals in 1963–64. Harry remembered, "He was the most naturally strong guy you could find. At my home in Jersey, we were tossing a football. I seen him throw one flatfooted about 60 yards."[3]

In his only game as a junior, Long twisted his knee handing the ball off. "I split the cartilage," he recalled in 2008. "That was when I had my first operation. It wound up becoming an accumulation of problems. They didn't have the medical technology back then—no arthroscopes or anything like that." He stayed off the gridiron in his senior year.

Baseball was where Jeoff really stood out, though. As a senior, the righty batted .590 while playing the outfield and pitching, where he had an impressive 8-1 record. "I played some catcher and third base too," he noted. "I always liked playing every day. I played church-league ball in the summer too."

Near midnight on June 19, 1959, Cardinals scouts Maurice "Mo" Mozzali and Eddie Lyons signed the seventeen-year-old hurler. Mozzali was a St. Louis farmhand from 1946 to 1958 who became a Cards coach in 1977–78 after nearly two decades as a scout. He was born in Louisville, so Kentucky was the base of his scouting zone. "He covered Indiana and Michigan too," Long observed. "Mo scouted Ted Simmons. I talked to all the teams pretty much, there were 16 back then. It came down to the Reds and Cards, the Reds being there at home, but I thought a lot of Mo. He was really good to me. It was a situation that I couldn't turn down."

It's something that Jeoff was very modest about, but St. Louis gave him a sizable bonus. The amount was reported at various points between $50,000 and $100,000, but the consensus is $70,000 (paid in four yearly installments). He downplayed it in 2008, much as he did in 1961: "Sure I like dollar bills, but all I was interested in was playing baseball. My dad handled most of the monetary details. He's a real good businessman, and got me the best possible deal. But truthfully, I didn't much care what the final figure was."[4]

Three days after he signed, the teenager reported to his first pro team, Wytheville in the Appalachian League. An emotional Pauline Long said, "He seems awfully young to be leaving home."[5] Jeoff played in Virginia just briefly (0-1, 6.00 in three games) before going to another Class D squad, Keokuk in the Midwest League. He formed a battery with another Cardinals bonus boy who signed around the same time out of Tennessee: Tim McCarver ($75,000). Two other young men got lavish money (for the time) from St. Louis. Jim "Charlie" O'Rourke ($60,000) got two at bats in St. Louis that June, and did not resurface for the remainder of his four-year pro career. Future University of New Orleans coach Tom Schwaner ($50,000) also lasted four years in the Minors but never made the big leagues.

Despite unimpressive stats with Keokuk (2-7, 5.10 earned run average, 67 walks in 67 innings across 12 starts), Long showed enough to win a promotion to Class B in 1960. With Winston-Salem in the Carolina League, he went 0-6, with a 7.64 ERA in 15 games (8 starts). Wildness—55 more walks in 48⅓ innings—remained a major factor. However, Jeoff said that arm problems ended his days as a pitching prospect. "I pitched a 13-inning game in the district championship my senior year. I got twinges in my shoulder, and it hung with me. The arm just wasn't what it should have been. I just didn't have the stuff.

"I asked my manager at Winston-Salem, Chase Riddle, if there was anything else I could do to help." Thus, the organization looked to convert him to a position player.

As the experiment took shape, Long dropped

RORY COSTELLO

back a level to Winnipeg (Class C Northern League) to start 1961. Despite suffering a cracked wrist bone in May, he hit strongly (.299, 14 home runs, 45 runs batted in in just fifty-five games). He was still raw in the field—and a cutup off it, observed Don Blanchard, a columnist for the *Winnipeg Free Press*. "'Big Joe' will go on imitating people . . . television announcers, army generals, and the Hunchback of Notre Dame . . . but he'll bear one objective in mind. That is to make the grade at bat and in [the] field."[6] Blanchard later noted, "You can't teach an individual to plant bat on ball and send the pellet orbiting 500 feet."[7] "Blanchie was a great character," Jeoff remembered. "He called me the Kentucky Clouter."

Long credited Goldeyes manager Grover Resinger for his development, but to round out his fielding skills, Mo Mozzali was also on hand for part of that season. Don Blanchard reported in mid-July that "the ex-first baseman . . . has been hitting ground balls at the big guy until he hates the sight of them. 'Jeoff needs a lot of work,' admitted Mo, 'but when he learns to play first, they're going to have a hard time holding him down.'"[8]

Shortly after, "the apple-cheeked kid with the big bat, weak glove, and, we suspect, faked nonchalant attitude toward baseball" (as Blanchard described him) jumped to the Double-A Texas League.[9] "The Cardinals . . . are highly interested in finding out what the big guy can do against tough company," wrote Blanchard, who suggested that the organization might look to recoup some of its investment via the Rule 5 or expansion drafts.[10] Jeoff hit 7 homers and drove in 25 runs in thirty-seven games for the Oilers, though his average was just .225 as he adjusted.

The twenty-year-old had a torrid start in 1962, cracking 16 homers in the Oilers' first thirty-one games. Inevitably he cooled off after that, but he still finished with 30 home runs, 80 RBIs, and a .284 average. He added 4 more round-trippers in the playoffs as Tulsa swept Albuquerque, 3–0, and

knocked off Austin, 3–1, en route to the American Association title. Meanwhile, pal Harry Fanok's Atlanta Crackers had won the Little World Series. To celebrate their success, the young men spent two weeks in Stuttgart, Arkansas—the duck-hunting capital of the world—pursuing their favorite hobby.

After a stint in the Instructional League, Long was promoted again for the 1963 season, joining the Crackers in the International League. In eighty-six games, he had 43 RBIs while batting .274—but he hit just 5 homers. There was a good reason for the drop-off, though. Jeoff noted, "They'd removed the inner cyclone fence, and that made it a lot deeper for a right-handed batter." Indeed, Atlanta general manager Joe Ryan had removed the four-foot wire fence in July 1962,[11] restoring old Ponce de Leon Park's former cavernous dimensions (365 feet to left field and 448 to straightaway center, up from 330 and 410).

At the time, he met the big club's needs, and so St. Louis summoned him on July 28. "The Redbirds, desperate at times for a right-handed pinch-hitter, called up Jeoff Long. Duke Carmel, a left-handed swinger . . . was sent to the Mets in a waiver deal to make room for Long."[12]

Jeoff made his debut on July 31 as a pinch hitter for Bob Gibson, striking out against the Reds' Jim O'Toole. Over the next month, he pinch-hit four more times without appearing in the field. In his last at bat that year, on August 27, Long got his first Major League hit—a single off Jack Sanford of San Francisco. He remained with the Cards through the end of the season but saw no more action.

Long then went once again to the Instructional League. He remembered in particular being on the field when the assassination of President John F. Kennedy was announced. There were happier memories of his autumns in Florida, though.

"One year we had a great team—we won the league over Detroit, which had guys like Willie

Horton and Jim Northrup. But my favorite memory is from an NL vs. AL all-star game. Eddie Stanky was the manager, and he wanted me to pinch-hit. I couldn't find my bat, and Pete Rose said, 'Here, take this one—it's got a lot of hits in it.' Sure enough, I lined a single, and when I came back to the dugout, Pete said, 'See, I told you!'" Of course, Rose's bats wound up with 4,256 big-league hits in them.

Jeoff proceeded to win a roster spot with the Cards in the spring of 1964. Two old St. Louis stars who knew the prospect from Tulsa remarked on his promise. "'He's built like Jimmie Foxx and can hit a ball a mile,' said old Gashouser [and Drillers coach] Pepper Martin. . . . Said [manager] Whitey Kurowski, 'He hit one ball at Tulsa that would have landed at the Fairgrounds Hotel if he had been swinging at Busch Stadium.'" Sheldon "Chief" Bender, associate director of player development, added, "Remember that at Atlanta last year, he was shooting at a 450-foot alley in left-center."[13]

Long remembered, "I had a good spring. I hit a few homers, did real well [.319], and after one big game against the Mets, I was on Howard Cosell's show as star of the game. I had a double off the right-center wall against Sandy Koufax the first time I faced him.

"Then in my first regular-season at-bat that year, Opening Night, in front of over 50,000 fans [at Dodger Stadium], I got another hit off Sandy. I remember it was a drive off the 410 mark in dead center, over Willie Davis's head. I thought, 'Gee whiz, this is terrific stuff.'" Long settled for a single and then left for a pinch runner, but his performance against Koufax remains "one of my biggest thrills in the game. I always hit lefties well."

Still, the rookie played only sporadically over the season's first few months. His career highlight came on May 15, against the Milwaukee Braves in his second career start. Bill White's streak of 284 consecutive games played, then the longest cur-

rent run in the National League, ended with a muscle strain. Batting fifth, Long hit his only Major League homer, off knuckleballer Bobby Tiefenauer. The two-run shot in the seventh inning was "a towering drive that bounced off the top of the scoreboard in left field, over 400 feet away."[14] It snapped a 6–6 tie, and St. Louis went on to win, 10–6.

Jeoff remembered, "Yep, it was a knuckleball. It was one of the longest shots at the old Busch Stadium, off the top of the Redbird, to the left of the eagle."

Long got five more starts during May, two at first base and three in right field. From Memorial Day on, though, he saw only pinch-hitting duty. On July 7 the Cardinals sold him to the White Sox for an undisclosed amount to make room for Mike Shannon. It was a pivotal move for the team during its run to the championship, as Shannon took over right field. Lou Brock, who had arrived from the Cubs a few weeks before, and Shannon flanked Curt Flood in a revamped outfield.

"I was shocked to leave the Cardinals," said Long. "It was my organization, who I signed with, where my heart was. And it was a great team."

The Sporting News stated that Long "could be a big help for the Sox, who are sorely lacking in punch from the right side of the plate."[15] Less than a week later, though, as Jeoff pointed out, "they made a deal with the Senators for Moose Skowron and put him at first base. Al Lopez asked me if I'd mind moving to left field. It was a rainy night in Boston [July 15], it was a wet field, and I slipped. I hurt my knee again."

Jeoff had to leave the game after the mishap on Frank Malzone's single. He missed five days and started just twice over the rest of the season. "I also got hit in the back by a foul ball in Detroit and cracked a rib. Things just didn't go my way physically."

Long collected only 5 singles in 35 at bats for the White Sox, driving in 5 runs. Together with his 10-for-43 mark for St. Louis, he hit .192. A start

RORY COSTELLO

against the Los Angeles Angels on September 23 proved to be Jeoff's last game in the Majors. He finished with a lifetime average of .193.

The Cardinals voted Long a half share, $4,311.64, of the winners' World Series money. (However, it appears his name may have been left out of the published lists by mistake!) He also got a half share of American League second-place cash, $733.01, from the White Sox. On December 1 Chicago traded pitcher Ray Herbert to Philadelphia for Danny Cater. As part of the deal, Long was swapped for future Major League manager Lee Elia. He went from Indianapolis (Chicago's top farm club) to Arkansas (then a Phillies affiliate in the Pacific Coast League).

A rash of injuries—instep, hand, ankle, and knee—kept Long sidelined for most of spring training in 1965.[16] He appeared in only fourteen games for the Travelers, going hitless with one RBI in eighteen at bats. In May, after the knee flared up again, the Travs invoked a condition in the deal to return the first baseman to the Chicago organization, which assigned him to Double-A Lynchburg. After hitting .195 in twenty-four games there, he was released—but the Cardinals picked him up and assigned him to Triple-A Jacksonville (.250 in eight games). Chief Bender said in Jeoff's defense, "He's had water on the knee since high school and people have thought he's been dogging it."[17]

That off-season, though he'd considered Instructional League, Long tried to get his bum knee fixed. In 1969 he remarked, "It wasn't worth a darn the whole season of 1965, so I decided to have it cut. Well, I had some bad luck. There were some complications, infection and hemorrhaging, so I had it done all over."[18] When spring 1966 rolled around, though, he still wasn't right. Said Chief Bender, "The operation did not relieve the stiffness in the knee and I doubt that Long will be able to play much, if at all." Jeoff had been assigned to Double-A Arkansas but would have had the opportunity to make Tulsa's squad.[19]

However, he wound up missing not only that season but also the next two. He went back to work in the family business and underwent another operation in 1967 "to try to loosen up the frozen joint. I went back to winter ball in 1968—I think it was George Silvey with the Cardinals who gave me the chance."

Jeoff started the 1969 season with Arkansas (Double-A). Travelers manager Ray Hathaway told *The Sporting News*, "He's had I don't know how many operations and he's paid for them himself. He loves the game that much. People who saw him before say he's 50 percent improved."[20] In the same article, Long observed as he rubbed his scarred right knee, "I've got a motion problem. It pulls quite a bit. You see that? That's as far back as it will go, but it seems to be giving a little. I'm here just trying it out. I don't know how much I'll be able to do."[21]

Even though Long hit only .162 in eighteen games for the Travelers, he still got the call from Triple-A Tulsa to replace the injured Willie Montañez on May 9. Back with the Oilers for the first time in seven years, he batted .263 with 2 homers and 18 RBIs and even pitched a little again (he'd also relieved once in Little Rock). Manager Warren Spahn used him to mop up for a few innings in a blowout on May 29, commenting, "Long showed me he could get the ball over the plate. And on this staff, that means a lot."[22]

Ultimately, though, the physical problems were too much. "I never regained but about 60 percent of the motion in that knee," said Long in 2008. "I just couldn't get it back. I could hit, but I couldn't do much with the wheels. So it was involuntary retirement."

After that he rejoined Cincinnati Drum, becoming a foreman. Jeoff married Katherine "Kathy" Martin in June 1975; they had one daughter, Lindsay, who became a national champion diver at Southern Methodist University.

Just before his wedding, Jeoff made national

news in a different game, showing that he was still a *long* hitter. With a blast of 322 yards 28 inches, he won the first National Open Long Driving contest at Butler National Golf Club in Oak Brook, Illinois. Looking back, *Golf Digest* noted in 1999, "Jeoff Long, a 15-handicap amateur from Fort Mitchell, KY . . . defeated a host of PGA Tour pros, including fourth-place finisher Jim Dent, who would go on to lead the senior tour in driving distance six consecutive years (1989–94)."

Long won a prize of $12,000, but he turned it over to the PGA Junior Golf Fund because he would have had to turn pro to accept. "I could have used the money," Long said. "I'm getting married this weekend. . . . I got started when I was playing with the Cards. Some of us would just get together and go out to the driving range and beat on some balls."[23]

Harry Fanok offered a jovial memory of those days. "The long driving deal started when Jeoff and I were in spring training. After the workouts, we'd head on out to a place called Ted Peters Smoked Mullet [a Tampa institution]. They had the good food there. Then we'd hit the driving range to see who could smoke the ball the farthest. He'd always win. Sometimes we'd be there at night time. There was a movie drive-in right next to the driving range. Bad idea! We'd shank many a ball amongst the folks trying to watch a flick or make out."[24]

Long was runner-up in the 1976 contest and competed through 1984. "I never could find the fairway again," he observed. "I was lucky to find it that first time!"

Jeoff remained in management at Cincinnati Drum for many years, but in 2010, "We decided to sell our business, it was a family decision. We still have a small real estate deal we are part of." He still follows baseball, and his original team remains in his heart. "I was glad the Cardinals won the World Series," Long said in November 2011. "I believe they were the best team, although Texas deserves a lot of credit."

Long looked back on his brief big-league career fondly in 2008. In a mild Kentucky drawl, he said, "I don't want to brag, but barring the physical situation, I think I'd have done fine. It didn't work out, but it was an enjoyable trip. I got to play the game I dreamed of playing for a little while, and I love the time I was involved in it and the people. That was the main thing, just being a Cardinal."

Chapter 25. **Dal Maxvill**

Loretta Donovan

AGE	G	AB	R	H	2B	3B	HR	TB	RBI	BB	SO	BAV	OBP	SLG	SB	GDP	HBP
25	37	26	4	6	0	0	0	6	4	0	7	.231	.231	.231	1	0	0

In the history of the St. Louis Cardinals, there have been many wonderful shortstops. Think of the flamboyant Leo Durocher, the slick-fielding MVP Marty Marion, and the Hall of Famer Ozzie Smith. To their number add Charles Dallan Maxvill, who went from barely making the team to building a Major League career that lasted fourteen years, most of them with his beloved Cardinals. He earned four world championship rings and became a trusted Major League coach and finally the general manager of the Cardinals. Dal Maxvill lived a young boy's baseball dream.

The Cardinals had been Dal's favorite team since he was a youngster growing up in a St. Louis suburb, Granite City, Illinois, where he was born on February 18, 1939, to Harold and Eileen Maxvill. Harold was a steelworker. His parents took him to Sportsman's Park, where he saw the Cardinals legends of the 1940s and early '50s, including the seven-time All-Star shortstop. When he was eleven years old, Dal wanted to play in the Khoury League, a youth baseball organization centered in the St. Louis area. Most of his friends' fathers were too busy working in the steel mills to coach his team, so Eileen volunteered to be the manager. Dal rode the handlebars of her bicycle taking the team's gear to the practices and games. Dal was always underweight, so his family tried to help him gain a few pounds. His grandmother financed a series of shots intended to improve his appetite. "But all I got out of the shots was a sore arm," he said.[1]

Dal played baseball at Granite City High School. A five-foot-eleven, 135-pound infielder when he got out of school, he received baseball

Dal Maxvill played thirty-seven games and posted a .231 batting average. He substituted for Javier in the World Series. He later became a Cardinals GM.

scholarship offers from the University of Missouri and Northwestern University.[2] He turned them down to attend Washington University in St. Louis, which had a good engineering school. The fact that his girlfriend, Diana Sinclair, was in St. Louis helped him make his college choice. Maxvill financed part of his college education by working at Granite City Steel as a laborer for several summers. He eventually received an academic half-scholarship and graduated in 1960, after three and

Maxvill jumps over Tom Tresh as he completes a double play in Game Seven of the 1964 World Series.

a half years, with a degree in electrical engineering and a senior-year .350 batting average on the Bears' university baseball team.

The Major League scouts considered Maxvill too small, but Irv Utz, his college coach, arranged a tryout with the Cardinals. By chance, one of the St. Louis affiliates needed a defensive infielder, so scout Joe Monahan signed him. Bing Devine, the Cardinals' general manager, was also a Washington University graduate, and he assigned Maxvill to Winnipeg, a Cardinals affiliate in the Class C Northern League. He received a $1,000 bonus and a promise of $1,000 more if he lasted the full season. He did last the season, playing in seventy-four games and batting .257 as the Goldeyes won the Northern League pennant. Maxvill began the 1961 season in Winnipeg, but was moved up to the Cardinals' Triple-A team in Charleston, West Virginia (International League), in time to play eighty games there.

The Cardinals moved Maxvill to Double-A Tulsa (Texas League) to start the 1962 season, but

brought him up after he batted .348 and fielded well in forty-eight games. He played in seventy-nine games for the Cardinals and batted .222. In 1963 he started only five games at shortstop because Dick Groat, acquired from Pittsburgh and the regular shortstop, was having another All-Star year. At the beginning of 1964 the Cardinals sent Maxvill to Triple-A Jacksonville, where he fielded well but hit an anemic .140 in thirty-eight games. The Cardinals sent him on loan to Indianapolis, a White Sox farm team, in June. While traveling to report to Indianapolis, Maxvill thought about quitting baseball and going home to work at Bussmann Fuse Company, his off-season employer. At the airport in Chicago he spoke by phone to his wife, Diana, who encouraged him to continue in baseball, and Maxvill decided to report to Indianapolis.

He made the right decision, because after playing in forty-five games for Indianapolis, batting .285, and continuing to field well, he was called up by the Cardinals. After playing in only a half-

LORETTA DONOVAN

dozen games as a backup to Groat, and getting only six hits in twenty-six at bats, Maxvill started at second base in the all-important last game of the season against the New York Mets. Julián Javier, the regular second baseman, was out with a bruised hip. The Cardinals had lost the first two games of the three-game series in St. Louis. If they lost this game, there could be a three-way tie for the lead in the National League, or they could lose the pennant if the Reds won their game. A Cardinals win would give them the pennant, if the Reds lost to the Phillies.

Manager Johnny Keane told Maxvill the night before the big game that he would be the second baseman for the pivotal game. "All I could think was if somebody hit the ball to me, I wanted to get them out," Maxvill said after the game.[3] He got the hitters out, but he also got two big hits in the game. He came up in the fourth with the score tied, 1–1, two out, and Groat on second. Maxvill singled to center off Galen Cisco, the Mets hurler, to give the Cardinals the lead. The Mets went ahead, 3–2, in the top of the fifth. In the bottom of the inning the Cardinals went ahead, 4–3, and Maxvill came to bat again. He got another run-scoring single, scoring Boyer to make it 5–3. The Cardinals eventually won, 11–5, to clinch their first National League pennant since 1946 (Philadelphia had already defeated Cincinnati).

Next came the World Series and the New York Yankees with Roger Maris and Mickey Mantle. Maxvill started every game at second base. (He was pinch-hit for in the late innings of three games.) Maxvill batted only .200 (4 for 20), but Keane was pleased with his play and the way the youngster handled the pressure. In Game Seven, Maxvill singled home Shannon in the fourth inning to make the score 3–0, and he caught the ninth-inning pop-up by Yankee Bobby Richardson that ended the game and gave the world championship to the Cardinals.

But 1965 was a different season. Javier had

healed and Groat was still the Cardinals' regular shortstop. As a result, Maxvill had only eighty-nine at bats in sixty-eight games. No matter that in spring training general manager Stan Musial had called him the "take-charge leader of the Cardinals' infield."[4]

Maxvill continued to use his engineering degree by working in the off-season for Bussmann Fuse Company. He usually traveled around the country demonstrating and selling fuse systems.

Groat was traded after the 1965 season, but Maxvill did not automatically inherit the shortstop position in 1966. In spring training, Jerry Buchek, Jimy Williams, and Phil Gagliano were his biggest competition. Coach Dick Sisler worked with Maxvill to improve his hitting, spending extra time in the batting cage with him. "Dick got me to wait on the ball better and hit to right field more consistently," Maxvill said. "He had me moving around better at the plate so I could handle certain pitches better."[5]

Finally, in early June, Maxvill became the regular shortstop. Red Schoendienst, his manager, felt that his defensive abilities made the infield stronger. Pitchers, especially Bob Gibson, wanted Maxie, as he became known, to be fielding behind them in every game. Although he batted only .244 for the season, Maxvill delivered numerous key hits and drew thirty-seven walks to tie Shannon for most on the team. After the season Maxvill was selected Khoury Major Leaguer of the Year, beating out ten other Major Leaguers who started their baseball careers in the Khoury League organization.

Maxvill began spring training of 1967 knowing he was the starting shortstop. He was pleased, telling a sportswriter, "Not many players like to be picked up, or substituted for. I don't. I want to play every day, all the time. It's an old story in baseball—rest two days and maybe you rest five years."[6]

Things went well for regular shortstop Maxvill

and the 1967 Cardinals. He played in 152 games and had 14 runs batted in during September. His fielding percentage at shortstop, .974, was tied for second best in the league. He also appeared in 7 games at second base, where he did not make an error.

The Cardinals again went to the World Series, this time against the Boston Red Sox. The Series went down to the seventh game at Fenway Park. Jim Lonborg, the Red Sox's starter, had won twenty-two games in the regular season and was the Cy Young winner in the American League. Lonborg had also won Games Two and Five with commanding complete-game efforts. Maxvill led off the third inning with a triple off the center-field wall and scored the Cardinals' first run when Flood drove him in with a single. With nobody out in the ninth inning, Maxvill grabbed a hard ground ball in the hole and teamed with Javier for a rally-killing double play. The Cardinals went on to win, 7–2, to claim their eighth world championship.

The 1968 season was another good one for Maxvill and the Cardinals. He was the National League Gold Glove winner at shortstop, and his .253 batting average was the highest of his Major League career. Maxvill was the only Cardinal who started every game in the club's stretch of fifty-nine games in fifty-six days after the All-Star break.[7] The Cardinals went to the World Series again that year, this time losing to the Detroit Tigers in seven games. Maxvill was 0 for 22 at the plate, a World Series record for futility.

The Cardinals had the highest payroll in baseball, in those pre-free-agency days that brought criticism of the organization from elsewhere in baseball. But manager Schoendienst and general manager Devine defended the players. "Some highly placed baseball people believe that by paying so well the Cardinals are undermining the very structure of baseball," a *Sports Illustrated* writer said just before the World Series, adding a com-ment from Devine: "Almost every place I go . . . someone will ask me how Dal Maxvill can be making $37,500. It really seems to bother people, but if you have seen the way he has played short-stop this year and how he gets himself involved in the good things we do, his salary won't sur-prise you."[8] Indeed, Maxvill's salary went up to $45,000 in 1969.

High salaries and all, the 1969 and 1970 sea-sons were forgettable for Maxvill and the Cardi-nals. The team finished in fourth place both years, thirteen games behind the division winners in the NL East. One bright spot for Maxvill came on April 14, 1969, when he hit the first Major League grand-slam home run in Canada during a Cardi-nals–Montreal Expos game at Parc Jarry. But in the 1970 season he tied a record for least home runs in a season when he failed to hit a homer in 152 games and 399 at bats. The Cardinals did bet-ter in 1971, winning ninety games but finishing in second place, seven games behind the Pittsburgh Pirates.

Maxvill was respected and popular among his teammates, who named him their union represen-tative. The responsibility put Maxvill in a tough spot during the players' strike in the spring of 1972. He thought the fans did not understand the players' side of the squabble, which erased the first week of the season. On August 28 he was named Sportsman of the Year by the Southside Kiwanis Club in St. Louis. Two days later he was traded to the Oakland Athletics for two Minor Leaguers. He was hitting .221 at the time, but the trade was somewhat of a surprise.

Maxvill played in most of the remaining games for his new club, usually at second base. He wanted to play every inning of every game, but the Oakland manager, Dick Williams, used a rotating second baseman system. Williams used ten short-stops/second basemen that season. Most of the time, the second baseman who started the game would not be around to finish it. He would usually be taken out for a pinch hitter early in the game. On September 28 Maxvill was the fourth second baseman the A's used against Minnesota. He batted in the bottom of the ninth with the game tied and a runner on first. His double to left field won the game, 8–7, and gave Oakland a six-game lead in the American League West. The A's finished five and a half games ahead of the Chicago White Sox for the West Division title, going on to beat the Detroit Tigers in the American League Championship Series. Maxvill played in every game of that ALCS, starting three of them at shortstop. He was ineligible for the World Series, in which the A's beat the Cincinnati Reds, but was awarded a World Series ring and was voted a half share of the World Series money.

Maxvill played only sporadically for the A's in 1973, and on July 7 he was sold to the Pirates, who ended up in third place, two and a half games behind the Mets. He started the 1974 season with the Pirates but was released on April 20 and went home to St. Louis to help operate Cardinal Travel, an agency he and former Cardinals teammate Joe Hoerner, along with other investors, had started in 1969. He did not stay there long, as the Athletics came calling on May 10, and he signed with them. He played in sixty games and had fifty-two at bats and ten hits for the A's. The A's again won the AL West, and played Baltimore in the league championship series. Maxvill appeared in one game in the ALCS, with only one at bat, in which he struck out. The A's went to the 1974 World Series and beat the Los Angeles Dodgers in five games. Maxvill played in two games, with no at bats, and received his fourth World Series ring and a full World Series share. He was released after the season but re-signed as a coach and utility infielder, at a salary of $40,000. He played in twenty games in 1975 and had two hits in ten at bats.

In November 1975 Maxvill retired from baseball. By this time he was thirty-six and ready to settle down in St. Louis and put his talents to work at the travel agency. In a few years, however, he was back in baseball, as Joe Torre, now the manager of the Mets, signed him to coach third base for the 1978 season. Torre respected Maxvill's knowledge of the fundamentals of baseball, and thought that his former Cardinal roommate could help improve the play of his infielders. Maxvill resigned after the season, again to be closer to home and his travel business. But baseball called again, and quickly. In October he and Red Schoendienst were hired as coaches for the Cardinals under manager Ken Boyer. Fans reacted favorably because both lived in St. Louis and were well liked in the baseball community. By that time Maxvill had four children and appreciated the opportunity to have a baseball job close to home. He coached for the Cardinals in 1979 and 1980. Whitey Herzog became the Cardinals' manager in June 1980 and hired his own coaches, and in 1981 Maxvill became a Minor League instructor.

When Torre became manager of the Atlanta Braves in 1982, Maxvill again became a coach for his good friend. After the 1984 season, Torre was fired and Maxvill was the only coach retained by the Braves.

The Cardinals fired their general manager, Joe McDonald, in January 1985. In February, during the Braves' spring training, the Cardinals came calling again, asking Maxvill to interview for the position of general manager. The team was looking for someone with a good head for business and a working knowledge of baseball and of the Cardinals organization. Maxvill and team owner August Busch Jr. talked on Busch's yacht off St. Petersburg. After the meeting, Maxvill, now forty-six, walked along the beach for a half hour until he was offered the position. He was officially named general manager on February 25, 1985. Maxvill was now the GM for Herzog, the man who had sent him down to coach in the Minors.

Maxvill was enthusiastic about the opportunity to help shape the team he had followed since he was a boy. "It would be awfully nice to be humble," he said, "but I can handle the job. It will be fun, a challenge. If I thought I couldn't do the job, I wouldn't have talked to them when they approached me."[9] His contract would be for one year at a time. The team's chief operating officer, Fred Kuhlmann, would be in charge of business matters. Everything would have to be approved by the executive committee and then by Busch.

Maxvill's rookie season as general manager was a good one. In his first trade, on April 2, 1985, he acquired Jose Oquendo from the Mets for Angel Salazar. For ten years Oquendo proved to be a valuable utility player for the Cardinals, and he became a popular coach in 1999. In a surprising turn of events, the 1985 Cardinals, whom many picked to finish last in the NL East before the season started, won 101 games and defeated the Dodgers in the NLCS. They battled Kansas City in what became known as the I-70 World Series, for the interstate highway that connected the two cities. The Cardinals were two outs away from winning the Series in Game Six before the Royals rallied to win that game and then Game Seven. The next season, 1986, the Cardinals finished three games under .500 and ended the season twenty-eight and a half games behind the Mets, but in 1987 they again won the NLCS, this time over the Giants, before losing the World Series to the Minnesota Twins in seven games. In 1988 St. Louis ended in fifth place, ten games under .500, in the NL East.

As general manager Maxvill often voiced his concern about escalating salaries in baseball. He had to contend with a manager, Herzog, who freely offered his ideas on ways to improve the team. Before the 1989 season pitchers Danny Cox and Greg Matthews were injured. Herzog wanted Mark Langston, a left-handed starting pitcher for Seattle. Even though Maxvill and Herzog agreed that the price for Langston was too high, the manager kept insisting on acquiring Langston. "When you're a manager, you want to have a club that can compete, that has a fair shake when you go out there. Last year we didn't have that from day one," Herzog said.[10] Langston went to the Expos in a July trade, and Herzog continued to have issues with the pitching.

The Cardinals finished the 1989 season in third place, seven games behind the division-winning Chicago Cubs. In late September the Cardinals also lost their primary backer at the brewery when August Busch Jr. died at the age of ninety. There was a restructuring of the team's top brass. Kuhlmann became the president and CEO, and August Busch III, who had no interest in baseball, was the chairman of the board.

Another example of the difficulties escalating salaries posed for Maxvill was his contract negotiations with Cardinals third baseman Terry Pendleton, who had been awarded a Gold Glove in 1989 and batted .264. The issue went to arbitration, and Pendleton was awarded $1.85 million, the second-highest amount given to a player in arbitration to that point. As much as he would have liked to keep Pendleton a Cardinal, Maxvill could not afford to sign him to a long-term deal at that price, and Pendleton went to the Braves as a free agent after the 1990 season.

By June 1990 the Cardinals were last in the National League in batting with a .235 average. Maxvill insisted that he would not make changes just to "shake things up." He was in a bind because eleven of the players were going to be free agents at the end of the season. The management did give Maxvill an endorsement by extending his contract another year, even though the team lost thirty-nine of its first sixty-six games.

On July 6, 1990, Herzog resigned as manager. The team was close to last place and playing poorly. Herzog could not motivate them and no trade was imminent. The number of free agents also bothered Herzog. Joe Torre eventually became the new manager, but the Cardinals finished in last place in the NL East, twenty-five games out. During the winter they lost several players to free agency. Maxvill had to work within the conservative budget of the brewery to try to put a winning team on the field. He had to find inexpensive young talent to replace the expensive free agents they had to let go.

For the next two seasons, the Cardinals sang the familiar refrain. They would not go after free agents. After the 1992 season, they had ten players who could apply for free agency. They re-signed Ozzie Smith but let the others leave. The Cardinals finished in third place in 1993, ten games behind the Phillies. After the season Maxvill admitted that the team needed pitching help but added, "Unfortunately, we are looking for a pitcher who doesn't make a lot of money."[11]

The 1994 season quickly disintegrated. The team was having trouble winning games, and then the Major League players went on strike on August 11, wiping out the remainder of the season. In August, Mark Lamping, a former Anheuser-Busch executive, was hired as president of the Cardinals. In September, he fired Maxvill. Dal continued to draw his salary through 1995, doing some specialized scouting. He was fifty-five years old. He did some scouting for the Yankees for a while. Otherwise, he stayed away from baseball.

Maxvill has been out of baseball for a long time, but fans who saw him consider him to be among the best defensive shortstops to wear a Cardinals uniform. Some remember a time in the 1960s when a feisty little shortstop would never make an error, because he wanted to win for his Cardinals.

Chapter 26. **Tim McCarver**

Dave Williams

AGE	G	AB	R	H	2B	3B	HR	TB	RBI	BB	SO	BAV	OBP	SLG	SB	GDP	HBP
22	143	465	53	134	19	3	9	186	52	40	44	.288	.343	.400	2	8	1

For those who saw Tim McCarver break in with the St. Louis Cardinals more than forty years ago, it is probably a surprise that he is now better known for his broadcasting career than for his days as a catcher. Not that he wasn't always articulate and glib, and that his finding a home in the broadcast booth is a shock; it's just that he was a pretty good ball player who was a major contributor on championship teams.

James Timothy McCarver was born October 16, 1941, in Memphis, Tennessee. A police officer's son, he had three brothers and one sister. Surprisingly, it is his sister Marilyn that he gave much of the credit to for his early development. She turned him into a left-handed hitter and worked with young Tim on his fielding. By the time he graduated from Christian Brothers High School in 1959, he was a three-sport athlete, shining in football and baseball. He was all-state in both sports as well as captain of both squads. His football team was a powerhouse that won twenty straight games. Tim was a standout at linebacker and was recruited by both Tennessee and Notre Dame. He played American Legion ball for Tony Gagliano, uncle of Phil Gagliano, who also later played with Tim in St. Louis.

McCarver was signed by Cardinals scout Buddy Lewis for $75,000. The New York Yankees were also interested in him. His first assignment was at Keokuk of the Midwest League, where Brent Musburger served as home plate umpire in Tim's first professional game. One can only imagine the in-game chatter between those two future broadcast legends. He hit .360 in 275 at bats and then was promoted to Rochester of the International

Tim McCarver led all Cardinals hitters in the 1964 World Series, hitting .478. He later became a national TV baseball announcer and commentator.

League, where he hit .357 in 70 at bats. This earned Tim a late-season promotion to the Majors and his first look at big-league pitching: he had 4 hits in 24 at bats (.167).

In 1960 McCarver had a big year at Memphis of the Southern Association. He batted .347—good for second in the league. This earned him another late-season call-up to the big leagues. He appeared in ten games for the Cards and batted .200 with 2 hits in 10 at bats. The year 1961 would not be so kind, however. He stumbled to a .229 average while playing for San Juan/Charleston of the International League. Another promotion to the Cards saw him get his first significant playing time in the Majors. Tim appeared in twenty games and had 67 at bats. The results weren't overwhelming, as he batted just .239, but he did hit his first home run on July 13, a solo shot to right field off Tony Cloninger of the Braves.

The year 1962 would be the last he would see of the Minor Leagues. He played for Atlanta of the International League and had a solid season with a .275 average, 11 homers, and 57 RBIS. Because Atlanta was in the playoffs, McCarver played in the Minors into early October; he had to wait until the next spring to see the Majors again. When he did, he was there to stay and impressed from the start. Despite his youth, he exhibited leadership skills, and St. Louis liked him enough to trade starting catcher Gene Oliver, who clubbed 14 homers for them in '62, in a trading deadline deal for Lew Burdette of the Milwaukee Braves. The trade officially anointed McCarver as the starting catcher and he responded with a .289 average, 4 homers, and 51 RBIS. He also had 7 triples. In 1966 his 13 triples tied him with Johnny Kling (1903) for the post-1900 record for triples by a catcher.

Showing rare speed for a man of his position, McCarver displayed some in a June game against the Mets when he hit his first career grand slam, a rare inside-the-park grand slam. McCarver hit a shot at the Polo Grounds that Mets center fielder Rod Kanehl slipped going after, and McCarver raced around the bases before Kanehl could recover. McCarver was also a popular player in the clubhouse. Not surprisingly, he was viewed as a cerebral player who liked to pick at the nuances of the game, but he also had a very keen sense of humor. He was noted for his dead-on impersonation of Frank Fontaine, who was the rubber-faced funnyman Crazy Guggenheim on the very popular *Jackie Gleason Show.*

A July 22, 1967, article in *The Sporting News* recapped some pretty heady praise McCarver inspired in his rookie season. Wally Schang, known both for his days as a catcher with Connie Mack's Philadelphia Athletics and for the first three Yankees pennant-winning teams, said, "The kid reminds me of Mickey Cochrane. I don't know if McCarver will hit with Cochrane, but he's got Mickey's same aggressiveness and speed. And as a kid, McCarver's a pretty good hitter right now." The legendary Branch Rickey was quoted in the same article as comparing McCarver to Bill DeLancey, catcher from the 1934 Cardinals' Gas House Gang: "DeLancey had the stronger throwing arm, but Tim's arm is strong enough. McCarver's a solid .280 hitter. He could hit .300 and he can run faster than DeLancey could. He has the same aggressiveness and baseball intelligence."

Success did not go to his head, and 1964 would prove to be a big year for Tim and the St. Louis Cardinals. He followed his strong rookie campaign with another good season as he batted .288 with 9 homers and 52 RBIS. He hit 3 triples, a fall-off from 7 the year before. The Cards found themselves in a tight pennant race in September 1964, a season that is known for the collapse of the Philadelphia Phillies. On September 21, with a six-and-a-half-game lead and World Series tickets already printed, the Phillies dropped ten consecutive games and found themselves in a four-way race along with St. Louis, San Francisco, and Cincinnati. Despite losing two straight games to the lowly Mets on the final weekend of the season, the Cards pulled out the pennant when they finally beat the Mets in the last game while the Reds, with manager Fred Hutchinson dying of cancer, lost to the Phillies.

St. Louis would head off to the World Series to play the New York Yankees. McCarver was a standout. In the critical Game Five, with the Series squared at two games apiece, Bob Gibson had the Yankees shut out until Tom Tresh hit a two-run homer in the bottom of the ninth inning to knot the score, 2–2. McCarver then hit a three-run homer in the top of the tenth inning and the Cards held on for a 5–2 victory and the Series lead. St. Louis won the Series in the seventh game and had its first world championship since 1946. McCarver batted .478 with 11 hits in 23 at bats, knocking in 5 runs and scoring 4. He also tied a Series record by hitting safely in all seven games. It was quite a year for a young man who turned twenty-three the day after the Series ended. He capped the year by marrying his high school sweetheart, Anne McDaniel, on December 29, 1964. The McCarvers would eventually have two daughters, Kelly and Kathy.

The year 1965 began inauspiciously as he broke a finger in spring training and missed the first week of the regular season. Battling injuries all season that limited him to 113 games, he was still productive at the plate, finishing with 11 homers, 48 RBIs, and a .276 average. The Cardinals slumped to a seventh-place finish as several key players—most notably Ken Boyer, Ray Sadecki, and Curt Simmons—had significant drop-offs in performance. The club improved only slightly to a sixth-place finish in 1966, but McCarver had another fine season at the plate. He improved to 12 home runs, 68 RBIs, and a .274 average, and set a Major League record for catchers with a league-leading 13 triples. He stayed injury-free and was a workhorse behind the plate, catching in 148 games.

The 1966 All-Star Game was held in St. Louis, and McCarver was selected for the first time to represent the National League. On a very hot day, McCarver began a game-winning rally in the bottom of the tenth with a single. He was sacrificed to second by Ron Hunt and scored on a single by Maury Wills, beating Tony Oliva's throw to the plate.

There was also an interesting incident in April 1966 that sheds some light on the relationship between players and management, pre–Marvin Miller. McCarver and veteran pitcher Bob Purkey represented the players in a meeting with management in a dispute over compensation for appearances for pregame and postgame shows. The players were not being compensated and they wanted $25 for radio and $50 for television appearances. Management pointed to small print in the player's contract stipulating that they agree to "cooperate with the club and participate in any and all promotional activities of the club and league." That was the end of that.

The year 1967 was big for McCarver and the Cardinals. Buoyed by a near-MVP season from first baseman Orlando Cepeda, St. Louis won the pennant by a comfortable ten-and-a-half-game margin over the San Francisco Giants. McCarver was batting .348 at the All-Star break and earned a second, and final, trip to the midseason classic. His average tailed off to .295, but he still finished with career highs in home runs (14) and RBIs (69). The Cardinals went into the 1967 World Series to face the "Impossible Dream" Boston Red Sox. Boston, which had finished ninth the season before, was led by Triple Crown winner Carl Yastrzemski and pitcher Jim Lonborg, who won twenty-two games. The Series was hard fought, and finally the Cardinals rode the strong arm of pitcher Bob Gibson to a seven-game victory. McCarver did not have the same outstanding performance as he did in the 1964 Series, batting only .125 with 3 hits in 24 at bats.

The last year in the great run for the St. Louis Cardinals was 1968. They captured their third pennant in five years, again finishing comfortably ahead of the San Francisco Giants. The year 1968 was also known as the Year of the Pitcher, and St. Louis was carried by Bob Gibson's historic 1.12 ERA and twenty-two victories. McCarver saw his average dip to .253, but he atoned for his poor performance in the 1967 Series with a very good 1968 Series. He batted .333, and among his nine hits was a three-run home run in the fifth inning of Game Three off Pat Dobson that put the Cards ahead and spurred them on to a 7–3 victory. Alas, things did not turn out as well for the Cards as it had in 1964 and 1967. St. Louis stormed out to a 3-games-to-1 lead before the Tigers mounted a comeback and took three games in a row to win the world championship.

McCarver ended his first tour of duty with the Cardinals in 1969 with another solid season: 7 home runs, 51 RBIs, and a .260 average. The club slumped to fourth place, thirteen games behind the first-place "Miracle Mets." In a historic trade, McCarver was sent off to the Philadelphia Phillies along with Curt Flood in a seven-player trade that also saw the enigmatic Dick Allen go to St. Louis. Flood refused to report to the Phillies and took his case all the way to the Supreme Court. This was the precursor to all the player/management labor issues in the '70s that changed the baseball landscape forever.

This also began the vagabond part of McCarver's career. He began the 1970 season as the Phillies starting catcher, but in a microcosm of all the troubles that befell the Phillies in those days, McCarver broke his finger on a foul ball off the bat of Willie Mays in early May. In the very same inning, backup catcher Mike Ryan suffered a similar injury and both were shelved for a good part of the season. McCarver already possessed a less-than-powerful arm, and the broken finger did not heal straight. The effect was that his throws moved like a cut fastball.

McCarver returned to form with the Phillies in 1971. He appeared in 134 games and again produced solid offensive numbers, with a .278 average to go along with 8 round-trippers and 46 RBIs. An interesting incident with his former Cardinal teammates took place in September. It began when McCarver dropped a pop-up near the St. Louis dugout. Cardinal players began riding him and really got under his skin when they began yelling from the dugout, "There he goes!" with the slow-footed Joe Torre on first base—the implication

being that his throwing problems would not even allow him to catch a pedestrian Torre on a stolen-base attempt. When Lou Brock was at the plate, he was brushed back by pitcher Manny Muniz on two consecutive pitches. Brock made a comment and the two former teammates and current friends began to scuffle. Umpire Al Barlick ejected McCarver.

The two teams met again the following week. Brock was on third when Torre lifted a shallow fly ball to right field. Brock tried to score and Willie Montanez's throw easily beat him to the plate, leaving him no choice but to bowl over McCarver. There was a brief moment when it appeared that the previous week's fight would resume, but Brock picked up McCarver's hat and handed it to him, which put an end to the hostility.

McCarver's first stint with the Phillies ended in 1972 with a deadline trade to the Montreal Expos. Of the trade, McCarver said, "Being traded is something I'm acclimated to, but it would be easier to accept if the people being traded and their families were treated with respect." Two things bothered him: one is that he never heard from general manager Paul Owens, who traded him; and the other was that he just put $1,100 down on an apartment in Philadelphia.

His time in Montreal was brief, but for the first time in his big-league career he played other positions besides catcher. He appeared in six games as a third baseman and fourteen as an outfielder. The 1973 season saw McCarver return to his baseball roots in St. Louis. He appeared in 130 games—77 of those were at first base—and he hit a respectable .266. The 1974 season saw another move: McCarver was sold to the Boston Red Sox in a stretch-drive move aimed at strengthening the bench for their pennant battle with the Baltimore Orioles. He was not much help as he batted only .250 with one run batted in, and the Red Sox fell short in their bid to unseat Baltimore as American League Eastern Division champions.

It was expected that Boston would release him after the season, but they held on to him. A spring training talk with manager Darrell Johnson convinced him that his chances of making the team were good and he would be counted on to contribute. He was quoted in the *Boston Globe* on March 15, 1975: "I'm not here to be a fill in. . . . I have a little pride with the good years I have had behind me." Unfortunately, things did not work out so well for McCarver. He appeared in four May games but didn't start until June; he was released soon after despite a .381 batting average when Carlton Fisk was reactivated.

Thinking his playing days were over, McCarver did some audition tapes at various Philadelphia television stations. Before anything came of it, the Phillies signed him to a contract and his career continued. There would prove to be some productive times ahead. In 1975 with Phillies ace Steve Carlton struggling, manager Danny Ozark began having McCarver catch Carlton on his turn through the rotation, with good results. In 1976, with Carlton off to a slow start, Ozark paired the two again, and Lefty won four starts in a row with McCarver behind the dish. He became Carlton's personal catcher and the Phillies won the Eastern Division, making the postseason for the first time since 1950. McCarver showed he could still hit as he batted .277. Philadelphia lost the NLCS to the eventual World Series champion Cincinnati Reds.

An unfortunate McCarver incident occurred on July 4 as the nation celebrated its bicentennial. He hit a grand slam into the right-field seats in Pittsburgh's Three Rivers Stadium, and on his way around the bases he inadvertently passed teammate Garry Maddox. He was called out for passing the base runner and received credit for a single and three RBIs.

Another good year for the McCarver-Carlton tandem and the Phillies was 1977. Carlton went 23-10 en route to his second Cy Young Award while McCarver batted .320. The Phillies won

their second consecutive division title, but again lost in the NLCS, this time to the Los Angeles Dodgers.

McCarver's playing days wound down in 1978 and 1979. He still caught Carlton regularly, but some of his starts were handled by regular catcher Bob Boone. He retired at the end of the 1979 season and was hired into the broadcast booth by the Phillies. He immediately took to the job, and a second career was born. His playing days were not quite finished, as he returned to the playing field in September of 1980 to become one of the few players, and the first twentieth-century catcher, to play in four decades. He moved over to the New York Mets broadcast booth in 1983 and would soon receive national recognition as an insightful analyst.

Just days before the 1985 World Series, ABC fired Howard Cosell, and McCarver was invited to share the booth with Al Michaels and Jim Palmer. He was an instant success on the national stage. In an October 19, 2003, *Boston Globe* article, McCarver said, "I was nervous, very nervous. Broadcasting a World Series was not even close to playing in one. As a player, you have a chance to do something about the outcome. . . . From a player's standpoint you think you know about 85 percent of the game. Then you go upstairs and find out you're wrong about that."

If that is the case, then McCarver has certainly proved that he has learned about the game. Opinionated, studious, and witty, McCarver has survived in the booth for longer than he was a player. He broadcast the Mets from 1983–98, the Yankees from 1999–2001, and the Giants in 2002, and hosted a weekly syndicated television interview that drew more than 90 million viewers. As a testament to his longevity as the top analyst in the sport, McCarver has now done more World Series telecasts than any other announcer in baseball history.

Blues Stadium in Memphis was renamed Tim

McCarver Stadium for the 1978–99 seasons, before it was replaced. McCarver won four Telly Awards and six national Emmys as Best Sportscaster/Analyst, and he has authored six books on baseball. In 2012 he was honored by the National Baseball Hall of Fame with its Ford C. Frick Award, granted annually for broadcasting excellence.

Chapter 27. **Joe Morgan**

Rory Costello

AGE	G	AB	R	H	2B	3B	HR	TB	RBI	BB	SO	BAV	OBP	SLG	SB	GDP	HBP
33	3	3	0	0	0	0	0	0	0	0	2	.000	.000	.000	0	0	0

There have been two big leaguers named Joe Morgan—and it's not hard to tell them apart. Joseph Michael Morgan played fractions of four seasons in "The Show," finishing with three games for the 1964 Cardinals. He is white. Joe Leonard Morgan's Hall of Fame career ran from 1963 to 1984. He is black. Joe L., who became a broadcaster, talks more than much of his audience would like to hear. Joe M., who became a manager, does not. Harry Fanok, a Minor League teammate, said, "He didn't say a hell of a lot, but he was one tough dude!"[1]

But when Walpole Joe speaks, his Boston roots are audible. Despite nearly forty years in pro ball, Joseph Michael Morgan is best remembered as manager of the Red Sox, whom he led from July 1988 through 1991. His teams won the American League East in 1988 and 1990, although the Oakland A's swept the playoffs both times. Yet even before the Red Sox finally wiped away eighty-six years of disappointment by winning the 2004 World Series, Morgan was a local blue-collar hero. He is also a classic salty raconteur with a well of stories; this brief career overview cannot do them justice.

Joe Morgan was born on November 19, 1930, in Walpole, about eighteen miles southwest of Boston. This town has always been industrial; Joe's father, William Morgan, was an engineer for Kendall Mills. William and his wife, Mary Kennedy Morgan, had four other children: sons Billy and Jim, and daughters Mary and Theresa.

Morgan was a two-sport star at Walpole High School and Boston College. Longtime Red Sox announcer Joe Castiglione called him one of the two best high-school hockey players in Boston area history, and he became an All-American cen-

In mid-September 1964 the Cardinals promoted the veteran Joe Morgan to the big leagues. Joe pinch-hit in three games. He later managed the Red Sox for several years. (Photo by Allied Photocolor Imaging Center)

ter at BC.[2] In 2009 Morgan said, "If I was born in Canada, I would have played in the NHL for a long, long time. That's the way I see it. I had the ability; all I needed was more ice time growing up."[3]

Instead, the shortstop went with Boston's other big-league baseball franchise back then, the Braves. In June 1952 Lucius "Jeff" Jones, the team's chief scout for New England, signed both Morgan and catcher Mike Roarke. Roarke, a fellow Boston College Eagle, later played and coached in the Majors too (he also worked for Joe as pitching coach at Pawtucket, the Red Sox's top farm team).[4]

Jones no doubt also saw both men as they played in the Blackstone Valley League, a local semipro circuit. In 1988 Joe remembered his days as shortstop for Hopedale (1949–51). "It was a pretty good league, with a lot of guys who went on to Triple-A and some [like Walt Dropo] who played in the majors. I know I struggled to hit .270. The league folded after 1952 because of economics."[5]

New Yorkers on the Hopedale team also coined a nickname for Joe: Mumsy. In 1988 Morgan explained, "Every time I went out in the sun, I'd burn. So I never got any sun. I was as white as a mummy."[6] The label stuck into the '60s.

Morgan played in seventy-two games at Hartford (Class A) in 1952, but batted just .229 and dropped back to Class B for 1953 (when he graduated from BC). He then spent the rest of 1953 through 1955 in the U.S. Army, "mostly at Fort Sill, Oklahoma," Morgan said. "I played service ball with Daryl Spencer and other big-leaguers."

Joe resumed his pro career in 1956, hitting .300 at Jacksonville (Class A). That year he also married Dorothy "Dot" Glebus. "She was from Walpole also—we met in church."

The lefty swinger hit .316 at Atlanta (Double-A) in 1957. He reached Triple-A in 1958, but Johnny Logan remained a fixture at shortstop in Milwaukee, where the Braves had moved in 1953. Morgan shifted to third base that season, and his hitting declined to .251 at Wichita. The following spring, *Baseball Digest* wrote that he "didn't bridge [the] gap." Its scouting report read, "Could fill in for some major league club but no chance to make it as a regular. Good arm but average in running and short of power at the plate."[7]

Joe made the Major League roster to begin the 1959 season, mostly pinch-hitting but also starting four games at second base. In early June the Braves sent him down to Louisville, where he mainly played the outfield. On August 20 the Kan-

sas City Athletics purchased his contract, and he spent the rest of the season there. He did almost nothing but pinch-hit, appearing just twice at third base in twenty games with the A's. With the two teams, he hit for a combined .205 average.

In April 1960 Kansas City returned Morgan to Milwaukee. He started that season with Louisville, but on June 23 he went to the Philadelphia Phillies in exchange for Alvin Dark, then in his final season. Joe played a lot at third base over the next several weeks, but in early August the Cleveland Indians bought his contract. Morgan got his only two big-league homers with the Tribe that year. His .192 average for the year, however, was even lower than the year before.

Morgan appeared in four games for the Indians early in 1961, but in May, Cleveland dealt him to St. Louis. He did not resurface in the Majors for nearly two and a half years. Instead, Joe provided veteran leadership for the 1962–63 Atlanta Crackers, the Cardinals' Triple-A affiliate in the International League. "Apparently I was a little too old for expansion clubs," he said in 2010.

Mumsy became a player-coach in 1964. He set a fine example, becoming the International League's Most Valuable Player as Jacksonville won the league pennant. In mid-September 1964 the Cards called up Morgan; he made his last three big-league appearances as a pinch hitter. He struck out the first two times and grounded into a force out the third time. All told, Morgan hit .193 in 187 at bats over his eighty-eight games in the Majors. Although he was not eligible for the '64 World Series, the team did vote him one-eighth of a winning share (he did not get a ring).

Morgan spent one more season at Triple-A in 1965 for the Cardinals. He then went to Class A in 1966 for his last year as a player—and first as a manager. "Harry Walker, who I played for in '63 and '64, got me the job with the Pirates in Raleigh, North Carolina." Walker had become Pittsburgh's manager in October 1964.

Joe remained in the Pirates chain through 1973, managing in Single-A, Double-A, and Triple-A ball. He guided his teams to three first-place finishes in the regular season (1967, '69, and '73), though without any championships. He spent 1972 as infield/batting coach with the big club under Bill Virdon, but he had to step back down again because the Pirates made retiring star Bill Mazeroski a coach.[8]

In the winter of 1973 Morgan heard of an opening with the Pawtucket Red Sox, Boston's top farm club. He seized the opportunity to get back to New England. "Filling out loading slips at his brother-in-law's sand and gravel business in Walpole," Joe called Boston general manager Dick O'Connell at home and asked for the job. Said O'Connell, "A lot of people want that job. I have a long list, but the job is yours."[9]

In his nine years with the PawSox, Morgan won a club-record 601 games and guided many future big leaguers. He was International League Manager of the Year in 1977, when Pawtucket won the regular-season championship (though the team lost the playoff finals).[10] Among other things, he was ejected in the twenty-second inning of the longest game in pro baseball history, the thirty-three-inning marathon with the Rochester Red Wings that started on April 18, 1981. For a while Joe watched from a peephole behind the backstop—though he later recalled, "Sand was flying through at an enormous rate, so I bailed out!"[11]

Another nickname—Turnpike Joe—came from this period. For ten winters, from 1976 through 1985, he drove a snowplow on the Massachusetts Turnpike (a stretch that included the record-setting blizzard of February 1978). This perfectly captured the man's no-frills approach. He joked, "The side benefit was the money you'd find in snowbanks. But about all I got was cat food, mayonnaise and salad dressing."[12]

In 1980 Morgan was a candidate to succeed Don Zimmer as manager in Boston, but Ralph Houk was hired instead. Joe said, "Sure, I'd like to manage the Red Sox. I've spent all my life in the minors. It's that simple. I'm in the game for that reason, to get to the majors." He added, "It is a little frustrating, but, still, if you love baseball like I do, it's not all that tough. I don't mind bus rides." Morgan joked about the "good fresh air out on the Pike" but turned prophetic when he said, "I'm only 49 years old. There's all kinds of time."[13]

Joe also turned down an opportunity to join Joe Altobelli as a coach in San Francisco in the late 1970s. In 1982 he said, "It would have meant moving west and would have cost me money. Still, if I'd done it I might be managing in the majors right now." That story called Morgan daring and innovative, noting his love of tactics such as five-man infields and the hidden ball trick.[14]

In early January 1983 the Red Sox bumped up two other Minor League managers and made Morgan a "special assignment scout." The noted baseball commentator Peter Gammons, then a Boston sportswriter, thought the demotion hurt Joe's chances of qualifying for his Major League pension (he was one and a half years short at that time). Nonetheless, Morgan loyally served scouting director Eddie Kasko as a cross-checker.

In October 1984 John McNamara replaced the retiring Houk, although Morgan was again considered.[15] Joe joined McNamara's staff. He coached first base in 1985, the bullpen in 1986 (finally quitting the Mass. Pike that winter after receiving his World Series runner-up share), and third base in 1987 and early 1988.

The '88 Red Sox were underachieving. A shakeup came at the All-Star break. As Morgan recalled in 2003, "I saw [co-owner] Haywood Sullivan going into John McNamara's office in one door. Then in the other door [general manager] Lou Gorman was coming in and he walked over to me and he said we're going to make a managerial change and you'll be the interim manager. That's the story."[16]

Joe became the first Boston-area native to lead

the club since Shano Collins in 1932. The Red Sox promptly reeled off twelve straight wins and nineteen out of twenty, as well as nineteen straight at home—a run called "Morgan's Magic."

Boston had considered many other managers, including old Boston College mate Mike Roarke. Yet Joe declared to a reporter, "Interim, sir, is not in my vocabulary."[17] After his seventh game, at Fenway Park on July 20, the tag was removed.

That game showed how Mumsy's toughness remained intact—slugger Jim Rice found out who was boss. Rice was furious after Morgan dropped him in the batting order and then pinch-hit for him with Spike Owen. He pulled Morgan into the runway and a confrontation ensued. Said Red Sox outfielder Mike Greenwell, "The amazing thing was that Joe didn't back down. If Jimmy wanted to fight, Joe was willing to fight."[18]

"A flushed and furious Morgan returned to the bench alone and announced, 'I'm the manager of this nine!'"[19] This line, with its old-timey flavor that is a Morgan trademark, immediately entered Red Sox lore. Then, in the bottom of the eleventh inning, Boston came back to win, 9–7. Co-owner Mrs. Jean Yawkey said, "Give that guy a contract for the rest of the year."[20] In fact, just a couple of weeks later the team extended his contract through 1989. Mrs. Yawkey said, "Joe has rekindled the enthusiasm and optimism of the players and the fans."[21]

Jean Yawkey, who was as generous as her late husband, Tom, rewarded Morgan further after the season, despite the playoff sweep by Oakland. As Joe Castiglione recalled, "Mrs. Yawkey had a dinner [at a Walpole restaurant] to show her support for Joe. . . . [She] came in and gave Joe a manila envelope. He put it in his pocket unopened. Mrs. Yawkey said, 'Joe, I think you should open that now.' So he did: inside was his bonus for having such a great half season: $50,000. He couldn't believe it."[22]

As a manager Morgan played hunches. He relied on his knowledge of talent and superb memory; computers were not his thing. He always told it like he saw it.

The Red Sox finished third in 1989 but won their division again in 1990, as Joe got the best out of a low-scoring lineup and thin pitching staff. However, they faded late in 1991, a season marred by injuries and discord. Despite getting his third straight one-year contract extension that June, Morgan lost his job two days after the last game. He "took the news hard. He knew he'd been fired because he managed without regard to the size of players' contracts, and it had cost him. In the free-agent era, the manager was not necessarily the most powerful man in the clubhouse."[23]

Joe's final meeting with Haywood Sullivan and other team executives featured typically blunt and memorable parting words: "Your team is not as good as you think it is."[24]

Morgan retired, turning down an offer to become a special assistant to Lou Gorman. "I didn't want to manage anymore," he said in 2003. "I did plenty of roaming around this country. In and out of hotels and planes and all that jazz. Plus I was old enough the following year to take my pension, which I did. Without that pension plan, I'd probably still be working somewhere."[25]

Joe and Dottie have lived in the same house in Walpole—two blocks from where Joe grew up—since 1958.[26] They had four children (Cathy, Joseph, William, and Barbara Jean) and now enjoy six grandchildren (Anthony, Ashley, Rachel, Paige, Jake, and Michael). Joe still enjoys his long-cherished pastimes, gardening, candlepin bowling, and golf. The nineteenth annual Joe Morgan Celebrity Golf Tournament, which benefits the Walpole Scholarship Foundation, took place in 2010 as usual, on the first Monday in October. His hometown also dedicated Joe Morgan Memorial Field in 1989.

Almost twenty years after he left the Red Sox, people still remember a Morgan catchphrase, "Six, two, and even." Many fans were baffled by what this meant—even Joe himself didn't really know. Humphrey Bogart said it in *The Maltese Falcon*, but Morgan picked it up from his old Minor League manager, Joe Schultz (who was also full of little sayings).[27]

"[Schultz] used to say, 'six, two, and even' all the time and when I'd ask him what it meant, he'd just shake his head. It wasn't until I was out of baseball about 15 years that I met this old guy, he was 94, who was a bookmaker in the 1920s." It refers to betting odds on horse races.[28]

Joe Castiglione summed up this man aptly. He said, "Joe is a very honest, down-to-earth, upbeat guy who can talk with anybody about anything. . . . I learned (and continue to learn) more about the game of baseball from Joe Morgan than from anybody else."[29]

Chapter 28. **Gordon Richardson**

John Harry Stahl

AGE	W	L	PCT.	ERA	G	GS	GF	CG	SHO	SV	IP	H	BB	SO	HBP	WP
25	4	2	.667	2.30	19	6	6	1	0	1	47	40	15	28	1	1

Three great passions shaped Gordon Richardson's career in baseball: his family, his southwest Georgia farm, and his dream of becoming a big-league pitcher.

Richardson (nicknamed Gordie) once characterized his fastball as "not overpowering." Instead, he was a control specialist with good breaking stuff and an excellent change-up.[1] He acknowledged that he had to hit his "spots" or he could quickly be in big trouble. "Baseball is a cat-and-mouse game," Richardson once said. "You have to outsmart the hitter."[2]

After seven years pitching in the Minors, Richardson joined the 1964 Cardinals in late July. He stayed with the team the rest of the season, contributing to several key victories during the pennant race, and pitched in the World Series. He subsequently spent two years with the New York Mets before retiring in 1966.

Gordon Clark Richardson was born on July 19, 1939, in Colquitt, Georgia. Colquitt is a small town (population 1,934 in 2009) in Miller County in southwestern Georgia. Farming is important to the area's economy, and Gordie's father was a farmer. Richardson recalled that he started pitching because his father managed a "cow pasture" team in a Sunday League. He said he was the "only left-hander around."

Richardson graduated in 1957 from Miller County High School, where he played baseball, basketball, and football, as well as American Legion ball. He said he did not get much attention from scouts; only the Milwaukee Braves, the Chicago White Sox, and the Cardinals showed any interest.

Gordon Richardson joined the 1964 Cardinals from the Minors in late July. He made significant contributions during the pennant race and pitched in the 1964 World Series.

Cardinals scout Mercer Harris signed the six-foot-one, 185-pound Richardson to a contract in 1957. Richardson jokingly remembered that he got no signing bonus from the Cardinals, just a "pat on the back" and a "you can do it, kid" pep talk.

The Cardinals initially assigned the eighteen-year-old to their Wytheville (Virginia) team in the short-season Appalachian League, where he went

5-5 with a 3.73 earned run average. Late in the season they moved him to the nearby Albany (Georgia) team in the Class D Georgia-Florida League, where he pitched thirteen innings and went 0-1. At Albany in 1958 he won thirteen games and lost four with a 2.93 ERA. One of his Albany teammates was seventeen-year-old Mike Shannon, who also played on the 1964 Cardinals. At the end of July, the Cardinals promoted Richardson to Houston in the Texas League, where he pitched in just two games before coming down with back trouble that required him to go on the disabled list for the remainder of the season.[3] After the season he played for the Cardinals' team in the Florida West Coast Instructional League.[4]

The Georgian spent all of the 1959 season pitching for Winston-Salem in the Class B Carolina League, where he won eleven games and lost eight. On January 16, 1960, he married Patsy Kimbrel.[5]

Richardson moved up to Double-A Tulsa in the Texas League in 1960. Under manager Vern Benson, the Oilers won the Texas League playoffs and the subsequent Pan Am playoffs. (Benson was the third-base coach for the 1964 Cardinals.[6]) Richardson posted an 8-7 record and a 4.50 ERA. He experienced control problems, however, walking 89 in 140 innings. He was back with Tulsa in 1961, posting a 10-8 record with a 3.38 ERA. He cut his walks to 78 in 165 innings while striking out 114. He ended his season early (August 24) after signing up for a six-month hitch in the army.

Richardson returned to the Oilers in 1962 and led the Texas League in several key pitching categories. He had nine complete games and posted a league-best winning percentage of .684 (13-6) and ERA (3.18). He made the league All-Star team and the Double-A All-Star team, and was voted the Texas League's 1962 pitcher of the year. He established two career highs by pitching 198 innings and striking out 153 batters. In the Major League draft after the season, the Los Angeles Angels drafted Richardson. He went to spring training with the Angels but ended up idle for most of it, pitching only six innings. The Angels wanted to send Richardson back to the Minors, but the Cardinals exercised their right to buy him back; they assigned him to Atlanta and then sent him back to Tulsa. Though he may have been disappointed at not starting the 1963 season in the Major Leagues with the Angels, Richardson nevertheless took up where he left off in 1962. On May 5, perhaps wanting to show both teams they had made a mistake, he pitched a two-hit masterpiece, winning 1–0. For the season he pitched 187 innings and posted a 12-8 record with a 3.85 ERA and 171 strikeouts.

At the start of the 1964 season, the Cardinals sent Richardson to their Jacksonville Suns affiliate in the Triple-A International League. This was to be a pivotal season for him. He gave himself a deadline. If he wasn't a Major League pitcher by the time he was twenty-five, he would retire to the family farm in Georgia. In July 1964 he would turn twenty-five.

Richardson got off to a great start at Jacksonville. "I learned a lot from (Suns manager) Harry Walker, either you do or you don't. You give it your best shot," he said. In early July he pitched a four-hit shutout over Columbus, making his record 9-3 with a 1.55 ERA in 116 innings, and got the call-up from the Cardinals.[7]

"We're counting on Richardson as a starter right now," said Cardinals manager Johnny Keane as Richardson arrived in St. Louis. "He'll start in one game of Sunday's doubleheader."[8] And on July 26 Richardson made his first Major League appearance, starting for the Cardinals against the league-leading Philadelphia Phillies in the first game of a doubleheader at Connie Mack Stadium in Philadelphia. He was nervous at the start as he walked lead-off hitter Tony Gonzalez. He was missing the strike zone, a bad sign for a control pitcher. Ken Boyer then made a key intervention. After Richardson went 2-0 on Cookie Rojas, Boyer went to the mound and told him simply to "calm down." Richardson got Rojas to pop up to short. Gonzalez was then caught trying to steal second. Johnny Callison ended the inning by popping up to first base. Richardson ended up pitching a complete-game 6–1 victory, allowing five hits, walking three, and striking out five.

The Phillies were not impressed. "I had to see that kid beat us to believe it," Philadelphia manager Gene Mauch quipped after the game. "Ugh," said Phillies star Callison. "He didn't throw hard at all and his curve wasn't much."[9]

Richardson was ecstatic. "It's a dream come true," he gushed after the game. "The seven years in the minors was pretty distressing at times, but it was worth all the heartaches and troubles and moving the family around." He credited the Cardinals' defense. "The fielding helped too," he said. "You don't have defense like this behind you in the minor leagues."[10]

Richardson contributed significantly to the Cardinals' pennant push in late September. On the 25th at Pittsburgh he started and won, 5–3, helping the Cardinals move up from three and a half games behind the Phillies to two and a half. On September 30 he recorded a save against the Phillies to help the Cards move to first place for the first time in the season. From the end of July to the end of the season, Richardson pitched forty-seven innings and posted a 4-2 record with a 2.30 ERA.

While the Cardinals won the 1964 World Series, Richardson did not fare well. He pitched in two games. In Game Two he entered in the top of the ninth inning and gave up two runs in a third of an inning as the Cardinals lost, 8–3. In Game Six he entered in the top of the eighth inning and gave up a grand slam to Joe Pepitone. For the Series, he finished with an astronomical 40.50 ERA. His Cardinals teammates awarded him a three-quarters share ($6,486.64) of their World Series player pool money.[11]

The Cardinals asked Richardson to pitch winter ball in the Dominican League. At first he agreed, but he and his wife were expecting their second child in December, and the doctor advised him not to leave. So Richardson told the Cardinals he could not play winter ball. The baby was born on December 4. Three days later, Cardinals general manager Bob Howsam called Richardson and told him the Cardinals had traded him to the New York Mets.[12]

Before 1965 spring training, the Mets greatly reduced Gordie's chances of becoming a starting pitcher by purchasing Warren Spahn. Then, during spring training, he injured his leg and the Mets sent him to their Triple-A club in Buffalo. Shortly before leaving the Mets camp, he and Gary Kroll combined to pitch an exhibition game no-hitter.

Initially, the Bisons used Richardson as both a starter and a reliever. He got off to a poor start. His usual good control eluded him. He wasn't walking a lot of hitters, but he wasn't hitting his spots. The results were bad. As the season progressed, Buffalo began using Richardson exclusively in relief. He responded with outstanding pitching. The Mets took notice and called him up on July 8. In his last twenty relief appearances for Buffalo, he had posted a 1.17 ERA. Reflecting his early struggles, his Buffalo record shows that he pitched eighty-seven innings, posting a 2-8 record with a 3.31 ERA.

Back in the big leagues, Richardson continued exclusively as a relief pitcher. After he made six strong relief appearances in eight days (July 25–August 1), acting manager Wes Westrum praised him for his endurance, calling him "rubber-armed." When asked about the tag, Richardson drawled, "I guess if I had to, I could work every day."[13]

For the 1965 Mets, Richardson pitched fifty-two and one-third innings, all in relief, posting a 2-2 record with a 3.78 ERA.

Richardson started 1966 with the Mets. He impressed Westrum in spring training. "If you really want to know," he said, "Richardson was the best pitcher down here." For the first time in his career, Richardson went north with a Major League team after spring training. When a reporter asked him how it felt going north, he quipped, "I don't know. I've never gone north before."[14]

For the 1966 Mets, Richardson posted an 0-2 record in eighteen and two-thirds innings with a 9.16 ERA. On June 5 he entered a game against the Los Angeles Dodgers in the seventh inning. In what would be his last Major League game, he gave up six runs on six hits. Soon after, the Mets sent him to Triple-A Jacksonville.[15] In his three-year Major League career, he pitched 118 innings and posted a 6-6 record with a 4.04 ERA.

At Jacksonville for the rest of 1966, Richardson pitched sixty-one innings, finishing 6-3 with a 3.25 ERA. At the end of the season, he retired. He was thirty-two years old. His first child was ready for school, and the itinerant nature of baseball life would not make it easy on her. The 750-acre family farm, which raised soybeans, peanuts, and cotton, also needed him. Richardson rented out the farm while he played baseball. After examining his options, he decided to take over the farm.

With their expanding family, Patsy and Gordie decided to build a new house on the farm in 1968. They eventually added a swimming pool, tennis courts, and an indoor garden. The grounds also included a small pond. Richardson enjoyed quail hunting. All six family members worked on the farm, and the family later added a meat-packing business.

Summing up his professional ball-playing experience, Richardson once reminisced, "I don't regret playing and I don't regret quitting. I enjoyed it and got to see a lot of places a country boy wouldn't have been able to."[16]

Chapter 29. **Ray Sadecki**

Justin Murphy

AGE	W	L	PCT.	ERA	G	GS	GF	CG	SHO	SV	IP	H	BB	SO	HBP	WP
23	20	11	.645	3.68	37	32	2	9	2	1	220	232	60	119	1	7

Frank Sadecki, the son of Polish immigrant parents, spent his childhood working in the family grocery store rather than playing baseball. As a result, his greatest wish for his son Ray from the beginning was to be "left-handed, (to) like baseball, and become a major leaguer."[1] Frank's wish was granted as his son, after just a brief Minor League apprenticeship, burst into the big leagues with the St. Louis Cardinals in 1960, the start of a long and successful career in baseball.

Raymond Michael Sadecki was born on December 26, 1940, in Kansas City, Kansas, to Frank and Josephine Sadecki. Frank Sadecki, a sheriff who worked out of the U.S. marshal's office in Kansas City, often had the task of escorting prisoners to the federal penitentiary in Terre Haute, Indiana, and he sometimes took Ray along, stopping on the return trip to catch Cardinals and Browns games in St. Louis. Ray began to garner serious attention as a player while at Ward High School in Kansas City (where he was also an excellent student). Not long after graduating in 1958, Sadecki, just seventeen years old, signed with Cardinals scout Runt Marr for a $50,000 bonus plus another $18,000 over the first three years. While in high school, Sadecki had also attracted the attention of a cheerleader named Diane Rush. The two married on July 13, 1960.

Sadecki said he never regretted forgoing college for baseball. "College probably wasn't as big a deal, just in life," he told an interviewer in 2009. "We were still postwar people who thought, 'Hey, go get a job.'"[2]

Sadecki began his professional career with the Winnipeg Goldeyes of the Class C Northern

In 1964 Ray Sadecki posted a 20–11 record. His twenty-win total was the highest in his eighteen-year career. He also won Game One of the '64 World Series.

League, posting a 9-7 record. This earned him a promotion to Triple-A Omaha for 1959, where he continued to excel, with a 13-9 record. He began the 1960 season in Triple-A Rochester under manager Clyde King. He was settling in comfortably in the International League, winning two of his first three decisions with a 1.76 earned run average, when the call came from St. Louis manager Solly Hemus. The Cardinals were short on left-handed pitching and had decided that the nineteen-year-old had gotten enough Minor League seasoning.

By 1960 the Cardinals had already assembled much of the talent that would eventually lead them to the pennant in 1964. But the youngsters — Sadecki, Bob Gibson, Curt Flood, Tim McCarver — needed time to develop, and they got it on the Major League roster. As Sadecki later recalled, it was an ideal proving ground: "If you join a first place ballclub you sit on the bench. But the Cardinals were in fourth or fifth place in 1960, back when it was an eight-team league. . . . The fact that the Cardinals weren't going anywhere, they gave me the ball, and I got to pitch. I kind of struggled through a nine and nine year, but it was enough to get my feet wet."[3]

Sadecki made his big-league debut on May 19, starting against the Pittsburgh Pirates. He was the losing pitcher as the Pirates won, 8–3. Taken out after two and two-thirds innings, he gave up eight hits and five runs, though three were unearned after an infield error. He started again on the 28th against the San Francisco Giants and lost again, 8–0, giving up five runs in six innings. (He was lifted for pinch hitter Stan Musial.) Sadecki spent the rest of the 1960 season in the starting rotation, alternately dazzling scouts with his fastball and maddening his manager with a troubling lack of control. At year's end, his record stood at 9-9, with a 3.78 ERA, 95 strikeouts, and 86 walks in 157⅓ innings.

As a twenty-year-old bonus baby on a second-division team, Sadecki was pretty much assured of a spot in the rotation for 1961. He led the team with 222⅔ innings pitched, going 14-10 with a 3.72 ERA. His walks-per-nine-innings ratio dropped from 4.92 in 1960 to 4.13 in 1961, but his strikeout ratio followed a similar trajectory, falling from 5.43 to 4.61.

On the strength of this modest success, Sadecki attempted to negotiate for more money in spring training of 1962, staying away from camp for several weeks before finally signing on March 2. When the season began, Sadecki's performance was abys-

mal. In his seven starts in April and May, he posted an inflated 6.69 ERA, giving up 52 hits and 19 walks in thirty-seven and two-thirds innings, and was bumped from the starting rotation.

On June 5 things went from bad to worse. Sadecki came in to pitch the sixth inning against the Cincinnati Reds. Five batters later, he left with an ugly line: zero outs recorded, five runs on three hits, and two errors of his own.

After the game, manager Johnny Keane called Sadecki's performance "the poorest exhibition of effort I've ever seen on a major-league diamond" and fined him $250. Stung, the lefty compounded the problem by showing up late the following evening. This in turn led to an indefinite suspension for what general manager Bing Devine termed a "flagrant abuse of a rule."

The suspension was lifted, but Sadecki continued to pitch poorly. Over his next ten appearances, from June 15 to July 28, he allowed an average of more than a hit an inning and walked nearly as many as he struck out, while compiling a 3-5 record and a 4.56 ERA. Keane went from a six- to a four-man rotation, and Sadecki was exiled to the Atlanta Crackers of the International League.

Sadecki's tribulations in 1962 had two lasting effects. First, it earned him a reputation as a malingerer that would persist, fairly or not, for several years, until he joined the Mets. Don Landrum, his teammate in 1962 and again in 1966, later offered an outside perspective on the situation. "If you watch him pitching, he's the kind of guy who doesn't look like he's exerting himself. He looks lackadaisical, but he isn't. Ray tried as hard as anybody on that [1962] staff. The trouble was they weren't using him."[4]

The 1963 season was not an unqualified success, but Sadecki showed improvement in every aspect of his game, including his maturity. His walks-per-nine-innings rate went down, his strikeout rate went up, and he remained in the starting rotation for the entire season. Still only twenty-two years old, he joined Ernie Broglio, Bob Gibson, and Curt Simmons with double digits in victories (ten, against ten losses). The team finished in second place with ninety-three wins, six games behind the Los Angeles Dodgers, who won the pennant and World Series.

In the off-season, Cardinals general manager Devine seriously considered shipping Sadecki to the San Francisco Giants for Felipe Alou, but eventually decided against it. The young pitcher responded in the 1964 pennant chase with one of his best seasons. Starting on May 11 and continuing through mid-June, Sadecki won ten games in twelve starts, including five complete games. After stumbling slightly in late July, he then put together a streak even more impressive than his first, one that carried him until the end of September. In fifteen starts, he won ten games with a 2.38 ERA, allowing just a .244 batting average against.

The Cardinals reached the World Series and faced the Yankees. Since ace Bob Gibson had pitched three times in the season's final seven days, the assignment for Game One at home against the Yankees' Whitey Ford fell to Sadecki. The best part of being in the World Series, he later said, was "pitching against a team you hadn't pitched against before. I knew nothing about the Yankees—no clue. I'm not saying the scouting reports were good or bad, it's just your own knowledge."[5]

The twenty-three-year-old got in trouble in the second inning, giving up a two-run homer to Tom Tresh and an RBI single to pitcher Ford. Tresh added another run in the fifth by doubling home Mickey Mantle, giving the visitors a 4–2 lead. Ray's teammates roared back in the bottom of the sixth, plating four runs and leaving him in line for a victory when he came out in the bottom of the frame. St. Louis went on to win, 9–5; Sadecki gave up four runs on eight hits in six innings, walking five and striking out two. He also started Game Four, but got knocked out after allowing three runs on four hits to the only four batters he faced.

The Cardinals came back to win that game, too, and took the Series in seven games.

Though he established a career high for victories, 1964 was not Sadecki's best. His defense-adjusted ERA was 4.89, a mark he topped in six other seasons. He later attributed his high win total to a combination of luck and offensive support: "It's only natural that everybody reflects back, 'You won 20 games. That must have been a great year. You must have been a great pitcher.' Well, it's not necessarily true. I won ballgames that year where they pinch hit for me in the fifth, and they'd get the hit that puts you ahead, and then the bullpen would hold them."[6]

The 1965 season was a reversal of 1964. Sadecki lost fifteen games and won only six with a 5.21 ERA as the Cardinals fell to seventh place in the ten-team league, though only one game under .500 (80-81). He got off to a slow start, and bounced back and forth between the crowded starting rotation and the bullpen. In the first half of the season he was 2-8 with a 7.20 ERA and gave up seventeen home runs in seventy-five innings. He was better in the second half of the season, going 4-7 with a 3.69 ERA and giving up nine home runs in ninety-seven innings.

Sadecki started the 1966 season with the Cardinals but was traded on May 8 to San Francisco for first baseman Orlando Cepeda. "It was probably the best opportunity I ever had," recalled Sadecki, "and then turned out to be the worst year I ever had." Under intense scrutiny in San Francisco, where Cepeda had been wildly popular, the lefty went 3-7 with a 5.40 ERA, even worse than in 1965. "When they gave up Cepeda to get me," Sadecki said, "they had to live with it. They had to keep running me out there. I was asked a hundred times if I felt the pressure of the Cepeda thing, which I didn't believe I did, and denied it all the time. But sometimes you reflect back and you wonder. . . . I was throwing the ball as well as I ever did or ever have, but I was pitching poorly."[7]

As a result, he was slotted into the bullpen at the beginning of the 1967 season. By the end of June, however, he'd earned a spot in the rotation, and he finished the season strong with six wins in September. For the season, he established career bests in earned run average, walks and hits per nine innings, strikeouts, and fewest walks per nine innings.

With renewed confidence and some success to build on, Sadecki got off to an uncharacteristically hot start in 1968, posting a 0.25 ERA in four April starts. It may have been partly due to a new pitch he had developed before the season, which he described as "a sort of a slip pitch—a half-speed curve, if you want to call it that."[8] Apart from a short midsummer slide, 1968 was Sadecki's best season statistically—an accomplishment obscured by his record of 12-18. The eighteen losses were the most for a pitcher in a season since the Giants moved to San Francisco. Sadecki received shockingly poor run support; in his thirty-six starts, the Giants scored one or no runs sixteen times. Still, he posted career highs in innings pitched (253⅔), shutouts (6), and strikeouts (206, a huge leap from his previous high of 145).

In 1969 Sadecki pitched two shutouts in his first three starts, but was demoted to long relief after a disastrous May. There he floundered, and after the best earned run averages of his career in 1967 and 1968, he posted a 4.23 ERA in 1969.

In December of 1969 Sadecki and outfielder Dave Marshall were traded to the Mets in return for spare parts Bob Heise and Jim Gosger. In New York he was a spot starter and long reliever in 1970, with nineteen starts in twenty-eight appearances. He pitched well but found it tough to break into a rotation that included Tom Seaver and Jerry Koosman. After his career ended, Sadecki lamented, "I was 29, feeling good. I'd finally learned how to pitch, but I couldn't get out on the mound anymore."[9] His overall line in six seasons with the Mets: a 3.36 ERA and 30-25 record in

165 appearances, including 62 starts. He pitched four times in relief for the Mets in the 1973 World Series against the Athletics, allowing one run and five hits while striking out six in four and two-thirds innings.

In this context it is interesting to reexamine two labels that haunted him throughout his career, the first being his reputation as a precocious troublemaker, stemming mainly from his troubles in 1962. As a veteran pitcher on a staff full of young talent, Sadecki seemed to grow into the role of Mr. Reliable. Indeed, California Angels general manager Harry Dalton referred to him as a "staff saver" when he tried to trade for him in 1973.

Second was the idea that Sadecki was never able to overcome the pressure placed on him after the Cepeda trade, a deal that is often characterized as one of the most lopsided in history. Cepeda went on to lead St. Louis to a pair of pennants in 1967 and 1968, but to relegate Sadecki to the level of an Ernie Broglio or Larry Andersen, pitchers in deals gone sour, is to ignore his yeoman service for a decade in San Francisco and New York.

A good example of Sadecki's utility with the Mets is his 1974 season. When relief ace Tug McGraw struggled in the first half, Berra plugged Sadecki into the bullpen, where he bent but did not break. Later on, starters George Stone and Craig Swan had arm troubles, and Sadecki was shuffled into the starting rotation, where he ran off four straight wins in August and September.

No matter: Sadecki was traded in the off-season to his first team, the Cardinals, in exchange for Joe Torre. Sadecki, who became available after the emergence of young pitchers Randy Tate and Hank Webb on the Mets, was pleased to return to St. Louis, where he could be nearer to his family.

Despite this encouraging development, 1975 was a topsy-turvy year for Sadecki. After just eight relief appearances for the Cardinals, he was traded to the Atlanta Braves as part of a package for starting pitcher Ron Reed. By this point Sadecki was thirty-four years old, with his prime firmly behind him, and he couldn't have been happy to be traded to a noncontender, away from his family. He appeared in twenty-five games for the Braves, starting five of them. Then, on September 4, he was gone as quickly as he'd come, completing an earlier trade between the Braves and the Kansas City Royals.

Back home again, Sadecki appeared in five games for the Royals at the end of 1975 and three at the beginning of 1976 before being released. He was then signed by Milwaukee and stayed with the Brewers for the remainder of the season.

With the Brewers, Sadecki appeared in thirty-six games, all in relief. Among his teammates were forty-two-year-old Hank Aaron, in the last season of a Hall of Fame career, and twenty-year-old Robin Yount, at the onset of his own. (During his career Sadecki was a teammate of sixteen Hall of Famers.)

After being released at the end of the 1976 season, Sadecki requested and received a spring training invitation from the Mets, who were looking for a left-handed specialist in the bullpen. His arrival was cheered in the New York clubhouse, where he remained popular. He made the squad for Opening Day 1977 and pitched four times in April, but he was released on May 2 to make room for young right-hander Jackson Todd.

Of the end of his career, Sadecki said, "I was cheap help [for the Mets], $25,000, and by the time the Mets released me I didn't even try to find something else. My arm was healthy but I was done. . . . I said goodbye and I had no gripes."[10]

The five-foot-eleven, 180-pounder left with a Major League record of 135-131 and a career 3.78 ERA, compiled over 2,500⅓ innings spanning eighteen seasons.

Sadecki worked for an office supply company from 1977 until 1990, then signed on with the Chicago Cubs as a Minor League coach and roving instructor. He worked for Chicago until 1993,

then spent a year as a roving instructor for the Giants before leaving that job in the aftermath of the 1994 players strike. Sadecki called his departure from the Giants a mutual decision, partly because of the economic uncertainty coming out of the strike and partly because he wasn't really in tune with the players — he said he didn't really understand that the game had changed since he played.

Sadecki's son, Steve, born in 1970, played baseball at Vanderbilt and made it as far as Triple-A in the Rangers organization. He also has a daughter, Susan Rae, born in 1966. He was divorced in 1990 and remarried in 1996. As of 2010 he lived in Mesa, Arizona.

Chapter 30. **Barney Schultz**

John Harry Stahl

AGE	W	L	PCT.	ERA	G	GS	GF	CG	SHO	SV	IP	H	BB	SO	HBP	WP
37	1	3	.250	1.64	30	0	22	0	0	14	49.1	35	11	29	0	0

"Eleven saves in two months. That's more than Schultz had in his whole big-league career," fumed Gene Mauch in September 1964. "He never saw the day he could get us out before," continued the frustrated Philadelphia manager.[1] In the last sixty games of the Cardinals' 1964 season, Barney appeared thirty times, all in relief, winning once and saving fourteen games as the Cardinals rushed past Mauch's Phillies and captured the National League pennant. After Barney's successful appearance in Game One of the 1964 World Series, Cardinals manager Johnny Keane declared, "Without him, we wouldn't be here."[2]

George Warren Schultz was born in Beverly, New Jersey, on August 15, 1926, the third of four sons born to Leo and Madeline Schultz. His father was a steelworker; his mother was born in Northern Ireland.[3] An uncle gave him the nickname Barney.[4] Growing up in South Jersey, Barney constantly played baseball, once noting that he "always seemed to have a ball and glove." An older kid next door introduced him to the knuckle ball, and he was immediately hooked on its bizarre, unpredictable movement. "He could make it dance," remembered Schultz admiringly.[5]

Although the "knuckler" is inherently hard to grip, Schultz found his fingers could do it, and so he began throwing it. Later, as a star pitcher for his Burlington High School team, Schultz still fiddled with the knuckle ball, using it as a change of pace when he was well ahead in the count. He showed enough promise that in 1944 he was signed by the Philadelphia Phillies organization.

Schultz spent the next six years pitching in the low Minor Leagues. Hampered by a sore arm, he

Called up at the end of July, knuckle-ball specialist Barney Schultz appeared in thirty of the last sixty Cardinals games. He logged fourteen critical saves.

never pitched above Class B. In 1950 he finally moved up to the Class A Minor League level, pitching in the South Atlantic League for the Macon Peaches. This was the first season since 1945 that Schultz's arm felt completely pain-free. He pitched a career-high 237 innings in 36 games, both starting and relieving. He allowed 189 hits and 94 earned runs. His win-loss record hovered around the .500 mark all season, and he finished with a 13-14 record. He struck out 168 while walking 123 and posted a 3.57 earned run average.

In 1951 Schultz began with the Des Moines Bruins in the Class A Western League. With the Des Moines mayor throwing out the first pitch, Barney started the Bruins' home opener and hurled a complete-game 9-1 victory over Sioux City, walking 6 hitters. On July 5, with a 4-6 record, 48 walks, and 49 strikeouts in 94 innings, Schultz was put on waivers by Des Moines. Bob Howsam, the young, aggressive general manager of the Western League's Denver Bears, brought Schultz to Denver.

Surrounded by a confident, winning organization, Schultz improved. His control reappeared, as he walked only 43 while striking out 78 in 104 innings. Although his 7-8 record was modest, his 2.75 ERA was the lowest among Denver's starting pitchers for the season.

Schultz began the 1952 season clearly established as a starting pitcher for Denver. He won his first three games and by the end of May had a 4-2 record with a 2.87 ERA. Throughout a very competitive pennant race, Schultz emerged as one of the Bears' leaders. He started the pennant-clinching game and watched in awe as Denver's fans "went berserk," celebrating the Bears' first Western League pennant since 1913.[6] Denver defeated Sioux City and Omaha to win the postseason playoff. Against Omaha, Schultz contributed a masterful 3-1 complete-game playoff victory, as his knuckle ball was "fluttering over the plate with rare consistency."[7] At season's end he had a 17-9 record, leading the team in innings pitched (239), strikeouts (148), and ERA (3.18).

After spending spring training with the Triple-A Hollywood Stars, Schultz again pitched for Denver in 1953, finishing 13-7 with a 4.16 ERA in 173 innings. In 1954 Denver sold him to St. Louis Cardinals, who assigned him to the Triple-A Columbus Red Birds managed by Johnny Keane.

On February 20, 1954, Schultz married Frances Elder, an avid baseball fan. They had three children, George Jr., Barbara, and Paul.

During the first half of the 1954 season, used as both a starter and a reliever, Schultz got off to a poor 1-5 start. Beginning in July, Keane began using him strictly as a reliever, and Schultz quickly turned his season around, helping Columbus reach an unexpected playoff berth. He had a string of 34 consecutive scoreless innings. Schultz finished the season with an 8-8 record in 119 innings, striking out 69 while walking 44.

During spring training in 1955, the twenty-eight-year-old Schultz pitched his way onto the Opening Day roster as a relief specialist. He saw action early, relieving in the Cardinals' 14-4 Opening Day loss in Chicago and several days later in the home-opening 12-11 victory over the Cubs. Then he suffered several bad outings, and on June 16 was sent down to Double-A Houston.[8] With the Cardinals he got into 19 games, compiled a 1-2 record, pitched 29⅔ innings, and finished with an ERA of 7.89.

Schultz failed to make the Cardinals' roster in 1956 and 1957. Both seasons the Cardinals assigned him to Johnny Keane's Triple-A Omaha Cardinals. As a reliever in 1956 (with 10 starts), he posted a 9-12 record, pitching 118 innings with a 4.19 ERA. In 1957 he appeared in 44 games (3 starts), posting an 8-7 record and pitching 121 innings with a 2.83 ERA. He struck out 86 while walking only 39.

Schultz began 1958 with Omaha, but on May 25 he was traded to the Triple-A Charleston Senators for a Minor League outfielder. Schultz posted an 8-5 record in 97 innings at Charleston, a Detroit affiliate. He finished the season with a 3.62 ERA, walking only 26 hitters while striking out 72.

Opening 1959 again with the Senators, Schultz again quickly established himself as a reliable fireman. He appeared in twenty-seven of the team's first fifty-two games. The Tigers brought up the thirty-two-year-old Schultz on June 7. In early July the Tigers sent him back to Charleston, where he spent the rest of the season. In April 1960, Detroit sold Schultz to the Chicago Cubs, who sent the thirty-three-year-old Schultz to their Triple-A affiliate, the Houston Buffs. Although a Chicago affiliate, Houston's organization had strong St. Louis connections. Marty Marion, a former star shortstop for the Cardinals, together with a St. Louis businessman had purchased a substantial share of the Buffs in late 1959. Marion hired former Cardinal and future Hall of Famer Enos Slaughter as manager. Schultz quickly became a favorite of Slaughter's and saw plenty of work in 1960. By season's end he had appeared in 53 of Houston's 154 games, all but three in relief, worked 146 innings, and posted a 3.02 ERA. He struck out 103 and walked just 41. Schultz earned another serious look by the big leagues, this time with the Cubs in 1961.

The 1961 Cubs employed an unusual "college of coaches" framework with the manager, or "head coach," periodically rotating from the Minor League system. In 1961 the head coach position rotated eight times among four coaches.[9] Within this fluid and highly distracting environment, Schultz tried to earn a relief spot on the Cubs' roster. After a brief start in the Minors, the team called him up.

For the first time in his now seventeen-year baseball career, Schultz played most of his season in the big leagues. He became the Cubs' third reliever, appearing forty-one times, recording seven saves, and posting a 7-6 record. He pitched sixty-six and two-thirds innings and had a 2.70 ERA, the lowest among Cubs relievers. The Cubs stayed with their college of coaches framework again in 1962. This time, the head coach position rotated three times among three coaches. Again a weak staff of starting pitchers provided plenty of work for Chicago's relievers. Schultz was now thirty-five years old, and the Cubs affectionately nicknamed him Mr. Old Folks.[10]

Mr. Old Folks promptly went out and pitched even more in 1962, exceeding his prior-year totals for appearances and innings pitched. Schultz

appeared in fifty-one games, logging a 5-5 record with five saves. He pitched seventy-seven and two-thirds innings with a 3.82 ERA, the second lowest among Chicago's relievers. He tied Elroy Face's Major League record for consecutive game appearances with nine.

In early 1963 the Cubs changed their coaching rotation experiment. Bob Kennedy was the coach/manager for the entire season. Schultz was once again in the Cubs' bullpen at the start of the season, but on June 24 the Cubs put him on waivers. He had pitched twenty-seven and one-third innings in fifteen games with a 1-0 record, two saves, and a 3.62 ERA.

At the urging of Johnny Keane, who was now the Cardinals' manager, Cardinals general manager Bing Devine traded for Schultz. When Barney rejoined the Cardinals, he found a crowded bullpen. Bobby Shantz and Ron Taylor both appeared in more than fifty games in 1963 and pitched a combined 212 innings. For his part, Schultz pitched in twenty-four games, finishing with a 2-0 record and a 3.58 ERA.

After the season Devine placed Schultz on waivers. No Major League team claimed him. Although disappointed, he again persevered. He told the author of a book published in 1991 that as an incentive to encourage him to report in 1964 to the Cardinals' Triple-A Jacksonville affiliate, the team offered him work with the organization after he retired as a player.[11] So Schultz began the 1964 season as a Jacksonville Sun. Working out of the bullpen, he started the season on fire. In his first thirteen appearances, covering twenty-six innings, he did not allow an earned run. By mid-June, Schultz had extended his scoreless streak to thirty-two and two-thirds innings in fifteen relief appearances. By mid-July, Schultz's pitching numbers showed thirty-five appearances, seventy-four innings pitched, a 6-4 record, and a microscopic 0.85 ERA. At that point the Suns occupied first place with a 59-38 record.

As Schultz and the Suns surged forward, the parent St. Louis club seemed to be in a holding pattern around the .500 mark. Searching for players to help spark the club, Keane pressed Devine to promote Schultz. Finally yielding to Keane's persistence, Devine returned Schultz to the Major Leagues.[12]

Schultz was recalled on July 31. The Cardinals were starting a three-game series at home against Cincinnati. The Cardinals had just won six of seven but were in sixth place with a 53-49 record, trailing first-place Philadelphia by seven games. Sixty games remained.

Keane used Schultz immediately; in the Cardinals' first ten games after Barney's return, Keane pitched him five times. After one game, Keane asked Schultz about his control. "Do you know where that knuckleball is going when you throw it," Keane asked, "or are you just hoping it will fool them?" Schultz deadpanned, "John, when I have my stuff, I know where the ball is going on four out of five pitches." Keane smiled.[13] Schultz quickly became the closer in the Cardinals' bullpen.

On August 17, however, Busch shocked the players by asking for Bing Devine's resignation. Busch immediately replaced Devine with Bob Howsam, whom Schultz knew from his time with the Denver Bears.

Suddenly the 1964 Cardinals jelled. Twelve victories in a fifteen-game home stand in late August and early September catapulted the club from the doldrums back into contention. Keane used Schultz in six of the fifteen games. By the end of the home stand, the club had improved its record to 77-61 and was tied for second place.

Schultz appeared eight times during the subsequent eighteen-game road trip, as the Cardinals posted a 12-6 record. They finished the trip by winning five games in a row at Pittsburgh. As the Cardinals came home for their final six games, the club stood in third place behind Philadelphia and Cincinnati.

St. Louis began its last six home games by sweeping a three-game series from the Phillies, who faded out of contention with a ten-game losing streak. Schultz saved two of the games. Then the last-place Mets came into town for the final three-game series of the season and proceeded to win the first two games. When Cincinnati lost to Philadelphia on Friday night and both teams had Saturday off, the 1964 National League pennant race came down to the last game. Cincinnati lost 10–0 to the Phillies, and the Cardinals were beating the Mets. With an 11–4 lead and one out in the ninth, Keane fittingly summoned Schultz to finish the Cardinals' final victory.[14]

This was Schultz's thirtieth appearance in the Cardinals' last sixty games. He appeared in seven of the Cardinals' last nine games. He finished 1964 with one win, fourteen saves, and a 1.64 ERA. The Cardinals ended in first place with a 93-69 record.

At the team's victory party, Schultz overheard Keane proclaiming, "I am the happiest man in the world." Schultz quickly corrected him: "I started playing for Keane back in 1954, but I have to disagree with him. *I'm* the happiest man in the world."[15]

St. Louis hosted Game One of the 1964 World Series. Schultz pitched three effective innings in relief of Ray Sadecki as the Cardinals defeated the New York Yankees, 9–5. After the game Schultz again gave Keane full credit for his success. "He's the one who made me a relief pitcher," Barney said. "He's the one who had faith in me. He's done more for me than any man in baseball.[16]

The Yankees won Game Two, 8–3. Schultz did not fare as well in Game Three, at Yankee Stadium. He entered the 1–1 game in the ninth inning. On Schultz's first pitch of the inning, Mickey Mantle blasted a game-winning home run. The towering homer reached the third tier of the right-field stands. Mantle later listed the home run as one of the top five thrills of his baseball career.

In the Cardinals' locker room after the game,

Schultz seemed stunned. He spoke briefly with reporters before he disappeared into the trainer's area. "The ball I threw was down the well," Schultz said sadly. "It was knee high and across the plate. It didn't break."[17]

Fran Schultz was also stunned by the blast. She had proudly stood with her camera in hand waiting to take a picture of Schultz's first pitch in Yankee Stadium. As he warmed up, Fran noticed a well-known movie star sitting nearby. As she momentarily turned her camera toward the star, she missed the first and only pitch Schultz would ever throw in Yankee Stadium. She could only watch as Schultz trudged off the field.

Schultz's reaction to the devastating home run impressed his catcher, Tim McCarver, who said, "Was [Schultz] screaming at my bad call? Was he bitching about what a lousy catcher I was? Was he blaming me for calling for his knuckler? Nope. Not Schultz."[18]

The Cardinals eventually won the World Series in seven games. Schultz pitched in four of the games, giving up nine hits and eight earned runs in four innings. His ERA was a lofty 18.00.

In 1965 Schultz was with the Cardinals until late August, when he was sent back to Jacksonville. He rejoined the Cardinals briefly at the end of the season. In all he made thirty-four appearances, pitched forty-two and one-third innings, and had a 3.83 ERA. His record was 2-2 with two saves. At Jacksonville, he was 0-1 with a 4.20 ERA in fifteen innings.

In 1966 the Cardinals made Schultz a player-coach with their Tulsa Oilers affiliate in the Pacific Coast League. For the first half of the season, Schultz was used strictly as a coach. His friendly yet detail-oriented nature made him a natural at the position. During the second half of the season he returned to the bullpen, and found he could still pitch effectively. Tulsa made the playoffs. Schultz finished 1966 with a 2-0 record, twenty-five appearances, twenty-five innings pitched, and a 3.24 ERA.

The Cardinals made Schultz their Minor League pitching instructor in 1967. Late in the season, he joined the Cardinals as a coach so he could pick up time toward a pension. The Cardinals won the World Series and Schultz got another World Series ring, but he ended up about three days short of the pension requirement.

In 1968 Schultz resumed his duties as a Minor League pitching instructor and finally, in his twenty-fourth year in professional baseball, met the pension requirement, when the Cardinals again added him as a coach. He remained a Cardinals Minor League pitching instructor through 1970.

In 1971 Schultz became the Cardinals' pitching coach, and remained in that position through 1975. In 1977 he was the pitching coach for the Chicago Cubs. For the next three seasons he was a special-assignment coach for the Cubs. After that, Schultz finished his coaching career in Japan with the Osaka Hawks.[19]

In 1982 Schultz retired from professional baseball. After playing in more than twenty-five states and three countries, he retired to Edgewater Park in southern New Jersey. In 1988 he was elected to the South Jersey Baseball Hall of Fame. In his eighties, still in awe of the game he devoted his life to and continued to love, he said, "I'd have to say I owe everything to baseball."[20]

Chapter 31. Timeline, July 1–July 31

John Harry Stahl

July 1 —CARDINALS 6, BRAVES 1 —The Cardinals began a ten-game road trip at County Stadium. Javier hit a three-run home run in the third inning and had four RBIS as Simmons pitched a complete game. Brock made a spectacular play on a Rico Carty drive to the left-field wall to end the game. Braves manager Bobby Bragan said afterward, "Brock must have jumped nine feet for that ball. I didn't think he had a chance to get it."

July 2 —CARDINALS 4, BRAVES 3 —Sadecki won his ninth game by overcoming home runs by Carty and Gene Oliver. Javier led the Cardinals' attack as he hit a home run in the fourth and scored on a James double in the seventh. Cardinals reliever Bob Humphreys pitched the last three innings and held the Braves hitless and scoreless.

July 3 —REDS 4, CARDINALS 1 —The Reds' Tsitouris pitched a complete game and struck out ten. Gibson dropped to 6-6 for the season. Vada Pinson was the Reds' hitting star, going 3 for 4 and driving in three runs. In the third, with runners on first and third and one out, Boyer hit into a double play, ending the Cardinals' best run-scoring threat.

July 4 —REDS 3, CARDINALS 2 —Jim O'Toole pitched eight strong innings to get the win. Reliever Billy McCool pitched out of ninth-inning trouble. In the ninth, Boyer led off with a double. McCool then struck out both White and James. With two out, the Reds' shortstop made an error on Javier's ground ball. Boyer scored and Javier ended up at second base. With the tying run on second, McCool struck out McCarver.

July 5 —CARDINALS 3, REDS 1 —Craig won his fifth game as he pitched a complete game and scattered ten hits. Run-scoring singles by Skinner and McCarver drove in the deciding runs in the seventh.

July 6–8 —ALL-STAR BREAK —Cardinals players Ken Boyer, Curt Flood, Dick Groat, and Bill White were selected to play on the 1964 NL All-Star team. At the break, the Cardinals' record stood at 39-40. They were tied for fifth place and ten games behind league-leading Philadelphia.

July 6 —General manager Bing Devine summarized the 1964 Cardinals' current situation: "What the Cardinals need badly right away is a hot streak. But we haven't done that yet, and we haven't shown signs that we are going to do it."

July 7 —The Cardinals sold infielder/outfielder Jeoff Long to the Chicago White Sox and recalled outfielder Mike Shannon from Jacksonville (Triple-A).

July 9 —METS 4, CARDINALS 3 —The Cardinals continued their road trip in New York. Leading 3–2 with two outs and a Mets runner on first base in the ninth inning, Cardinals starter Simmons gave up a walk-off home run to Mets pinch hitter Frank Thomas. Al Jackson pitched a complete game for his fifth victory.

July 10 —CARDINALS 3, METS 1 —Gibson pitched a complete game for his seventh victory. Cardinals hitting stars included Shannon, who drove in two runs with a fourth-inning single. Flood, Groat, and White each had two hits.

July 11 — CARDINALS 11, METS 4 — Six Mets errors and eleven Cardinals hits gave Sadecki the victory. Three Cardinals hitters had multi-hit games: Brock went 2 for 4, scoring two runs with two RBIs; Boyer went 3 for 5, scoring three runs with one RBI; and Shannon went 2 for 3, scoring one run with three RBIs. The victory brought the Cardinals back to the .500 mark for the season (41-41).

July 12 — No game scheduled.

Bill White publicly blamed himself for the Cardinals' disappointing first half of the season. "I'm what's happened to the ball club," he said. "Your 3-4-5 hitters have to hit. A year ago this time I had 60 RBIs, to 30 now. If I had been hitting the way I should, maybe a kid like [Johnny] Lewis wouldn't have had to leave the club."

July 13 — CARDINALS 5, PIRATES 4 (12 innings) (game one) — The Cardinals pounded fifteen hits off three of five different pitchers, finally winning the game in the twelfth inning. Initially, the Cardinals were poised to win the game in the ninth inning. However, a Willie Stargell triple and a Donn Clendenon double sent the game into extra innings. In the tenth, after White's home run had given the Cardinals the lead, Bob Bailey hit a home run with two out to tie the game again. In the twelfth, the Cardinals scored another run on Javier's single and Taylor retired the Pirates in order.

July 13 — CARDINALS 12, PIRATES 5 (game two) — The Cardinals' twenty hits combined with Pittsburgh's six errors led to a lopsided Cardinals victory. Six Cardinals had two or more hits, led by White (3 for 6 with four RBIs), Javier (4 for 5 with two RBIs), and Brock (4 for 6 with three runs scored). Cuellar pitched seven and one-third innings for the victory.

July 14 — CARDINALS 8, DODGERS 7 — Losing 7–4 in the bottom of the ninth, the Cardinals used three walks and two singles to score four runs. The game-winning hit was Skinner's walk-off two-run single with two outs. Through the top of the fourth, the Dodgers, with Koufax pitching, led 6–0. Cardinals relief pitcher Taylor got the win.

July 15 — DODGERS 13, CARDINALS 3 — The Dodgers hit four home runs and the Cardinals made two costly errors to send Gibson to his seventh loss. Tommy Davis, Willie Davis, and Ron Fairly (two) hit home runs to lead the Dodgers.

July 16 — DODGERS 10, CARDINALS 2 — The Dodgers scored four runs off Sadecki in the first inning and never trailed. Fairly went 3 for 4 with four RBIs. Tommy Davis went 2 for 5 with three RBIs.

July 17 — CARDINALS 9, METS 8 — In his third relief appearance, Gibson entered the game in the ninth with two outs and retired pinch hitter Hawk Taylor with the tying run on third. The Cardinals got twelve hits, including a two-run home run by White. Groat went 3 for 4 with three RBIs. Brock went 3 for 4 with a walk and scored three runs. He also stole his twentieth base.

July 18 — CARDINALS 15, METS 7 — Although the Mets scored five runs in the first inning, the Cardinals scored a single-inning season-high eleven runs in the eighth inning to win the game. During that inning, the Cardinals hit back-to-back-to-back home runs. Boyer's grand slam was followed by home runs from White and McCarver. Shannon then lined a double high off the left-field wall to just miss a fourth consecutive homer. Boyer went 2 for 4 with four RBIs. White went 4 for 4 with four RBIs.

July 19 — METS 3, CARDINALS 2 (game one) — Jack

Fisher pitched a complete game, allowing eight hits and holding the Cardinals scoreless for the last three innings. Flood, Groat, and Shannon each had two hits. Simmons suffered his eighth defeat.

July 19 — CARDINALS 7, METS 6 (game two) — Trailing 6–3, the Cardinals stunned three Mets pitchers by scoring four runs on six consecutive hits in the ninth to win the game. Warwick's pinch double started the ninth. Singles from Flood, Brock, and White followed. Boyer's double tied the game and Groat's single won it. Both Flood and Groat went 4 for 5. Gibson pitched a complete game, allowing ten hits and six earned runs but striking out eleven.

July 20 — No game scheduled.

July 21 — PIRATES 8, CARDINALS 4 — Leading 1–0, the Pirates scored five in the fifth inning sparked by a Jerry Lynch grand slam and added two more runs in the sixth to top the Cardinals. Flood led the Cardinals going 4 for 5, and Boyer was 3 for 5. Shannon hit a three-run home run in the eighth inning.

July 22 — PIRATES 13, CARDINALS 2 — The Pirates scored four runs in the first and never trailed. Pittsburgh banged out eighteen hits, including home runs by Stargell, Bill Mazeroski, and Jerry Lynch. Stargell went 4 for 4, scored two runs, and had three RBIs. Veale pitched a complete game. Brock and Groat had two hits each for the Cardinals.

The Cardinals purchased pitcher Gordon Richardson from Jacksonville (Triple-A), recalled infielder Ed Spiezio from Tulsa (Double-A), and optioned infielder Phil Gagliano to Jacksonville (Triple-A) and pitcher Dave Bakenhaster to Winnipeg (Single-A).

July 23 — PIRATES 8, CARDINALS 5 — The Pirates completed a three-game sweep of the Cardinals,

who ended their ten-game home stand with a 4-6 record. The two teams combined for twenty-nine hits. Bailey and Virdon each had three hits, with both hitting home runs. Five Cardinals had a multi-hit game.

July 24 — PHILLIES 9, CARDINALS 1 — The Cardinals lost their fourth game in a row as Chris Short pitched a complete game while striking out eight. After scoring two runs in the first inning, the Phillies never trailed. Gibson lost his eighth game. The Cardinals made four errors that led to three unearned runs. The Cardinals' season record dropped to 47-48 for seventh place, ten games behind Philadelphia.

July 25 — CARDINALS 10, PHILLIES 9 — The Cardinals broke their four-game losing streak. Boyer led their attack with two home runs, including his second grand slam of 1964. White and Shannon each had three hits. The Phillies scared the Cardinals by scoring seven runs in the ninth on four hits and four walks. With the score 10–9, Gus Triandos popped out to second base to end the game.

July 26 — CARDINALS 6, PHILLIES 1 (game one) — Rookie Gordon Richardson made his first Major League start and pitched a complete game, striking out five. The Cardinals banged out fifteen hits. Flood led the way with three hits and four RBIs.

July 26 — CARDINALS 4, PHILLIES 1 (game two) — Sadecki won his eleventh game with a complete-game victory. Boyer had three hits as the Cardinals swept the doubleheader.

July 27 — No game scheduled.

July 28 — CARDINALS 12, CUBS 7 (10 innings) — In Chicago, the teams combined for thirty-three hits. Ernie Broglio started for the first time against his former teammates. Tied 7–7 at the end of nine innings, the Cardinals scored five runs in the tenth. Flood's triple drove in two runs to key the Cardinals' scoring. Cuellar pitched a scoreless tenth for the Cardinals. Every Cardinal starting player (with the exception of the pitcher) had at least one hit. Shannon, McCarver, and White all hit home runs.

July 29 — CARDINALS 9, CUBS 1 — Simmons pitched a complete game for his eleventh victory. The Cardinals scored seven runs in the seventh inning to take command of the game. Brock led the Cardinals, going 4 for 5 with an RBI, a run scored, and a stolen base. Flood, Boyer, White, and Javier each had two hits.

July 30 — CARDINALS 5, CUBS 2 — The Cardinals completed a three-game sweep of the Cubs as White led the attack with two hits and four RBIs. Sadecki went eight innings to get his twelfth victory. Entering the game in the ninth with two on and no outs, Craig allowed only one run to score.

July 31 — REDS 7, CARDINALS 6 — The visiting Reds scored five runs in the second and two more in the fifth to beat Richardson. Pinson, Robinson, Don Pavletich, and Leo Cardenas had two hits apiece. Brock, Groat, Javier, and McCarver each had two hits for the Cardinals.

The Cardinals acquired relief pitcher Barney Schultz from Jacksonville (Triple-A), recalled shortstop Dal Maxvill from Indianapolis (Triple-A), and sent pitcher Glen Hobbie to Jacksonville (Triple-A).

Cardinals July win-loss record: 17-11.
Cardinals year-to-date win-loss record: 53-49.

Standings, July 31, 1964

	W	L	T	PCT	GB
Philadelphia Phillies	59	41	0	.590	—
San Francisco Giants	59	44	0	.573	1½
Cincinnati Reds	56	47	1	.544	4½
Pittsburgh Pirates	53	45	0	.541	5
Milwaukee Braves	53	48	0	.525	6½
St. Louis Cardinals	53	49	0	.520	7
Los Angeles Dodgers	50	50	2	.500	9
Chicago Cubs	48	52	0	.480	11
Houston Colt .45s	45	60	0	.429	16½
New York Mets	32	72	1	.308	29

Chapter 32. **Mike Shannon**

Kevin D. McCann

AGE	G	AB	R	H	2B	3B	HR	TB	RBI	BB	SO	BAV	OBP	SLG	SB	GDP	HBP
24	88	253	30	66	8	2	9	105	43	19	54	.261	.310	.415	4	7	0

For more than fifty years, Mike Shannon has been a fixture in the Cardinals organization. He played for his hometown team and was a member of three pennant-winning teams and two World Series champions. He became a hometown hero with a game-tying home run at Busch Stadium that helped win the first game of the 1964 World Series. A selfless player, he gave up his personal comfort for the betterment of the team when he learned to catch and later switched from the outfield to third base. His playing career was prematurely ended by a life-threatening kidney ailment, but it led to a successful forty-year broadcasting career with the Cardinals.

Thomas Michael Shannon was born in St. Louis on July 15, 1939, the first child of Thomas W. and Elizabeth (Richason) Shannon, and attended Epiphany of Our Lord parish school. Growing up, he played various sports depending on the time of year. His father was a police officer working his way through law school, but still he took time to help Mike improve his skills. Shannon developed into an exceptional three-sport athlete at Christian Brothers College (high school) in nearby Clayton, Missouri. As a senior, he was the starting quarterback for the undefeated football team and was voted a high school All-American. He won Missouri prep Player of the Year honors in football and basketball, the only player to receive both awards in different sports in the same year.[1]

Shannon felt he was a better football player than baseball player, but at the time it was baseball, not football, that offered the best opportunity for a professional career. "Back then, there wasn't any money in football," he recalled. "If

Mike Shannon played in eighty-eight games and batted .261 in 1964. Defensively, he provided one of the strongest throwing arms in the NL. He later became a popular announcer for the Cardinals.

there would have been, I would have stayed with football." His baseball talent was "really raw," by his own admission, and no team offered him more than an $8,000 signing bonus. Stan Musial, whose son Dick was Shannon's high school teammate, told Shannon that the rule requiring players with large bonuses to be on the Major League roster for two years would soon change. Shannon decided to attend college and wait for a better offer. He was offered football scholarships by colleges across the country and accepted the one from the University of Missouri.[2] But in June 1958 Shannon signed with the Cardinals for a bonus of close to $50,000. "I liked football, but baseball was always my first love," he later said.[3] The Cardinals sent the seventeen-year-old to play for Albany (Georgia) of the Class D Georgia-Florida League. Playing center field in his debut, he drove in the winning run in the first game of a double-header and helped win the second with a four-hundred-foot double. Shannon batted .322, hit six home runs, and was named to the postseason All-Star team, even though injuries limited him to sixty-two games — "I dislocated a shoulder diving back into second base, I was hit on the head by a ball when I stole third base and I got a broken nose diving for a line drive," he recalled. After hitting a home run in the 1964 World Series, he recalled hitting a longer one for Albany, in Dublin — "Dublin, Georgia, of course. I really shillaleghed that one."[4]

Shannon married his high school sweetheart, Judith Ann Bufe, in St. Louis on February 7, 1959. She traveled with him to spring training and through the Minor Leagues even after their children (three sons and three daughters) were born. "It was Judy who took care of the family and made it possible for me to enjoy my career," he said.[5] By 1960 he was playing in Double-A and in 1961 he was in Triple-A, with Portland in the Pacific Coast League. There he earned the nickname Moonman for the way he dodged out of the way of a pitch behind his back. "It looked like I was floating in mid-air," Shannon recalled; a teammate thought he "looks like a moon man." Future teammates, however, believed there was a quirkier reason behind it. "He'll talk 15 minutes and when he's through you'll go away scratching your head and wondering what he said," Bob Gibson remarked. "He may start a conversation about baseball and end up with insurance after going through 45 other topics. You still don't know what he said."[6]

Shannon was among four Minor League pros-pects invited to the Major League camp for spring training in 1962, but he was sent back to Triple-A when camp broke. He spent the first half of the season with the Atlanta Crackers in the International League, then was traded in August to the Seattle Rainiers, the Boston Red Sox's Triple-A club in the Pacific Coast League, where he batted .311 in seventy-six games. The Cardinals reclaimed him and brought him up to St. Louis, where he made his Major League debut in right field against the Cincinnati Reds at Busch Stadium on September 11, 1962. In his second at bat he hit a single to left field. "You always remember that first at-bat and first hit," Shannon said. "Mine came against a pitcher [Bob Purkey] who was one of the best in the majors at the time" — Purkey went 23-5 that season — "and it was a confidence builder to be successful."[7] The Cardinals thought enough of his potential to place him on the forty-man roster and invite him to play in the Florida Winter Instructional League.[8]

The 1963 season was a difficult one for Shannon. He made a poor showing in spring training and was sent down to Triple-A Atlanta. His wife, Judy, pregnant with their fourth child and seriously ill, was bedridden and couldn't care for their three young children. Shannon missed the first half of the season, and though he returned to Atlanta in early July, he considered quitting until his wife was better. To allow him to stay close to home, the Cardinals promoted him to the Major League roster on July 21 and he stayed with the team the rest of the season, getting twenty-one at bats as an outfield defensive replacement for Stan Musial and others.[9] Before his last Major League game, on September 29, Musial pointed to former Cardinal Joe Medwick and said, "This is the guy I replaced as regular left fielder 22 years ago." Then he motioned to Shannon and fellow outfielder Gary Kolb, sitting on either side of him: "And these are my protégés who'll replace me next year."[10]

In the off-season St. Louis offered Shannon to

KEVIN D. MCCANN

the Milwaukee Braves in a deal for reserve catcher Bob Uecker, but the deal was not made, and Shannon went north with the Cardinals after spring training.[11] After three weeks riding the bench with little playing time, he was sent down to Triple-A Jacksonville. Now out of options and subject to the Minor League draft if the Cardinals did not bring him back by the end of the season, Shannon decided to make the most of his demotion. "I made up my mind to work as hard as I could to improve my hitting. . . . I had to," he said. "I've got a wife and four kids at home." He also gave himself a deadline for returning to the Majors. "I figured, if I don't come up by this date, I'm kidding myself. I'd better find a job and go to work someplace." Batting lead-off for Jacksonville, Shannon hit .278 with eleven home runs in seventy games; on July 9 he returned to St. Louis. "I just beat the mark, that's all," he said of his deadline. "By about a week or 10 days, I beat it." He became the starting right fielder for a team poised to make a remarkable comeback.[12]

When Shannon joined the Cardinals they were in sixth place in the ten-team National League with a record of 39-41 and eleven games behind the Philadelphia Phillies. He batted .351 in July with 17 RBIS, but cooled to a .203 average and 9 RBIS in August as the team climbed into fourth place, seven and a half games behind Philadelphia. Shannon proved adept at gunning out base runners and notched seven outfield assists. The Cardinals surged in September, winning twenty-one games to place themselves back in contention. A ten-game Phillies losing streak down the stretch coincided with the Cardinals' longest winning streak of the season—eight games—to lift St. Louis past the Cincinnati Reds into first place on September 30. Two losses to the last-place New York Mets left the Cardinals in a first-place tie with the Reds. In the second inning of the crucial final game of the season, Shannon singled Tim McCarver home with the first run against the Mets. Later the Cardinals

bounced back from a 3–2 deficit for an 11–5 win which—coupled with Cincinnati's 10–0 loss to Philadelphia—clinched the pennant for St. Louis.[13]

In the World Series, the Cardinals faced the New York Yankees. It was a dream come true for Shannon, though he had only six hits for a .214 average and struck out five consecutive times in the seven-game Series. But one of those hits was pivotal in the team's 9–5 victory in Game One at Busch Stadium. With one out in the sixth inning, Ken Boyer on second base, and the Cardinals behind 4–2, he faced Whitey Ford, who was pitching in his twenty-second and final World Series game. Ford hung a slider and Shannon belted it over the left-field wall and against the top of the seventy-five-foot-high scoreboard, striking the *U* in the Budweiser sign and tying the contest. St. Louis scored twice more in the inning and won, 9–5. "That homer gave me the biggest thrill of my life," he said at the time. Twenty-five years later, he recalled, "I was a hometown boy in front of the hometown crowd, and I hit a home run off Whitey Ford in the World Series. You can't hardly top that."[14] Before Game Two, Shannon found out that it would cost more than $4,000 to repair the sign. He walked to owner August Busch's box seat and apologized for the damage. Busch laughed and said he didn't care if Shannon hit a couple more off the sign during the Series. Shannon hit no more home runs but had two outfield assists, and in Game Seven he and McCarver pulled off a double steal for the second run; then Shannon scored on a single by Dal Maxvill as the Cardinals went on to defeat the Yankees and win the Series.

Shannon's line-drive bat and strong throwing arm earned him the right-field berth in 1965. He hit well in spring training, but he struggled at the plate during the season and ended with a .221 average. "I just put myself in a slump by pressing," he said. "I'd keep saying to myself, 'I got to get a hit this time. I got to get a hit this time.' I worried that if I didn't get the hit, I probably wouldn't get to play the next game." On September 25, at Dodger Stadium in Los Angeles, he fell victim to Sandy Koufax's 350th strikeout, which set a Major League single-season record. (Koufax finished with 382 strikeouts.[15])

While disappointed with Shannon's bat, new Cardinals manager Red Schoendienst was impressed with his versatility. Former manager Johnny Keane had tinkered in 1964 with the idea of the rifle-armed Shannon being an emergency catcher, but it didn't come to fruition until August 8, 1965. McCarver was injured, and Bob Uecker, starting in his place, split his right thumb on a foul ball in the first inning against the San Francisco Giants. Shannon was called upon to replace him. "When they handed me Uecker's mitt, an ounce or two of blood spilled out of it," he recalled. "That's when I wasn't so sure I wanted to go out there and catch."[16] Despite a few mishaps — like putting shin guards on the wrong legs and "sticking my hand straight down, instead of holding it against the inside of my leg" when giving signals to the pitcher — Shannon did a good job handling five pitchers (including knuckle-ball reliever Barney Schultz) and turned a double play by tagging out Willie Mays trying to score on Jim Ray Hart's double and then throwing out Hart advancing to third.[17]

At the end of the season, Shannon went to the Florida Instructional League to learn catching fundamentals and work on his hitting. "We're figuring him as an outfielder yet, but this gives him a chance to do many things," said general manager Bob Howsam. It was a tumultuous off-season as the Cardinals traded stalwarts Ken Boyer, Bill White, and Dick Groat and acquired outfielder Alex Johnson from Philadelphia. Johnson was considered the favorite to win a starting job and Shannon hoped that if he was blocked from an everyday role in the outfield, he might be a reserve catcher. "I feel that I sharpened up enough at catching that I could step in right now and do a good job in a

regular season game," he said after the Instructional League season ended.

Once again, Shannon made a good showing with the bat in spring training, but he found himself on the bench to start the 1966 season. When the highly touted Johnson slumped early in the season, Shannon got the opportunity to play more often. In the last game played at Busch Stadium (formerly Sportsman's Park), on May 8, his fifth-inning solo home run against San Francisco was the last one hit there by a Cardinal; Willie McCovey and Willie Mays homered later for the Giants at the historic ballpark. When Busch Stadium II opened, on May 12, he had the first Cardinal hit, a single; the next night he hit the first Cardinal homer, a solo shot in the fourth inning. Still, he was unhappy being part of an outfield platoon with Johnson and rookie Bobby Tolan, and considered playing football again (he had been invited to try out with the Atlanta Falcons). But a torrid hitting streak in July that led teammates to nickname him the Cannon quelled his gridiron aspirations and made it hard for him to sit on the bench. He batted .395 with 45 hits and 23 RBIs for the month, including a 4-for-5 performance with 3 runs scored at Cincinnati on his twenty-seventh birthday; a week later in Chicago he went 5 for 5 with a home run, double, and 3 runs scored. "Shannon has been a big reason for our team's recent improvement," Schoendienst said. Though the Cardinals finished in sixth place, he enjoyed his best Major League season to date, batting .288 with 16 home runs and 64 RBIs in 124 games.[18]

Shannon's breakout performance convinced the team that he should be an everyday player, but with the added challenge of learning yet another position. Schoendienst was confident that Shannon could make the transition to third base and make room in right field for Roger Maris, acquired over the winter from the New York Yankees. (He and Maris became close friends, and Shannon was a pallbearer at his funeral in 1985.) Though his

KEVIN D. MCCANN

strong, accurate throwing arm made him one of the top outfielders in the league, he agreed to the switch and fielded countless bunts and ground balls during the winter and spring training to prepare for it. "Listen, nobody has to tell me about how I play third," Shannon candidly admitted about his defense. "Nobody playing the game looks worse than I do when I'm going badly. But over the long haul I think I can do the job." Though his batting average fell to .245 and he committed 29 errors at the hot corner, he contributed 12 home runs and 77 RBIs (second on the club behind National League MVP Orlando Cepeda) despite injuries and illness in spring training and during the first half of the 1967 season. General manager Stan Musial said Shannon's willingness to move to third enabled him to add more offense to the team: "There's no question but that Shannon agreeing to take a shot at third base set up our club," Musial said. The Cardinals captured the pennant and faced the Boston Red Sox in the World Series. In Game Three, his second-inning two-run homer (the first-ever hit in the postseason at Busch Stadium II) put St. Louis ahead 3–0 in the Cardinals' 5–2 victory over Boston. Shannon batted just .208 in the Series, but St. Louis won it in seven games. "Every time we win a pennant, I have to play a new position," he joked. "I hope that I'm pitching next year if we win."[19]

Fortunately for Shannon, there was no new position for him to learn in 1968. His fielding at third base improved, with fewer errors, but more important, he had his best season at the plate, leading the Cardinals in RBIs (79) and finishing seventh in the MVP voting while batting .266 with 15 home runs (second best on the club). The team won the pennant again and played the Detroit Tigers in the World Series. Shannon enjoyed his best postseason performance with 8 hits in 29 at bats and 4 RBIs, but St. Louis dropped the Series in seven games. Shannon's ninth-inning home run at Busch Stadium (giving him a homer in each

World Series he played in) was the only blemish on Detroit left-hander Mickey Lolich's 4–1 victory in Game Seven. Afterward, the Cardinals embarked on an eighteen-game goodwill tour of Japan and won thirteen games against the host teams. Shannon, Lou Brock, and Orlando Cepeda led the team with five home runs each.[20]

Coming off their second straight pennant, the Cardinals were the favorites to win it again in 1969. Shannon and his teammates did well in spring training, but they struggled when the season began and were fifteen and a half games behind the Chicago Cubs in the East division standings on July 4. A midsummer resurgence wasn't enough to overcome the Cubs or the division-winning Mets, however, and the team finished in fourth place. Shannon's numbers dropped from the previous season to a .254 batting average and 12 home runs, while his RBI total fell to 55.[21]

There were rumors over the winter that he might be dealt to the California Angels, but Shannon was still a Cardinal when spring training began in 1970. During the players' physical exams, it was discovered that he had glomerulonephritis, a potentially life-threatening condition that prevents the kidneys from filtering waste properly. The team physician, Dr. Stan London, told the thirty-year-old Shannon that he might miss the entire season. "The severity of exercise could be injurious to his health," London said. "His condition could have been aggravated by his playing baseball." Before his diagnosis, the Philadelphia Phillies were interested in Shannon to replace Curt Flood (who had refused to be traded) in the deal that sent Dick Allen to the Cardinals. "He was that close to not making it," remembered Cardinals broadcaster Jack Buck, spreading two fingers slightly apart on his hand. "A lot of people thought he was going to die." After a month of medication and rest at Jewish Hospital in St. Louis, Shannon was allowed to begin workouts for a possible comeback. "I've got a clean bill of health," he announced upon his return to the club. "There's nothing wrong with me that a few base hits won't cure." He made his season debut as a pinch hitter against the Pittsburgh Pirates in a home game on May 14 and got a standing ovation. The comeback was understandably difficult, and Shannon batted just .213 in 193 plate appearances with no home runs and 22 RBIs. On August 14 Dr. London determined that his condition had worsened and he would have to resume treatments and not play the rest of the season.[22]

A possible return in 1971 was ruled out before spring training, and Shannon accepted an offer from the Cardinals to serve as assistant director of promotions and sales in the front office. "There's not much difference" between his new position and being on the field, he said. "Now, I'm just promoting the game from behind a desk instead of from behind third base." After the season, general manager Bing Devine offered him the chance to manage the Cardinals' Triple-A Tulsa club or be a Major League coach, but he turned both down for financial reasons and to stay close to his family.[23]

Rather than attempt a second comeback at thirty-two years old, Shannon accepted a new challenge. He became the color commentator on the Cardinals' radio and TV broadcasts alongside announcer Jack Buck for the 1972 season. "It was an easy decision because I had six small children, and I had to educate them," he recalled. "I thought the opportunity was better in broadcasting. So I worked as hard as I could to become the best broadcaster I could. It turned out to be the right decision." Eventually he began sharing the play-by-play duties with Buck. There were times when the transition was not a smooth one as he learned the intricacies of calling a game, but Buck was a patient teacher and Shannon an eager student. "Good Lord of mercy, I don't know what I would have done without him," Shannon said. "That man helped me so much. I didn't have to go to broadcasting school—working with Jack was like having a private tutor [and] on-the-job training." In 1985 Shannon received a regional Emmy Award for sports broadcasting, and in 1999 he was inducted as a broadcaster into the Missouri Sports Hall of Fame.[24]

Shannon was still broadcasting in 2011, with a unique broadcasting style that included clichés and distinctive phrases. Games "at the old ballpark" consisted of healthy doses of "stee-rike call!" during a pitch count; "Get up, baby, get up! Oh yeah!" when a Cardinal home run was hit; and "Ol' Abner has done it again" for a dramatic moment late in the game. Sometimes "deuces are wild" on a 2-2 count, and when a pitch was down the middle of the plate, it was "right down central." An opponent's drive into the gap with runners on was "a peck of trouble." Then there were his sometimes off-the-wall remarks that fans affectionately called "Shannon-isms." Here is a sampling:

"He knew he was out when he heard that right hand go up."

"It's raining so hard that I thought it was going to stop."

"You can't argue with the weather."

"Well, he did everything right to get ready for the throw, but if ya ain't got the hose, the water just won't come out."

"This big standing-room-only crowd is settling into their seats."

"It's Mother's Day today, so to all the mothers out there, 'Happy Birthday.'"

"How'd you like to be a bug in Whitey Herzog's head this week?"

During an unusual exchange with Jay Randolph on a televised game in 1987, Shannon remarked on the rarity of winning streaks by the Pittsburgh Pirates. "Winning streaks in Pittsburgh have been about as common as 600-acre lakes in the middle of the Sahara Desert," he said. "You mean, like an oasis," Randolph clarified. "Yeah, well, an oasis is what they're having here in Pittsburgh," Shannon replied.[25]

KEVIN D. MCCANN

Shannon and Buck worked together for thirty seasons. Shannon also became a partner in a downtown St. Louis restaurant called Mike Shannon's Steaks and Seafood. After Buck's death in 2002, Shannon became the primary play-by-play announcer. As of 2011, he shared the broadcast booth with John Rooney, his on-air partner since 2006, and had signed a contract to continue as the voice of the Cardinals until at least 2013.[26]

Mike Shannon became an enduring—and endearing—part of Cardinals baseball. Two generations of fans grew up listening to his unpretentious, down-to-earth, and entertaining play-by-play style on the radio. He overcame many obstacles in his personal and professional life—including the death of his wife, Judy, in July 2007—yet kept an optimistic outlook on life and was thankful for every new day. In September 2011 the Cardinals launched a campaign to encourage fans to nominate him for the 2012 Ford C. Frick Award, the highest honor for broadcasters presented by the Baseball Hall of Fame. It would be a fitting tribute to his forty-year broadcasting career. At seventy-one years old, he still delighted in the drama and excitement of baseball. "The greatest thing about my job," he said, "is that when you come to the ballpark, you never know what's going to happen." He once said that Stan Musial "is Cardinals baseball, it's as simple as that." The same could truly be said for Mike Shannon as well.[27]

Chapter 33. **Bobby Shantz**

Mel Marmer

AGE	W	L	PCT.	ERA	G	GS	GF	CG	SHO	SV	IP	H	BB	SO	HBP	WP
38	1	3	.250	3.12	16	0	10	0	0	0	17.1	14	7	12	0	1

Almost every scout considered him too short (5 feet 6½) to be a Major League pitching prospect. One scout was not deterred, however, and dared to sign the left-hander, setting Bobby Shantz off on a sixteen-year odyssey in the Major Leagues. Shantz reached the heights of success early in his career by winning the American League's Most Valuable Player Award in 1952. He also bore the depths, nearly quitting baseball in midcareer because of serious arm injuries.

During four seasons (1953–56) nursing those injuries, Shantz won just thirteen games against twenty-six losses. Traded by the Kansas City Athletics to the New York Yankees before the 1957 season, Shantz enjoyed success again working mostly as a relief pitcher. He pitched in two World Series, and except for a freakish bad break, he might have been a surprise hero of the 1960 Series. In 1964 his career came full circle when he returned to Philadelphia, where he had begun. Shantz figured in that season's dramatic conclusion, though hardly for the expected reasons.

Robert Clayton Shantz was born on September 26, 1925, to Wilmer and Ruth Eleanor (Ebert) Shantz in Pottstown, Pennsylvania, a city of twenty thousand people forty miles northwest of Philadelphia. His father worked at a Bethlehem Steel mill. In 1927 brother Wilmer Jr. (Billy) was born, and in 1929 the family moved to larger quarters in the suburbs with a big backyard where they could play sports.

Wilmer Sr. loved baseball and was considered a good semipro third baseman. Offered a Minor League contract by the Chicago White Sox, he was advised by his father, Clayton, to "turn it down,

A veteran left-handed relief pitcher with World Series experience, Bobby Shantz posted a 1–3 record with a 3.16 ERA in sixteen games. The Cardinals included Bobby in the Brock trade. (Photo by Allied Photocolor Imaging Center)

and play for the love of the game instead." Clayton had played baseball, too, and had had a bad experience as part-owner of a local baseball team.[1]

Wilmer taught his sons to play baseball and football when they were toddlers. One of Bobby's favorite games was devised by Wilmer to reward throwing strikes.[2] Perhaps this early training was responsible for the excellent control Bobby demonstrated in the Major Leagues; in nine of his sixteen seasons, he struck out more than twice as many batters as he walked.

At the age of six, Bobby suddenly became sick one day. He was sent to the hospital with a high fever and was not expected to live through the night. He survived, and his mother remained by his bedside for a week.[3] Bobby recovered completely and enjoyed a happy childhood. In addition to baseball and football, his favorite pursuits were fishing at nearby Sanatoga Lake, taking part in family snowball fights, and trapping small animals.[4]

Despite tough economic times, the Shantzes were able to obtain sports equipment by redeeming hundreds of cereal box tops given to them by a friend of the family, a cook at a local school.[5]

Young Bobby helped to organize a baseball team called the Sanatoga Pee Wees. As a four-foot-four teenager, he pitched for a neighborhood team, Lower Pottsgrove. The family took trips to Philadelphia to watch the Athletics play, and Bobby's only dream was to play baseball. Could he play baseball professionally one day, being so much smaller than the other boys?

Shantz made the Pottstown High School baseball team as an outfielder. His manager told him to forget about being a pitcher, because he was too small. He never showed off the snappy curve ball he'd been practicing for years with his brother in their backyard. He played well for the high school team, though it did not have a good record. He was also a fine diver on the varsity swim team.

Perhaps Bobby's serious childhood illness had impaired his growth, for when he graduated from high school in 1943 he was still under five feet tall. He got a job as a busboy in the cafeteria of the nearby Jacobs Aircraft plant, where he made the plant baseball team but sat on the bench.

The family moved to Philadelphia when Bobby's father took a job at a shipyard there. The family's relocation was a good break for Bobby and Billy. Their new neighborhood was a hotbed of sports activities and gave the brothers more opportunities to play ball. Bobby played sandlot baseball and Pop Warner football and continued to grow. In 1944 he got a $75-a-week job at the Disston Saw Company as a glazer, shining saws. His draft board called him in, but he was rejected for military service because he was one inch below the minimum five-foot height requirement. Though Bobby was short, his hands were comparatively large and strong, which helped him to excel at athletics.

In the spring of 1944 Bobby played for the Holmesburg Ramblers, a youth baseball team that played in the competitive Quaker City League. He played center field, and his brother Billy, who had dropped out of high school in the tenth grade, was a catcher.

One day Bobby threw batting practice, and the team's manager saw his fine overhand curve ball with its sharp downward break and immediately added him to the pitching staff.[6] Bobby compiled a 9-1 record and played the outfield in games he didn't pitch, batting .485 from the cleanup spot.

Shantz continued to excel in other sports besides baseball. "Shantz was a 'big star' in the neighborhood who could throw, kick, and run," according to Brud Williamson, the son of the Holmesburg Ramblers' coach. "Without question, he was the most modest guy I ever met. Boulevard Pools used to put on diving exhibitions with professional divers. We talked them into letting Bobby dive one summer, and he stole the show. He was a great gymnast too, and he could beat anyone in ping-pong or bowling, any sport he tried."[7]

Meanwhile, Shantz had grown an inch, enough to pass his army physical, and was sworn in on December 28, 1944.[8] After three months of basic training, he headed to Fort Knox, Kentucky, to be trained to drive tanks. But his feet barely reached the pedals, so he was transferred to a mortar outfit. In June of 1945, two months before the end of World War II, he arrived in the Philippines.[9] At camp in Batangas he played interdivisional ball, sharing pitching duties with the White Sox's Gordon Maltzberger. Later, he played against a team of touring Major Leaguers at Rizal Stadium in Manila. Shantz pitched and lost the game, 4–2, but his performance against established Major Leaguers helped to build his confidence.[10] Shantz also pitched well in games against the highly regarded service team the Manila Dodgers. (The Dodgers gave Shantz a tryout but rejected him, which only inspired him to work harder.[11]) Discharged from the army in 1946, Corporal Shantz had grown to 5 feet 6½ and weighed 139 pounds. He returned home to work at the saw company in the fall of 1946. He played quarterback and punted for a Pop Warner League football team, but after he hurt his back he quit football for good so he would not jeopardize his baseball career.

In 1947 Shantz signed to play sandlot baseball for the Souderton (Pennsylvania). His Nibs team, in the East Penn League, rated equivalent to a Class B Minor League team. He went 8-0, and 1-1 in the postseason. In the championship game, Shantz pitched a four-hitter, hit a double, and scored a run. Fans held a Bobby Shantz Day and showered him with cash and gifts. Shantz's reputation spread. Admirers arranged a game against a team featuring Curt Simmons, another highly touted left-handed pitcher who had just signed for a large bonus with the Philadelphia Phillies.[12]

Fans from the East Penn League and their counterparts from the Lehigh Valley League set up the match game for charity. Bobby and his team from the East Penn League faced Simmons and his former team from the Lehigh Valley League.

A left-hander from upstate Egypt, Pennsylvania, Simmons had recently signed with the Philadelphia Phillies for $65,000 and had spent the last few months in Class B ball. The Phillies had called him up the week before, and he had pitched a complete-game 3–1 win, a five-hitter, over the New York Giants.

On the big day, October 6, 1947, fans filed into the stadium. The exhibition game benefited a memorial park, and all 2,500 seats were sold out. Shantz had injured his wrist playing touch football the day before. It was swollen and he had difficulty throwing. Manager Glick worked on the wrist and bandaged it. Bobby asked Glick to warm him up out of sight of the fans, and said that if he felt okay, he'd try to pitch.[13] The thought of disappointing the fans who had come to watch him pitch made him uneasy. After warming up for a while, Shantz was ready to call it quits. Glick, however, got an idea. He produced a book and told Bobby to rest his hand on a flat surface. To Bobby's surprise, Glick lifted the book and thwacked Bobby's swollen wrist with it. "Perhaps he figured I had something like carpal tunnel syndrome, and that the sudden smack would fix it. I don't know. But, it worked! I was able to go out on the mound and pitch."[14] Shantz won the game, 4–1. He allowed 5 hits, struck out 14, and walked 1. Simmons allowed 8 hits, struck out 9, and walked 3. Bobby and Curt later became good friends and golf buddies.

Scouts from all of the Major League teams admired Bobby's competitiveness but passed him up because of his height. Phillies scout Jocko Collins liked Shantz very much but felt he was too small for the rigors of Major League baseball. "He thought I had one heck of a curve ball but was just too small," Shantz told a biographer. "When he met me years later, he apologized. 'I sure made a mistake with you, Shantzy,' he said. I told him I didn't blame him, that I had doubts myself."[15] The Tigers and Browns offered contracts to play in the Class D Minor Leagues, but Shantz was not interested in them. Tony Parisse, a former Athletics catcher and Bobby's batterymate on the Souderton His Nibs, warned him not to sign a "D-Ball contract," fearing that teams that offered that wouldn't take him seriously.[16] Tony recommended Shantz to A's scout Harry O'Donnell, as did Souderton's third baseman, Bill Hockenbury.

O'Donnell signed Shantz to an "A-Ball" contract in November 1947. Bobby convinced the A's that his brother Billy was a good catcher and that they should sign him, too, as a part of the deal. At least he wouldn't be lonely in Lincoln, Nebraska, in the Class A Western League. Bobby was twenty-two years old and Billy was twenty. The A's accepted. Billy was soon sent down to Class C ball, but Bobby wasn't lonely very long. He went out on a date with Shirley Vogel of Lincoln, a student at the University of Nebraska, and they hit it off very well. They married a year and a half later. The couple had four children: Bobby, born in 1954, followed by Kathy (1956), Teddy (1957), and Danny, born in 1965.

In his first year of professional baseball, with the Lincoln A's, Shantz was the talk of the league. He pitched 28 games and went 18-7 with a WHIP (walks and hits per innings pitched) of 1.093, struck out 212 batters in 214 innings, and had an ERA of 2.82. In a game against Des Moines, he faced 32 batters and threw only 17 pitches for balls.[17]

After just the one Minor League season, Shantz went north from spring training with Philadelphia in 1949. He was sent down for more experience but was quickly recalled when another pitcher was injured. After a brief relief appearance on May 1, Shantz relieved Carl Scheib on May 6 against the Detroit Tigers with the bases loaded and none out in the fourth inning and held the Tigers hitless for the next nine innings, though he walked seven. In the top of the thirteenth inning the A's went ahead, 5–3. Shantz allowed two hits and a run in the bottom half of the inning, but won his first Major League game, 5–4.

Shantz finished his rookie season with a 6-8 record and a 3.40 ERA. In 1950 he was 8-14 (the A's were 52-102). For the first half of 1951, he was a so-so 8-8, then won ten of his next twelve games, and was the American League's most effective pitcher for the second half of the season. He was chosen for the American League team in the All-Star Game, but he didn't get in the game.

In his first three Major League seasons, Shantz improved from year to year. He was doing very well with a fastball, curve, and change-up, but he felt he needed another pitch. That pitch was the knuckle ball. Shantz had experimented with it since he was a boy throwing to his father and brother in their backyard.[18] Athletics manager Connie Mack had forbidden him to throw the knuckler in a game, but when Jimmie Dykes succeeded Mack in 1952, he told Shantz, "Throw the knuckleball. I am not Mr. Mack."[19] Shantz credited A's catcher Joe Astroth with helping him perfect the pitch. Some contemporary writers assumed that Chief Bender, the Athletics' great pitcher, who was working with Shantz at the time, helped him with the knuckle ball, but Shantz said in an interview in 2011 that it wasn't true. "Mr. Bender helped me to become a more confident pitcher, Joe Astroth helped me with the knuckleball," he said.[20]

Shantz also threw a few varieties of the curve ball. He was best known for his classic over-the-top curve that broke sharply down, and as much as a foot across. But he also threw a tighter-breaking curve ball and, on occasion, what was then called a "nickel curve," thrown more from the side than a regular curve, and which came to be called a slider. Shantz once said he felt the slider was dangerous to throw because if it did not move as expected, it would come over the plate and be easy to hit.[21]

Shantz had a breakout year in 1952. After eighteen starts, he was 15-3. By his sixteenth complete game, he had racked up three shutouts. A person's size was fair game back then, and sportswriters referred to him in terms like "the midget southpaw" and "toy pitcher." The press speculated that he could become the first thirty-game winner in eighteen years.

Named to the American League All-Star team for the second time, Shantz pitched in the All-Star Game, played that year in Philadelphia. He entered the game in the bottom of the fifth inning and struck out Whitey Lockman looking, Jackie Robinson swinging, and Stan Musial looking. Shantz wanted to see if he could duplicate Carl Hubbell's 1934 feat of striking out the side twice in an All-Star Game, but rain came and washed out the game with the National League ahead, 3–2.

Shantz finished the season 24-7 and was named the American League MVP with 83 percent of the vote. Five days before the end of the season, on September 23, he broke his left wrist when he was hit by a fastball from the Senators' Walt Masterson. Connie Mack had warned Shantz that batting right-handed and leaving his pitching hand "exposed" could result in just such an injury.[22] Shantz had tried batting left-handed but gave up the idea because he could not control the bat as well. The injury healed during the off-season.

Shantz started 33 games, completed 27, and pitched 5 shutouts. In 279 innings he struck out 152 and allowed 77 earned runs, for a 2.48 earned run average.

On May 21, 1953, pitching against the Red Sox, Shantz injured his left shoulder. A tendon had separated from the bone, and it was the beginning of three difficult years. His shoulder eventually healed, but it would require treatment for the remainder of his career.

Among treatment possibilities, a novel experimental surgery was proposed: a tendon would be taken from another part of the body to replace the one that had separated. Shantz rejected this and opted to let nature take its course.[23] Until his body healed completely, it was rough going. Shantz made only sixteen starts in 1953 and was 5-9 with a 4.09 ERA.

On Opening Day 1954, Shantz had a 5–2 lead over the Red Sox when he reinjured his shoulder. He pitched in only one other game that season. In 1955, the Athletics' first year in Kansas City, he was 5-10, and in 1956, in which he pitched almost entirely in relief, he was 2-7. There were occasional flashes of brilliance. On April 29, 1955, Shantz pitched a shutout, his first since 1952, before 33,471

in Kansas City to defeat the Yankees, 6–0. On April 19, 1956, in one of only two starts he made that season, Shantz five-hit the Tigers and the A's won, 4–1. After that, he experienced pain in his right side, and manager Lou Boudreau made him a reliever. Trainer Jim Ewell wrapped hot water bottles around Shantz's arm between innings to prevent it from stiffening, which helped for a long time.

Before the 1957 season, Shantz was part of a thirteen-player trade between the Athletics and the Yankees. Yankees manager Casey Stengel intended to use him exclusively as a relief pitcher, but an injury to left-hander Whitey Ford forced him to use Bobby as a starter.

While Ford was out and other Yankees pitchers struggled, Shantz, healthy for the first time in years, kept the Bronx Bombers in contention. He had a record of 9-1 at the All-Star break with an ERA of 2.25. He completed seven games and earned his third selection as an All-Star, though he did not pitch in the game. Bobby finished the season with a record of 11-5 and led the American League in ERA at 2.45. He started twenty-one games, completed nine, and saved five. He was awarded the first Major League Gold Glove Award given to a pitcher.

Yankees pitching coach Jim Turner advised Shantz to throw the side-arm curve less often because it consumed too much energy, and to follow through more on his fastball. Most of all, Turner harped on Shantz to keep his pitches down. He also taught him to throw the sinker.[24]

In the 1957 World Series against the Milwaukee Braves, Shantz started the second game in Yankee Stadium. He struck out the side in the first inning, but gave up a run in the second and three runs in the fourth, and was the losing pitcher in the Braves' 4–2 win. In the bottom of the second inning with the score tied 1–1 and two men on base, Shantz drove a Lew Burdette pitch toward the left-field corner, but left fielder Wes Covington made a miraculous catch. Covington snared the ball backhanded to end the inning and change the complexion of the game. Shantz pitched in relief in two other games as the Yankees fell to the Braves in seven games.

Shantz was considered one of the game's finest fielding pitchers, "the kind that managers dream of and so seldom find. He goes with the Brecheens, Burdettes, and Haddixes," broadcaster Mel Allen said of him during the 1960 World Series.[25] He won the American League Gold Glove for a pitcher in 1958, 1959, and 1960. Traded to the National League, he won National League Gold Glove Awards in 1961, 1962, 1963, and 1964. After the award began, Shantz won it every year he played. Only pitchers Bob Gibson, Jim Kaat, and Greg Maddux won more.

Shantz pitched solely in relief in 1960, appearing in forty-two games and posting eleven saves. The Yankees won the pennant and Shantz figured in one of the most dramatic World Series games ever played. He pitched an inning in relief against Pittsburgh in Games Two and Four. Bob Turley started for the Yankees in Game Seven at Forbes Field. Shantz began warming up in the first inning in case he'd be needed. Turley was roughed up early and the Yankees trailed 4–0 when Shantz entered to begin the third inning. He held the Pirates to one hit for five innings as the Yankees took a 7–4 lead. (During the 1960 season, Shantz hadn't gone more than four innings in a game.) Leading off the bottom of the eighth, pinch hitter Gino Cimoli got the second hit off Shantz, a bloop single to short right-center field. Bill Virdon followed with a sure double-play ball toward shortstop Tony Kubek, but the ball took a bad hop and struck Kubek in the Adam's apple. Kubek went down, unable to make the play. Dick Groat drove in Cimoli with a single to left field. Jim Coates relieved Shantz and the Pirates eventually went ahead, 9–7. The Yankees tied it in the top of the ninth, but in the bottom of the inning, Bill Mazeroski hit his famous home run off Ralph Terry to win the World Series

for the Pirates. Instead of becoming a hero, Shantz had wound up responsible for three Pittsburgh runs. Ironically, after Stengel lifted Shantz, Coates failed to cover first base on a ground ball hit to the first baseman by Clemente. It was the type of play that Shantz routinely made, and which helped to earn him eight Gold Gloves. Coates then gave up a three-run home run to Hal Smith.

Still, Shantz said that, while his fondest memories were of his early career with the Athletics, his time with the Yankees was the most satisfying, because the team went to the World Series three of the four years he was there—1957, 1958, and 1960.[26] He did not participate in the 1958 World Series because of an injured finger.

The 1961 season found Shantz pitching for his erstwhile World Series foes. The Major Leagues held an expansion draft in the off-season and Shantz was left unprotected by the Yankees. He was selected by the new American League expansion Washington Senators, and two days later the Senators traded him to the Pirates. Shantz began the season in the bullpen, but between May 23 and July 22, he started six games. In the first start he was out-dueled by Lew Burdette of the Braves, 1–0. Shantz was 6-3 as the Pirates finished in sixth place.

Another expansion draft was held after the season and Shantz moved again, selected by the National League Houston Colt .45s. On April 10, 1962, he started Houston's first-ever game, defeating the Chicago Cubs with a complete-game five-hitter. After each inning, trainer Jim Ewell placed a steam-heated pad on Shantz's pitching arm to keep it from stiffening. A week later, on April 17, he had a no-decision against the Mets, and on the 27th he lost a 2–1 decision to the Braves in what turned out to be the last start of his career.

On May 7 Shantz was traded to the St. Louis Cardinals for pitcher John Anderson and outfielder Carl Warwick. Reunited with his buddy Curt Simmons, Shantz pitched out of the bullpen in twenty-eight games, with a 5-3 record, four saves, and a

2.18 ERA with the Cardinals. He pitched a season-high six innings on August 26, 1962, to earn a win over Pittsburgh. In 1963 Shantz made a career-high fifty-five appearances with a 2.61 ERA and eleven saves. He was adept at shutting down the opposition and was brought into crucial situations at any time in a game. Left-hander Shantz and twenty-five-year-old right-hander Ron Taylor were the mainstays of the Cardinals' dependable bullpen. The Cardinals won ninety-three games yet finished six games behind the Los Angeles Dodgers.

In January 1964 Bobby's father died suddenly on a bitterly cold night. Bobby was playing in an alumni/faculty basketball game at Pottstown High School. The PA announcer had just told the crowd a car in the parking lot had its headlights on. Wilmer Shantz realized it was his car and ran out to the lot to turn off the headlights. He ran back to the gym, settled into a seat, and collapsed with a fatal heart attack, in Bobby's arms.

Taylor and Shantz were not as effective in 1964 as they had been in 1963. Taylor regained his 1963 form for a while, but Shantz, now thirty-eight years old, did not, and starting pitchers were pressed into duty for relief chores. On June 15 Shantz was dealt to the Cubs in the six-player trade that netted the Cardinals speedy twenty-five-year-old outfielder Lou Brock.

Bobby did not pitch well for the Cubs. The team fell out of contention quickly, and Shantz was sold to the Phillies on August 15. The city where he began in the Major Leagues was gripped in pennant fever, and then disbelief as the Phillies blew a six-and-a-half-game lead down the stretch and finished in a tie for second place, one game behind the Cardinals.

Shantz's finest performance of 1964 came on September 17 when he defeated the Dodgers' Don Drysdale, 4–3. He relieved Rick Wise in the first inning and allowed just three hits and one run in seven and two-thirds innings. However, by exhausting Shantz in long relief, Phillies manager

Mauch left his bullpen short-staffed and had to use a left-hander just up from Triple-A two days later with dire results: a game-ending steal of home plate. During the Phillies' epic ten-game collapse, Shantz lost to the Braves on September 26, giving up a bases-loaded triple to Rico Carty in the ninth inning. Three days later he made what turned out to be his final appearance in Organized Baseball, pitching two-thirds of an inning in relief against the Cardinals.

Shantz was asked to return to the Phillies for 1965 but instead retired from baseball. His odyssey ended with a career record of 119-99 and a 3.38 ERA.

After his baseball career, Bobby managed a dairy bar and restaurant in Chalfont, Pennsylvania, next to the bowling alley he co-owned with his former A's catcher, Joe Astroth. The bowling alley was sold in 1966, but Shantz worked at the restaurant until he retired in 1986. After retiring, Shantz golfed regularly at a course owned by his friends Curt Simmons and Robin Roberts.

In 1994 Bobby received the first of a number of honors in his retirement. He became the forty-first member to be inducted into the Philadelphia Baseball Wall of Fame. His plaque hung in Veterans Stadium, Philadelphia, but is now located in the Philadelphia Athletics Historical Society in Hatboro, Pennsylvania. In 2009 Shantz was invited to attend the showing of a newly discovered film of the seventh game of the 1960 World Series, but he declined to attend, saying, "I'd rather face a tough hitter with the bases loaded than speak in public. It's not my forté."[27]

In 2010 Bobby received two additional honors. He was inducted into the Philadelphia Sports Hall of Fame, and Pottstown High School renovated its baseball field and dedicated it, in his honor, Bobby Shantz Field. A metal plaque with a photograph of Shantz can be seen by the entrance to the field.[28]

Chapter 34. **Curt Simmons**

Edward W. Veit

AGE	W	L	PCT.	ERA	G	GS	GF	CG	SHO	SV	IP	H	BB	SO	HBP	WP
35	18	9	.667	3.43	34	34	0	12	3	0	244	233	49	104	5	1

Curt Simmons left the visiting dugout and was moving through the bowels of Yankee Stadium toward the visitors' locker room when a roar erupted from the Yankee Stadium crowd. Simmons knew the third game of the 1964 World Series was over, but he had given the St. Louis Cardinals eight solid innings, allowing only four hits. Cardinals manager Johnny Keane had pinch-hit for Simmons in the top of the ninth inning. With the score tied 1–1 in bottom of the ninth, reliever Barney Schultz was now on the mound. Mantle remarked to an exhausted Jim Bouton, the Yankees' starter, "I'm gonna hit one outta here." Mantle hit Schulz's first pitch, a knuckle ball, into the third tier of the right-field stands. Simmons nonetheless could take some pride in his outing; at the age of thirty-five, he had finally pitched in the World Series. He'd missed out on one when he was twenty-one, the youngest of the Philadelphia Phillies' 1950 Whiz Kids.

In 1946 and 1947, nearly every Major League club was interested in signing Curtis Thomas Simmons, a schoolboy phenom born in Egypt, Pennsylvania, on May 19, 1929. Looking at what he did during his high school years, it was easy to see why. He had led his Whitehall High School team to three straight Lehigh Valley championships, and the Coplay American Legion team to two state championships.

During his senior year in high school, in 1947, Simmons batted .465 with 2 home runs, 3 triples, and 6 doubles. On the mound he struck out 102 batters and gave up only 12 hits in 43 innings. He threw 2 no-hitters, 3 one-hitters, and 2 four-hitters. In one game he struck out 20 of the 21 batters he retired.[1]

The thirty-five-year-old Curt Simmons posted an 18–9 record with a 3.43 ERA. He specialized in mixing speeds and excellent control.

Simmons also played high school basketball and football, but his father wouldn't let him play football in his senior year. Curt was disappointed, but his father, Larry Simmons, didn't want him to jeopardize his baseball promise by getting injured.

Simmons played in the Pennsylvania American Legion All-Star Game at Shibe Park (later Connie Mack Stadium), striking out seven of the nine batters he faced, and was the MVP of the East-West All-Star Game, played at the old Polo Grounds in New York. (Simmons showed the author a photo of him flanked by managers Ty Cobb and Babe Ruth.) Simmons pitched the first four innings before Ruth moved him to the outfield. He singled and tripled for the victorious East team. Having made a similar move in his own career, Ruth advised Simmons afterward to give up pitching and stay in the outfield.

By the spring of 1947, three teams—the Phillies, the Detroit Tigers, and the Boston Red Sox—were still in the running for the left-handed schoolboy. About a week before his high school graduation, his father and Phillies scout Cy Morgan organized an exhibition game that pitted Simmons and the Egypt town team against the Phillies. The Phillies players were not happy playing on an off day, but their lineup featured Jim Tabor, Emil Verban, Johnny Wyrostek, Howie Schultz, Lee Handley, and Del Ennis. Unknown at the time, the twenty-one-year-old Ennis was the first of the Whiz Kids. Simmons would soon be the second. In the exhibition game he struck out the first two batters, Jack Albright and Johnny Wyrostek. The game was tied, 4–4, when it was called because of darkness. Simmons struck out 11, walked 3, and gave up 7 hits. His team committed 5 errors and allowed 2 unearned runs.

After graduation Simmons signed with the Phillies for $65,000, becoming one of the first of the postwar bonus babies. The Red Sox had offered $60,000, but Larry Simmons had offered to let the Phillies match the offer. (Before Simmons signed, the New York Giants offered him $125,000, but the Simmons family kept to its promise.)

Curt Simmons grew up during World War II and before Little League. "We would play pickup games on open fields and behind the schools until we were old enough for American Legion ball," he recalled. "Some kids had bats, we used tire-tap balls or some kid had a real ball. I remember us walking four miles to play another town. We didn't have coaching then—my father was working in a cement mill and didn't have time for base-

ball. Times were different. A lot of my stuff comes natural to me." He credited much of his success to his high school coach, Bud Nevins, who had been a catcher in the Cardinals chain. Simmons's American Legion coach, Sam Balliet, had advised him against signing a $150 contract with the Allentown Red Birds while he was a high school sophomore.

Simmons signed his contract with the Phillies on June 16, 1947, and was assigned to the Wilmington Blue Rocks of the Class B Interstate League, where he posted a 13-5 record. The Phillies called him up after the Interstate League season ended. The eighteen-year-old Simmons's first Major League start was the last game of the 1947 season, against the home run–hitting New York Giants in Shibe Park. Giants slugger Johnny Mize, who was tied with Pittsburgh's Ralph Kiner for the league lead in home runs, was batting lead-off to perhaps get more at bats. Simmons walked six but kept the Giants from scoring for eight innings, gave up a scratch run in the ninth, and won a five-hitter, 3–1, with nine strikeouts. Mize got a broken-bat single in five attempts.

Because Simmons was a bonus baby, he was allowed only one year in the Minor Leagues before being placed on the Major League roster. When shortstop Eddie Miller, who was picked up in a trade, saw Simmons, he commented, "Kid, you signed for more than I made during my whole career." Simmons stuck with the Phillies through the next two seasons; they could best be described as learning years. Pitching coach George Earnshaw tried to change his delivery. Simmons stepped toward first base and threw across his body, and the coaches thought he would hurt his shoulder. After going 7-12 in 1948, then 4-10 in 1949, he was told to return to his old delivery.

For the Phillies, 1950 was magic; all the pieces were in place. Del Ennis and Jim Konstanty, Granny Hamner and Willie Jones, Dick Sisler and Curt Simmons—all had career years. By the end of August, Simmons had won sixteen games and Robin Roberts had won eighteen games, and the Phillies held a seven-game lead over second-place Brooklyn. But the pitching faltered, and in early September the Phillies were on the verge of collapse. Then, because the United States was fighting a war in Korea, Simmons's National Guard unit was activated. Bubba Church, who had eight wins, was slammed in the face with a ball off the bat of Cincinnati's Ted Kluszewski, and Bob Miller (eleven wins) developed back problems and was never again effective. Russ Meyer and Ken Heintzelman were not the same pitchers they had been in '49, Meyer winning nine and Heintzelman only three. Nonetheless, the Phillies won the pennant with last-day heroics from Richie Ashburn, Roberts, and Sisler. Simmons finished the season 17-8 with a 3.40 ERA.

In the World Series, the Yankees swept the Phillies. Simmons was on a ten-day pass from the service, but he was reduced to the role of spectator after baseball commissioner Happy Chandler ruled him ineligible for the Series.

What would have happened if Simmons had not been called into military service? How would that have affected the team? Maybe the September swoon would not have happened. Maybe the Yankees' sweep would never have happened. Simmons said in March 2009, "Right after I had been activated (in 1950) Phillies owner and club president Bob Carpenter said don't worry, he was going to get me out of it—it never happened."

The Phillies expected to win several more pennants during the 1950s, but Simmons spent all of 1951 on military duty, and the Phillies slid to fifth place with a 73-81 record. "Not having Curt Simmons all year really hurt us in 1951," manager Eddie Sawyer said. But Simmons returned from the service in 1952 and, without the benefit of spring training, went 14-8. He was the starting pitcher for the National League in the All-Star Game, giving up one hit in three innings as his team got a 3–2 victory in the rain-shortened game. (Bob Rush was the winning pitcher.) Sim-

mons posted a 2.82 ERA and led the league with six shutouts. The Phillies won no more pennants in the '50s, but with Roberts a habitual twenty-game winner and Simmons winning fourteen to sixteen a season, they stayed in the first division from 1952 through 1955.

In June 1953 Simmons cut off part of his left big toe while mowing his lawn and was out for a month. Three weeks before the accident, he had pitched perhaps the best game of his Major League career, a one-hit shutout of the Milwaukee Braves. Bill Bruton led off the Milwaukee's first with a single, then Simmons retired twenty-seven straight batters, striking out ten. Simmons returned to the Phillies' rotation in time to pitch one inning in the All-Star Game, and he finished the season with sixteen wins and thirteen losses (3.21 ERA). Simmons said of his injury, "I always felt the effect of that accident was exaggerated." The Phillies finished tied for third with St. Louis behind the Dodgers and Braves.

In 1954 Simmons posted the second-best earned run average of his career (2.81), ranking third in the National League—though his win-loss record was 14-15, reflecting the team's 75-79 fourth-place finish. Roberts was 23-15. The Whiz Kids began to fade away; Dick Sisler, the hero of the pennant-winning game in 1950, was traded after the 1951 season.

Simmons slipped to 8-8 in 1955, with an elevated 4.92 ERA. He rebounded to 15-10 in 1956 and cut more than a run and a half off his ERA (3.36). Simmons more or less replicated his 1956 performance the next year (12-11). He started the 1957 All-Star Game and had back-to-back starts (May 30 and June 5) in which he pitched ten innings. By 1958 the Phillies were back in the cellar, and arm woes had finally come to a climax for Simmons. He won only seven games and lost fourteen. After Richie Ashburn was traded to the Cubs on January 11, 1960, Roberts and Simmons were the last of the Whiz Kids still with the Phillies.

Much of the Phillies' downward spiral was blamed on several factors: Simmons's inability to become a twenty-game winner; owner Bob Carpenter's refusal to sign African American ballplayers (Roy Campanella, Junior Gilliam, and Hank Aaron were available for the asking in 1947 and 1948); and the drying up of the farm system once the Whiz Kids were promoted to the big leagues.

Simmons missed most of the 1959 season, healing from a sore shoulder and elbow surgery. Throwing across the body had caught up to him. Even in his good years, his arm was sore after every outing. But he went to spring training with the Phillies in 1960 with his arm feeling good. "After a year away, I was pressing like a kid," he said. He started the 1960 home opener, but he gave up two home runs in the first inning and was lifted in the second inning. He had three more rocky no-decision outings, and then, after thirteen years with his hometown team, was unceremoniously released while the Phillies were in San Francisco. He got the news from Robin Roberts, his roommate. He got coach fare back to Philadelphia and was soon on the telephone looking for a job. The Orioles wanted Simmons to come to Baltimore for a workout, and the Pirates offered him a job in Triple-A Salt Lake City. Cardinals manager Solly Hemus, a former Phillies teammate, asked about his arm and Simmons said it was fine. Hemus urged Cardinals general manager Bing Devine to sign Simmons. Devine agreed, signing Simmons for $25,000—$5,000 more than the Phillies were paying him.

At thirty-one, Simmons said, "I'm a pitcher now, no longer a thrower. I can pitch to spots and I don't give in to hitters." Hemus placed him in the starting rotation on June 19. Simmons won seven games and lost four for the Cardinals with a 2.66 ERA and after the season was voted the Comeback Player of the Year by the St. Louis baseball writers. In 1961 he finished third in the league with a 3.13 ERA. In 1962 he defeated the Los Angeles

Dodgers twice in the last ten days of the season to help force the Dodgers into a pennant playoff with the Giants. In the first of those two games, he was making an emergency start against the Dodgers' Sandy Koufax after Bob Gibson fractured his ankle during batting practice.

In late 1963, during a 19-of-20 Cardinals win streak, Simmons was 4-0 with three shutouts. He finished 15-9. Then he became a big winner in 1964, the year of the Cardinals' surge and the Phillies' great collapse. He was 11-8 at the end of July, then finished with an 18-9 record. His final 1964 win was the last game of the Phillies' ten-game losing streak. He no-hit the Phils into the seventh inning while the Cards gave him an 8–0 lead; he won, 8–5. This win, coupled with the Reds' extra-inning loss to Pittsburgh, propelled the Cardinals into sole possession of first place. Against the Phillies, Simmons was 19-6 since his release in 1960, and in 1964 he went 4-0 with one no-decision in a game the Cardinals won. Besides Game Three of the World Series, Simmons also started the sixth game. After getting a no-decision in Game Three, he was the losing pitcher in Game Six, giving up three runs in six and one-third innings before the Yankees plated five runs against two of the four St. Louis relievers to win, 8–3. The Cardinals bounced back the next day to win Game Seven.

Hank Aaron, a right-handed batter, hit 6 of his 755 home runs off left-hander Simmons, but he told a sportswriter that Curt was the hardest on him. "Speed had nothing to do with it," Aaron said. "It was that motion of his. He would turn his body, give me a view of his backside, then he would throw and I wouldn't see the ball until a split second before he would let it go . . . then it come floating in like plastic."

Simmons slumped to 9-15 (4.08 ERA) in 1965 and was 1-1 in 1966 when he was sold to the Cubs on June 22 (joining old teammate Robin Roberts). Simmons won seven games and lost fourteen for the Cubs during the rest of 1966 and the first four months of 1967 before Chicago sold him on August 7 to the California Angels. He was 2-1 with the Angels with a 2.60 ERA, but he wanted to retire, be with his family, and help restore a golf course in Pennsylvania that he and Roberts had purchased; so the Angels gave him his release after the season. During a twenty-year career, he won 193 games and lost 183 with an ERA of 3.54.

Simmons made one brief return to baseball, as part of the Phillies' Minor League instructional staff in March 1970. He spent most of his post-retirement career managing his and Roberts's golf course, the Limekiln Golf Club near Ambler, Pennsylvania (Robin Roberts Jr. later took over the reins of the club). In 2011 Simmons and his wife, Dorothy (Ludwig) Simmons, lived next to a fairway of the golf course.

When they were young, Dorothy lived across the street from the Simmons family, and she and Curt went to school together from the first grade on. "I was shy," Simmons said. "We never started dating until after I was out of high school." They were married on September 23, 1951. The couple raised two sons, Timothy and Thomas, and a daughter, Susan. Curt and Dorothy celebrated their sixtieth wedding anniversary in 2011.

In 1968 Simmons was inducted into the Pennsylvania Sports Hall of Fame. In 1993 he was made part of the Philadelphia Baseball Wall of Fame, with a plaque in Citizens Bank Park. In 1997 Simmons was inducted into the Brooklyn Dodgers Hall of Fame in the outstanding opponent category. In November 2011 he was inducted into the Philadelphia Sports Hall of Fame.

Chapter 35. **Bob Skinner**

Joseph Wancho

AGE	G	AB	R	H	2B	3B	HR	TB	RBI	BB	SO	BAV	OBP	SLG	SB	GDP	HBP
32	55	118	10	32	5	0	1	40	16	11	20	.271	.333	.339	0	0	0

After stagnating at the bottom of the National League for much of the 1950s, the Pittsburgh Pirates showed some life toward the end of the decade, finishing in second place in 1958 and in fourth place in 1959.

They began the 1960 season with an Opening Day loss at Milwaukee. They began the home portion of their schedule with a four-game series against Cincinnati starting on April 14. After splitting the first two games, the teams closed out the set with a doubleheader on the 17th, Easter Sunday. Bob Friend pitched a four-hit shutout in the opener as Pittsburgh won, 5–0. In the nightcap, Reds pitchers Don Newcombe and Raul Sanchez pitched their team to a 5–0 lead heading into the ninth inning, but the Pirates battled back in the bottom of the frame. They scratched for a run and after Hal Smith's pinch-hit three-run homer, the deficit was just one run. Then shortstop Dick Groat singled to center field and left fielder Bob Skinner homered to right off Reds reliever Ted Wieand, giving the Pirates a most improbable victory. Besides providing the winning margin in the second game, Skinner enjoyed a wonderful day at the plate, going 4 for 9 with two runs scored and two runs batted in. Those Pirates fans who remained among the announced Easter Sunday attendance of 16,196 left Forbes Field happy after witnessing a different type of resurrection before their very eyes.

For many baseball fans, the arrival of spring brings the promise of warm weather and hopes for a pennant in the autumn for their heroes. But even the most astute Pirates fan could not have imagined how Skinner's game-winning blast would

Acquired in June, the thirty-two-year-old Bob Skinner hit .271 in fifty-five games. Pinch-hitting exclusively, he went 2 for 3 in the World Series.

foreshadow how the Bucs' season would end in October.

Robert Ralph Skinner was born to Ralph and Lula Skinner on October 3, 1931, in La Jolla, California. At La Jolla High School he earned two varsity letters in baseball and was named to two all-star teams. Ralph, his father, was a Spanish teacher at the school and coached track and field. After high school Bob enrolled at San Diego Junior College, where he played basketball as well as baseball.

Pittsburgh scouts Tom Downey and Art Billings signed Skinner to a contract with the Pirates in 1951. Sent to Mayfield, Kentucky, of the Class D Kitty League, the nineteen-year-old Skinner played in twenty-nine games and smacked 50 hits in 106 at bats for an amazing .472 batting average. Moved up to Waco of the Class B Big State League, he cooled off, batting .283 in ninety-eight games. His combined average was .326 with 87 runs batted in, 107 runs scored, 15 home runs, and 31 doubles. The six-foot-four, 190-pound left-handed-hitting first baseman showed patience at the plate, accumulating 86 walks against 52 strikeouts.

The United States was fighting in the Korean War, and Skinner was drafted into the Marines. He spent two years at the San Diego Recruiting Depot, where he played for the base team. Toward the end of the 1953 Major League season, Pirates general manager Branch Rickey told manager Fred Haney to check Skinner out when he got back home to the West Coast.[1] Haney's report on Skinner prompted Rickey to invite the young player, who was about to be discharged, to the big-league camp the following spring.

On January 4, 1954, Skinner and Joan Phillips were married. The next month, he reported to spring training at Jaycee Park in Fort Pierce, Florida. In 1953 the Pirates had finished in last place, fifty-five games behind pennant-winning Brooklyn. (In '52 they had also finished in last place, fifty-four and a half games out.) Whatever the team's goals were, Skinner, in his first spring training camp, hoped to make the Pirates' top farm team. "I hoped to do well enough to be assigned to New Orleans," he said.[2]

The Pirates were high on Skinner's ability. Rickey called him "absolutely the best natural hitter I've seen in many years . . . who gets an awful lot of power into his swings. He does not seem to go for too many bad balls." Rickey predicted, "The boy has a tremendous future."[3]

Manager Fred Haney concurred with his boss. "He's destined to be one of the great hitters in baseball," he said. "He has a wonderful attitude too. He doesn't try to be fancy. I asked him the other day how he got so much power in that swing and he said, 'I dunno, I just go up there and swing.'"[4]

Though all he had hoped for in his first big-league camp was to be assigned to Triple-A, Skinner performed well enough to make the Pirates' roster. On the team's way north he received a call informing him that Joan had been in a head-on car accident in Oklahoma. Bob went to Oklahoma to be with her and was relieved to find out that she had not been badly injured. He was able to rejoin the team the day before the season opened.

Skinner started 116 games at first base in his rookie year, hitting .249 with 8 home runs and 46 RBIS. Just over a week into the season, on April 22, he got four hits in a 7–4 victory over the New York Giants, the first of several four-hit games in his twelve-year Major League career. At season's end the Pirates found themselves in last place for the third season in a row, forty-four games off the pace.

In 1955 the Pirates decided Skinner needed more seasoning and sent him to the New Orleans Pelicans of the Double-A Southern Association. After eighty-six games he was leading the league with a .346 batting average, but his season ended when he broke his left wrist. When he reported to spring training in 1956, Bobby Bragan was the manager; he had replaced Haney after another last-place showing by the Bucs in 1955.

Skinner made the team in 1956 but was supplanted at first base by Dale Long. He played only twenty-four games at first and thirty-six games in the outfield, bouncing between left field and right field, and he even played two innings at third. Skinner, who had never played in the outfield before, spent the season learning the nuances of being an outfielder. Because of that defensive focus, as is common with many part-time players, he was unable to establish a smooth flow in his offensive game. He hit .202 for the season as the Pirates left the cellar and moved up to seventh place.

Left fielder Lee Walls was traded to the Chicago Cubs at the beginning of the 1957 season, and Skinner replaced him against right-handed starters. Although the Pirates were still struggling in the standings, they were forming a good nucleus of ballplayers. Bill Mazeroski and Dick Groat were becoming a terrific keystone combination, Bill Virdon was solid in center field, and Bob Friend and Vern Law were leading a young pitching staff. But the player who brought it all together for the Pirates was Roberto Clemente. He could run, throw, and hit for power and average — the complete player. The Pirates were on the cusp of being a pennant contender.

The 1957 Pirates were 36-67 when Bragan was fired on August 4 and replaced by third base coach Danny Murtaugh, who would enjoy a long managerial career in Pittsburgh. The new manager informed Skinner, "You're playing left field until you play your way out of it."[5] And 1957 became Skinner's breakout year. Showing he was the hitter Rickey and Haney predicted he would be, Skinner batted .305 and hit 13 home runs. Almost half of his 118 hits came after the patient Murtaugh took the reins of the club.

The Pirates had slipped back to the cellar in 1957 but finished the 1958 season in second place, eight games behind Milwaukee. Skinner led the team in batting average (.321), on-base percentage (.387), and walks (58), and was second to Groat in doubles (33, to Groat's 36). He shined in his left-field position at Forbes Field, leading the league with 17 outfield assists. Skinner was the starter in left field for the National League in the 1958 All-Star Game in Baltimore. He went 1 for 3 with an RBI in a 4–3 loss to the American League.

Skinner was earning respect from his teammates for his hitting. He was being compared to St. Louis Cardinals great Stan Musial as the best left-handed hitter in the league. Teammate Dick Groat rated him the best left-handed hitter in the league after Musial. "And I'm not so sure he isn't about up with Stan," said the Pirates shortstop.[6]

Skinner said his approach at the plate was simple: "My objective is to meet the ball in a level swing. Then it has a chance to go some place whether you hit it in the air or on the ground."[7] Murtaugh, true to his word, penciled Skinner into the lineup and left him there. It didn't matter to Murtaugh which arm the opposing pitcher used to pitch. "He's a hard-working kid," said the manager. "He took up handball to help him get the angle of playing balls hit off the wall and that big scoreboard in left field in Pittsburgh."[8]

The Pirates finished the 1959 campaign in fourth place, nine games behind pennant-winner Los Angeles. Skinner's average dipped some, but he still batted a respectable .280, smacking 13 homers and driving in 61 runs. Both figures were good enough for second on the team behind first baseman Dick Stuart (27 HRs, 78 RBIs). Skinner led the team with 78 runs scored. In a four-game series in Cincinnati in late May, he was 7 for 16, with 5 home runs and 11 RBIs, including a grand slam in the finale. The Pirates stayed in the hunt throughout the season, and as the calendar turned to September they were only five games out of the top spot. An 8-14 record that month, however, sealed their fate, and they finished in fourth place, nine games out of first.

The Pirates brought it all together in 1960, clinching the pennant when the second-place Cardinals lost to the Cubs on September 24. They finished the year with a 95-59-1 record. (The tie was a 7–7 duel with San Francisco on June 28 that was never completed.) Skinner hit for an average of .273, with 15 home runs and 86 RBIs, a career high. He was chosen to start in left field for the National League in both of that year's All-Star Games.

Skinner missed five games of the epic seven-game World Series against the New York Yankees. He went 1 for 3 with an RBI and a run scored in Game One, but he jammed his thumb when he slid head-first into third base in the fifth inning, and then was hit by a pitch in the seventh. After that he was replaced by Gino Cimoli and didn't return to the Pirates' lineup until the seventh game, in Pittsburgh. Down 7–4 to the Yankees in the eighth inning, the Pirates scored five runs to take a 9–7 lead. During the rally, Virdon was on second and Groat on first when Skinner laid down a perfect sacrifice bunt along the third base line to move the runners up. After the Yankees tied the game with two runs in the top of the ninth inning, Bill Mazeroski won the Series with a dramatic home run off Ralph Terry that gave Pittsburgh its first world championship since 1925.

Success did not last for long. In 1961 the Pirates dropped to sixth place, eighteen and a half games off the pace. They were in third place at the All-Star break, but they started the second half with a 3-14 record. For the third straight year, Skinner's average dropped, this time to .268. Groat batted .275, down from .325, and no starter won more than fourteen games.

In 1962 the National League expanded by two teams, adding Houston and New York. That season Skinner rebounded at the plate with a .302 batting average. He led the team in home runs (20) and walks (76) and ranked second in doubles (29) and RBIs (75). The Pirates improved as well, finishing fourth with a record of 93-68. But in 1963 the team was dismal, finishing ahead of only the two expansion teams. Skinner was not there at the finish, as he became the fourth regular from the 1960 World Series winners to be shipped out of Pittsburgh. Groat, Stuart, and Hoak had all left before the trade that sent Skinner to Cincinnati for pinch hitter extraordinaire Jerry Lynch on May 23. The *Dayton Daily News* summarized the trade with the following headline: "Reds Get Regular for Lynch the Pinch." "I've got to like this deal," said Reds manager Fred Hutchinson. "Skinner can play more for us—he can do more things. Jerry has done a great job for us, but I'd rather have a guy who can play every day. It's nice to have a good bench, but not at the expense of the regular lineup."[9] Skinner had a similar take on the swap: "You always have a soft spot for the first team, but I'm real glad to come to this team. I'd been playing regular, but the last few days Willie Stargell and Ted Savage had been in the lineup for me and Clemente. So I kind of had an inkling that something might be going to happen."[10]

Skinner played regularly at first, but as the season wore on he was sitting on Hutchinson's bench. He was in the starting lineup for only ten games from July 11 to the end of the season. Skinner hit .253 for the Reds, to end up at .259 for the season. People started to think that perhaps the Pirates were following the adage of trading a player a year too early instead of a year too late. Skinner dismissed these criticisms, instead putting the onus on himself to work hard that winter and report to spring training in top shape.

Now thirty-two years old, Skinner was a part-time starter for the Reds as the 1964 opened. Hitting just .220 in fifty-nine at bats, he was dealt to the Cardinals on June 13, 1964, for a career Minor League catcher, Jim Saul. At first the move proved to be a bit of a rebirth for Skinner. He was inserted into the starting lineup by Cardinals manager Johnny Keane. He was also reunited with Groat, who had come to the Cardinals a year earlier. But on June 15 St. Louis pulled off a blockbuster trade, acquiring Lou Brock from the Cubs in a six-player deal, and by mid-July Brock was getting most of the starts in left field. Skinner was once again relegated to the bench, starting only on occasion for the rest of the season.

The Cardinals won the pennant with a remarkable late-season rush, aided by the Phillies' collapse. In the World Series their opponent was again the New York Yankees, whom Skinner and Groat had faced when they were with the Pirates four years earlier. This Series also went seven games, with the Cardinals winning. Skinner didn't play in the field; in four pinch-hitting appearances, he went 2 for 3 with a walk, a double, and an RBI.

In 1965 Skinner was used primarily in a reserve role by new St. Louis skipper Red Schoendienst. He spelled either Brock in left field or Mike Shannon in right. "Bob's still a good hitter—and good hitters are hard to find," Schoendienst said. "He can jump off the bench after a long layoff and do a real good job with the bat. And he's still dangerous as a long-ball threat."[11] In 152 at bats, Skinner hit .309, showing his professionalism by being ready when called on. He also started in twenty-eight games in the outfield. In 1966, though, Skinner was used strictly as a pinch hitter, forty-eight times, and not once seeing the field in a defensive position.

Skinner was released by the Cardinals after the season. He managed the San Diego Padres of the Pacific Coast League, the Philadelphia Phillies' Triple-A affiliate, in 1967 and 1968. He led the Padres to the PCL championship in his first season and was named Minor League Manager of the Year by *The Sporting News*. (Skinner was inducted into the San Diego Hall of Fame in 1976.) When Gene Mauch, manager of the Phillies, was fired in mid-June of 1968, Skinner was promoted from San Diego to replace him. When Mauch was fired, the Phillies were in fifth place, but only five and a half games out of first place. It was believed that difficulties with Richie Allen, the Phillies' star outfielder and a consistent discipline problem, led to Mauch's sacking. Nevertheless, Skinner was pleased with the promotion: "The organization has been great to me and it's a real thrill and pleasure to be able to manage the team," he said.[12]

The Phillies posted a 48-59 record under Skinner's watch in 1968, finishing twenty-one games out of first place. The 1969 season was a frustrating one for Bob and the Phillies. Although Skinner said all the right things about being positive and about the team having the proper attitude, it did not take long for the inevitable clash between the manager and the star. Allen skipped a double-header in New York on June 24. He was suspended for twenty-six games and did not play until July 24 in Houston. In addition to the suspension, it was reported that Allen was fined $450 each game he did not play, for a total of $11,700. On August 5, Allen informed Skinner that he had an agreement with Phillies owner Bob Carpenter and that he refused to accompany the team to Reading for an exhibition game against the Phillies' Double-A affiliate. Skinner resigned a few days later.

"Now I know what Gene Mauch went through," said Skinner. "You can fine Allen and he just laughs at you. He negotiates with the front office, makes his own private agreement and it's like handing the money right back to him. I don't want to go on managing this club under the circumstances."[13] The Phillies were 44-64 when Skinner resigned. Bob Carpenter said that Skinner really resigned because the Phillies wouldn't extend his contract past the 1969 season, but Carpenter's assertion largely fell on deaf ears. An article by New York columnist Jimmy Cannon was headlined "The Richie Allen Mess—Skinner: Class Guy." Cannon wrote of Skinner, "He isn't working, but he goes voluntarily for matters of pride. He went down with style because he refused to maim his dignity as a man. There aren't many men in baseball who would make this choice. The world is short of them. And that is why there is so much trouble."[14]

Skinner spent the next thirty years in a variety of posts. He coached for the Padres, Angels, Pirates, and Braves from 1970 through 1988. In 1979 he was the hitting coach for the Pirates, who won the World Series that year. One of Skinner's projects in 1979 was Tim Foli, the Pirates' light-hitting shortstop. By getting Foli to hold the bat parallel to the ground and choke up, Skinner

JOSEPH WANCHO

helped him raise his batting average that season by forty points over his career average. Foli proved valuable in the second position of the batting order behind speedster Omar Moreno.

Skinner managed the Tucson Toros, Houston's Triple-A affiliate, in 1989 and 1990. After that he stayed in the Houston organization as a special assignment scout until 2009.

As of 2011, Skinner and his wife, Joan, resided in the San Diego area. They had four sons, Robert, Craig, Andrew, and Joel. In 2002 Bob and Joel became only the second father-and-son combination (George and Dick Sisler were the first) to be Major League managers, when Joel became the Cleveland Indians' manager.

Chapter 36. **Ed Spiezio**

John Harry Stahl

AGE	G	AB	R	H	2B	3B	HR	TB	RBI	BB	SO	BAV	OBP	SLG	SB	GDP	HBP
22	12	12	0	4	0	0	0	4	0	0	1	.333	.333	.333	0	0	0

Strength, quick wrists, an open, positive demeanor, and unwavering confidence made young Ed Spiezio an outstanding baseball prospect. Cardinals Hall of Famer Red Schoendienst once told *The Sporting News* that Spiezio was the "the finest looking young hitter" he had ever seen.[1] In five seasons with the Cardinals (1964–68), Spiezio played on three National League championship teams and two World Series winners. In his nine-year Major League career, he also played for the San Diego Padres and the Chicago White Sox. Called up to the Cardinals in late July 1964, Spiezio appeared in twelve games as a pinch hitter. He did not play in the subsequent World Series.

Edward Wayne Spiezio was born on October 31, 1941, in Joliet, Illinois. Located about forty miles south of Chicago, Joliet has always strongly supported semiprofessional baseball. His father, Edward Wayne Spiezio Sr., an ironworker, was an all-around athlete. "Everything from ping-pong to hockey to boxing," Spiezio told the *St. Louis Post-Dispatch*.[2] In particular, his father loved baseball and played semiprofessionally. He instilled his love of the game into his son.

According to *Sports Illustrated*, Edward Sr. put a catcher's mask on his son at an "alarmingly young age," and stood him at the edge of the infield. He then hit blistering grounders over and over to his son. A daily two-hour session in the batting cage was also part of the training session. His father pitched and provided a running critique of his young son's hitting. "Coil like a snake," he instructed young Ed, "and then when the ball is close, explode."[3]

Young Spiezio supplemented these on-the-field

Called up in late July 1964, Ed Spiezio appeared in twelve games. He played on three NL champions and two World Series winners with the Cardinals.

sessions with weight training and began seriously studying some of baseball's greatest hitters at the time, including Stan Musial, Joe DiMaggio, and Ted Williams. Late in his career he was spotted still reading over a well-worn copy of Williams's book on hitting.

As a youngster Spiezio usually led his team in hitting wherever he played. After high school, at his father's insistence, he went to college. After initially spending a year at the University of Illinois at Urbana-Champaign, he transferred to Lewis College (now Lewis University) in Romeoville, about ten miles north of Joliet.

Spiezio played two seasons at Lewis for College Baseball Hall of Fame coach Gordie Gillespie, who in 1993 passed USC's Rod Dedeaux to become college baseball's winningest coach. In 1962 and 1963 Spiezio was a spectacular hitter. He established several Lewis hitting records that still stood in 2011, among them the highest season batting average (.491 in 1963); the highest career batting average (.445 over two years); the most total bases in a game (13); and the most home runs in a game (3). The National Association of Intercollegiate Athletics (NAIA) named him a first-team baseball All-American in both of his seasons.[4] During the summer of 1962, Spiezio played for Winner, South Dakota, in the summer college Basin League and was chosen by the league's managers as the all-star third baseman.[5] In 1981, in his first year of eligibility, he was elected to the Lewis University Hall of Fame.

After the 1963 season Spiezio was signed by Cardinals scout Joe Monahan and got a $25,000 signing bonus. He gave a substantial portion of his bonus to his father, who in 1957 had lost a leg in an accident at work.[6]

Spiezio broke in with the Cardinals' Brunswick (Georgia) team in the Class A Georgia-Florida League, where he played fourteen games at shortstop. After the season ended, he went to Tulsa in the Double-A Texas League, where he played third base, and in sixty-four games he hit .265, with 11 home runs and 37 runs batted in. Eight of the RBIS came in a game against El Paso, when he belted two home runs (one a grand slam), a double, and a single.[7] In the off-season, Spiezio became a student again, attending the University of Illinois and majoring in accounting.[8] On November 23, 1963, he married Verna June Fretty.

In 1964 Spiezio started the season with Triple-A Jacksonville (International League), but after hitting .190, he was sent back to Tulsa in late June.

There he hit .360 in thirty-two games, and in late July, the Cardinals brought him up to the Majors. His first Major League appearance was as a pinch hitter. After an all-night trip from Tulsa, a sleepy Spiezio sat in the Busch Stadium grandstand before the July 23 game with Pittsburgh. St. Louis bench coach Red Schoendienst spied him and told him to get into a uniform. Manager Johnny Keane later put him into the game to pinch-hit against veteran closer Roy Face and his famous forkball. With his knees "knocking," Spiezio managed a soft fly to center field that was caught by Bill Virdon for the final out in an 8–5 loss.

At that point St. Louis was in seventh place at 47-47, nine games behind league-leading Philadelphia. The Cardinals appeared to be adrift. If the team continued to languish, there might be plenty of late-season opportunities for a top prospect like Spiezio to gain some low-pressure Major League experience by occasionally subbing for Ken Boyer, the regular third baseman. Instead, the Cardinals began to click and became part of the hotly contested pennant race, eventually winning the pennant when the Phillies collapsed. Within this new environment, the first-year player rode the bench. He ended up appearing in twelve games, all as a pinch hitter, and got four hits, all singles, in twelve at bats. He did not play in the World Series, but the players voted him a quarter share (slightly over $2,100) of their World Series money,[9] and he got a World Series ring.

Spiezio's prospects for making the Cardinals team in 1965 were slight—after all, third baseman Ken Boyer had been voted the National League's Most Valuable Player. But Ed finished spring training with a .515 batting average, and the Cardinals took him north to open the season.[10] (His hitting in Florida earned him the nickname "the Joliet Jolter" from his teammates.) Spiezio played in only ten games before being sent back to Jacksonville in mid-April. There he was plagued by a series of injuries, including a badly sprained ankle, a heel injury, and a fractured right thumb, and he hit only .221. "It was a tough year all around for Spiezio," Cardinals Minor League director Sheldon "Chief" Bender said. "But we still like his bat."[11]

In the off-season the Cardinals traded the aging Ken Boyer to the New York Mets for veteran third baseman Charley Smith. Spiezio started the 1966 season with Tulsa (now in the Triple-A Pacific Coast League). He played in 112 games and hit .301 before the Cardinals called him up in early August. Spiezio pinch-hit in his first five plate appearances, but from September 4 on, he started at third base in nineteen of the team's twenty-one remaining games. He hit his first two Major League home runs on September 11 in Pittsburgh off Bob Veale and on September 30 at the then new Busch Stadium off Fergie Jenkins. With the Cardinals he hit .219.

Charley Smith was traded to the New York Yankees for Roger Maris in 1967, but instead of going for Spiezio, the Cardinals moved right fielder Mike Shannon to third base. Spiezio spent the entire season with the Cardinals, who won the pennant and the World Series, but his playing time actually diminished. During the Cardinals' 161-game season, he played in 17 games at third base, 4 games in right field, and 2 games in left field, and pinch-hit 29 times, batting .210 for the season. He had one appearance in the World Series, grounding out as a pinch hitter in Game Six. Although he spent most of the season on the bench, he remained a positive factor in the clubhouse. An accomplished accordion player, Spiezio often played for his teammates. With teammate Nelson Briles, he played in a musical group that occasionally made public appearances on off days.

The Cardinals won the pennant again in 1968 but lost to the Detroit Tigers in seven games in the World Series. Again Spiezio made just one appearance, getting a pinch single in Game Five. His playing time during the season had dropped again. He played in twenty-nine games, pinch-hitting seventeen times and playing third base twice. He hit .157. In December, Spiezio and three other Cardinals were traded to the San Diego Padres, an expansion team that would begin play in 1969.

In his five years with the Cardinals, Spiezio played in 132 games and recorded a .205 batting average. He pinch-hit in 72 games and played 41 games at third base. Although he played on three pennant winners, he may simply have been in the wrong place at the wrong time when it came to being the Cardinals' regular third baseman. Spiezio acknowledged his dilemma after he went to the Padres. He told *The Sporting News*, "I didn't have a future with the Cardinals. Mike Shannon's going to be around a long time. I'm 27 and I need to play every day if I'm going to make any money in baseball."[12]

Spiezio began the season as the Padres' regular third baseman. On Opening Day he got the franchise's first hit (a home run) and scored its first run.[13] On August 6 Spiezio hit a walk-off home run off Steve Carlton to beat the Cardinals. (It was his only hit off Carlton.) He played a career-high 121 games and hit .234. Spiezio's .939 fielding average in 98 games at third base was one of the lowest in the National League, and his limited fielding range troubled the Padres. By the end of the season, he faced stiff competition at third as the team tried other players.[14]

Spiezio took the competition seriously and spent the winter in Joliet fielding ground balls in a local field house. His winter regimen succeeded, as his fielding range significantly improved. Though he started the 1970 season splitting time with others at third base, in mid-July injuries hit his competition and he regained his role as the regular third baseman. For the season, Spiezio played in 110 games (93 at third base) and hit .285.

After the 1970 season Spiezio played winter ball for the first time, for a team managed by Padres first base coach Dave Garcia in the Venezuela

JOHN HARRY STAHL

League. He continued to work hard to improve his fielding. By season's end was among the league's leading hitters and was second in fielding among third basemen.[15]

Spiezio held out for a salary increase before the 1971 season, but he ended his holdout by reportedly agreeing to a $25,000 contract.[16] During the season he was plagued by injuries, including a pulled muscle in his side, a hand injury, strained knee ligaments, and injuries from being struck in the face by a bouncing ball. He played in ninety-seven games and hit .231. *The Sporting News* reported that his season all but eliminated him as a candidate for a starting job at third base.[17]

The 1972 season began contentiously for Spiezio. The Padres demanded that he take the maximum 20 percent allowable pay cut. When he refused, they assigned him to their Hawaii team in the Pacific Coast League. Spiezio played in five games there and went back to the Padres. Primarily pinch-hitting, he played in twenty games before the Padres traded him to the Chicago White Sox in early July to replace third baseman Bill Melton, who had suffered a season-ending herniated disc.[18] He ended up playing seventy-four games, all at third base, for the White Sox and hitting .238 for the season.[19] It was his final Major League season. In March 1973 the White Sox released him. His last at bat was on September 27 and Spiezio finished just as he had started in 1964, by being the last out in a 4–2 loss to the Kansas City Royals.

Spiezio retired in March 1973 after a brief spring-training trial with the California Angels. In his nine-year career he played in 554 games and finished with a .238 batting average. He played in 395 games at third base and 19 games in the outfield, and pinch-hit in 147 games. During the 1972–73 off-season, he and his wife, Verna, opened Spiezio's Furniture Inc., in Morris, Illinois, about sixty miles from Chicago.

Ed's son, Scott, was born on September 21, 1972. Using many of the same drills his father had used with him, Ed played a significant role in Scott's development as a baseball player, and Scott had a twelve-year career as a Major League infielder.[20]

In 2002 Scott Spiezio's Anaheim Angels team won the World Series. Scott hammered a three-run home run late in Game Six to help the Angels roar back from a 5–0 deficit. Ed Spiezio was in the stands for the Game Seven 4–1 victory over the San Francisco Giants. After the game, a reporter asked how he felt. "This is better," Ed said, comparing the celebration to his in 1964 and '67. "When it's your son, this is definitely the best."[21]

Scott Spiezio continued his baseball career and in 2006 played for a second World Series winner, the Cardinals. When the Cardinals handed out their world championship rings before their first 2007 home game, Scott received his ring from his father during a ceremony on the field. They had become the first father and son to each receive a World Series ring from the same team. "It's a super special moment," Ed said.[22]

Chapter 37. Jack Spring

Jim Price

AGE	W	L	PCT.	ERA	G	GS	GF	CG	SHO	SV	IP	H	BB	SO	HBP	WP
31	0	0	.000	3.00	2	0	0	0	0	0	3	8	1	0	0	1

Starting pitcher and reliever, high school phenom, and long-term professional, winning Minor League manager, state championship coach, and honored administrator — Jack Spring left few stones unturned in a baseball career that spanned almost half a century. Although he played eighteen seasons, a few in the big leagues and many in Triple-A, the Baseball Hall of Fame may be out of the question. Nonetheless, Spring has been named to three halls of fame. And if there were a shrine for matchmakers, he'd be a candidate for that as well.

At age seventy-eight in 2011, Spring had lived most of his life in Spokane, Washington, a city that has turned out several top athletes, including Ryne Sandberg, John Stockton, Super Bowl MVP Mark Rypien, and, decades ago, Boston Braves pitching star "Lefty" Ed Brandt. Sandberg has been inducted into baseball's Hall of Fame. Stockton, who spent his entire NBA career with the Utah Jazz, is a member of the Basketball Hall of Fame. Spokane-area high schools have produced nearly two dozen Major League ballplayers, most recently southpaw reliever Jeremy Affeldt.

Spring graduated from Lewis and Clark High School in 1951, played a season at Washington State University, turned pro with the Spokane Indians (Western International League), and zipped through the Philadelphia Phillies organization to make his Major League debut in 1955. Before the lean left-hander called it quits in 1969, he had played all or parts of eight big-league seasons with seven teams. A starting pitcher in his early Minor League years, Spring became a permanent reliever when he reached the prime of his career with the American League's Los Angeles Angels in the early

The Cardinals were the third team Jack Spring pitched for in 1964, but he had time to pose for a team photo. (Photo by Allied Photocolor Imaging Center)

1960s. During his Major League career, he put up a 12-5 record with a 4.26 earned run average. Helped by a decade as a young starter, he won 107 Minor League games with 104 losses and a 3.53 ERA.

When Spring retired from professional baseball, following a final season with the hometown Spokane Indians, he went into teaching and coaching, spending his entire career at West Valley High School, a few miles east of downtown Spokane.

Jack Russell Spring, the last of three children,

was born in Spokane on March 11, 1933. His father, Ralph Joseph Spring, a Michigan native, operated a shingle mill on the city's north side. His mother, a Spokane native born Marguerite Russell, was the daughter of a brick and tile factory manager. Ralph and Marguerite had married on June 6, 1925. Their first child, a boy named Ralph Eugene, was born the next year. James Douglas followed as the family settled into the Perry neighborhood, almost right behind Grant School, about a mile southeast of downtown on Spokane's South Hill.

Jack was a toddler of two and a half when his mother died of tuberculosis on October 9, 1935. She was only thirty. Young Ralph, known as June, and Jim stayed with their dad. But Jack went to live with his grandparents, the Russells, whose home was just a few blocks up the hill. "My mom's sister, Aunt Liz, took care of me and pretty much raised me," Spring said. "When my dad remarried, he moved to Sandpoint, Idaho. I went along and went to school there through the fourth grade. Then my dad was divorced, and I went back to Spokane to live with my grandparents."

Surprisingly, Spring didn't play a bit of organized baseball until the summer following the seventh grade. "I played first base in the park league at Grant Park, right behind the school," he said. "The park director, a man named John Goodman, recognized that I threw pretty good. But I didn't start to realize it until my freshman year at Lewis and Clark High School. I started playing American Legion ball that summer. And the next summer (on July 27, 1949), I threw a no-hitter (against Sedro Woolley) for the Oscar Levitch Jewelers team in the state tournament at Seattle."

Four more no-hitters followed over the next three years, including another in Legion play. As a sophomore, in 1949, he was Lewis and Clark's second pitcher behind Curt Bloomquist, a hard-throwing right-hander who bypassed professional baseball for the insurance business and regional stardom in the semipro ranks. Lewis and Clark shared the city championship in Spring's junior season. The Tigers went unbeaten the next year, when Spring, first baseman Ed Bouchee, and catcher Bill Farr were the team's three best players.

Spring and Bouchee were on their way to the Major Leagues. Farr didn't play as a pro, but the Los Angeles Dodgers chose his son, Ted, with the eighteenth pick in the 1973 draft. The younger Farr, also a catcher, hit with power and had a fine throwing arm. A persistent shoulder injury forced him to retire after five seasons in the Minors.

Lewis and Clark's coaches recognized Spring's all-around athletic ability. And Spring considered Elra "Squinty" Hunter, the school's immortal basketball coach, his greatest influence. "I wanted to teach and coach because of my admiration for Squinty," he said. "He made a big impact on me." As it turned out, Hunter, whose career encompassed four state championships and twenty-one league titles, kept his young charge on more than one career path.

Bouchee and Farr were good football players. Spring had tried the sport as a freshman and didn't like it. But as his senior year began, coach Hal Jones had nearly talked him into turning out for wide receiver when Hunter happened by.

"You bird dog"—Hunter's favorite expression—"get outta here," the popular old coach told him. "Scouts are looking at you. Only one thing can happen to you playing football, and that's bad. So why don't you go shoot some baskets?"

Spring backed away from football, earned All-City honors for Hunter's 18-2 basketball team, and opened his senior baseball season on April 19, 1951, with a 4–0 no-hit victory over Rogers that included nineteen strikeouts. He made All-City again.

By then, Spring, Bouchee, and Farr were close friends. With matchmaking assists from Spring and his future wife, they became married friends for life. Spring recalled that "at the end of my freshman year, I was out at Liberty Lake, which used to have a resort out in the Spokane Valley. We saw these girls. It turned out they went to North Central High. I liked the looks of one of them and, somehow, I got her phone number. Finally, she agreed to go to a movie. Later, I lined Ed up with one of her friends, and then she lined up Farr with another friend."

Farr and Ollie Hart married not long after they graduated from high school. Bouchee and Joanne Brand tied the knot almost a year later on May 17, 1952. Jack Spring and Vona Lee McLean married twenty-five days later, on July 11, 1952. Like Jack, Vona had lost a parent as a child. After her father died, her mother, Naomi, married Bob Nolan, who owned a taxi company. The Farrs, the Bouchees, and the Springs remained married to their original spouses, and, although the Bouchees, longtime Chicago residents, retired to Arizona, the six of them continued to talk and visit as often as they could.

In the summer of 1951, Spring, beginning to fill out to six feet one and 175 pounds, and Bouchee, broad-shouldered at 200-plus, agreed to play baseball at Washington State. Spring also planned to turn out for basketball. Because high school graduates couldn't play Legion ball in those days, the two of them and Farr joined the City Boosters in the semipro Twilight League. Spring and Bouchee also hired out on weekends with Troy, Montana, which fielded a team for a series of annual tournaments held across the border in Canada. In August, Troy won the state American Baseball Congress tournament, earning a trip to the Western regionals in Watertown, South Dakota. "We both did well, playing against several ex-pros, and we won that," Spring said. "That put us in the nationals at Battle Creek, Michigan, where we played Kalamazoo in a series for the championship."

The best-of-five series went six games. After each team won twice with one tie, Kalamazoo claimed its second title in three years with an 8–4

victory. "I won the opening game," Spring said, "but my arm was getting tired. In the final game, I tried pitching again. But I couldn't do it."

Spring and Bouchee then took up their studies. Spring played freshman basketball. Both lettered in baseball, one of the sports that allowed freshmen to participate in varsity competition. Spring won four games and lost four. Bouchee hit .302 and showed some power. Scouts were watching. On June 9 Bouchee signed a Spokane Indians contract. Longtime Minor League pitcher Don Osborn, the new manager of Spokane's unaffiliated entry in the Class A Western International League, signed Spring two days later for $375 a month and 25 percent of any future sales price.

The nineteen-year-old former Lewis and Clark High School stars were well established by the end of the season. Bouchee made his professional debut on June 10. Spring pitched for the first time in the final inning of a 6–5 home loss to Wenatchee on June 16. He made his first start five days later, dropping a 5–1 decision to Wenatchee, and didn't earn his first pro victory until July 27, when he defeated Lewiston 11–2 in the second game of a doubleheader. Although Spokane had a veteran staff that included Western International League standouts John Conant, John Marshall, and Dick Bishop, Spring worked ninety innings and finished with a 6-5 record and a 3.20 ERA. Bouchee, the regular first baseman, appeared in ninety-eight games and batted .319. The Indians, who had won the 1951 pennant, finished second, six games behind Victoria.

That winter, team owner Roy Hotchkiss, presumably prompted by Osborn, signed a partial working agreement with the Philadelphia Phillies. The deal included rights to local boys Spring and Bouchee as well as shortstop Wilbur Johnson, a third-year professional player and a Gonzaga University student. Johnson, who became known as Moose, later gained fame as a scout for the Phillies and the Toronto Blue Jays.

By spring, Hotchkiss had unloaded most of his older standouts to make room for Philadelphia prospects. Future big-leaguers Stan Palys and Jimmy Command headed the incoming talent, but the 1953 Spokane Indians needed ten pitchers to win seventy games. Spring, who attended Gonzaga classes during the day, emerged as the ace and won fourteen of them, going 14-8 with a 4.02 ERA. Although he walked 94 in 188 innings, his 157 strikeouts made him second in the league behind Marshall, who struck out 165 while winning twenty-one games for Lewiston.

With the WIL expanded to ten teams, Spokane struggled through the first half of a split schedule and wound up sixth with a 29-35 record, eleven and a half games behind Salem. Nonetheless, the Indians (46-32) won the tightly contested second half by finishing one game ahead of Lewiston. Then, with three straight late-inning victories, they downed Salem in the best-of-seven playoff series, 4 games to 2. Palys joined Spring on the all-league team. Recalling almost daily reports of his impending sale to Philadelphia, Spring, anticipating his 25 percent cut, said, "I could divide almost any number by four." Ultimately, Hotchkiss received $30,000.

Spring, now an official member of the Philadelphia Phillies organization, leapfrogged Double-A ball to Syracuse of the Triple-A International League in 1954. He had a tough time, starting thirteen times and working sixteen times in relief. In 118 innings, despite a 3.13 ERA, he won only three games and lost ten.

The next season, 1955, he came out of camp with the big club, one of the extra men during the thirty-day period when teams could carry twenty-eight players. The Phillies opened at home, where Robin Roberts pitched a 4–2 victory over the New York Giants on April 13. "I was in the bullpen," Spring said. "In the ninth, they told me to warm up. I could hardly stand up, let alone warm up." Three days later, on April 16, the Phillies faced the Giants again, at the Polo Grounds in New York. Rookie starter Jack Meyer and reliever Steve Ridzik were raked for ten hits, five of them home runs, in the first six innings.

"I came in and threw two hitless innings and struck out two," Spring said, "It was quite a thrill. Unfortunately, the next time I pitched [May 3] was against Cincinnati. I came into a tie game with two men on base and two out in the sixth inning and got out of it. But, in the next inning, Ted Kluszewski hit a long home run. A couple of batters later, somebody else [Chuck Harmon] hit another one." Spring took the loss and spent the rest of the year at Syracuse. With nineteen starts among thirty appearances, he put up a 7-8 record and a 4.00 ERA in 135 innings.

In 1956 Spring, Bouchee, and Osborn were reunited at Miami of the International League. Bouchee had spent 1953 and 1954 in the army and had hit .313 with twenty-two home runs playing for Osborn in 1955 at Schenectady of the Double-A Eastern League. With Miami, Bouchee prospered on a weak-hitting club, but Spring was lost in the shuffle on a staff that included top prospects Don Cardwell, Turk Farrell, and Jim Owens, as well as the apparently ageless Satchel Paige. Spring worked only ninety-three innings as a starter and reliever and finished 6-6, with a 4.06 ERA. Paige—"Oh, he was very impressive"—was about to turn fifty, but he went 11-4 and 1.86.

"Don Osborn was a first-class guy," Spring said. "He was easygoing, quiet and he knew the game and how to handle men. He helped me learn what professional baseball was about and how to deal with the ups and downs. Around midseason, I had two or three bad outings in a row and I was thinking about quitting. Don told me that I was still a prospect and said, 'You're not going anywhere.' My wife helped talk me out of it, too. Then I had a really good year the next year."

Despite Spring's reduced activity, Boston selected him that fall in the Rule 5 draft. He pitched just once for the 1957 Red Sox, a one-inning mop-up stint at Fenway Park in a 7–5 loss to Baltimore. He faced three batters and struck out two. Within days, he was optioned to the San Francisco Seals, where future Hall of Fame second baseman Joe Gordon led a mixture of prospects, Minor League veterans, and ex-big-leaguer Grady Hatton to the 1957 Pacific Coast League pennant. Spring joined the rotation and compiled an 11-9 record with a 3.19 ERA. It was the league's last season before the Major Leagues came west.

Boston sent Spring to Minneapolis of the American Association in 1958. On June 28, after he had put up a 1-3 record in forty-nine innings, the Red Sox traded him to Washington for reliever Bud Byerly. Spring started one game and finished two others for the Senators. Nursing a sore elbow, he was hammered for sixteen hits and eleven earned runs in seven innings. On July 11 the Senators sent him back to Boston. Several days later, the Red Sox traded Spring again, to Cleveland. The Indians farmed him out to the San Diego Padres of the PCL, where he was used as a starter. However, he completed only forty-eight innings for a 2-1 record.

Before the 1959 season, Cleveland shuffled Spring off to Dallas, which had joined the American Association with an eye toward attracting a Major League franchise. Spring stayed three years. In 1959 he responded with his finest season as a starter. On a losing club, he embellished a 15-13 record with a 2.87 ERA, twelve complete games, and six shutouts. At one stretch, he surrendered only three runs in fifty-one innings.

The franchise was renamed Dallas–Fort Worth in 1960. On March 10 the Kansas City Athletics acquired Spring's contract as part of a new working agreement. He had arm trouble and struggled to a 5-11 record. In 1961 the expansion Los Angeles Angels became the parent club. Spring recovered to go 8-7 in twenty-three starts, and in August, in his tenth professional season, he found himself back in the Major Leagues. After nine appearances, with one start, he made his second start on September 4 in the first game of a doubleheader at Kansas City. He pitched into the eighth inning and came away a 4–3 winner. Six days later, at Wrigley Field in Los Angeles, he beat the Chicago White Sox by the same score. His final start, at Chicago on September 16, resulted in an 11–4 victory, and he finished the season 3-0, with a 4.26 ERA.

The 1962 season was extraordinary. The Angels, eighth in their inaugural campaign, moved into newly constructed Chavez Ravine (Dodger Stadium) and improved to 86-76.

"We finished third with a bunch of guys rejected by somebody else," Spring said. "Just being part of the group stands out. . . . Leon Wagner, Albie Pearson, Dean Chance, Bo Belinsky, Ken McBride, Tom Morgan, Ryne Duren, and Earl Averill. We were really a close group and had a lot of fun, a camaraderie like I'd never seen in pro baseball before." Working exclusively in relief, Spring threw sixty-five innings in fifty-seven games and had a 4-2 record. Five relievers shared thirty-six saves. He had six of them.

Spring fondly recalls his first American League outing in New York. It was Tuesday, May 22. "I remember coming out of the bullpen at old Yankee Stadium," he said. "And I heard Bob Sheppard saying 'Now coming in to pitch for the Angels . . . is number 41 . . . Jack Spring.' And I thought, 'That's me.'" He went two and one-third scoreless innings in a game eventually won by the Yankees 2–1 in twelve innings.

"Among managers, Bill Rigney was my No. 1," Spring said. "He liked me, everybody knew their role, and he treated everybody alike. It didn't matter if you were a star or the last guy on the bench." Spring regarded Joe Gordon and Don Osborn, who spent several years as pitching coach for the Pittsburgh Pirates, as his other favorites.

In 1963 the Angels skidded back down the standings. Rigney mostly employed Spring as a situational reliever, often facing just one or two left-handed batters. Spring appeared in forty-five games but pitched only thirty-eight and one-third innings with a 3-0 record. "A guy [Brent P. Kelley] wrote that I was among the first to pitch more games than I had innings," he said. "Now, almost every team has a pitcher like that."

Spring told Kelley, in an interview for his book *The San Francisco Seals, 1946–57*, that Rigney had made a wise choice by moving him permanently to the bullpen. "I guess I wish that I would have made the transition sooner. Maybe I would have reached the major leagues sooner than I did and gotten in more years than I did. And I found out, kind of by accident, that I could pitch almost every day."

The 1964 season was barely three weeks old when the Angels sold Spring to the Chicago Cubs. Spring pitched two perfect innings in a lopsided loss to the New York Mets on May 26. Otherwise, he usually pitched less than an inning and, on June 15 the Cubs sent him to St. Louis in what has come to be regarded as one of baseball's most lopsided trades. The Cardinals also received outfielder Lou Brock and little-used pitcher Paul Toth in exchange for former twenty-game winners Ernie Broglio and Bobby Shantz and outfielder Doug Clemens. In time, Brock was elected to the Hall of Fame. Broglio and Shantz, it turned out, were near the end of their careers.

"When the trade was made, I was home in Chicago," Spring said. "My wife called out to me that they're talking about it on the TV. Brock and I flew to Houston, where the game had already started. I went to the bullpen. They told me to warm up and go into the game. The catcher was Tim McCarver. I got to the mound, and he said, 'Hi, Jack. I'm Tim. What do you throw?'"

Although the Cardinals defeated the New York Yankees that fall in the World Series, Spring wasn't with them. That first outing against the Colt .45s resulted in four runs, three unearned. His second, a two-inning stint in St. Louis against San Fran-

cisco, ended with five unearned runs. After that, Spring said, the Cards wanted to send him to Triple-A Jacksonville. He didn't want to go that far from home, refused to report, and moved his family back to Spokane. On July 9 the Cardinals sold his contract. "I was home about 10 days, when I got a call from the Angels. They had a farm team in Hawaii and wanted to beef the team up. I finished out the season and had a very good year."

After posting a 3-3 record and a 2.11 ERA, Spring went to Seattle, where the Angels relocated their Pacific Coast League affiliate in 1965. Then California sold him to Cleveland on June 14. This time, unlike 1958, Spring pitched for the Indians. He earned his final Major League victory on June 27, working five scoreless innings to complete a fifteen-inning, 10–7 victory over Kansas City. After fourteen appearances that resulted in a 1-2 record, Cleveland returned him to the PCL, where he finished the season with Portland. His combined PCL record was 5-3.

Spring spent three more seasons with the Beavers. In 1966 he pitched in fifty-nine games with a 4-1, 2.97 record. The next year, 1967, sixty-nine appearances produced a 10-5, 2.45 record. After a 2-5 record and 4.06 ERA in 1968, Cleveland assigned his contract to the American Association. Having returned to school at Eastern Washington State College, now Eastern Washington University, and not wanting to play far from home, Spring quit.

That winter Tommy Lasorda, who had been promoted to manage Spokane for the Los Angeles Dodgers, phoned to ask Spring if he was willing to pitch for him in 1969. Seventeen years after he started, Jack rejoined the hometown team. He put up a 5-6 record with thirteen saves for a group of prospects that included Bill Buckner, Bobby Darwin, Von Joshua, Fred Norman, and Bobby Valentine. "I could have played in 1970," Spring said, "but I was getting close to graduation and needed to do my student teaching."

He spent the 1970–71 school year at East Valley High School, close to the nearby Idaho state line, completed his degree work, and hired on that fall at West Valley, which had just fired its baseball coach. He coached for fourteen seasons, became the athletic director after the tenth, and remained so until he retired in 1995. As of 2011 Spring's 1978 club remained the only Spokane-area high school team to win a state baseball championship.

"We did it with a bunch of great kids and a lot of luck," he said. "We had a couple of good pitchers and good defense, and everything fell into place. In the championship game at Cheney Stadium in Tacoma, we beat a team [Capital] out of Olympia, 2–1. Shortstop Ron Soss, probably my best player, had the winning hit in the sixth inning." Kent Luedtke, a big right-hander whose father, Ed, a former West Valley star, had pitched for the Spokane Indians, threw a three-hitter.

Twice in his early coaching years, Spring accepted managerial jobs in the short-season Class A Northwest League. In 1972 he won a divisional title with Walla Walla, which finished with a 41-39 record. His 1976 Portland Mavericks won their division with a 40-32 record. Both teams lost in the postseason playoff series. Neither team included any serious prospects, but Spring managed actor Kurt Russell, who was his second baseman, in Walla Walla. Russell's father, Bing, who had become the owner, hired Spring to manage Portland.

Spring is a member of the Washington State Coaches Association Hall of Fame. In 1997 he was voted into the Washington Secondary Schools Athletic Administrators Association's Hall of Fame. And in 2005 he was inducted into the Inland Northwest Sports Hall of Fame in a class that included John Stockton.

Jack and Vona Spring had five children, daughters Vicki Spring Brown and Teresa Jordan and sons John, Mike, and Chris. Chris split a standout college baseball career between North Idaho College and Gonzaga. The Springs have six grandchildren.

Although he was diagnosed with Parkinson's disease in 2008, Spring continued to live an active life and followed baseball closely. Because he played during an era when players needed five years of Major League service to qualify for a pension, he was particularly interested in the 2011 decision to disburse up to $10,000 to nonqualifiers. Spring had a little less than four years.

"I certainly had a wonderful career," he said. "I don't think I would do it any different. I had a great time. I traveled all over the country, met a lot of wonderful people, and made a lot of friends. I didn't get rich financially, but I was very rewarded in other ways. It was a lot of fun."

Chapter 38. Ron Taylor

Maxwell Kates

AGE	W	L	PCT.	ERA	G	GS	GF	CG	SHO	SV	IP	H	BB	SO	HBP	WP
26	8	4	.667	4.62	63	2	31	0	0	7	101.1	109	33	69	1	1

A biography may be defined as a "remarkable odyssey through life and the lessons learned."[1] This description could have suited virtually anyone, but Bart Mindszenthy adapted it to introduce Ron Taylor before the Empire Club of Canada. Taylor's odyssey ranged from the University of Toronto (the only alumnus to play Major League baseball), to the Ontario Society of Professional Engineers, the Major League Baseball Players Association, and the Ontario Medical Association. His dry, self-deprecating sense of humor pervaded his multifaceted, half-century-plus career. When approached to deliver a twenty-minute autobiographical speech before the Empire Club in October 2004, Taylor replied, "Well, we've got the first five minutes covered."[2]

Ronald Wesley Taylor was not the first member of his family to lend numerous talents to a career that crossed geographical and interdisciplinary borders. His paternal grandfather worked in a variety of professions in urban and rural environments on both sides of the Atlantic. Walter Taylor and his wife, Elizabeth, immigrated to Canada from Ireland, settling in Flesherton, Ontario, as pioneer farmers. The Taylors eventually moved to Toronto, where Walter established a confectionery in the east end of the city. He took a second job as a streetcar driver for the Toronto Transit Commission in order to feed a family that grew to include five children. Tragedy struck the Taylor household in 1919 when Walter became one of millions to fall victim to the global influenza epidemic. Their son Wesley, at the age of thirteen, left school to support his family, accepting a job at Dunlop Tire and Rubber. Although his employer endured finan-

Ron Taylor pitched in two World Series games, four and two-thirds innings of hitless ball, earning a save in Game Four.

cial difficulties during the Great Depression, Wesley never lost his employment. Consequently, he remained at Dunlop out of loyalty for better than fifty years. Wesley married Maude Evans, a Welsh immigrant with a noteworthy family legacy of her own. Her father, William, was a cavalry soldier during the Boer War who fought the Battle of Mafeking under Colonel Robert Baden-Powell. After he died, his widow, Emily, led the family to immigrate to Canada — "their intended destination was Australia but they missed the ship."[3]

Ron Taylor was born on December 13, 1937,

a brother to older sister Carole.[4] He was raised in the north end of Toronto, joining the Leaside Baseball Association at the age of eight.[5] Although he was a natural left-hander, his mother feared that young Ron would suffer cardiovascular ailments from extensive use of his left arm, and insisted that he learn to pitch right-handed — "Insist? She tied my left hand behind my back!"[6] He played at Talbot Park, a facility of unusual configurations. As only 275 feet separated home plate from the left-field fence, commuter traffic on Eglinton Avenue often saw windows fall prey to home run balls. Meanwhile, a baseball could travel 400 feet to right field and remain in fair territory. Worse yet, there were two light standards in play. As Howie Birnie, longtime president of the Leaside Baseball Association, once remarked, "You have to be part mountain goat to play here."[7] To play there, candidates were required to either live in Leaside or be enrolled at St. Anselm Catholic School. Under ordinary circumstances, Taylor would have been disqualified. Had the school's recreational director, Phil Stein, not made an exception for Taylor, he might never have developed into a professional baseball player.

By 1954 Taylor had graduated to the Metropolitan Motors Club, where at sixteen he managed to baffle twenty-one-year-old hitters.[8] Often attending Taylor's games was Chester Dies, a sheet-metal worker and part-time scout for the Cleveland Indians. Despite Dies's rave reviews over Taylor's performances, his telephone calls to the Indians' area scout remained unanswered. Consequently, Dies took Taylor to Cleveland for an uninvited tryout at Municipal Stadium, even paying for the young pitcher's train ticket.[9] Although initially admonished for bringing a prospect without an invitation, Dies ultimately received permission for Taylor to throw in the bullpen.[10] Pitching coach Mel Harder, impressed by what he saw, invited Taylor to return the following day.[11] This time, he pitched to Al Lopez, the Indians manager, who

Taylor appeared in sixty-three games posting a 7–9 record with a 4.62 ERA. He relieved Roger Craig in Game Five of the World Series and pitched three scoreless innings.

had begun his career catching Walter Johnson some three decades earlier. Impressed, Lopez and Minor League director Laddie Placek offered Taylor a contract on the spot, signing the pitcher for $4,000, the maximum bonus allowed at that time without roster restrictions.[12] An airman with the Royal Canadian Air Force (Auxiliary 411) fighter squadron, Taylor had considered training to become a pilot until receiving his offer from the Indians.

Now eighteen, Taylor attended his first training camp with the Indians in 1956. Out of 250 players, he was assigned uniform No. 247.[13] Bewildered, he later remarked that "I knew that 'T' was low in the alphabet, but not that low."[14] Taylor was befriended by a Cleveland farmhand who wore No. 9, outfielder Roger Maris. Reporting to Daytona Beach of the Florida State League for the 1956 season, he went 17-11 with a 3.13 ERA in

MAXWELL KATES

227 innings. After the season Taylor decided he wanted to return to school to pursue his education. Although Placek offered to register him at the Case Institute in Cleveland, Taylor decided that he would rather return to Canada to finish grade 13 before enrolling as an engineering student at the University of Toronto. According to his plan, Taylor would pitch only during the summer, missing spring training for the duration of his education. Placek, though reluctant to accept, agreed to Taylor's conditions.[15]

By 1961 Taylor had risen through Cleveland's farm system, pitching for Fargo-Moorhead, Minot, Reading, and Salt Lake City. Pitching for Minot, he was one of the Northern League's three premier pitchers, along with Gaylord Perry and Bo Belinsky. Perhaps more important, he graduated from the University of Toronto in 1961 at the top in his class of engineers.[16] After the season Taylor asked Walter "Hoot" Evers, Cleveland's farm director, to guarantee him a spot on the rotation at Salt Lake City along with an invitation to the Major League training camp. Evers agreed and at spring training in Tucson, Taylor pitched twenty-three scoreless innings to earn a spot in the Major League rotation.[17]

Starting the second game of the 1962 season, Taylor faced Boston's Bill Monbouquette at Fenway Park on April 11. Through eleven innings, spectators saw nothing but zeroes on the Green Monster scoreboard as both pitchers were hurling extra-inning shutouts. However, Taylor surrendered a lead-off triple to Carl Yastrzemski in the bottom of the twelfth. After two intentional walks, he surrendered a grand slam to Carroll Hardy. Despite the loss, the *Cleveland Plain Dealer* called Taylor's performance "one of the most remarkable pitching performances in all baseball history."[18] He beat Dean Chance of the Los Angeles Angels, 3–2, on April 24 but was demoted to Jacksonville a month later. Tim McCarver, who caught for the Atlanta Crackers that season, described Taylor as "lights out that year." Pitching every three days, he won twelve and lost four with an ERA of 2.62 as Jacksonville won the International League pennant. Little did either Taylor or McCarver realize that both would return to the Major Leagues in 1963 — as teammates.

After the 1962 season, Taylor pitched for the San Juan Senadores of the Puerto Rican Winter League. When St. Louis Cardinals manager Johnny Keane saw him pitch, he immediately telephoned general manager Bing Devine. On the grounds that the Canadian hurler was "not afraid of the bat," Keane insisted on arranging a deal for him.[19] On December 15, 1962, Taylor was traded with infielder Jack Kubiszyn to the Cardinals for first baseman Fred Whitfield. Developing a sinker-slider to complement his fastball, Taylor won nine games and saved eleven with a 2.84 ERA in Stan Musial's farewell tour of the Major Leagues. His first save of the 1963 season was at the expense of the eventual world champion Los Angeles Dodgers on April 28. He struck out Frank Howard and got Ron Fairly to fly out to right before giving up a single to John Roseboro and fanning Moose Skowron to end the game. Meanwhile, Taylor returned to Toronto in the winter to pursue work as an electrical engineer.

Taylor remained productive in 1964, winning eight games in sixty-three appearances as the Cardinals won their first National League pennant in eighteen years. His quiet and reserved personality made him a contrast from a clubhouse full of future broadcasters. However, he was a fierce competitor on the mound as the situation warranted — as he demonstrated in Game Four of the 1964 World Series. Already trailing the New York Yankees 2 games to 1, the Cardinals appeared headed for another defeat when starter Ray Sadecki surrendered three runs in one-third of an inning. After Roger Craig pitched solidly in relief, the Cardinals claimed the lead in the sixth inning on a grand slam by Ken Boyer. Now leading by one run, manager Keane summoned Taylor from the bullpen. Taylor held the lead by pitching four no-hit innings against the Yankees, whose lineup included former Minor League teammate Roger Maris. The walk Taylor surrendered to Mickey Mantle in the eighth inning represented the only base runner he allowed. A loss would have given the Yankees a 3–1 Series lead, but instead the Cardinals forced a tie. Mike Shannon, one of the future broadcasters on the Cardinals, later said, "We shut down that powerful Yankee club. If we don't win that game, I don't even know if we're going back to St. Louis."[20] Back to St. Louis the Series went, where Bob Gibson pitched his legendary complete-game win in Game Seven to secure the championship.

The defending world champions disappointed in 1965, languishing in seventh place at the June 15 trading deadline. Satisfying the need for a left-handed reliever, general manager Bob Howsam acquired Hal Woodeshick from the Houston Astros at a cost of Taylor and pitcher Mike Cuellar. Immediately, Taylor knew it was "a bad deal for both clubs."[21] Unhappy in Houston, he saw his ERA soar to an astronomical 5.71 in 1966. After the season, his contract was sent outright to Oklahoma City. As he told Maury Allen of the *New York Post* years later, he became frustrated by the direction of his baseball career.

"I felt I wasn't used properly. I never had a chance to pitch, and in order to be effective, I needed to pitch a lot," Taylor said.[22] Meanwhile, Bing Devine had left the Cardinals to become general manager of the New York Mets. "Bing . . . asked me if I could pitch. I told him I was sound — 'Get me out of here!' He said that he thought he could make a deal."[23] The following day, February 10, 1967, Taylor's contract was purchased by the Mets' Triple-A affiliate at Jacksonville. A change of scenery may have been just what the doctor ordered for Taylor. He earned a spot on the Opening Day roster for the Mets in 1967, leading the team with eight saves in fifty games while setting a personal mark with a 2.34 earned run average. He allowed only one home run all season, to Pittsburgh's Manny Jimenez on April 17. (Taylor's homerless streak lasted ninety-two innings, well into the 1968 season, when he allowed a ninth-inning blast by the Dodgers' Ted Savage on June 23.)

"In New York, I really found a home. I worked hard and I pitched well," Taylor said.[24] The Mets, meanwhile, were ensconced as the doormat of the National League. The team lost 101 games in 1967 to finish in last place for the fifth time in its six-year history. "When there was a rainout, half the team held a victory party," Taylor said.[25] The Mets bade the cellar farewell in 1968 when they signed Gil Hodges as their manager. Although a record of 73-89 typically goes unnoticed, for the Mets in 1968 it was one small step in the right direction. Taylor contributed by tying Jack Hamilton's club saves record with thirteen and finished fourth among senior circuit hurlers with fifty-eight appearances.

After the 1968 season, Taylor joined several Major Leaguers on a tour of military hospitals in Guam, the Philippines, and Okinawa. The following year, he traveled to Saigon to visit soldiers in war-ravaged South Vietnam after the Tet Offensive. This second tour offered him "the chance to meet doctors and talk to them about what they were doing."[26]

As the Mets prepared to entertain the expansion Montreal Expos on Opening Day of 1969, the franchise had never finished higher than ninth place or won more than seventy-three games. Moreover, Taylor's two appearances in the 1964 World Series with the Cardinals marked the extent of postseason play among his teammates. Bookmakers in Las Vegas gave the Mets 100-to-1 odds to win the pennant, while in the Shea Stadium clubhouse, only Jerry Grote foresaw his team as contenders.[27] Ignoring the disbelievers, Gil Hodges assigned specific roles to his entire roster. Through a combination of natural talent and proper communication, Hodges foresaw his players contending in 1969.

"Everybody knew what their role was," Taylor remembered. "Everybody was quite happy with their role—even more so when we started to win."[28] Taylor was consistent once again, pitching in fifty-nine games out of the bullpen. In a dozen appearances from May 30 to June 24, he worked fifteen scoreless innings. By this point, the Mets were surprising even baseball experts as they stood in second place with a 38-28 record, five games behind the division-leading Chicago Cubs. While his 2.72 ERA was virtually identical to his 1968 record, Taylor went 9-4 for a team that won one hundred games to earn a National League East division title.

Taylor pitched two scoreless innings in Game One of the NLCS, preserving Tom Seaver's 9–5 victory over the Braves and earning the first save in League Championship Series history. He came on the next day to get the last out in the fifth inning and also threw a scoreless sixth to earn the win. Taylor, who was familiar with the Atlanta lineup, offered the following anecdote from the regular season that featured two of their Hall of Fame sluggers.

"Orlando Cepeda's in the on-deck circle and Henry's up. So Hodges comes up to me and says, 'I want you to put Henry on and face Cepeda.'"

Taylor, who had a history of trouble facing Cepeda, insisted, "No, I want Aaron."

"Hodges said, 'You *what*?' I knew he was angry. When he got angry, that jugular vein popped out of his neck. He said, 'You want to pitch to Aaron. You better get him out.'"[29]

Aaron grounded out to the infield.

After sweeping the Braves in the Championship Series, the Mets faced the Baltimore Orioles in the World Series. Taylor pitched in relief of Tom Seaver once again in Game One, limiting Baltimore to one base runner—a walk to Paul Blair—in two innings. Although the Mets were defeated by Mike Cuellar, Taylor's former St. Louis and Houston teammate, in the opener, they took a 2–1 lead in the second game. After retiring the first two Orioles in the bottom of the ninth, Jerry Koosman walked Frank Robinson and Boog Powell. With the tying run on second and Brooks Robinson at the plate, Hodges called Taylor from the bullpen to save the game and tie the Series at a game apiece.

"I got to 3 and 2 on him and they were off and running on the pitch; it was the worst possible situation for me," Taylor said.[30] In a classic case of role reversal, Robinson hit a grounder to third baseman Ed Charles, who threw the ball to Donn Clendenon at first for the final out of the game.

Taylor was sitting in the dugout at Shea Stadium four days later, on October 16, when Davey Johnson flied out to Cleon Jones in left field for the last out of the deciding Game Five. The Mets were world champions. For Taylor, the experience was both exhilarating and humbling: "After we won . . . we were riding down Broadway in that ticker-tape parade and the crowds were cheering and the paper was floating down from high above from those office buildings. I couldn't stop thinking that this was the path that MacArthur, Eisenhower, and Kennedy had ridden. I never felt so euphoric," Taylor said.[31]

Taylor remained a mainstay in Hodges's bullpen for two more seasons, becoming the Mets' first-ever Opening Day winner, over the Pirates at Forbes Field in 1970. The Canadian's contract was sold to Montreal on October 20, 1971, but rather than wearing the Expos' tricolor cap, Taylor found himself dressed in the all-yellow double-knits of the San Diego Padres.

The Expos released him on April 20, 1972, five days into the season, without having appeared in a game. He signed with San Diego on the same day. Taylor surrendered five home runs in four relief appearances, pitching for the last time on May 14 in relief of Clay Kirby at Montreal's Jarry Park.

The final batter he faced was a Mets teammate only one season earlier—Ken Singleton. At thirty-four, Taylor knew it was time to call it a career.

If there were a chance of Taylor spending any more time in a Major League clubhouse, it would be more likely as a doctor than as a baseball player. During that road trip to Montreal, Taylor took a sojourn to his hometown for an interview with the dean of student affairs at the University of Toronto medical school. Hank Aaron and Orlando Cepeda now paled by comparison as Taylor faced the dean in an interview.

"You graduated in engineering in 1961. What have you been doing for the past 11 years?"

"Playing major league baseball."

"What's *that*?"

Taylor knew he was in trouble. After providing a response, the associate dean explained what the odds were against the former world champion.

"We very rarely accept people over 30. We don't want people changing careers."

"My career died a natural death," Taylor pleaded. "My arm went dead."

The dean then asked to see his transcript. Scanning the grades, he turned to Taylor and asked, "Are these *yours*? With these grades, if you were 25, you'd be in. What I suggest to you is to go back and enroll in an honors course in all the pre-med courses—organic chemistry, microbiology. If you get the same grades, we'll consider you."

Taylor asked, "What are the odds?"

"Depends on the personality of the registrar. About 50-50."

"Those sound like good odds to me."

"I moved back into my old bedroom. I was single at the time and didn't have any responsibilities," Taylor said.[32] His daily routine would appear draconian even to a Rhodes scholar. He attended classes daily from 8 a.m. to 5 p.m., would sleep for four hours, and study until 7 the next morning.

Asked to produce references, Taylor offered a glowing letter of recommendation from Mets president and Montreal native M. Donald Grant. Excelling academically as expected, Taylor overcame all probabilities as his candidacy was accepted. He spent the summer of 1973 managing the Lethbridge Lakers of the semiprofessional Alberta Major League. Under Taylor's tutelage, the Lakers advanced to represent Alberta at the national finals held in New Brunswick. Taylor also returned to Shea Stadium that summer to make an appearance at Old Timers Day.

He remembered the astonishment of his classmates that a middle-aged student was in their midst. As he told members of a baseball class at Seneca College in Toronto, "They just assumed I was the maintenance man. They were looking for my tool kit."[33]

Hardly a janitor or a volunteer patient, Taylor persisted for four years and graduated from medical school in 1977. He was appointed team physician to the Toronto Blue Jays in 1979, and also pitched batting practice for several years at Exhibition Stadium. Taylor began a general practice in midtown Toronto, working six days a week, often exceeding twelve hours a day at the office. Two evenings a week, he operated the S. C. Cooper Sports Medicine Clinic at Toronto's Mount Sinai Hospital.

Mount Sinai was significant for Taylor on several counts. Not only did he practice there during his residency, but it was also where he met the mother of his children. Rona Douglas was a nurse when she met Taylor, and they married on September 26, 1981. Their oldest son, Drew, was born in August 1982, while younger son Matthew was born in April 1984. Matthew pursued studies in history and film while Drew decided to follow in his father's footsteps. Which footsteps? Baseball or medicine? After graduating from the University of Michigan, Drew was signed by the Blue Jays in 2006. He pitched at the Rookie League level for two seasons. He pitched in the independent Frontier League in 2008.

Although Ron Taylor's schedule left no room for hobbies, he amassed an impressive collection of rings over the years. They include his wedding ring, two for his world championships as a player, two earned as team doctor for the world champion Blue Jays in 1992 and 1993, and another to commemorate the All-Star Game held at Sky-Dome in 1991. However, pointing to the engineering ring on his left hand, Taylor said, "It's the only one you see." He was inducted into the Canadian Baseball Hall of Fame in 1985, and into Canada's Sports Hall of Fame eight years later. In 2006 he was inducted into the Order of Ontario by Lieutenant Governor James K. Bartleman for his work in medicine.

Into his seventies, he showed little inclination toward retirement. John Koopman of the Empire Club of Canada described Taylor's life as "a power of will." Before the era of free agency, Taylor served as his own agent. Without the deal with Laddie Placek, he would never have attended spring training. In the absence of a subsequent deal with Hoot Evers, his Major League career may have ended before it began. Finally, if his negotiations to enter the University of Toronto medical school had not succeeded, he would not have practiced medicine. His baseball career remained an important component of his career, which he explained as follows: "I might be able to name ten doctors in my graduating class and perhaps fifteen engineers. But I can name all my World Series teammates, both with the Mets and the Cardinals. The pressures we went through . . . when you win championships like those, you're like brothers for life. That how we are, we're all brothers."[34]

Chapter 39. Timeline, August 1–August 31

John Harry Stahl

August 1—REDS 6, CARDINALS 5—The Cardinals scored two runs in the first, highlighted by a double steal with Brock stealing home as White stole second base. Brock's steal brought his season total to twenty-three (ten with the Cubs). In the seventh inning, the score was 3–1 Cardinals when the Reds scored five runs. Pinch hitter Mel Queen's three-run home run was a key hit in the rally. The Cardinals also scored two runs in the seventh but left the bases loaded as Boyer struck out and White popped to the shortstop. Gibson's season pitching record dropped to 8-9.

August 2—CARDINALS 5, REDS 4—Deron Johnson hit two home runs and drove in four runs for the Reds, but the score was 4–4 in the bottom of the eighth. With the bases loaded and one out, Warwick hit a sacrifice fly off Reds reliever Sammy Ellis to provide the winning run. Taylor pitched a scoreless ninth.

August 3—No game scheduled.

August 4—CUBS 4, CARDINALS 0—Traded by the Cardinals to the Cubs earlier in the year, Burdette scattered ten hits while pitching a complete-game shutout for his eighth victory. Billy Williams hit a two-run home run in the sixth and Joey Amalfitano hit a two-run single in the seventh to account for all of the Cubs' scoring.

August 5—CARDINALS 4, CUBS 2—Surviving a shaky first inning, Richardson won his second game with relief from Humphreys. White hit a three-run home run in the fifth to key the Cards'

scoring. Brock, White, Boyer, and Flood each had a multi-hit game.

August 6—CARDINALS 5, CUBS 3—Groat went 3 for 4, scoring two runs and driving in two more. White hit a key double in the third inning, driving in two runs. Gibson won his ninth game with help from Schultz. Entering the game in the ninth with the bases loaded and two outs, Schultz struck out Ernie Banks to end the game.

August 7—CARDINALS 4, COLT .45s 0—Simmons pitched a complete-game, five-hit shutout for his twelfth win. White hit a solo home run in the first, and Brock's single scored two more runs in the fifth inning. Brock, White, Boyer, and Groat each had two hits. McCarver went 3 for 3 and scored two runs.

August 8—COLT .45s 4, CARDINALS 3—Houston scored two runs in the second and two more in the seventh to take a 4–1 lead into the bottom of eighth. Boyer hit a two-run home run in the bottom of the inning, making the game 4–3 into the ninth. With the tying run on third base and one out, reliever Jim Owens struck out White and retired Boyer on a grounder to the shortstop. In a rare start, Ron Taylor was the loser.

August 9—CARDINALS 8, COLT .45s 2—Sadecki pitched a complete game for the victory. The Cardinals had fourteen hits and continued their aggressive base running. They pulled off a double steal in the eighth when McCarver stole home as Shannon stole second. Brock also stole a base and Boyer was caught trying to steal.

August 10 — CARDINALS 2, GIANTS 1 — Gibson won his tenth game with significant help from relief pitcher Schultz and outfielders Shannon and Brock. On Lanier's single in the fifth, Shannon's throw nailed Tom Haller at the plate for the third out. In the seventh, Gibson gave up a home run and two consecutive singles. Although Schultz was greeted with a double steal, putting runners on second and third with no outs, he retired the side with no runs scoring. In the eighth, after two outs, Cepeda was on second base when Haller hit a ground ball single to left. Cepeda tried to score the tying run without sliding and was out on Brock's throw to McCarver. Schultz retired the Giants in order in the ninth.

August 11 — GIANTS 6, CARDINALS 3 — The Giants jumped out to an early 5–0 lead by scoring three runs in the first and two more in the third. Cepeda and Mays each hit two-run home runs to spark the scoring. Cardinal starter Simmons lasted only two and one-third innings, giving up five hits and five runs. Shannon hit a two-run home run in the ninth.

August 12 — CARDINALS 6, GIANTS 4 — The teams combined for twenty-one hits. Thanks to six singles, the Cardinals scored four in the third inning. The Giants scored four runs in the top of the seventh, including a three-run home run by Mays. Three singles and a wild pitch by Giants reliever Billy O'Dell led to two Cardinal runs in the bottom of the seventh inning. Schultz pitched a scoreless ninth. White led the Cardinal hitters by going 3 for 4 with a double, two runs scored, and an RBI.

August 13 — No game scheduled.

August 14 — CARDINALS 4, DODGERS 3 — The Cardinals scored all of their runs in the fourth inning on a walk, three singles, a two-run triple by Javier, and a throwing error caused by Brock's

speed on the base path. McCarver and Javier each had two hits.

August 15 — DODGERS 4, CARDINALS 3 — The Dodgers came from behind, scoring three runs in the seventh inning. A bases-loaded single by Dick Tracewski was the key hit. Brock led the Cardinal attack, going 2 for 3 with a walk, stealing two bases, and scoring two runs.

August 16 — DODGERS 3, CARDINALS 0 (game one) — Sandy Koufax dominated the Cardinals, pitching a complete-game shutout and striking out thirteen. Brock and White struck out three times apiece. James added two more. The Dodgers scored two of their three runs in the fifth on a combination of singles, walks, a stolen base, a wild pitch, and a Cardinal fielding error. Brock threw out John Roseboro at the plate to end the fifth-inning scoring. Tommy Davis hit a solo home run in the sixth. Koufax ended his season after this game due to recurring left elbow problems. In five starts versus the Cardinals in 1964, he was 3-1, with three complete-game shutouts, a 1.77 era, and thirty-two strikeouts.

August 16 — CARDINALS 4, DODGERS 0 (game two) — Simmons pitched a complete-game shutout. The Cardinals scored one run the first inning and three more in the fourth to account for all of the scoring. Flood led the offense, going 4 for 5. He scored a run and drove in two more.

August 17 — CARDINALS 3, COLT .45s 1 — The Cardinals scored all their runs in the ninth inning to spoil the thirty-nine-year-old Hal Brown's bid for a shutout. Four singles, two Houston errors, and a ground out accounted for the Cardinal runs. Schultz retired the last two batters to end the game.

Cardinals owner August A. Busch Jr. asked for and received the resignations of both general manager Bing Devine and longtime business manager

Art Routzong. In a subsequent newspaper interview, Busch took full responsibility for the shake-up. "I felt it was time for a change," he said. "Bing has been in charge for seven years. We have not won a pennant in that time and we are nine games away from one now. It was my feeling that we are not making any progress." On Branch Rickey's recommendation, Busch immediately brought Bob Howsam in to replace Devine.

August 18 — CARDINALS 5, COLT .45s 2 — Sadecki pitched six and two-thirds innings for his fifteenth win. The Cardinals scored two runs in the fourth, one in the seventh, and two more in the ninth for the victory. Schultz held Houston scoreless and hitless for the final two and one-third innings.

August 19 — COLT .45s 8, CARDINALS 7 (10 innings) — Trailing 6–3 in the ninth, the Cardinals came back to take the lead on a two-out Groat bases-loaded double and a Skinner single. However, Houston tied the game in the ninth on an Aspromonte single and won in the tenth on a Nellie Fox single, scoring Al Spangler from second base. Brock went 2 for 4, scored two runs, and stole two bases. Schultz was the loser.

August 20 — No game scheduled.

August 21 — CARDINALS 6, GIANTS 5 — Trailing 5–3 in the ninth, the Cardinals again came back to take the lead on consecutive two-out singles by Maxvill and Shannon and an error. Schultz pitched a scoreless ninth in relief. Cepeda and Jim Ray Hart each hit home runs for the Giants. Flood went 3 for 5 and scored two runs, and Boyer had three RBIs.

August 22 — GIANTS 4, CARDINALS 2 — Bob Bolin pitched a complete game, registering eleven strike-outs. Although Brock stole two bases, he struck out four times. Javier also struck out three times.

August 23 — GIANTS 3, CARDINALS 2 (10 innings) — With the game tied 2–2 after nine, the Giants scored the winning run in the tenth on an error by Maxvill. White went 2 for 5 and Brock hit a home run tying the game in the eighth. The loss put the Cardinals eleven games behind first-place Philadelphia.

August 24 — CARDINALS 5, PIRATES 1 — The Cardinals started a fifteen-game home stand as Gibson dominated the Pirates with a complete game while striking out twelve. Both White and Boyer hit home runs and had two hits and two RBIs each. Brock also had two hits and stole his twenty-fifth base as a Cardinal.

August 25 — CARDINALS 7, PIRATES 6 (13 innings) — The Cardinals jumped out to a 4–0 lead in the second on a combination of two walks, two singles, a two-run double by Bob Uecker, and a Pirates error. The Pirates tied the game with three runs in the seventh. Tied 4–4 after nine, the Pirates took a two-run lead in the twelfth on a bases-loaded pinch-hit single by Smoky Burgess. The Cardinals again tied the game (6–6) in the twelfth on three singles and a double. Brock hit a walk-off home run to win the game in the thirteenth. The game took 3 hours and 54 minutes.

August 26 — CARDINALS 4, PIRATES 2 — Cuellar pitched his first and only complete game of the season, holding the Pirates to six hits and two runs. The Pirates' two runs came on home runs by Gene Alley and Donn Clendenon in the fifth inning. A Brock-Javier relay throw to McCarver got Alley at home plate to end a Pirate rally in the eighth. With the exception of Cuellar, every Cardinal starting player had at least one hit. Boyer went 2 for 3 with three RBIs. Brock also hit a solo home run for the Cardinals.

August 27 — No game scheduled.

August 28—CARDINALS 5, DODGERS 3—Overcoming a two-run home run by Willie Davis in the first inning, Sadecki pitched a complete game and struck out six. The Cardinals scored all of their five runs in the third inning on a combination of three hits (including a three-run home run by White), two walks, and a throwing error by Maury Wills.

August 29—CARDINALS 4, DODGERS 1—Gibson pitched a complete game as the Cardinals scored all of their runs in the second inning. A double, a single, a fielder's choice (one run scored), and a three-run home run by pinch hitter Skinner produced all the runs Gibson needed.

August 30—CARDINALS 5, DODGERS 1—Simmons pitched the Cardinals' fourth consecutive complete-game victory. Trailing 1–0 in the sixth, the Cardinals used three doubles to score two runs and take the lead. In the eighth, Shannon hit a three-run double to provide some insurance.

August 31—DODGERS 12, CARDINALS 3—Behind 2–0 after the first inning, Don Drysdale went on to pitch a complete game and struck out twelve. The Dodgers took the lead for good in the fourth by scoring five runs on a combination of three runs, two walks, two singles, and an error by Boyer.

Cardinals August win-loss record: 18-10.
Cardinals year-to-date win-loss record: 71-59.

Standings, August 31, 1964

	W	L	T	PCT	GB
Philadelphia Phillies	78	51	0	.605	—
Cincinnati Reds	73	57	1	.562	5½
San Francisco Giants	73	59	0	.553	6½
St. Louis Cardinals	71	59	0	.546	7½
Milwaukee Braves	66	64	0	.508	12½
Pittsburgh Pirates	66	64	0	.508	12½
Los Angeles Dodgers	63	66	2	.488	15
Chicago Cubs	60	70	0	.462	18½
Houston Colt .45s	57	75	0	.432	22½
New York Mets	44	86	1	.338	34½

Chapter 40. **Bob Uecker**

Eric Aron

AGE	G	AB	R	H	2B	3B	HR	TB	RBI	BB	SO	BAV	OBP	SLG	SB	GDP	HBP
29	40	106	8	21	1	0	1	25	6	17	24	.198	.315	.236	0	1	1

When Bob Uecker was sent down to the Minor Leagues in 1961 after breaking camp with the Milwaukee Braves, manager Charlie Dressen told him, "There is no room in baseball for a clown."[1] Dressen could not have been more wrong. While no one would dispute that professional baseball is a business, Bob Uecker has spent more than a half century in the game reminding us that the national pastime should also be about fun. "Mr. Baseball," as he is known to both casual and diehard baseball fans alike, has been a player, broadcaster, coach, actor, all-around ambassador for the game, and, yes, comedian. Beloved for his self-deprecating humor, he would be the first person to make fun of his rather unremarkable playing career, particularly his offensive statistics. "Uke," *Sports Illustrated*'s William Taaffe once said, "is the man who made mediocrity famous."[2]

In six seasons (1962–67) as a Major League catcher (almost all of them as a backup), Uecker batted exactly .200. In 297 games (217 starts) he got 146 hits, hit 14 home runs, and drove in 74 runs. "Anybody with ability can play in the big leagues. . . . But to be able to trick people year in and year out the way I did, I think that was a much greater feat," he once said.[3] In truth, he was a solid defensive catcher, with a career fielding percentage of .981. He played for the Milwaukee/Atlanta Braves, St. Louis Cardinals, and Philadelphia Phillies. In the Cardinals' world championship season of 1964, he was the backup to Tim McCarver. He did not play in the World Series. In 2003 he was honored by the Baseball Hall of Fame with the Ford C. Frick Award, presented annually to a broadcaster.

Bob Uecker played in forty games and batted .198. He provided tension-breaking humor throughout the 1964 season. Uecker later became a popular baseball announcer. (Photo by Allied Photocolor Imaging Center)

The first Milwaukee native to be both signed and traded by the Braves, Uecker joked that the highlight of his Major League career was when he "walked with the bases loaded to drive in the winning run in an intersquad game in spring training."[4] Another time he said of his career highlights, "I had two. I got an intentional walk from

Sandy Koufax [he also hit a home run; both came on July 24, 1965, at Dodger Stadium], and I got out of a rundown against the Mets."[5] On being intentionally walked by Koufax, he joked, "I was pretty proud of that until I heard that the commissioner wrote Koufax a letter telling him the next time something like that happened, he'd be fined for damaging the image of the game."[6]

Robert George Uecker was born on January 26, 1935, in Milwaukee, Wisconsin, although he jokes to the contrary: "My mother and father were on an oleo margarine run to Chicago back in 1934, because we couldn't get colored margarine in Milwaukee. On the way home, my mother was with child. Me. And the pains started, and my dad pulled off into an exit area, and that's where the event took place. . . . There were three truck drivers there. One guy was carrying butter, one guy had frankfurters, and the other guy was a retired baseball scout who told my folks that I probably had a chance to play somewhere down the line."[7]

His parents, Gus and Sue Uecker, were Swiss immigrants who came to Wisconsin in the 1920s. Gus was a tool and die maker. He played soccer in his native Switzerland. "That's where I got my talent," Uecker said.[8] Even during the Great Depression, Gus was able to support his wife, son, and two daughters, earning $3 to $4 a day working on cars.[9] Uecker called his father a great family man who never let him down. He said, "In the minors, when I was making $250 a month and the money ran out, he was there."[10] Gus had a circulation problem in his legs. The conditioned worsened over the years, and by the end of the 1962 season, his legs had to be amputated. He died a few years later.

Uecker attended a technical high school in Milwaukee, where he played baseball and basketball. He would ride his bike eight blocks to Borchert Field, home of the Minor League Milwaukee Brewers, where he would see his idols Alvin Dark, Johnny Logan, Heinz Becker, and Danny Mur-

taugh play. He made his baseball team as a pitcher after a scout saw how hard he could throw. The story goes that at the age of eighteen, he became a catcher when a teammate handed over his gear to him, asking if he could do any better.[11] In his joking fashion, he gave a different version of his switch: "My first game, my parents and everybody was there, my friends, and the manager came out to take me out of the game. I didn't want to come out because I was embarrassed. I said, 'Let me face this guy one more time, because I struck him out the first time I faced him.' He said, 'I know, but it's the same inning. I've got to get you out of here.' And that was my move to catching."[12]

Uecker didn't finish high school, and in 1954, at the age of twenty, he enlisted in the army. He hoped to avoid going overseas by playing military baseball with soldiers who had played in the Minors or in college. At the time he had done neither, so he made up a college and lied. He claimed he had played at Marquette, given that it was a college in his native Milwaukee. "Marquette didn't have a team, but they never checked," he said.[13] He played at Fort Leonard Wood in Missouri, and later at Fort Belvoir, Virginia, where he teamed with shortstop and future Cardinals teammate Dick Groat.

Coming out of the service, he signed with his hometown Braves in 1956 for $3,000. "I could have signed with the Phillies or the Pirates. The Yankees were also interested at that time."[14] He bounced around the Minors for six years, playing for Braves affiliates at all levels and showing decent batting ability and some power. In 1956, his first year, he played for two teams in Class C, Eau Claire (Northern League) and Boise (Pioneer League). Between the two clubs, he hit nineteen home runs. Appearing in fifty-three games for Boise, he also had a .312 average. With Eau Claire, Evansville, and Wichita in 1957, he hit fifteen homers. He kept moving up the ladder, and with Boise and Atlanta (Southern Association) in 1958, he hit twenty-two home runs. In 1959 he played for Jacksonville and Wichita, and in 1960 he was with Triple-A Louisville and Indianapolis. He spent 1961 with just one team, Louisville, where he hit .309 with fourteen home runs, and began the next season with the Brewers.

Uecker made his Major League debut on April 13, 1962, grounding out as a pinch hitter against the Los Angeles Dodgers' Don Drysdale at Dodger Stadium. His hometown debut came on April 19 at Milwaukee's County Stadium. Facing the San Francisco Giants and Juan Marichal, he was the starting catcher, going 0-3 with two strikeouts and a walk. His first Major League hit came on May 3 at Connie Mack Stadium in Philadelphia. He replaced Joe Torre and singled to left off Art Mahaffey.

After a season of backing up Torre and Del Crandall, Uecker finished the 1962 season on a high note. On September 29 he caught Warren Spahn in the left-hander's 327th victory, which broke Eddie Plank's record for the most victories by a left-hander. Uecker went 3 for 4 with three singles, driving in two runs in the 7–3 triumph over the Pittsburgh Pirates in Milwaukee. The next day was the last day of the season. Uecker caught again, and he hit his first Major League home run, off Pittsburgh's Diomedes Olivo. Uecker got into thirty-three games that season and hit .250. He started the 1963 season with the Brewers but got into only nine games as the third-string catcher before being sent down in June to Triple-A Denver, where he batted .283 in fifty-two games.

While Milwaukee manager Bobby Bragan always liked Uecker defensively, catchers Joe Torre and Ed Bailey made Uecker expendable, and on April 9, 1964, he was traded to the St. Louis Cardinals for two Minor Leaguers, catcher Jimmie Coker and outfielder Gary Kolb. During his two years in St. Louis, Uecker was used sparingly. Neither manager Johnny Keane nor his successor, Red Schoendienst, stuck with him very long. He

was pulled if he wasn't hitting well and generally played only when another catcher was injured or a late-game substitution was made. The primary receiver Uecker backed up during those years was Tim McCarver. Uecker had just 106 at bats and hit .198 in the World Series season, but McCarver (who also made a successful second career as a broadcaster) praised him for helping to keep the World Series team loose. He said, "If Bob Uecker had not been on the Cardinals, then it's questionable whether we could have beaten the Yankees."[15]

The 1964 National League pennant race was one of the closest and most exciting of all time. After going 21-8 in September, the 93-69 **Cardinals** finished just one game ahead of both the Phillies and the Reds, who along with the Giants were all alive going into the season's final weekend. Gene Mauch's Philadelphia team had a six-and-a-half-game lead with twelve games remaining, but blew the pennant by losing ten straight. As for the NL champs, Uecker called them "the loosiest, goosiest team ever to come from ten games behind to reach the World Series."[16]

McCarver played every inning of the World Series, hitting .478. "Sat my way through it," Uecker wrote. "Called it from the bullpen. Yankee fans threw garbage at us, and I picked it up and threw it back."[17] Bob did, however, contribute in his own way, through his usual antics. During pregame ceremonies before Game One in St. Louis, he found a neglected marching band tuba in the outfield. He picked it up and started shagging fly balls with pitcher Roger Craig.

McCarver broke his finger early in the 1965 exhibition season and Uecker was the Opening Day receiver, catching ace Bob Gibson against the Chicago Cubs. The game was the kind of contest Uecker would joke about while doing his post-career shtick. It was a 10–10 tie at Wrigley Field, which didn't have lights yet, and was called by the umpires after eleven innings on account of darkness. Uecker was injured in the sixth inning after slamming into a wall while attempting to catch a foul ball. He had been picked off trying to steal home the previous inning, apparently crossed up on coaching signs. Gibson had one of the worst outings of his career, going only three and one-third innings and giving up five runs on six hits. (Future Hall of Famer Steve Carlton made his Major League debut in the game, walking the only batter he faced.)

Uecker hit .228 in fifty-three games, and after the season he was traded to the Phillies with short-stop Groat and first baseman Bill White for catcher Pat Corrales, outfielder Alex Johnson, and pitcher Art Mahaffey. The 1966 season was the closest he came to being a primary catcher. He had 237 plate appearances, platooning with Clay Dalrymple, who had 404 plate appearances. Always quick to discuss his own futility, Uecker summed up his experiences as a hitter for the Phillies: "With Philadelphia, I'd be sitting on the bench and [manager] Gene Mauch would holler down 'grab a bat, Bob, and stop this rally.'"[18]

Uecker's favorite line about his time in Philadelphia was when he was once fined by a police officer for being intoxicated on the street. "They fined me $50 for being intoxicated and $400 for being on the Phillies."[19] "My managers didn't want me in the game. Heck, they didn't want me on the bench. Kids ask which club I played for. Nobody, but I sat for a lot."[20] Ironically, his best offensive season was in 1966. As a Phillie, he hit seven of his fourteen career home runs while establishing a career high in hits with forty-three.

On June 6, 1967, Uecker was traded by the Philadelphia Phillies to the Atlanta Braves for utility man Gene Oliver. The Braves wanted Uecker specifically to catch Phil Niekro's knuckle ball. "I had caught [knuckle ballers] Bob Tiefenauer in Milwaukee and Barney Schultz in St. Louis, so I had a basic idea of how to survive back behind the plate."[21] In fifty-nine games he caught for the Phillies, he had twenty-five passed balls, and he led the

National League with twenty-seven overall. Two weeks after the trade he hit his only Major League grand slam, off Ron Herbel of San Francisco.

During 1968 spring training, Uecker and his Atlanta teammates Deron Johnson and Clete Boyer were involved in a nightclub fight in West Palm Beach, Florida, on March 21, 1968, at the Cock 'n Bull Restaurant. Uecker was struck on the head with a beer bottle and required forty-eight stitches to close the wound. On the field he reaggravated an injury suffered in a motorcycle accident. He was released as a player and coach on April 2. His final Major League game had been on September 29, 1967.

Capitalizing on his gift as a storyteller, Uecker became a public-relations ambassador for the Braves. "I did stand-up, weird and ignorant stuff about my career—anything for a laugh," he said.[22] In 1969 Uecker's broadcasting career began with WSB-TV, on which he did television work with Ernie Johnson and Milo Hamilton. His career as a personality in television and movies took off after he did an opening act for Don Rickles at jazzman Al Hirt's Atlanta nightclub.[23] Beginning in 1970 Uecker made close to one hundred appearances on Johnny Carson's *Tonight Show*, doing three to five shows a year.[24]

He said Carson was the first to refer to him as "Mr. Baseball." Carson "didn't know that much about baseball but as we went along he let me do whatever I wanted," Uecker recalled. "As a matter of fact, when I started doing the shows in New York, you get a script to follow and promote whatever you want to talk about. After about the tenth time I did the show Johnny said, 'Do you need this stuff?' and I said, 'No, I thought you did.' So from then on we pretty much just ad-libbed and went along and whatever he said I just jumped in and went along with it."[25] His on-air relationship with Carson concluded with Carson's retirement from late-night television in 1992.

As he continued his entertainment career,

Uecker was lured back to his native Milwaukee by Brewers owner Bud Selig. The 1970 Brewers were in their inaugural season, a franchise purchased by Selig after the Seattle Pilots went bankrupt after their first season. Uecker initially signed with the Brewers as a scout before becoming the club's radio voice. "Worst scout I ever had," Selig said. "We sent him up to the Northern League, and the next thing I know [general manager] Frank Lane comes raging into my office asking what kind of scout I hired. The report was smeared with gravy and mashed potatoes."[26] "Yeah, I did scouting, if you could call it that," Uecker said. "For every guy, I wrote, 'Fringe major leaguer,' so in case he made it nobody could say, 'How'd you miss that guy?'"[27]

Clearly his talent lay behind the microphone, and on September 4, 1971, the Brewers announced that Uecker would broadcast games on TV and radio. "I've never signed a contract with the Brewers since I've been broadcasting and I never will," he said in 1999. "Whatever we agree on, we have a talk and a handshake, and I don't even think that I have had a handshake the last ten years."[28] On radio station WTMJ he first partnered with friend and colleague Merle Harmon. Tom Collins filled in as well. "Merle Harmon helped me from the start," Uecker wrote. "I'd never done [radio] baseball when I joined him in the booth, not unless you count my play-by-play into beer cups in the bullpen. Beer cups don't criticize, [but] people do. . . . Merle and Tom Collins let me do color, then play-by-play, and saved me if I screwed up."[29]

While achieving quick fame as a buffoon on TV, Uecker slowly grew as a play-by-play announcer on radio. "It's amazing to think of now, given his ability, but Bob's problem then was in finding stuff to ad-lib," recalled Tom Collins. "He'd constantly repeat the count and the score, and swing his legs like a pendulum, and smoke cigarette after cigarette."[30] Uecker honed his craft with hard work. "I had everything to learn and I spent ten years learning it. . . . I didn't try to wisecrack my way through

it."[31] In a rare moment of seriousness, he said he never spoke badly of or criticized a player on the air, reasoning, "I know how hard this game is to play."[32] Uecker, who became the main play-by-play man in 1980, said he preferred radio over television: "You paint a picture in the mind. It's a kick to make baseball come alive to a guy hundreds of miles away who's never seen your home park."[33]

Uecker was serious behind the mike. The only time he let loose in the booth was in a blowout at Miller Park, said former broadcast partner Jim Powell (1996–2008). "It's a 9–1 game, that's when the buttons at home get pushed [off]. That's when everyone tunes in. . . . When it's 9–1, Bob becomes Uke. It's a lopsided game where he really gets going."[34]

While continuing his radio work with the Brewers in the '70s, Uecker went national and helped telecast play-by-play for ABC's *Monday Night Baseball* from 1976 to 1982. During his tenure there, which included All-Star Games, League Championship Series, and World Series games, he teamed up in the booth with an initial crew of Bob Prince, Warner Wolf, and Howard Cosell. Cosell in particular had great chemistry with Uecker, playing the straight man while Bob was his comedic foil. Cosell once teased him on the air, saying that he didn't know what the word "truculent" meant. "Sure I do," Bob said one night in Minneapolis. "If you had a truck and I borrowed it, that would be a truck-u-lent." Cosell paused and said to the national audience, "Need I say any more?"[35]

Uecker cohosted a variety of television shows in the 1970s and '80s, among them ABC's *The Superstars*, *Battle of the Network Stars*, and *Bob Uecker's Wacky World of Sports*. He also appeared in a number of commercials. The ones he is best remembered for were for Miller Beer, both starring himself and as part of the ex-jock Miller Lite All-Stars. In his first ad he appeared outside a tavern only to be locked out because a fan asks him if he is Bob Uecker. In a sequel, he gets into the bar by claiming that he is actually Yankees pitching legend Whitey Ford. "So I lied," he says as he looks into the camera.[36] A popular Ueckerism was born in another Miller ad when he thinks that management has given him the best seats in the ballpark. Ready to sit down close to behind home plate, he is escorted elsewhere by an usher while bragging, "I must be in the front rooow."[37] He has in fact been placed way up in the nosebleed seats, as animated and excited as ever.

While his career as the radio voice of the Brewers continued, Mr. Baseball landed his first major acting gig in 1985. It was a new ABC sitcom about a family in suburban Pittsburgh. *Mr. Belvedere* was based on a 1949 Gwen Davenport novel, *Belvedere*, which first was made into films starring Clifton Webb. The small-screen version was similar in story to the Hollywood films. Christopher Hewitt played Lynn Belvedere, who was hired as a nursemaid for the family's three children. Uecker was the patriarch of the family, a sportswriter named George Owens. "A lot of his character was picked up from my own," Uecker said.[38] To do the show, the Brewers granted him permission to shoot episodes in Hollywood in the late summer and early fall. He continued to make Miller Lite commercials and make appearances on the *Tonight Show*. He even hosted *Saturday Night Live* once, on October 13, 1984. *Mr. Belvedere* was by all accounts a successful show, running for six seasons from 1985 to 1990.

In 1989 Uecker's acting career reached new heights when he appeared in the comedy movie *Major League*, starring Tom Berenger, Wesley Snipes, and Charlie Sheen, with a plot about a woman who inherits the Cleveland Indians from her late husband. She wants to move the team to a warmer climate, yet the only way she can get out of a contract is by fielding a bad team with low attendance. The players foil her plans by making the playoffs. Uecker played the gregarious yet often inebriated team broadcaster Harry Doyle.

Many of the film's scenes were shot in Milwaukee's County Stadium.

With the release of the film, Uecker made himself a household name while introducing himself to a new generation of fans. The Harry Doyle line of "Juuuuuust a bit outside," which described a wild pitch, became a piece of baseball popular culture. It has become an oft-quoted phrase like "There's no crying in baseball" (from *A League of Their Own*), or "Chicks dig the long ball" (from a late-1990s Nike commercial with pitchers Tom Glavine and Greg Maddux). Uecker reprised his role as Harry Doyle in two sequels. He enjoyed making the first two movies, but as for *Major League 3: Back in the Minors*, he said, "Three stunk. . . . It was on airplanes the day after we finished it."[39] Upon the first *Major League*'s twentieth anniversary in 2009, Uecker said, "It seems to be playing more now than when it originally came out. . . . Every day I run into someone at the ballpark or on the street and they say, 'Hey, I saw you in that movie . . . it was on again today.' I mean, I go into clubhouses all the time and these players today are playing it in clubhouses before the game."[40]

At one point Uecker considered leaving broadcasting to concentrate full time on acting, doing commercials, making movies, and appearing on television. It was not helping that Milwaukee was fielding some consistently bad teams. Such an example was the 1984 Brewers, who finished last in the American League East, thirty-six and a half games behind the World Series champion Detroit Tigers. In the end he decided to stay put, declaring, "I could have left there a long time ago, but no matter what I do, I'm staying. All the television stuff, the movies, the sitcoms, the commercials, that's all fun. All I wanted to do is come back to Milwaukee every spring to do baseball."[41]

Over the years Uecker has called some of the biggest games in Brewers history. He was behind the mike on July 20, 1976, when former teammate Hank Aaron hit his 755th and final home run.

He was there when the "Harvey's Wallbangers" Brewers clinched their first and only American League pennant in 1982 (the team switched to the National League's Central Division in 1998), and he called Juan Nieves's April 15, 1987, no-hitter, as of 2011 the only one in franchise history, and Robin Yount's 3,000th hit, on September 9, 1992.

In the 1990s Uecker helped call the 1995 and 1997 World Series on NBC-TV alongside Bob Costas and Joe Morgan. In 2003 he received the prestigious Ford C. Frick Award, denoted by a plaque at the Hall of Fame. Even in accepting the award, he couldn't resist a few jokes. He thanked all the people he worked with in the booth over the years: "I remember working first with Milo Hamilton and Ernie Johnson. And I was all fired up about that, too, until I found out that my portion of the broadcast was being used to jam Radio Free Europe. And I picked up a microphone one day and it had no cord on it, so I was talking to nobody."[42]

He also didn't forget to thank his family for sticking with him over the years: "My family is here today." (Uecker, who has been married and divorced twice, has two daughters, Leann and Sue Ann, and two sons, Bobby Jr. and Steve.) "My kids used to do things that aggravate me, too. I'd take them to the game and they'd want to come home with a different player. . . . But my two boys are just like me. In their championship Little League game, one of them struck out three times and the other one had an error allowing the winning run to score. They lost the championship, and I couldn't have been more proud. I remember the people as we walked through the parking lot throwing eggs and rotten stuff at our car. What a beautiful day."[43]

In addition to winning the Frick Award, Uecker has been named Wisconsin Sportscaster of the Year five times by the National Sportscasters and Sportswriters Association. He was named to the Wisconsin Performing Artists Hall of Fame in 1993 and inducted into the Wisconsin Athletic Hall of Fame in 1998. He was elected into the National Radio Hall of Fame in 2001.

In 2006, Uecker's fiftieth year in professional baseball, the Brewers placed a No. 50 in their "Ring of Honor," near the retired numbers of Hall of Famers Robin Yount and Paul Molitor. Three years later, on May 12, 2009, Uecker's name was also added to the Braves Wall of Honor inside Miller Park. In March 2010, in an honor likely no other Major League baseball player will ever claim, Uecker was inducted into the WWE Wrestling Federation's Hall of Fame for participating in *Wrestlemania III* and *IV* in the 1980s.

Finally, the words of his famous home-run call— "Get up! Get up! Get outta here! Gone!"—were inscribed in the lights above Miller Park. Perhaps more fittingly, there are 106 obstructed-view seats in the upper terrace level above home plate that cost only $1 in honor of Uecker's Miller Lite "Front Row" commercial. As of 2011 he could still be heard calling Brewers games on WTMJ-AM radio with partner Cory Provus. "It's been great," he said in a 2005 ceremony marking fifty years in baseball. "I'd like to do this again 50 years from now when I get to 100. Wherever I am, dig me up. Bring me back here. A couple times around the warning track and take me back to the hole where you picked me up."[44]

Chapter 41. **Carl Warwick**

Thomas Ayers

AGE	G	AB	R	H	2B	3B	HR	TB	RBI	BB	SO	BAV	OBP	SLG	SB	GDP	HBP
27	88	158	14	41	7	1	3	59	15	11	30	.259	.306	.373	2	2	0

To many baseball fans, especially those in St. Louis, Carl Warwick will be best remembered for being a hero off the bench in the 1964 World Series. After spending the regular season as a reserve outfielder and bat off the bench, Warwick excelled in the postseason and whacked a record-tying three pinch hits that played key roles in two of the Cardinals' victories as they vanquished the New York Yankees in seven games.

Carl Wayne Warwick was born on February 27, 1937, in Dallas, Texas. The son of an auto mechanic, he began playing organized baseball at the age of nine and was always an outfielder, except for a short stint at first base in high school.[1] After graduating from Sunset High School in 1955, Warwick attended Texas Christian University on an athletic scholarship.

More famous as TCU's football coach, Dutch Meyer coached the baseball team for one season during Warwick's freshman year and led the Horned Frogs to the Southwest Conference championship. That season, Warwick was named to the All-Conference team and the NCAA All-American third team. As a sophomore, Warwick led TCU with a .321 batting average and attracted the attention of Los Angeles Dodgers scout Hugh Alexander.

Warwick turned to Meyer for advice after the Dodgers promised him a $25,000 signing bonus before his senior year.[2] Meyer advised Warwick to accept the money, as it was a significant amount at the time, and said Warwick need not feel any obligation toward the university. After spending two weeks struggling with the decision, Warwick decided to forgo his senior season and signed with the Dodgers.

In 1964 Carl Warwick hit .259 in eighty-eight games. In the World Series, he had a record-tying three pinch hits leading to two Cardinals victories.

Despite his five-foot-ten, 170-pound frame, Carl began to cultivate a reputation as a power hitter during his first Minor League season. Playing for Macon of the South Atlantic League in 1958, Warwick hit .279 with 29 doubles and led the Sally League with 22 homers. The following year, starring for the Victoria Rosebuds, Warwick was named the Texas League's Most Valuable Player. The Dallas native hit .331 and led the league in home runs (35), total bases (324), and runs scored (129), and was second in stolen bases (18). War-

Warwick singles to left field to drive in Tim McCarver in Game One of the 1964 World Series.

wick didn't rest during the off-season, traveling to the Dominican Republic where he played in the winter league for Escogido.

Warwick earned a promotion to St. Paul of the American Association for the 1960 season. He hit .292 with 27 doubles, 11 triples, 19 home runs, 75 RBIS, and 18 stolen bases. Warwick also had a fine year defensively and led the league's outfielders in put-outs and assists.

Warwick was invited to spring training with the Dodgers in 1961 and had an impressive camp, hitting over .400. There appeared little chance to break into the veteran Dodger outfield of Wally Moon, Willie Davis, and Frank Howard, and the Dodgers also had strong reserves in Tommy Davis, Ron Fairly, and Duke Snider. However, Warwick overcame these odds and was named to Los Angeles's Opening Day roster. He made his Major League debut on April 11, 1961, against the Philadelphia Phillies at the Los Angeles Memorial Coliseum. With the Dodgers leading 5–2, manager Walter Alston sent Warwick to pinch-hit for Moon in the eighth inning. Facing Philadelphia reliever Ken Lehman, Warwick singled to left field, scoring Willie Davis. He would always remember this hit as his favorite Major League thrill, although later

he would recall in an interview, "Funny thing, I can't remember the pitcher's name."[3]

Playing time was in short supply with the Dodgers' deep roster and Warwick was used primarily as a pinch runner or defensive replacement for Moon, appearing in nineteen games but only registering that first hit in eleven at bats. On May 30, 1961, Los Angeles traded Warwick to the St. Louis Cardinals with shortstop Bob Lillis for shortstop Daryl Spencer. Warwick later reflected, "I was just there at the wrong time. The Dodgers started the year with three outfielders and all three did well, so naturally they were hesitant to make a change. I don't have any complaints about the way I was treated by the Dodgers."[4]

His debut for the Cardinals came the same day he was acquired, as Carl didn't have to travel very far to reach his new teammates—only across the halls of Memorial Coliseum to the visitor's clubhouse. Warwick came into the game in the bottom of the seventh inning as a defensive replacement for right fielder Joe Cunningham. He came to bat in the ninth and drew a walk off former teammate Stan Williams.

The Cardinals demonstrated their faith in Warwick immediately, as they thrust him into the starting lineup, usually in center field, for the team's next twenty-two games, which included four doubleheaders. He hit his first Major League home run on June 3 to deep left against Bob Buhl of the Milwaukee Braves during a 9–3 loss. However, playing time dwindled as the season progressed. To keep him fresh, the Cardinals sent Warwick to San Juan/Charleston of the International League, where he hit .289 in 204 at bats. He returned to St. Louis in mid-September and went 8 for 18, finishing with a .239 batting average, .317 on-base percentage and 4 home runs.

Warwick began the 1962 season on a hot streak, going 8 for 23 (.348), but would not have another hit for the Cardinals for nearly two years. On May 7 he was dealt to Houston with relief pitcher John Anderson for pitcher Bobby Shantz. Warwick wasn't displeased at the move, feeling he was in St. Louis "at the wrong time" given the presence of Curt Flood, Charlie James, and Stan Musial in the outfield.[5]

With the expansion Colt .45s, Warwick became an everyday starter for the first time in his Major League career. He finished the season batting .264 and totaled 17 doubles, 17 home runs, and 64 RBIs. Warwick's 16 homers for the Colt .45s were second on the team, and his season total of 17 was more than half his career total of 31. However, he believed he focused too much on hitting for power and admitted, "I wanted to hit 20 home runs and it probably cost me 20 or 30 points on my batting average."[6] He was popular with teammates and coaches in Houston, and Colt .45s manager Harry Craft praised Warwick's willingness to listen and learn, calling him "a darned good subject."[7]

Warwick finished his career with thirty-one home runs, but in his mind it would have been thirty-two if not for a missed call on May 3, 1963. In the top of the fifth inning, Warwick hit a double and went to third on the throw to the plate. According to an article that appeared in *The Sporting News* two weeks later, Harvey Pinsk, a Philadelphia high school student sitting in the front row at Connie Mack Stadium, admitted he tried to catch Warwick's line drive and it deflected off his hand back onto the field. Pinsk stated, "Sure, it was a home run. I leaned over to try and catch the ball, but it hit my hands and then glanced off the stands before falling back on the field."[8] Warwick didn't score and the Colts went on to lose the game, 4–3.

On February 17, 1964, Warwick was traded back to the Cardinals in exchange for first baseman/outfielder Jim Beauchamp and pitcher Chuck Taylor. Warwick's defensive reputation appeared to have decreased over the past few seasons, as Cardinals general manager Bing Devine only characterized it as "adequate," but he was hopeful Warwick could contribute more offensively in St. Louis than he did in Houston, as Colt Stadium was a difficult park for hitters, due to long fences, imperfect lighting, and the fatigue of playing in the Texas heat during the summer.[9] Devine was optimistic about the way the Cards could utilize him, saying, "Warwick could play full time or part time, he could be platooned or he could be valuable as a pinch-hitter."[10] That latter comment would prove to be very prescient.

As in 1963, Warwick began 1964 on a tear at the plate. However, a tragedy struck the family, when his wife's seventeen-year-old sister died of an unexpected heart attack in a Houston high school on May 20.[11] Carl left the team to be with the family and didn't play again for a week. As the season progressed, Warwick's playing time dwindled as the starting outfield solidified with the arrival of Lou Brock in a trade and Mike Shannon's emergence as the everyday right fielder. After playing six full games between June 2 and June 12, Warwick only played three complete games during the rest of the season, as he fell behind Charlie James on the depth chart and was confined to the corner outfield positions and pinch-hitting appearances. On September 27, he had his cheekbone fractured on a fungo hit by reliever Ron Taylor and had it promptly operated on in a St. Louis hospital.

Warwick finished the season with a .259 batting average in 158 at bats, going 11 for 41 as a pinch hitter with a pair of walks and a pair of sacrifices. He credited his success in those situations to a new aggressive approach, developed with the help of two of his teammates. "I seem to carry a different attitude up there coming off the bench. I wouldn't call it confidence. I come up there swinging. You've only got three swings. I don't want to pass up an opportunity." He continued, "Early in the year I was nervous pinch hitting. Then I got talking with Red Schoendienst and Jerry Lynch. . . . Both of them agreed you've got to be ready to attack the ball. Now I enjoy it. I begin to sense on the bench when my time is coming and I get anxious. When the time comes, I'm swinging."[12] Pinch-hitting success had eluded the Cardinals during their previous nine World Series appearances, however, as Cardinals batters were 8 for 42 in pinch-hit at bats during that time.

Warwick was on the bench for Game One of the World Series as Ray Sadecki faced Whitey Ford of the New York Yankees. With the score tied 4–4 in the bottom of the sixth inning, Warwick was summoned to hit for Sadecki with the go-ahead run on second base and two down. Warwick drove a single to left off Al Downing that scored Tim McCarver and gave St. Louis a lead it would not relinquish, as Barney Schultz picked up a three-inning save in a 9–5 victory.

Bob Gibson faced Mel Stottlemyre in Game Two at Busch Stadium I. With the Yankees leading 4–1 in the bottom of the eighth, Warwick led off the frame by batting for Dal Maxvill and singled off Stottlemyre. Warwick eventually scored on a grounder by Brock. However, New York won the game, 8–3.

The Series shifted to New York for Game Three, and St. Louis's Curt Simmons faced Jim Bouton. The pitchers' duel was tied 1–1 when Warwick was again called on to hit for Maxvill in the ninth, with McCarver standing on second and one

out. Warwick coaxed a walk off Bouton, but St. Louis didn't score in the inning, and New York won the game in the bottom of the frame with a walk-off home run by Mickey Mantle.

Warwick's contribution in Game Four didn't change the game as obviously as his hit in Game One, but it was an important at bat in the most crucial inning of the game. The Cardinals fell behind 3–0 early, but reliever Roger Craig pitched four and two-thirds innings of scoreless relief. In the sixth inning, manager Johnny Keane chose to pull Craig and summoned Warwick to pinch-hit. Warwick singled off Downing, who had only allowed one bloop single in the game until that point. Curt Flood singled, Dick Groat reached on an error, and Ken Boyer unloaded a grand slam that gave the Cardinals a 4–3 lead. Ron Taylor combined with Craig to hold the Yankees to one single over the last eight innings, and the Cardinals won 4–3. While Boyer had won the game with a grand slam, Bob Skinner said, "[Warwick's single] began to turn the game around."[13]

Warwick's third pinch hit tied the record for pinch hits in a World Series, held by Bobby Brown and Dusty Rhodes. (Since then the record has also been tied by Gonzalo Marquez and Ken Boswell.) However, even his feat didn't eclipse the memory of his first big-league hit, as Warwick still harkened back to "Opening Day, 1961, before 60,000 in the Coliseum" as his favorite memory.[14]

For the first time all Series, Warwick didn't make it off the bench in Game Five, as Gibson threw ten strong innings in an extra-inning 5–2 victory. The Yankees forced a seventh game with an 8–3 victory in Game Six, and in that game they were finally able to keep Warwick off the bases in his fifth plate appearance of the Series. Warwick hit for Maxvill in the seventh inning but fouled out to third base off Bouton. Gibson was brought back on two days' rest to start Game Seven, and he pitched another complete game. The Cardinals scored three runs in the bottom of both the fourth and the fifth inning on their way to a 7–5 victory and a World Series championship. Afterwards, Keane praised Warwick's pinch-hitting ability and said he was better suited to coming off the bench, because he was more aggressive as a pinch hitter but took too many pitches as a starter.

Following that spectacular end to the season, Warwick returned to Houston, where he and his family lived in the off-season. During the winter Warwick had a career as a manufacturer's representative for a paint company, but he was grateful he was able to spend more time with his wife, the former Nancy Hemsler, and their daughters, Karla and Julie.[15] Nancy was active in several charity ventures, such as when she teamed up with other baseball wives to produce the 1966 Houston Pinch-Hitters charity dinner, dance, style show, and revue benefit for the Council for Minimally Brain Injured Children. The charity venture was held at the Houston Club, with Nancy heading the models' committee and Carl participating in a skit.[16]

As the 1965 season began, Warwick appeared ready to serve as the primary outfield reserve with the ability to start in right field should Mike Shannon falter. His strong World Series performance was fresh in everyone's mind and Warwick also offered defensive versatility and a positive attitude, as he did not complain over a lack of regular playing time.

However, as well as the 1964 season finished, 1965 began that poorly. Warwick struggled from the beginning and Tito Francona, an off-season acquisition from the Cleveland Indians, and Bob Skinner jumped ahead of him on the depth chart. Warwick found consistent playing time was difficult to come by. After playing the entire game at first base on May 7, Carl played in only seven full games over the next two and a half months, and six of those came between June 9 and 14.

On July 24, hitting only .156, Warwick was sold to the Baltimore Orioles for cash considerations.

Manager Hank Bauer tabbed Warwick to be one of Baltimore's primary pinch hitters and said that he might get some starts against left-handed pitching. Although the Cardinals were in Los Angeles at the time of the trade, Warwick made it to Baltimore for that evening's game against Minnesota, where he made a pinch-hitting appearance.

However, Warwick's only stint in the American League was perhaps the least enjoyable of his big-league career. He was hitless in fourteen at bats, although he drew three walks and scored three runs. He made only three starts and went 0 for 6 as a pinch hitter. Warwick spent the last month and a half of the season on the end of the Orioles bench; his only playing time after August 13 was one pinch-hit appearance.

Warwick thought Baltimore would move him after the 1965 season. In an October interview he said, "I guess [Baltimore] will get rid of me." He recounted a conversation with his manager: "I asked Bauer what his plans were for me and he said I'd be the fifth or sixth outfielder. I asked him if I'd get a chance to play in spring training and he said, 'No.'" Warwick was upset, remarking at the time, "This is the first club I've ever been on where I won't even get a chance to try and win a job in spring training. I don't know why they bought me if they didn't intend to use me."[17]

The trade Warwick was waiting for eventually arrived, as Leo Durocher acquired him for the Cubs on March 31 for catcher Vic Roznovsky. Warwick was acquired to provide competition for George Altman in left field and solidify Chicago's bench. Durocher spoke glowingly about Warwick's defensive versatility, stating, "He gives us insurance at both [center and left]" and also praised his speed and throwing accuracy.[18] At this point, Warwick was the only Major Leaguer listed to bat exclusively right-handed and throw left-handed.[19]

Despite Durocher's comments, it soon became evident that Warwick would be utilized solely as an outfield reserve and a pinch hitter. He started four games in April, all in center field, and finished the month with two singles in thirteen at bats. He appeared in three games in May and struck out in both of his at bats. After going 2 for 7 in early June, Warwick entered his final big-league game on June 12, as the Cubs visited the Astrodome. He replaced Adolfo Phillips in center field with one out in the bottom of the sixth, immediately after Rusty Staub had hit an inside-the-park homer to center. His final big-league at bat came in the eighth against Dave Giusti, and Warwick singled and later scored. On June 15, 1966, three days after his final hit, he was optioned to Dallas–Fort Worth and never played in the Majors again. He hit just .140 as a pinch hitter during 1965 and 1966 after his three hits in the 1964 World Series.

Warwick played forty-three games with Dallas–Fort Worth and hit .248 with 6 home runs and 26 RBIs. On August 1 he was assigned to the Tacoma Cubs of the Pacific Coast League, where he struggled, hitting .212 in 113 plate appearances with a pair of homers. At the end of September, the Cubs assigned Warwick outright to the Jacksonville Suns. Warwick signed a Minor League contract with the Mets in the off-season and was invited to spring training. However, he chose to retire on March 1, 1967, just a few days before he was to report to Florida.

After his career ended, Warwick returned to Houston and started a real estate company named Carl Warwick & Associates. Later, he started a travel company called Questar Travel, dealing mostly with corporate travel, which he continues to own and operate. Warwick also served as chairman of the Executive Committee of the Major League Baseball Alumni Association, which raises funds for charity.

Warwick's retirement has been busy, as he is also active in the baseball community at the local and state level. He is involved with the Karl Young Baseball League, an MLB-sanctioned summer base-

ball league for college-age baseball players, and is involved with college baseball in Houston—such as when he arranged a meeting between former Astro Terry Puhl and the vice president of the University of Houston-Victoria, which led to Puhl being hired as the university's head baseball coach.[20] Warwick also serves as a board member for the Harris County–Houston Sports Authority and as an advisory board member for the Texas Baseball Hall of Fame. He founded and chairs the Milo Hamilton Golf Classic, honoring the Astros broadcaster. Warwick was elected to the Texas Baseball Hall of Fame in 1990 and the Texas Christian University Lettermen's Association Hall of Fame in 1959.

In one survey of Major League players, Carl listed his favorite hobbies as golfing and fishing, although he also mentioned he enjoyed playing the piano and trumpet, and also noted that he did all of these activities right-handed.[21] His hobbies continued into retirement, and he also finds pleasure working with Little League baseball players. However, his favorite activity is spending time with his wife, Nancy, and their two children and four grandsons.

Chapter 42. **Ray Washburn**

Tim Herlich

AGE	W	L	PCT.	ERA	G	GS	GF	CG	SHO	SV	IP	H	BB	SO	HBP	WP
26	3	4	.329	4.05	15	10	3	0	0	2	60	60	17	28	5	0

A. L. "Shorty" Hardman, the late sports editor of the *Charleston (WV) Gazette*, extolled Ray Washburn just as the lanky right-hander was to attend his first Major League spring training camp in 1962: "Ray must be considered the best investment the Cards have made since they signed Stan Musial to a contract back in the late '30s."[1]

While this assessment seems preposterous in retrospect, given Washburn's modest 72-64 lifetime win-loss record, the fact is that he appeared to be on his way to fulfilling those lofty expectations until he suffered a devastating shoulder injury in 1963. With grit and determination, the Washington State native came back from this debilitating ailment to compile a respectable ten-year career, capped by a historic no-hit pitching performance in 1968. All but one of those years was as a member of the St. Louis Cardinals.

Ray Clark Washburn was born on May 31, 1938, in Pasco, Washington, and grew up in the nearby small town of Burbank, at the confluence of two mighty rivers of the West, the Snake and the Columbia. His grandmother traveled by buckboard wagon from Kansas City to Moscow, Idaho, where she met Ray's grandfather. Together they homesteaded a wheat farm in the area known as Horse Heaven Hills near Kennewick, Washington. His father, Chet, made a meager living as a truck driver, while his mother, Bernice, raised three boys and two girls. Ray was the oldest son. Life was pretty simple in rural America immediately after World War II. "Being in a small town, there were all kinds of vacant lots—that's how we played all the time," Washburn recalled. "We'd scrape out an area, build our own field, and round up some-

Limited by a serious shoulder injury, Ray Washburn pitched sixty innings and compiled a 3–4 record. Although eligible, he did not appear in the 1964 World Series.

thing we'd make a backstop out of."[2] By the time he was fourteen, Ray was bicycling into Pasco four times a week to play organized ball. Upon graduation from tiny Burbank High School in 1956, he became the first member of his family to attend college, receiving an athletic scholarship from Whitworth College, a small Presbyterian institution in Spokane, Washington.

Washburn was a standout basketball player in college, but he always knew that baseball was his game. He honed his skills by playing in regional semipro leagues each summer. In 1958 he pitched

227

for Bellingham in the semipro National Baseball Congress tournament in Wichita, Kansas, and won three games against the likes of future Major Leaguers Earl Wilson and Floyd Robinson, who played for the San Diego Marines team. In 1959 Washburn toiled through a 152-pitch no-hitter in which he walked eight batters, and helped Lethbridge win the Southern Alberta Baseball League pennant. One of his teammates was Steve Schott, who would take a different path to the Major Leagues from Ray, becoming part-owner of the Oakland Athletics in 1995.[3]

In his senior year at Whitworth, Washburn led the Pirates to the 1960 National Association of Intercollegiate Athletics (NAIA) championship in Sioux City, Iowa. In what can be described simply as a Ruthian performance, he struck out thirty-seven batters in nineteen innings and socked two home runs.[4] In the tournament semifinal game, Washburn fanned future teammate and Hall of Famer Lou Brock three times in a 4–0 shutout of defending champion Southern University.[5] He was voted the tournament's Most Valuable Player and was named to its All-Star team.[6]

At the recommendation of St. Louis scout Charlie Frey, Washburn was flown to Pittsburgh, where the Cardinals were playing, for a tryout at Forbes Field. After an impressive workout, the Redbirds signed the six-foot-one right-hander to a contract with a $50,000 bonus, payable in installments, and assigned him to their top farm club, in Rochester, where he posted a 5-4 record.

One of Washburn's most memorable teammates was the forty-four-year-old former Negro League and American League first baseman Luke Easter. "He didn't know your name. He just called everybody Bub," Washburn recalled with a laugh. After the season Washburn enlisted in the army for a six-month tour of duty. After his active duty, he reported to the Cardinals' Minor League camp in Homestead, Florida.

Pitching for San Juan–Charleston in 1961 (the team began the season playing in Puerto Rico and was transferred to Charleston in May), Washburn led the International League with sixteen victories and a 2.34 earned run average, and was promoted to the parent club in September, going 1-1 with a complete-game victory over the Philadelphia Phillies. On November 25, 1961, Ray wed the former Beverly Anderson of Seattle, whom he had met at Whitworth College. He was invited to the Redbirds' 1962 spring training camp and earned a spot in manager Johnny Keane's starting rotation. Washburn finished his rookie campaign with a 12-9 record in 175⅔ innings, and he was chosen for the John B. Sheridan Rookie Award by the St. Louis chapter of the Baseball Writers Association of America.

"I felt I probably threw in the mid to upper 90s at one time," the fireballer remembered about his fastball, in an era before radar guns. "I developed a good slider. I could throw it up there at probably 89, 90, like Mariano Rivera. He calls it a cut fastball." Washburn was basically a two-pitch pitcher. "I could throw a sinker or a curve, but I was probably doing them a favor." After the 1962 season, Washburn was sent to the Florida Instructional League to work on his curve ball and change-up, and he excelled with a 7-1 record and a 1.71 ERA.

After pitching brilliantly in Florida, Washburn joined Bob Gibson and Ernie Broglio at the top of the Cardinals' rotation in 1963. He began the season with a shutout of the New York Mets at the Polo Grounds in New York on April 10, and followed with complete-game victories over Pittsburgh and Houston. On April 27 in Los Angeles, Washburn took a perfect game into the seventh and a no-hitter into the eighth inning and shut out the Dodgers, 3–0, on a three-hitter. He returned home on May 2 to beat Chicago, 4–3, holding the Cubs hitless until the seventh and striking out a career-high ten batters. Mixing an occasional off-speed pitch with his two-seam fastball and hard slider, the sensational Washburn was 5-0 and

TIM HERLICH

leading the Major Leagues in victories, complete games, and strikeouts.

Then his season, and nearly his career, started to unravel. Washburn lost his next three starts and began feeling discomfort in his pitching shoulder. After several ineffective appearances, he was optioned to Tulsa on June 17 to work out the soreness. Ultimately, it was discovered that the intensely competitive Washburn had torn his triceps muscle. Washburn said in a 2010 interview that he didn't know when it happened. Cardinals manager Johnny Keane and the team physician, Dr. I. C. Middleman, felt it may have happened during his victories over the Dodgers and Cubs, in which he took no-hitters deep into both games. "He was really bearing down," said Keane. "He was throwing too hard."[7] "If I'd only known," the hard-throwing right-hander said. "If I learned something more off-speed . . . when I hurt my arm, it probably was because I was throwing too hard, too long."

Trainer Bob Bauman said Washburn tore the shoulder twice, the second time in Tulsa, noting that "he had discoloration from his elbow to his belt."[8] Many years later, underscoring the severity of the injury, Bauman said he'd never seen a worse tear, and he counted his rehabilitation of Washburn among his greatest accomplishments.[9] Washburn's sophomore year ended with a 5-3 record in eleven starts with St. Louis, plus 1-1 in four games at Tulsa, as the second-place Cardinals fell just short of winning the National League pennant.

The road back to health was not an easy one for Washburn. After the season he began an arduous rehabilitation program. He worked out with a three-pound iron ball the size of a baseball, developed by Bauman, and used wall pulleys to stretch the arm muscles. He reported to camp in 1964 ready to throw.

Washburn pitched well in exhibition games but was optioned to Jacksonville to get more work under the warm Florida sunshine. After pitching twice at Jacksonville, he was recalled to St. Louis on May 5 and pitched eight strong innings in a 2–1 victory over Philadelphia. Over the next six weeks, Washburn started eight games and posted a 3-4 record and 3.12 ERA for a Cardinals team that was struggling to play .500 ball. But his return from serious injury gave general manager Bing Devine the reassurance he needed to deal starting pitcher Ernie Broglio to the Cubs in the celebrated six-player trade for left fielder Lou Brock on June 15. Had Washburn not returned, it is doubtful that Devine would have made the trade. "We wouldn't want to deal Bob Gibson, Ray Washburn, or Ray Sadecki," the general manager said. "Broglio thus seemed to be the most logical to deal."[10]

It turned out that Washburn's comeback was short-lived. In his tenth and last start of the year, on June 29, he was pulled in the third inning after developing a blister on his pitching hand.[11] He made only five more appearances, all in relief, the rest of the season. On July 23 the Cardinals placed Washburn on the disabled list after a calcium deposit formed at the point of his previous shoulder injury. At the time, the club was tied for seventh place in the standings, nine games behind the league-leading Phillies. Washburn rejoined the team in September, when rosters were expanded beyond the twenty-five-man limit, and pitched in a mop-up role in two games. He finished the 1964 season at 3-4 with just sixty innings, and he did not factor in the Cardinals' pennant surge.

Perhaps as a reward for his effort to rebound from injury, Washburn was added to the World Series roster by manager Keane. However, he did not make an appearance in the Series.[12] Keane never even had him warm up. "I knew the circumstances, I wasn't 100 percent," Washburn remembered. He said he wished he could have contributed more to the pennant drive, although without his encouraging mound comeback in May that paved the way for the Broglio-Brock trade, there might well have been no pennant drive.

In 1965 Washburn continued on his road to recovery under the watchful eye of Bauman and new manager Red Schoendienst. "I had to change to a different type of pitcher," he recalled. "I could still throw pretty well, but not ever to the over-powering [degree] that I did before. That's when I came up with more of an off-speed curveball. It made my fastball look better than it did before."

The Cardinals' field staff proceeded cautiously with Washburn the next two years. Gradually he came around, going 9-11 in 117 innings as a spot starter/reliever in 1965, and improving to 11-9 in 170 innings as a full-time starter in 1966. On May 12, 1966, he started the first game at the new downtown Busch Stadium. From May 31 through July 27, Washburn won eight of nine decisions with an ERA of 1.99. It was around that time that he was given the nickname "Deadbody" by team-mate Bob Gibson, because "he moved as if every particle of life had been sucked out of him."[13] He accepted this moniker gracefully, as almost every-one in the close-knit clubhouse had one.

While he did not complete games as often as most starters of his day, Washburn had proved his durability by not missing his turn in the rotation throughout 1966. For the first time since 1963, he reported to spring training in 1967 free from spec-ulation over the condition of his shoulder. On May 3 he hurled a two-hit shutout over the first-place Cincinnati Reds, matching Gibson's performance the previous night. The Cardinals overtook the Reds for the top spot by mid-June, and Washburn continued to take his regular turn until a chip frac-ture of his right thumb during the game on June 21 landed him on the disabled list. He returned to action on July 16, the day after Gibson suffered a broken leg after being nailed by a line drive off the bat of Roberto Clemente. With Gibson out for an extended stretch, Washburn and the rest of the Cardinals starters stepped up to the challenge. By the time Gibson returned on September 7, the team had all but clinched the pennant. Washburn

finished the season at 10-7, tying for second on the club with twenty-seven games started and for third with 186⅓ innings pitched. Unlike in 1964, Wash-burn did see action in the World Series this time, throwing 2⅓ scoreless innings in two relief appear-ances. His parents saw him pitch Major League ball for the first time during the 1967 World Series. His mother passed away the following spring, and his father died soon after.

The next season, 1968, will forever be known as the Year of the Pitcher. It was also the year Ray Washburn finally achieved his full potential, jus-tifying the $50,000 bonus and patience bestowed by the Cardinals organization. He posted career highs in victories (14), games started (30), com-plete games (8), shutouts (4), innings pitched (215⅓), and strikeouts (124), while spinning a 2.26 ERA, eighth best in the league.

From the All-Star break on, the thirty-year-old veteran was sensational. In sixteen starts cov-ering 127⅓ innings, Washburn allowed just nine-teen earned runs for a microscopic 1.34 ERA, while pitching six complete-game victories and three shutouts. But he was also a bit of a hard-luck hurler, twice going ten innings without giving up an earned run, yet coming away with no decision in either game. On the afternoon of September 18 in San Francisco, Washburn reached the pinna-cle of his career. After Gaylord Perry had no-hit the Redbirds the night before, Washburn twirled a no-hitter of his own against the Giants. It was the first time in Major League history that consec-utive no-hitters had been tossed in the same ball-park. Washburn scattered five walks but knew he had a no-hitter going all along. In the bottom of the ninth, he retired Ron Hunt and Willie Mays on ground balls, and then faced the dangerous Wil-lie McCovey. "I got the ball in on McCovey and he pulled it way foul down out there towards the Bay," Washburn recalled. "The next pitch he hit a high fly to center field." It was only the second time a ball had left the Cardinals' infield that day. When

Curt Flood tracked down the deep drive, the no-hitter was secured. Washburn threw 138 pitches, of which 42 were curve balls that kept the Giants off-balance. "I never saw a guy throw a curve much better," Mays said at the time. "It floated, but you couldn't hit it."[14] Washburn's no-hit gem was the first by a Cardinals pitcher in twenty-seven years.

Washburn started Game Three of the World Series in Detroit, drawing Earl Wilson, his old adversary from the National Baseball Congress tournament a decade earlier, as his mound opponent. Washburn came away with a 7–3 victory despite struggling with control of his curve ball. In his next start, in Game Six, Washburn was ineffective in the Tigers' 13–1 drubbing of the Redbirds.

Because of his strong showing in 1968, the Cardinals kept the soon-to-be thirty-one-year-old Washburn on the protected list from the 1969 expansion draft. But his pitching career quickly came to an end. He tumbled to a 3-8 record as the Cardinals failed to keep pace with the Miracle Mets in the first year of division play. After the season he was traded to the Cincinnati Reds for pitcher George Culver. He pitched poorly in middle relief in 1970, but he earned one more World Series check with the Reds before being given his unconditional release. After an unsuccessful tryout with the California Angels in 1971, Washburn retired.

During his Major League career, Washburn worked full time during the off-season at a sporting-goods store in Seattle. In 1963 he picked up the necessary credits for his college degree. In 1964 he and Beverly bought a home in suburban Seattle, where they raised a family of two daughters and a son. In 1972 he managed the Seattle Rainiers, a co-op team in the Class A Northwest League, before accepting a teaching position the following year at Bellevue Community College. On nights and weekends, Washburn earned a master's of education administration degree at Seattle University. Eventually he became chairman of the department of physical education and the athletic director at Bellevue College. He retired from full-time duties in 2003. He also coached the baseball program there for twelve years. He continued to teach part-time at the school, which became Bellevue College. Washburn is a member of the NAIA Hall of Fame, the Inland Empire Hall of Fame, and the Washington State Sports Hall of Fame.

It is tempting to dwell on how Washburn's career might have turned out had he not severely injured his shoulder. "I was fortunate to have the career I had," he reflected in 2010, without bitterness on what might have been. "I was fortunate to play with a lot of great players."

Chapter 43. **Bill White**

Warren Corbett

AGE	G	AB	R	H	2B	3B	HR	TB	RBI	BB	SO	BAV	OBP	SLG	SB	GDP	HBP
30	160	631	92	191	37	4	21	299	102	52	103	.303	.355	.474	7	6	1

Bill White spent fifty-one years in a game he didn't love. The five-time All-Star became the first black play-by-play broadcaster for a Major League team and the first black president of a major sports league. He railed against racism in baseball, though he acknowledged that, even as National League president, he couldn't do much about it.

William DeKova White was born on January 28, 1934. In his autobiography White gives his birthplace as Paxton, Florida, a crossroads town in the state's panhandle near the Alabama border. Baseball encyclopedias say he was born in Lakewood, another hamlet just three miles east. White never knew his father, Penner White, and was raised by his grandmother, Tamar Young, and his mother, Edna Mae Young. His first home was a shack with no electricity or indoor plumbing. When Bill was three years old, his mother joined the black migration northward, moving to Warren, Ohio, where several relatives worked at the Republic Steel plant. The family lived in a segregated public housing project. His mother worked as a housecleaner until she went to secretarial school and got a civilian job with the U.S. Air Force. While her work moved her around the country, she left her son in Warren with his grandmother.

Bill attended the mostly white Warren G. Harding High School. When he was elected senior class president, the principal ended the tradition of having the president dance with the prom queen, because the queen was white. Bill lettered in football, basketball, and baseball, but he said later, "I was first string in nothing. I was about the third-string halfback in football, and in basketball I was the tenth man on a ten-man team."[1]

Bill White hit .303 with 103 RBIS in the 1964 season. He also had a .996 fielding average. Bill was a vocal supporter of team integration, and he later became president of the National League.

Despite his later memory, he attracted two football scholarship offers. Instead, he went to tiny Hiram College in Hiram, Ohio, because he liked the school's pre-med program and was offered an academic scholarship. A left-handed first baseman, White called himself an average baseball player in college. But he hit two home runs in the championship game of the National Amateur Baseball Federation tournament at Cincinnati's Crosley Field. A bird-dog scout for the New York Giants, Alan

Fey, invited White to Pittsburgh to work out for manager Leo Durocher. He hit a few balls over Forbes Field's right-field wall before Durocher hustled him into the locker room so Pirates general manager Branch Rickey wouldn't spot him. To his surprise, White was offered a contract with a $1,000 bonus. He said no. His family had always preached the importance of a college education and he didn't want to disappoint them. When Durocher was called in to close the deal, the eighteen-year-old said he needed $2,500 to finish college. "Okay, kid, you've got it," the manager replied. He also threw in a new pair of spikes.[2] White's mother agreed to let him sign only after he promised to finish college.

Durocher took White to spring training with the big-league club in Phoenix in 1953 and made the professional rookie his personal project. Some other players called him "Leo's little bobo." White remembered his first encounter with segregation when he tried to go to a movie. The theater manager turned him away because the building had no balcony. He didn't know that black patrons were only allowed to sit in the balcony in many theaters. His roommate, the veteran Monte Irvin, counseled him, "Don't rock the boat. Someday all this is going to change."[3]

The Giants sent White to Danville, Virginia, where he was the only black player in the Class B Carolina League. That made him a target for some white fans; he said it was the first time he had been called "nigger" to his face. He asked to be transferred to a team in the North, but he was leading Danville in hitting and the manager wouldn't part with him.[4] His temper erupted one night in Burlington, North Carolina, when he flashed his middle finger at an abusive crowd. His white teammates escorted him to the bus behind a shield of bats, and the Danville club left town in a hail of rocks. He recalled that year as "probably the worst time of my life."[5] He answered the abuse with his bat, hitting twenty home runs with a .298 average.

White planned to give baseball three or four years and go for his medical degree if he didn't make the Majors. Promoted to the Class A Western League in 1954, he hit thirty homers and stole forty bases for Sioux City Iowa, then followed with twenty homers for Dallas in the Double-A Texas League the next year. He had returned to Hiram College every fall, but in 1955 he played winter ball and left school for good, to his mother's everlasting disappointment.

During spring training in Arizona in 1956, veteran umpire Jocko Conlan, a former Major League outfielder, offered some advice: "If a pitcher misses [with] the first pitch when you're hitting, look for a fastball on the second pitch." White recalled, "And that's the way I hit for fourteen years."[6] He was playing for the Triple-A farm club at Minneapolis when the Giants called him up in May. In his first time at bat, in St. Louis on May 7, he slammed a home run off right-hander Ben Flowers. He added a single and a double later in the game but went 1 for 16 before he hit his second home run, off Don Newcombe six days later. He homered twice off Robin Roberts on the last day of the season to bring his total to twenty-two, with a .780 on-base plus slugging percentage (OPS).

That bought White a ticket to the army. His draft notice spurred the Giants to trade for Jackie Robinson to play first base, but Robinson retired. Before White was inducted, he married his high school sweetheart, Mildred Hightower, on November 20, 1956. They would have five children before they divorced in the 1980s.

The army assigned White to the supply room at Fort Knox, Kentucky. He played for the post baseball team until he was refused service in a restaurant. Most of his white teammates went on with their meal, and White, angry at their indifference, quit the team at the end of the season. He supplemented his army pay by playing semipro ball for $50 a game.

When White rejoined the Giants in July 1958,

the team had moved to San Francisco and he had lost his job. Orlando Cepeda was playing first base, becoming a favorite of Bay Area fans on his way to the Rookie of the Year Award. The Giants had another first baseman, twenty-year-old Willie McCovey, in Triple-A. Newspapers immediately began speculating that White was trade bait. The next spring, manager Bill Rigney said he would keep White as a pinch hitter and occasional first baseman when Cepeda moved to third. White wanted no part of that; he told a reporter, "You can't make the big money unless you're a top-ranking major-league regular."[7] On March 25, 1959, the Giants traded him to St. Louis with third baseman Ray Jablonski for pitchers Don Choate and Sam Jones, the latter a three-time National League strikeout leader.

White had wanted to be traded, but not to St. Louis. The Cardinals had *three* first basemen, all left-handed: Joe Cunningham, George Crowe, and Stan Musial, who was moving to first to rest his thirty-eight-year-old legs. Besides, black players did not feel welcome in St. Louis; the Cardinals were the last Major League team to integrate seating at their ballpark. Looking back, White said, "Eventually it would turn out to be one of the best moves of my life."[8] He played primarily in the outfield in 1959, and acknowledged that he was terrible at it, but he batted over .350 for most of the first half. Players and managers elected him to his first All-Star team as a left fielder. He tailed off to finish at .302 with an .814 OPS. The next year White spent most of his time at first base, winning the first of seven Gold Gloves, and by 1961 he was the Cardinals' everyday first baseman.

Fourteen years after Jackie Robinson's debut, baseball's spring training sites in Florida were still segregated in 1961. In St. Petersburg the Cardinals' black players stayed with local families. The pioneering black sportswriter Wendell Smith had raised the issue and a few major newspapers took up the story. That spring the St. Petersburg Chamber of Commerce invited only white players to its annual "Salute to Baseball" breakfast. White complained to a reporter, "When will we be made to feel like humans?"[9] He was one of the few black players—if not the only one—to speak up publicly.

A St. Louis–area newspaper called for a black boycott of Cardinals owner August A. Busch Jr.'s beer. Busch was no liberal, but he was a dedicated capitalist. He ordered his staff to make the problem go away. By the next spring a St. Petersburg businessman had bought two motels and made them available to the team. Stars including Musial and Ken Boyer, who usually stayed with their families in rented beach houses, moved into the motels in a show of solidarity. Several players manned grills at dinnertime, and White's wife, Mildred, conducted classes for the children. Locals would drive by to watch black and white families frolicking together in the pool, a sight unprecedented in the Deep South.

In 1962 White began a five-year run as one of the NL's elite players. He posted an adjusted OPS (adjusted for park and league average) above 120 every year (100 is defined as the league average) while winning Gold Gloves. In '62 his .868 OPS and .324 batting average were career bests. The next year he registered career highs with 200 hits, 106 runs, 27 home runs, and 109 RBIs. Along with Julián Javier, Dick Groat, and Ken Boyer, White was part of the all-Cardinal starting infield in the 1963 All-Star Game. (He also won the Cardinals' horseshoe-pitching tournament.) The team won nineteen of twenty games to close within one game of the first-place Dodgers in September, finishing second.

In pursuit of "the National League pennant nobody seemed to want,"[10] White, like several of his teammates, stumbled through the early months of 1964, then came on strong in the second half. After the All-Star break he raised his batting average from .263 to .303 and his OPS from .704 to

WARREN CORBETT

.829. In the season's final game, when the Cardinals had to win or go home, White singled in the fifth inning and scored the go-ahead run, then added a two-run homer in the sixth as the Cardinals beat the Mets to clinch the pennant. He finished third in the Most Valuable Player voting, behind teammate Boyer and Philadelphia's Johnny Callison. White said the 1964 Cardinals were a close-knit team: "There's no way to quantify the spirit that a group of men share, but in baseball, as in the military, that spirit can sometimes make the difference between victory and defeat."[11]

White batted only .111 in the World Series, but he contributed two hits and scored a run in the Game Seven victory over the Yankees. That night he showed up to speak at a St. Louis church banquet, as he had promised months before when the Cardinals appeared to be out of the pennant race. After fulfilling his commitment, he joined his teammates at Stan Musial's restaurant for a celebration.

After St. Louis fell to seventh place in 1965, general manager Bob Howsam traded three-fourths of his pennant-winning infield: White, Boyer, and Groat, the only players in the lineup over thirty years old. White, not yet thirty-two, was the youngest of them, but Howsam told reporters he thought the first baseman was actually older. (There is no evidence that he was.)

White and Groat went to the Phillies with backup catcher Bob Uecker for pitcher Art Mahaffey, catcher Pat Corrales, and outfielder Alex Johnson. White did not like his new manager, Gene Mauch: "He was a control freak. The way to win is to let players play."[12] He didn't care for the tough Philadelphia fans, either, but he bought a house and made the area his permanent home.

White gave the Phillies a standout performance in 1966, with 22 home runs and 103 RBIs, but he went into a sudden decline after he tore his right Achilles tendon while playing paddleball. In 1967 he was able to start only ninety games as his bat-

ting average fell to .250. He said the Philadelphia trainers would shoot him up with novocaine, in addition to dispensing amphetamines. His average dropped to .239 in 1968 and he was traded back to St. Louis, where he wound up his career in 1969 primarily as a pinch hitter. "I gave it 16 years of my life and never less than 100 percent on the field," he said. "So we're even."[13] Later he wrote, "I didn't love baseball. Because I knew that baseball would never love me back."[14] The Cardinals offered White a Triple-A managing job, but he had already chosen his next career.

When White chided Harry Caray about how easy his broadcasting job was, Caray invited him to try it. While playing for the Cardinals, he worked part-time for KMOX radio in St. Louis. In Philadelphia he hosted a pregame radio show and worked in the off-seasons as a sports reporter on local television. One of his early assignments was a hockey game; inevitably, he referred to the puck as the ball. After retiring, he became a full-time sports anchor for WFIL-TV and studied with a New York voice coach to improve his performance.

White had met Howard Cosell before the sportscaster became famous and respected him for his coverage of racial issues. Cosell recommended him to the Yankees for their play-by-play job. In 1971 he became the first African American broadcaster for a Major League team—although, despite his radio and TV experience, he had never called a baseball game. The plan was to let White start as a color analyst and break him in slowly on play-by-play. But as he broadcast his first spring training game with Phil Rizzuto, the Scooter spotted Joe DiMaggio in the stands and bolted out of the booth to greet his old teammate, leaving White on his own. White survived to start a rewarding partnership with Rizzuto.

The former shortstop was a famously casual broadcaster, plugging his favorite restaurants, especially those that supplied free cannoli, and leaving games in the seventh inning so he could beat the traffic home to New Jersey. It was said that the most frequent entry in his scorebook was "ww," for "wasn't watching." White blossomed as his on-air foil and straight man. Rizzuto always called him "White," never "Bill." They worked side by side for eighteen seasons and became friends. When Rizzuto was dying in 2007, White visited him in the hospital and silently held his hand. White said, "I loved Phil Rizzuto."[15]

White said Yankees owner George Steinbrenner twice offered him the job of general manager, but he knew better than to work directly for "The Boss." In 1989 the fifty-five-year-old White had decided to leave the Yankees. He had earned enough respect in broadcasting circles to call several World Series for the CBS Radio Network, but the Yankees had switched most of their games to cable, leaving only about sixty each season for White on WPIX-TV. He thought it was a good time to retire.

Los Angeles Dodgers president Peter O'Malley invited White to interview for the job of National League president, but he said he was not interested. O'Malley called again and White agreed to talk to the search committee. He understood what was going on; less than two years earlier, Dodgers general manager Al Campanis had ignited a firestorm when he said blacks might lack "the necessities" to be managers or general managers. Baseball had a public-relations problem, one that only a high-profile African American could fix. White later acknowledged, "Let's face it, they wanted a black National League president."[16] Token or not, "Bill had no choice but to accept that job," his friend Bob Gibson said. "Not for himself, but for other people."[17]

In addition to being the first black league president, White was the first former player to head the National League since John Tener seventy years earlier. (Former shortstop Joe Cronin had served as president of the American League.) The president's duties included supervising the umpires and disciplining players. White also had to deal with Marge Schott, the Cincinnati Reds owner whose drunken rants and racist comments repeatedly embarrassed Major League Baseball. White said she never showed her racist side to him; in fact, she thanked him for treating her more respectfully than her fellow owners did.

White and Richie Phillips, the leader of the umpires union, despised each other. Phillips said White still thought like a player and took their side against the umps.[18] Not all players agreed. White suspended Cincinnati pitcher Rob Dibble twice in one season. When the Phillies' John Kruk was named to the 1991 NL All-Star team, he remarked, "That's the first time I got a letter from Bill White where I didn't have to pay a fine."[19]

White believed his most important accomplishment as league president was helping to guide the expansion that awarded teams to Denver and Miami. Even that came with controversy. The American League owners demanded a share of the entry fees paid by the new teams, and Commissioner Fay Vincent sided with them, although the AL had not shared its windfall when it expanded in 1977. White protested that Vincent was butting in on a National League matter. He also accused Vincent of interfering on disciplinary issues that were the league president's prerogative.

Before the expansion cities were chosen, White thought he had exacted a promise from the new Colorado Rockies that they would interview minorities for front-office jobs. When they didn't, he said he was "surprised and disappointed" that the team had broken its word. This time Vincent joined in the criticism of the Rockies' owners.[20]

White had made his living by talking, but his major shortcoming as president, his critics said, was his silence. He seldom went to ballgames and refused most interviews. He did not speak out on his passionate conviction that baseball needed to integrate the ranks of managers and executives. "It's the same for all of us in positions we've

WARREN CORBETT

achieved," said Frank Robinson, then one of two black managers in the Majors. "If we don't speak up and speak out, who will?"[21] White contended he could best serve the cause of equal rights by doing his job well, but he admitted that minorities in baseball made little progress during his tenure.

White shed his reserve in a 1992 speech to the Black Coaches Association—preaching to the choir before a non-baseball audience. He said he was bitter about the racism he faced in his job, adding, "I deal with people now who I know are racists and bigots."[22] He praised Commissioner Vincent for hiring minority executives in Major League Baseball's central office, but he and Vincent could not persuade teams to integrate their front offices.

Despite his differences with the commissioner, White thought the owners destroyed the independence of the commissioner's office when they forced Vincent out in 1992. With Milwaukee owner Bud Selig installed as acting commissioner, White said, "No longer was there even the pretense that an objective 'outside baseball' authority was watching over the best interests of the game."[23] He soon realized that Selig intended to concentrate power in his own hands and abolish the position of league president. White retired in 1994. When the owners wanted to give him a farewell dinner, he told his successor, Leonard Coleman, "You can tell the owners I said the hell with them." He believed the owners "understood the *business* of baseball. But I don't think they ever truly understood the game."[24]

White filled his retirement with fishing and trips in his motor home, accompanied by the woman he called his "lady friend," Nancy McKee. He guarded his privacy until the 2011 publication of his autobiography. He titled it *Uppity*. "I use 'uppity' as a point of pride," he said. "I demanded to be recognized for what I accomplished, nothing more. If people thought that was uppity—and many did—so be it."[25]

Chapter 44. **Johnny Keane**

John Harry Stahl

"He was, in fact, the closest thing to a saint that I came across in baseball," remembered Hall of Fame pitcher Bob Gibson about his 1964 St. Louis Cardinals manager, Johnny Keane.[1] Maintaining a quiet, patient demeanor, punctuated with occasional well-timed outbursts of Irish temper, Johnny drew on his seventeen-year Minor League managerial experience to guide the 1964 Cardinals to the National League pennant and a World Series victory over the favored New York Yankees.

John Joseph Keane had a long career as a Minor League infielder but never played in the Major Leagues. He was born on November 3, 1911, in St. Louis. His father regularly took young Johnny to Cardinals games. Johnny later joined the Cardinals' Knot Hole Gang, a group of youthful fans. As a teenager, he played shortstop for a team in the St. Louis Muny League. He also enrolled in the St. Louis Preparatory Seminary to begin study for the Catholic priesthood. For a brief time, he tried to pursue both baseball and the priesthood but quickly chose baseball.

In 1930 he signed a Minor League contract offered to him by Cardinals scout Charlie Barrett.[2] After a rookie season (and a .304 batting average) with Waynesboro (Pennsylvania) in the Class D Blue Ridge League, he moved up in 1931 to Springfield (Missouri) in the Class C Western League, playing 126 games and hitting .285. He batted .312 in 1932 and .324 in 1933 as the Western League moved up to Class A. In 1934 the Cardinals sent him to Houston in the Double-A Texas League, where he came down with malaria after a few games. Upon recovery he was sent to Elmira (New York) in the Class A New York–Pennsylva-

The Sporting News's 1964 National League Manager of the Year, Johnny Keane managed Cardinals Minor League teams for seventeen seasons before reaching the Majors.

nia League, where he again hit .300 and earned a late-season promotion back to Houston. Keane seemed to be establishing himself as a definite Major League prospect.

In 1935, after a three-game stay with Rochester of the International League, the Cardinals again placed Johnny at Houston, where he was the club's scrappy starting shortstop by midseason. Then, in a game against Galveston on July 22, tragedy almost struck. Galveston pitcher Sigmund "Jack" Jakucki, who later pitched for the St. Louis Browns, was

Johnny Keane with Bill White (*left*) and Julián Javier (*right*).

wild. In the bottom of the fourth inning, he hit the first batter. The next hitter sacrificed, bringing up Keane, who hit Jakucki well. Jakucki's first pitch hit Keane on the head, knocking him unconscious. His teammates carried him off the field.[3]

At the hospital the attending physician told the *Houston Post* that Keane "was very fortunate that the blow caused a long fracture (seven inches) and if there had been a depression, an operation would have been essential." Keane was unconscious for six days and in the hospital for six weeks.[4] The upset Houston team, which had been surging, fell back into the second division.[5]

During spring training the following season, Keane later recalled, Houston tested him to see if the beaning made him gun-shy, making him bat against the wildest pitcher in camp.[6] Keane passed the test and played the full 1936 season with Houston, hitting .272 in 534 at bats.

The 1937 season was a watershed year in Keane's career. He met and married his wife,

Lela Reed.[7] Lela became a key source of support for Johnny throughout his baseball career. Keane played the entire season with Houston, hitting .267 in 595 at bats. At the end of the season, Houston sent Keane back to Springfield, and *The Sporting News* reported a rumor that he would become player-manager there.[8]

Instead of Springfield, the Cardinals offered to make Keane the player-manager of their Albany, Georgia, team in the Class D Georgia-Florida League. A disappointed Keane reportedly balked at the move and the Cardinals abruptly released him.[9] Then cooler heads prevailed. With Lela's full support, Johnny accepted the Albany post.[10]

Keane was an immediate success as a manager. In 1938 and 1939 he led Albany to first-place finishes. Describing his 1938 season, *The Sporting News* wrote, "The fighting Irishman from Texas led an inspired band of players to a walk-away in the Georgia-Florida League."[11] In 1940 the Cardinals moved Keane up to Mobile in the Class B

Southeastern League, where his team finished in third place and lost in the first round of the league playoffs. In 1941 he moved back to Class D, to New Iberia in the Evangeline League, again leading his team to first place.

At the beginning of World War II, Johnny volunteered for military service. His 1935 skull fracture prohibited him from serving in the armed forces, so he joined the Brown Shipbuilding Company in Houston, supervising fifty employees in its procurement operations, and managing the company's semipro baseball team. It was an important business-related experience for Keane, giving him an appreciation for both the operations and needs of large organizations. Lela later recalled Johnny's pride in his work at Brown.[12]

In late 1945, as the Minor Leagues prepared to resume their operations, the Houston club hired Keane as its manager. In 1946 he suffered the first losing season of his career, as Houston went 64-89 and finished sixth. He rebounded sharply in 1947; Houston finished in first place, won the league playoffs and the Dixie Series (over Mobile, his old Southern Association club), and smashed all Houston attendance records. He achieved this despite having to use a patched-up lineup most of the season. Keane later recalled the year as his top thrill as a Minor League manager. In 1948 Houston finished third with an 82-71 record and lost in the first round of the playoffs. After the season Keane was named manager at Triple-A Rochester.

The Red Wings finished second in 1949, first in 1950 (they lost to Baltimore in the playoff finals) and second in 1951. In 1950 the team set an attendance record. Keane's consistent Minor League success caught the eye of Cardinals owner Fred Saigh, who was looking for a new manager. Saigh interviewed Keane, but the job went to former St. Louis shortstop Marty Marion.

At Rochester, Keane worked for general manager Bing Devine. They meshed immediately, forming a highly successful career-long friendship.

Reminiscing years later, Devine wrote that he was most impressed by Keane's friendly demeanor and his intense work ethic.[13]

In 1952 the Cardinals reassigned Keane to their other Triple-A team, the Columbus Red Birds. The franchise had finished last and reportedly lost an estimated $151,000 in 1951. Armed with young prospects, Keane needed to quickly turn the team around and at least break even.[14] He accepted the challenge, noting, "It's my job to develop players but it's also my job to win pennants and to lure fans through the gates."[15] But Keane experienced the three worst seasons (1952–54) in his Minor League career, posting a three-year record of 209-251 and finishing seventh, seventh, and fourth.

In 1954, after two dismal years, Keane rallied Columbus to a fourth-place finish, qualifying for the American Association playoffs for the first time. *The Sporting News* took note of his ability to develop low-cost talent into skilled, marketable players, showing a number of examples where he had taken castoffs from other organizations and enhanced either their trade or their playing value to the parent club. One of the examples cited was Barney Schultz, who became a hero with the 1964 World Series winners.

While Keane was managing at Columbus, major changes were taking place in the Cardinals' front office. In 1953 the prison-bound (for tax evasion) Fred Saigh sold the franchise to August A. Busch Jr.[16] In 1955 the Columbus team was moved to Omaha, Nebraska, and manager Keane moved with it.[17] In 1956 general manager Frank Lane interviewed Keane for a Cardinals coaching position, and was shocked when Keane asked to stay at Omaha. From 1955 through 1958, the Omaha Cardinals finished second, third, fifth, and fifth and reached the league playoffs twice.

Trader Lane (who once reportedly tried to trade Stan Musial) was fired in 1957 and was succeeded by Keane's friend Bing Devine. Eventually the GM persuaded Keane to join new manager Solly

JOHN HARRY STAHL

Hemus's coaching staff for 1959. Under Hemus the Cardinals were 71-83 in 1959 and 86-68 in 1960. In the first half of 1961, when the team started slowly (33-41) Busch replaced Hemus with Keane, who finished the second half with a 47-33 record.

Both Devine and Keane set about building a confident, contending team. They continued the development of key young players who would be 1964 stars: Bob Gibson, Ray Sadecki, Curt Flood, Bill White, Tim McCarver, and Julián Javier. Devine signed Curt Simmons as a free agent and added Dick Groat and Roger Craig via trades. These veterans were essential to the 1964 team.

Perhaps the most important issue facing the organization was how to effectively use future Hall of Famer Stan Musial. Starting in 1961, the Cardinals carefully monitored the forty-year-old Musial's playing time throughout the notoriously hot, muggy, and draining St. Louis summers, making sure he remained fresh. Musial responded by remaining a positive contributor to the team throughout his final three years (1961–63) as a player. At the end of the 1963 season, Musial became a Cardinals vice president.[18]

In late October 1962, Busch threw another ingredient into the Cardinals management mix by hiring the eighty-year-old baseball front office legend Branch Rickey as a special personnel consultant to the team.[19]

Unfortunately for the Cardinals in 1963, the Los Angeles Dodgers had the best starting pitchers in baseball: Sandy Koufax (25 wins, 311 innings pitched, 1.88 ERA) and Don Drysdale (19 wins, 315 innings pitched, 2.63 ERA). The Dodgers won 99 games and swept the Yankees in the World Series. The 1963 Cardinals were also a formidable team, winning 93 games. Their spirited effort simply wasn't enough.

With the high expectations established by their second-place finish, the Cardinals started the 1964 season sluggishly, as Philadelphia jumped to a large early lead. Seeking a spark to propel the team, Devine and Keane made a bold move. They traded starting pitcher Ernie Broglio to the Chicago Cubs for the immensely talented but largely unproved Lou Brock. When a cautious Devine asked Keane's opinion on the potential trade, Johnny replied, "What are we waiting for?" Brock was eventually installed as the everyday left fielder. His speed, coupled with Keane's willingness to use it, added a key ingredient of unpredictability to the St. Louis offense. A second important move was the July recall of Mike Shannon and installing him as the everyday right fielder. Shannon provided defensive prowess and additional hitting power.

Even with these Cardinals moves, Philadelphia remained comfortably in the lead. At the beginning of August, the Phillies led the sixth-place Cardinals by seven games. Based on Keane's strong recommendation, the Cardinals then made a seemingly innocuous but critical last move; they summoned journeyman reliever Barney Schultz from Triple-A Jacksonville. St. Louis began to creep closer to tiring Philadelphia. In mid-August the Dodgers' hopes for a repeat received a crushing blow when Sandy Koufax suffered a season-ending injury to his elbow while sliding into second base.[20]

Fearing a repeat of the 1963 near-miss, a deeply disappointed Busch began planning for the post-Devine/Keane era. On August 17, with the Cardinals still nine games behind Philadelphia, Busch asked for and received Devine's resignation. Based primarily on the recommendation of Rickey, he hired Bob Howsam to replace Devine.

Citing the availability of Leo Durocher, sportswriters speculated that Keane would be the next to go. Seeing the fate of his career-long friend Devine and uncertain that with all the off-the-field distractions the club could overtake Philadelphia, Keane feared for his job. Anticipating his dismissal, Johnny carried a resignation letter with him during the last frantic weeks. Both Lela and their daughter, Pat, helped him draft the letter.

Keane's fears proved correct. Busch and Durocher held a clandestine meeting in late August to discuss Durocher's becoming manager in 1965. Busch always denied offering Durocher the job, but Durocher said, "When a man says to me 'Do we have a deal,' and I answer, 'We have a deal,' and we shake hands on it, what does that mean?"[21]

Amid this swirl of front-office activity and uncertainty, the pennant race momentum shifted dramatically away from Philadelphia and toward St. Louis. Leading by six and a half games with twelve games to play, the Phillies lost ten games in a row, including three to the Cardinals.

The Cardinals played their last six high-pressure games at home. At every game, Lela sat at field level by the Cardinals dugout within Johnny's view. As she had for so many games throughout his managerial career, she kept score. When they won the pennant on the last day of the season, the couple celebrated with an emotional embrace and a kiss. As cheering fans watched, she broke down and cried.[22]

After the Cardinals unexpectedly beat the favored Yankees in the World Series, Keane had one more surprise to offer. On October 16, during a post-Series news conference, Keane politely refused the hefty new contract Busch had offered him and resigned. On the same day, the Yankees fired their manager, Yogi Berra, and four days later they hired Keane. It came to light later that toward the end of the season, as Keane's job was reportedly in jeopardy, he had opened a line of communication with the Yankees. *The Sporting News* subsequently named Keane the National League Manager of the Year and Devine the National League Executive of the Year.

In 1965 Keane began his new career as the manager of the Yankees. He took over an aging team that suffered some key injuries during the season and finished 77-85, a disappointing sixth in the American League. In his book *Ball Four*, pitcher Jim Bouton strongly criticized Johnny's frantic effort to energize the veteran Yankee club. However, he also points out that the players always considered Keane an outsider and

resisted him from the start. As he pushed them, their resistance quickly turned to hate. Their whispered criticisms became personal.[23] Through it all, Keane, with Lela and Pat's unwavering support, remained focused on trying to get the team's course corrected.

The Yankees fired Keane in early May of 1966 after the Yankees started slowly.[24] The Yankees were 4-16 at the time. It was the first time he had been fired in his twenty-two years as a manager. He and Lela spent the rest of 1966 in Houston enjoying their two young and boisterous grandsons. Late in the year, on the day his Yankees contract expired, he was hired by the California Angels as a special assignment scout beginning in 1967. Unexpectedly, on January 6, 1967, Keane suffered a fatal heart attack in his Houston home.[25] He was fifty-five years old. Lela died in 1992.

As a Major League manager for six seasons, Johnny's cumulative record stands at 398 wins and 350 losses. His seventeen-year Minor League managerial record stands at 1,357 wins and 1,166 losses.[26]

Upon his death, members of the Cardinals and Yankees who played under Keane reflected on his lifelong love of baseball. "Johnny was one of the finest guys that ever happened to be in baseball," said Stan Musial. "He was a gentleman and a real credit to the game." "There isn't a thing I know that you can say bad about him," said Ken Boyer. "As a manager, he demanded respect and he got it. He expected a lot from his ballplayers, and rightly so. He was not an easy man on players, but he was a good manager." Whitey Ford, whom Keane had managed for a little over a season, called him "a true gentleman and a fine baseball man." "He was a fine gentleman," remembered Elston Howard. "He'll be missed by people in all fields of sports."

"Johnny," reflected Bing Devine, Johnny's Cardinal mentor, "was like one of the family. I have never known a finer man."[27]

Johnny and Lela are buried together in Houston, Texas.

Chapter 45. **Vern Benson**

Rory Costello

"For a man who wants to stay in baseball, being a utilityman is the best training he can get. Much better than being a regular. The fellow who's on the bench, if he applies himself, has an opportunity to study every facet of the game, and to learn more about it than the regular."[1]

That was Vern Benson in 1968. Fifteen years before, the infielder-outfielder's modest Major League career (.202 in 104 at bats over fractions of five seasons spread over eleven years) had ended. Yet he stayed in the game for decades, passing on his knowledge. Although he served just briefly as an acting manager in the Majors, he was a skipper for eight and a half seasons in the Minors and seven more in winter ball. Benson was also a big-league coach during eighteen summers, and though he stepped down from that role after the 1980 season, he remained active as a scout until 1996.

Perhaps the greatest testimonial to Benson's impact as a teacher came from Bob Gibson. As author Tom Van Hyning wrote, "Benson remembers a thank-you note he received from Gibson after the pitcher's retirement from baseball. 'I wouldn't want to take any credit for the success Gibson had after that [their winter together in Puerto Rico in 1961–62], but that tells me something.'"[2]

Vernon Adair Benson was born on September 19, 1924, in Granite Quarry, North Carolina, of Swedish and Irish descent. His father, William Luther Benson, was a brick mason. His mother, born Ruth Elizabeth Foster, was a homemaker. Vern's one brother, William Luther Jr., became an accountant.

The 1964 Cardinals' third base coach, Vern Benson began in the Major Leagues as a utility man. He coached for eighteen years in the big leagues.

When he wasn't on the road with baseball, Benson did not stray far from his native soil, living in either Granite Quarry or neighboring Salisbury. He and his wife, Rachael Lyerly Benson, were married for more than sixty-one years—from October 23, 1946, until she died in April 2008. The Bensons had two daughters, Bonnie and Robin. In addition to Benson's seven grandchildren, he has become a great-grandfather.

Growing up, Benson played baseball and basketball at Granite Quarry High School. After high school he entered Catawba College in Salisbury in 1942, where he focused on baseball. Records he set include a streak of sixteen games with a run scored. The Catawba Sports Hall of Fame inducted him as part of its second class in 1978.

Few men alive in 2010 could talk about what it was like to play under Connie Mack, and Benson was one of them. After his sophomore year, Benson played for the Salisbury Aggies in the Carolina Victory League, a local semipro circuit that sprang up during World War II. Ira Thomas, who played for the Philadelphia Athletics from 1909 to 1915, scouted the Victory League for the A's. Owner/ manager Mack, in need of reserves amid the war, assessed a group of youngsters up from Catawba.[3]

Benson was the only one who impressed the Tall Tactician enough to get a contract. He signed on July 29, 1943 (he never did go back and get his degree). Two days later the eighteen-year-old made his big-league debut at Philadelphia's Shibe Park. He flied out as a pinch hitter for pitcher and future big-league manager Lum Harris.

Days later, however, the army drafted Benson. He missed the rest of 1943 plus all of the 1944 and 1945 seasons in the service. He was stationed at Fort Bragg, North Carolina, where he played ball for two years. He also went to France and Germany.

When he returned to professional baseball in 1946, Benson had a new position. A brief AP news report from spring training that March said, "Vernon Benson, a 21-year-old outfielder, is putting smiles on Connie Mack's face. The Philadelphia Athletics' manager says Benson — once an infielder — 'may be the man we're looking for.' He has a good arm, is fast and can hit."[4]

Although Benson made the roster to start the season, he saw little action. Of his seven appearances, four came as a pinch runner. He was hitless in five at bats and went back to the Minors in early May — at his own request — to play regularly. He would not resurface in the Majors for five years.

After the 1946 season, Benson was released by the Athletics and joined the St. Louis Cardinals chain. Future Cardinals general manager Bing Devine, then GM of the Columbus, Georgia, farm team, recommended him. "He saw me at Savannah," Benson said. He played most of the next five seasons at Triple-A, spending a stretch at Double-A in 1949. The 1951 season was easily his best as a pro: For Columbus he batted .308 with 18 homers and 89 RBIs, and drew 111 walks. All were career highs.

As a result, the Cardinals recalled Benson after the American Association season ended. He got into thirteen games, and more than eight years after his Major League debut, he finally recorded his first base hit. Nine days later, on September 18, the left-handed hitter stroked his first big-league home run, at Sportsman's Park off Brooklyn's Ralph Branca — fifteen days before Branca served up Bobby Thomson's "Shot Heard 'Round the World."

During the winter of 1951–52, Vern went to play in Cuba. He was the shortstop for the Havana Reds, who won the league championship thanks to Benson's bases-loaded triple. As a result, he got to play in the Caribbean Series in Panama. Against Venezuela on February 21, teammate Tommy Fine threw the only no-hitter in the tournament's history. Benson (at third base) made one of two great defensive plays that preserved it.

Benson started the 1952 season back at Columbus, but he returned to St. Louis in July and spent the rest of the year with the Cardinals as a backup third baseman. He had nine hits in forty-seven at bats over twenty games, including his two other homers in the Majors. Both homers, hit off the Pirates' Murry Dickson and the Braves' Jim Wilson, also came at Sportsman's Park.

Another moment from that year echoed for much longer, though. On August 25 Benson hit a little sinking liner to Dodgers left fielder Dick Williams, who dived for it and missed, injuring his shoulder badly. Williams credited that injury with starting him on the path to becoming a manager. Like Benson, he became a student and observer of the game.

Benson made the Cardinals' roster out of spring training in 1953, but he remained at the end of the bench. From Opening Day through May 30, he got into just thirteen games—eight as a pinch runner and five as a pinch hitter. In early June, St. Louis signed its first bonus baby, eighteen-year-old Dick Schofield, and optioned Benson to Houston in the Texas League.[5] He never got back to the Majors.

Benson returned to winter ball in 1953–54, hitting .346 in sixty games for Pastora in the Venezuelan League, and again played in the Caribbean Series. The following winter, he appeared in twenty-two games for Santa Marta. A quarter-century later, he would return as a manager.

He made his transition to coaching in 1954 with Rochester, under GM Bing Devine, and two years later he was named manager of Winnipeg in the Northern League in 1956. For his first three years as a skipper, he remained a playing manager, finally playing in his last two games in 1959, with the Tulsa Oilers.

In 1961 Benson began the season managing Portland in the Pacific Coast League. Then, on July 6, St. Louis fired Solly Hemus as manager and replaced him with Johnny Keane. The Cardinals reassigned coach Darrell Johnson and, at Keane's request, brought Benson up to the big-league staff. Keane had managed Benson for several years in Triple-A, going back to 1949. "I said, 'I won't come as a yes-man,'" Benson recalled in 2010. "And I didn't."

During the early 1960s Benson coached winter-ball teams in Puerto Rico and the Dominican Republic. In the winter of 1961–62, he managed the Santurce Cangrejeros to the Puerto Rican Winter League championship as well as to victory in the subsequent Inter-American Series tournament. He brought down several young Cardinals for seasoning, including Bob Gibson. "[Benson] was familiar with player turnover, the lack of pitching depth, and other winter challenges."[6] For example, he reached out to the Dominican Republic and got another Cardinal, Julián Javier, to fill in at second base for a while.

Two winters later (1963–64), Benson managed successfully in his only season in the Dominican Republic, at the helm of the Licey Tigres. The Tigres were just 28-30 in the regular season but came together in the playoffs. In the best-of-five first round, they lost the first two games but then came back and won; in the finals, they dropped the first three before running the table. Again young Cardinals were present, such as Phil Gagliano.

When Benson joined Johnny Keane's staff, he likely served as the first base coach, given that Harry Walker was the batting coach, Howie Pollet was the pitching coach, and Red Schoendienst was a player-coach. Keane, who had been the third base coach under Solly Hemus, continued to coach third while managing the club through 1962, although Benson spelled him on occasion that year.[7] When Keane moved full-time to the dugout, Benson took over the third base lines. He also got a chance to manage the Cardinals during a doubleheader on May 12, 1963, when Keane was out with gastritis.

In 1964 the Cardinals won it all. During the World Series against the Yankees, Benson's insights helped St. Louis come out on top. In the opener, against Whitey Ford, he told Lou Brock to ask for a new ball because he knew that catcher Elston Howard was helping Ford load up. "He would act like he'd lost his balance and screw the ball into the dirt," Benson said. The crafty Ford would then turn the dirt into mud on the mound.

In Game Four, with Roger Craig in long relief, Benson asked Keane in the fifth inning, "Who are you gonna use to hit for Craig?" Keane replied, "The way he's pitching, I may just let him go." But after Keane reconsidered, Carl Warwick's lead-off single in the sixth inning paved the way for Ken Boyer's game-winning grand slam.

Despite the Cardinals' championship, the 1964 season left an unpleasant taste for Benson, following the firing of GM Devine in August. After the Series, Benson followed Keane to the New York Yankees as his right-hand man. When he arrived, Whitey Ford greeted him by saying, "You caught me, didn't you?" As Jim Bouton recalled in *Ball Four*, Vern also got the nickname Radar because he was not only the first base coach (Frank Crosetti was at third) but also Keane's eyes and ears in the clubhouse.

"I didn't like it in New York," Benson recalled, "the city or the situation. I said, 'That ball club's getting old.'" When the Yankees fired Keane in May 1966, it was not surprising that Benson went too.

He wasn't out of work long, though. "The Angels offered me a job even before I'd left town. Bing Devine [by then GM of the New York Mets] found a spot for me in rookie ball at Marion, Virginia." When the Cincinnati Reds made Dave Bristol their manager in July 1966, he hired Benson, whom he had known since 1957 (when Bristol was playing for Wausau, Wisconsin, in the Northern League). "I got paid by three clubs that year—but I don't recommend doing it that way!" Benson said.

He remained the Reds' third base coach until Bristol was fired after the 1969 season. Although Bristol succeeded Joe Schultz as manager of the Seattle Pilots (shortly thereafter to become the Milwaukee Brewers), Benson did not go with him. In late October, Devine—who had returned to the Cardinals in December 1967—brought Benson back into the St. Louis organization. Benson was a general instructor in the Minors, in charge of infielders and base running. He rejoined the big club in July 1970 and remained on Red Schoendienst's staff through the 1975 season.

In 1976 Dave Bristol got a new managing job with the Atlanta Braves. He brought Benson aboard as third base coach. "Atlanta was close to home," Benson recalled, "and I could get home more often." He served as acting manager whenever Bristol served suspensions. He said, "When you're with Dave Bristol you get a lot of chances to manage."[8]

Benson's record-book entry as a big-league manager consists of one game. It came under unusual circumstances. On May 11, 1977, with the Braves mired in a sixteen-game losing streak, mercurial owner Ted Turner put Bristol on a ten-day "special assignment" and became skipper himself. National League president Chub Feeney forced Turner out of the dugout after one game, in which Benson and another coach, Chris Cannizzaro, actually made the strategic decisions. Benson took over on May 12. The Braves won, ending the losing streak, and Bristol was back the next day.

When the Braves fired Bristol after the 1977 season, Benson went to manage the Syracuse Chiefs, the top farm club of the Toronto Blue Jays, for two seasons. The Chiefs were 50-90 in 1978, but they bounced back to second in the International League in '79. They lost the Governor's Cup to Columbus in the ninth inning of Game Seven. *The Sporting News* named Benson its Minor League Manager of the Year.

"'I've never had more satisfaction from a club,' Benson remarked at the close of the season. 'They worked hard. I couldn't have gotten any more out of them. They're why I got Manager of the Year. It's not that I was smarter than anybody else.'" The article described Benson as "humble, extremely patient . . . firm but fair."[9]

One of the Chiefs was his son, pitcher Vernon Randall "Randy" Benson, whose Minor League career lasted from 1972 to 1980. Both Bensons went down to Venezuela that winter, as Vern took a job managing Cardenales de Lara. He led the club through the winter of 1982–83, reaching the finals in three of his four seasons.

Benson had expressed interest in managing the Blue Jays when Roy Hartsfield was dismissed after the 1979 season. The Jays offered him a coaching position instead, which he turned down. He said, "I don't feel like I lost anything because I never had it, but I'd be less than honest if I said I wasn't disappointed. If I didn't merit the job after this season, then I'd reached the end of the road there."[10] In early October, Benson joined Dave Bristol once more. He coached third base for the San Francisco Giants in 1980.

Bristol found himself out of a job again in December 1980, and so in February 1981 Benson came back home—literally and figuratively. He became the Cardinals' scouting supervisor for the Carolinas, which allowed him to work out of Granite Quarry. His reports prompted St. Louis to draft several men who made it to the Majors, the most notable being Cris Carpenter, pitcher from 1988 to 1996. It became a father-and-son operation starting in 1994; Randy also worked as a regional scout (and eventually scouting supervisor) for the Cardinals.

Looking back over his life in baseball, Benson said, "I was in the game 56 years and I never missed a payday. I never made much money, but just about every year was enjoyable."

Chapter 46. Howie Pollet

Warren Corbett

Left-hander Howie Pollet was a pitching prodigy, but arm injuries stunted his career. Howard Joseph Pollet was born in New Orleans on June 26, 1921. The family name is French, but they pronounced it "pol-LET" rather than "poh-LAY." His father, Joseph King Pollet, was a railroad detective; his mother was Elodie Cecile (Wilson). Growing up in New Orleans, his next-door neighbor was Mel Parnell, who became a left-handed pitching star for the Boston Red Sox. Their fathers, both railroad men, were close friends.

Joseph Pollet died when Howard was fifteen, leaving his widow with two younger sons, Wilson and Lloyd, and a daughter, Shirley. Howard worked in a gas station to help support the family. He also pitched for Fortier High School and American Legion Post 197. His Legion junior team played in the national championship game in 1937, but lost to a team from East Lynn, Massachusetts.

Pollet's boss at the gas station, Texaco executive Hugh McConaughey, recommended him to a friend in the oil business, Eddie Dyer, a former big-league pitcher also born in Louisiana and a longtime manager in the Cardinals' farm system. Dyer was named Houston's manager for the 1939 season and signed the teenager for a $3,500 bonus, beating out a half-dozen other clubs. Dyer became Pollet's mentor and lifelong business partner. Pollet later said he had used part of his baseball bonus to buy the Harvard Classics book collection.

The seventeen-year-old joined the Houston Buffaloes, a Cardinals farm club in the Class A Texas League, in 1939, but he was soon sent down to New Iberia, Louisiana, in the Class C Evangeline League. He pitched a no-hitter in August and

Howie Pollet enjoyed a fourteen-year Major League pitching career before he became a pitching coach. He was a friend of fellow Houston resident Johnny Keane.

followed that with a one-hitter in his next start. He struck out 212 batters in 163 innings, a phenomenal accomplishment in that era. (No Major League starter struck out one batter per inning until twenty-six years later.) He was deemed ready for the fast Texas League in 1940.

He was ready. Pollet won his first twelve decisions for Houston, celebrating his nineteenth birthday during the streak. He posted a 21-7 record with a 2.88 ERA. He lost one game to Dizzy Dean, who was trying to come back from arm trouble with Tulsa.

Despite that strong showing, Pollet returned to Houston in 1941. The Cardinals had the Majors' largest farm system and usually required their prospects to serve a long apprenticeship. He opened the season with three straight shutouts, the middle one a no-hitter against Shreveport. In August he won his twentieth game, with a league-record 1.16 ERA. Cardinals general manager Branch Rickey watched that twentieth win and broke his rule against calling up players in mid-season, because Houston was twenty-four games in front of its nearest rival on the way to a third straight pennant.

The Cardinals were locked in a tight pennant race with the Brooklyn Dodgers. Manager Billy Southworth immediately put Pollet into the rotation. In his first start he was nursing a 3–2 lead over the Boston Braves when he let the potential tying and winning runs reach base in the ninth. Southworth came out to relieve him, but the rookie protested, "Hell, I'm not in a spot, Mr. Southworth. I like spots like this." He stayed in the game and won.

Pollet started eight times down the stretch, winning five, losing two, and posting a 1.93 ERA. *The Sporting News* publisher J. G. Taylor Spink dubbed him "the eleventh-hour sensation of this red-hot N.L. race." Despite his late-season heroics and those of twenty-year-old outfielder Stan Musial, who batted .426 in twelve games, St. Louis finished two and a half games behind the Dodgers.

Rickey characteristically had plenty to say about the rookie: "He has inherent intellect. He was born with it and it shows in his pitching. What I mean is that he knows how to pitch and can put the ball just about where it should be pitched. . . . No, Howard hasn't the greatest fastball, but it's a good one. It's the variations of his speed and curves that count. He uses three speeds on his fast one and his curve comes up at different paces. The sameness of his delivery also is a fine asset. He has a technique all his own."

Dick McCann of *The Sporting News* described the twenty-year-old as "a soft-spoken, mild-mannered, honestly modest and quite model young man." Shortstop Marty Marion, who roomed with Pollet for a time, remembered him as "a good Catholic boy . . . the calmest person I ever saw."

After the season Pollet married eighteen-year-old Virginia Clark, a Houston girl he had met at a skating rink. Described as "a vivacious blonde" known as Ginger, she was studying piano at Loyola University in New Orleans. Howard (the name he preferred over "Howie") spent the off-season working as a department-store detective in New Orleans.

Pollet developed a sore arm during 1942 spring training and was in and out of the starting rotation in the first half of the season. He didn't start a game for seven weeks in July and August, but by mid-September was taking his regular turn. He pitched twenty-seven times, only thirteen of them starts, and registered an excellent 2.88 ERA and a 7-5 record.

The 1942 Cardinals won 106 games but barely edged out Brooklyn in a classic pennant race. Another rookie, Johnny Beazley, joined veteran Mort Cooper as the aces of the pitching staff. In the World Series against the Yankees, Pollet relieved in the sixth inning of Game Four with the score tied and threw one pitch to retire the side. He was replaced by a pinch hitter as the Cardinals staged a winning rally in the top of the seventh.

Pollet was the pitcher of record when his club took the lead, but the three official scorers awarded the win to Max Lanier, who held the Yankees scoreless over the final three innings. The Cardinals won the Series in five games, and each player took home a full share of $6,192.53, much more than Pollet's annual salary.

World War II was under way and draft calls were claiming more and more ballplayers. Pollet went to work in a Houston defense plant in the off-season. When his draft board summoned him for a physical, he appealed for a deferment from military service because he was supporting his widowed mother and sister. (Being married didn't matter under the draft rules at the time unless a man had a child born before Pearl Harbor.)

Pollet's 1943 season showed every sign of living up to his promise. In July he had an 8-4 record with five shutouts. He had pitched three straight shutouts and twenty-eight consecutive scoreless innings. He was chosen for the All-Star team, but his draft board had classified him 1-A, available for immediate induction. On the day the All-Star Game was played, he enlisted in the Army Air Force. At the end of the season he was named the league's ERA champion at 1.75. (Ten complete games were required to qualify for the championship; Pollet completed twelve in his half season.)

His military training took him to Miami Beach, Santa Ana, California, and Las Vegas, but he washed out of advanced gunnery school and never received a commission. In 1944 Private Pollet won eleven of thirteen games for the San Antonio Aviation Cadet Center team. Sergeant Enos Slaughter, his Cardinal teammate, was San Antonio's star with a .414 average. Pollet went to the Pacific with military all-star teams in 1945 and continued to play exhibitions for the troops after the war ended. There is no mention in contemporary accounts of any combat service before he was discharged in November 1945.

Eddie Dyer had been named the Cardinals' manager for 1946. Pollet had settled in Houston, his wife's hometown as well as Dyer's. The men were so close that Pollet had given Dyer his power of attorney while he was in military service. When he rejoined the Cardinals in spring training, teammates called him "Eddie's boy."

He was Eddie's main man on the mound. In his first start he tacked seven more scoreless innings onto the twenty-eight-inning streak he had left behind when he went into the army three years earlier.

The Cardinals had a turbulent season. St. Louis had ten pitchers of prime age returning from military service, but two of them, Howard Krist and Johnny Grodzicki, never recovered from their war wounds. Left-hander Ernie White, a seventeen-game winner in 1941, had fought through a freezing winter in the Battle of the Bulge and had come home with a dead arm. None of those three ever won another big-league game. Johnny Beazley, the rookie sensation of 1942, had ruined his arm pitching for an army team in an exhibition against the Cardinals; his career was effectively over. Another prewar prospect, Hank Nowak, had been killed in action.

Two other pitchers, Max Lanier and Fred Martin, and second baseman Lou Klein defected to the Mexican League, which was tempting big-league players with fat salary offers. The Cardinals survived a scare when their superstar, Stan Musial, turned down a reported $50,000 signing bonus from the Mexicans, nearly four times his big-league salary.

After Lanier and Martin jumped the team, rookie manager Dyer said, "I felt like our pennant chances had been shot out from under us." As Dyer recalled it, Pollet came to his hotel room and said, "'Skipper, we're all going to have to carry a little extra load. I'll do my part. Give me a day's rest after I start a game and I can relieve if you need me. Then another day of rest and I can start again.' . . . Howie wasn't a robust fellow, but his heart was stout and I'll never forget it."

Pollet's friend Dyer took him up on that offer, and may have ruined his career. Pollet started thirty-two games, relieved in eight more, and pitched a league-high 266 innings. His 2.10 ERA led the league as he finished 21-10. In August he was rushed into a game in relief without a proper warm-up and strained muscles behind his shoulder, but he didn't miss a start.

Two teams built by Branch Rickey, the Cardinals and the Dodgers, finished tied for the

National League lead. Both clubs had a chance to win the pennant on the final day, but both lost.

Pollet started the first playoff game in Major League history in a best-of-three series. With just two days' rest, he beat Brooklyn 4–2. In game two, fifteen-game-winner Murry Dickson and his roommate Harry Brecheen put the Dodgers away to send St. Louis to the World Series for the fourth time in five years.

Pollet opened the Series against the Boston Red Sox on four days' rest. He took a 2–1 lead into the ninth inning, but gave up the tying run with two out. Dyer sent him back to the mound in the tenth. Red Sox first baseman Rudy York had been embarrassed in his first three at bats, but he told his teammates, "He's gonna throw me a changeup one time, and when he does, I'm gonna hit it." Pollet did and York did. His homer gave Boston a 3–2 victory.

During the game, it was reported, Pollet was digging his fingernails into his palm to fight the pain in his shoulder. He said he lay awake all night afterward, hurting. The Series was tied at two games apiece when he started Game Five. Three of the first four Red Sox batters got base hits, and Pollet was relieved after throwing only ten pitches. The Cardinals won the Series in seven games on Enos Slaughter's fabled "mad dash" from first to home with the winning run.

Pollet finished fourth behind Musial in the National League Most Valuable Player voting, but his future was in doubt at age twenty-five. At a dinner in Houston after the Series, Dyer said, "There was a lot of kidding among the Cardinals about Pollet being 'Eddie Dyer's boy.' Well, that suits me and I think it suits Howard, for Pollet is the type of man I'd like to have as a son or as a brother."

Doctors treated Pollet's shoulder during the off-season and Dyer reported he was recovering. But he lost his first three starts in 1947 and uncharacteristically walked eight batters in his first victory.

Later he said, "Every pitch hurt. I began to pitch with a half motion, using my elbow instead of my back . . . and I began to feel a lump in my elbow. It frightened me. I was afraid I was through." He started twenty-four games, winning nine and losing eleven, and his ERA more than doubled to 4.34. After the season, surgeons removed a bone spur from his elbow.

By this time Pollet had gone to work for Dyer's Houston insurance agency and was taking insurance courses at the University of Houston in the off-season. Another member of the 1946 championship team, utility infielder Joffre Cross, also began a long career with the firm. Cardinal pitcher George Munger later worked for Dyer in the winters.

A 1948 spring training headline in *The Sporting News* asked, "Will Pollet and Musial Regain '46 Form?" Stan the Man had suffered from appendicitis and had batted "only" .312, 53 points below his MVP performance of 1946.

Musial rebounded with the best season of his career, leading the league in practically every batting category and falling just one home run short of the triple crown. Pollet's comeback attempt was not nearly as successful. He won his first four decisions, but was dropped from the rotation for nearly three weeks in July. Although he finished with a 13-8 record, his 4.54 ERA was 10 percent worse than the league average.

The 1949 season started no better. He was battered for eleven runs in his first six innings and was sent to the bullpen. Dyer, who had been sticking up for him, now said, "You've started your last game until you throw the damn ball hard." He waited two and a half weeks for his next start, and soon began to look like the 1946-model Pollet. In one stretch he won four straight games and allowed just three runs in thirty-five innings.

"I think I was too cautious about my arm last year," he told reporters. "I didn't dare try to break off my sharp curve until July. Now I throw hard and give it the full snap of my wrist without thinking. Most important though is that I have my control."

Back in top form, Pollet appeared in his only All-Star Game in July, but the American Leaguers torched him for three runs in his only inning. The Cardinals were in first place from August 17 until the last week of the season, when they lost four in a row and finished one game behind the Dodgers. Pollet apparently ran out of gas in September; he didn't start for twelve days before he won his twentieth in the season's final game. He finished 20-9 with a league-leading five shutouts and a 2.77 ERA, third-best in the league. *The Sporting News* named him the NL Pitcher of the Year.

Pollet was a left-handed stylist rather than a power pitcher, known for his sharp control and a fine change-up. His catcher in his early years with the Cardinals, Walker Cooper, said, "Pollet's change actually moved up and in on a right-handed hitter." Jackie Robinson credited him with "the best changeup in the league." Joe Garagiola, who caught Pollet on three teams, called him "an intelligent pitcher." In pregame meetings, Garagiola remembered, "He didn't say how he'd pitch the hitter, or what he'd throw him, but where to play the batter."

In a purple flight of fancy, longtime St. Louis writer Bob Broeg described Pollet as having "the sensitive features of a symphony violinist." Broeg soared on: "The virtuoso of variable velocities, he can throw his fast ball and curve at several disconcerting degrees of speed, keeps batters off stride constantly and he's got the courage to throw his change of pace and get it over the plate when he's behind in the ball and strike count."

He earned a raise to a reported $25,000 in 1950, but he had to hold out until the first week of spring training to get it. His 3.29 ERA was 30 percent better than the league average, but his record slipped to 14-13 as the Cardinals dropped to fifth place. That cost Eddie Dyer his job. St. Louis's

attendance had fallen by three hundred thousand and Saigh cut salaries across the board. When Pollet balked at a pay cut, Saigh called him "unreasonable" and pointed out, accurately, that twelve of the left-hander's fourteen victories had come against losing teams. Pollet held out until just before Opening Day, and Saigh put him on the trading block.

After an 0-3 start in 1951, he was swapped to the last-place Pirates a few days before his thirtieth birthday with reliever Ted Wilks, outfielder Bill Howerton, and infielder Dick Cole for outfielder Wally Westlake and left-hander Cliff Chambers. He joined a former teammate, right-hander Murry Dickson, who had been sold to Pittsburgh in 1949.

On June 22, 1951, Pollet was warming up to start against Brooklyn when several lights in the Forbes Field outfield blinked out. After repairs were made, he delivered the first pitch at 10:44 p.m. The game was interrupted by rain after midnight, but Pollet came back to the mound after a thirty-six-minute delay. Brooklyn won 8–4, with the last out recorded at 1:56 a.m. It was the latest completed game in Major League history to that point.

The highlight of his season came on August 28, when he stopped the Giants' sixteen-game winning streak with a six-hit shutout. The Giants were surging from behind to catch the Dodgers and win the pennant on Bobby Thomson's "Shot Heard 'Round the World." At the other end of the standings, Pollet went 6-10 for Pittsburgh after the trade with an ugly 5.04 ERA. Dickson's twenty wins helped boost the Pirates to next-to-last. Sportswriter Milt Richman wrote that Pollet was "now considered strictly a junk pitcher."

Pittsburgh reclaimed last place in 1952 as Pollet lost 16 games against 7 wins, with a 4.12 ERA. Dickson went from 20 wins to 21 defeats for a team that lost 112 games.

In June 1953 Pollet's ERA was above 10 when he was traded to another perennial loser, the Chicago Cubs, in the biggest deal of the year. Branch Rickey sent Pittsburgh's best player, Ralph Kiner, along with Pollet, catcher Joe Garagiola, and outfielder George Metkovich to Chicago for outfielder Gene Hermanski, catcher Toby Atwell, first baseman Preston Ward, third baseman George Freese, outfielder Bob Addis, pitcher Bob Schultz, and cash estimated at $100,000 to $150,000. Kiner had won or shared the NL's home run championship in each of his first seven seasons, but Rickey wanted to dump his $65,000 salary. Rickey had told him, "We can finish last without you." He was right.

St. Louis Post-Dispatch writer J. Roy Stockton said, "Pollet is well over the hill." He was thirty-two. He served as a spot starter and reliever for the Cubs over the next two and a half seasons until the club released him in the fall of 1955.

His former Cardinal teammate Marty Marion, manager of the White Sox, gave him a tryout the next spring. Chicago released him in May, but re-signed him a week later after trading two pitchers. The White Sox dropped him for good in July, but he caught on with the Pirates. He wasn't ready to quit, as he told a reporter: "I have six children to support and they cost money. Our milk and food bill alone is $225 a month. And with September coming up, they'll all need new clothes." The Pirates were still where he had left them, in last place. He pitched creditably in relief but was released after the season and retired. He had won 131 games and lost 116; his 3.51 ERA was 13 percent better than the league average.

He returned to full-time work with the Eddie Dyer Insurance Agency. Dyer made Pollet and former Cardinal Joffre Cross partners in the business. Pollet's teammates had recognized his business knowledge; they elected him player representative for the Cardinals, Pirates, and Cubs. In those days the Players Association was a tame company union that did not even call itself a union. The player rep's job involved pressing such complaints as poor showers and inconvenient scheduling, according to historian Charles P. Korr.

Pollet went back to baseball in 1959 when the Cardinals' new manager, Houston resident Solly Hemus, named him pitching coach. In spring training *The Sporting News* credited him with "a new idea": counting pitches instead of innings in his pitchers' exhibition outings. Pitcher Jim Brosnan wrote, "Howie is a quiet, soft-spoken gentleman, a type not ordinarily given to accepting coaching jobs." Longtime reliever Lindy McDaniel said Pollet switched him from a side-arm delivery to overhand, enabling him to put more movement on the ball.

Hemus, a firebrand in the Leo Durocher mold, alienated many of the players and was fired midway through the 1961 season. His successor, Johnny Keane, was also a Houston resident and Pollet's friend. Keane led St. Louis to the world championship in 1964, but it was a year of tumult. Bing Devine, the general manager who built the championship team, was fired in midseason and the owner, August A. Busch Jr., was planning to replace Keane with Durocher until the club got hot late in the season. After the Cardinals beat the Yankees in the World Series, Keane abruptly quit to become the pinstripes' new manager.

Pollet left the Cardinals to join the Houston Astros as pitching coach in 1965, then went back to the insurance business. Eddie Dyer had died in 1964, and Pollet, Cross, and Eddie Dyer Jr. ran the agency.

Howard Pollet died at age fifty-three on August 8, 1974, after a long illness. He was survived by Virginia (his wife of nearly thirty-three years), five sons, and two daughters.

Chapter 47. Timeline, September 1–September 30

John Harry Stahl

September 1 — CARDINALS 5, BRAVES 4 — Uecker hit a home run and a game-winning single in his best offensive game of the season. Boyer also went 2 for 4 with a two-run home run and a double. Tied 4–4 with one out in the ninth, Uecker singled to left field, scoring Javier to end the game. Taylor got the win by relieving Sadecki in the third and pitching six and two-thirds innings of scoreless relief.

St. Louis baseball icon Stan Musial collapsed at the game. Dehydration and exhaustion were subsequently cited as the causes. The forty-three-year-old Musial was rushed to a hospital, where he stayed for several days. The doctors advised him to cut back on his rigorous schedule.

September 2 — CARDINALS 6, BRAVES 2 — Striking out eight, Gibson pitched a complete game. Brock, Flood, and Boyer starred for the Cardinals. Brock went 3 for 4 (two singles and a double) and scored two runs. Once again, Brock showed his aggressive base-running style by easily scoring from third base on a short pop fly beyond the infield caught by the second baseman. He took off after the infielder caught the ball, dropped his hands, and began running to the infield. Flood went 2 for 4 with two RBIS and threw out a runner attempting to advance after his catch. Boyer went 1 for 3 (triple) with two RBIS.

September 3 — BRAVES 7, CARDINALS 0 — Wade Blasingame pitched a complete-game shutout and struck out seven. Leading 1–0, the Braves scored six runs in the seventh inning on a walk, four singles, a triple, and a sacrifice fly. Hank Aaron hit a solo home run for the only other score.

September 4 — CARDINALS 8, CUBS 5 — The Cardinals scored three runs in the ninth on a two-out Boyer home run to get the victory. Led by a multi-hit game from Flood, Brock, and Groat, each Cardinal starter (except the pitcher) had at least one hit. Aggressive Cardinal base running again helped produce runs with a double steal. In the eighth, Maxvill stole second while Shannon stole home. Shannon's steal was called "spectacular," as he faked to the right and then slid to the left, avoiding the catcher's tag.

September 5 — CUBS 8, CARDINALS 5 — With the score tied, 1–1, the Cubs scored seven runs after two outs in the second inning to secure the victory. Banks started the inning with a solo home run. The Cubs used five singles, a double, and a walk to produce the runs.

The Cardinals recalled Phil Gagliano from Jacksonville (Triple-A).

September 6 — CARDINALS 5, CUBS 4 (11 innings) — Cubs starter Broglio was set to earn a win over his former teammates. Behind 4–2 in the ninth, the Cardinals tied the game by scoring two runs on a double by McCarver, a single by rookie Ed Spiezio, a ground out, a run-scoring ground out, and a two-out single by White. The Cardinals won in the eleventh on a game-winning single with two out by Brock. Humphreys got the win in relief. McCarver had three hits and scored three runs.

September 7 — CARDINALS 3, REDS 2 (game one) — Gibson threw a complete game and struck out eight. Tied 2–2 in the ninth with two runners on and one out, McCarver lofted an easy pop foul that Reds third baseman Chico Ruiz dropped for an error. Given a second chance, McCarver singled in Boyer with the winning run. Boyer hit a two-run home run, walked twice, and scored two runs.

September 7—CARDINALS 3, REDS 2 (game two)—Tied 2–2 in the ninth, Flood hit a one-out single scoring Javier from second with the winning run. McCarver went 3 for 4 with a game-tying home run in the seventh. In relief, Schultz pitched four innings of shutout ball.

The Cardinals completed their fifteen-game home stand with twelve wins and three losses and embarked on their longest (eighteen games) and final road trip of the regular season.

September 8—No game scheduled.

September 9—CARDINALS 10, PHILLIES 5 (11 innings)—The two teams combined for thirty-four hits in one of the most important games of the season for the Cardinals. Behind 5–3 in the ninth, Brock produced a series of spectacular plays that led to a tied game. Caught in a rundown between first and second, he drew first baseman Danny Cater closer to second and then blew by him safely back to first. "It was the first time I ever stole first base," he said later. Brock later stole second and ended up scoring the tying run on Boyer's two-out single. In the eleventh, the Cardinals scored five runs to win the game. Brock was the Cardinal star, going 5 for 6 with a home run and four runs scored. White had two hits and three RBIS. The win moved the second-place Cardinals to five games behind Philadelphia, and gave the club a sense that they just might have a chance to catch the Phillies. Cardinal captain Boyer, who had three hits and three RBIS, said after the game, "I got a feeling right now that they might be peeking back at us."

September 10—PHILLIES 5, CARDINALS 1—Short

dominated the game with a complete-game, twelve-strikeout performance. Callison hit a two-run home run as the Phillies scored all of their runs in the second inning. The Cardinals committed five errors.

The Cardinals purchased veteran infielder Joe Morgan from Jacksonville (Triple-A).

September 11—CARDINALS 5, CUBS 0—Gibson pitched a complete-game, two-hit shutout against the Cubs. The Cardinals scored two in the first (Boyer two-run home run) and three in the ninth (Gibson run-scoring single and Brock two-run triple). Flood (three), Brock (three), and Boyer (two) each had a multi-hit game.

September 12—CUBS 3, CARDINALS 2—Bob Buhl pitched a complete game for the win. St. Louis scored in the first on a Brock two-run home run for all of their scoring. Banks hit a two-run home run for the Cubs.

Tim McCarver's dad, police detective Lt. Grover Edward McCarver, announced his retirement from the Memphis police department. "I want to be in a position to go to all [Cardinals] ball games when I feel like it," he said.

September 13—CARDINALS 15, CUBS 2—The Cardinals banged out eighteen hits and scored in every inning of the game. Brock, Javier, and Shannon hit home runs. Flood (three), Brock (two), Groat (four), Boyer (two), Shannon (two), and Javier (three) each had a multi-hit game. Groat went 4 for 5 with three RBIS and scored two runs. Shannon had four RBIS. The Cubs committed seven errors. Simmons won his fifteenth game.

September 14—Rained out. Rescheduled for September 15.

Groat, former NL MVP, discussed Boyer's 1964 performance. "Kenny Boyer never swung a better bat," he said. "Without him this year, we're a second division club—easily. If we finish first or second, he should be given strong [MVP] consideration."

September 15—CARDINALS 11, BRAVES 6 (game one)—The Cardinals scored four in the fourth and five in the seventh to beat the Braves. Shannon hit a three-run home run to anchor the scoring in the fourth. A combination of walks (two), singles (three), sacrifice flies (two), and a Braves error produced the runs in the seventh. White went 4 for 5 and scored three runs. Continuing their aggressive base running, the Cardinals pulled a double steal of home (Javier) and second base (Flood) in the third. Schultz pitched two and two-thirds innings in relief.

September 15—CARDINALS 3, BRAVES 1 (game two)—Gibson pitched a complete game and struck out twelve for the victory. Javier's two-run home run in the seventh was the key hit of the game.

September 16—BRAVES 3, CARDINALS 2—The Braves scored all of their runs in the third inning on a three-run home run by Menke. The Cardinals scored in the eighth on a pair of doubles and a sacrifice fly.

September 17—No game scheduled.

September 18—Rained out. Rescheduled for September 19.

September 19—REDS 7, CARDINALS 5 (game one)—Frank Robinson hit a three-run home run with two out in the ninth inning to give the Reds a come-from-behind victory to beat Gibson. Boyer and Shannon hit home runs as the Cardinals scored all of their runs in the third to take a 5–0 lead.

September 19—CARDINALS 2, REDS 0 (game

two)—Schultz entered a 2–0 game with a runner on first and Robinson coming to the plate. He successfully retired the side with no runs scoring. Using aggressive base running, the Cardinals scored all their runs in the second. As Shannon struck out, White broke for third as Javier broke for second. Both scored on a throwing error by the Reds' catcher.

September 20—REDS 9, CARDINALS 6—Behind 6–0 in the top of the fourth, the Reds stormed from behind to win the game. Pete Rose (two), Vada Pinson (two), Robinson (two), Marty Keough (two), and Johnny Edwards (two) each had a multi-hit game. Shannon, Brock, and Groat hit home runs for the Cardinals. In a losing cause, Brock went 4 for 4, scored two runs, and had one RBI.

September 21—No game scheduled.

Owner August A. Busch Jr. publicly announced he was "unsure" whether Keane would manage the club next year.

September 22—CARDINALS 2, METS 1—Simmons pitched a complete game. The Cardinals scored both of their runs in the fourth inning. Boyer's triple scored one run and Groat's sacrifice fly scored Boyer.

September 23—METS 2, CARDINALS 1—Both teams scored all their runs in the seventh inning. White hit a solo home run for the Cardinals' run. The Mets scored two runs on two doubles and an error. White went 2 for 4 for the Cardinals.

September 24—CARDINALS 4, PIRATES 2 (game one)—Gibson pitched a complete game and struck out eleven. The Cardinals scored in the first (one), the second (one), and the fifth (two). Flood went 4 for 5.

September 24—CARDINALS 4, PIRATES 0 (game

two) — Sadecki pitched a complete-game shut-out and struck out ten Pirates. Brock went 2 for 5 (home run and triple) scoring two runs and driving in another. Shannon also hit a home run.

September 25 — CARDINALS 5, PIRATES 3 — The Cardinals scored all their runs in the first and seventh innings. White went 2 for 3 with two walks. He scored one run and drove in another. Richardson went five and one-third innings for his fourth win. Schultz pitched two scoreless innings.

Eddie Stanky, the director of player development, resigned.

September 26 — CARDINALS 6, PIRATES 3 — The Cardinals scored four runs in the fourth inning. A key hit was a Shannon bases-loaded single scoring three runs. The Cardinals also scored one run in the sixth and ninth innings for the victory. Groat, White, McCarver, and Shannon had two hits. Simmons went eight and two-thirds innings for the victory. Schultz got the final out to preserve the win.

September 27 — CARDINALS 5, PIRATES 0 — Craig pitched seven and two-thirds scoreless innings for the victory. The Cardinals scored two in the first, one in the fifth, and two in the ninth. McCarver, Javier, and Shannon each had two hits. Schultz pitched a scoreless final one and one-third innings. The game ended the longest road trip (eighteen games) of the season with twelve wins and six losses, in third place, one and a half games behind first-place Cincinnati.

An estimated crowd of five thousand welcomed the Cardinals home when they returned to St. Louis.

September 28 — CARDINALS 5, PHILLIES 1 — Gibson pitched eight innings for the victory. White went 3 for 4, drove in one run, and scored two more. Boyer went 2 for 4 (two doubles) and scored

Standings, September 30, 1964

	W	L	T	PCT	GB
St. Louis Cardinals	92	67	0	.579	—
Cincinnati Reds	91	68	1	.572	1
Philadelphia Phillies	90	70	0	.566	2½
San Francisco Giants	88	70	0	.557	3½
Milwaukee Braves	84	73	0	.535	7
Pittsburgh Pirates	79	78	0	.503	12
Los Angeles Dodgers	78	80	2	.494	13½
Chicago Cubs	73	85	0	.462	18½
Houston Colt .45s	65	93	0	.411	26½
New York Mets	51	107	1	.323	40½

two runs. Schultz entered the game with two runners on and none out in the ninth. A double play and an infield pop fly ended the game without any additional scoring.

September 29 — CARDINALS 4, PHILLIES 2 — Sadecki went six and two-thirds innings for his twentieth victory of the season. The Cardinals scored in the first, second, and sixth innings. Both White and Javier went 2 for 4 and scored a run. Schultz shut out the Phillies over the final two and one-third innings to preserve the win. The win, coupled with Pittsburgh's 2–0 defeat of Cincinnati, put the Cardinals into a first-place tie with the Reds.

The New York Mets hired Bing Devine as an assistant to club president George Weiss. The Mets also hired Eddie Stanky to become their new director of player development.

September 30 — CARDINALS 8, PHILLIES 5 — The Cardinals jumped to an 8–0 lead before the Phillies scored their first two runs. Flood, Boyer, and Groat each had three hits. McCarver hit a two-run home run in the second inning. In addition to the Cardinals' fourteen hits, the Phillies made four errors. Simmons won his eighteenth game of the season. It was the Cardinals' eighth consecutive win (their longest winning streak of the season) and the Phillies' tenth consecutive loss. After Cincinnati lost to Pittsburgh, 1–0, in sixteen innings, the Cardinals were in sole possession of first for the first time this season.

Chapter 48. **Red Schoendienst**

Kristen Lokemoen

On October 28, 2011, the St. Louis Cardinals won their eleventh World Series championship. Among those celebrating with the team was eighty-eight-year-old Red Schoendienst, who had first tasted World Series victory as a young second baseman for the Cardinals in 1946.

Sixty-five years after he savored his first World Series win, Schoendienst was still an integral part of the Cardinals organization. Officially listed as Special Assistant to the General Manager, at heart he was still a coach, donning a uniform for pre-game practice at home games, at which he routinely hit fungoes to infielders.

Albert Fred "Red" Schoendienst was born on February 2, 1923, in Germantown, Illinois, a village of about eight hundred residents forty miles east of St. Louis. He grew up in a large Catholic family with five brothers and a sister. Three of his brothers would go on to play in the Minor Leagues.

Schoendienst never saw a Major League game until he played in his first game for the Cardinals in 1945, but the sport was central to his life almost from birth. His father, Joe, had been a catcher in the Clinton County League. By the time his sons were growing up, Joe often came straight from his coal-mining job to umpire a game.

Red's mother, Mary, a homemaker, made baseballs out of sawdust for her sons and their friends. The balls made it through only a few pitches before they disintegrated. The ingenious young players also used items like corncobs, hickory nuts, and rocks as balls and dried pieces of wood to serve as bats.

St. Louis sportswriter Bob Broeg (the Baseball Hall of Fame J. G. Taylor Spink Award winner in

Inducted into the Hall of Fame in 1989, Red Schoendienst played in 2,216 games, mostly at second base. Replacing Johnny Keane in 1965, he managed the Cardinals for twelve years.

1979) compared Schoendienst to Mark Twain's classic character Huckleberry Finn. Never a big fan of school, young Al cared mainly about baseball and fishing—and, in the winter, some hunting. And with all of those brothers and friends, there were always plenty of boys around for a baseball game.

There were two Major League teams in St. Louis while Schoendienst was growing up, and the Germantown boys were split between Browns fans and Cardinals fans. Red favored the Cardinals, but both teams seemed very distant to him. Few games were broadcast on the radio in those days and little was known about their players.

Red preferred playing the game to watching it, anyway. Many of the towns had their own teams in the Clinton County League and the Germantown team's manager, Ed Roach, helped the young player learn baseball fundamentals. Schoendienst said, "He was always telling us how important it was to think when we were on the field, to know where the base runners were and how many outs there were. He always made certain we knew what inning it was and what the score was."

By the age of sixteen, Schoendienst had had enough of school. He got his Social Security card and joined the Civilian Conservation Corps, one of President Franklin Roosevelt's programs to put the country back to work after the Depression. Schoendienst and two friends were assigned to a camp in nearby Greenville, Illinois, where they made a dollar a day planting trees or working on roads or other projects.

Each camp had its own baseball team. Red and his pal Joe Linneman were only sixteen and most of the players were in their early twenties, but Red won the position at shortstop and Joe pitched, winning seventeen games and losing only one. Both boys had dreams of playing professional ball, but soon Red's dream would be threatened. He and Joe were building fences one day. Red held the wire tight and Joe hit a staple with his hammer. The staple ricocheted off the post into Red's left eye. He termed it "the most intense pain I've ever felt in my life." His worst fear was losing the eye and not being able to play baseball. He spent five weeks in a St. Louis hospital. The doctors' opinion was that the eye would have to be removed. But Schoendienst found one doctor willing to work with him on exercises to save the eye. His vision gradually improved, but continued to be a problem for him.

When World War II broke out, the CCC was disbanded and some of Schoendienst's brothers went off to fight. Red wanted to play ball as long as he could and took a job at Scott Field (now Scott Air Force Base) in Belleville, Illinois. He heard in 1942 that the Cardinals were holding tryouts and that the prospects could watch a Cardinals game free. That was incentive enough for Red, Joe, and another friend, none of whom had ever seen a Major League game.

The three would-be players hitched a ride into St. Louis. Nearly four hundred young men showed up at Sportsman's Park for the tryouts. Red and Joe passed the first round and were asked to come back the next day. Joe spent the night at his aunt's house, but Red, too proud to admit he had nowhere to go, didn't go with him. With a quarter in his pocket, he spent ten cents on a hot dog at a diner and later, after being driven off a park bench by rain, his last fifteen cents for a room in a fleabag hotel—literally. He woke up with bites all over his body.

The Cardinals kept Schoendienst at the camp the rest of that week, but at the end of the week sent him home without offering him a contract. But the Cardinals soon asked him to come back to St. Louis. Their head scout, Joe Mathes, had had to leave town before the camp was finished. When he returned and found Schoendienst unsigned, he rectified that quickly. The Cardinals sent the nineteen-year-old to their Union City (Tennessee) farm team in the Class D Kitty League. His salary was $75 a month.

Schoendienst gave himself three years to see if he could make a career as a ballplayer. He timed things perfectly, even though he feared that his professional career might end after just one game. He had a good night at the plate, getting four hits. But he made two errors on one key play late in the game. To make things worse, Cardinals general manager Branch Rickey happened to be at the game. Rickey approached his newest hire at his locker and, to Red's relief, consoled him.

KRISTEN LOKEMOEN

"Young man," Rickey said, "this is your first time away from home. You signed your first contract, and you played your first game. That would make anybody nervous. You made a couple of errors tonight. You're a fine ballplayer. But let me tell you something. You're going to make a few more errors before you get out of this game. You look like you could be a pretty good ballplayer. Go out and get them tomorrow."

Schoendienst played just six games for Union City. The Kitty League folded in June, as other Minor Leagues did in that wartime season. The Cardinals sent Schoendienst and his friend Joe Linneman to another Class D team, Albany, Georgia, of the Georgia-Florida League. Because Schoendienst's injured left eye created problems at the plate against right-handed pitchers, he became a switch hitter. In the field he made twenty-seven errors in sixty-eight games.

In 1943 the Cardinals moved Schoendienst up to Lynchburg of the Class B Piedmont League. He played mostly at shortstop, but he also gained experience at both second base and third base. After just nine games, in which he got seventeen hits and batted .472, he was promoted to Rochester, one of the Cardinals' top two farm teams, where the starting shortstop had been hurt.

Playing for manager Pepper Martin, a veteran of the Cardinals' Gas House Gang teams of the 1930s, Schoendienst led the International League in hitting with a .337 average. He was the youngest player to lead the league in hitting since Wee Willie Keeler in 1892 (when it was called the Eastern League).

After playing twenty-five games at Rochester in 1944, Schoendienst was drafted. After basic training, he was sent to Pine Camp, New York, where he hurt his right shoulder while playing for the camp's baseball team. The recoil from firing weapons aggravated the injury, which would plague Schoendienst throughout his career. Eventually he got a medical discharge because of his eye and shoulder problems. The Cardinals promoted him to the Major Leagues for 1945, which, because so many Major Leaguers were in the service, was baseball's worst wartime season. But it was the opportunity of a lifetime for Schoendienst. The Cardinals already had an excellent shortstop in Marty Marion. Schoendienst didn't mind, however. He didn't care where they played him, just so they let him play. He started the season in left field, replacing the service-bound Stan Musial, and got his first Major League hit, a triple, on Opening Day. (He also made his first Major League error.) Schoendienst finished his rookie season with a .278 batting average and a league-leading twenty-six stolen bases.

By the 1946 season, the war was over and most of baseball's stars had returned. Musial reclaimed his position in left field. Marty Marion was still at shortstop. Lou Klein had been expected to be the regular second baseman, but he jumped to the Mexican League in May and Schoendienst took over that position. He played in 128 games at second base, and a few games at shortstop and third base. His place on the team was solidified and he had found the position where he would play for the bulk of his career. He batted .281 that season and started at second base for the National League in the All-Star Game. (It was the first of his ten All-Star Game appearances.) The Cardinals defeated the Dodgers in a playoff for the 1946 NL pennant. Schoendienst then played in his first World Series, with the Cardinals defeating the Boston Red Sox in seven games.

Schoendienst was now a seasoned Major Leaguer, a valued part of the Cardinals, and Musial's roommate. They became friends off the field, especially after Schoendienst married Mary O'Reilly, whom he had met on a streetcar while going home after a game in 1945. Wed on September 20, 1947, they had three daughters and a son. The son, Kevin, played two years of Minor League ball.

After their 1946 pennant season, the Cardinals finished second in 1947, 1948, and 1949. Schoendienst settled in at second base, continually improving both defensively and as a hitter. Some tips came from his baseball-savvy wife, Mary, who also was able to negotiate better contracts for him.

The most memorable moment in Schoendienst's ten All-Star Game appearances came in 1950 at Comiskey Park in Chicago. Before the game, he and some other players were kidding around and making predictions on how long a hit they might get. Red pointed to the upper deck in right field and said he was going to hit a ball there. For someone who hit only eighty-four career home runs, it was a bold statement. But in the top of the fourteenth inning, Schoendienst came to bat against left-hander Ted Gray. Now that he would bat right-handed, he told his teasing teammates that he'd have to hit the ball into the left-field stands. He did just that—and on the first pitch, providing the winning margin for the National League and laughing all the way around the bases.

Schoendienst reached his peak at the plate in 1953, setting personal highs in batting average (.342), runs (107), home runs (15), and RBIS (79). In early June he was hitting .378 but fell off, and as the season wore on he battled Brooklyn's Carl Furillo for the batting title. Furillo broke his hand and missed the last three weeks of the season, leaving his average stuck at .344. A mild slump pushed Schoendienst down to .329. He continued to battle and ended the season with a .342 average, knowing that two more hits somewhere during the season would have made the difference.

Those early '50s Cardinals teams were not particularly good. Manager Eddie Dyer left after 1950, and there were several managers during the period. Changes in managers and players didn't seem to make much difference. In 1953 the team was sold to August A. Busch Jr., the owner of the Anheuser-Busch Brewery, in a deal that prevented the team from moving to another city. After the

1955 season, Busch hired Frank Lane, noted for the frequency of his trades, as general manager. Driving to the ballpark on June 14, 1956, Red heard that he had been traded to the New York Giants. It was part of an eight-player deal that brought Alvin Dark to the Cardinals. Mary had been notified at home and said she "just about fell over" from the shock. Musial called losing his friend to another team his "saddest day in baseball." The Schoendienst family had just moved into a new home and had no desire to move from St. Louis. Red went to New York alone. In his first game he hit a pinch-hit home run.

In 1957 the family leased a home in New York so they could be together through the season, but they'd hardly had time to settle in when Schoendienst was traded, again in June, this time to the Milwaukee Braves, for outfielder Bobby Thomson, infielder Danny O'Connell, and pitcher Ray Crone. The Braves were a team loaded with talent—Eddie Mathews, Henry Aaron, Warren Spahn, Lew Burdette, Joe Adcock, Del Crandall, Johnny Logan. When Red donned a Braves uniform, Aaron said, "it made us all feel like Superman. We knew he was going to mean so much to our ballclub that wouldn't show up in the box score. . . . He definitely became the leader of that ballclub." Sure enough, the Braves won the pennant and defeated the Yankees in seven games in the World Series. Schoendienst batted .278 in five games but had to sit out the last two games with a groin injury. The Braves won the pennant again in 1958, but they lost the World Series to the Yankees in seven games.

During that season Schoendienst was concerned about his health. He played in only 106 games and wasn't hitting well or feeling like himself. After the World Series and the birth of his son, Kevin, he went to the doctor. The examination's results showed that Schoendienst had tuberculosis and that he had probably been playing with it for years. Red had noticed that his energy would lag

KRISTEN LOKEMOEN

in the second half of the season and that a few days off always helped him. Ahead of him now were months of rest at Mount Saint Rose Sanatorium in St. Louis. He determined to do all he could to get healthy and return to the game. By the end of 1958 he had received more than ten thousand letters and cards, including one from President Dwight Eisenhower, who told him that "anyone with the competitive spirit that you have so often demonstrated can lick this thing."

To speed his recovery, he had surgery to remove part of his lung. The Braves gave him a contract for the 1959 season not knowing whether he would play at all. Schoendienst left the hospital on March 24, 1959, feeling better than he had in years and wondering how much better his career could have been had he been truly healthy throughout it. He didn't return to action until September, when he got a huge ovation from the eighteen thousand fans at Milwaukee County Stadium when he came out to pinch-hit. Schoendienst had only three at bats that season, but he was back in the game and that felt good. He was the honorary chairman of the National Tuberculosis Association's Christmas Seal campaign that year.

The Braves' 1960 season started with a new manager. Charlie Dressen had replaced Fred Haney, and Schoendienst called Dressen "the only difficult manager I ever played for." Red had worked out all winter with Musial, Ken Boyer, and other players in St. Louis and was in great shape for spring training. But when the season started, Schoendienst found his playing time cut drastically. Never one to question a manager's decision, he reluctantly rode the bench. He played in just sixty-eight games, hitting .257. He knew the Braves were trying to ease him out to make way for someone younger, so it came as no surprise when the team released him at the end of the season. But he still wanted to play. Bing Devine, the Cardinals' general manager, offered Schoendienst a chance to go to spring training in 1961 to try

to make the team. Haney, now general manager of the expansion Los Angeles Angels, guaranteed him the Angels' second-base job. But Schoendienst felt that St. Louis was a better place to raise his family. It was home. He also felt confident enough to feel that he'd get a place on the Cardinals.

He did, of course, make the team, and more than fifty years later, he would still be wearing a Cardinals uniform. He knew his role would be as a utility player and he was fine with that. Sitting on the bench allowed him to learn more about what the manager and coaches did. He played in seventy-two games in 1961 and hit .300.

As the 1962 season came around, Schoendienst signed a contract to coach rather than play. Part of the reason was that each team had to provide players to the expansion New York and Houston franchises. As a coach he was protected from being sent to one of the new teams. He was put on the active roster when the season started.

Schoendienst enjoyed playing out his career with his friend Stan Musial, who was winding down his Hall of Fame career. Both retired as players after the 1963 season. Schoendienst had signed as a coach for 1963 but was reactivated in late June. His last at bat was on July 7 in San Francisco. He grounded out, just as he had in his first Major League at bat eighteen years earlier.

Schoendienst's first full season of coaching, 1964, was an exciting year in Cardinals history. A June 15 trade with the Cubs brought them Lou Brock, who provided a spark that helped take the Cardinals back to the World Series for the first time since 1946. Their opponent was the Yankees, and the Cardinals beat them in seven games. In a surprise move, manager Johnny Keane resigned three days after the Series. He had written his resignation letter before the end of the season, after learning that August Busch wanted to bring in Leo Durocher to manage the Cardinals in 1965.

As it turned out, Durocher didn't get the Cardinals job. Red Schoendienst did. Teams rarely change managers after winning the World Series (although the same thing happened in St. Louis in 2011). Expectations are high after a championship season, making it especially tough on an untested skipper. Some of his veteran players—Ken Boyer, Bill White, Dick Groat, and Curt Simmons—were nearing the end of their careers. The Cardinals finished the 1965 season in seventh place. Still, Gussie Busch believed in Red enough to bring him back for a second season. After a rough start in 1966, St. Louis finished sixth. But they acquired Orlando Cepeda from the Giants and moved into Busch Stadium II during the season.

In 1967 Musial was general manager, Roger Maris was obtained from the Yankees, and Mike Shannon (with Schoendienst's help in spring training) switched from the outfield to third base. The Cardinals won the pennant by ten and a half games. The Boston Red Sox were again trying for their first championship since 1918. Again they were disappointed, as the Cardinals won in seven games, led by Gibson, who won three games, and Brock, who hit .414.

The team stayed essentially the same in 1968 and repeated its trip to the World Series, this time playing the Detroit Tigers. The Tigers took the Series in seven games, after St. Louis had a 3-games-to-1 lead.

Schoendienst continued to manage the Cardinals through the first half of the 1970s, but those teams did not enjoy the same success. After a ninety-loss, fifth-place finish in 1976, Red was fired. Not knowing any other business, he knew he wanted to stay in baseball, thinking he might even come back to the Cardinals one day. His next job, though, would be in Oakland.

Charlie Finley had just hired Jack McKeon as the Athletics' manager. McKeon hired Schoendienst for his coaching staff. It was Red's first and only foray into the American League. The Athletics were a bad team in 1977, losing ninety-eight games and finishing thirty-eight and a half games

out. McKeon was fired and replaced by Bobby Winkles. Later, Winkles was also fired. Schoendienst was offered the job, but he had no desire to manage for Finley.

After two years in Oakland, Schoendienst had a chance to go back to the Cardinals in 1979, serving as hitting coach for new manager Ken Boyer, who inherited a team in upheaval. The Cards won eighty-six games that year, but Gussie Busch wanted more. On June 8, 1980, with the Cardinals in last place, Boyer was fired and Whitey Herzog became the new manager.

Red and Whitey had grown up about thirty minutes apart in southwestern Illinois. Though they didn't know each other well, they would work together for the next decade. Busch gave Herzog the added role of general manager so that he could obtain the players he wanted to build the kind of team he wanted to manage. Schoendienst stepped in to manage for the last thirty-seven games of the 1980 season so that Herzog could watch the team and scout the Cardinals' Minor League teams for prospects. Red returned to his coaching duties in 1981.

Herzog moved players in and out over the 1981 season and by 1982 had the team he wanted. His teams won National League pennants in 1982, 1985, and 1987. They defeated the Milwaukee Brewers in the 1982 World Series but lost to Kansas City in 1985 and to Minnesota in 1987.

Schoendienst was elected to the Baseball Hall of Fame by the Veterans Committee in 1989. In his induction speech he spoke of the day he and his pals had hitchhiked to St. Louis to try out for the Cardinals, commenting, "I never thought that milk truck ride would eventually lead to Cooperstown and baseball's highest honor." He also spoke about his attitude toward playing the game: "I would play any position my manager asked. Whatever it took to win, I was willing to do. All I ever wanted was to be on that lineup card and become a champion."

KRISTEN LOKEMOEN

Another honor came on May 11, 1996, when the Cardinals retired Red's No. 2. (Technically it wasn't retired, because Schoendienst continued to wear it.)

Mary Schoendienst died on December 11, 1999. She was seventy-six years old and had loved the game of baseball almost as much as her husband. She was known for reaching out to new players' wives, helping them adjust to life with a Major Leaguer. Mary sang the National Anthem before many Cardinals games, and she organized the wives' charity group, the St. Louis Baseball Pinch Hitters.

Schoendienst stayed involved with the Cardinals throughout Tony LaRussa's sixteen-year tenure as manager, there in uniform for most home games. His love of the game never faltered. Nor did the respect and love of fans, players, and managers for him. In his autobiography, Schoendienst said, "What makes baseball so great is you can't hold the ball for 24 seconds and take the last shot or run the clock down and kick a field goal. You have to get 27 outs, one way or the other. Time doesn't run out until you get that 27th out. Everything I have in my life I owe to baseball. I've been lucky in so many ways, making a career out of something I loved to do as a kid. It's been a great ride, and I'm not ready to end it yet."

Stan Musial probably summed up his friend best: "A lot of guys had the privilege of playing with or for Red over the years, and I'm proud I was one of them. He is one of the kindest, most decent men I've ever known in my life. Even more important than having been his teammate or roommate, however, is having been his friend for so many years. They don't come any better."

Chapter 49. **Joe Schultz**

Rory Costello

Joe Schultz, a catcher in his playing days, spent over forty years in professional baseball. His career included five full seasons and parts of four others as a fringe reserve in the Majors. That paved the way for thirteen years as a Minor League manager and another fourteen as a big-league coach. He was there for all three pennants that the Cardinals won in the 1960s. Yet Jim Bouton's classic *Ball Four* is what made the manager of the 1969 Seattle Pilots famous to generations of fans.

"Who could have created Joe Schultz?" said the pitcher-turned-author in 1990. "You couldn't dream up those guys."[1] Although many perceived Schultz as a figure of fun in the diary, the comedy was often intentional. Bouton also said, "I think Joe Schultz knows the guys get a kick out of the funny and nonsensical things he says, so he says them deliberately. . . . There's a zany quality to Joe Schultz that we all enjoy and that contributes, I believe, to keeping the club loose."[2]

Joseph Charles Schultz Jr. was born on August 29, 1918, in Chicago. His father, Joe "Germany" Schultz, was a Major Leaguer from 1912 through 1925. Joe Sr.'s cousins, Hans and Frank Lobert, were also big-leaguers. Mrs. Josephine Schultz (née Doyle) had three other children after Joe Jr.: two daughters, Pauline and Josephine, and a son named John.[3] As a child, Joe was nicknamed "Dode" by his parents—although the boy "had no idea what it meant, if anything."[4]

Germany Schultz became a manager in the Cardinals' Minor League chain. In 1932 he was skipper of the Houston Buffaloes in the Texas League (whose star pitcher was Dizzy Dean). On the last day of the season against Galveston, he sent his

Joe Schultz was a backup catcher in the Major Leagues before he began coaching. His eighteen-year big-league coaching career included six seasons (1963–68) with the Cardinals.

fourteen-year-old son—the team mascot and bat-boy—up as a pinch hitter. As Joe recalled in 1975, "They had a left-handed pitcher, Hank Thor-mahlen, who'd been with the Yankees. . . . The pitcher didn't throw hard and I hit a single through the box."[5] The eighth-grader became the youngest "man" ever to get a base hit as a pro. He then stole second and third and scored.[6]

Young Joe attended St. Louis University High, a Jesuit prep high school for boys founded in 1818.

He was a member of the Class of 1936. His real Minor League career began that summer, shortly after graduation. By that time, his father was one of Branch Rickey's most trusted scouts. Joe Jr. started with Albany in the Georgia-Florida League (Class D), one of the Cardinals' many outposts. He had very little power, and his arm was not strong either, but he typically hit for a high average (.304 over his career in the Minors). Overall, Schultz did enough on the field to climb the ladder successfully in three years.

At the tail end of the 1939 season, Joe Jr. made it to the Majors for the first time, playing four games with the Pittsburgh Pirates, who bought the young catcher's release from the Houston Buffaloes, where he had arrived almost seven years after that first hit. The break came courtesy of his father, who had become the Pirates' farm director in December 1937.[7]

Pittsburgh manager Frankie Frisch kept Schultz as an extra receiver at the beginning of the 1940 season, largely to send a wakeup call to Ray Mueller. "I'm not going to waste my time with his type, especially with a kid like Schultz around," Frisch snapped.[8] At the end of May, though, the Pirates obtained catcher Eddie Fernandes from Portland in the Pacific Coast League. In exchange, they sent Joe to Portland on option, recalling him on August 31. The same year, Schultz began to study law at St. Louis University,[9] but he attended for only two years.

Before the 1941 season, the *Pittsburgh Press* wrote, "Frisch thinks Joe Schultz needs another year of steady work in the minors and with Al Lopez and Spud Davis around, the youngster couldn't hope to be used much in Pittsburgh."[10] Germany Schultz would not influence the decision; on April 13, two days before Opening Day, he passed away after a brief illness. Nonetheless, Joe Jr. did stay until May 13, making (as expected) just two appearances. The Pirates then picked up catcher Bill Baker on waivers, and with the dead-line looming to get down to the twenty-five-man roster limit, they sent Joe back down to Portland.

Joe again spent the rest of the season with Portland. As of early September, reports indicated that the Bucs wanted him to report to spring training in 1942—but at the end of the month, they released him outright to Memphis in the Southern Association. This completed a deal for yet another catcher, Vinnie Smith (who played a mere sixteen games for Pittsburgh in 1941 and 1946). Schultz saw no big-league action at all in 1942.

That November, the St. Louis Browns drafted him from the Pittsburgh organization, and he served as their third-string catcher for most of the next six years (he never appeared in more than forty-six games or got more than 102 at bats in a season). In August 1943 the army rejected Joe for military service.[11] Despite the reprieve, he got into just three games for the Brownies' one and only pennant-winning team: the 1944 squad, which featured assorted other 4-FS. On May 11, 1944, his bad throw lost a game at Washington. Manager Luke Sewell sent Joe down to Toledo; although he was recalled in September, he saw no further action.

The 1946 season was Joe's pinnacle: though he caught in just seventeen games, he went 22 for 57 (.386) with 14 RBIS, also drawing 11 walks to bring his on-base percentage close to .500. In both 1947 and 1948, although he was on the roster for the full year, Schultz did not get into a game behind the plate at all. The lefty swinger served exclusively as a pinch hitter and bullpen catcher. Joe hit his only big-league homer on August 11, 1947, at Comiskey Park off Pete Gebrian of the Chicago White Sox. The Browns released him in October 1948; his career batting average was .259 in 328 at bats.

Schultz spent 1949 as a "battery coach" for the Browns.[12] Then, from 1950 through 1962, he was a Minor League manager. He started with Wichita (Class A) in the Browns organization, and remained in that city when the franchise became affiliated with the Cleveland Indians. After that came four years in the Cincinnati chain—in 1953 he was mentioned as a possible candidate to succeed Rogers Hornsby with the Reds—and two with Baltimore. These jobs were at the Double-A level.

Schultz then joined the Cardinals organization. He spent three of the next five seasons in Triple-A ball. In 1961 he started the season in San Juan, but the team was uprooted to Charleston, West Virginia, in May. Joe was runner-up for Manager of the Year honors as the Marlins finished second in the International League, though they lost in the first round of the playoffs.

Schultz went to the new top affiliate, the Atlanta Crackers, in 1962. He boosted the club with many speaking engagements before spring training, noting that Atlanta was a future Major League town, especially if it got a new stadium. Introduced at one talk as "one of the best umpire baiters in the world," Joe said, "I finally gave up arguing with the umpires the last couple of years. I was getting myself real excited for nothing and besides, I haven't won a decision yet."[13] He never fully reformed, though, getting ejected on nine occasions to come as both Major League manager and coach.

Harry Fanok, a Cards prospect with Atlanta in 1962, recalled, "Joe Schultz was famous for his beer and cold cuts. Cold cuts is all he talked about when the time was appropriate."[14] The Crackers finished the regular season in third place in the International League with a modest 83-71 record. Yet they came back from a poor first half to win thirty-four out of their last forty-nine games, closing with a 20-6 run. Then they won the league playoffs, overcoming two-game deficits against both Toronto and Jacksonville. To cap it all, they conquered Louisville in the Little World Series. Joe, who again was second in the voting for IL Manager of the Year, said, "I've managed about 20 clubs in 13 years, counting winter leagues,

and I've never had a team make such a terrific comeback."[15]

Even so, for Schultz the success was sour—news of his firing broke before the season ended. Atlanta journalist Lee Walburn, who later became PR director for the Braves, remembered it as the first real scoop of his newspaper career.[16] Another leading Atlanta sportswriter, Furman Bisher, said it happened because the Cardinals were dissatisfied with how young players had developed under Joe (the winning squad was heavy on veterans).[17]

Schultz wound up switching spots with St. Louis coach Harry Walker. He remained on the big-league staff for the next six seasons (1963–68). Aside from his duties in the coaching boxes (both first and third base), he remained a mentor to Tim McCarver, as he had been in the Minors. He also joined Clete Boyer in recommending Roger Maris to manager Red Schoendienst, who recalled, "[Schultz] said, 'Maris can help us.' That was good enough for me."[18]

Among other things, Joe was credited by long-time Cardinals announcer Jack Buck with labeling the 1967 Cardinals team "El Birdos."[19] That sounds correct, because at one point in *Ball Four*, Joe said, "Hey, I want to see some el strikos thrown around here." A little Spanish must have rubbed off on him while managing in winter ball. Schultz was a skipper in the Dominican Republic (including the 1958–59 champion Licey Tigres), Venezuela, and Puerto Rico.

Another clubhouse anecdote about Schultz and his love of food came from Tim McCarver. The team had noticed Joe's habit of setting up a choice plate in advance from the postgame spread, and then hiding it under a towel. So they ate his fried chicken and then replaced the bones under the towel. Joe reacted with a stricken wail, "Who the f——did that?"[20]

Schultzie's fondness for beer reportedly cost him one of the World Series rings that he won in St. Louis. "[He] was said to be out drinking with friends one night when he tossed a beer from the open car window, only to have the ring fly off with the can of suds. 'He and some others came back and looked for it the next day,' [St. Louis memorabilia collector Jerry] McNeal laughed. 'And they found it along the road, but it had been run over so many times it was ruined.'"[21]

Late in the 1968 season, it became an open secret that the Seattle Pilots, one of the new expansion teams for 1969, wanted Schultz to become their manager. Seattle's general manager, Marvin Milkes, and Joe were friendly from their days together in San Antonio (1956–57). When asked how long it took him to make the decision, Joe said, "About thirty seconds, maybe less than that. . . . My association with the Cardinals has been great. It's the finest organization in baseball. I think I've learned some things from the players. So I had to take the job. I owed it to myself."[22] Tim McCarver wished Joe well, saying, "Joe Schultz deserves a chance to manage in the majors." He also prefigured Jim Bouton by remarking, "[Joe] knows how to keep a team loose."[23]

Bouton's gift for turning a phrase was on display as he described his manager in the spring of 1969. "He's out of the old school, I think, because he looks like he's out of the old school, short, portly, bald, ruddy-faced, twinkly-eyed." Joe's salty sayings (including his own special expletives) and love of brew amply supported this belief.

Schultz was optimistic that his team would do well, predicting a third-place finish in the AL West.[24] As of August 13, the Pilots were indeed in third (albeit twenty games off the lead at 48-66). However, they then lost ten in a row and sixteen of seventeen, falling to the cellar. That was where they finished, and Milkes fired Joe on November 19, 1969.

In his book about the Pilots, author Kenneth Hogan got firsthand views of Schultz from many team members. While everybody agreed that Joe was a nice and entertaining guy, opinions of him as a manager were mixed. To select just two, Wayne Comer said, "I thought he got a raw deal. He didn't have a whole lot to work with." On the flip side, pitcher Dick Baney saw the Peter Principle at work. "He didn't create a winning atmosphere. I don't think he had full control on the field, he was definitely better as a third base coach."[25]

A 2006 feature in the *Seattle Times* also showed the pros and cons of "the rollicking, lovable skipper" and his easygoing approach. "'Schultzie was the right guy for that job,' said [Mike] Hegan. 'He had a great sense of humor, a great personality, and he was very patient. He knew what he was dealing with.' 'Everyone loved Joe,' said [Greg] Goossen. 'That's why he only managed a year. If the players like you, watch out. Your days are numbered.'"[26]

Joe "stoically described his dismissal as 'part of the game.'"[27] With that in mind, he landed on his feet. The Twins reportedly considered him to succeed Billy Martin, whom they had fired; oddly enough, there were also rumors that Billy might head to Seattle. Instead, Joe joined the staff of the Kansas City Royals in late November. Royals GM Cedric Tallis said, "Schultz is a fine baseball man. Now that he has been released by the Pilots this will give us a chance to talk to him."[28] However, Joe spent only the 1970 season in Kansas City; he then moved on to the Detroit Tigers, where Martin had become manager. Schultz remained in the Motor City for the next six seasons.

In the wake of *Ball Four*'s publication, Schultz remained in comical character. He said, "I wouldn't dignify Jim Bouton by reading his book. Besides, a lot of the things he put in there weren't true." In the end, though, he said, "What the s——. The more I think about it, it's not so bad." In Bouton's view, if there were ever to be a movie made of *Ball Four*, only Joe Schultz could play Joe Schultz (though in the short-lived 1976 sitcom version, short, portly, bald character actor Jack Somack played the character of "Cappy").[29]

In 1972 Joe still did the bidding of his boss, Billy Martin, by running Bouton (then an ABC TV reporter) off the field.[30] No doubt the revelations about Mickey Mantle in *Ball Four* peeved Billy, Mantle's old bar buddy. Martin did not reward Schultzie's loyalty, though, as Tigers outfielder Jim Northrup recalled. "He'd go after those coaches with all of us around. Joe Schultz especially took a horrible beating. No man should have to put up with what Joe Schultz took. No matter what Joe did, it was wrong."[31]

On August 31, 1973, American League president Joe Cronin suspended Billy for ordering two of his pitchers to throw Vaseline balls to retaliate against Cleveland's Gaylord Perry. Schultz ran the team in his absence, but just a couple of days later, the Tigers dismissed Martin for assorted "policy infractions." As interim manager for the rest of the season, Schultz won fourteen and lost fourteen. That brought his mark as a big-league skipper to 78-112 (.411).

In September 1976 the Tigers announced that Schultz would not be rehired. No reason was given. Joe then retired from baseball and went back to St. Louis. His wife, Mary Grace Tesson (whom he married on September 2, 1940), died in 1981 at the age of sixty-two. Grace, as she was known, and Joe had two children: Mary Jo (born 1944) and Thomas (born 1950).

As of 1984, the widower was working as a salesman for a company that supplied parts for railroad freight cars.[32] Five years later, age seventy, he was still on the road with that business. The *Milwaukee Journal* interviewer recalled how Joe cheerfully encouraged his players, "Pound that ol' Budweiser!" Schultz responded, "I have one in my hand right now." He said about the Pilots, "You had to be a humorist out there," and mused about how he would have liked Milwaukee if he had made it for the club's move. "I would have been in a good town with all that beer."[33]

Joe Schultz passed away from heart failure on January 10, 1996. He was seventy-seven years old. Among his many comical sayings, one in particular endures: "Well, boys, it's a round ball and a round bat and you got to hit it square."

Chapter 50. **Bing Devine**

Mark Armour

Vaughan Pallmore "Bing" Devine, a soft-spoken, modest man, spent more than a quarter century as a baseball executive and played a major role in building four National League champions and three World Series winners. Devine left his biggest mark as the general manager of the St. Louis Cardinals, whose owner fired him in 1964 just as his years of work and patience were finally paying off. He made some of the most famous deals in baseball history, acquiring Lou Brock, dealing Steve Carlton, and trading Curt Flood, an event that changed baseball forever. Through it all, Devine maintained the respect of his peers and the knowledgeable people around the game who twice named him Executive of the Year.

Devine was born on March 1, 1916, in the St. Louis suburb of Overland, Missouri, to Grover W. and Pearl P. Devine. His younger sister, Barbara Alice, died at the age of two of scarlet fever, so he grew up an only child. His lifelong nickname, Bing, was given to him by his Aunt Daisy, who noticed the way he threw things around when he was a baby, making them go "bing" and "bang." "He's a binger!" she concluded.[1] He was called Bing throughout his childhood, but the name faded away for several years until a college reporter told him he didn't like calling him Vaughan in the paper. Devine confessed to his old nickname, and it returned for the rest of his life. Bob Broeg, longtime sports editor with the *St. Louis Post-Dispatch*, called his friend "Der Bingle."

Devine's love of baseball, and all sports—he would have liked to play them every minute of the day—was no doubt influenced by his father, a big baseball fan who took his family on vaca-

Despite his being replaced in August 1964, *The Sporting News* chose Bing Devine as their 1964 National League Executive of the Year. He returned as the Cardinals' GM from 1968–78.

tions often centered around St. Louis Cardinals road trips. Before his senior year at University City High School in St. Louis he attended a four-week baseball camp in Hot Springs, Arkansas, that he later said was an important time in his life. "I got an inkling that maybe I wasn't as good as I thought I was," he recalled.[2]

He played baseball and basketball at Washington University in St. Louis, and is a member of their Sports Hall of Fame for his basketball exploits. While in college he edited the school newspaper and also wrote for the *Watchman Advocate*, a newspaper in the St. Louis suburb of Clayton. After his college years he still played amateur baseball around the city.

Upon Devine's graduation in 1938, his father helped him get a job interview with the Cardinals, who hired him as a part-time publicity man. In reality he did whatever needed to be done around the office, along with occasionally pitching batting practice. These were the Cardinals of Sam Breadon and Branch Rickey, though Devine's menial work did not get him much face time with his famous bosses. In 1941 the twenty-five-year-old Devine became the general manager for one of the Cardinals' many Minor League teams, an Appalachian League club in Johnson City, Tennessee. Faced with a roster shortage due to the military draft, Devine signed himself to a player contract and played twenty-seven games at second base. After hitting just .118, with no extra-base hits, and committing 9 errors in 139 chances in the field (.935), he hung up his uniform.

While in Johnson City he managed to scout himself a life partner, meeting his future wife, Mary. At the time Mary was dating one of his players, whom Devine soon got rid of (or, at least, that's how he often related the story). After the season, on October 25, 1941, Devine and Mary were married, and they honeymooned in Fresno, California, where Devine's career took him next. In 1942 he ran the Fresno club in the California League. When the league folded, Devine finished the season in Decatur, Illinois.

After three years in the navy, all spent in Hawaii, Devine returned to the Cardinals organization, spending two seasons running the club in Columbus, Georgia (Single-A South Atlantic League), and seven more in Rochester, New York (Triple-A International League). In Rochester, Devine worked not only with many future Major League players but also with managers Johnny Keane and Harry Walker, both future big-league managers with whom Devine would remain close. After a successful run in Rochester, including two league championships, Devine was promoted to the Cardinals in 1956 as general manager Frank Lane's assistant. This role did not give Devine much to do, since Lane did not involve advisors in his deal making. "If Frank Lane didn't make a deal in a month," recalled Devine, "he'd be nasty, just like a smoker who needed a cigarette."[3]

After the 1957 season Lane resigned and owner August "Gussie" Busch hired Devine to replace him. Devine held the job for nearly seven years. Lane had worked out a final deal in which the Cardinals would give up Ken Boyer, who Lane thought was soft. Devine nixed the deal, one of the best decisions he made in his career. Boyer went on to earn MVP honors in 1964, win five Gold Glove Awards, and retire with the third-highest slugging average by a third baseman.

In his memoirs, Devine credited Lane for instilling in him the willingness to take a chance, to be aggressive in making trades. Devine would never be the deal maker that Lane was, but he thought Lane's example allowed him to not be afraid to make a trade that might be unpopular. Devine outlined his four rules for making a good trade:

You've got to need the player.

You've got to have good reports from your scouts and talent evaluators.

You've got to have the guts to make the deal.

You've got to get lucky.[4]

Unlike Lane, Devine sought and received a lot of input, and he credited other people for his successful deals. Eddie Stanky became an important Devine advisor, as did Harry Walker and whoever the team's manager happened to be. Devine then had to consult with Busch's assistant, Dick Meyer, who would run everything past Busch. Unlike Lane, Devine developed a good relationship with Meyer and they became close friends. Devine felt that Busch had every right to want to be notified on possible deals, and the owner rarely interfered. In fact, if Busch expressed any misgivings, Meyer would likely as not lobby on Devine's behalf to get the deal approved.[5]

Devine made his first trade in December 1957, when he dealt three pitchers—only one of whom, reliever Willard Schmidt, had Major League experience—to the Cincinnati Reds for outfielder Joe Taylor and infielder-outfielder Curt Flood. Both acquisitions had limited Major League experience, but each had shown promise—Taylor as a slugger, Flood as a hitter and defensive player. Flood was just nineteen at the time of the deal and had not yet played higher than Single-A. He would be slow to develop, but would turn into a good hitter and a great defensive center fielder.

Before the 1959 season, Devine acquired first baseman–outfielder Bill White from the San Francisco Giants. White was caught in a logjam with the Giants—after a fine rookie year in 1956, he spent most of the next two seasons in the army. When he returned, he had lost his first base job to Orlando Cepeda, and he asked for a trade. Also arriving in 1959 was Bob Gibson, a fireballing right-handed pitcher the Cardinals had signed from Creighton University. Like Flood and White, Gibson was African American, and the three men helped the Cardinals become a proudly integrated club filled with strong personalities, both white and black.

In 1959, at Busch's insistence, Devine hired Solly Hemus to manage the club, then experienced three difficult years filled with player turmoil. Midway through the 1961 season, Devine was finally allowed to hire his own manager, and he chose Johnny Keane, a longtime friend and veteran of the Cardinals organization. Devine continued to remake the roster, acquiring infielder Julián Javier from the Pirates in early 1960 and Dick Groat from the Pirates after the 1962 season.

Busch was frustrated that the club did not contend and began to put more pressure on his general manager. Notably, in late 1962 he hired Branch Rickey as an adviser who would report directly to the owner. One evening shortly after Rickey had joined the club, he asked Devine, "Are we going to have trouble if I'm here to run the club?" Devine boldly replied, "Mr. Rickey, we're not *going* to have trouble. We *have* trouble right now." Devine knew that his career was on the line, but he had no interest in playing second fiddle after so many years in charge. According to Devine, he and Rickey did not speak much after that. When a writer asked about the reported feud, Dick Meyer said, "Bing Devine is still the general manager."[6] As it happened, Rickey advised Busch to veto the Groat trade, but Busch did not.

Despite the distractions in the front office, the Cardinals finally took a step forward in 1963, finishing second at 93-69. They drew to within one game of the Dodgers with twelve to play, but lost three straight to Los Angeles on the way to losing six in a row, and they finished six games out. The team's success was largely credited to Devine, whose trades were seen as the key to the team. This was especially on display in the All-Star Game, which featured all four Cardinals infielders (White, Javier, Groat, and Boyer) starting the game for the National League—three of them acquired by Bing Devine. After the season he was named baseball's Executive of the Year by *The Sporting News*.

The Cardinals began the 1964 season playing well, and were just one game behind the first-place San Francisco Giants on May 22. The team then slumped badly, however, dropping seventeen of twenty-three games to fall seven games behind the front-running Phillies by the June 15 trade deadline. During the weeks leading up to the deadline, Devine looked desperately for outfielders to acquire. The man he most wanted was Chicago Cubs outfielder Lou Brock, and Devine finally pulled off a deal: he sent pitchers Ernie Broglio and Bobby Shantz, and outfielder Doug Clemens to the Cubs for Brock and pitchers Jack Spring and Paul Toth. It became the most famous trade of Devine's career, and perhaps the best in Cardinals history. In Bob Gibson's words, "Presto, we were transformed." Batting second behind Flood, Brock hit .348 with 42 extra-base hits in 103 games to finish out the season.

Despite providing the final piece to his team, Devine would not be on the scene when the Cardinals tasted glory. On August 17 Busch fired Devine and hired Bob Howsam, longtime Minor League operator in Denver, at Rickey's suggestion. One thing that might have helped trigger the dismissal was an incident involving Keane and Groat in July. Keane had given Groat the freedom to call a hit-and-run play when he was batting, but after it failed a few times early in the season, Keane revoked the privilege. According to Gibson, Groat stopped talking to Keane and their feud divided the team for a while. Devine told Keane to hold a team meeting to air out the problem; Keane confronted Groat, and Groat apologized to the team, putting the issue to rest. Busch heard about the problem, though (weeks after it had been solved), and took it as a sign that there were problems on the team that Devine was keeping from him.[7]

Devine, for one, believed he was dismissed mainly because of Busch's frustration over the performance of the team. Devine had been running the ball club for nearly seven years and only once, the previous season, had it won more than eighty-six games. Now, with 1963's fine second-place finish appearing more like a fluke than a real step forward, Busch reconsidered the leadership of his team.

The 1964 Cardinals' final record, 93-69, was unchanged from 1963, though it was enough to win a thrilling pennant race; they went on to beat the Yankees in the World Series. When the season finished, Devine's role in creating the club began to take over the narrative. Keane, Devine's friend and hand-picked manager, resigned shortly afterward.

The Sporting News named Devine the Major League Executive of the Year, as it had in 1963. Busch was humbled by the experience, and ordered Howsam to fire Rickey early in the off-season.

Devine spent the next three years with the New York Mets, two as George Weiss's assistant before becoming team president in 1967. In reality, he acted as the team's general manager for all three years, helping build the team that would win the World Series in 1969. A key to the Mets' eventual success was the acquisition of Tom Seaver. In early 1966 Commissioner William Eckert ruled that the Atlanta Braves had improperly signed Seaver, a pitcher for the University of Southern California, to a contract after the college season had begun. Eckert ruled that any team that wished to assume the terms of the contract, including a $50,000 bonus, could enter into a drawing. Devine successfully lobbied Weiss to enter, and the Mets were eventually selected among the three interested teams. Devine made important moves to further help the team, trading for Jerry Grote, Tommie Agee, and Art Shamsky, while keeping the organization focused on player development. He also lured Gil Hodges from the Senators to manage the club. Although the team was not yet winning, the pieces were falling into place.

Meanwhile, back in St. Louis, Howsam left the Cardinals for the Reds after the 1966 season and was replaced by Stan Musial. After the Cardinals won the World Series again in 1967, Musial resigned his post and Dick Meyer suggested to Busch that he hire Devine to replace him. Busch had long regretted his decision to fire Devine, and quickly agreed. Convincing Devine was not difficult—he had been born and raised in St. Louis, and his wife and three daughters had remained there while Devine commuted to New York for three years. Devine eagerly agreed. He made few changes to the championship club that won another pennant in 1968, and he remained at the helm for another ten years.

One of Devine's least popular deals took place just prior to the 1969 season when he dealt first baseman Orlando Cepeda to the Atlanta Braves for Joe Torre. Cepeda was considered one of the leaders of the recent Cardinals squads, though Torre had more production left in him. After the season Devine then pulled off his most famous deal, a seven-player swap with the Phillies that sent Curt Flood and Tim McCarver to Philadelphia for slugger Dick Allen. Flood refused to accept the deal, however, and instead filed suit against baseball, a suit that he ultimately lost in the U.S. Supreme Court in 1971.

While Devine built a championship team during his first tenure with the Cardinals, his second tenure saw the team head in the opposite direction. One reason for the decline was Busch's inability to deal with the growing independence of his players, which led Devine to make several ill-conceived trades in the early 1970s. After winning twenty games in 1971, left-hander Steve Carlton asked for a big raise, and the negotiations were too much for the owner. Busch demanded that Devine trade him, and badgered him every day until he did—to the Phillies for Rick Wise. A few weeks later, Devine traded pitcher Jerry Reuss (to the Astros for Lance Clemons and Scipio Spinks) at Busch's insistence, reportedly because Busch did not like Reuss's facial hair. Carlton and Reuss went on to win a combined 450 games after their banishments.

Although the Cardinals remained on the fringe of contention for a few years in the early 1970s, they dropped to 72-90 in 1976 and then to 69-93 in 1978, despite new organization-developed stars like Ted Simmons, Keith Hernandez, and Bob Forsch. After the 1978 season Devine was fired again, this time for good.

Devine worked as a special-assignment scout for the Giants in 1979, and as vice president of player development for the Montreal Expos in 1980 and 1981. In 1981 he became the general manager of the St. Louis (and later Arizona) football Cardinals, a job he held for six years. He worked for the St. Louis Sports Commission for several years, but eventually he returned to baseball's Cardinals as a special advisor in 2000.

Bing and Mary Devine raised three daughters—Joanne, Janice, and Jane—and stayed in Bing's beloved St. Louis. In 2004 Mary reflected on her then sixty-two years of marriage, and admitted to the sacrifices they had made while Bing traveled for half of the year. "We missed you, the girls and I, but we were proud of you. So has life in baseball been easy? Heck no! But has it been good? Definitely yes!"

Devine died at the age of ninety on January 27, 2007, in St. Louis. He was survived by Mary, his three daughters, eight grandchildren, and three great-grandchildren. What's more, he left behind an impeccable reputation around the game, especially in his native city. "Bing Devine put this organization on top," recalled Mike Shannon, who played for Devine's team and later worked in the broadcast booth for the club. "The Cardinals are class because of his class."[8]

Chapter 51. **Bob Howsam**

Mark Armour

Bob Howsam would consider himself one of the last of a breed. A protégé of Branch Rickey, who believed in scouting, player development, and the art of making a deal, Howsam built—just before the advent of free agency—one of history's greatest teams, the 1975–76 Cincinnati Reds, a ball club that reflected that same Rickey-like approach. With the introduction of free agency, however, Howsam, who was greatly disturbed by it, believed future champions would be built mostly by having the most money, not through the traditional scouting, player development, and deal making.

Robert Lee Howsam was born on February 28, 1918, in Denver, Colorado, to Lee and Mary Howsam. Lee had emigrated from Canada as a child, and Mary was a native of Colorado. Lee was a partner in a beekeeping business, harvesting and selling honey.

When Howsam was eight years old, his family moved to La Jara, a town 250 miles south of Denver in the San Luis Valley, just north of the New Mexico border. He attended high school in La Jara, where he starred for the basketball team. He also played first base for an American Legion baseball team, and often told the story of being struck out by Satchel Paige on one of the famed Negro League star's barnstorming trips through the West.

After high school Howsam attended the University of Colorado in Boulder, intending to learn enough to help his father run the family business. In 1936 Howsam ran into Janet Johnson, whom he had met briefly on a double date in high school. The two began dating and a few years later were married, on September 15, 1939. Johnson was the

Bob Howsam replaced Bing Devine as the Cardinals' GM in mid-August 1964. Several years later, Howsam went to Cincinnati and built the 1975–76 Reds.

daughter of Edwin "Big Ed" Johnson, who served Colorado as either governor or U.S. senator for twenty-five years. Big Ed would become one of the most important people in Howsam's life.

After a few years at Boulder, with World War II approaching, Howsam enrolled in a flight-training program in Alamosa, Colorado, and then moved to a more advanced one in Parkersburg, West Virginia. Eventually he became a flight instructor. In 1943 he joined the navy and became a test pilot, checking out new planes before delivering them to naval air stations around the country. During this time Janet lived in La Jara with Howsam's parents. She gave birth to two sons, Robert Jr. in 1942, and Edwin in 1944. After the war, Howsam returned to La Jara to help run the beekeeping business, which became highly profitable in the late 1940s.

Howsam didn't stay with the family business long, though, for in late 1946 he left for Washington DC to be Senator Johnson's administrative assistant. It was while working for Johnson that he got his start in Organized Baseball. It came about when the Western League, a Single-A circuit disbanded in 1937, was revived in 1947 in Denver, Pueblo, Sioux City, Des Moines, Omaha, and Lincoln, and Senator Johnson was asked to be the unpaid president of the league. He asked Howsam to move to Lincoln to be the league's executive secretary. In this role Howsam more or less ran the league—he wrote a constitution and bylaws, drafted a schedule, hired an umpiring crew, and worked with local operators in the six league cities. He spent most of the summer of 1947 driving his car throughout this vast area.

After one season the Denver owners wanted to sell out. Howsam approached his brother and father, who agreed to put up the money from their business, recently sold, to buy the Denver team for $75,000. With that, Howsam, at thirty years old, became the owner of the Denver Bears. As he still had to run the league, the rest of the family helped run the team. Lee Howsam, his father, was the president, Mary and Janet collected tickets, even boys Robert and Edwin helped out by raking the field. Howsam later claimed this experience was invaluable—it taught him how to run every aspect of a baseball franchise.

One of Howsam's first moves was to buy an old dump site in the city and build a new stadium, naming it Bears Stadium when it opened in August 1948. It was later to become Mile High Stadium, and it would be the principal outdoor facility for baseball and football in Denver for more than fifty years.

The Bears led the league in attendance in 1948, and would for the rest of their tenure in the league. In 1949 the Bears drew nearly five hundred thousand fans, more than the St. Louis Browns of the American League and one of the highest attendance totals in Single-A history. In 1951 Howsam was named *The Sporting News* Single-A Executive of the Year. The next year the Bears won their first league championship, and they copped a second in 1954.

After the 1954 season Howsam bought the Kansas City Blues of the American Association and moved them to Denver, where they became the New York Yankees' Triple-A affiliate and replaced the Single-A Bears. The move had been precipitated by the Blues themselves being displaced in Kansas City by the Philadelphia Athletics' move there for the 1955 season. Howsam's great success continued, as the new Bears led the American Association in attendance during their first three years in the league. Howsam won the *The Sporting News* Triple-A Executive of the Year Award in 1956, then watched his Bears win the league title and the Little World Series in 1957.

Howsam often credited two men in particular for his baseball success. One was Branch Rickey, whom Howsam got to know when Denver was a Pirates affiliate in the early 1950s. Howsam watched Rickey run tryout camps and team drills in the spring, and thought him baseball's greatest talent evaluator. He also considered Rickey a great speaker and motivator. Some of Rickey's lessons—about the importance of speed and the importance of youth—show up in Howsam's own Major League teams later.

Howsam's other main influence was former Yankees president George Weiss, whom Howsam worked closely with when the Bears became the Yankees' top Minor League team. Weiss's roots were like Howsam's—he spent years running hugely successful Minor League teams before joining the Yankees in the 1930s as farm director. Weiss was not a baseball man in the sense that

Rickey was (Rickey had both played and managed in the Major Leagues), but Weiss knew how to run an organization. He surrounded himself with baseball people he could trust, and he listened to their advice.

By the late 1950s Howsam had reason to feel that he had conquered Minor League baseball, with a celebrated ballpark, three championships in eleven years, and two prestigious executive awards. To that end, he spent a couple of years on two unrelated efforts—bringing professional football and Major League baseball teams to Denver. Howsam was one of the leaders behind the Continental League, a proposed rival to the American and National Leagues that planned to open in 1961 with teams in Denver, New York, Minneapolis, Houston, Dallas/Ft. Worth, Toronto, Atlanta, and Buffalo. The league wanted to be part of the established order, and attempted to work within the existing Major Leagues for approval. After the league was announced in 1959, the effort fell apart in August 1960 when the two Major Leagues countered, announcing plans to expand.

Howsam got involved in football at the behest of Dallas oil magnate Lamar Hunt. Hunt wanted to own a football team and thought his best option was to start his own league. The National Football League tried to lure away some of the owners with expansion franchises, but Hunt ultimately got the league off the ground in 1960. Howsam's family-owned business, Rocky Mountain Empire Sports, owned the Denver team, called the Broncos, who played in Bears Stadium and began play in September 1960. The club finished just 4-9-1 in its debut and reportedly lost $1 million for Howsam and his family. At the end of the season, Howsam sold his business, which meant he lost not only the Broncos but also the Bears and the stadium. He saved his family's financial situation, but he was now out of work. For the Howsam family it was a heartbreaking time. Howsam and a friend spent the next three years selling mutual funds.

In August 1964 baseball called again. The St. Louis Cardinals were in the midst of a disappointing season and had fired their general manager, Bing Devine. August "Gussie" Busch, the chairman of Anheuser-Busch, owned the club, and over the past couple of seasons had employed Branch Rickey as a senior adviser. Most observers felt that Rickey had undermined Devine, publicly questioning many of the trades he had made. With Devine dismissed, Rickey turned down the job himself and instead recommended Howsam. Busch agreed, and when Rickey called Howsam in Denver to offer him the job, Howsam took it.

Although the club had started the 1964 season poorly, by the time Devine was fired the team had been playing well for two months, thanks in no small part to his brilliant acquisition of Lou Brock in June. It took a while for the Cardinals to make up any ground on the first-place Philadelphia Phillies, who had opened up a big lead and maintained it late into the season. However, beginning on September 21 the Phillies lost ten consecutive games, and the Cardinals stepped into the void ahead of the Reds, Phillies, and Giants to win their first pennant since 1946. Howsam, who did not change the personnel at all during this time, always credited Devine for building the team. After the season Devine was in fact named the Executive of the Year by *The Sporting News* for the second consecutive season.

The change in general managers was not popular in St. Louis. Devine was popular with the fans, players, and media, all of whom blamed Rickey for his dismissal. Howsam's style, meanwhile, differed greatly from Devine's. Whereas Devine had been personal friends with many of the players and spent time on the field before games, Howsam mostly stayed away, other than occasionally sending word that someone was not wearing his uniform properly. Soon after firing Devine, however, Busch realized he had made a mistake, so he told Howsam to in turn fire Rickey. Howsam did so, but Rickey

MARK ARMOUR

had to talk him out of resigning himself. Howsam stayed to run the defending champions, aware that his place might not be terribly secure.

Although Howsam greatly respected Devine as a player evaluator, and grew to admire Busch as an owner, many things about the Cardinals operation bothered him. He felt his Denver clubs, as well as his own business outside baseball, were better run, and he made changes accordingly. Surprised that the Cardinals had no promotions or season-ticket sales, for instance, he implemented a plan to organize those. Also, in 1965 he ordered the resodding of old Busch Stadium's playing field, which was a mess, even though the club would move into a new facility in 1966. And as in Denver, Howsam demanded that his ballpark be clean, that park employees be friendly, and that the field be well cared for. There was natural resentment among front-office people and other club employees, many of whom resisted the changes. Given their resistance, and having discovered some had been leaking news to the press, while others had been grafting tickets, Howsam replaced many of those employees.

The Cardinals' front office presented a further challenge for Howsam. While Busch spent most of his energies running his brewery, he employed Dick Meyer as his personal representative with the team. All important decisions, including trades, had to first be run past Meyer, who would talk to Busch. Devine, whose entire professional life was with the Cardinals, did not mind this setup—he figured Busch owned the team and had the right to have final say. In fact, Devine and Meyer became close friends, and Meyer had tried to intervene to save Devine's job. Howsam, used to complete control, chafed under the arrangement and resented Meyer's interference. In his memoirs, Howsam did not point to any particular decision that was ever overruled; he seemed to object to the relationship in principle.

Taking a page from George Weiss, Howsam

identified two key assistants who would help him. Dick Wagner, who had operated the Lincoln club in the Western League when Howsam was in Denver, was hired as Howsam's assistant. Wagner ran the business side, organizing the club's promotions and setting up its season-ticket operation. Howsam also promoted Sheldon "Chief" Bender to farm director. Howsam wanted people who would be loyal to him and his vision. In return, he granted complete trust in his subordinates. These men would work with Howsam for twenty years.

Howsam spent two full years in St. Louis. He was immediately faced with a major decision when manager Johnny Keane resigned just days after winning the World Series (partly because of the firing of his friend Devine). Busch had wanted to hire Leo Durocher and had talked with him even before the season had ended. Howsam did not approve of Durocher's off-field lifestyle, and he advised Busch that his best chance to get the fans back on his side (after the unpopular departures of Devine and Keane) was to hire longtime favorite Red Schoendienst to manage the club. Busch agreed, and Schoendienst took over.

After the team fell to seventh place in 1965, Howsam made several successful moves. In a style similar to that of his mentor Rickey, he traded his three aging regulars—Bill White, Dick Groat, and Ken Boyer. Although the moves were not popular, Howsam was correct that all three were near the end of the road. In May 1966 he traded pitcher Ray Sadecki to the San Francisco Giants for first baseman Orlando Cepeda, who would win the MVP Award for the Cardinals in 1967. In December 1966 Howsam sent third baseman Charlie Smith to the Yankees for right fielder Roger Maris. These two acquisitions helped transform the team: Maris and Cepeda became the numbers three and four hitters for the club that would win the next two pennants and the 1967 World Series. But before any of that happened, Howsam had moved on.

In late 1966 the Cincinnati Reds were sold

by Bill DeWitt to an eleven-man group headed by Francis Dale, the publisher of the *Cincinnati Enquirer*. DeWitt was a longtime baseball man, previously the general manager with the Browns, Reds, and Detroit Tigers, before buying a majority stake in the Reds in 1962. DeWitt had wanted to build a ballpark in the suburbs, and the group that bought him out did so primarily to save the team for the city. The men did not know baseball, and they needed someone who did. They contacted Howsam and offered him complete control over the ball club, a substantial raise, and a three-year contract. Howsam was happy with the Cardinals and felt they were moving in the right direction, but he could not turn down either the money or the total freedom.

Once again Howsam found the organization and performance of the front office not to his liking. He again hired Dick Wagner to run the business side of the team, and brought Chief Bender from St. Louis to run the Minor League operation. The new owners had much more money than DeWitt had, and Howsam was able to hire many more scouts and expand the farm system. He also replaced much of the office staff, focusing more on advance ticket sales and upkeep of Crosley Field and its environs.

He inherited some talent in Cincinnati. After a surprising pennant in 1961, the Reds had nearly won in 1964, losing on the final day to the team Howsam had taken over in St. Louis. Though the Reds had fallen to 78-84 in 1966, their worst finish since 1960, the farm system had recently produced Pete Rose, Tony Perez, and Lee May, and in 1967 would offer up Johnny Bench. Howsam did not make any big trades until the end of the season, when he dealt Deron Johnson to the Atlanta Braves for Mack Jones to open up first base for May. Then in February 1968, he traded starting catcher Johnny Edwards to the Cardinals, creating a spot for Bench.

Still in 1968, Howsam made two of his best deals. In June he traded pitcher Milt Pappas, who Howsam felt was a bad clubhouse influence, and two journeymen to the Braves for shortstop Woody Woodward and pitchers Clay Carroll and Tony Cloninger. All three would be key members of the team for a few years. After the season he dealt center fielder Vada Pinson to the Cardinals for outfielder Bobby Tolan and relief pitcher Wayne Granger. This last deal was classic Howsam. Pinson had been a star for many years, but Howsam saw him as fading and Tolan, seven years younger, as a rising star. He got the Cardinals to throw in Granger, who anchored the Reds' bullpen for three years.

In Howsam's first three years in charge, the Reds won eighty-seven, eighty-three, and eighty-nine games, respectively, finishing only four games out in 1969. After that season Howsam replaced manager Dave Bristol, whom he had inherited, with thirty-five-year-old Sparky Anderson, who had five years of Minor League experience. The choice was met with derision, but Anderson proved to be one of history's greatest skippers. In his first season the Reds finished 102-60, losing the World Series to the Baltimore Orioles. The Reds had acquired the nickname "The Big Red Machine" and were led by offensive stars Bench, Rose, May, Perez, and Tolan.

One highlight of the 1970 season for Howsam was the opening on June 30 of Riverfront Stadium, which hosted the All-Star Game just two weeks later. The park was already being planned when Howsam got to Cincinnati, but he had typically insisted upon the spotless facility, friendly and clean employees, and efficiency everywhere. He also had artificial turf installed, part of the ongoing trend with new facilities. Howsam, like Rickey, believed in team speed—an element that helped on both offense and defense. This would be especially important, Howsam believed, on artificial turf.

In 1971 a number of Reds had off years, and the team fell to 79-83 and a tie for fourth. Bobby

MARK ARMOUR

Tolan, who had hit .316 with fifty-seven steals in 1970, injured himself playing basketball in the winter and missed the entire season. In Howsam's view, it was the loss of Tolan that hurt the team the most at bat and in the field, and he and Anderson determined that they needed more team speed to return to the top. In December 1971 Howsam pulled off his most famous deal, trading slugging first baseman Lee May, second baseman Tommy Helms, and utility man Jimmie Stewart to the Astros for second baseman Joe Morgan, infielder Denis Menke, outfielders Cesar Geronimo and Ed Armbrister, and pitcher Jack Billingham. Billingham and Geronimo were key members of the upcoming teams, while Morgan, an unappreciated star in Houston, became the best player in the game. Howsam also added outfielder George Foster and pitcher Tom Hall through trades in 1971.

The trades paid dividends, as the 1972 Reds won ninety-five games and returned to the World Series. Tolan's return and Morgan's arrival gave the team even more firepower, and it was a surprise when they lost the Series to the Oakland Athletics. In 1973 pitcher Fred Norman was added, further strengthening the team, but their season ended in even more of a surprise than did the 1972 team's—the club won ninety-nine games, the best record in baseball, but lost in the NLCS to a Mets team that had won just eighty-two. Still, Howsam's achievements were recognized with *The Sporting News* Executive of the Year Award in 1973.

After the 1973 season, Howsam traded Bobby Tolan, one of his favorite players, to San Diego. Tolan had just suffered a disastrous season, hitting .206, and had sulked and feuded with Anderson and his teammates. The loss of Tolan, however, did not slow the Reds down. In 1974 they won ninety-eight games; they were bettered only by the Dodgers, who kept them from winning their own division and making the playoffs. The Reds seemed destined to be a great team that could not quite take the final step.

During this time, in an era of increasing facial hair in the culture and in baseball, the Reds stood out for their short hair and lack of facial hair. Howsam had very conservative views about the image of the game and his players. He was insistent that they wear their uniform a certain way—not too baggy, socks visible up nearly to the knee, low stirrups, black shoes—and the uniforms were clean and pressed each day. While the Cardinals players had chafed at Howsam's old-fashioned sensibilities, the Reds players, starting with the leaders like Rose and Bench, went along. One notable exception was Ross Grimsley, a young star pitcher who was traded to the Orioles in 1973 for very little. To Howsam, looking and performing as a team was part of the formula for success.

Ultimate success finally came to the Reds in 1975 and 1976. They won World Series titles both years and are considered among the greatest baseball teams ever. The 1976 team swept the Yankees in the World Series, the crowning achievement of Howsam's career. He later said that he felt some sadness knowing that no team would ever again be put together the way his team had. Howsam was referring to the onset of free agency in baseball, which would take place in the upcoming offseason for the first time. Howsam was one of baseball's most vocal hawks on labor matters, speaking out for holding the line during the 1972 strike and the 1976 lockout. Howsam had more power than most general managers, as both Francis Dale and later Louis Nippert (who bought controlling interest in 1973) let him represent the club at ownership meetings.

Howsam and the Reds did not adjust well to the changing landscape. They lost star pitcher Don Gullett to free agency that fall, and lost several other free agents in the coming years, foremost among them Rose and Morgan. After a slow start in 1977, Howsam acquired pitcher Tom Seaver from the Mets. Despite Seaver's great second half, the Reds could not catch the Dodgers. After the season Howsam resigned, taking a position as vice chairman of the board, while appointing Dick Wagner as his successor. Wagner's regime was contentious, as he became the scapegoat with the fans and the press for the loss of the well-known players and for the deteriorating performance of the team. The club contended for a few years before falling to last place in 1982.

Midway through the 1983 season, Howsam returned as general manager, a position he held for two years. Howsam's biggest move was to reacquire Rose in August 1984 and make him player-manager. Rose helped turn the team around—beginning in 1985, it finished second for four straight seasons. Howsam retired, as planned, effective July 1, 1985. His insistence on keeping to his retirement date was solidified by the sale of the team in late 1984 to Marge Schott, with whom Howsam did not get along. While Howsam had stayed busy with the team during his five years as vice chairman, this parting was a real retirement. Howsam's baseball career had ended.

He and Janet split their retirement years between their homes in Glenwood City, Colorado, and Sun City, Arizona. The Howsams had been a devoted baseball couple—Howsam had it written into his contract that Janet could travel with him on any of his business trips, and she often had. The entire family remained very close. Howsam's parents lived long enough to attend the World Series in 1970. His children, Edwin and Robert Jr., each had success in other pursuits before finding work with the Reds while their father ran the team—Edwin as a scout, Robert Jr. in marketing.

Howsam was named to the Cincinnati Reds Hall of Fame in 2004. He has been a perennial candidate for the Baseball Hall of Fame, but as of 2012 he had not yet attained that honor. He died of heart failure on February 19, 2008, in Sun City, just nine days shy of his ninetieth birthday. He was survived by Janet, his wife of sixty-nine years, and their two sons.

MARK ARMOUR

Chapter 52. **Branch Rickey**

Andy McCue

Branch Rickey was "a man of strange complexities, not to mention downright contradictions," wrote the *New York Times*'s John Drebinger. The great decision to break baseball's policy of excluding blacks, for which he is justly praised, has, in recent decades, tended to overwhelm the highly negative image he had earned before that decision. He went from "El Cheapo" to moral beacon in just a few years, and richly deserved each characterization.

He was deeply religious, sowing biblical quotations and religious axioms like Johnny Appleseed sowed apple seeds.

He was a tightwad. "Rickey believes in economy in everything except his own salary," wrote the *New York Daily Mirror*'s Dan Parker. *Daily News* columnist Jimmy Powers tagged him "El Cheapo" after Rickey dumped a number of the Dodgers' older, and better-known, players soon after taking over.

He was politically and socially conservative. He preached on the temperance circuit as a young man and, as an older man, would regularly attack Communism, Communists, and liberal politicians.

He preached courage and honesty, yet he was devious. Bob Broeg of the *St. Louis Post-Dispatch* dubbed him "Branch Richelieu." When a decision by Commissioner Kenesaw M. Landis deprived Rickey of a promising player, he could actively work to subvert the decision through fake transfers. Rickey could "think up many a little scheme that, while not dishonest, still will not leave Rickey & Co. holding the sack on the snipe hunt," wrote Bill Corum in the *New York Journal-American*.

He could bring Jackie Robinson to the Majors,

In 1964 Branch Rickey served as a consultant to August Busch and recommended Bob Howsam to replace the fired Bing Devine. The Hall of Fame inducted Rickey in 1967.

and tell stories of being deeply moved when an African American player he coached in college sought to rub off his skin color to escape the prejudices of white America, but he could also relate dialect jokes. He made anti-Catholic remarks at the dinner table and characterized a potential Dodgers purchaser as being "of Jewish extraction and characteristics."

He was articulate, if inclined to overdo the rhetoric and the vocabulary. "Rickey's natural element is the pulpit," wrote Red Smith. "He talks with such pontifical oratory that he could and would make a reading of batting averages sound as impressive and as stirring as Lincoln's Gettysburg Address," said the *New York Times*'s Arthur Daley. Players who stumbled out of salary-negotiating sessions were amazed at the verbal rings that had been run around them, and at the salaries they had accepted.

He was absent-minded, often tossing lighted matches into trash cans filled with paper and acknowledging defeat when his five daughters all wound up with fingers next to their noses, the family code that somebody was talking too much. Jane Moulton Rickey, whom he met when she was twelve, proposed to a hundred times, and married at twenty-four, could note, "Mr. Rickey is not, and never has been, one of the ten best-groomed men in America."

He was fearsomely intelligent, well read, and thoughtful.

Wesley Branch Rickey was born on December 20, 1881, in the hamlet of Flat in Scioto County, Ohio. His parents, Jacob Franklin "Frank" Rickey and Emily Brown Rickey, worked a small farm. Branch had an older brother, Orla, born in 1875, and a younger brother, Frank, born in 1888. As Branch's first name would indicate—John Wesley was the founder of Methodism—it was a pious, Methodist household. Rickey finished grade school in Lucasville, Ohio, but then farm labor called. With help from a sympathetic retired educator, he read as widely as the resources of Scioto County allowed in the 1890s. He educated himself enough to become the teacher at the local grade school, saving money for college. Eventually, he went off to Ohio Wesleyan University. For the next decade, Rickey's life was a welter of sporadic academics, sports, and, eventually, coaching.

He played baseball and football at Ohio Wesleyan and, realizing he could make money to pay for his studies, entered baseball's semipro summer circuit in 1902 and began to coach the university team the next spring. That summer, he moved to the Minor Leagues, playing in Terre Haute, Indiana; LeMars, Iowa; and Dallas, Texas. In 1904, after graduation, Rickey returned to Dallas and was purchased by the Cincinnati Reds near the end of the season.

He spent parts of the next three seasons in the Majors, earning a reputation as a marginal catcher, a poor hitter, and an odd duck for refusing to play baseball on Sundays. In Cincinnati his refusal to play on Sundays infuriated manager Joe Kelley, who released him back to Dallas before he appeared in a league game. For the winter, Rickey moved to Allegheny College, in Meadville, Pennsylvania, where he served as football and baseball coach.

That winter the Chicago White Sox purchased Rickey's contract, but they sent him to the St. Louis Browns after deciding they could not afford a catcher who took Sundays off and would not report until his college coaching duties were done. He made his Major League debut on June 16, 1905. That one appearance was it for the year, as his mother became ill and Rickey went back to Lucasville. As her recovery progressed, he went back to Dallas before heading to Allegheny for another year of coaching. There, he became disillusioned with the semiprofessional character of college football and left before the baseball season began.

When the 1906 season did begin, Rickey was back with the Browns. He had his best year that summer, playing in sixty-five games and hitting .284. The left-handed-hitting Rickey had his first Major League safety, a single, on April 23 off Detroit southpaw Ed Killian at Sportsman's Park. The offensive highlight of his career came on August 6 against the New York Yankees. Rickey hit a two-run homer in the bottom of the second inning to chase Jack Chesbro and extend the

Browns' lead to 5–0. He then hit a "fluke" inside-the-park home run off reliever Walter Clarkson in the sixth inning to make the score 6–2. But by the end of the summer, his arm was hurting. He returned to Ohio Wesleyan to coach and complete the courses he needed to enter law school. In late winter, the shoulder pain returned.

During the off-season, Rickey had been transferred to the Yankees. Despite a spring training visit to Hot Springs, Arkansas, his arm did not improve. Rickey played sporadically and the league noticed his inability to throw. On June 28, 1907, the Washington Senators stole thirteen consecutive bases against him, and Rickey had stopped bothering to throw by the end of the game. It's a record that stands a century later. Offensively, his average fell to .182 in 52 games. He would make a cameo two-game appearance for the Browns in 1914, but otherwise his playing career was finished. In all, he played in 120 games over four seasons and had a .239 lifetime batting average.

After marrying Jane in Lucasville in June 1906, he had turned to a laundry list of jobs. He was Ohio Wesleyan's athletic director, while also coaching football, basketball, and baseball. He was secretary of the Delaware, Ohio, YMCA, and he taught beginning law classes even while taking other law classes as a student. As 1908 rolled in, Rickey threw himself into William Howard Taft's campaign for the presidency and the work of the Anti-Saloon League. By the end of 1908, perhaps run down from his schedule, Rickey was diagnosed with tuberculosis, the biggest medical killer of the time.

He spent much of 1909 in a sanatorium in upstate New York, leaving only to begin his first semester at the University of Michigan law school in the fall. By early 1910, his health had improved enough for him to supplement his savings by coaching the university's baseball team.

In 1911, nearing age thirty, Branch Rickey graduated from law school and chose Boise, Idaho, as the site of his law office. He was, by his own accounts, a miserable failure, gaining one client, who did not even want a lawyer. The impressions he had made as a baseball player and coach came to his rescue. Even while in Boise, he had spent his summer scouting for Robert Hedges, owner of the St. Louis Browns, who had been impressed with Rickey's intelligence and articulate presentations when he was a player. After his second unsuccessful winter in Boise, Rickey was only too happy to respond to Hedges's request for a meeting in Salt Lake City to discuss a full-time job with the Browns. He borrowed the train fare from Hedges and began a half century of life in professional baseball.

Rickey's initial role was somewhere between scout and general manager. With the help of full-time scout Charley Barrett, Rickey evaluated and tracked players from the Midwest and South. In the winter of 1912, he produced a list of players the Browns could draft from Minor League teams, and 30 of the 105 players chosen that winter were taken by the Browns. By mid-1913, Rickey was the field manager of the Browns. He began teaching his players with a blend of lectures, heart-to-heart talks, and drills. He also began his lifelong fascination with statistical analysis, hiring a young man to sit behind home plate and keep track of how many bases each player made for himself and advanced his teammates. The team improved in 1914, but slid back in 1915 amid accusations that Rickey was too intellectual in dealing with his players.

That winter, Hedges sold the Browns to Phil Ball, after granting Rickey a long-term contract. Ball, however, was contemptuous of Rickey's religious views and his approach to the game. He brought in Fielder Jones as field manager while Rickey chafed in his former role of finding players for the Browns. By the spring of 1917, a new ownership group for the National League's St. Louis team persuaded Ball to let Rickey out of his contract to become the Cardinals' president.

While he was still in St. Louis with his growing family, running the Cardinals was not a dream job. The new ownership was undercapitalized. The team had finished in the top half of the league once in the previous quarter century. Rickey and Cardinals manager Miller Huggins clashed over Rickey's "theoretical" approach to the game. The 1917 Cardinals struggled to their best record since 1891, but it was good only for third place. After the season, Huggins was lured away by the New York Yankees, and Rickey hired Jack Hendricks to take his place.

In August 1918 Rickey joined the Army Chemical Corps, then a new field with cachet. He was commissioned a major and joined a unit with Captains Ty Cobb and Christy Mathewson. In the weeks leading to the November 11 armistice, Rickey's unit supported a number of American attacks on the Germans. He was back in the United States on December 23 and in Lucasville with the family for Christmas.

The Cardinals team he returned to was in serious financial trouble. Rickey borrowed Jane's family heirloom rugs to make his barren office look respectable, and made himself manager to save a salary. But he was building the foundation that would make the Cardinals a dominant team for the next three decades.

Rickey's record as manager of the Cardinals was mediocre. For his first three years, he increased the win totals each year, and the Cardinals reached third place by 1921. But by 1923 the team had slipped to fifth, then sixth, before he was replaced early in 1925. Angry and humiliated, he contemplated quitting, but eventually decided to remain as general manager. For those who questioned Rickey's ability to lead and motivate players, they had their prejudices confirmed when Rogers Hornsby took the Cardinals to the 1926 pennant and their first World Series championship.

While the critics savaged Rickey as a manager, no one doubted his abilities in the front office. It was only when Rickey was kicked upstairs from the Cardinals' dugout that he found his true role. "Rickey practically created the office of business manager as it is understood today," wrote the *New York Times*'s John Drebinger in 1943.

Rickey's first great innovation was the farm system. "When the Cardinals were fighting for their life in the National League, I found that we were at a disadvantage in obtaining players of merit from the minors," Rickey said. "Other clubs could outbid. They had money. They had superior scouting machinery. In short, we had to take what was left or nothing at all. . . . Thus it was that we took over the Houston Club for a Class A proving ground in 1924. . . . Still, I do not feel that the farming system we have established is the result of any inventive genius—it is the result of stark necessity. We did it to meet a question of supply and demand of young ballplayers," he told *The Sporting News*'s Dick Farrington.

The Cardinals eventually created a chain of Minor League teams so they could sign players cheaply, winnow the good from the great, win pennants, and make money. Rickey would sell the good to others and keep the great for the Cardinals.

Rickey proved a cold-blooded judge of talent, and a man with the knack for nurturing what talent he had. He was not the sentimentalist to hang on to an aging player who had contributed greatly to the team's past success. It is better to trade a man a year too early than a year too late, he preached. He created the concept of the "anesthetic ballplayer," the one who is good enough to be a Major Leaguer, but not good enough to help win a pennant or a World Series. Trading the anesthetics and the fading stars filled holes the farm system could not. And in the Minors, Rickey was an innovator not just in creating, but in teaching.

He came up with sandpits to teach players to slide; a set of strings to define the strike zone and help pitchers with their control; the batting tee to help hitters hone their swings, and chalk talks. After World War II, when Rickey was with the Dodgers, he expanded on the statistical analysis he had first tried with the Browns. He hired Allan Roth as the first full-time team statistician.

Rickey was observant in a way that amazed even other baseball men. There was the story of one pitch — a foul ball — while Rickey was sitting behind the plate one day. After the pitch he turned to an aide and dictated the following notes: The center fielder had failed to get a jump on the ball, the pitcher had an unbalanced motion and would not be able to field his position, and the catcher had blinked as the batter swung, causing him to miss the foul tip.

Rickey's player-evaluation skills built the Cardinal machine that dominated the National League, winning nine pennants and six World Series between 1926 and 1946. This machine, built on the ownership of Minor League clubs, did not run smoothly. Baseball commissioner Landis did not like to see minor leagues or teams run simply as talent suppliers for the Major Leagues. He wanted them to act as independent businesses. He wanted players to have the fullest freedom to exploit their talent, and not get stuck in the Minor League systems of talent-rich organizations. Rickey, whose plan had been followed by the other Major League teams, argued that Major League ownership had allowed the Minor Leagues to survive the Depression of the 1930s.

In 1938, in what became known as the Cedar Rapids decision, Landis freed at least seventy-four Cardinals farmhands. Landis found that the Cardinals had relationships with more than one team in some leagues, meaning it could affect pennant races by moving players between these teams. He offered no evidence that they had done so. The one released player of unusual talent was Pete Reiser, and Rickey set out to subvert Landis's decision by making sure his protégé, Larry MacPhail of the Brooklyn Dodgers, picked up Reiser with a prom-

ise to return him to the Cardinals once the hullaballoo calmed down. Reiser, however, performed so well in spring training that press and public pressure to keep the young outfielder led MacPhail to renege on his promise.

In public, Rickey's reputation as a shrewd executive and motivational speaker grew. He was asked to speak often, and he was never afraid to tie his conservative religious and political beliefs to his baseball success. He befriended political figures, usually conservative Republicans. He was approached to run for governor of Missouri. He was described as one of Republican presidential candidate Thomas Dewey's closest friends and supporters and touted as his successor as New York governor if Dewey were elected president.

By late 1942 Rickey's relations with Cardinals owner Sam Breadon had become strained. The two were fighting over Rickey's bonus payments and Breadon's dismissal of Rickey protégés in the farm system. Rickey reportedly was upset at Breadon's refusal to back him over the Cedar Rapids decision and with Breadon's paying a large bonus to himself while cutting Rickey's budget for salaries. Rickey was considering a top executive post with a large insurance company.

In 1937, when Brooklyn Dodgers board member James Mulvey had first approached him, Rickey had not been prepared to leave a comfortable life in St. Louis. By late 1942, he was. The wooing was relatively quick. The *New York Times* first reported Brooklyn-Rickey talks on October 4, 1942. The move was announced on October 29, a day when Rickey was introduced as the new general manager at a lunch at the Brooklyn Club. At that lunch, Rickey also was introduced to Walter O'Malley, a thirty-nine-year-old lawyer who shared the Brooklyn Trust table with him.

In Brooklyn, Rickey saw a different team than the press and the fans. The fans and the reporters saw the 1941 pennant winner and a 1942 team that had finished second. Rickey saw a team that was old, with a roster about to be ravaged by the needs of military service. It was the disposal of aging stars that earned him the nickname "El Cheapo." It was his response to World War II that would build the foundation of the Boys of Summer.

With the draft in place, most teams cut back on signing players, bowing to the uncertainties of wartime. In response, the number of Minor Leagues shrank to ten in 1944 from the forty-one of 1941. Rickey simply figured the war would end some day and he signed talent in buckets, seeking to repeat his success in building the Cardinals' Minor League system. Players like Gil Hodges would make token appearances in the Major Leagues before disappearing into boot camp, then emerge after the war to stock baseball's richest farm system. Rickey earned another nickname, "The Mahatma," after sportswriter Tom Meany read a portrait of Indian political leader Mohandas "Mahatma" Gandhi that described Gandhi as a combination of "your father and Tammany Hall."

In the years immediately after the war, Rickey blended prewar players like Dixie Walker, Hugh Casey, and Pee Wee Reese with the results of his player-development program. That program had led to another Rickey innovation — the spring training complex. With more than seven hundred players under contract, the Dodgers needed a large facility if they wanted to ensure uniform training and easy analysis of their prospects. In 1947 Rickey struck a deal with the town of Vero Beach, Florida, for the use of the former U.S. Navy pilot training base on the west edge of town. Using a complex system of colors and numbers, the Minor Leaguers were sorted, trained, analyzed, graded, and eventually assigned to their Minor League teams, all according to the Rickey methods.

Except for the Vero Beach facility, which would become a model for other teams, the methods were those Rickey had developed with the Cardinals. But in Brooklyn, he took another step, one that

would raise him from talented baseball executive to sainted agent of progress.

Rickey's decision to seek black baseball talent came fairly soon after he joined the Dodgers. His pursuit of black players was a typical combination of motives and methods. It was a product of his religious beliefs; of his desire to win and draw fans; and of his ability to see baseball in the context of American society. It was conducted not by looking for just the best baseball talent, but for the best combination of on-field talent, maturity, and intelligence. For his African American torchbearer, he chose a college-educated man who would be twenty-seven before he played even one game in the white Minor Leagues. He chose Jackie Robinson in part because he was from California, in whose milder racial climate he had played most of his life on integrated athletic teams. Rickey encouraged him to marry his fiancée, a move he felt always helped a ballplayer's career. Robinson went on to justify Rickey's gamble in every way and cement a lifelong relationship between the two men.

But his relationships with his partners were not so strong. By 1950 Rickey knew his lucrative contract would not be renewed, and he began the steps that would put O'Malley in control of the Dodgers and himself at the general manager's desk in Pittsburgh.

In Pittsburgh, Rickey set out to build the kind of dominant organization he had constructed in St. Louis and Brooklyn. But he started in an even bigger hole than he had in St. Louis, and he made few concessions to even putting a respectable team on the field. The Pirates finished in last place in the National League every year from 1952 through 1955. As he told Ralph Kiner during salary negotiations, the team could finish last without him. Kiner led the league in home runs every year from 1946 through 1952. Rickey traded him while laying out enormous sums for unproven talent. Some of Rickey's bonus babies, such as Dick Groat and

Bill Mazeroski, would pay dividends in the Pirate World Series winners of 1960, but the overall talent would take a long time to flower. Rickey's one original move in Pittsburgh came too late to save him. In 1955 he sent Howie Haak, his best scout, to begin scouring the Caribbean for talent. This move would bear immense fruit for the Pirates in the 1960s, but by then Rickey was gone.

After the 1955 season, Rickey stepped down as general manager, saying he would spend the rest of his ten-year contract as a senior consultant to the team. But it was clear that consulting was a cover for being at loose ends, a situation that did not change until late in 1958, when Rickey began talking with a New York lawyer named William Shea. In the wake of the Dodgers' and Giants' departures for the West Coast, New York City mayor Robert Wagner Jr. had asked Shea to head an effort to bring National League baseball back to New York. Shea turned for advice to George V. McLaughlin, a New York banker and civic luminary who had brought O'Malley to the Dodgers in 1940. McLaughlin suggested that Shea talk to Rickey. Rickey, who had apparently been mulling the idea for a while, suggested a third league.

For the next two years, Rickey headed the Continental League. He wooed ownership groups, promised his league would find players even while honoring Major League baseball's reserve clause, and worked through Congress to bring pressure to limit the Major Leagues' control of their players. The league collapsed in late 1960, when both the National and American leagues committed to expansion.

For two years, Rickey puttered, a period punctuated by the April 1961 death of his only son, Branch Jr., then the vice president in charge of the Minor Leagues for the Pirates. In late October 1962, he jumped at owner Gussie Busch's offer to return to the Cardinals as a "senior consultant." It was an awkward relationship. General manager Bing Devine felt threatened by owner Gussie

Busch's hiring of Rickey. Rickey's opposition to a trade that brought Groat to the Cardinals worsened the situation. And when a strongly worded memo urging Stan Musial's forced retirement leaked to the press, Rickey's status became fragile. He was not helped when Busch decided to fire Devine August 1964, a move that was interpreted as interference by Rickey. The move embarrassed Busch as the Cardinals rallied to win the pennant with a team Devine had assembled. After the World Series, won by the Cardinals, Busch fired Rickey as well.

In 1965 Rickey finished his work on *The American Diamond: A Documentary of the Game of Baseball*, the closest thing to an autobiography Rickey would do. It contained portraits of a group Rickey called the sports immortals, as well as reflections from his years in the game.

Rickey died in late 1965 — still pushing himself, still talking. On November 13, despite having been in the hospital for tests for several days, he checked out to attend a luncheon and a football game and then drive to Columbia, Missouri, where he was to be inducted into the Missouri Sports Hall of Fame. He began his acceptance speech, on "Courage," but fifteen minutes into his talk, he paused, then said, "I don't believe I'm going to be able to speak any longer." He collapsed into a chair and was rushed to the hospital, where the doctors diagnosed a heart attack. He lingered until December 9. He was buried in Rushtown, Ohio, just across the Scioto River from Lucasville. Jane Rickey died on October 16, 1971, and was buried next to him.

Branch Rickey was inducted into the Baseball Hall of Fame in 1967.

Chapter 53. **Stan Musial**

Jan Finkel

Every team has at least one player who is the face, heart, and soul of the franchise—an icon, a legendary, even mythic figure—a man often known simply by his first name or an epithet. Think of the Red Sox and Ted comes immediately to mind. Some teams have more than one. The Pirates gave us Roberto and The Flying Dutchman. Can anyone imagine the Orioles without Brooks and Cal? The Yankees have a small army running from Babe Ruth through Lou Gehrig to Joe DiMaggio to Mickey Mantle, Yogi Berra, and on to today. Willie? Ernie? Hank? Do you really have to ask?

Say "The Man" in St. Louis and everybody knows you're taking about Stan Musial.

They know the name came from Brooklyn Dodgers fans who had to watch him wreak havoc on their beloved Bums. "Here comes that man again!" It's a simple name, almost modest, but it and all the great baseball epithets have something in common: they're earned titles.

Besides being great enough to gain election to the Hall of Fame, what do these legends share?

There's often a compelling story. Musial fills that requirement. Born on November 21, 1920, in Donora, Pennsylvania, he was the fifth of six children and the first boy. Stan's father, Lukasz Musial, came to the United States from Poland; his mother, the former Mary Lancos (primarily of Czech descent but with a Hungarian name), was born in New York City, the daughter of immigrants from Austria-Hungary. Stan married his high school sweetheart, Lillian Labash, the daughter of Russian immigrants. It's a basic American story: a young man rises from humble beginnings and goes on to fortune and greatness.

A St. Louis icon, Stan Musial was both President Johnson's national physical fitness advisor and a Cardinals vice president in 1964. The Hall of Fame inducted Stan in 1969.

About twenty-five miles south of Pittsburgh along the Monongahela River in what Western Pennsylvanians call the Mon Valley, Donora was once a thriving town made up of hard-working Eastern Europeans, Italians, and African Americans. People got along and worked in the local steel and zinc plants. Of tough, hardy stock, they produced a disproportionate number of world-class athletes. Dan Towler went from nearby Washington and Jefferson College to the old Los Angeles Rams, where he led the NFL in rushing. Arnold

Galiffa quarterbacked two undefeated Army teams under the tutelage of Red Blaik. Buddy Griffey didn't get to the Major Leagues, but his son (Ken) and grandson (Ken Jr.) did all right. And above them all is Stan Musial.

It wasn't easy. Signed by Cardinals scout Ollie Vanek while still in high school, Stan went off to Williamson, West Virginia, and struggled. He hit only .258 with little power and went 6-6 on the mound with a high ERA and entirely too many walks. He improved over the next couple of years, and during the summer of 1940 everything seemed to be going well. Stan was hitting and pitching well, manager Dick Kerr and his wife had taken a shine to him and Lil, standing up with them at their wedding in May—but it all came crashing down on August 11. Playing the outfield when he wasn't pitching, Stan dove for a sinking fly ball and landed awkwardly on his left shoulder. Suddenly he was facing a dead arm, a fresh marriage, and impending fatherhood.

Adversity leads to a comeback for a legend, however, and Musial was no exception. Kerr and Cardinals general manager Branch Rickey realized the obvious, that Stan Musial's future wasn't as a pitcher. It was as a hitter. In 1941 he hit hard everywhere he played, be it Class C Springfield in the Western Association (.379-26-94), Double-A Rochester in the International League (.326-3-21), or National League St. Louis (.426-1-7), where he made his debut on September 17.

He was in St. Louis to stay, for twenty-two years, a record for tenure with the same club when he retired. Carl Yastrzemski and Brooks Robinson have since broken it, each with careers of twenty-three years. A legend stays awhile, not bouncing around from one city to another for more money or because he's worn out his welcome. With one exception, icons like Gehrig, Williams, and Ripken stayed put or had a cup of coffee elsewhere. The exception, as he always tends to be, is Ruth; he had some success as a pitcher in Boston before

he became a Yankee, and he hit his last six homers with the old Boston Braves. Not coincidentally, the Red Sox and Yankees won big with him in their lineups.

In addition to the longevity that contributes to being a legend, the player's numbers certainly bear it out as well.

When Stan retired in 1963, he owned much of the National League and Major League record books. He had seven batting titles to his name, three Most Valuable Player Awards, and at least one title in every major offensive category except stolen bases (even so, one of his nicknames was the Donora Greyhound) and home runs (his thirty-nine in 1948 was one behind league leaders Ralph Kiner and Johnny Mize). He produced runs by the boatload—1,949 scored (atop the National League then, fifth now, ninth overall), 1,951 driven in (third in National League history, sixth overall, first in 1963). He helped his teams win, appearing in the World Series each of his first four full seasons (1942–44 and 1946), a mark he shares with Joe DiMaggio (1936–39). He led the league in doubles so frequently that a common image of Musial is a wicked line drive off the wall and Stan going into second standing. He was durable, once holding the National League record for consecutive games played. His 1,377 extra-base hits stood as the Major League record until Hank Aaron and Barry Bonds came along; he's still third. He was first in total bases with 6,134; now he's second, behind Aaron. Finally, he accumulated 3,630 hits, the National League record in 1963 and second to Ty Cobb's 4,189. Only Pete Rose and Aaron have surpassed him.

About those 3,630 hits—he got 1,815 at home and 1,815 on the road. (That had to take years of planning, and it did, with Stan rapping two sharp singles of Cincinnati fireballer Jim Maloney in his final two at bats.) He didn't care where he hit or who was pitching; he just hit. Dispelling the conventional wisdom that left-handed hitters have trouble with southpaws, he made three first-rate lefties among his top home run victims — Warren Spahn, Preacher Roe, and Johnny Antonelli. On September 29, 1963, Musial's No. 6 was the first number ever retired by the Cardinals.

Legend that Musial was, he was consistent in his production. Over the ten-year period from 1948 to 1957, his average season was .340 batting, .431 on-base percentage, .600 slugging, 196 hits, 40 doubles, 9 triples, 31 homers, 111 runs, and 112 RBIs. What manager wouldn't love to assume those numbers year after year?

Musial's extra-base hits tell their own story. His 475 home runs are certainly impressive, ranking seventh when he retired, but he's not in the top 25 anymore. Especially eye-popping are his 725 doubles and 177 triples. The triples are the most of anyone who played his entire career from 1940 on. Taken together, Musial's doubles and triples tell you that he was going full-tilt the instant he left the batter's box.

Dodgers broadcaster Vin Scully, who's seen every National League player for almost sixty years, summed up Musial perfectly. "How good was Stan Musial?" he asked rhetorically. "He was good enough to take your breath away."

A legend also plays the game right. That's not as easy or simple as it sounds. There are really only two ways to play the game, right and wrong, and they're not the same thing as well and poorly. Many utility infielders who hit .240 with no power still play the game right. They run out every ground ball, navigate the bases intelligently, and dive for grounders. They get their uniform dirty and help their team win. Conversely, a number of players hitting .340 play the game wrong. They loaf on ground balls, run their team out of an inning, and make a bullfighter's pass on a ball hit to their backhand. They've been known to drive in two and let in three.

Stan Musial played the game right. He played hard, followed the rules, and treated opponents and umpires with respect. A situation that never turned up in the box score or record books exemplifies this trait.

As everybody knows, Jackie Robinson made his debut in 1947. And, as everybody knows, all hell broke loose, most of it on Robinson's head. He dealt with indescribable viciousness, and most of the time he had to bear it alone. A rare exception came in a game with the Cardinals. A Cardinal hitter (name withheld to protect the guilty) was running out a ground ball, but his intention wasn't as much to get a hit as to harm Robinson, who was playing first. His intent to spike Jackie was crystal clear. Robinson was under strict orders from Dodgers president and general manager Branch Rickey not to fight back or retaliate — no easy task. Later, still seething, Robinson reached first base and mumbled to fellow first baseman Musial what he'd like to do to the offending Cardinal. To Robinson's surprise, a sympathetic Musial quietly replied, "I don't blame you." He knew right from wrong, how to play the game, and wouldn't deviate from what is ultimately an unwritten code of fair play to defend the bad act of a teammate.

Life off the field has been much the same for Musial. He does things right. When he retired from the game, it was said that he had more money and more friends than anyone up to that time. The money part may or may not be true, but the friends part is spot-on. Musial was confident without being arrogant, knowing he played the game better than just about anybody who ever picked up a bat. He played enthusiastically; treated everyone well, from fellow stars to clubhouse attendants; signed autographs — and all with a smile. He joined the Society for American Baseball Research and listed his expertise as "hitting a baseball," said with tongue firmly in cheek but nonetheless true. In addition to a variety of business enterprises, he's worked on behalf of the USO, Boy Scouts, Senior Olympics, President's Council on Physical Fitness, and Crippled Children's Society of St. Louis. As

Joe Posnanski put it in *Sports Illustrated*, he makes people happy.

The honors continue to come in. On November 17, 2010, the White House announced that Stan would receive the most prestigious honor that can be awarded to a civilian, the Presidential Medal of Freedom. The medal is given "for especially meritorious contribution to the security or national interests of the United States, world peace, cultural or other significant public or private endeavors." Cardinals official Ron Watermon remarked, "Thanksgiving has come early to Cardinals Nation," and called the award an "early birthday present for Stan." As a recipient of the award Musial joins previous winners — Negro leagues ambassador Buck O'Neil and Hall of Fame greats Hank Aaron, Roberto Clemente, Joe DiMaggio, Frank Robinson, Jackie Robinson, and Ted Williams.

If you go to the Cardinals' team store in Busch Stadium at the corner of Clark and Eighth streets, you'll be greeted by statues of Cardinal greats Rogers Hornsby, Bob Gibson, Ozzie Smith, Dizzy Dean, Lou Brock, Enos Slaughter, and Red Schoendienst, broadcaster Jack Buck, Browns immortal George Sisler, and Negro leagues star Cool Papa Bell.

You'll find Stan Musial's statue there, too, but it's on the west side of the stadium at the Gate 3 entrance in an area named Stan Musial Plaza — alone. It's appropriate because, as great as the others were, Stan is in a league of his own. The statue reminds all who go to Cardinals games that Stan Musial was "the perfect warrior, the perfect knight" — a fitting tribute to the Western Pennsylvania native, the son of Eastern European immigrants, the embodiment of the American dream.

Chapter 54. **Jack Buck**

Kristen Lokemoen

Jack Buck teamed with Harry Caray to broadcast the Cardinals' 1964 season. Jack received the Ford C. Frick Award from the Hall of Fame in 1987.

On the night of September 17, 2001, a frail white-haired man in a red blazer walked to a microphone on the field of Busch Stadium II in St. Louis. In his shaking hands was a piece of paper on which he had written a poem for the occasion. It was Major League Baseball's first day back to playing the game after the terrorist attacks of September 11.

Five hundred firefighters and policemen from the St. Louis area stood on the white lines of the diamond. A huge American flag was unfurled, but all eyes were on the seventy-seven-year-old white-haired man, Jack Buck, the St. Louis Cardinals' longtime, beloved play-by-play radio announcer. In recent years Buck had been assailed by numerous medical ailments, including Parkinson's disease. That accounted for the shaking and the wobbly walk to the mike. When Buck started to speak, however, his voice was strong and determined. He ended his poem, titled "For America," with these words:

> Everyone is saying the same thing and praying
> That we end these senseless moments we are living
> As our fathers did before, we shall win this
>   unwanted war
> And our children will enjoy the future we'll be
>   giving.

Baseball commissioner Bud Selig said that Buck's poem and his steadiness that night were what brought baseball back. ESPN rated the moment number 98 on its list of the 100 most memorable moments in sports of the past twenty-five years.

For those who were at Busch Stadium that night, it was an experience that would never be forgotten. Sadly, but perhaps fittingly for such a patriot, it turned out to be Jack Buck's last major moment in the spotlight. Shortly after the Cardinals' 2001 season ended with a loss to the Arizona Diamondbacks in Game Five of the National League Division Series, Buck entered Barnes-Jewish Hospital in St. Louis for lung cancer surgery. He left the hospital for a period, but reentered it during the winter for treatment of various conditions. He remained there until his death on June 18, 2002.

John Francis Buck was born on August 21, 1924, in Holyoke, Massachusetts, the third of seven children born to Earle and Kathleen Buck. Earle was an accountant for the Erie Railroad and commuted to his job in Hoboken, New Jersey, each week. The elder Buck was a good enough baseball player that he had a tryout with the New York Giants, but a dispute with manager John McGraw kept Earle from becoming a professional player. (In his autobiography, *That's a Winner!*, Buck said that his father never told his family what the dispute was about. "He never told us exactly what happened, but he and manager John McGraw had some sort of disagreement and that was the end of his professional dream," Buck said.)

Holyoke was ninety miles from the Red Sox in Boston and from Jack's favorite player, Jimmie Foxx. Jack said that he learned about baseball from hanging out in the drugstore across the street from his home. Three men there assisted young Jack with writing a letter to the Red Sox manager, Joe Cronin, in which he suggested a lineup for the team. Cronin answered his letter and a few days after that used Buck's lineup, and the Red Sox won the game.

Like most boys during the 1930s, Buck and his friends lived baseball during the warmer months of the year. They listened to games on the radio, talked about it, and played it whenever and wherever they could. "We all played baseball every spring and summer day," wrote Jack in *That's a Winner!* "I bet I've played more baseball games than half the people I'm watching now in the major leagues. We settled everything among ourselves, and we did it through sports. That's the essence of sports. You learn who you are, what you can do and where you belong."

Also, like many boys during the Depression of the 1930s, Jack tried to help out his family financially in any way he could. He hawked newspapers on street corners and said that that experience helped him develop the voice that would sustain him through his broadcasting career. (He also cited his time as a drill instructor in the army and forty years of smoking Camel cigarettes.)

Jack's baseball loyalty switched to the Cleveland Indians when the family moved to the Cleveland area in 1939 for his father's job. They bought their first house and relished being together. But Earle suffered from high blood pressure, and he died at the age of forty-nine not long after the move to Ohio. Jack was just fifteen.

Kathleen Buck went to work in a sewing machine factory to support her seven children, and each of them helped as much as they could. In addition to selling newspapers, Jack also become a soda jerk at the Franklin Ice Cream Shop, where he met his first Major Leaguer, Oscar Grimes, a utility player with the Indians.

The young Buck enjoyed listening to the Indians' announcer, Jack Graney, who late in life would live in Bowling Green, Missouri, and listen to Buck's broadcasts. Other favorites included Red Barber and Mel Allen in New York, Bob Elson in Chicago, and late-night Spanish broadcasts from Cuba. Jack had unthinkingly been calling games since his days in Holyoke, when he'd give play-by-play during games with his friends. He did the same when he and his brother, Earle Jr., attended Indians games. His brother would eventually tell Jack to "shut up" or Earle would move elsewhere in the stadium.

Buck graduated from Lakewood High School in January 1942. The month before, he had been working at the ice cream shop one Sunday afternoon when word came over the radio about the Japanese attack on Pearl Harbor. Jack knew that meant his future was uncertain. After graduation he and a friend went to work on ore boats on the Great Lakes. He spent the next two years working on the boats as a porter, night cook, painter, and deckhand.

Buck was drafted into the army in July 1943. He trained in anti-aircraft at Fort Eustis, Virginia. He stayed there as an instructor and was promoted to corporal. Buck said this happened "because of my voice, and I was really good at close-order drill. You could hear me all over the area."

Buck was transferred to Camp Stewart in Georgia, where he continued as an instructor. Then he shipped out for Europe on the liner-turned-troopship *Mauretania* in February 1945. The ship landed in Liverpool, England, and Buck was sent on to France and eventually Belgium. On March 7, 1945, he crossed the Ludendorff Bridge at Remagen, one of the few bridges remaining across the Rhine, and the site of a fierce battle a few weeks before.

Buck was wounded on March 15 when Germans started shelling his position. Shrapnel pierced his left arm and leg, but missed hitting the hand grenade hanging from his belt. A medic bandaged him. Years later he and the medic met again at a banquet in St. Louis. The medic was Frank Borghi, goaltender for the 1950 U.S. World Cup team that defeated England 1–0 in Brazil in one of the greatest upsets in World Cup history.

When Buck was released from the hospital, after receiving the Purple Heart, he was given a two-day pass to Paris. That's where he was on May 8, 1945, when the war in Europe ended. He remained in Europe until April 1946, spending much of his time either playing in or coordinating various sporting events for the soldiers.

The G.I. Bill allowed Buck to enter Ohio State University in Columbus in the fall of 1946. He planned to major in radio speech with a minor in Spanish. He did his first broadcast in 1948 on the campus radio station, WOSU. While still in college, he went to work for a commercial station, WCOL. With absolutely no experience, Buck did play-by-play of Ohio State's basketball games.

"I didn't know how to do these things, I just did them," wrote Buck. "It was the ultimate example of learning by experience and I'm glad there were no tape recorders around to immortalize how bad some of those first shows and broadcasts must have been."

After Buck did his first basketball game, his class was assigned to listen to him and critique his performance. The most devastating criticism came from his professor, who told him, "You'd better find something else to do for a living." Buck ran into the professor in 1970 en route to New Orleans to broadcast the Super Bowl. Point made!

In 1948 Buck eloped to Kentucky with fellow student Alyce Larson. They would have six children—Beverly, Jack Jr., Christine, Bonnie, Betsy, and Danny—before divorcing in 1969. With his second wife, Carole Lintzenich, he had two more children—Joe and Julie.

Buck graduated from Ohio State in December 1949. He remained with WCOL, which started broadcasting the games of the Columbus Red Birds, the Cardinals' Triple-A farm team. Buck had to audition for the Columbus general manager, Al Banister, to be allowed to do the games. His audition consisted of re-creating an entire baseball game from a play-by-play account in *The Sporting News*. He got the job and, for the first of many times, headed to Florida for spring training.

As Buck prepared to broadcast his first baseball game, he wondered how he should approach the job. He asked Rollie Hemsley, the Columbus manager and a former Major League catcher, for advice. Hemsley's words stuck with Jack: "If somebody doesn't catch the ball, and you couldn't have caught it either, keep your mouth shut. If they didn't catch it and you could have caught it, give 'em hell."

Buck did manage a coup that spring back in Columbus when the Red Sox came through to play an exhibition game on their way home to Boston. He snagged a media-resistant Ted Williams for a thirty-minute interview, which Buck termed more of a speech. He was glad to have it, however, as it pleased his bosses.

WCOL was sold in 1952 and the new owner wasn't interested in sports. Buck was out of a job, but within three days was on television at WBNS. As a father with three young children, Buck was glad to have another job so quickly. However, he quickly realized that "even in those early days of TV, I knew I was going to be the sort of broadcaster who would be better off on radio."

Buck missed doing sports, but baseball reentered his life in 1953 when he got the job of broadcasting the games of the Rochester Red Wings, the Cardinals' International League farm team. Then the Anheuser-Busch Brewery bought the Cardinals, including its farm teams. "The timing was exquisite," said Buck. D'Arcy, the advertising agency for Anheuser-Busch, hired the baseball announcers. Buck auditioned for the chance to join Harry Caray in the Cardinals booth by having him broadcast a game between St. Louis and the New York Giants at the Polo Grounds. He waited for weeks to hear if the job was his, and finally the word came. In 1954 he would be broadcasting in the big leagues.

Buck felt that he might be doomed from the start when he received a tape of Caray's work from the Cardinals and was told, "This is the way we want you to broadcast." Any good broadcaster knows that he has to develop his own style, and Buck's and Caray's were not at all alike. Their personalities didn't blend really well either, especially since Caray had wanted someone else for the job.

The third man in the booth that first year was Milo Hamilton. He and Jack split road and home duties and did as many innings on the Cardinals' broadcasts as Caray would allow. Almost sixty years later, Hamilton, still in the business with the Houston Astros, referred to Jack as "probably my best friend in the industry."

The Cardinals' broadcasts were on KMOX, the CBS affiliate in St. Louis. At the time, St. Louis was the westernmost city with a Major League baseball team, and the Cardinals' fan base extended well beyond that of most teams.

All three men in the KMOX booth in 1954 would go on to receive the Ford C. Frick Award, giving them a plaque in the Baseball Hall of Fame—Buck in 1987, Caray in 1989, and Hamilton in 1992. But 1954 was the only year all three worked together. Joe Garagiola, a St. Louis product who caught for the Cardinals, Pirates, Cubs, and Giants, replaced Hamilton in 1955 and become Caray's protégé.

While Buck was excited to be doing Major League games, his situation was also frustrating, as Caray pretty much controlled the booth and decided who did what. Harry didn't like to have anyone else be on the mike when something exciting happened, and since that was impossible to predict, he did most of the innings.

With Garagiola traveling on all the road trips with Caray in 1955, Buck was left behind in the St. Louis studio to do commercials and update incoming baseball scores. However, the time allowed him to expand into other sports. He did bowling, soccer, and wrestling on the radio.

As the 1950s rolled along, the Cardinals were not winning any pennants and Buck was still the odd man out in the broadcast booth. After the 1959 season, when former Cardinals player Buddy Blattner was added to the team, Buck was out totally. He got the word that he was fired just before Christmas.

"We had just built a six-bedroom house with a swimming pool and had bought all new furniture, on credit of course," wrote Buck in *That's a Winner!* "I had to find a job quickly, or I'd have to sell the kids." Enter Bob Hyland.

In St. Louis the name Bob Hyland is legendary for his masterful management of KMOX Radio, which was the king of the St. Louis airwaves and often the top-ranked station in the country. Hyland persuaded Buck not to go after a baseball job in another city, feeling certain that he would eventually get his job back with the Cardinals. In the meantime, he had plenty of ways to use the announcer's talents.

Buck did a nightly show from Stan Musial and Biggie's Restaurant, playing records and doing interviews. He did other sporting events as well as an interview show called *At Your Service*, which became key in radio history. Hyland decided to do away with musical programming and go all-talk. KMOX was the first station to do this, creating a brand-new format that remains popular today.

Jack also started doing public appearances and became the most sought-after emcee in St. Louis for banquets and other events. Many of the events were for charity, such as the Cystic Fibrosis Association, one of Buck's top priorities. One year he appeared at 385 events.

To satisfy his sports interest, Buck did baseball games for ABC-TV, as well as the Big Ten Basketball Game of the Week. He was one of the first announcers to do American Football League games and created the Pro Bowlers Tour with Chris Schenkel. He did minor-league hockey for the St. Louis Braves and then announced the first games for the National Hockey League St. Louis Blues in 1967.

Where Buck really wanted to be, of course, was back in the Cardinals' broadcasting booth. Blattner had moved on to the expansion Los Angeles Angels, and Caray and Garagiola had had a falling out. Joe moved on to NBC and Harry again needed a partner. While Caray was still the dominant figure, he and Buck got along better this time.

Buck wrote, "When Harry and I were doing the games together, we were as good a team as there ever was. His style and mine were so different, that it made for a balanced broadcast. The way we approached the job, with the interest and love both of us had for the game, made our work kind of special."

It was an exciting time in St. Louis. Gussie Busch, owner of the brewery and the Cardinals, built a new stadium in downtown St. Louis that opened in 1966. The 1960s were also great years for the team. St. Louis played in three World Series during the decade, beating the Yankees in 1964 and the Red Sox in 1967, but losing in 1968 to the Tigers.

After the many years of being Caray's unappreciated sidekick, however, Buck was ready to move on as the '60s came to a close. His salary had been stuck at $20,000 a year and he felt stuck as well. Then Caray failed to follow an instruction from Busch and was fired. Buck was offered Caray's contract. Finally, after sixteen difficult years, the booth would be his.

Buck needed a partner for the 1970 season, and his first choice was the retired Red Barber. Barber, the longtime Dodgers announcer, had been fired by the Yankees four years before and was interested in getting back in the game, "but my wife would kill me," he said. The job eventually went to Jim Woods, an uneasy fit, and Woods left after two years. In the spring of 1972, former Cardinals outfielder Mike Shannon, a novice at broadcasting, became Buck's partner and would remain that for the rest of Buck's baseball career. Shannon, a St. Louis native, had been a popular player but was forced to retire early because of a kidney ailment.

Talking about those early days, Shannon said, "I had absolutely no experience and I knew that I was going to walk into a situation where I needed to learn. But because of Jack, I knew I had a person that was the best in the business."

Buck continued to do pro football for a number

of years, including broadcasting the memorable Ice Bowl game in Green Bay in 1967. Although he did some TV work, most of his football coverage was also on radio. He and former coach Hank Stram did radio coverage of the Monday Night Football games for CBS for almost two decades.

As to why he fit better on radio than TV, Buck once said, "In television all they want you to do is shut up. I'm not very good at shutting up." He also felt that television coverage of baseball and other sports was more centered on the analyst, not the play-by-play man.

Probably the greatest example of Buck's discomfort with TV came in 1975, when he became host of a new studio sports show on NBC called *Grandstand*. It meant giving up his job with the Cardinals, at least in 1976. *Grandstand* was a failure pretty much from the beginning. It was badly produced, which made it difficult for Buck ever to get comfortable with the format. He was eventually fired and went back to broadcasting baseball.

The 1970s had been another bad time for the St. Louis Cardinals. The team had gotten sloppy and Buck was often embarrassed by how the players dressed for flights and by how they acted. Manager Red Schoendienst was fired after the 1976 season, but things didn't improve—until Whitey Herzog came to town.

Buck wrote, "I was immediately impressed with Whitey and the way he went about his business. He is the smartest person I've ever met in baseball." Herzog guided the Cardinals to three more World Series in the 1980s. They beat the Milwaukee Brewers (then in the American League) in 1982, but lost to the Kansas City Royals in 1985 and the Minnesota Twins in 1987.

One of Buck's most famous calls came in 1985, when the Cardinals were playing the Dodgers in Game Five of the National League Championship Series in St. Louis. Cardinals shortstop Ozzie Smith, not exactly a power hitter, hit his first home run left-handed to win the game for the Cards.

Buck's call went like this: "Smith corks one into deep right field, down the line. It may go . . . Go crazy, folks! Go crazy! It's a home run, and the Cardinals have won the game, 3–2, on a home run by the Wizard! Go crazy!"

Equally memorable was his call on CBS Radio during the 1988 World Series when Kirk Gibson, though hobbled by injuries, smashed a pinch-hit home run to win Game One. "Unbelievable! The Dodgers have won the game on a home run by Kirk Gibson! I don't believe what I just saw!" Even though that was a radio call, it is often played when Gibson's trot around the bases is shown on TV.

In 1990 Buck made one more foray into television, when CBS hired him to do the number two game on its new Saturday baseball broadcast. Before the season even started, however, he was moved up to the number one game when Brent Musburger was fired. Jack was teamed with Tim McCarver, whom he knew well from McCarver's playing days with the Cardinals. As had happened before, Buck was relegated to second place and the duo never quite clicked. He was fired in 1992.

One of the greatest joys of Jack Buck's life was the arrival in the broadcast booth of his youngest son, Joe. As a boy, Joe had spent a great deal of time with Jack in the booth, going on road trips, and he took it all in as a very proud son. On Joe's eighteenth birthday, Jack and Mike Shannon felt the young man was "ready for prime time" and left him alone in the broadcast booth to do an inning of a Cardinals game. He didn't let them down. As Jack's health deteriorated in the 1990s, Joe became a regular part of the KMOX team on the Cardinals' broadcasts. Starting in 1995, Jack cut back on the travel and Joe was Shannon's partner on road games.

When Mark McGwire was vying for the home run record in 1998, it was Jack Buck who was at the microphone to call number 61, which tied McGwire with Roger Maris. As Busch Stadium went crazy on that Labor Day afternoon, September 7, Buck said, "Pardon me while I stand up and applaud. What a Cardinal moment this is. What a baseball moment this is." It was Joe who delivered the national television call for number 62 one night later.

When the millennium came, Jack Buck had been a baseball broadcaster for fifty years, all but a few of those with the Cardinals. He had been dealing with Parkinson's disease for several years. He also had a pacemaker and had diabetes, cataracts, and other ailments. *Sports Illustrated*'s Rick Reilly wrote, "Herking and jerking in his seat, his face contorting this way and that, he still sends out the most wonderful descriptions of games you've ever heard."

Joe said, "I have no idea how, but his voice has been stronger lately. It's like he's putting every ounce of energy God can give him into those three hours of the broadcast." And Cardinals fans did not want to let him go. Buck had the knack for making the game real, "like talking baseball with the guy across the backyard fence," wrote Reilly.

On the evening of June 18, 2002, the Anaheim Angels played in St. Louis, the first time the two teams had ever played each other. Darryl Kile was on the mound for the Cardinals in what would turn out to be his last game before his sudden death from a heart attack four days later in Chicago. With Joe Buck broadcasting, the Cardinals won the game, 7–2, a win that put St. Louis into first place in the National League Central.

Joe rushed from the broadcast booth to the hospital to tell his dad. Apparently, that was the news Jack had been waiting for. After months in the hospital, after several surgeries, after losing the ability to speak (Joe compared the last indignity to being like "a great pianist with broken hands"), Jack Buck died just an hour after the game ended. His Cardinals were in first place and he'd let the angels take him home.

Joe called KMOX with the news and a make-shift memorial quickly started to grow around Jack Buck's monument outside Busch Stadium II. The radio station that had invented the call-in talk show format put it to good use over the next few days. Tributes poured in from around the country and from all kinds of people. No matter how famous or ordinary the person, they all loved Jack Buck because he loved them.

A month after Buck's death, Mike Shannon talked about his longtime broadcast partner: "Jack was so good to so many people, you'll never know. He thought about people and their situations and their walks of life. He would go out of his way to talk to the guy who parked his car, the bellhop, the guy serving the dinner—and he learned a lot [from them]."

Tony La Russa, who had come to St. Louis in 1996 to manage the Cardinals, became friends with Jack and said, "Most fans knew him for his broadcasting, and he was a super talent as a broadcaster. But that was the smallest part of why he was so special. He was a great man in so many ways."

A ceremony to honor Jack Buck was held at Busch Stadium two days after his death, with his coffin resting at home plate. A Budweiser Clydesdale stood guard nearby. The funeral was held the next day. Many baseball and other sports figures attended.

The title of Jack Buck's memoir, *That's a Winner!*, was the phrase he developed to announce a Cardinals win to his radio audience. It also summed up the way he felt about his life. Jack ended his book with these lines: "Carole once asked me what I would say if I met the Lord and my answer then is the same as it is now. I want to ask Him why He was so good to me."

In 2009 Joe Buck was recording a public service announcement about Parkinson's disease with actor Michael J. Fox, who was hit with the disease at a relatively young age. Fox turned to Joe and said, speaking for countless baseball fans, "I miss your dad's voice. It was so iconic."

October 1 — No game scheduled.

October 2 — METS 1, CARDINALS 0 — Al Jackson pitched a complete-game shutout for his eleventh victory. The Mets' lone run came on a single by Ed Kranepool in the third inning. The Cardinals had good opportunities in both the fourth inning and the eighth but could not score. In defeat, Gibson pitched a strong eight innings and struck out seven. He worked out of a bases-loaded, one-out situation in the first inning and a bases-loaded, nobody-out situation in the fourth. "Jackson was just too good," said Keane after the game.

The Phillies ended their ten-game losing streak by coming back from a 3–0 deficit to beat the Reds, 4–3. The Cardinals' lead was a half game over Cincinnati and one and a half games over Philadelphia. The San Francisco Giants were two games behind the Cardinals.

October 3 — METS 15, CARDINALS 5 — The Mets pounded eight Cardinals pitchers for seventeen hits. Five Mets hit home runs (George Altman, Charley Smith, Kranepool, Bobby Klaus, and Joe Christopher). The Cardinals also made five errors. Boyer and White hit back-to-back home runs for the Cardinals.

Philadelphia and Cincinnati had the day off. The Reds were now tied with the Cardinals, and the Phillies were one game behind. The San Francisco Giants were eliminated from the National League pennant race when they lost, 10–7, to the Chicago Cubs.

August A. Busch Jr. reportedly offered a one-year contract with a substantial raise to Johnny Keane to manage in 1965.

Final Standings

	W	L	T	PCT	GB
St. Louis Cardinals	93	69	0	.574	—
Cincinnati Reds	92	70	1	.568	1
Philadelphia Phillies	92	70	0	.568	1
San Francisco Giants	90	72	0	.556	3
Milwaukee Braves	88	74	0	.543	5
Los Angeles Dodgers	80	82	2	.494	13
Pittsburgh Pirates	80	82	0	.494	13
Chicago Cubs	76	86	0	.469	17
Houston Colt .45s	66	96	0	.407	27
New York Mets	53	109	1	.327	40

October 4 — CARDINALS 11, METS 5 — On one day of rest, Gibson won his nineteenth victory by pitching four innings in relief of starter Simmons. Every Cardinal in the starting lineup (with the exception of the pitcher) had at least one hit. White and Flood each hit home runs. Schultz got his fourteenth save of the season when McCarver caught Kranepool's foul pop for the final out. With Philadelphia having already defeated Cincinnati, the Cardinals' victory clinched the National League pennant for the first time since 1946.

Ken Boyer finished the 1964 regular season with an NL-leading 119 RBIS. He was later named the Most Valuable Player in the National League. Curt Flood finished the regular season with 211 hits, tying him for the NL lead with Roberto Clemente. Lou Brock finished his combined (Chicago/St. Louis) 1964 regular season with a .315 batting average, 200 hits, 111 runs scored, and 43 stolen bases. In his 103 games with St. Louis, he had a .348 batting average, 146 hits, 81 runs scored, and 33 stolen bases. In a postseason interview, Johnny

Keane again said that the Cardinals became contenders that day in June when Devine brought
Brock to the club.

Cardinals September–October 4 win-loss record:
22-10.
Cardinals year-to-date win-loss record: 93-69.

Chapter 56. Harry Caray

Matt Bohn

"The taxi driver, the bartender, the waitress, the man in the street, those are my people," Harry Caray once said.[1] Caray was a larger-than-life figure who loved the game and broadcast it with enthusiasm. He was respected by colleagues for his play-by-play ability, but unlike many sportscasters, he never hesitated to editorialize. A typical moment from Harry's play-by-play: "Egan tries to pick the runner off first, and he throws the ball into right field! Now if he could only hit it that far."[2] Caray had fun with the game, handing out bottles of beer to fans in the bleachers, singing "Take Me Out to the Ballgame" and (sometimes purposely) mispronouncing players' names on the air. "Let's face it, a broadcaster has to be an entertainer. The game isn't all balls and strikes," Harry said in 1979. "You have to have a sense of humor and believe me, there's nothing like having fun at the old ballpark."[3] In over a half century of broadcasting, Caray led the fun in St. Louis, Oakland, and Chicago, describing the games of the Browns, Cardinals, Athletics, White Sox, and Cubs.

Caray kept his early life shrouded in mystery. Even his birthdate was not clear. Various sources differ on his year of birth, putting it at anywhere from 1915 to 1920. When asked about it, Caray would generally shrug off the question of his age. After his death in 1998, it was reported that, according to St. Louis city health records, Harry Christopher Carabina was born on March 1, 1914, on Olive Street in St. Louis. His father, Christopher Carabina, left around the time of Harry's birth. Harry never met his father and never knew anything about him. According to his autobiography, Harry's mother, the former Daisy Argint,

The emotional Harry Caray worked with Jack Buck broadcasting the Cardinals in 1964. In 1989 Harry received the Ford C. Frick Award from the Hall of Fame.

remarried when Harry was about five or six years old and died when he was about seven or eight. (A search of Missouri marriage records shows a marriage between Daisy Argint and Sam Capuran in September 1926, when Harry would have been twelve. Missouri records also show that Daisy Capuran died in April 1928 of lobar pneumonia at the age of thirty-seven.) After his mother's death, he was raised primarily by an aunt, Doxie Argint.

Coming from a poor family, Harry went to work selling newspapers at the age of eight. One of the brightest parts of his childhood was being able to watch the games of the St. Louis Cardinals. Whenever he was able to afford it, young Harry attended games at Sportsman's Park. At Webster High School in Webster Groves, a St. Louis suburb, Harry played second base and shortstop and played well enough that he was offered a baseball scholarship by the University of Alabama. Unable to pay for the expenses for room and board or books, he did not accept the scholarship.

Working odd jobs after completing high school, Harry picked up additional money by playing semipro baseball on the weekends. Playing for such teams as the Smith Undertakers and the Webster Groves Birds, he attracted the attention of some scouts and was invited to participate in a tryout camp for the Cardinals in Decatur, Illinois. Harry didn't have the physical skills to make the tryout, but through a friend on the Webster Groves baseball team, he landed a steady job as an assistant sales manager with a company that manufactured lockers, gymnastic equipment, and other products.

Harry continued to attend Cardinals games as often as possible. However, he noticed that the games he saw in person were invariably more exciting than the play-by-play descriptions he heard when he listened to the games at home on the radio. Convinced that he could do a better job broadcasting Cardinals games himself, he brashly sent a personal letter to the home address of Merle Jones, general manager of radio station KMOX asking for the job. Impressed with Harry's drive and enthusiasm, Jones arranged for him to audition for the station. Jones thought Harry had a great voice but needed some experience. He helped Harry to land a job as a sports announcer at a Joliet, Illinois, radio station, WCLS.

By the spring of 1940, Harry was working on WCLS covering sporting events like high school and junior college basketball games, summer softball league games, and bowling league events. At the suggestion of WCLS station manager Bob Holt,

Harry changed his last name from Carabina to Caray.

After a year and a half working at WCLS, Caray was hired as sports director of WKZO in Kalamazoo, Michigan, where he worked with the young newscaster Paul Harvey. The station carried Harry Heilmann's broadcasts of Detroit Tigers games, and Caray hosted locally produced pregame and postgame shows. He also provided play-by-play of Western Michigan University basketball and football. During his stint at WKZO, Caray also got his first experience with baseball play-by-play, broadcasting a semipro tournament in Battle Creek, Michigan.

Caray later claimed that it was during the broadcast of this semipro tournament that he first uttered two phrases he would employ throughout his career. When a player hit a home run, Caray exclaimed, "It might be . . . it could be . . . it *is* . . . a home run!" Another expression he claimed to have first used during this early broadcast was "Holy cow!" Caray later explained, "I knew the profanity that had been used up and down my street wouldn't go on the air. So I just trained myself every time I was excited to say 'Holy Cow' instead of some profanity."[4] The expression itself was not unique to Caray's broadcasts; it had been used over the air by Minnesota sportscaster Halsey Hall as early as the 1930s and was later picked up by New York Yankees announcer Phil Rizzuto. Harry later said, "Not that it's so unique—everybody uses 'Holy Cow.' The unique part was that I finally did it on a major-league broadcast, in 1945, with a lot of radio stations across the country listening to it."[5]

Rejected for military service because of bad eyesight, Caray moved back to St. Louis, where he was working at radio station KXOK by early 1944. Working first as a staff announcer, Caray soon had a fifteen-minute nightly sports show. Unlike other radio sports show hosts of the day, he not only provided sports news but also editorialized and criticized. His controversial approach won a lot of attention in a year when both St. Louis teams met in the World Series. In the fall of that year, Caray was hired to do play-by-play of the minor-league St. Louis Flyers hockey team, college basketball, and other sports events sponsored by the Griesedieck Brothers Brewery on station WIL.

Griesedieck Brothers were planning on sponsoring broadcasts of Cardinals and Browns home games in 1945 and were looking for a famous sportscaster to handle the play-by-play duties. Caray went directly to brewery president Edward J. Griesedieck to lobby for the job. Griesedieck initially turned him down, explaining that he preferred to hire an announcer in the style of veteran St. Louis broadcaster France Laux. Laux, Griesedieck explained, described the action in a way that allowed a person to listen and yet read the newspaper undisturbed. At this, Caray exploded. "You're spending hundreds of thousands of dollars to sponsor baseball, and when your commercial comes on, when your handpicked announcer is selling your product, you're busy reading the paper!" Caray continued, "You need someone who's going to keep the fan interested in the game. Because if they're paying attention to the game, they'll pay attention to the commercial!"[6] Convinced by Caray's argument, and certain that Caray could keep the fans interested, Griesedieck hired him immediately.

Starting in the spring of 1945, Harry was teamed with former catcher and manager Gabby Street to broadcast the home games of the Cardinals and the Browns on WIL. In St. Louis at the time, there were no exclusive broadcast rights. Several local St. Louis radio stations aired the baseball games in direct competition with one another through the 1930s and into the mid-1940s. Caray and Street were competing with such established St. Louis announcers as France Laux and Johnny O'Hara as well as colorful former pitcher Dizzy Dean. Between the enthusiasm of Caray and the analysis and expertise of Street, the duo built a following in the St. Louis area. As the Cardinals won the National League pennant in 1946, Caray and Street gained increasing recognition and popularity from St. Louis fans. Caray's only regret about the 1946 season was that he did not get the opportunity to broadcast the World Series, which the Cardinals won in seven games.

In 1947 Cardinals president Sam Breadon granted exclusive broadcast rights to Griesedieck Brothers. This meant that Caray and Street would be the only broadcasters for all of the Cardinals' home and road games. The Cardinals radio network was baseball's largest network, with fifty-four affiliate stations in 1948. The network included ninety-one stations by 1954, introducing listeners in states like Oklahoma and Mississippi to Caray's play-by-play descriptions. By 1954 Caray had survived changes in Cardinals ownership (August A. Busch Jr. bought the team in 1953) and a change in broadcast sponsors (from Griesedieck to the Anheuser-Busch Brewery). Caray and Street worked together until the former catcher died in 1951. Caray's later broadcast partners in St. Louis included Joe Garagiola and Jack Buck.

Caray's style was viewed by many as controversial. He said in 1977, "You can't be controversial by design because it comes off as phony. It has to be spontaneous. I'm like a fan. If I see something on the field I don't like, I react the way a fan does. If I think a player isn't hustling I'll say so. If I think a manager is making mistakes platooning I'll say so. When I was with the Cardinals I was always in the hot box with managers like Eddie Stanky and Eddie Dyer. I've always said the managers and owners don't like me, but the people love me."[7] Stan Musial said of Caray years later, "He said it like it was. I guess some of the ballplayers were perturbed, but he was a fan. . . . He didn't mean anything by it. A little later he'd be rooting for you. He wanted the ballplayers to do well."[8]

One of the highlights of Caray's broadcasting

career came on October 3, 1951, in a game that did not involve the Cardinals. Harry shared a booth with Russ Hodges (separated by a curtain) for a special broadcast back to St. Louis of the National League playoff game between the New York Giants and the Brooklyn Dodgers. Caray was one of many announcers at the microphone as Bobby Thomson hit his famous home run to win the pennant for the Giants. Another exciting moment came in May 1958 as Harry broadcast the play-by-play when Stan Musial got his three thousandth hit. A rather memorable moment occurred on April 17, 1964, as Caray excitedly announced a surprise second-inning double by pitcher Roger Craig by saying, "I can't believe it! Roger Craig just hit the left-center field fence! The Cardinals are going to win this pennant!"[9] Caray made this statement during the fourth game of the season. His enthusiastic call turned out to be prophetic, as the Cardinals (who were never in first place until the final week of that season) would clinch their first pennant in eighteen years. Harry broadcast the World Series over NBC radio and TV as the Cardinals beat the Yankees in seven games. Caray also had NBC network announcing duties as the Cardinals went to the World Series in 1967 and 1968, and he broadcast the All-Star Game in 1957 (on NBC radio).

When not broadcasting, Caray enjoyed partying and mingling with fans at local taverns. He said in 1996, "Everywhere I'd go, if I didn't know anybody at the bar I'd make a friend out of the bartender in two minutes. If there were two people at the bar, I'd say, 'Give the house a drink, and be sure to lock the front door so nobody else gets in.'"[10] Spending so much time on the road with the Cardinals and celebrating with fans afterward took a toll on Caray's personal life. In 1949 Dorothy Caray, his wife of twelve years, divorced him. Their ten-year-old son, Skip, remembered being devastated as he learned of the divorce when he saw it headlined on the front page of a newspaper as he walked to school. After the divorce, Skip and his brother, Christopher, and sister, Patricia, would see even less of their father as he kept up the grueling travel schedule of a professional sportscaster.

Caray's career and his life nearly came to an end on November 3, 1968. "I was walking across the street leaving a St. Louis hotel at 1:15 in the morning when I was hit by a car," he said in 1970. "The driver was a 21-year-old veteran just back that morning from Vietnam. He had no driver's license . . . no insurance. The car knocked me 35 feet in the air. I suffered two broken legs, a broken shoulder and a broken nose. They said I would be in the hospital for seven months. But I wound up walking out after 3½ months. I never missed a game."[11]

Caray recovered and returned for his twenty-fifth season with the Cardinals in 1969. It turned out to be his last in St. Louis, as he was fired at the end of the season. Rumors circulated that Caray was involved in an affair with Susan Busch, wife of August Busch III. Caray himself would never deny the rumors, commenting that it was good for his ego for people to believe such a thing to be true. He wasn't unemployed long. In 1970 he was hired to broadcast the games of the Oakland Athletics.

"I've criticized the Cards and got into hot situations with the management, and I'll tell the truth about the club here, too," Harry said as he introduced himself to Oakland in 1970. "The biggest thing I must have as an announcer is believability."[12] Harry didn't change anything about his broadcasting style in Oakland. (Athletics owner Charlie Finley tried to persuade Caray to change his trademark expression from "Holy cow" to "Holy mule" in honor of the team mascot, but Harry rejected the suggestion.[13]) By now married to his second wife, Marian, Harry claimed to enjoy his time in Oakland but refused to move there. "St. Louis is still my home," he said in June of that year. "I have a nice home in Ladue, a suburb, and I didn't want to give it up. And Marian and I didn't want to take our daughters, Michelle and Elizabeth, out of school."[14] Missing the Midwest, after one year Harry left Oakland for Chicago.

Replacing legendary broadcaster Bob Elson, Caray became the voice of the White Sox in 1971. The White Sox under owner John Allyn were experiencing difficult financial times. Unable to offer Caray a salary as high as the one he earned in Oakland, the White Sox offered an attendance clause in Harry's salary. Knowing that Caray had a reputation for promoting the game and drawing fans, the White Sox offered Caray a $10,000 bonus for every hundred thousand spectators the Sox drew over six hundred thousand. (More than eight hundred thousand fans came to see the White Sox play that year.) Beginning in 1973, Caray added television to his duties, providing play-by-play on WSNS-TV for the first and last three innings and switching to radio play-by-play for the middle three. By the mid-1970s, all of the White Sox home games and most of the road games were televised, and Harry was becoming one of the most popular figures in Chicago.

Caray loved Chicago and he tried to provide fun for the fans, as he had in other cities. He would occasionally take a cooler of beer to the outfield bleachers at White Sox Park (passing bottles of beer to the fans) and broadcast the game from there. He continued to mingle with the fans in area taverns celebrating into the early-morning hours after the games. He soon became known as "the Mayor of Rush Street." As much as he cheered on the White Sox when they did well, he remained unafraid to criticize them when he felt it was warranted. His criticisms often put him at odds with players such as third baseman Bill Melton and manager Chuck Tanner. By the end of the 1975 season, owner John Allyn had heard enough of Caray's criticisms and was going to fire him. However, in December 1975 a group of investors led by Bill Veeck bought the team. Veeck, knowing the popularity Caray had with the fans, kept him on.

It was because of Veeck that another one of Caray's trademarks began. One night Veeck noticed Caray singing "Take Me Out to the Ballgame" in the booth during the seventh-inning stretch. Inspired, the next night Veeck secretly installed a public-address microphone in the booth and turned it on when Caray began singing the song. Caray was surprised to hear his voice singing over the PA system. He recalled in 1996, "When the game was over I walked up to Veeck and said, 'What the hell was that all about?' He said, 'Harry, I've been looking for 45 years for the right man to do this, sing this song.' I began to puff up with flattery. 'Yes,' he said, 'everybody, no matter where they were sitting, as soon as they heard you, they knew they could sing better than you, so they'd join in.'"[15] Thus began the tradition of Caray leading the fans in an off-key rendition of "Take Me Out to the Ballgame."

After working with a series of partners in Chicago, Caray was teamed primarily with former center fielder Jimmy Piersall beginning in 1977. Piersall was even more outspoken in his commentary than Caray. Caray loved working with Piersall. Though they often said things on the air that angered players or management, the White Sox broadcasts became more popular than ever with the public. By 1981 the team was sold to a group led by Jerry Reinsdorf and Eddie Einhorn.

By late 1981 Reinsdorf and Einhorn were planning on putting the White Sox telecasts on a subscription-only pay TV channel. Caray felt strongly that asking the White Sox fans to pay a subscription to watch the televised games would not work. Caray, who already had reservations about working for Reinsdorf and Einhorn, contacted the Chicago Cubs and asked if they would be interested in hiring him to replace retiring TV announcer Jack Brickhouse. They were. In November 1981 it was announced that Harry Caray would be the new voice of the Cubs.

With Caray working the first and last three

innings on television (and the middle three on radio), the games were telecast on superstation WGN, which was seen in thirty million homes by the late 1980s. Caray became even more of a celebrity than he had been when broadcasting on a large radio network with the Cardinals. Caray made the jump from the South Side to the North Side of Chicago seamlessly. At the time of his crosstown move, Caray quipped, "Moving to the Cubs and day baseball shouldn't be too hard. I hear the bars on Rush Street are going to start closing at 2 a.m. soon anyway. It's those 4 a.m. and 5 a.m. nights that give you a headache."[16] At Wrigley Field he continued the tradition of occasionally broadcasting games from the outfield bleachers and led the fans in singing "Take Me Out to the Ballgame."

On February 17, 1987, Caray suffered a stroke while playing cards with friends in Palm Springs, California. It was uncertain whether he would work again. Well-wishes were sent by fans all over the United States. "I couldn't move my leg, I couldn't move my arm, I couldn't control my speech," Caray said. "And then I got boxes of mail, expressions of love in letters and flowers from people I didn't know, and it breathed a little more hope into me."[17] He worked with a therapist to improve his speech so that he could return to the broadcasts. Caray wasn't able to be back with the team by Opening Day, so the Cubs used a series of guest broadcasters in his place, including sportscaster Brent Musburger, columnist George Will, and comedian Bill Murray. On May 19, 1987, Caray made his return to Wrigley Field. During the game he received an on-air phone call from President Ronald Reagan welcoming him back to the booth. (It wouldn't be the last time Caray received greetings from the White House. Reagan visited him in the Wrigley Field booth on September 30, 1988, and broadcast part of the game. In 1994 First Lady Hillary Rodham Clinton joined Harry in leading the singing during the seventh-inning stretch.)

Caray broadcast for some exciting teams in Chicago, as the Cubs won the National League East title in 1984 and 1989. However exciting the game might have been on the field, though, Caray made sure to have fun in his broadcasts as well. Partner Steve Stone recalled how when Caray thought the game was moving too slowly, he would pronounce players' names backwards. He would also mispronounce the names of players, sometimes on purpose. On Caray's broadcasts, Rafael Palmeiro became "Palermo." Delino DeShields became "Delino DeSanders."[18] Five years after the stroke, Harry admitted, "I'm not as sharp as I used to be. I mispronounce a lot of names, I know. I'll never be able to say the name of the Cubs' catcher [Hector Villanueva]. I say Valenzuela. I say Villanova. But people should understand that I've never been able to pronounce names correctly—even when I was younger."[19]

Toward the end of his life, Harry reflected, "If I had to do it over again, I wouldn't have missed my kids' growing up. I missed a lot, and I have regrets. But I think I've made up for that now and I have a wonderful family."[20] By the early 1990s, that family included three generations of Carays broadcasting baseball. His son Skip worked to establish his own name in the business and became the voice of the Atlanta Braves in 1976. Skip's son Chip Caray would begin broadcasting the games of the NBA Orlando Magic in 1989 and would join his father in the Braves booth two years later. On May 13, 1991, Harry, Skip, and Chip Caray were together at the microphone as the Braves and Cubs played at Wrigley Field. Both Skip and Chip were present during another proud moment in 1989 as Harry received the Ford Frick Award from the Baseball Hall of Fame. Another of Harry's grandsons, Josh Caray, has worked as a Minor League Baseball broadcaster.

During a road trip in Miami in June 1994, Harry collapsed and was hospitalized. Doctors discovered that he had an irregular heartbeat. He returned to broadcasting the games a month later, but cut back greatly on his travel schedule. Doctors ordered Harry to restrict his alcohol consumption as well. "I'm reduced to drinking O'Doul's," Caray said. "Can you imagine Harry Caray unable to drink a martini? Without a cold Budweiser? It's not me."[21] By now twice divorced, Harry had found a lasting partnership with his third wife, Dutchie. After his stroke, Harry insisted that Dutchie accompany him on road trips. As the years went on, Dutchie's presence on the road became more important to him. "I don't want to die alone in a hotel room like my friend Don Drysdale did," Harry said.[22]

Shortly before the 1998 season, Harry's grandson Chip was hired to announce the Cubs games with him. Harry was excited at the prospect of working with his grandson. Sadly, it was not to be. On Valentine's Day 1998, Harry collapsed while having dinner with Dutchie at a restaurant in Rancho Mirage, California. He never regained consciousness and died four days later of cardiac arrest with resultant brain damage. Harry's Funeral Mass was held at Holy Name Cathedral in Chicago. He was buried at All Saints Cemetery in suburban Chicago.

On Opening Day 1998, Dutchie Caray led the Wrigley faithful in singing "Take Me Out to the Ballgame." It's a tradition that still continues on the North Side of Chicago with "guest conductors" filling Harry's place as leader of the seventh-inning stretch. After Harry's death, a statue of him was dedicated outside the entrance of Wrigley Field. In 2010 the statue was moved to the outfield bleacher entrance. Cubs owner Tom Ricketts explained the move, saying, "As a real fan, he was always comfortable in the bleachers. He liked the atmosphere in the bleachers."[23] Harry probably would have agreed. He himself said in 1975, "I don't mind being known as a fan. Listen, baseball is part of Americana and no one is going to supplant it. And no other sport can match it. . . . I'm a fan, a fan's announcer."[24]

Chapter 57. **August A. Busch Jr.**

John Harry Stahl

Gussie Busch with National League president Warren Giles.

For nearly a quarter century, Gussie Busch simultaneously led a nationwide brewing company and the St. Louis Cardinals franchise. Nicknamed "The Big Eagle," Gussie lived life to its fullest. His enemies called him profane, tyrannical, hot-tempered, a philanderer, and a huckster. His friends saw him as soft-hearted, congenial, open, personable, philanthropic, and loyal.

In 1953 he convinced his brewery, Anheuser-Busch, to buy the financially struggling St. Louis Cardinals.[1] After eleven years of frustration, Busch won his first world championship with the 1964 Cardinals. Starting that year, Gussie subsequently left a baseball legacy of six National League champions and three World Series winners.

Born in St. Louis on March 28, 1899, August Anheuser Busch Jr. was the second son of August A. Busch Sr. and the former Alice Ziesemann. Already immensely wealthy, Gussie's family also included five sisters. His grandfather Adolphus Busch Sr. cofounded the Anheuser-Busch brewery and became a legendary figure in St. Louis.

Gussie idolized his highly successful grandfather. Adolphus set the standard for the legendary Busch family work ethic. He once described the secret of his success as a willingness "to work double the time I was paid for."[2]

In 1903 Gussie's father acquired the 245-acre Grant's Farm in south St. Louis County; he later built a hunting lodge and a French chateau on the

310

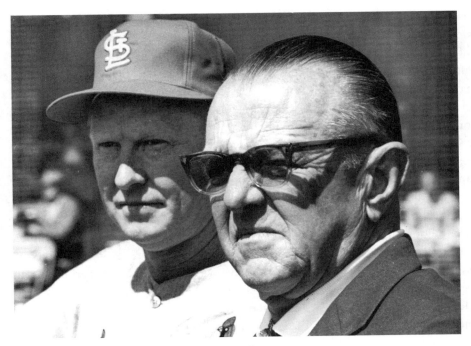

Red Schoendienst and Busch. The 1964 Cardinals team was Busch's first World Series winner. He left a legacy of five National League champions and three World Series winners. (Collection of Bill Nowlin)

property and moved his family to the country. The chateau had twenty-six rooms and fourteen baths. The farm, which subsequently grew to 281 acres, was opened to the public in 1955 and featured a menagerie of exotic animals, including the famous Clydesdales. Gussie transformed this tract into a very popular tourist attraction to craft the image of his brewery.

Young Gussie spent his youth learning to ride, shoot, and enjoy the life of wealth provided by his doting parents. He also drove horse coaches competitively and enjoyed both horse riding and boxing. He traveled extensively, accompanying his grandfather on several trips to Germany. For a brief time he tried rodeo riding in Wyoming, where he met Will Rogers. As later reported in *Time* magazine, Gussie remembered, "A kid just couldn't have had more."[3]

Although he subsequently gave millions to various educational institutions and received honorary degrees from several universities, Gussie initially shunned formal education. He attended the public Tremont School in St. Louis and the private Smith Academy but never graduated from high school. "Without a doubt," Gussie later remembered, "I was the world's lousiest student. I never graduated from anything."[4]

During World War I, Gussie served for fourteen months as a "stable sergeant" for the Home Guard. In 1918 he married the beautiful twenty-two-year-old Marie Christy Church. She bore Gussie two daughters before dying of pneumonia in 1930.

Gussie started his working life in a family-owned bank and then moved on to a railroad company where the family owned a significant share of the stock. At age twenty-four, he started working in the brewery. He began at the very bottom, initially scrubbing beer vats and performing menial tasks throughout all of the brewery's operations. His dad subsequently appointed him the general superintendent of brewing operations.[5]

As would be expected, the advent of Prohibition devastated the legal brewing industry. The Busch family faced a decision. They could go out of business and sell their $30 million brewery for scrap.

At ten cents on the dollar, the family could retire from the brewing business and still walk away with a sizable amount of money.

Instead, they doggedly kept turning out other products such as baker's yeast, malt syrup, and grape-flavored pop to try to keep the operation open. They achieved only limited success. As a last resort, his dad sent Gussie to meet with gangster Al Capone. They reached a deal where Busch would legally supply Capone with the raw ingredients for his illegal brewing operations.

As Gussie later recalled, "We ended up as the biggest bootlegging supply house in the United States. Every goddamn thing you could think of. Oh, the malt syrup cookies! You could no more eat the malt syrup cookies. . . . They were so bitter. . . . It damn near broke Daddy's heart."[6]

When Prohibition ended at midnight on April 6, 1933, the brewery gates swung open and the big brewery trucks rolled though the St. Louis streets delivering the beer to a thirsty public. The *Saturday Evening Post* subsequently reported Gussie's reaction: "It was the greatest moment in my life," he said. "The greatest, I guess that I will ever know."[7]

In September 1933 Gussie married his second wife, Elizabeth Overton Dozier. The two apparently had an affair before the death of his first wife and the marriage occurred only two weeks after Elizabeth's divorce from her husband. She subsequently bore Gussie both a daughter and a son.

Less than a year later, the Busch family suffered a significant setback when August A. Busch Sr. died on February 13, 1934. Mr. Busch, who was sixty-eight years old, suffered intense pain for more than six weeks from a complication of heart disease, gout, and dropsy. During his painful ordeal, Gussie reportedly tried to cheer him up by riding a horse into the house and up a staircase to his father's second-floor bedroom.[8]

His recovery efforts did not result in any significant improvements. Using a revolver he kept by his bedside, Busch killed himself with one shot under his heart. Busch left an unsigned note on a night table beside his bed. On a plain sheet of paper it read, "Good-bye, precious mommy and adorable children." In the tradition of the Busch family, the presidency of the brewery passed on to the eldest son, Adolphus.[9]

The forty-three-year-old Gussie volunteered for service in the army in June 1942 and received the rank of lieutenant colonel with an assignment to the Pentagon. He oversaw ammunition production, won promotion to colonel in 1944, and received the Legion of Merit for his service.[10] Throughout his time in the army, he continued to add to his reputation as someone who liked to party and flirt with the girls. Remembering his military experience, Gussie later confided, "Jack Pickens (an old friend) was in the service with me. We used to smell powder together—that is women's face powder." When Adolphus died on August 29, 1946, Gussie became president of the company.[11]

Returning home after his service, Gussie also found that all was not well between him and his second wife. A lady of queenly disposition, Elizabeth did not share his love of hops, horses, hunting, and singing German party songs. He quickly moved out of the family's town house back to Grant's Farm. Instead of living in the main mansion (his mother still used the residence), he moved into a nearby eighteen-room apartment. Gussie dealt with his loneliness by hosting spectacular parties.[12]

On a subsequent trip to Switzerland in 1949, Gussie met the beautiful twenty-two-year-old Gertrude (Trudy) Buholzer. After a nasty $1 million divorce settlement with Elizabeth, he married Trudy in 1952 at the Busch family cottage in Little Rock, Arkansas. Trudy bore him seven children between 1954 and 1966.[13]

In February 1953 Fred Saigh, the Cardinals' owner, faced a prison sentence for tax evasion. Rumors flew that out-of-towners would buy the team and move it to Milwaukee. Gussie and his brewery stepped in, bought the struggling team for $3.75 million, and pledged never to move the team out of St. Louis. At the time of the sale's announcement, Gussie vowed, "Come hell or high water, I will bring a baseball World Championship to St. Louis before I die."[14]

The local press lauded him as the savior of the team. However, the primary reason for buying the team was to sell more beer. The Cardinals and Anheuser-Busch quickly became enmeshed. From a personal viewpoint, after saving the Cardinals, the flamboyant Busch family also finally gained full access to the upper echelon of St. Louis society.[15]

Gussie soon discovered he was now a national personality. On a trip to New York, shortly after buying the club, he decided to meet baseball reporters at a luxurious restaurant. Anticipating that a small group would attend, a stunned Gussie ended up meeting over three hundred baseball journalists. He never forgot the incident. The volume of his incoming mail also skyrocketed. He marveled, "Not many people wrote to me when I was just a brewery president, but as owner of the Cardinals . . . I began to receive thousands of letters."[16]

Gussie quickly found he had several formidable obstacles to overcome before the brewery would reap the enormous potential of his acquisition. Including the team's initial selling price, the brewery poured an estimated $6 to 7 million into the Cardinals franchise. It bought and completely refurbished the dilapidated stadium where the ball club played (Sportsman's Park).

Initially, Gussie also attempted to rename the ballpark Budweiser Stadium. However, baseball commissioner Ford Frick would not approve the name due to the commercialization of a product. In memory of his grandfather, father, and brother, Gussie adjusted the name to Busch Stadium. Then, he ordered his brewery to create a new line of beer with the name Busch on the label. He also began to restore the Cardinals' withering farm system.

Gussie wanted to quickly make the team competitive. Not surprisingly, his initial baseball personnel decisions tried to both improve the Cardinals and sell more beer. Essentially, he tried to buy a pennant by throwing money at the other owners to obtain stars like Willie Mays, Ernie Banks, and Gil Hodges. The other owners successfully rebuffed his efforts, forcing Gussie to make a number of embarrassing efforts to purchase overrated players.[17]

In early 1953 Gussie went to his first Cardinals spring training camp in St. Petersburg, Florida. He arrived at the wheel of his specially outfitted bus. Costing $75,000, the bus had an Anheuser-Busch emblem on the back. Inside, it had six berths, a galley, a bar, a bathroom, and a lounge.[18] He mingled with his new team, even donning his own Cardinals uniform. Although his trip generated nationwide publicity for the brewery, the 1953 Cardinals finished third.

The brassy Busch approach of simultaneously promoting beer and professional baseball angered some in Congress. Sen. Edward Johnson from Colorado sponsored a bill that made baseball clubs owned by beer or liquor subject to antitrust laws. In addition, he called Gussie "a personable and able huckster" who regarded baseball as "a cold-blooded, beer-peddling business." Gussie subsequently testified successfully before the Senate Judiciary Committee against Johnson's bill. The bill went nowhere.[19]

In 1954 Gussie, with his characteristic flourish, updated his transportation to Cardinal road games. The Wabash Railroad delivered a $300,000 custom-built "rail business car" to Gussie. He named the eighty-eight-foot streamlined car the *Adolphus*. The exterior of the stainless steel car featured a St. Louis Cardinal emblem on one end and an Anheuser-Busch emblem on the other. Inside accommodations included four bedrooms that could be converted into meeting rooms, a dining room, two bathrooms with showers, two service personnel quarters, and an observation lounge fully stocked with Anheuser-Busch beer.[20]

Sometimes, Gussie attached the luxurious *Adolphus* to the train that carried the Cardinals on their road trips. As the Cardinals reached their destinations, Gussie could and did use the car to hold meetings with his beer wholesalers and retailers in the area. When he traveled with the team, his parties featured gin playing (his favorite card game) and heavy drinking. In 1955 he spent nearly the entire year traveling the country on the *Adolphus* meeting with the brewery's nine hundred wholesalers.[21] Impatient for success, Gussie employed five managers between 1953 and 1959 — Eddie Stanky, Harry Walker, Fred Hutchinson, Stan Hack, and Solly Hemus. During the same period he employed three general managers: Dick Meyer (a brewery executive), Frank Lane, and Bing Devine. The changes made no difference. After the 1953 third-place finish, the team finished in the second division four times through 1959. In January 1958 Musial agreed to a salary of $91,000, but Gussie increased the pact to make Stan the first $100,000 per year NL player.

In the early 1960s, GM Devine began accumulating a group of young, talented black players who would form the strong nucleus for several future winning teams. For many years the Cardinals held their spring training in St. Petersburg, Florida. Reflecting the local social norms of the times, St. Petersburg discouraged racial interaction. Black players stayed in different quarters than the whites. Those whites who did not agree with the practice rented private houses.

Cardinals first baseman Bill White publicly criticized the situation, and both the Cardinals and the brewery issued statements denouncing the practice. Gussie bluntly told local officials to fix it or the team would train at some other site.

Local officials quickly found a way to lodge the entire team together. Several of the white players had traditionally stayed with their families in beachfront cottages during spring training, but when Musial and Boyer gave up their private accommodations to move in with the rest of the team — blacks included — the Cardinals successfully broke down the local custom. The Cardinals' motel became a tourist attraction. People would drive by to see the white and black families swimming together or one of the famous team barbecues, with Howie Pollet making the salad and Boyer, Larry Jackson, and Harry Walker grilling up the steaks and hamburgers. As Bob Gibson later remembered, "The camaraderie on the Cardinals was practically revolutionary in the way it cut across racist lines." Gussie's strong show of support for equality within the entire team created the environment necessary for future Cardinal successes.[22]

During the 1963 season, Cardinals icon Stan Musial announced he would retire at the end of the season. In addition, under Devine's and Johnny Keane's leadership, the Cardinals were now serious contenders. Gussie wanted an NL pennant for both himself and Stan, the man who had remained steadfastly loyal to him throughout his ownership. The 1963 Cardinals won ninety-three games, but Sandy Koufax and the Los Angeles Dodgers won the pennant. After the season, *The Sporting News* recognized Devine's efforts by naming him their NL Executive of the Year.

After the profoundly discouraging near-miss finish in 1963, a volatile Gussie demanded a pennant in 1964. He publicly threatened to tear down the current Cardinal management structure and start over again. Branch Rickey, whom Gussie hired as a special consultant in October 1962, encouraged him. Engaged in a behind-the-scenes power struggle with Devine, Branch wanted to bring in his own GM.

Throughout his career, Gussie would never accept dishonesty or disloyalty from any of his employees. During the 1964 pennant race, he sincerely believed Devine both lied to and betrayed him by not telling him about a disagreement within the team. When he felt Devine subsequently covered up the incident, he impulsively fired both Devine and their longtime business manager, Art Routzong. Privately, he also made plans to fire manager Johnny Keane. At Rickey's recommendation, Bob Howsam became the new Cardinals GM.[23]

Amid all the management upheavals, the 1964 Cardinals unexpectedly rallied in September. The pennant race came down to the last game of the season. When St. Louis fell behind early, Gussie left his seat and went up to his private box, called the Redbird Roost. Angry and frustrated that the team might again come close and lose again, he kicked a hole in the wall of the Roost.[24] The team rallied, beat the Mets, and won the 1964 NL pennant by one game over Philadelphia and Cincinnati. After the game, a beaming Gussie could hardly contain himself as he walked around the clubhouse hugging the ballplayers. The Cardinals went on to beat the Yankees in the 1964 World Series. In a final irony, *The Sporting News* again named the fired Devine their NL Executive of the Year.[25] Then, at an October 16 press conference to publicly offer a new contract to Keane, Johnny presented Gussie with his resignation letter dated September 28. The Cardinals quickly selected Red Schoendienst as their new manager.

In addition to bringing a world championship to St. Louis, Gussie led a drive to replace his refurbished old stadium with a privately funded new one. On May 12, 1966, the new Busch Memorial Stadium opened in downtown St. Louis. The stadium led to a revitalization of the entire area. The new stadium became the last major sports complex to be built solely with private funds.

By the end of 1966, with Howsam's help, a strong restructured Cardinals team emerged. Howsam then left St. Louis for an offer from Cincinnati. In January 1967 the loyal Gussie again

reached out to his longtime friend Stan Musial and persuaded him to become the new Cardinals GM. This action brought Schoendienst and Musial together again.

The 1967 Cardinals won both the NL pennant and the subsequent World Series against the Red Sox. Orlando Cepeda, a May 1966 Howsam acquisition, won the NL Most Valuable Player Award. The Cardinals also went over two million in home attendance for the first time.

Off the field, Gussie continued to party hard during the 1967 World Series. He, his wife, and a group of close friends thoroughly enjoyed themselves when they traveled to root for the Cardinals in Boston. At one Boston hotel, their food fights and chandelier-swinging mayhem caused an estimated $50,000 worth of party-related damages. When presented with the bills, Gussie reportedly told his employees to put the expenses in the advertising account.[26]

In November 1967 Stan Musial, who was never really comfortable behind a desk, told Gussie he no longer wanted to be the Cardinals' GM. Surprisingly, Gussie rehired Bing Devine. He publicly admitted he had made a mistake in letting Devine go in 1964, and he attributed the mistake to "impatience and misunderstanding."[27]

The Cardinals easily won the 1968 NL pennant, as Bob Gibson was the NL Most Valuable Player and the Cy Young Award winner. After leading 3 games to 1, the team faltered in the World Series, losing to the Detroit Tigers.

The 1960s teams won three championships, and Gussie rewarded them handsomely. By 1970 he had become the first team owner in history to have a payroll in excess of $1 million.[28]

However, Gussie and his Cardinals fell on hard times starting in 1969. Much to his chagrin, Gussie found his paternalistic approach toward player relations now being publicly portrayed as one-sided and akin to slavery. Curt Flood's vocal support of these positions and his public salary squabble with the club irked Gussie. Right or wrong, Gussie sincerely believed he had saved Flood from baseball oblivion earlier in his career, and he now felt Flood had betrayed his loyalty. The Cardinals' subsequent trade of Flood to Philadelphia prompted Curt to declare himself a free agent.[29]

Near the end of 1974, Gussie and Trudy tragically lost their youngest daughter, Christina Martina Busch. Described as a "beautiful blue-eyed blonde child," and nicknamed "Honey Bee" by Gussie, Christina died on December 17 from injuries she suffered in a December 6 traffic accident while returning from school. The crash, on a busy St. Louis expressway, killed their chauffeur instantly. The other passenger in the Volkswagen bus, her brother Andrew, survived. The loss deeply affected both Gussie and Trudy.

In 1975 his son Augustus Busch III successfully convinced the Anheuser-Busch board of directors to force his seventy-six-year-old father's retirement as the head of the company. Gussie relinquished day-to-day brewery control, becoming an honorary chairman of the board of directors. As a part of the deal, he retained control of the Cardinals.[30]

In 1978, frustrated by nearly ten years without a pennant-winning ball club and going through a messy divorce with Trudy, Gussie fired Bing Devine a second time. He also employed three field managers that season: Vern Rapp, Jack Krol, and 1964 (NL) MVP Ken Boyer.

In 1980, after an unsuccessful decade, Gussie made another outstanding baseball decision by hiring Whitey Herzog as both his GM and his on-the-field manager. Gussie and Herzog clicked immediately. Both Whitey and Gussie shared German ancestry and loved beer. Whitey enjoyed a direct line of communication with Gussie. For his part, Gussie later said, "He's [Whitey] not only a great manager but a helluva guy. He and I talk the same language." In his eleven years with the team, the Whitey-led Cardinals won one world cham-

pionship and three NL championships.[31] In 1987 the Cardinals went over the three million mark in home attendance for the first time. Gussie also started a new St. Louis postseason tradition before each NLCS and World Series home games during the 1980s when he would ride into Busch Stadium on the Budweiser Clydesdales' wagon waving a red cowboy hat. The Cardinals' fans went wild and Gussie loved the attention.

In 1981 Gussie married Margaret Snyder, his one-time personal secretary. Six years before, she had become the first woman to serve on the board of directors of Anheuser-Busch. In the same year, the St. Louis Cardinals also named her to its board. In August 1988 she suffered a pulmonary embolism and died at the age of seventy-two in a St. Louis hospital.

In 1982 Gussie reportedly played a key role in the dismissal of then baseball commissioner Bowie Kuhn. At various times during Kuhn's tenure, Gussie publicly clashed with him over a variety of baseball and business issues. Ultimately, Gussie sided with just enough other owners to deny Kuhn's continuation as the commissioner.[32]

In 1984 the Cardinals retired No. 85 in honor of Gussie's eighty-fifth birthday.

In 1989, after a hospitalization for pneumonia, the ninety-year-old August A. Busch Jr. died at his St. Louis home. A sister, one former wife, nine children, twenty-seven grandchildren, and nine great-grandchildren survived him.

When asked if he ever regretted his baseball ownership experience, Gussie replied, "Hell, I'd do it all over again."[33]

Chapter 58. A Three-Way Tie for the Pennant?

Russell Lake

In 1946 the St. Louis Cardinals participated in the first-ever regular-season baseball playoff to decide the pennant. At the end of that season, on September 29, the Cardinals and the Brooklyn Dodgers were tied for the National League lead with 96-58 records after both teams had lost their final regular-season games. Baseball commissioner Happy Chandler and National League president Ford Frick had already set up a best-of-three-games playoff to determine the pennant winner, and St. Louis defeated Brooklyn 2 games to 0 to advance to the World Series, which finally started on October 6.

Over the next eighteen years, from the Cardinals' World Series appearance in 1946 to their next appearance, in 1964, the Major Leagues witnessed several more regular-season playoffs. In 1948 the Cleveland Indians and Boston Red Sox had a one-game playoff to decide the American League pennant. Three more National League pennant playoffs followed. In 1951 a best-of-three playoff between the New York Giants and the Dodgers was climaxed by Bobby Thomson's "Shot Heard 'Round the World" home run. In 1959 the Los Angeles Dodgers swept the Milwaukee Braves in two games. In 1962 the San Francisco Giants defeated the Dodgers 2 games to 1 in a dramatic series to win the pennant.

In 1964, having played in all four of the National League's regular-season playoffs so far, the Dodgers fell too far back in the standings in September and were officially eliminated from the pennant race on September 18. In fact, with only fourteen games left on the schedule at that point, and the Philadelphia Phillies at thirty games over

.500 (89-59) and comfortably ahead of the second-place Cardinals by six games, another National League playoff seemed unlikely.

The American League showed much more potential to have a pennant-deciding playoff that season. As the race came down to the wire, three teams were fighting for the pennant. On September 17 the New York Yankees (.593) were two percentage points ahead of the Baltimore Orioles and the Chicago White Sox (each .591). But over the next week the Yankees pulled away, and on the 24th they had a four-game lead over the Orioles and White Sox. The race tightened up again, but when the season ended on October 4, the Yankees had won the pennant by one game over the White Sox and two games over the Orioles.

While the American League race was ebbing and flowing, the National League race had suddenly become much tighter. The Philadelphia Phillies, who had led the league by six and a half games with two weeks to go, were reeling in a losing streak that would reach ten games, while Cincinnati, St. Louis, and San Francisco were transforming their goals from a "Let's finish second!" to a "Hey, we can win this thing!" position.

On the morning of Thursday, October 1, three days before the end of the season, the Cardinals were in first place by one game over Cincinnati, two and a half games over the Phillies, and three and a half games over San Francisco. On that day, at a meeting in Cincinnati, National League president Warren Giles and team officials set up a number of playoff scenarios. If two teams finished the regular season tied, the best-of-three format used in 1946, 1951, 1959, and 1962 would apply. However, a three- or four-team tie would certainly require a playoff format that was different and complicated.

For four teams, pairings and sites would be determined by lot. Both pairs would play a one-game playoff, and the winners would meet in a best-of-three series to decide the pennant.

For three teams, there would be a round-robin. Lots would be drawn to designate Teams 1, 2, and 3. On Monday, October 5, the day after the regular season ended, Team 2 would play at Team 1's ballpark. On Tuesday Team 3 would play at Team 2's ballpark, and on Wednesday Team 1 would play in Team 3's ballpark. After those three games, any team with two losses would be eliminated, and the two teams remaining would draw lots to determine the site of the fourth contest. If a fifth game became necessary, the visiting team in the fourth game would select the site for the deciding game.

But if the teams each had one win and one loss after the first three games, lots would be drawn once more to determine new numbers for each team. (New) Team 2 would play in Team 1's ballpark. The winner of this contest would play Team 3 with the location again to be decided by lot. The winner of that game would be the pennant winner.

By Friday, October 2, both leagues were still looking at possible pennant playoffs. In the American League the Yankees' lead had been trimmed to two and a half games over both the White Sox and the Orioles. In the National League the third-place Phillies came out of their slump and beat the second-place Reds, who had now lost three out of four at Crosley Field. The first-place Cardinals, who had won eight straight games, were shut out in St. Louis by the last-place New York Mets. The fourth-place Giants were two games back with two to play after defeating the eighth-place Chicago Cubs, so the best they could hope for was a tie.

Warren Giles told New York sportswriter Dick

Young that he preferred a three-team playoff to a four-team showdown. "If there had been a four-way playoff, I'd have been a basket case," said the sixty-eight-year-old National League president.[1]

Games on Saturday, October 3, the next-to-last day of the regular season, clarified the playoff picture sharply. The possibility of a playoff in the American League disappeared entirely when the Yankees defeated the Indians and clinched their fifth-straight pennant. In the National League, the possibility of a four-way tie disappeared when the Giants lost to the Chicago Cubs, 10–7, and were eliminated from the pennant race. In St. Louis, the Mets hit five home runs to pummel the Cardinals, 15–5. The loss dropped the Cardinals into a first-place tie with Cincinnati, with Philadelphia one game behind. (Both the Reds and the Phillies had an off day that day.)

On October 4, the final day of the regular season, a Cardinals win and a Reds loss would give the Cardinals the pennant, while a Cardinals loss and a Reds win would give Cincinnati the pennant. If both teams won, they would face each other in a best-of-three playoff, starting the next day in Cincinnati. For the season to end in a three-way tie, the Phillies would have to beat the Reds and rely on the Mets topping the Cardinals.

In St. Louis on Sunday, broadcaster Harry Caray's guest on his pregame show was the seventy-four-year-old peripatetic manager of the Mets, Casey Stengel. After Caray raised the possibility that the lowly Mets might help to decide the pennant race, Stengel declared that either the Cardinals or Cincinnati would have the best chance against the Yankees in the World Series. Whichever National League team won, he said, it would be in trouble in the World Series, with or without a playoff, because it had had to stretch its pitching so much during the past two weeks.

With number two man Jack Buck on a pro football assignment, Caray would do the play-by-play for the Cardinals game by himself. Jerry Gross would be in the booth to announce the starting lineups and offer limited commentary. The game in St. Louis would be on radio with no national or regional television coverage. There would be periodic information from Roy May, who was at the Phillies-Reds game, so Caray could update his listeners on what was happening in Cincinnati. This type of in-depth reporting was not easy during the hectic pennant chase. A few games earlier, Caray had committed this gaffe on the KMOX airwaves: "... and now for the latest in Cincinnati. The Reds have runners on first and third with one out in the eighth inning. ... Oh, just a minute. That's our game!"[2]

In the Reds-Phillies game, Cincinnati's John Tsitouris (9-12) and Philadelphia's Jim Bunning (18-8) were the starting pitchers. For the Cardinals, Curt Simmons (18-9) would go against the Mets' Galen Cisco (6-18). Cisco was 1-1 against the Cardinals with a 3.45 ERA. Simmons was 1-2 with a 2.48 ERA against the Mets with all three games decided by one run. Dal Maxvill replaced the injured Julián Javier at second base in the St. Louis lineup. The weather was excellent in both cities, with bright sunshine and 15–20 mph winds from the left-field corner to right field. Capacity crowds had filed into the stadiums to see what part of baseball history they might witness.

In the top of the first inning, Caray asked his Busch Stadium listeners if they had brought their transistor radios with them. The resounding roar from the grandstand answered that many had done just that. With his thoughts leaning to the game in Cincinnati, Caray mixed up his call after the first inning ended by saying, "At the end of one in St. Louis, the Phillies ... er, the Cardinals nothing, the Mets nothing." Caray noted a half inning later that even the scoreboard operator in left field was apparently nervous, as he placed the zero for the Mets in the top of the second into the bottom of the frame.

After four innings, the Cardinals had scratched

out a 2–1 lead. Promising news came from Cincinnati that the Phillies had a 4–0 lead on the Reds. However, the top of the fifth put anxiety back into the thirty-thousand-plus Busch Stadium spectators. Simmons had not been sharp as he faced Bobby Klaus with one out and the tying run on second base. Klaus lifted a short pop fly that Caray described this way: "There's a high pop fly to right. That should be caught by somebody. Maxvill is there, he's under the ball ... Oh ... he lets it drop! And, here's the runner around third holding up. Klaus winds up at second. Shannon could have caught the ball, but Maxvill called for it ... and the wind grabbed it—c'mon Mike ... take those kind! Gee! An easy pop fly ... and now they have the leading run at second, the tying run at third."

The next batter, Roy McMillan, who was a good clutch hitter and ended up with a .328 career batting average against Simmons, put the Mets in front with a double into the left-field corner. With the Mets up 3–2, Caray was beside himself: "Well ... if everything stays the way it is now, there will be a triple tie starting tomorrow in Philadelphia." Cardinals manager Johnny Keane summoned Bob Gibson from the bullpen to replace Simmons. Gibson would be pitching on one day's rest (he had lost to the Mets, 1–0, on Friday night), so he would be going more on adrenaline than his best stuff. Cardinals owner August A. Busch Jr. was exasperated as he moved from his field-box seat to his private owner's box. He simply could not believe that the Cardinals might lose to the cellar-dwelling Mets again, and he became so angry that he kicked a hole in a wall.

With the Phillies in command in Cincinnati, if they won and the Cardinals lost, the three-team playoff would begin the next day, and this would be the schedule for the first three games:

Monday: Cincinnati at Philadelphia
Tuesday: St. Louis at Cincinnati
Wednesday: Philadelphia at St. Louis

There had been no official announcements, but the pitching match-ups could have been the following:

Monday: Jim Maloney (15-10) of the Reds versus Chris Short (17-9) of the Phillies
Tuesday: Ray Sadecki (20-10) of the Cardinals versus Jim O'Toole (17-7) of the Reds
Wednesday: either Dennis Bennett (12-14) or Jim Bunning (19-8) of the Phillies versus Curt Simmons (18-9)

A Cardinals rally put an end to that speculation. After Gibson got out of the top of the fifth inning with no more runs scored, the Cardinals fought back from the one-run deficit with three runs in the bottom of the inning to take a 5–3 lead. Gibson walked in a run to make it 5–4 in the sixth inning, but after Lou Brock's one-out double in the St. Louis sixth, Bill White hit a two-run home run to increase the Cardinals' lead to 7–4. In Cincinnati, the Phillies had opened up a 9–0 lead over the Reds with Bunning on his way to a complete-game 10–0 shutout. After White's smash, the Cardinals scored four more runs to finish the game. In the ninth inning Barney Schultz took over for an exhausted Gibson to get the final two outs in the 11–5 victory, his fourteenth save since August 6. The Cardinals had won the pennant, and the need for a playoff in the National League was put to rest.

If a three-team playoff had been necessary and had gone the maximum number of games, the World Series would not have started until October 10 in the city of the National League pennant winner. It is difficult to imagine how much more discussion the 1964 baseball season would be subject to had a playoff in either league been added to it.

Chapter 59. **The 1964 World Series**

John Harry Stahl

October 4

The Cardinals clinch the 1964 National League (NL) pennant, one game ahead of the Cincinnati Reds and the Philadelphia Phillies with a 93-69 regular season record. The club played at a .718 clip from August 23. For the Cardinals organization, it was their first NL pennant in eighteen years.

The Cardinals' players were ecstatic about being in the World Series. In late September as they were battling for the pennant, Cardinals All-Star third baseman and team captain Ken Boyer told a reporter he would give "ten years off my life" to play in a World Series. "This is the greatest thing that ever happened to me," he said after the pennant-clinching victory.

Boyer's thoughts were echoed by Cardinals field manager Johnny Keane. "This is the happiest day of my life," Keane told reporters after the game.

October 5

Julián Javier, the Cardinals' second baseman, bruised his left hip during a collision at first base on Saturday (October 3) against the Mets. Dal Maxvill replaced him in the regular season finale, but Javier was reported to be ready for the World Series.

Boyer pulled a hamstring muscle during the season finale but looked forward to playing against his younger brother (Yankee Clete Boyer) in the World Series.

October 6

The Yankees entered the 1964 World Series with a clear advantage over the Cardinals in World Series participation experience. Dick Groat (one), Bob

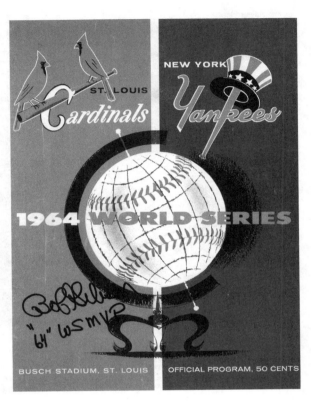

Official program for the '64 World Series. This copy is signed by series MVP Bob Gibson. (Courtesy of John Harry Stahl)

Skinner (one), and Roger Craig (three) were the only Cardinals with prior experience. By contrast, many of the Yankees players had already appeared in previous World Series: Mickey Mantle (eleven), Whitey Ford (ten), Elston Howard (eight), Bobby Richardson (six), Tony Kubek (five), and Roger Maris, Hector Lopez, Johnny Blanchard, Clete Boyer, and Ralph Terry (four). For several other Yankees, this would be either their second or third

Ray Sadecki throws the first pitch of the 1964 World Series at Busch Stadium. (Photo by Allied Photocolor Imaging Center)

time in the Series. In addition, Yogi Berra, the first-year Yankees manager and former resident of the St. Louis "Hill District," appeared in fourteen World Series while he was a player.

Kubek, the regular Yankees starting shortstop, sprained his wrist trying to break up a double play two weeks before the Series and was ruled unavailable for the entire Series. The Cardinals and the Yankees agreed to let him sit in civilian clothes in the New York dugout for all the games.

October 7 — Game One / Busch Stadium / Cardinals 9, Yankees 5

Ray Sadecki started against Whitey Ford. For Ford, it was his twenty-second start in a World Series game and his eighth start in an opening game, both World Series records.

The Cardinals scored in the first inning as Brock singled, went from first to third on a Groat single, and scored on a Ken Boyer sacrifice fly. Cardinals 1, Yankees 0.

Tom Tresh hit a two-run home run in the second inning, as the Yankees scored three runs on five hits. On Bobby Richardson's single to left, Ford was thrown out at the plate by Brock's strong throw. Yankees 3, Cardinals 1.

Shannon scored another Cardinals run in the second inning as he came home from second base on Sadecki's single. Yankees 3, Cardinals 2.

In the fifth, Tresh doubled home Mickey Mantle for another Yankees run. Yankees 4, Cardinals 2.

A turning point in Game One came in the Cardinals' sixth. St. Louis scored four runs and

JOHN HARRY STAHL

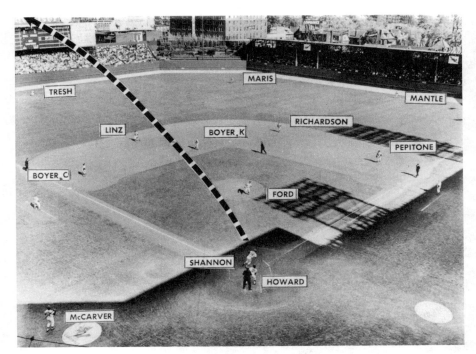

A diagram depicting the trajectory of Mike Shannon's sixth-inning homer off Whitey Ford in Game One of the '64 Series.

knocked out Ford. Shannon hit a long (estimated between 475 and 500 feet) two-run home run high off the left-field scoreboard to tie the game. After Tim McCarver doubled to right, Al Downing relieved Ford. Pinch hitter Carl Warwick singled through the hole into left to score McCarver. Pinch runner Julián Javier scored when Curt Flood hit a triple to left field that Tresh momentarily lost in the sun. Cardinals 6, Yankees 4.

Javier played second base in both the seventh and the eighth inning before leaving for a pinch hitter. Because of his injured hip, though, it would be his only appearance in this World Series.

Barney Schultz entered the game at the start of the seventh inning. In the eighth, the Yankees scored a run on a Richardson single. Cardinals 6, Yankees 5.

The Cardinals ended the scoring with three runs in the eighth as Flood hit a run-scoring single and Brock drove in two runs with a double. Cardinals 9, Yankees 5.

October 8 — Game Two / Busch Stadium / Yankees 8, Cardinals 3

Bob Gibson opposed twenty-two-year-old rookie Mel Stottlemyre in the second game. During the regular season, Gibson led St. Louis starting pitchers from August 24 through the last game of the season. He started ten times and pitched eight complete games.

Gibson began the game by striking out six of the first nine Yankees he faced.

In the bottom of the third, the Cardinals began the scoring. With runners on second and third and one out, Flood grounded out to the shortstop and Shannon scored. Cardinals 1, Yankees 0.

In their fourth, the Yankees tied the score on a Clete Boyer sacrifice fly. Cardinals 1, Yankees 1.

After a walk and a line out, a controversial play occurred in the sixth inning when Joe Pepitone checked his swing at a low curve ball and plate umpire Bill McKinley ruled that it hit Pepitone's left thigh. The Cardinals claimed his bat hit the

Overhead photo of Busch Stadium, first game of 1964 World Series. (Photo by Allied Photocolor Imaging Center)

ball before it hit his leg. After a heated argument, Pepitone went to first base, putting runners on first and second. The next batter, Tresh, hit a run-scoring single. Yankees 2, Cardinals 1.

The Yankees added two runs in the seventh on an RBI single by Richardson and a Mantle ground out. Yankees 4, Cardinals 1.

The Cardinals scored one run in their eighth on Brock's run-scoring ground out. Bob Skinner pinch-hit for Gibson. Gibson pitched eight innings and struck out nine. Yankees 4, Cardinals 2.

Phil Linz greeted reliever Schultz with a solo home run. After one out and a Roger Maris single, Gordon Richardson relieved Schultz and gave up run-scoring hits to Mantle and Pepitone, two walks, and a sacrifice fly. Yankees 8, Cardinals 2.

The Cardinals scored one run in the ninth on a Groat triple and a McCarver single. Stottlemyre struck out pinch hitter Charlie James for the final out. Yankees 8, Cardinals 3.

October 9 — Travel Day

Professional oddsmakers announced the Yankees as 8–5 favorites for Game Three and 2–1 favorites to win the World Series.

Game Three would be the twenty-seventh time in the forty-two-year history of Yankee Stadium that the World Series was contested there.

As the Cardinals practiced at Yankee Stadium, Pepitone teased them by slowly limping across the field heavily favoring one leg, and then limping as he started back favoring the other leg.

JOHN HARRY STAHL

Ticket for World Series Game One at Busch Stadium, October 7, 1964. (Courtesy of John Harry Stahl)

October 10 — Game Three / Yankee Stadium / Yankees 2, Cardinals 1

Cardinals veteran left-hander Curt Simmons started against the Yankees' Jim Bouton.

The Yankees began the scoring in the second inning on a two-out double by Clete Boyer. Yankees 1, Cardinals 0.

In the Cardinals' fifth inning, McCarver singled and advanced to second on Mantle's error. With two outs, Simmons singled off Clete Boyer's glove to drive in McCarver. Cardinals 1, Yankees 1.

With the scored tied 1–1 in the bottom of the ninth inning, Schultz entered the game. On his first pitch, Mantle hit a tremendous home run into the third tier of the stadium in right field to end the game. As Mantle rounded third base, he was joined by a group of young fans and Yankees third base coach Frank Crosetti. In ten World Series, it was Mantle's sixteenth home run in sixty-one games. Mantle later listed the home run as one of his ten greatest thrills in his baseball career. Yankees 2, Cardinals 1.

"The ball I threw was right down the well," Schultz said. "It was knee-high and across the plate. It didn't break." Trying to counter the gloomy atmosphere in the clubhouse, Keane, when asked if Barney's knuckle ball to Mantle had anything on it, said, "Yes, I guess it did — when it came off Mantle's bat."

October 11 — Game Four / Yankee Stadium / Cardinals 4, Yankees 3

Sadecki, the winner of Game One, faced New York's Downing. Berra had scheduled Ford to start the game but reported that he had suffered an injury and could not pitch. Ford did not appear again in the 1964 Series.

In the first inning, the Yankees scored three runs on five hits and an error. Roger Craig relieved Sadecki, and as Craig left the bullpen, his wife and two sisters intercepted him and planted kisses on his cheek for good luck. After allowing a run-scoring single to Elston Howard, he got the final two outs. Yankees 3, Cardinals 0.

Craig pitched four and two-thirds innings, allowing no runs and striking out eight. Warwick pinch-hit for him in the sixth inning and singled. Flood followed with another single. With one out, Richardson made an error on a potential double-play ground ball hit by Groat, and Ken Boyer came to the plate with the bases loaded. After taking a low and outside fastball, Boyer guessed right as Downing followed with a change-up and hit a grand slam down the left-field line. When asked later if the home run was his greatest baseball experience, Boyer said, "Our winning the pennant was. I'll never recapture that." Cardinals 4, Yankees 3.

Ron Taylor entered the game in the Yankees'

Hitting in the house that Ruth built: the Cardinals survey Yankee Stadium while taking batting practice.

sixth inning and pitched the last four innings, allowing no hits and no runs. "It was the greatest thrill of my life to help win the game," Taylor said later.

"That has to be the finest relief work we've had," said Keane after the game. "It couldn't be improved upon. Craig and Taylor were splendid."

October 12 — Game Five / Yankee Stadium / Cardinals 5, Yankees 2 (10 innings)

In a repeat of Game Two, Gibson again opposed Stottlemyre. After four scoreless innings, the Cardinals scored two runs in the fifth with the help of a single by Gibson followed by an infield error, a run-scoring single by Brock, and a run-scoring ground out. Cardinals 2, Yankees 0.

In the Yankees' ninth inning, Mantle batted first and grounded to Groat, who bobbled the ball for an error. Howard struck out. Pepitone then hit a sharp grounder off Gibson's right hip. Gibson scrambled after the ball as it rolled toward the third base line, grabbed it, and fired it to White to retire Pepitone on a close play. On Gibson's next pitch, Tresh hit a four-hundred-foot two-run home run to the right-center-field bleachers to tie the game. Cardinals 2, Yankees 2.

In the Cardinals' tenth, with runners on first and third and one out, McCarver hit a home run to right field, driving in Groat and White. McCarver later explained the winning home run was almost accidental as all he was trying to do was hit a fly ball to score the runner on third base. "It was the biggest hit in my life," McCarver later told reporters. Cardinals 5, Yankees 2.

Aided by a great catch from Ken Boyer on a foul pop by Maris to end the game, Gibson pitched a scoreless tenth for a complete-game victory. He struck out thirteen, a total exceeded only twice in prior World Series. He threw 133 pitches.

October 13 — Travel Day

Ten thousand fans and a brass band greeted the returning Cardinals at Lambert Airport in St. Louis.

JOHN HARRY STAHL

Dick Groat and Bob Gibson embrace as the Cardinals win the World Series.

Asked how he felt after pitching twelve innings in the final regular-season series against the Mets and now eighteen innings against the Yankees, Gibson replied, "I feel as though I'd just come out of a 10-round bout."

October 14 — Game Six / Busch Stadium / Yankees 8, Cardinals 3

In a rematch of Game Three, Simmons and Bouton squared off to start Game Six.

In their first inning, the Cardinals scored on two singles and a double play. Cardinals 1, Yankees 0.

The Yankees tied the game in the fifth inning on a two-out single by Bouton. Yankees 1, Cardinals 1.

During the sixth inning, the Yankees scored twice on back-to-back home runs by Maris and Mantle. Maris's home run went down the line and barely fair over the right-field roof. Mantle's landed on the pavilion roof in right-center field. Yankees 3, Cardinals 1.

Taylor replaced Simmons to get the final two outs of the seventh inning. Schultz replaced Taylor to start the eighth inning. With two outs and two on, Schultz gave up a run-scoring single to Howard. A walk to Tresh loaded the bases. The Cardinals brought in Richardson to pitch to Pepitone, who hit a grand slam. Yankees 8, Cardinals 1.

The Cardinals scored one in the eighth on a ground out and one in the ninth on a pinch single by Skinner. Flood ended the game by grounding into a double play. Yankees 8, Cardinals 3.

October 15 — Game Seven / Busch Stadium / Cardinals 7, Yankees 5

Gibson faced Stottlemyre in the Series finale. Both hurlers were pitching on only two days' rest.

The Cardinals began the scoring in the bottom of the fourth inning by scoring three runs on three hits, a walk, and an error. A highlight of the inning was a double steal with Shannon stealing second and McCarver stealing home. Cardinals 3, Yankees 0.

The Cardinals added three more runs in the fifth. Brock hit a solo home run and the Cardinals added two more on a single by White, a double by Ken Boyer, a run-scoring ground out, and a sacrifice fly. Cardinals 6, Yankees 0.

In the sixth, Mantle hit a three-run home run, setting a new record for most World Series home runs (eighteen). Cardinals 6, Yankees 3.

In the seventh, Ken Boyer hit a two-out solo home run off Yankees reliever Steve Hamilton. Cardinals 7, Yankees 3.

In the ninth, both Clete Boyer and Linz hit solo home runs around two strikeouts before Richardson popped out to second base to end the game. According to *Sports Illustrated*, as second baseman Maxvill waited for the ball to come down, shortstop Groat yelled over and told him not to let the descending ball "hit him on the coconut."

For the second time in the Series, Gibson pitched a complete-game victory. He struck out nine, raising his total World Series strikeouts to thirty-one. In three games, Gibson logged twenty-seven innings with a 3.00 ERA. It was the seventh World Series championship for the St. Louis Cardinals.

Post 1964 World Series

Gibson won the tenth annual Sport Magazine Corvette Award as the World Series's outstanding player. He was lauded as exhibiting all the "courage" and "physical stamina" that could be asked from a man.

On October 16, Keane resigned as the manager of the St. Louis Cardinals and Berra was fired as the New York Yankees' manager.

On October 20, Keane agreed to manage the New York Yankees in 1965.

Epilogue

John Harry Stahl

The dramatic late-season comeback by the 2011 world champion Cardinals sparked comparisons with the 1964 team's accomplishments. Both teams faced daunting regular-season challenges. Both the 2011 and 1964 teams won the National League championship on the last day of the season. Both beat highly favored opponents (the Texas Rangers and the New York Yankees) to subsequently win their World Series.

The 1964 Cardinals' success also laid the foundation for the 1967 world champion and 1968 National League champion Cardinal teams. Bob Gibson, Lou Brock, Tim McCarver, Curt Flood, Mike Shannon, Bill White, Julián Javier, Dal Maxvill, and Ed Spiezio played on all three teams. Red Schoendienst coached the 1964 team and managed the 1967 and 1968 teams. Stan Musial was a Cardinal vice president in 1964, the Cardinal general manager in 1967, and a Cardinal vice president in 1968.

In mid-November 2011, the St. Louis Sports Hall of Fame honored the 1964 Cardinal team with the St. Louis Award. The citation said, in part, "For some 18 years St. Louis had been without a World Series champion before the 1964 edition of the Redbirds pulled off one of the most remarkable comebacks in Major League history." Other individual inductees have included Lou Brock, Bob Gibson, August A. Busch Jr., Stan Musial, and Red Schoendienst.

Between 1965 and 2011, the Missouri Sports Hall of Fame selected Bob Gibson, Jack Buck, Branch Rickey, Ken Boyer, Lou Brock, Bing Devine, Mike Shannon, Tim McCarver, and Red Schoendienst, citing their career accomplishments.

After their playing days, Stan Musial, Bob Gibson, Lou Brock, and Red Schoendienst were all selected to the National Baseball Hall of Fame as players. In 1965 the Hall of Fame selected Branch Rickey in the baseball executive category. Tim McCarver, Harry Caray, Bob Uecker, and Jack Buck have each won the Ford C. Frick Award for Excellence in Broadcasting, awarded annually by the Hall of Fame.

Notes and References

1. Dave Bakenhaster

1. The photograph also appears in the March 5, 1964, editions of the *Morgantown (WV) Post* and the *Fitchburg (MA) Sentinel*; the March 9, 1964, edition of the *Montana Standard*; the March 18, 1964, edition of the *Hope (AK) Star*; and the April 2, 1964, edition of the *Biddeford (ME) Journal*.

2. Johnny Stewart, "Bakenhaster to Cardinals for Substantial $$ Bonus," undated 1963 article from the *Columbus (OH) Citizen-Journal*, in the archives of the National Baseball Hall of Fame and Museum, Cooperstown NY.

3. All statistics for Dave Bakenhaster come from Baseball-Reference.com, http://www.baseball-reference.com/players/b/bakenda01.shtml.

4. Interview with Carolyn Bakenhaster, February 4, 2011. (Dave Bakenhaster declined to talk to the author of this article.)

5. Carolyn Bakenhaster interview.

6. Stewart, "Bakenhaster to Cardinals."

7. Stewart, "Bakenhaster to Cardinals."

8. Interview with Tim Saunders, February 4, 2011. At the time of the interview, Saunders was in his twenty-fifth year as the high school baseball coach at Bakenhaster's old school and was also the coordinator of the high school's athletic Hall of Fame.

9. Interview with Craig Duffey, February 8, 2011.

10. Duffey interview.

11. Saunders interview.

12. "Cards Tell of Signing Pitcher," *Greeley (OH) Tribune*, June 10, 1963.

13. "Cards Tell of Signing."

14. Fritz Howe, "Glenville Favored to Take Crown," *Steubenville (OH) Herald-Star*, May 25, 1963.

15. Saunders interview.

16. S. Sgt. Ron Flechtner, "Bullseyes Rarin' to Play," *Pacific Stars and Stripes*, May 6, 1968.

17. http://www.baseball-reference.com/minors/player.cgi?id=bakenh001dav.

18. "Scouting Reports," *Baseball Digest*, March 1964, 123.

19. Game details from Retrosheet.org, http://www.retrosheet.org/boxesetc/1964/B06200SLN1964.htm.

20. Game details from Retrosheet.org, http://www.retrosheet.org/boxesetc/1964/B07220SLN1964.htm.

21. Fred Collins, *Winnepeg Free Press*, August 6, 1964.

22. Collins.

23. Associated Press, "Cards Recall 13 Players," September 5, 1964.

24. St. Louis Cardinals player questionnaire, in the archives of the National Baseball Hall of Fame and Museum, Cooperstown NY.

25. Ancestry.com, *Ohio Divorce Index, 1962–1963, 1967–1971, 1973–2007* [database online] (Provo UT: Ancestry.com Operations, Inc., 2010).

26. Clifford Kachline, "Small Park Shrinks Cards Series Pot—40 Share in Swag," *Sporting News*, November 7, 1964.

27. E-mail to author from Carolyn Bakenhaster, February 8, 2011.

28. Carolyn Bakenhaster interview.

29. Burt Graeff, "The Winner Was a Loser," *St. Petersburg Independent*, May 19, 1966.

30. St. Louis Cardinals official news release, April 29, 1971, in the archives of the National Baseball Hall of Fame and Museum, Cooperstown NY.

31. Carolyn Bakenhaster interview.

32. Carolyn Bakenhaster interview. For Dave, it was a second marriage, his first one in the 1960s being short-lived.

33. Saunders interview.

34. Rich Marazzi and Len Fiorito, "Dave Bakenhaster," in *Aaron to Zipfel* (New York: Avon Books, 1985).

2. Ken Boyer

Gillette, Gary, and Pete Palmer. *The ESPN Baseball Encyclopedia*, 5th ed. New York: Sterling, 2008.

Golenbock, Peter. *The Spirit of St. Louis: A History of the St. Louis Cardinals and Browns*. New York: HarperCollins, 2000.

Halberstam, David. *October 1964*. New York: Villard, 1994.

Rains, Rob. *The St. Louis Cardinals, 1892–1992*. New York: St. Martin's, 1992.

Thorn, John, Phil Birnbaum, and Bill Deane, eds. *Total Baseball*, 8th ed. New York: Sport Classic Books, 2004.

New York Times, September 8, 1892.
Sporting News.
St. Louis Post Dispatch.

BaseballLibrary.com.
BaseballProfilesnl.info.
Baseball-Reference.com.
Biographicon.com.
KenBoyer.net.
Retrosheet.org.
StartSurfing.com.
TheBaseballPage.com.
TheStLCardinals.com.
TripAtlas.com.
Web.archive.org.

3. Lou Brock

1. David Halberstam, *October 1964* (New York: Fawcett Books, 1994), 133.

2. Halberstam, *October 1964*, 134.

3. Lou Brock and Frank Schulze, *Stealing Is My Game* (Upper Saddle River NJ: Prentice-Hall, 1975), 30.

4. Lou Brock player file, National Baseball Hall of Fame Library, Cooperstown NY, credit to *New York Post* article by Maury Allen, September 11, 1974, 90.

5. Brock file, *Post* article.

6. Brock and Schulze, *Stealing*, 37.

7. Brock and Schulze, *Stealing*, 37.

8. Brock and Schulze, *Stealing*, 38.

9. Brock file, *Post* article.

10. Brock and Schulze, *Stealing*, 39.

11. Halberstam, *October 1964*, xiii.

12. Brock file, quote not credited.

13. Brock and Schulze, *Stealing*, 56.

14. Brock and Schulze, *Stealing*, 56.

15. Halberstam, *October 1964*, 355.

16. Brock and Schulze, *Stealing*, 132.

4. Ernie Broglio

1. Unless otherwise indicated, all remarks by Ernie Broglio come from correspondence with him.

2. Rains, *Cardinals*, 64–65.

3. Rains, *Cardinals*, 65.

4. Citation from Castle and Rygelski, *I-55 Series*, 175.

5. Rains, *Cardinals*, 65.

Broeg, Bob. *Memories of a Hall of Fame Sportswriter*. Champaign IL: Sagamore, 1995.

———. *Redbirds: A Century of Cardinals' Baseball*. St. Louis: River City Publishers, 1981.

Castle, George, and Jim Rygelski. *The I-55 Series, Cubs vs. Cardinals*. Champaign IL: Sports Publishing, 1999.

Cohen, Richard, and David Neft, eds. *The Sports Encyclopedia: Baseball*, 14th ed. New York: St. Martin's, 1994.

Halberstam, David. *October 1964*. New York: Villard Books, 1994.

Rains, Rob. *Cardinals, Where Have You Gone?* Champaign IL: Sports Publishing, 2005.

———. *The St. Louis Cardinals, 1892–1992*. New York: St. Martin's, 1992.

Thorn, John, Phil Birnbaum, and Bill Deane, eds. *Total Baseball*, 8th ed. New York: Sport Classic Books, 2004.

Tiemann, Robert L. *Cardinal Classics*. St. Louis: Baseball Histories, 1982.

Broeg, Bob. "On Cards' Trade." *St. Louis Post-Dispatch*, October 8, 1958.

Braun, Kevin. "Where Are They Now: Ernie Broglio." BaseballSavvy.com. March 5, 2009. www.baseball-savvy.com/w_broglio.htm (accessed October 31, 2010).

Baseball-Reference.com.
Retrosheet.org.

St. Louis Cardinals Yearbooks, 1960–64.

5. Jerry Buchek

All quotations from Jerry Buchek come from an interview on January 3, 2011, and subsequent e-mail correspondence. The author relied on Baseball-Reference.com and the Ultimate Mets Database at http://ultimatemets.com, as well as the *1968 Mets TV Radio Press Guide* and the *New York Times*.

6. Lew Burdette

1. Allen, "Biggest Froggy," 30.
2. Driver, "Pride of Nitro," 59.
3. "Burdette Sees Life on 'Outside.'"
4. Haudricourt, "Obituary," C1.

Buege, Bob. *The Milwaukee Braves: A Baseball Eulogy.* Milwaukee: Douglas American Sports, 1988.

Mumau, Thad. *An Indian Summer: The 1957 Milwaukee Braves, Champions of Baseball.* Jefferson NC: McFarland, 2007.

Schoor, Gene. *Lew Burdette of the Braves.* New York: G. P. Putnam's Sons, 1960.

Sutter, L. M. *Ball, Bat, and Bitumen: A History of Coalfield Baseball in the Appalachian South.* Jefferson NC: McFarland, 2009.

Vincent, Fay. *We Would Have Played for Nothing: Baseball Stars of the 1950s and 1960s Talk about the Game They Loved.* New York: Simon & Schuster, 2008.

Allen, Phil. "Biggest Froggy, Biggest Pond: The Lew Burdette Story." *Baseball Digest*, December 1957, 29–33.

Chen, Albert. "The Greatest Game Ever Pitched." *Sports Illustrated*, June 1, 2009, 63–67.

Driver, David. "The Pride of Nitro: Baseball Star Lew Burdette." *Goldenseal* (Fall 1998): 56–62.

Haudricourt, Tom. "Obituary; Lew Burdette 1927–2007; Farewell to a Hero: Crafty Right-Hander Led Braves to Glory in '57 Series." *Milwaukee Journal-Sentinel*, February 7, 2007, C1.

Baseball-Reference.com.

"Burdette Sees Life on 'Outside.'" Unattributed clipping in Lew Burdette player file, National Baseball Hall of Fame Library, Cooperstown NY.

7. Timeline, April 14–April 30

Unless otherwise indicated, all direct quotations come from the *St. Louis Post-Dispatch*.

Baseball-Reference.com.
Retrosheet.org.

8. Doug Clemens

1. Allen Lewis, "Clemens Hopes to Muscle into Phils' Outfield," *Sporting News*, April 2, 1966, 7.
2. Fran Zimniuch, *Phillies: Where Have You Gone?* (Champaign IL: Sports Publishing, 2004), 166–69.
3. Allen Lewis, "Ah, Peace at Last—Noisy Wes Departs; Quiet Doug to Phils," *Sporting News*, January 29, 1966, 22.
4. BasinLeagueHistory.com.
5. John Thorn, Pete Palmer, and Michael Gershman, eds., *Total Baseball*, 7th ed. (Kingston NY: Total Sports Publishing, 2001), 1481.
6. Neal Russo, "Big Noise in Minors, Clemens Bat Could Crash Card Lineup," *Sporting News*, March 7, 1964, 16.
7. Lewis, "Clemens," 7.
8. Baseball-Reference.com, Doug Clemens Minor League Statistics and History.
9. Melissa Yerkov, "Memoirs of a Major Leaguer," *Northeast Times*, November 2008, www.northeast-times.com.
10. "Pilots Select Seven Amarillo Players for Texas All-Stars," *Sporting News*, July 12, 1961, 38.
11. J. Roy Stockton, "Speedy Birds Revive Hope for New Model of St. Louis Swifties," *Sporting News*, March 28, 1962, 28.
12. Oscar Kahan, "Capsule Comments Pinpoint '62 Eye-Poppers," *Sporting News*, April 18, 1962, 10.
13. International Items, *Sporting News*, August 11, 1962, 40.
14. Yerkov, "Memoirs."
15. Johnny Carrico, "Crackers Cap Merriwell Feats with JWS Triumph," *Sporting News*, October 13, 1962, 29.
16. "Unassisted DP by Outfielder," International Items, *Sporting News*, September 28, 1963, 25.
17. Zimniuch, *Phillies*, 168.
18. Ray Kelly, "Phils Keep Clemens out of School," *Philadelphia Evening Bulletin*, September 22, 1967, 57.

19. Kelly, "Phils Keep Clemens."

20. Allen Lewis, "Phils' Clemens Rips Fringe Label with Clouting Spree," *Sporting News*, September 21, 1968, 13.

21. Zimniuch, *Phillies*, 168.

9. Roger Craig

Craig, Roger, and Vern Plagenhoef. *Inside Pitch: Roger Craig's '84 Tiger Journal.* Grand Rapids MI: Eerdmans, 1984.

Lee Sinins' Complete Baseball Encyclopedia. http://www.baseball-encyclopedia.com (accessed October 30, 2009).

Treder, Steve. "Humm Baby!" BaseballAnalysts.com. January 11, 2007. http://baseballanalysts.com/archives/2007/01/humm_baby_1.php (accessed October 30, 2009).

Shook, Richard L. Telephone interviews with Roger Craig, October 5, 2009; July 15, 2010.

10. Mike Cuellar

1. Eisenberg, *33rd Street.*

2. *Sporting News*, June 19, 1957.

3. *Sporting News*, October 7, 1959; October 14, 1959.

4. *Sporting News*, October 7, 1959; October 14, 1959.

5. Gene Freese, *St. Louis Post Dispatch*, August 27, 1964.

6. Eisenberg, *33rd Street*, 201.

7. Eisenberg, *33rd Street*, 204.

8. Weaver, *It's What You Learn*, 239.

Eisenberg, John. *From 33rd Street to Camden Yards—An Oral History of the Baltimore Orioles.* Chicago: Contemporary Books, 2001.

Weaver, Earl, and Berry Stainback. *It's What You Learn after You Know It All That Counts.* New York: Doubleday, 1982.

Thornley, Stew. "Minneapolis Millers vs. Havana Sugar Kings." *National Pastime* (Society for American Baseball Research), no. 12, 1992.

Jorge Colon Delgado and Alberto "Tito" Rondon of SABR's Latino Baseball Committee.

Clippings from Mike Cuellar player file, National Baseball Hall of Fame Library, Cooperstown NY.

11. Dave Dowling

1. Mah, 1961 season recap.

2. Colton, *Goat Brothers*, 9.

3. Martin, "Road to the Majors," K18.

4. "Cardinal Prospect Picked," 18.

5. "Cards Sign UCLA [sic] Hurler," B4.

6. Ferguson, "Dowling," 35.

7. Ferguson, "Dowling."

8. Polner, *Branch Rickey*, 247.

9. Russo, "'Here Comes the Judge,'" 9.

10. Russo, "Redbirds Mine Pair," 6.

11. Associated Press, "Big Leaguers Sit Around."

12. Russo, "'Here Comes the Judge.'"

Colton, Larry. *Goat Brothers.* New York: Doubleday, 1993.

Polner, Murray. *Branch Rickey: A Biography.* Jefferson NC: McFarland, 2007.

Associated Press. "Big Leaguers Sit Around, Dread News." May 11, 1965.

Ferguson, John. "Dowling, Cal Chemistry Student, Concocts Heady Victory Potion." *Sporting News*, July 4, 1964.

Martin, Danny. "Road to the Majors before They Became Big-Leaguers." *Anchorage Daily News*, July 11, 1993.

Russo, Neal. "'Here Comes the Judge,' Redbirds Hum When Steve Raps for Order." *Sporting News*, June 15, 1968.

———. "Redbirds Mine Pair of Hill Nuggets in Dowling, Briles." *Sporting News*, October 24, 1964.

"Cardinal Prospect Picked as Sandlot Star of Year." *Sporting News*, December 28, 1963.

"Cards Sign UCLA [sic] Hurler." *Los Angeles Times*, September 13, 1963.

Mah, Jay-Dell. 1961 season recap. Western Canada Baseball. http://www.attheplate.com/wcbl/1961_1.htm.

Baseball-Reference.com.

Goldpanners.com.

NewspaperArchive.com (in particular, the *Centralia Chronicle*).

Retrosheet.org.

VirtualWall.org (Bob Dowling memorial).

Grateful acknowledgment to Dave Dowling for his memories (telephone interview, July 18, 2010).

12. Harry Fanok

Grateful acknowledgment to Harry Fanok for his enthusiastic collaboration, including the loan of his personal scrapbooks. Along with the scrapbooks, the Retrosheet website (www.retrosheet.org) enabled fact-checking. Some minor revisions to Harry's account resulted. Thanks also to Joe M. Morgan.

Capezzuto, Tom. "Harry Fanok's Cup of Coffee . . . It Was High Octane." *Barnstorming: New Jersey's Baseball Magazine* (Winter 1993–94): 14–17.

Russo, Neal. "Bandmaster Fanok Tunes Up Redbird Mudcat Memories." *Sporting News*, November 30, 1963, 10.

———. "Fanok, the Whippany Fireman, Almost Got Burned by Tigers." *St. Louis Post-Dispatch*, April 25, 1963.

———. "Redbirds Just Wild about Harry—Hard-Firing Beaut of Bullpen." *Sporting News*, May 4, 1963, 10.

Statistics courtesy of Pat Doyle, developer of the Professional Baseball Players Database.

13. Curt Flood

1. Flood and Carter, *The Way It Is*, 11.

2. Flood, *The Way It Is*, 8. Flood biographer Stuart Weiss argues that Flood's childhood environment was not as deprived as Flood might have his readers believe. See Weiss's *Curt Flood Story*.

3. Among Powles's protégés were Billy Martin, Frank Robinson, Vada Pinson, Chris Cannizzaro, and Joe Morgan, in addition to Flood.

4. Flood and Carter, *The Way It Is*, 14.

5. Flood and Carter, *The Way It Is*, 15.

6. Some doubt has arisen in recent years about Flood's oil portraits. According to Brad Snyder's *A Well-Paid Slave*, Flood did not paint the oil portraits. Instead, he would send photographs of his subjects to one Lawrence Williams in Los Angeles, who would do the portraits and ship them back to Flood, allowing Flood to take all of the credit for the paintings. This includes the Martin Luther King portrait for which Flood was so widely acclaimed. Snyder asserts that the portrait was signed by someone else, although he doesn't say who. Weiss disagrees with Snyder's claims as they relate to the portraits done while Flood was still playing baseball. Both agree, however, that by the 1980s, when Flood tried to resuscitate this source of income, he could not possibly have done the portraits attributed to him at that time because of the effects of his alcoholism. A female companion of Flood's at the time supposedly confirmed that he did not actually paint those portraits.

7. Gross, "Curt Flood," 70.

8. When Powles died in 1987, Flood was the only one of his former big leaguers to attend the funeral.

9. Flood and Carter, *The Way It Is*, 22.

10. Flood and Carter, *The Way It Is*, 24.

11. Flood and Carter, *The Way It Is*, 24. The manager was Bert Haas.

12. Flood and Carter, *The Way It Is*, 25.

13. Flood and Carter, *The Way It Is*, 51. For those seeking a somewhat more detailed summary of Hemus's treatment of his black players, see the profile of Bob Gibson elsewhere in this volume.

14. Weiss argues that Hemus's failure to use Flood more regularly stemmed as much from his desire to find a power-hitting outfielder to boost the Cardinals' offense as it did from Hemus's supposed racism.

15. Flood and Carter, *The Way It Is*, 92.

16. Weiss asserts that the divorce decree was never finalized.

17. Weiss's *The Curt Flood Story: The Man Behind the Myth* is the best source of detailed information about Flood's financial obligations arising from his divorce.

18. Flood's relationship with Marian Jorgensen was the subject of widespread speculation by people in St. Louis who knew him. By his own account the relationship was completely platonic.

19. "What Ever Happened," 55.

20. Among other roles, Judy Pace played the wife of Gale Sayers (Billy Dee Williams) in *Brian's Song*.

21. Flood and Carter, *The Way It Is*, 145–51.

22. Flood and Carter, *The Way It Is*, 158.

23. Flood and Carter, *The Way It Is*, 114.

24. Over the years, many observers have incorrectly

stated that the court in *Federal Baseball* said baseball was a *sport*, not a business, and therefore not subject to antitrust laws. The court never made that distinction.

25. A number of players publicly criticized Flood's lawsuit and the executive committee's decision to fund it. Among those voicing opposition were Carl Yastrzemski, Harmon Killebrew, and Frank Howard. Prominent former players also voiced opposition, including Ted Williams, Ralph Kiner, Joe DiMaggio, and Joe Garagiola. Garagiola, in fact, testified against Flood in the district court trial.

26. The selection of Goldberg turned out to be a disaster. He embarked on a campaign for governor of New York shortly after accepting the Flood case (and after promising Miller he had no intention of running for office). Goldberg was ill prepared when the case came to trial in May 1970, although it is doubtful that his performance had anything to do with the final outcome.

27. Interview with Howard Cosell on ABC's *Wide World of Sports*, January 3, 1970.

28. Justice Lewis Powell recused himself from the case because he owned stock in Anheuser-Busch, the parent company of the Cardinals.

29. Goldberg argued Flood's appeal before the Supreme Court. As was the case in the district court, he was woefully unprepared and stumbled through a presentation that was painfully embarrassing both for him and for the members of the court. It was the last case Goldberg ever argued before the Supreme Court.

30. Miller and the union never claimed that abolition of the reserve clause was the only way to satisfy the players' grievances. In fact, Miller and the union recognized the owners' need to have some control over players they had developed and invested in. Miller always expected that negotiation would be the means by which the reserve clause would be modified. Flood's lawsuit arose precisely because the owners had failed to negotiate in good faith after the 1968 Basic Agreement, which created a joint committee to examine possible changes in the system.

31. According to Weiss, with the exception of a very brief period of time in 1982, Flood stopped making child support and alimony payments in October 1968. His ex-wife filed another lawsuit after his death trying to identify assets that might be confiscated in partial payment of his arrears.

32. Originally, Flood and Short agreed to a two-year contract at $100,000 per year without a reserve clause. Short readily agreed to Flood's demands, but Bowie Kuhn later told Short he would reject any contract that did not contain the reserve clause.

33. Snyder, *Well-Paid Slave*, 132.

34. Weiss characterizes Flood's autobiography as an "apologia" for the lawsuit. Weiss paints a darker picture of Flood's emotional state and motivations for his decision to sue baseball. He says Flood resorted to a "victimization" mentality to justify his inability or unwillingness to deal with the troubles in his life, including his failed marriage and resulting financial pressures, the guilt he felt from his gaffe in the 1968 World Series, and the volatile state of his relationship with the St. Louis front office during the 1969 season. He says the lawsuit was Flood's irrational way of lashing out and blaming others for his troubles, despite the hardships his actions would place on his family and himself.

35. Snyder, *Well-Paid Slave*, 219.

36. Snyder and Weiss both suggest that Flood started drinking again two or three years after leaving rehab.

37. Weiss claims that an investigation after Flood's death showed the Curt Flood Youth Foundation to be of questionable viability. It was based in the Flood home in Los Angeles. It had scant financial resources. Judy Flood had been using foundation funds to pay the utility bills. Aside from one letter suggesting the foundation had found summer jobs for thirty-five youths, there was no evidence of significant assistance provided to anyone.

38. Chass, "Forgotten Man," 63.

39. Gibson supported his friend privately but recognized, as did other players, that supporting Flood publicly would put a target on his own back. Gibson and others were not willing to sacrifice their livelihoods for the cause. Gibson did visit Flood in his hotel in New York during the trial when the Cards were in town playing the Mets.

40. Snyder, *Well-Paid Slave*, 2–3.

41. Will, "Dred Scott."

Flood, Curt, with Richard Carter. *The Way It Is.* New York: Pocket Books, 1971.

Korr, Charles P. *The End of Baseball As We Knew It:*

The Players Union, 1960–81. Champaign: University of Illinois Press, 2002.

Kuhn, Bowie. *Hardball: The Education of a Baseball Commissioner.* New York: McGraw-Hill, 1988.

Miller, Marvin. *A Whole New Ballgame: The Sport and Business of Baseball.* New York: Birch Lane Press, 1991.

Snyder, Brad. *A Well-Paid Slave: Curt Flood's Fight for Free Agency in Professional Sports.* New York: Plume, 2007.

Weiss, Stuart L. *The Curt Flood Story: The Man behind the Myth.* Columbia: University of Missouri Press, 2007.

Chass, Murray. "Curt Flood—Baseball's Forgotten Man." *Baseball Digest,* January 1977.

Gildea, William. "Curt Flood—Baseball's Angry Rebel." *Baseball Digest,* February 1971.

Gross, Neil. "Curt Flood—His Teammates Call Him Rembrandt." *Ebony,* July 1968.

"What Ever Happened to . . . Curt Flood?" *Ebony,* March 1981.

Will, George. "Dred Scott in Spikes." Syndicated newspaper article from November 21, 1993. Reprinted in Will's *Bunts: Curt Flood, Camden Yards, Pete Rose and Other Reflections on Baseball.* New York: Scribner, 1998.

Baseball-Reference.com.
Retrosheet.org.

14. Phil Gagliano

1. Interview with Phil Gagliano on December 4, 2009. All quotations not otherwise attributed derive from this interview. In a 1967 profile on Tony Gagliano, the same publication informed readers that he had led his American Legion team to nine of the preceding ten Tennessee championships. In 1933 Tony's team won the state championship and also the Tri-State Legion championship against teams from Mississippi and Arkansas as well as Tennessee. He remained active in semipro baseball, first as a batter and then as a coach, winning six championships in eight years, twice going to the semifinals of the National Amateur Baseball Federation tournament.

2. *Sporting News,* July 31, 1965, which reported Gagliano's bonus as $15,000. The "gold dust twins" line appears in many publications.

3. *Christian Science Monitor,* July 8, 1961. Russ Lake points out that Gagliano played 143 games at second base, while Jerry Buchek was the primary shortstop.

4. *St. Louis Post-Dispatch,* March 24, 1964.

5. In early June the Cleveland Indians signed Ralph Gagliano for a $40,000 to $60,000 bonus, beating out offers from sixteen other Major League clubs, several times what Phil had received five years earlier. Ralph became a cup-of-coffee Major Leaguer, appearing in only one game—September 21, 1965, for the Indians. Ralph was drafted and spent three years in military service during the heart of the Vietnam War. He came back to two more years in the Minors, 1970 and 1971, but he'd missed his prime years. Baseball was good to younger brother Paul as well. He never played professionally, but he did earn a full-ride scholarship that put him through Vanderbilt University.

6. *St. Louis Post-Dispatch,* May 7, 1965.

7. *Chicago Tribune,* May 18, 1965.

8. *Sporting News,* July 3, 1965.

9. *Sporting News,* June 7, 1969.

10. *Sporting News,* July 31, 1965.

11. *Sporting News,* September 14, 1968.

12. *Chicago Tribune,* March 25, 1964.

13. *Sporting News,* August 7, 1971.

14. *Sporting News,* March 18, 1972.

15. *Sporting News,* March 18, 1972; and *Hartford Courant,* February 26, 1972.

16. *Sporting News,* April 28, 1973.

17. *Sporting News,* October 6, 1973.

18. *New York Times,* October 11, 1973.

19. Rob Rains, *Cardinals, Where Have You Gone?* (Champaign IL: Sports Publishing, 2005).

In addition to the sources cited in this biography, the author consulted the Phil Gagliano player file at the National Baseball Hall of Fame Library, Cooperstown NY, the online SABR Encyclopedia, Retrosheet.org, and Baseball-Reference.com.

15. Timeline, May 1–May 31

Unless otherwise indicated, all direct quotations come from the *St. Louis Post-Dispatch.*

Baseball-Reference.com.

Retrosheet.org.

16. Bob Gibson

1. Gibson and Wheeler, *Stranger to the Game*, 101. Unless otherwise noted, the shorter quotes in this text are taken from the same source.

2. McCarver and Robinson, *Oh, Baby I Love It!* 58–59.

3. Gibson and Wheeler, *Stranger to the Game*, 166–67.

4. He did not care for the name "Pack," and later had it legally dropped.

5. Gibson and Wheeler, *Stranger to the Game*, 10–11.

6. Information about Gibson's basketball career at Creighton can be found at www.gocreighton.com.

7. Gibson and Wheeler, *Stranger to the Game*, 52–53.

8. Gibson and Wheeler, *Stranger to the Game*, 62.

9. Flood and Carter, *The Way It Is*, 51–52.

10. Flood and Carter, *The Way It Is*, 53–54.

11. Gibson and Wheeler, *Stranger to the Game*, 66.

12. McCarver and Robinson, *Oh, Baby I Love It!* 61.

13. Flood and Carter, *The Way It Is*, 68–69.

14. Gibson and Wheeler, *Stranger to the Game*, 82–83.

15. At least one researcher argues that Gibson's fielding ability was overstated. See Knox, "The 100 Top Fielding MLB Pitchers," 49.

Angell, Roger. "Distance." In *Late Innings: A Baseball Classic from the Best Writer in the Game*. New York: Fireside Books, 1982.

Flood, Curt, with Richard Carter. *The Way It Is*. New York: Pocket Books, 1972.

Gibson, Bob, and Reggie Jackson, with Lonnie Wheeler. *Sixty Feet, Six Inches: A Hall of Fame Pitcher and a Hall of Fame Hitter Talk about How the Game Is Played*. New York: Doubleday, 2009.

Gibson, Bob, with Lonnie Wheeler. *Stranger to the Game: The Autobiography of Bob Gibson*. New York: Penguin Books, 1994.

Halberstam, David. *October 1964*. New York: Villard Books, 1994.

Kahn, Roger. *The Head Game: Baseball Seen from the Pitcher's Mound*. San Diego: Harcourt Press, 2000.

McCarver, Tim, with Ray Robinson. *Oh, Baby I Love It!* New York: Dell Publishing, 1987.

Knox, John. "The 100 Top Fielding MLB Pitchers, circa 1900–2008." *Baseball Research Journal* (Summer 2009): 49.

MacCarl, Neil. "Pilots Tab Nelson 'Most Dangerous.'" *Sporting News*, September 10, 1958, 29.

Weber, Al. "Cards' Big Four of Future Polishing at Rochester." *Sporting News*, July 16, 1958, 33.

Baseball-Reference.com.

Retrosheet.org.

17. Dick Groat

1. *Sporting News*, April 2, 1966, 7.

2. Jeremy Anders, article dated July 22, 2007, located at http://www.baseballhall.org.

3. *Boston Herald*, August 13, 1978.

4. Huhn, *The Sizzler*, 18–27, 270–71.

5. Lowenfish, *Branch Rickey*, 529–30.

6. Lowenfish, *Branch Rickey*, 529–30.

7. *Sports Illustrated*, August 8, 1960, 26.

8. *Sporting News*, November 24, 1962, 29.

9. *Pittsburgh Press*, November 20, 1962.

10. *Sports Illustrated*, July 22, 1963, 34.

11. Halberstam, *October 1964*, 334.

12. Phil Pepe, undated article in Groat file.

13. *Sporting News*, May 21, 1966, 20–21.

Halberstam, David. *October 1964*. New York: Random House, 1994.

Huhn, Rick. *The Sizzler*. Columbia: University of Missouri Press, 2004.

Lowenfish, Lee. *Branch Rickey: Baseball's Ferocious Gentleman*. Lincoln: University of Nebraska Press, 2007.

http://minors.sabrwebs.com/cgi-bin/index.php.

http://pittsburghpanthers.cstv.com/sports/m-baskbl/pitt-m-baskbl-body.html.

http://pittsburgh.pirates.mlb.com/index.jsp?c_id=pit.

www.basketball-reference.com/players/g/groatdi01.html.

www.collegebasketballexperience.com/inductees.aspx?alpha=all.

www.goduke.com.
www.pittsburghpanthers.com/genrel/111907aad.html.
www.retrosheet.org.

Pepe, Phil. Undated article in Dick Groat player file, National Baseball Hall of Fame Library, Cooperstown NY.

18. Glen Hobbie

1. Interview with Glen Hobbie, December 7, 2011.
2. *Sporting News*, December 10, 1958.
3. *Sporting News*, April 29, 1959.
4. http://articles.chicagotribune.com/2007-03-25/sports/0703250019_1_cubs-wrigley-field-pirates.
5. Lew Freedman, *Chicago Cubs: Memorable Stories of Cubs Baseball (Game of My Life)* (Champaign IL: Sports Publishing, 2007).
6. Freedman, *Chicago Cubs*.
7. *Sporting News*, September 21, 1963.
8. *Sporting News*, September 21, 1963.
9. *Sporting News*, March 28, 1964.
10. *Sporting News*, March 28, 1964.
11. *Sporting News*, June 13, 1964.
12. *Sporting News*, June 20, 1964.
13. *Sporting News*, June 20, 1964.
14. *Sporting News*, January 16, 1965.
15. *Sporting News*, February 13, 1965.

In addition to the sources noted, the author also consulted Retrosheet.org, Baseball-Reference.com, and http://ontheoutsidecorner.wordpress.com/2011/05/13/glen-hobbie.

19. Bob Humphreys

1. Bob Humphreys player clippings file, National Baseball Hall of Fame Library, Cooperstown NY, accessed September 2010. Material from the file is used throughout this chapter.
2. "Humphreys Discards Glove with 'Pep-Up' Inscription," *Sporting News*, July 18, 1964, 17.
3. Neal Russo, "Humphreys Makes a Hit without Even Going to Bat for Cards," *St. Louis Post-Dispatch*, June 2, 1963.
4. Hampden-Sydney College Athletics website, www.hscathletics.com.
5. Humphreys's comments on earlier draft of this biography, February 4, 2010. His comments resulted in clarifications, deletions, and additions to the draft biography. In each case involving his MLB performance, the author verified the data using various analyses of Humphreys's career on Baseball-Reference.com.
6. Watson Spoelstra, "Lary Will Skip Japan Trip to Exercise Wing at Home," *Sporting News*, October 27, 1962, 15.
7. Bill James and Rob Neyer, *The Neyer/James Guide to Pitchers*, 251; Rob Neyer phone interview with Humphreys on October 1, 2002.
8. Larry Whiteside, "Knuckler Puts Humphreys on Victory Track," *Sporting News*, July 11, 1970, 29.
9. James and Neyer, *Guide to Pitchers*.
10. Humphreys file.

20. Charlie James

1. Broeg, "Cards' Signing."
2. Murphy, "Cardinal Legend."
3. Russo, "Sadecki Twirls."
4. Russo, "James Boy Rides Again."
5. Murphy, "Cardinal Legend."
6. Rains, *Cardinals*, 162, 163.
7. Rains, *Cardinals*, 162, 163.

Broeg, Bob. *Memories of a Hall of Fame Sportswriter*. Champaign IL: Sagamore, 1995.
Rains, Rob. *Cardinals, Where Have You Gone?* Champaign IL: Sports Publishing, 2005.

Lewis, Allen. "Comeback for O'Toole Would Do It for Reds." *Baseball Digest*, April 1966, 40.
Stockton, J. Roy. "Charley the Champion." *Mizzou Magazine* (Summer 2009): 42.

Broeg, Bob. "Cards' Signing of College Flyhawk Draws Fire from Mizzou Coaches." *Sporting News*, January 15, 1958, 7.
Kahan, Oscar. "Redbirds Feather Flag Nest with Two Fledgling Phenoms." *Sporting News*, August 10, 1960, 17.
Russo, Neal. "James Boy Rides Again—as Cards' Headline Bandit." *Sporting News*, July 14, 1962, 23.
———. "Sadecki Twirls First Route Job of '62 in Stopping L.A." *Sporting News*, June 2, 1962, 14.

———. "Slugger Altman Sees Card Wall as Choice HR Target." *Sporting News*, October 27, 1962, 11.

Stockton, J. Roy. "Bing Weighs Plus, Minus Signs, Sees Redbird Rise." *Sporting News*, April 5, 1961, 17.

———. "Former Cardinal Calls It Quits in Pro Baseball." *Ogden (UT) Standard-Examiner*, April 17, 1966, 2C.

Murphy, Megan. "A Cardinal Legend among Us." July 28, 2010. www.komu.com/news/a-cardinal-legend-among-us (accessed January 5, 2011).

Baseball-Reference.com.

Retrosheet.org.

St. Louis Cardinals Yearbooks, 1960–64.

21. Julián Javier

1. Neal Russo, "Javier Something Special with Bat as Well as Glove," *Sporting News*, September 2, 1967.

2. Herbert Simons, "Scouting Reports on 1960 Major League Rookies," *Baseball Digest*, March 1960.

3. Jack Herman, "Cards Find Comet in Swifty Javier," *Sporting News*, June 15, 1960.

4. Jack Herman, "Redbirds Boost Firepower with Changed Lineup," *Sporting News*, June 8, 1960.

5. Neal Russo, "Swift Keystoner Rated Key Man in Redbirds Future; Cuts Down on Strikeouts," *Sporting News*, August 23, 1961.

6. Neal Russo, "Hoolie's Hot Bat Fuels Redbird Takeoff," *Sporting News*, May 6, 1967.

7. "Boozer-Wine-Old Taylor Knocks Cards on Ears," *Sporting News*, July 8, 1967.

8. "Dominican Republic Gives Hero's Welcome to Javier," *Sporting News*, November 4, 1967.

9. Fernando Viscioso, "Pirates Defeat Native Stars before 19,152," *Sporting News*, November 4, 1967.

10. Neal Russo, "$84,320 U.S. Tax Liens Brought against Javier," *Sporting News*, October 17, 1970.

11. Neal Russo, "Javier Figures in '71 Redbird Plans," *Sporting News*, January 30, 1971.

12. "Bunts and Boots—Javier Tax Settlement," *Sporting News*, April 3, 1971.

13. "Baseball's Week," *Sports Illustrated*, July 8, 1963.

14. Neal Russo, "Hoolie's Hot Bat Fuels Redbird Takeoff," *Sporting News*, May 6, 1967.

15. Neal Russo, "Redbird Phantom Striking Dread in Hearts of Enemies," *Sporting News*, August 23, 1969.

16. Lyle Spatz, ed., *The SABR Baseball List and Record Book* (New York: Scribner, 2007).

17. "Baseball's Week," *Sports Illustrated*, May 25, 1964.

18. "Baseball's Week," *Sports Illustrated*, July 21, 1969.

19. Russo, "Redbird Phantom."

20. Bob Broeg, "All-Star Team of Switch-Hitters," *Sporting News*, February 17, 1979.

21. A. S. "Doc" Young, "Ashford Was One Ump with Box-Office Appeal," *Sporting News*, December 26, 1970.

22. Joe Falls, "The Ump GETS This Decision," *Baseball Digest*, July 1966.

22. Johnny Lewis

1. Milton Gross, "Cardinals' Johnny Lewis: He Remembers Tragedy," *Des Moines Register*, April 14, 1964, 30.

2. Bob Broeg, "Lewis Listens to Stan," *St. Louis Post-Dispatch*, Johnny Lewis player file, National Baseball Hall of Fame Library, Cooperstown NY.

3. Jack Herman, "Cardinals Dust Off 'Oh, Johnny' Lyrics, Croon 'Em for Lewis," unattributed clipping in Lewis file.

4. "Fracture Idles Suns' Lewis," *Sporting News*, August 12, 1964.

5. *Sporting News*, November 21 and 28, 1964.

6. Barney Kremenko, "Lewis Forecast: Less Pressure, More Base-Hits," *Sporting News*, January 9, 1965.

7. Kremenko, "Lewis Forecast."

8. "Lewis Uncorks Rifle Throws," *Sporting News*, May 1, 1965; "Mets' Lewis Belongs," Lewis file.

9. Til Ferdenzi, "Funny Mets No Joke to Maloney," unattributed clipping in Lewis file.

10. Ferdenzi, "Funny Mets."

11. *Sporting News*, October 30 and November 23, 1965.

12. Larry Fox, "Foster, Lewis Derail Mets' Salary Express," and "Lewis Agrees to 15 G," Lewis file.

13. "New Stance for Lewis," *Sporting News*, Lewis file.

14. "Lewis Joins Suns, Irked by Demotion," unattributed clipping in Lewis file.

15. "Buffs Win Twinbill from Suns," *Port Arthur (TX) News*, August 15, 1967.

16. Cardinals press releases, December 23, 1969, and December 8, 1971, Lewis file.

17. "Lewis Back in Uniform," unattributed clipping in Lewis file.

18. "Cards Demote Batting Coach," unattributed clipping in Lewis file.

19. "Johnny Lewis Calgary," unattributed clipping in Lewis file.

23. Timeline, June 1–June 30

Unless otherwise indicated, all direct quotations come from the *St. Louis Post-Dispatch*.

Baseball-Reference.com.
Retrosheet.org.

24. Jeoff Long

Grateful acknowledgment to Jeoff Long for his personal memories (telephone interviews on March 20 and 21, 2008; e-mail update on November 2, 2011). Thanks also to Harry Fanok.

1. "Schoolboy Gets $70,000 Bonus," 5D.

2. Blanchard, "He Came to Play," 44.

3. E-mail from Harry Fanok to the author, June 7, 2007.

4. Blanchard, "He Came to Play."

5. "Mom Wept," 2.

6. Blanchard, "He Came to Play."

7. Blanchard, "Trial of Jeoff Long," 48.

8. Blanchard, "Cards' Silvey Arrives," 47.

9. Blanchard, "Trial of Jeoff Long."

10. Blanchard, "Trial of Jeoff Long."

11. "Too Many Visitors' Homers," 38.

12. Russo, "Flashy Flood's Sock Shower," 8.

13. Russo, "Cardinals Look to Longshot," 19.

14. "Cubs, Giants Cut Short All-Star Rest," 10-M.

15. "Cards Slug to 10–6 Win," 12.

16. "Injuries Hamper Jeoff Long," 30.

17. Russo, "Jeoff Long Undergoes Knee Surgery," 20.

18. Wirth, "Do-or-Die Season," 39.

19. "Jeoff Long Doubtful," 34.

20. Wirth, "Do-or-Die Season."

21. Wirth, "Do-or-Die Season."

22. "Cisco Sets Trend," 36.

23. "Blast of 322 Yards," 14.

24. E-mail from Harry Fanok to the author, February 11, 2008.

Blanchard, Don. "Cards' Silvey Arrives, Goldies' Lucky Charm?" *Winnipeg Free Press*, July 12, 1961.

———. "Goldeye Glints: He Came to Play." *Winnipeg Free Press*, May 3, 1961.

———. "Goldeye Glints: The Trial of Jeoff Long." *Winnipeg Free Press*, July 22, 1961.

Russo, Neal. "Cardinals Look to Longshot Long as Long Ball Hope." *Sporting News*, February 22, 1964.

———. "Flashy Flood's Sock Shower Helps Whet Cards' Flag Appetite." *Sporting News*, August 10, 1963.

———. "Jeoff Long Undergoes Knee Surgery; Slugger Stakes Claim to Redbird Job." *Sporting News*, December 6, 1965.

Wirth, Ned. "Do-or-Die Season for Guindon and Long." *Sporting News*, May 10, 1969.

"Blast of 322 Yards Wins Long Driving Championship." *Greeley (CO) Tribune*, June 25, 1975.

"Cards Slug to 10–6 Win Over Braves." *Syracuse Post-Standard*, May 16, 1964.

"Cisco Sets Trend." *Sporting News*, June 14, 1969.

"Cubs, Giants Cut Short All-Star Rest." *Manitowoc (WI) Times-Herald*, July 8, 1964.

"Injuries Hamper Jeoff Long." *Sporting News*, April 24, 1965.

"Jeoff Long Doubtful." *Sporting News*, April 2, 1966.

"Mom Wept When Cards' $70,000 Long Left Home." *Sporting News*, July 15, 1959.

"Schoolboy Gets $70,000 Bonus." *Corpus Christi Caller-Times*, June 21, 1959.

"Too Many Visitors' Homers, Atlanta Takes Down Fence." *Sporting News*, August 4, 1962.

Baseball-Reference.com.
CincinnatiDrumService.com.
PaperofRecord.com.
ProBaseballArchive.com.
Professional Baseball Players Database v6.0.
Retrosheet.org.
SABR Minor League Database.

25. Dal Maxvill

1. Russo, "Dal Maxvill."
2. Russo, "Little Maxie."
3. Gross, "Dal Maxvill No Bat Boy."
4. Herman, "Musial High on Maxvill."
5. Russo, "Alley Route Best for Me."
6. Mann, "Pickup Man Who Made Good."
7. Bob Harlan, St. Louis National Baseball Club, Inc., press release, February 18, 1970.
8. Leggett, "Manager of the Money Men."
9. Herman, "Rookie Executive."
10. *Sporting News*, March 27, 1989.
11. Rick Hummel, *Sporting News*, November 8, 1993.

Feldmann, Doug. *St. Louis Cardinals Past and Present.* MVP Books, 2009.

Goold, Derrick. *100 Things Cardinals Fans Should Know and Do before They Die.* Chicago: Triumph Books, 2010.

Leggett, William. "Manager of the Money Men." *Sports Illustrated*, October 7, 1968.

Allen, Maury. "Cards' New GM Rarin' to Rebuild." *New York Post*, April 11, 1985.

Daley, Arthur. "Sports of the Times." *New York Times*, March 28, 1969.

Gross, Milton. "Dal Maxvill No Bat Boy." *Chicago Daily News*, October 5, 1964.

Herman, Jack. "Musial High on Maxvill." *St. Louis Globe Democrat*, March 11, 1965.

———. "Rookie Executive." *St. Louis Weekly*, July 19, 1985. Article from Dal Maxvill player file, National Baseball Hall of Fame Library, Cooperstown NY.

Mann, Jimmy. "Pickup Man Who Made Good." *St. Petersburg Times*, 1967.

Russo, Neal. "Alley Route Best for Me, Says Maxvill." *Sporting News*, January 7, 1967.

———. "Dal Maxvill: Classy Card Minute-Man." *Sporting News*, January 30, 1965.

———. "Little Maxie Getting Big Cardinal Hits." *Sporting News*, August 24, 1968.

St. Louis Post Dispatch.

Baseball-Reference.com.
Retrosheet.org.

National Baseball Hall of Fame Library, Cooperstown NY.

New York Mets Scorebook, 1978.

St. Louis Mercantile Library at University of Missouri–St. Louis.

26. Tim McCarver

The Baseball Encyclopedia, 10th ed.

2005 ESPN Baseball Encyclopedia.

Boston Globe.
New York Times.
Sporting News.
St. Louis Post-Dispatch.

Tim McCarver player archive, National Baseball Hall of Fame Library, Cooperstown NY.

27. Joe Morgan

1. E-mail from Harry Fanok to author, May 9, 2007.
2. Castiglione and Lyons, *Broadcast Rites*, 336.
3. McGourty, "'Walpole Joe.'"
4. Crehan, *Red Sox Heroes*, 375.
5. Trust, "Red Sox March into Second."
6. "Former 'Mumsy,'" 4C.
7. "Scouting Reports," 87.
8. Hairston, "Old Friend Joe Morgan," 1-C.
9. Cafardo, "Timing Has Proven."
10. Borges, *The Pawtucket Red Sox*, 25.
11. Drawn from Morgan interview (which contains several other funny lines) on the Internet feature "The Longest Game in History."
12. Gammons, "Red Hot."
13. Associated Press, "Houk Named New Boston Red Sox Manager."
14. Hackenberg, "Red Sox Fans," D3.
15. Associated Press, "McNamara May be Heading for Boston."
16. Browne, "Where Have You Gone?"
17. Castiglione and Lyons, *Broadcast Rites*, 256.
18. Gammons, "Red Hot."
19. Stout and Johnson, *Red Sox Century*, 418. To his credit, Rice issued a genuinely chastened apology after serving a three-game suspension.
20. Browne, "Where Have You Gone?"
21. McAdam, "Joe Morgan's Success," D-13.

22. Castiglione and Lyons, *Broadcast Rites*, 257.

23. Stout and Johnson, *Red Sox Century*, 423.

24. Castiglione and Lyons, *Broadcast Rites*, 258.

25. Browne, "Where Have You Gone?"

26. Gammons, "Red Hot"; Browne, "Where Have You Gone?"

27. Shaughnessy, "'Six, Two and Even,'" 41.

28. McGourty, "'Walpole Joe'"; Crehan, *Red Sox Heroes*, 381.

29. Castiglione and Lyons, *Broadcast Rites*, 256.

Borges, David. *The Pawtucket Red Sox*. Charleston SC: Arcadia Publishing, 2002.

Castiglione, Joe, and Douglas B. Lyons. *Broadcast Rites and Sites*. Lanham MD: Taylor Trade Publishing, 2004.

Crehan, Herb. *Red Sox Heroes of Yesteryear*. Boston: Rounder Books, 2005.

Stout, Glenn, and Richard A. Johnson. *Red Sox Century*. New York: Houghton Mifflin, 2005.

Gammons, Peter. "Red Hot." *Sports Illustrated*, August 1, 1988.

"Scouting Reports on 1959 Major League Rookies." *Baseball Digest*, March 1959.

Associated Press. "Houk Named New Boston Red Sox Manager." October 28, 1980.

———. "McNamara May be Heading for Boston." October 10, 1984.

Cafardo, Nick. "Timing Has Proven to Be Everything for Joe Morgan." *Quincy Patriot Ledger*, July 16, 1988.

Hackenberg, Dave. "Red Sox Fans Would Love Daring, Innovative Morgan." *Toledo Blade*, August 8, 1982.

Hairston, Jack. "Old Friend Joe Morgan Deserved Big-League Job." *Gainesville Sun*, July 24, 1988.

McAdam, Sean. "Joe Morgan's Success Breeds New Contract through 1989." *Providence Journal*, August 4, 1988.

Shaughnessy, Dan. "'Six, Two and Even'—Huh?" *Boston Globe*, July 27, 1988.

Trust, Dick. "Red Sox March into Second." Patriot Ledger Sports Service, August 3, 1988.

"Former 'Mumsy.'" *USA Today*, October 5, 1988.

Browne, Ian. "Where Have You Gone, Joe Morgan?" www.mlb.com. July 28, 2003.

"The Longest Game in History." http://web.minorleaguebaseball.com/team1/page.jsp?ymd=20080904&content_id=454286&vkey=team1_t533&fext=.jsp&sid=t533.

McGourty, John. "'Walpole Joe' a legend of Boston athletics." www.nhl.com. December 24, 2009.

www.baseball-reference.com.

www.retrosheet.org.

www.walpolescholarshipfoundation.org.

Grateful acknowledgment to Joe Morgan for his memories (letter to author, June 2010).

28. Gordon Richardson

1. Neal Russo, "Richardson Applies Balm, Cards' Shell-Shocked Hill Staff Recoils," *Sporting News*, August 8, 1964.

2. Gordon Richardson clippings file, National Baseball Hall of Fame Library, Cooperstown NY.

3. "Erickson Sets Oilers Hill Mark," *Sporting News*, August 27, 1958.

4. Fred Lieb, "Gem by Cardinals Features Opening of Florida League," *Sporting News*, October 22, 1958.

5. *The Sporting News Baseball Register*, 1965.

6. John Ferguson, "Young Hurlers Lead Oilers to Texas Loop Playoff Title," *Sporting News*, September 28, 1960.

7. Richardson file.

8. "Help! Redbirds Send for Southpaw Hurler," *St. Louis Post-Dispatch*, July 23, 1964.

9. Richardson file; George Kiseda, "Et tu, Gordon Richardson?" *Philadelphia Evening Bulletin*, July 2, 1964.

10. Russo, "Richardson Applies Balm."

11. *Sporting News*, November 7, 1964.

12. Richardson file.

13. Barney Kremenko, "Workhorse Gordie Pulls Mets Out of Jams," *Sporting News*, August 14, 1965.

14. Richardson file; Vic Ziegel, "Going North at Last," April 10, 1966.

15. "A Team That Can Make a Man Cry," *Sports Illustrated*, June 27, 1966.

16. Richardson file; "Family Is Richardson's First Priority," *Sporting News*, April 3, 1965.

29. Ray Sadecki

1. *St. Louis Post-Dispatch*, August 30, 1964.
2. Telephone interview with author, October 1, 2009.
3. Mandel, *Giants*, 154.
4. *St. Louis Post-Dispatch*, May 11, 1966.
5. Telephone interview with author.
6. Mandel, *Giants*, 155.
7. Mandel, *Giants*, 156.
8. *Sporting News*, April 13, 1968.
9. Mandel, *Giants*, 157.
10. Telephone interview with author.

Mandel, Mike. *San Francisco Giants: An Oral History.* Self-published, 1979.

New York Times.

Baseball-Reference.com.
Ultimate New York Mets Database (www.ultimatemets .com).

Ray Sadecki player file, National Baseball Hall of Fame Library, Cooperstown NY.

30. Barney Schultz

1. Fedo, *One Shining Season*, 123.
2. "Schultz Is Cardinal Hero."
3. *U.S. Census, 1930.*
4. Schultz file.
5. Fedo, *One Shining Season*, 124.
6. Haraway, "Bears End 39 Year Draught."
7. Haraway, "Bears Win Series Opener."
8. "Birds Send Moford, Schultz Down."
9. Puerzer, "The Chicago Cubs' College of Coaches."
10. Enright, "Landrum Holds Monicker Crown."
11. Fedo, *One Shining Season*, 123.
12. "Maxvill Elated at Promotion."
13. Burnes, "The Bench-Warmer."
14. Addie, "Cards Take Pennant."
15. Russo, "We Had Differences."
16. "Schultz Is Cardinal Hero."
17. "First Pitch," S5.
18. Golenbock, *The Spirit of St. Louis*, 465.
19. Fedo, *One Shining Season*, 131, 132.
20. http://www.hotstovers.org/index.php.

Fedo, Michael. *One Shining Season.* New York: Pharos Books, 1991.

Golenbock, Peter. *The Spirit of St. Louis: A History of the St. Louis Cardinals and Browns.* New York: HarperCollins, 2000.

Puerzer, Richard J. "The Chicago Cubs' College of Coaches: A Management Innovation That Failed." In *The National Pastime: A Review of Baseball History*, 3–17. Cleveland: Society for American Baseball Research, 2006.

Addie, Bob. "Cards Take Pennant, Wallop Mets." *Washington Post*, October 5, 1964.

Burnes, Bob. "The Bench-Warmer." *St. Louis Globe-Democrat*, October 1, 1964.

Enright, James. "Landrum Holds Monicker Crown—Three Nicknames." *Sporting News*, June 1, 1963.

Haraway, Frank. "Bears End 39 Year Drought, Grizzlies Take Flag in Finale." *Denver Post*, September 12, 1952.

———. "Bears Win Series Opener, 3–1, Rain Washes Out, Tonight Game Here Saturday." *Denver Post*, September 19, 1952.

Russo, Neal. "We Had Differences, But I Respect Him." *St. Louis Post-Dispatch*, October 10, 1964.

"Birds Send Moford, Schultz Down, Get Woolbridge, Wright." *St. Louis Globe-Democrat*, June 16, 1955.

"First Pitch in the Last of Ninth 'Didn't Break and Mantle Acted.'" *New York Times*, October 11, 1964, S5.

"Maxvill Elated at Promotion, Loses No Time Joining Birds—Club Drops Hobbie, Buys Schultz." *St. Louis Globe-Democrat*, August 1, 1964.

"Schultz Is Cardinal Hero with Three Innings of Effective Relief Pitching." *New York Times*, October 8, 1964.

U.S. Census, 1930, Population Schedule, New Jersey, Burlington, Beverly City, 2nd District, Sheet 9A, Line 37.

Barney Schultz player file, National Baseball Hall of Fame Library, Cooperstown NY.

31. Timeline, July 1–July 31

Unless otherwise indicated, all direct quotations come from the *St. Louis Post-Dispatch*.

Baseball-Reference.com.
Retrosheet.org.

32. Mike Shannon

1. Mike Shannon player file, National Baseball Hall of Fame Library, Cooperstown NY; Neal Russo, "Shannon's Backyard Ballpark," *St. Louis Post-Dispatch*, September 28, 1967; Neal Russo, "'Finishing School' Gives Shannon Start," *St. Louis Post-Dispatch*, July 25, 1966.

2. David Craft and Tom Owens, *Redbirds Revisited: Great Memories and Stories from St. Louis Cardinals* (Chicago: Bonus Books, 1990), 206; Dan Caesar, "Tiger QB Saw Future in Cards," *St. Louis Post-Dispatch*, August 11, 1991.

3. "Mike Shannon Is Signed by Cards for Big Bonus," *St. Louis Post-Dispatch*, June 12, 1958; Shannon file; *Sporting News*, June 18, 1958, 19; Russo, "Shannon's Backyard Ballpark."

4. *Sporting News*; Russo, "Shannon's Backyard Ballpark."

5. Dan Caesar and Pat Bolling, "Mike's Going 'Silver,'" *Cardinals Magazine*, October 1995, 23.

6. Bob Gibson with Phil Pepe, *From Ghetto to Glory: The Story of Bob Gibson* (New York: Popular Library, 1968), 128.

7. Bob Kuenster, "Players Recall Their Major League Debut," *Baseball Digest*, July 2009, 74.

8. *Sporting News*, October 6, 1962, 32; November 17, 1962, 23.

9. Neal Russo, "Shannon Shaping Up as Strong Candidate for Card Picket Post," *Sporting News*, October 19, 1963, 9.

10. *Sporting News*, May 11, 1963, 8; July 20, 1963, 39; August 3, 1963, 9; October 12, 1963, 19; Bing Devine with Tom Wheatley, *The Memories of Bing Devine* (Champaign IL: Sports Publishing, 2004), p8–9, 11; "Too Young to Remember Series," *Dayton (OH Daily News*, October 8, 1964, in Shannon file.

11. Neal Russo, "'Great Experiment' Recalls Cards Almost Goofed," *Sporting News*, February 3, 1968, in Shannon file.

12. "Mike Shannon . . . Survivor," *St. Louis Globe Democrat*, July 4, 1979, in Shannon file.

13. John Snyder, *Cardinals Journal: Year by Year & Day by Day with the St. Louis Cardinals Since 1882* (Cincinnati: Emmis Books, 2006), 475–77.

14. David Halberstam, *October 1964* (New York: Villard Books, 1994), 320; Russo, "Shannon's Backyard Ballpark"; Dan O'Neill, "A Storybook Season—Rekindling Memories of 1964," *St. Louis Post-Dispatch*, January 29, 1989.

15. Neal Russo, "Shannon Has New Name—The Cannon!" *Sporting News*, July 23, 1966, 15.

16. Neal Russo, "Shannon's Backyard Ballpark," *St. Louis Post-Dispatch*, September 28, 1967.

17. James K. McGee, "An Irish Comeback," *San Francisco Examiner*, June 17, 1967; Russo, "Shannon's Backyard Ballpark."

18. Neal Russo, "Cards on Wing with Shannon, Buchek Hitting," *Sporting News*, May 28, 1966; Russo, "Shannon Has New Name," 15, 20; Sandy Ramras, "Player of the Week," *Sports Illustrated*, August 1, 1966.

19. Neal Russo, "Switch or Fight? A New Post Spurs Sweating Shannon," *Sporting News*, August 5, 1967, 7; Neal Russo, "Redbirds Saved by Swaps They Failed to Make," *Sporting News*, September 9, 1967, 10; Ralph Ray, "Briles Drives Second Nail into Fading Bosox' Coffin," *Sporting News*, October 21, 1967, 9.

20. Dick Kaegel, "World Champion Bengals Shower with Champagne," *Sporting News*, October 26, 1968, 8.

21. Neal Russo, "Cards Flout Laws of Nature, Rise in West and Set in East," *Sporting News*, August 30, 1969, 4.

22. *Sporting News*, November 8, 1969, 40; December 13, 1969, 44; December 27, 1969, 38; "Ailing Shannon Takes Batting, Fielding Drills," *Sporting News*, May 16, 1970; Shannon file; Tim Moriarty, "Mike Is Back with Will," *Newsday*, May 27, 1970; Phil Pepe, "Mike Kicked K-Kidney Ailment," May 29, 1970, unidentified clipping in Shannon file; "Cards Ram Pirates 11–7—Shannon a Pinch-Hitter," May 15, 1970, unidentified clipping in Shannon file; Dan Caesar, "Shannon Scores: 20 Years Later, Broadcast 'Project' is a Pro," *St. Louis Post-Dispatch*, August 11, 1991; Neal Russo, "Cards Told Shannon Is Out for Season," *Sporting News*, February 27, 1971; Shannon file; "Docs Sideline Mike Shannon," unidentified clipping in Shannon file.

23. Bing Devine with Tom Wheatley, *The Memories of Bing Devine* (Champaign IL: Sports Publishing, 2004), 13; "Shannon Joins Redbirds' Promotions-Sales Staff," *Sporting News*, May 1, 1971.

24. Dan Caesar, "From Field to Booth—Eight from 1964 Cardinals Become Broadcasters," *St. Louis Post-Dispatch*, January 31, 1989; Neal Russo, "Shannon Selects Broadcast Booth," *St. Louis Post-Dispatch*, November 5, 1971; "Mike Shannon Joins Buck on Cards' Radio-TV Team," *St. Louis Post-Dispatch*, November 20, 1971, 47; Dan Caesar, "Shannon Scores," *St. Louis Post-Dispatch*, August 11, 1991.

25. Mike Smith, "Eye Openers," *St. Louis Post-Dispatch*, September 16, 1989; Bernie Miklasz, "Mike Shannon's Not Polished, But He's Real," *St. Louis Post-Dispatch*, August 6, 1989; Mike Eisenbath, "Sunny Side Up: Mike Shannon Likes to Fully Embrace Life," *St. Louis Post-Dispatch*, August 11, 1996; "The Mike Shannonisms Quiz," *St. Louis Post-Dispatch*, stltoday.com.

26. Dan Caesar, "Cards Re-Sign Radio Broadcasters," *St. Louis Post-Dispatch*, February 4, 2011; Spencer Engel, "Press Club Honors Mike Shannon as Media Person of the Year," *St. Louis Beacon*, September 30, 2010, stlbeacon.org (accessed September 13, 2011).

27. Rick Hummel, "Cards Start 'Like Mike' Campaign for Shannon," *St. Louis Post-Dispatch*, September 1, 2011; Dan Caesar, "Cards Re-Sign Radio Broadcasters," *St. Louis Post-Dispatch*, February 4, 2011; Dan O'Neill, "What Made Stan 'The Man'?" *St. Louis Post-Dispatch*, April 3, 2009.

33. Bobby Shantz

1. Shantz, *Story*, 21.
2. Shantz, *Story*, 26.
3. Shantz, *Story*, 26.
4. Shantz, *Story*, 27.
5. Shantz, *Story*, 28.
6. Shantz, *Story*, 34.
7. Gordon and Burgoyne, *Movin' On Up*, 93.
8. Shantz, *Story*, 36.
9. Shantz, *Story*, 36.
10. Shantz, *Story*, 37.
11. Shantz, *Story*, 38.
12. Shantz, *Story*, 44.
13. Personal interview with Bobby and Shirley Shantz, January 13, 2011.
14. Telephone interview with Bobby Shantz, January 20, 2011.
15. Shantz, *Story*, 51.
16. Shantz, *Story*, 51.
17. *Sporting News*.
18. Personal interview.
19. Personal interview.
20. Personal interview.
21. *Baseball Digest*, September 1957, 50.
22. Personal interview.
23. Personal interview.
24. *Baseball Digest*, September 1957, 44.
25. *Pittsburgh Pirates Baseball's Greatest Games*.
26. Personal interview.
27. Personal interview.
28. www.philadelphiaathletics.org/event/shantzfieldupdate.htm.

Delaney, Ed. *Bobby Shantz, Most Valuable Player Series*. New York: A. S. Barnes, 1953.
Gordon, Bob. *Game of My Life: Memorable Stories of Phillies Baseball*. Champaign IL: Sports Publishing, 2008.
Gordon, Robert, and Tom Burgoyne. *Movin' On Up: Baseball and Philadelphia, Then, Now, and Always*. Moorestown NJ: Middle Atlantic Press, 2004.
Reiser, Jim. *The Best Game Ever: Pirates vs. Yankees, October 13, 1960*. New York: Carroll & Graf Publishers, 2007.
Shantz, Bobby. *The Story of Bobby Shantz as Told to Ralph Bernstein*. Philadelphia: J. B. Lippincott, 1953.

"Shantz Field." *Berks-Mont News*, December 22, 2010.
Christian Science Monitor, July 18, 1952.

Baseball-Reference.com.

Pittsburgh Pirates Baseball's Greatest Games: 1960 World Series Game 7. Major League Baseball Productions. A&E Home Video, 2010. DVD.
SABR Oral History, Bobby Shantz, 1991, by Bob Ulster.

34. Curt Simmons

1. Data in Rogers, "Day the Phillies Went to Egypt," 9–12. Some of the games may have been shortened by a mercy rule, hence the unusually low number of innings.

Bryant, Howard. *The Last Hero: A Life of Henry Aaron*. New York: Pantheon Books, 2010.

Clayton, Skip, and Jeff Moeller. *50 Phabulous Phillies.* Champaign IL: Sports Publishing, 2000.

Halberstam, David. *October 1964.* New York: Villard Books, 1994.

Leavy, Jane. *The Last Boy: Mickey Mantle.* New York: HarperCollins, 2010.

Linn, Ed. "The Tragedy of the Phillies." In *The Phillies Reader*, 104–21. Philadelphia: Temple University Press, 2005.

Roberts, Robin. *My Life in Baseball.* Chicago: Triumph Books, 2003.

Roberts, Robin, and C. Paul Rogers III. *The Whiz Kids and the 1950 Pennant.* Philadelphia: Temple University Press, 1996.

Spatz, Lyle, ed. *The SABR Baseball List and Record Book.* New York: Scribner, 2007.

VanLindt, Carson. *Fire and Spirit: The Story of the 1950 Phillies.* New York: Matabou Publishing, 1998.

Bisher, Furman. "Hank Aaron Tells a Secret." *Baseball Digest*, November 1971.

Broeg, Bob. "Season's Biggest Dollar's Worth." *Baseball Digest*, November 1962.

Eck, Frank. "Simmons' Feet Get Twisted Up." *Baseball Digest*, June 1948.

Rogers, C. Paul, III. "The Day the Phillies Went to Egypt." *Baseball Research Journal* (Fall 2010).

"What Ever Became of . . . Curt Simmons." *Baseball Digest*, March 1970.

Interviews with Curt Simmons conducted by the author in March 2009 and September 2011.

35. Bob Skinner

1. *Pittsburgh Press*, June 1, 1958.
2. *New York Times*, April 19, 1959.
3. Skinner file.
4. Skinner file.
5. *New York Times*, April 19, 1959.
6. *Baseball Digest*, June 1959.
7. *Baseball Digest*, June 1959.
8. *Baseball Digest*, June 1959.
9. *Dayton Daily News*, May 24, 1963.
10. *Dayton Daily News*, May 24, 1963.
11. Skinner file.
12. Skinner file.
13. Skinner file.
14. Skinner file.

Ranier, Bill, and David Finoli. *When the Pirates Won It All.* Jefferson NC: McFarland, 2005.

Peterson, Richard. *The Pirates Reader.* Pittsburgh: University of Pittsburgh Press, 2003.

The Pittsburgh Pirate Encyclopedia. Champaign IL: Sports Publishing, 2003.

Sporting News.

U.S. Census, 1930.

http://minors.sabrwebs.com/cgi-bin/index.php.
www.baseballlibrary.com/homepage.
www.retrosheet.org.
www.sdhoc.com.

Bob Skinner player clippings file, National Baseball Hall of Fame Library, Cooperstown NY.

36. Ed Spiezio

1. Lowell Reidenbaugh, "A Delectable Taste of Spring Training," *Sporting News*, April 10, 1965.
2. Bob Broeg, "Meet Ed Spiezio, the Joliet Jolter," *St. Louis Post-Dispatch*, March 25, 1965.
3. Tom C. Brody, "Please, Please, Ed Spiezio, Won't You Please Pop Up?" *Sports Illustrated*, April 12, 1965.
4. Lewis University Flyers, Men's Sports, Baseball, Lewis Baseball Record Book, http://www.lewisflyers.com.
5. Don Linder, "Cowboys Trim Huron to Grab Playoff Crown," *Sporting News*, September 10, 1962.
6. Jack Herman, "Keep Eye on Spiezio—That's Stan's Tip," *Sporting News*, April 28, 1964.
7. "Rookie Spiezio Drives in Eight Runs to Pace Tulsa," *Sporting News*, July 27, 1963.
8. Herman, "Keep Eye on Spiezio."
9. Clifford Kachline, "Small Park Shrinks Cards' Share in Swag," *Sporting News*, November 7, 1964.
10. Jack Herman, "Cards Count on Boyer Bat for Big Edge," *Sporting News*, April 24, 1965.
11. Neal Russo, "Card Clan Gathers To Finger Culprits; Vets See Ax Falling," *Sporting News*, October 2, 1965.
12. Paul Cour, "Padres Eye Spiezio Bat to Lead 'Em," *Sporting News*, March 22, 1969.

13. Paul Cour, "After 33 Years in Wing, San Diego on Majors' Stage," *Sporting News*, April 26, 1969.

14. Paul Cour, "Spiezio Heats Up at Padres Hot Sack," *Sporting News*, August 29, 1970. As to Spiezio's fielding, see *Sporting News*, June 28, 1969.

15. Paul Cour, "Who Said Iron Glove? Spiezio Sharp in Field," *Sporting News*, January 30, 1971.

16. Ed Spiezio clippings file, National Baseball Hall of Fame Library, Cooperstown NY. Sent via e-mail by Bill Francis on June 13, 2011.

17. Paul Cour, "14 Original Selectees Still Wear Padre Garb," *Sporting News*, November 27, 1971.

18. Jerome Holtzman, "Back Injury Shelves Melton Rest of the Year; Spiezio Purchased as Replacement," *Sporting News*, July 22, 1972.

19. Edgar Munzel, "Ex-Padre Spiezio Answer to Chisox Prayer," *Sporting News*, November 2, 1972.

20. Julia Dankovich, "Like Father, Like Son," *Chicago Tribune*, July 12, 1996.

21. Paul White, "After a Generation Circle Complete for Angels, Spiezios," *USA Today Baseball Weekly*, October 29, 2002.

22. Daniel Berk, "Special Night as Cards Get Their Rings," Cardinals.com, April 4, 2007.

37. Jack Spring

Kelley, Brent P. *The San Francisco Seals, 1946–57*. Jefferson NC: McFarland, 2002.

Dallas Times-Herald.
Spokane Daily Chronicle.
Spokesman-Review.

Baseball-Almanac.com.
Baseball-Reference.com.
ESPN.go.com.
MLB.com.
Retrosheet.org.
smws.us/champions.htm.
www.digitalarchives.wa.gov.
www.wilbaseball52.blogspot.com.

Face-to-face and telephone interviews with Jack Spring, various years.

"Indians: A Century of Baseball in Spokane." Unpublished manuscript by Jim Price.

Washington State University Sports Information Department.

38. Ron Taylor

Thanks to Wanda Chirnside, Eric Cousineau, Scott Crawford, Alan Gans, Bill Humber, Anthony Kalamut, Ben Kates, Nanda Lwin, Kelly McNamee, T. Kent Morgan, Ron Taylor, Rona Taylor, Dan Turner, Tom Valcke, Max Weder, Eric Zweig.

1. Bart Mindszenthy, introduction to Ron Taylor Keynote Speech at the Empire Club of Canada, October 1993.

2. Mindszenthy, speech introduction.

3. Interview with Ron Taylor, November 8, 2007.

4. "Ron Taylor," 183.

5. Turner, *Heroes*, 104.

6. Taylor interview.

7. Elliott, *Northern Game*, 137.

8. Elliott, *Northern Game*, 136.

9. Turner, *Heroes*, 104.

10. Elliott, *Northern Game*, 138.

11. Elliott, *Northern Game*, 138.

12. Elliott, *Northern Game*, 138.

13. Elliott, *Northern Game*, 138.

14. Taylor interview.

15. Elliott, *Northern Game*, 138.

16. Turner, *Heroes*, 105.

17. Elliott, *Northern Game*, 139.

18. Turner, *Heroes*, 106.

19. Turner, *Heroes*, 106.

20. Elliott, *Northern Game*, 141.

21. Taylor interview.

22. Taylor interview.

23. Allen, *After the Miracle*, 42.

24. Taylor interview.

25. Taylor interview.

26. Elliott, *Northern Game*, 144.

27. Bock and Jordan, *Fan's Almanac*, 65.

28. Markusen, *Tales*, 44.

29. Markusen, *Tales*, 44–45.

30. Taylor interview.

31. Allen, *After the Miracle*, 45.

32. Allen, *After the Miracle*, 44.

33. Taylor interview.

34. Taylor interview.

Allen, Maury. *After the Miracle: The Amazin' Mets —Two Decades Later.* New York: St. Martin's, 1989.

Bock, Duncan, and John Jordan. *The Complete Year-By-Year N.Y. Mets Fan's Almanac.* New York: Crown, 1992.

Elliott, Bob. *The Northern Game: Baseball the Canadian Way.* Toronto: Sport Classic Books, 2005.

Markusen, Bruce. *Tales from the Mets Dugout.* Champaign IL: Sports Publishing, 2005.

Turner, Dan. *Heroes, Bums, and Ordinary Men.* Toronto: Lester & Orpen Dennys, 1988.

Weissman, Harold. *The Mets Official 1967 Year Book.* Flushing NY: Metropolitan Baseball Club, Inc., 1967. [The yearbooks through 1974 were also referenced.]

Daley, Arthur. "The Two Managers." *New York Times,* September 26, 1954.

Baseball-Reference.com.
Retrosheet.org.

"Ron Taylor." Brooklyn: Topps Chewing Gum Inc., 1964.

39. Timeline, August 1–August 31

Unless otherwise indicated, all direct quotations come from the *St. Louis Post-Dispatch.*

Baseball-Reference.com.
Retrosheet.org.

40. Bob Uecker

1. Bob Uecker and Mickey Herskowitz, *Catcher in the Wry: Outrageous but True Stories of Baseball* (New York: Jove Books, 1982), 25.

2. Curt Smith, *Voices of Summer: Ranking Baseball's 101 All-Time Best Announcers* (New York: Carroll & Graff, 2005), 269.

3. Uecker, *Catcher in the Wry,* 4.

4. Curt Smith, *Voices of the Game: The Acclaimed Chronicle of Baseball Radio and Television Broadcasting from 1921–Present* (New York: Simon & Schuster, 1992), 420.

5. Larry Stewart, "Just a Bit Outside the Bounds of Reality," Inside Track Morning Briefing, *Los Angeles Times,* May 23, 2006.

6. "A Life of Detours: Confessions of a Feather-Hitter," *Christian Science Monitor,* July 24, 1961.

7. Uecker, *Catcher in the Wry,* introduction.

8. Smith, *Voices of Summer,* 266.

9. Uecker, *Catcher in the Wry,* 12.

10. Uecker, *Catcher in the Wry,* 12.

11. Michael Hiestand, "Broadcaster Spin Years: Punchless Former Catcher Casts Out Baseball's Best Punchlines," *USA Today,* October 14, 1997.

12. Adam McCalvy, "Brewers Celebrate Native Son Uecker; 'Mr. Baseball' Honored as Milwaukee's First Home-Grown Player," MLB.com, May 12, 2009, http://mlb.mlb.com/news/article.jspymd=20090512&content_id=4686608&vkey=news_mlb&fext=.jsp&c_id=mlb&partnerId=rss_mlb.

13. Hiestand, "Broadcaster Spin Years."

14. Chuck Greenwood, "As Voice of the Brewers, Uecker 'Just Started Talking,'" *Sports Collectors Digest,* February 5, 1999.

15. Andrew Milner, *The St. James Encyclopedia of Popular Culture* (Gale Group, 2000).

16. Uecker, *Catcher in the Wry,* 31.

17. Richard Sandomir, "World Series, as Told by Bob Uecker," *New York Times,* October 15, 1995.

18. "A Life of Detours."

19. Smith, *Voices of Summer,* 267.

20. Smith, *Voices of Summer,* 267.

21. Greenwood, "As Voice of the Brewers."

22. Peter Carlson, "They Locked Bob Uecker Out of the Bar, but They Can't Keep Him Out of the Announcer's Booth," *People,* September 19, 1983.

23. Smith, *Voices of Summer,* 411.

24. Greenwood, "Voice of the Brewers."

25. Bob Costas interview with Bob Uecker, MLB Network, September 28, 2010.

26. Richard Sandomir, "Bob Uecker Returns to the Booth," *New York Times,* August 13, 2010.

27. Sandomir, "Uecker Returns."

28. Greenwood, "Voice of the Brewers."

29. Dan O'Donnell and Jay Sorgi, "Remembering Merle Harmon," NBC Milwaukee, May 18, 2009, http://www.todaystmj4.com/news/local/45359962.html.

30. Smith, *Voices of the Game,* 412.

31. Carlson, "They Locked Bob Uecker Out."

32. Costas interview.

33. Curt Smith, *The Storytellers. From Mel Allen to Bob Costas: Sixty Years of Baseball Tales from the Broadcast Booth* (New York: Macmillan, 1995), 267.

34. Shannon Ryan, "Finally, the Front Row: Baseball's Funnyman Gets a Seat in the Hall," *Philadelphia Inquirer*, July 23, 2003.

35. Uecker, *Catcher in the Wry*, 113.

36. Bob Uecker Miller Lite commercial, 1984, http://www.youtube.com/watch?v=_Ql7m9LQULM&feature=related.

37. Smith, *Voices of Summer*, 269.

38. Lauren Simon, "Uecker to Star in New TV Sit-Com," *USA Today*, March 6, 1985.

39. Costas interview.

40. Ben Platt, "Popularity of 'Major League' Remains: Classic Baseball Comedy Celebrates Its 20th Anniversary," MLB.com, April 7, 2009, http://mlb.mlb.com/news/article_entertainment.jsp?ymd=20090407&content_id=4147526&vkey=entertainment&fext=.jsp.

41. Michael Hunt, "Uecker Heading for Hall," Milwaukee Journal-Sentinel, March 14, 2003.

42. Bob Uecker, Ford Frick Award presentation speech, National Baseball Hall of Fame, July 27, 2003.

43. Uecker, Frick Award speech.

44. Drew Olson, "Uecker Celebrates Golden Anniversary," *Milwaukee Journal-Sentinel*, August 27, 2007.

Statistics and game information found through BaseballReference.com and Retrosheet.org.

41. Carl Warwick

1. Jerry Wizig, "It's Warwick Wielding That Hot Bat," *Houston Chronicle*, May 21, 1963.

2. Bob Broeg, "Warwick Was Ready for War on Yanks When Keane Said 'Scramble,'" *St. Louis Post-Dispatch*, October 12, 1964.

3. Broeg, "Warwick Was Ready."

4. Wizig, "Hot Bat."

5. Wizig, "Hot Bat."

6. Wizig, "Hot Bat."

7. Wizig, "Hot Bat."

8. Allen Lewis, "Warwick Claims HR Despite Veto by Ump," *Sporting News*, May 18, 1963.

9. Lewis, "Warwick Claims HR."

10. Neal Russo, "Warwick's Return Bolsters Cardinals' Outfield Corps," *St. Louis Post-Dispatch*, February 29, 1964.

11. Broeg, "Warwick Was Ready."

12. Joe Donnelly, "Alas, Warwick, the Yanks Know Him," October 12, 1964. Red Schoendiest set the NL record for pinch-hits in a season with twenty-two in 1962—and he could have had twenty-three except for a base-running mistake.

13. Donnelly, "Alas, Warwick."

14. Broeg, "Warwick Was Ready." The actual attendance has been reported as 50,927.

15. Jack Gallagher, "Big Timers Pick Hearths in Houston," *Sporting News*, December 5, 1964.

16. Gallagher, "Big Timers."

17. Associated Press, "'No Chance to Try,' Says Warwick," October 16, 1965.

18. Richard Dozer, "Cubs Trade Roznovsky for Warwick," *Chicago Tribune*, April 1, 1966.

19. Dozer, "Cubs Trade."

20. Bob Boughton, "Interview with Team Canada/Houston-Victoria Head Coach Terry Puhl," *College Baseball Blog*, August 25, 2008, http://thecollegebaseballblog.com/2008/08/25/interview-with-team-canadahouston-victoria-coach-terry-puhl/ (accessed August 2009).

21. Broeg, "Warwick Was Ready."

42. Ray Washburn

1. Hardman, "Card Brass Stamps," 16.

2. Interviews with Ray Washburn, March 10 and October 27, 2010. All quotations from Washburn are from his interviews with the author in 2010 unless otherwise noted.

3. www.attheplate.com.

4. Russo, "Washburn's Hit No Surprise," 23.

5. Burnes, "Rookies Cashing In," 4.

6. "Ray Washburn's Uniform Retired," 16.

7. Burt, "Rickey," 1-C.

8. Russo, "Cards' Patience Pays Off," 7.

9. Dorr, "'Rebuilding' of Washburn," 5-B.

10. Russo, "Redbirds Label Speedy Brock," 12.

11. Russo, "Birds Flutter," 21.

12. Other Cardinals who did not appear in the 1964 World Series were pitcher Mike Cuellar, catcher Bob Uecker, and infielder Ed Spiezio.

13. Gibson and Wheeler, *Stranger to the Game*, 129.

14. Russo, "Gay, Ray Play No-Hit," 22.

Feldman, Doug. *El Birdos, the 1967 and 1968 St. Louis Cardinals.* Jefferson NC: McFarland, 2007.

Gibson, Bob, with Lonnie Wheeler. *Stranger to the Game.* New York: Penguin, 1994.

The Official Baseball Guide. Sporting News, 1961–72.

Burnes, Bob. "Rookies Cashing In on 'Chance of a Lifetime.'" *Sporting News*, April 25, 1962.

Burt, Lonnie. "Rickey: If Ray Is Sound, We're In." *St. Petersburg Times*, March 14, 1964.

Dorr, Dave. "'Rebuilding' of Washburn." *St. Louis Post-Dispatch*, November 7, 1989.

Hardman, A. L. "Card Brass Stamps 'Can't-Miss' Tag on Whizzer Washburn." *Sporting News*, January 24, 1962.

Russo, Neal. "Birds Flutter, Start Flirting with 9th Spot." *Sporting News*, July 11, 1964.

———. "Cards' Patience Pays Off Big in Washburn Case." *Sporting News*, May 18, 1968.

———. "Gay, Ray Play No-Hit Tit for Tat." *Sporting News*, October 5, 1968.

———. "Redbirds Label Speedy Brock Hot Asset for Present, Future." *Sporting News*, June 27, 1964.

———. "Washburn's Hit No Surprise to His Old Coach." *Sporting News*, June 19, 1965.

"Ray Washburn's Uniform Retired." *Tri-Cities Herald*, June 15, 1960.

Google Archives.

Retrosheet.org.

43. Bill White

1. *All Things Considered*, NPR, May 11, 2011.

2. Bill White with Gordon Dillow, *Uppity: My Untold Story about the Games People Play* (New York: Grand Central Publishing, 2011), 7.

3. White, *Uppity*, 29.

4. Larry Moffi and Jonathan Kronstadt, *Crossing the Line: Black Major Leaguers, 1947–1959* (Iowa City: University of Iowa Press, 1994), 161.

5. White, *Uppity*, 38.

6. Moffi and Kronstadt, *Crossing the Line*, 160.

7. United Press International, *Chicago Defender*, March 21, 1959, 23.

8. White, *Uppity*, 60.

9. White, *Uppity*, 73.

10. *Chicago Tribune*, October 5, 1964, D1.

11. White, *Uppity*, 90.

12. *Philly Post*, April 21, 2011, http://blogs.philly-mag.com/the_philly_post/2011/04/21/the-former-phillie-everyone-should-know/ (accessed September 30, 2011).

13. Stan Hochman, "Bill White Keeps His Promises," *Baseball Digest*, January 1969, 39.

14. White, *Uppity*, 47.

15. White, *Uppity*, 147.

16. Claire Smith, "Baseball's Angry Man," *New York Times Magazine*, October 13, 1991, 53.

17. Smith, "Baseball's Angry Man," 56.

18. Smith, "Baseball's Angry Man," 31.

19. "They Said It," *Sports Illustrated*, July 15, 1991.

20. *New York Times*, September 28, 1991.

21. Smith, "Baseball's Angry Man," 30.

22. "NL Prexy Bill White Cites Baseball Racism," *Jet*, June 15, 1992, 46.

23. White, *Uppity*, 282–83.

24. White, *Uppity*, 7.

25. *Philly Post*.

44. Johnny Keane

1. Gibson and Wheeler, *Stranger to the Game*, 43.

2. Lyons, "New Post Challenge to Keane."

3. Layer, "Keane Hurt."

4. Lyons, "New Post Challenge to Keane."

5. Lyons, "Sports Chatter."

6. Lyons, "New Post Challenge to Keane."

7. Frantz, "Keane, John Joseph"; Gabriel Schecter, research associate, National Baseball Hall of Fame, e-mail to author, August 26, 2008.

8. "Caught on the Fly."

9. "Brief Bits of Gossip."

10. Asinof, "The Word for Johnny Keane."

11. "Johnny Keane Reappointed."

12. Eck, "Life's Never Dull."

13. Devine with Wheatley, *Memoirs of Bing Devine.*

14. Gillespie, "Cardinals' Farm System Revamped."

15. Young, "Cardinal Chain $650,000 in Hole."

16. United Press, "Busch, Brewer."

17. "Columbus Group."

18. Gillespie, "Keane Sparked My Comeback."
19. Russo, "Birds Toss Flag Eggs."
20. "Digest of 1964 Diamond Highlights."
21. Burnes, "Matthews-Busch Marriage."
22. Reichier, "Johnny Keane's Wife."
23. Bouton, *Ball Four.*
24. Koppett, "Emotion, Not Strategy."
25. "Johnny Keane Dies." So that he could do his scouting job, Keane had just purchased a new automobile during the morning of the day he died.
26. "Johnny Keane."
27. Durso, "Keane's Death Shocks Baseball."

Bouton, Jim. *Ball Four.* New York: Wiley, 1990.
Brock, Lou, and Frank Schultze. *Stealing Is My Game.* Englewood Cliffs NJ: Prentice-Hall, 1976.
Devine, Bing, with Tom Wheatley. *The Memoirs of Bing Devine.* Champaign IL: Sports Publishing, 2004.
Gibson, Bob, and Lonnie Wheeler. *Stranger to the Game: The Autobiography of Bob Gibson.* New York: Penguin Books, 1994.
Gibson, Bob, with Phil Pepe. *From Ghetto to Glory: The Story of Bob Gibson.* Englewood Cliffs NJ: Prentice-Hall, 1968.
Golenbock, Peter. *The Spirit of St. Louis: A History of the St. Louis Cardinals and Browns.* New York: HarperCollins, 2000.
Halberstam, David. *October 1964.* New York: Villard Books, 1994.
The Sporting News Official Baseball Guide. St. Louis: The Sporting News, 1965–68.
Thorn, John, Pete Palmer, and Michael Gershman, eds. *Total Baseball*, 7th ed. Kingston NY: Total Sports Publishing, 2001.

Asinof, Eliot. "The Word for Johnny Keane Is: Patience." *New York Times*, May 30, 1965.
Burnes, Bob. "Matthews-Busch Marriage Recalls Card '64 Hassle." *St. Louis Globe Democrat*, February 26, 1977.
Durso, Joseph. "Keane's Death Shocks Baseball." *New York Times*, January 8, 1967.
Eck, Frank. "Life's Never Dull for the Keane Family." *Pacific Stars and Stripes*, February 3, 1965.
Gillespie, Ray. "Cardinals' Farm System Revamped to Curb Losses." *Sporting News*, February 20, 1952.

———. "Keane Sparked My Comeback, Stan Tells Fans." *Sporting News*, December 1, 1962.
Koppett, Leonard. "Emotion, Not Strategy, Fired Keane." *Sporting News*, May 21, 1966.
Layer, Bruce. "Keane Hurt When Hit by Pitched Ball." *Houston Post*, July 23, 1935.
Lyons, Johnny. "New Post Challenge to Keane." *Sporting News*, December 5, 1951.
———. "Sports Chatter." *Houston Post*, July 27, 1935.
Reichier, Joe. "Johnny Keane's Wife Felt Pennant Pressure." Associated Press, October 7, 1964.
Russo, Neal. "Birds Toss Flag Eggs in B.R.'s Basket." *Sporting News*, November 10, 1962.
United Press. "Busch, Brewer, Buys the Cardinals; Pays $3,750,000 for St. Louis Club." *New York Times*, February 21, 1953.
Young, Clarence. "Cardinal Chain $650,000 in Hole for '51, Says Saigh." *Sporting News*, February 13, 1952.
"Brief Bits of Gossip." *Sporting News*, December 23, 1937.
"Caught on the Fly." *Sporting News*, October 28, 1937.
"Columbus Group Pledges Advance Sale of $200,000." *Sporting News*, November 17, 1954.
"Digest of 1964 Diamond Highlights." *Sporting News*, January 2, 1965.
"Johnny Keane Dies; Managed Yanks and Cards." *New York Times*, January 8, 1967.
"Johnny Keane Reappointed as Pilot of the Albany Travelers." *Sporting News*, February 5, 1939.

Frantz, Joe B. "Keane, John Joseph." *The Handbook of Texas Online.* Texas State Historical Association, Austin, Texas, June 6, 2001.
"Johnny Keane." BR Bullpen, Year-by-Year Managerial Record, www.baseball-reference.com (accessed December 6, 2007).
SABR Minor League Database, John Keane (accessed February 3, 2008).

Johnny Keane file, vertical files, Barker Texas History Center, University of Texas at Austin (accessed 2008).
National Baseball Hall of Fame and Museum.

45. Vern Benson

1. Burick, "Utility Role Is Best Training," 89.
2. Van Hyning, *Puerto Rico's Winter League*, 181.

3. Utley, Peeler, and Peeler, *Outlaw Ballplayers*, 188.

4. Associated Press, "Benson Pleases Connie."

5. International News Service, "Cards Sign Bonus Star."

6. Van Hyning, *The Santurce Crabbers*, 87.

7. Associated Press, "Keane of Cards to Quit Coaching."

8. Leslie Timms, *Spartanburg (SC) Herald-Journal*, September 10, 1976, B2. Bristol was ejected fourteen times while Benson was coaching for him.

9. Bellinger, "Benson Hailed," 45.

10. Bellinger, "Benson Hailed."

Bjarkman, Peter C. *Baseball with a Latin Beat.* Jefferson NC: McFarland, 1994.

———. *Diamonds around the Globe: The Encyclopedia of International Baseball.* Westport CT: Greenwood Press, 2005.

Figueredo, Jorge S. *Cuban Baseball: A Statistical History, 1878–1961.* Jefferson NC: McFarland, 2003.

———. *Who's Who in Cuban Baseball: A Statistical History, 1878–1961.* Jefferson NC: McFarland, 2003.

The Sporting News Baseball Register, 1965.

Utley, R. G., and Tim Peeler, with Aaron Peeler. *Outlaw Ballplayers.* Jefferson NC: McFarland, 2006.

Van Hyning, Thomas. *Puerto Rico's Winter League.* Jefferson NC: McFarland, 1995.

———. *The Santurce Crabbers.* Jefferson NC: McFarland, 1999.

Burick, Si. "Utility Role Is Best Training for Embryo Pilot." *Baseball Digest*, December 1968.

Associated Press. "Benson Pleases Connie." March 12, 1946.

———. "Keane of Cards to Quit Coaching." January 18, 1963.

Bellinger, Chuck. "Vern Benson Hailed as No. 1 Minor Pilot." *Sporting News*, December 8, 1979.

International News Service. "Cards Sign Bonus Star, Option Benson." June 4, 1953.

Rachael Benson obituary. *Salisbury Post*, April 8, 2008.

Baseball-Reference.com.
CardenalesDelara.com.
GoCatawbaIndians.com.
Licey.com.
Retrosheet.org.

Grateful acknowledgment to Vern Benson for his memories (via mail and a telephone interview on June 27, 2010).

46. Howie Pollet

Brosnan, Jim. *The Long Season.* New York: Harper & Row, 1960.

Giglio, James N. *Musial: From Stash to Stan the Man.* Columbia: University of Missouri Press, 2001.

Golenbock, Peter. *The Spirit of St. Louis: A History of the St. Louis Cardinals and Browns.* New York: HarperCollins, 2000.

James, Bill, and Rob Neyer, *The Neyer/James Guide to Pitchers.* New York: Fireside/Simon & Shuster, 2004.

Korr, Charles P. *The End of Baseball As We Knew It.* Urbana and Chicago: University of Illinois Press, 2002.

Moffi, Larry. "Mel Parnell." In *This Side of Cooperstown.* Iowa City: University of Iowa Press, 1996.

Turner, Frederick. *When The Boys Came Back.* New York: Henry Holt, 1996.

Associated Press, stories in the *New York Times*, *New York World-Telegram*, *Washington Post*, and *Chicago Tribune*.

Sporting News, various issues, 1939–74.

U.S. Census, 1920, Orleans Parish, Louisiana.

Unidentified clippings in Howie Pollet file, National Baseball Hall of Fame Library, Cooperstown NY.

47. Timeline, September 1–September 30

Unless otherwise indicated, all direct quotations come from the *St. Louis Post-Dispatch*.

Baseball-Reference.com.
Retrosheet.org.

48. Red Schoendienst

Broeg, Bob. *Memories of a Hall of Fame Sportswriter.* Champaign IL: Sagamore, 1995.

Hunstein, Jim. *1, 2, 6, 9 . . . and Rogers.* St. Louis: Stellar Press, 2004.

Schoendienst, Red, with Rob Rains. *Red: A Baseball Life.* Champaign IL: Sports Publishing, 1998.

St. Louis Globe-Democrat.

St. Louis Post-Dispatch.

www.baseballhall.org.
www.stlouis.cardinals.mlb.com.

49. Joe Schultz

1. Peary, *Baseball's Finest*.

2. Bouton, *Ball Four*, 117, 159.

3. Associated Press, "Pirates Lose Executive."

4. Skipper, *Baseball Nicknames*.

5. Green, "Memories of the Beloved St. Louis Browns," 50.

6. Charlton, *The Baseball Chronology*, 269. This event has often been cited as occurring in 1931, but that does not appear correct. See "Darrow Gets 15th and Hank 21st." Note also that on July 19, 1952, a twelve-year-old African American batboy, Joe Relford, grounded out as a pinch hitter.

7. "Pirates Take Scout's Advice," 23.

8. Biederman, "Mueller May Be Farmed," 21.

9. United Press, "Collegians Add Names."

10. Biederman, "Handley Demoted," 27.

11. Associated Press, "Army Rejects Joe Schultz." Detail on the reason for rejection is still pending; this article mentioned only the usual "extensive physical examinations."

12. Associated Press, "Brownies' New Acquisitions." The headline refers to a conversation between Schultz and Red Sox coach John Schulte.

13. "Schultz Sees 'Heck of a Club,'" 8.

14. E-mail from Harry Fanok to the author, May 16, 2007.

15. "Crackers Tabbed 'Miracle' Club," 28.

16. Walburn, "This Old House," 84.

17. Bisher, "Crackers Rule as Comeback Kings," 49.

18. Clavin and Peary, *Roger Maris*, 311.

19. Buck, Rains, and Bob Broeg, *That's a Winner!* 105.

20. McCarver, *Oh, Baby, I Love It!*

21. Muller, "Rudy's Rings."

22. Burnes, "Thirty Seconds," 47–48.

23. Mann, "Schultz Eager to Tackle Big Test," 3-C.

24. "Schultz Is Happy," 36.

25. Hogan, *The 1969 Seattle Pilots*, 159, 157.

26. Stone, "Endearing and Enduring."

27. Associated Press, "Dave Bristol Plans."

28. Associated Press, "Joe Schultz KC Prospect."

29. Bouton, *I'm Glad You Didn't Take It Personally*, 153.

30. Spoelstra, "Schultz Savors Edict," 42.

31. Falkner, *The Last Yankee*, 169.

32. Blanchette, "Where There's Low Smoke," D1.

33. Clines, "The Pilots," 18C.

Bouton, Jim. *Ball Four*. Paperback ed. New York: Dell Publishing, 1971.

———. *I'm Glad You Didn't Take It Personally*. Paperback ed. New York: Dell Publishing, 1971.

Buck, Jack, with Rob Rains and Bob Broeg. *That's a Winner!* Champaign IL: Sports Publishing, 1999.

Charlton, James, ed. *The Baseball Chronology*. New York: Macmillan, 1991.

Clavin, Tom, and Danny Peary. *Roger Maris: Baseball's Reluctant Hero*. New York: Simon & Schuster, 2010.

Falkner, David. *The Last Yankee*. New York: Simon & Schuster, 1992.

Hogan, Kenneth. *The 1969 Seattle Pilots*. Jefferson NC: McFarland, 2007.

McCarver, Tim. *Oh, Baby, I Love It!* New York: Villard, 1987.

Peary, Danny, ed. *Baseball's Finest*. North Dighton MA: JG Press, 1990.

Skipper, James K. *Baseball Nicknames: A Dictionary of Origins and Meanings*. Jefferson NC: McFarland, 1992.

The Sporting News Baseball Register, 1948.

The Sporting News Official Baseball Guide, 1968.

Burnes, Robert L. "Thirty Seconds and Joe Schultz Jumped Cardinals to Seattle." *Baseball Digest*, February 1969.

Green, Jerry. "Memories of the Beloved St. Louis Browns Still Linger." *Baseball Digest*, December 1975.

Associated Press. "Army Rejects Joe Schultz." August 21, 1943.

———. "Brownies' New Acquisitions Will Help, Predicts Schulte." January 21, 1949.

———. "Dave Bristol Plans to Talk with Seattle." November 20, 1969.

———. "Joe Schultz KC Prospect." November 15, 1969.

———. "Pirates Lose Executive." April 14, 1941.

Biederman, Lester. "Handley Demoted; Deb [*sic*] Garms Gets Chance at Third." *Pittsburgh Press*, April 1, 1941.

———. "Mueller May Be Farmed As Pirate 'Wake Up' Measure." *Pittsburgh Press*, April 8, 1940.

Bisher, Furman. "Crackers Rule as Comeback Kings after Playoff Victory." *Sporting News*, October 6, 1962.

Blanchette, John. "Where There's Low Smoke, There's Joe Schultz." *Spokane Spokesman-Review*, September 16, 1984.

Clines, Frank. "The Pilots." *Milwaukee Journal*, April 9, 1989.

Mann, Jimmy. "Schultz Eager to Tackle Big Test." *St. Petersburg Times*, October 15, 1968.

Muller, Rich. "Rudy's Rings Are Latest Twist in World Series Lore." *American Chronicle*, May 11, 2007.

Spoelstra, Watson. "Schultz Savors Edict to Ban Bouton." *Sporting News*, April 1, 1972.

Stone, Larry. "Endearing and Enduring: The 1969 Seattle Pilots." *Seattle Times*, July 9, 2006.

United Press. "Collegians Add Names to Pirate Roster." January 8, 1940.

Walburn, Lee. "This Old House." *Atlanta*, November 2001.

"Crackers Tabbed 'Miracle' Club." *Sporting News*, September 29, 1962.

"Darrow Gets 15th and Hank 21st as Bucs Win Two." *Galveston Daily News*, September 12, 1932.

"Pirates Take Scout's Advice; And His Son, Too." *Chicago Tribune*, September 7, 1939.

"Schultz Is Happy." *Spokane Daily Chronicle*, May 27, 1969.

"Schultz Sees 'Heck of a Club' for Crackers." *Rome (GA) News-Tribune*, February 21, 1962.

Ancestry.com.

Catholic Cemeteries of the Archdiocese of St. Louis, records, www.archstl.org/cemeteries.

Retrosheet.org.

St. Louis University High School website, www.sluh.org.

Detroit Tigers Press Guide, 1971.

50. Bing Devine

1. Bing Devine, *The Memoirs of Bing Devine: Stealing Lou Brock and Other Brilliant Moves by a Master G.M.* (Sports Publishing, 2004), 112.

2. Devine, *Memoirs*, 116.

3. Devine, *Memoirs*, 62–82.

4. Devine, *Memoirs*, 4.

5. Bob Burnes, "Why Solly Hemus?" *Sport*, April 1959, 18.

6. *New York Times*, October 30, 1962, 55; Devine, *Memoirs*, 14–16; *Washington Post*, November 6, 1962, A17.

7. Peter Golenbock, *The Spirit of St. Louis: A History of the St. Louis Cardinals and Browns* (New York: HarperCollins, 2000), 457–58.

8. Devine, *Memoirs*, 13.

51. Bob Howsam

In writing this article, the author primarily relied on Howsam's memoir, *My Life in Sports*, written with Bob Jones (self-published, 1999), as well as Daryl Smith's *Making the Big Red Machine* (Jefferson NC: McFarland, 2009). For the Cardinals phase of his career, Peter Golenbock's *The Spirit of St. Louis: A History of the St. Louis Cardinals and Browns* (New York: HarperCollins, 2000) was the main reference. Howsam's extensive clipping file from the Baseball Hall of Fame in Cooperstown was also used.

52. Branch Rickey

Current Biography 1945, 497.

Lowenfish, Lee. *Branch Rickey: Baseball's Ferocious Gentleman.* Lincoln: University of Nebraska Press, 2007.

Polner, Murray. *Branch Rickey.* New York: Atheneum, 1982.

Chamberlain, John. "Brains, Baseball, and Branch Rickey." *Harper's*, April 1948.

Dexter, Charles. "Brooklyn's Sturdy Branch." *Collier's*, September 15, 1945.

Fitzgerald, Ed. "Sport's Hall of Fame: Branch Rickey, Baseball Innovator." *Sport*, May 1962.

Holland, Gerald. "Mr. Rickey and the Game." *Sports Illustrated*, March 7, 1955, 38.

Rice, Robert. "Profiles: Thoughts on Baseball." *New Yorker*, May 27 and June 30, 1950.

Farrington, Dick. "Branch Rickey, Defending Farms, Says Stark Necessity Forced System." *Sporting News*, December 1, 1932, 3.

The Branch Rickey Papers at the Library of Congress.

53. Stan Musial

Giglio, James N. *Musial: From Stash to Stan the Man*. Columbia: University of Missouri Press, 2001.

Lansche, Jerry. *Stan the Man Musial: Born to Be a Ballplayer*. Dallas: Taylor Publishing, 1994.

Posnanski, Joe. "Stan Musial." *Sports Illustrated*, August 2, 2010, 48–54.

"A Look at Musial, Year by Year." *St. Louis Post-Dispatch*, November 21, 2010.

"90 Things to Love about The Man." *St. Louis Post-Dispatch*, November 21, 2010.

"10 Greatest Living Baseball Players." *St. Louis Post-Dispatch*, November 21, 2010.

Finkel, Jan. "Stan Musial." SABR Baseball Biography Project. www.sabr.org.

Baseball-Almanac.com.

Baseball-Reference.com.

Retrosheet.org.

54. Jack Buck

Buck, Carole, Joe Buck, and Julie Buck. *Jack Buck: Forever a Winner*. Champaign IL: Sports Publishing, 2003.

Buck, Jack, with Rob Rains and Bob Broeg. *That's a Winner!* Champaign IL: Sagamore Publishing, 1999.

Reilly, Rick. "The Spirit of St. Louis." In *Great Baseball Writing*, edited by Rob Fleder, 231–33. New York: Sports Illustrated Books, 2007.

Lokemoen, Kristen. "So Long, for Just a While." *Show-Me Missouri Magazine* (Fall 2002): 12–14. Content used with permission from the publisher.

Caesar, Dan. "Buck Didn't Shine in TV Spotlight Like He Did on Radio." *St. Louis Post-Dispatch*, June 19, 2002.

Sandomir, Richard. "Actor Remembers Announcer Who Shared Struggle." *New York Times*, April 20, 2009.

Fallstrom, R. B. "Final Respects Paid to Jack Buck." BaseballWeekly.com. June 21, 2002.

Martzke, Rudy. "Joe Buck Reflects on Fallen Father." USAToday.com. June 19, 2002.

Weinberg, Rick. "98: Jack Buck's Tribute to America."

Interview with Ernie Hays, July 16, 2002.

Interview with Mike Shannon, July 16, 2002.

Interview with Milo Hamilton, November 29, 2011.

Interview with Ron Jacober, November 22, 2011.

Interview with Tony LaRussa, July 17, 2002.

55. Timeline, October 1–October 4

Unless otherwise indicated, all direct quotations come from the *St. Louis Post-Dispatch*.

Baseball-Reference.com.

ESPN.com.

Retrosheet.org.

56. Harry Caray

1. Logan, "Caray's Epitaph."
2. Luecking, "Harry Caray."
3. Associated Press, "Caray Ignores Critics."
4. Gay, "Holy Cow!"
5. Gay, "Holy Cow!"
6. Caray and Verdi, *Holy Cow*, 58–59.
7. Dolgan, *Plain Dealer*.
8. Luecking, "Harry Caray."
9. Kaegel, "Holy Cow!"
10. Kaegel, "Holy Cow!"
11. Levitt, "Caray Nets New Job."
12. Levitt, "Caray Nets New Job."
13. Craig, "SporTView."
14. Scott, "Oakland Is A-Okay."
15. Gay, "Holy Cow!"
16. Nordlund, "Caray Moves."
17. Berkow, "All Is Right."
18. Stone and Rozner, *Where's Harry?*
19. York, "Baseball Can Be Fun."
20. Rozner, "Caray Talks Freely."
21. Associated Press, "Harry Back in Booth."
22. Rozner, "Caray Talks Freely."
23. Miles, "Caray Statue Moved."
24. Langdon, "Radio's Cosell."

Caray, Harry, and Bob Verdi. *Holy Cow*. New York: Berkley Books, 1989.

Hodges, Russ, and Al Hirshberg. *My Giants*. Garden City NY: Doubleday, 1963.

Hughes, Pat, and Bruce Miles. *Harry Caray: Voice of the Fans*. Naperville IL: Sourcebooks, 2008.

Poindexter, Ray. *Golden Throats and Silver Tongues: The Radio Announcers*. Conway AK: River Road Press, 1978.

Silvia, Tony. *Fathers and Sons in Baseball Broadcasting: The Carays, Brennamans, Bucks and Kalases*. Jefferson NC: McFarland, 2009.

Smith, Curt. *Voices of Summer*. New York: Carroll & Graf, 2005.

Stone, Steve, and Barry Rozner. *Where's Harry? Steve Stone Remembers His Years with Harry Caray*. Dallas: Taylor Publishing, 1999.

Thornley, Stew. *Holy Cow! The Life and Times of Halsey Hall*. Minneapolis: Nodin Press, 1991.

Alesia, Mark. "'He Was the Life of Baseball'; Friends Remember Caray's Colorful Life On, Off Microphone." *Daily Herald* (Arlington Heights IL), February 19, 1998.

Associated Press. "Caray Ignores Critics; Plays to His Doting Fans." *Daily Herald* (Arlington Heights IL), July 17, 1979.

———. "Cards Snub Dean, Browns in New Broadcast Policy." *Waterloo (IA) Daily Courier*, January 12, 1947.

———. "Harry Back in Booth; Cubs Win." *Rockford (IL) Register-Star*, July 23, 1994.

———. "Harry Caray Suffers Stroke." *Rockford (IL) Register-Star*, February 20, 1987.

———. "Sportscaster Must Pay $575 Monthly Alimony." *Rockford (IL) Register-Republic*, November 11, 1949.

Berkow, Ira. "All Is Right at Wrigley Again." *New York Times*, May 20, 1987.

Brands, Edgar G. "Two Stations to Air St. Louis Tilts; Gabby Street to Return, Dean Out as Play Gabber." *Sporting News*, March 22, 1945.

Craig, Jack. "SporTView." *Sporting News*, May 15, 1971.

Cunningham, Pat. "'Classless Bunch Deserves to Lose.'" *Rockford (IL) Register-Star*, September 18, 1981.

Dolgan, Bob. *Cleveland Plain Dealer*, May 7, 1977.

Gay, Nancy. "Holy Cow! A Conversation with Legendary Broadcaster Harry Caray." *San Francisco Chronicle*, April 27, 1996.

Glennon, Ed. "First Lady Returns to Friendly Confines." *Rockford (IL) Register-Star*, April 5, 1994.

Jones, Todd. "Despite Limelight Caray Remains a Mystery; Baseball Voice an Institution among Fans in Chicago." *Toronto Globe and Mail*, April 29, 1994.

Kaegel, Dick. "'Holy Cow!' The Voice of Caray Has a Tight Grip on Cards Fans." *Sporting News*, July 2, 1966.

Langdon, Jerry. "'Fan' Carey [*sic*] Is Radio's Cosell." *Rockford (IL) Register-Republic*, July 29, 1975.

Levitt, Ed. "Harry Caray Nets New Job as Voice of Athletics." *Sporting News*, February 7, 1970.

Logan, Bob. "Caray's Epitaph: 'You Can't Beat Fun at the Old Ballpark.'" *Daily Herald* (Arlington Heights IL), February 19, 1998.

Luecking, Dave. "Harry Caray: 1914–1998." *St. Louis Post Dispatch*, February 19, 1998.

Miles, Bruce. "Caray Statue Moved to Bleacher Entrance." *Daily Herald* (Arlington Heights IL), September 2, 2010.

Munzel, Edgar. "White Sox Sign Caray as New Radio Voice." *Sporting News*, January 23, 1971.

Nordlund, Jeff. "Caray Moves into House That Jack Built." *Daily Herald* (Arlington Heights IL), November 17, 1981.

O'Donnell, Jim. "Addition of Brock Greases Skids for Piersall." *Daily Herald* (Arlington Heights IL), June 21, 1981.

———. "Caray's Doctor Maintains Positive Approach." *Daily Herald* (Arlington Heights IL), February 26, 1987.

Rocky Mountain News Wire Service. "Services to be Held for Caray in Calif., Chicago." *Rocky Mountain News*, February 20, 1998.

Rozner, Barry. "Caray Talks Freely about His Age, His Life." *Daily Herald* (Arlington Heights IL), February 16, 1998.

Scott, Jim. "Oakland Is A-Okay, Claims a Contented Caray." *Sporting News*, June 27, 1970.

Spink, J. G. Taylor. "Broadcasting Awards Won by Allen and Caray." *Sporting News*, October 6, 1948.

Tucker, Tim. "'. . . This Is Something I Was Born to

Do.'—Josh Caray, Rome Braves Announcer." *Atlanta Journal Constitution*, May 5, 2007.

York, Marty. "Baseball Can Be Fun When You're Carayed Away." *Toronto Globe and Mail*, April 28, 1992.

"Air Lanes." *Sporting News*, October 6, 1954.

"Back Home at KXOK." *Sporting News*, January 13, 1944.

"Caray Makes Ticker Talk Sound Like Park Aircast." *Sporting News*, July 30, 1947.

"City Health Records Divulge the Secret of Harry Caray's Age." *St. Louis Post-Dispatch*, February 19, 1998.

"People . . . in Sports." *Rockford (IL) Register-Star*, November 23, 1972.

Ancestry.com.
http://www.sos.mo.gov/archives/resources/deathcertificates/.

57. August A. Busch Jr.

1. Lawrence O. Christensen, William E. Foley, and Kenneth H. Winn, "Busch, August A. Jr., (1899–1989)," in *Dictionary of Missouri Biography* (Columbia: University of Missouri Press, 1999), 138.

2. August A. Busch Jr. clippings file as of July 2010, National Baseball Hall of Fame Library, Cooperstown NY, *Time Magazine*, July 11, 1953, 85.

3. Busch file.

4. Busch file.

5. Roy Malone, "Gussie Busch: Soft Heart with a Hard Nose," *The St. Louis Post Dispatch*, August 25, 1975, 13A; William H. Kester, "Gussie, 'The Boss,' Built an Empire with His Beer," *St. Louis Post-Dispatch*, August 27, 1975, 4G.

6. Peter Golenbock, *The Spirit of St. Louis: A History of the St. Louis Cardinals and Browns* (New York: HarperCollins, 2000), 403.

7. Harold H. Martin, "The Cardinals Strike It Rich," *Saturday Evening Post*, June 27, 1953, 22–23, 70, 74–75, 78.

8. Robert McG. Thomas Jr., "August A. Busch Jr., Dies at 90; Built Largest Brewing Company," Obituaries, *New York Times*, September 30, 1989.

9. Golenbock, *The Spirit of St. Louis*, 404.

10. Benita W. Boxerman and Burton A. Boxerman, *Ebbets to Veeck to Busch: Eight Owners That Shaped Baseball* (Jefferson NC: McFarland, 2003), 179.

11. Golenbock, *The Spirit of St. Louis*, 404–5.

12. Martin, "Cardinals Strike It Rich," 78.

13. Martin, "Cardinals Strike It Rich," 78.

14. Thomas, "August A. Busch Jr."

15. Golenbock, *The Spirit of St. Louis*, 405.

16. Peter Hernon and Terry Ganey, *Under the Influence: The Unauthorized Story of the Anheuser-Busch Dynasty* (New York: Avon Books, 1992), 215.

17. Leonard Koppett, "Busch, Beer and Baseball," *New York Times*, April 11, 1965.

18. Busch file; John Gardner, "Gussie's No Buscher," April 21, 1954; and Martin, "Cardinals Strike It Rich," 23 and 70.

19. Hernon and Ganey, *Under the Influence*, 213; and "Busch Rejects Charges by Sen. Johnson That Cards Are Used to Help Beer Sales," *New York Times*, February 24, 1954.

20. Busch file, "$300,000 Rail Business Car for Card President Busch," January 12, 1955.

21. Kester, "Gussie, 'The Boss,'"; and Hernon and Ganey, *Under the Influence*, 216.

22. Golenbock, *The Spirit of St. Louis*, 440–41.

23. Bob Broeg, "The 'Big Eagle' Never Was Able to Buy a Pennant," *St. Louis Post-Dispatch*, August 29, 1975, 5B.

24. Roy Malone, "Busches: Too Flamboyant for St. Louis High Society," *St. Louis Post-Dispatch*, August 26, 1975, 10A.

25. Ed Wilks, "Devine Acclaimed as Executive of the Year," *Sporting News*, October 24, 1964, 1.

26. Hernon and Ganey, *Under the Influence*, 249.

27. Malone, "Busches"; and Kester, "Gussie, 'The Boss.'"

28. Broeg, "Big Eagle."

29. Boxerman and Boxerman, *Ebbets*, 506, 507.

30. Ted Schafers, "Grand Old Man of Brewing Steps Aside as Chief Executive," *St. Louis Globe-Democrat*, May 9, 1975; and Boxerman and Boxerman, *Ebbets*, 195.

31. Golenbock, *The Spirit of St. Louis*, 528.

32. Martin, "Cardinals Strike It Rich," 200–202.

33. Malone, "Busches."

58. A Three-Way Tie for the Pennant?

1. Young, "Young Ideas."
2. Young, "Young Ideas."

Anderson, Dave. *Pennant Races*. New York: Galahad Books, 1994.

Gibson, Bob. *Stranger to the Game*. New York: Penguin Group, 1994.

Halberstam, David. *October 1964*. New York: Villard Books, 1994.

Schoendienst, Red. *Red: A Baseball Life*. Champaign IL: Sports Publishing, 1998.

Turner, Frederick. *When the Boys Came Back*. New York: Henry Holt, 1996.

Young, Dick. "Young Ideas." *Sporting News*, October 17, 1964, 16.

"NL Boss Giles Calls Confab on Playoff Pattern." *Sporting News*, October 10, 1964, 16.

Baseball-Reference.com.

Retrosheet.org.

SABR Baseball Biography Project. http://bioproj.sabr.org (accessed January 11, 2012).

Contributors

MARK ARMOUR grew up in Connecticut but now writes baseball from his home in Oregon. He is the author of *Joe Cronin: A Life in Baseball*, coauthor of *Paths to Glory*, the director of SABR's Baseball Biography Project, and a contributor to many websites and SABR journals. He resides with Jane, Maya, and Drew.

ERIC ARON has lived in Boston since getting his master's degree in history from Northeastern University in the late 1990s. He became a SABR member when the annual convention came to town in 2002, and he has been hooked ever since. A regular contributor to the BioProject "team" publications, he has written pieces on Cecil Cooper, Dick Williams, and Alvin Dark. Eric grew up a Mets fan in his hometown of Rye, New York, and now roots for the local nine. In addition to baseball, he likes movies, reading, and soy hot chocolate.

THOMAS AYERS is a lifelong Blue Jays fan who was born and raised in Toronto. He is currently a law student at the University of Toronto and is in the process of completing his third postsecondary degree. This is his third contribution to the SABR Biography Project. He found the latter trio much more enjoyable than the former.

MATT BOHN is a Detroit Tigers fan living in Oregon at the time of this writing. A native of Hemlock, Michigan, he is a graduate of Saginaw Valley State University. Besides following the Tigers and listening to the great play-by-play voices of the game, Matt enjoys participating in theater and researching his family history.

BURTON A. BOXERMAN is a retired high school history and government teacher and a diehard Cubs fan. He and his wife, Benita, a Cardinals fan, have written three books published by McFarland: *Ebbets to Veeck to Bush: Eight Owners Who Have Shaped Baseball*; *Jews and Baseball*, vol. 1, *Entering the American Mainstream, 1871–1958*; and *Jews and Baseball*, vol. 2, *The Post-Greenberg Years, 1949–2008*.

WARREN CORBETT is a contributor to SABR's Biography Project and the author of *The Wizard of Waxahachie: Paul Richards and the End of Baseball as We Knew It*. He lives in Bethesda, Maryland.

RORY COSTELLO lives in Brooklyn, New York, with his wife, Noriko, and their three-year-old son, Kai. He hopes that Kai will also grow up as a Mets fan. Rory has always enjoyed the rivalry between the Mets and Cardinals, especially in the mid-1980s, and he respects the rich franchise history in St. Louis.

LORETTA DONOVAN started life in a family that followed the St. Louis Browns. When the team left St. Louis, it was not hard for her to embrace the Cardinal tradition. Loretta taught elementary school in the Hazelwood School District in suburban St. Louis for thirty years. She has been a member of SABR for about five years. She enjoys the insights she gets from the other SABR members during the Bob Broeg Chapter monthly meetings. This is the first article she has written for SABR.

A retired English professor, JAN FINKEL has been a member of SABR since 1994. He has contributed several articles to various SABR projects, including the BioProject, where he serves as chief editor. He was born and grew up in Pittsburgh, where he saw Stan Musial destroy the Pirates. Jan and his wife, Judy, live on Deep Creek Lake in the westernmost part of Maryland.

PAUL GEISLER JR. grew up in San Antonio, Texas, and has been a Lutheran pastor for more than thirty years. He lives in Lake Jackson, Texas, with his wife, Susan, and their three children: Sarah, Brydon, and Johanna. He loves anything baseball—playing, watching, coaching, researching, and writing.

TOM HEINLEIN grew up in Connecticut and has moved around during adulthood, first to Baltimore and then to Europe for ten years before moving back to the United States in 2001 to the Boston area, where he resides today with his wife and two sons. Tom follows the local team, the Red Sox, but with the paternal side of his family all residing in southern Illinois, he has also followed the Cardinals over the years, as well as the Orioles from having lived in Baltimore, a time he counts as the most exciting of his lifelong love of following the game. Currently a marketing manager at an engineering firm, he has served in various writing and editorial roles during his career. In addition to his work as associate editor for this volume, he has contributed a bio on Dave Pope for the upcoming book on the 1954 Indians and is leading a project about the 1979 Orioles.

TIM HERLICH has been a lifelong fan of baseball and a member of SABR since 1996. He received the Doug Pappas Award for best oral presentation—titled "21*," a tribute to single-game strikeout record holder Tom Cheney—at the SABR Annual Conference in Washington DC in 2009.

Tim resides in Seattle and roots for the Mariners, but his favorite team is (gulp!) the 1964 Philadelphia Phillies.

MAXWELL KATES is an accountant working for a downtown Toronto firm. The director of marketing for the Hanlan's Point Chapter of SABR, he has contributed to the biographical projects *Sock It to 'Em, Tigers, From Go-Go to Glory*, and *The Miracle Has Landed*, along with four issues of *The National Pastime*. He attended his first Cardinals home game in 2007, a contest accentuated by a third-inning rain delay. This was two days after a guide on a tour of Busch Stadium advised his group that "it never rains during our games."

ALEX KUPFER is originally from Milwaukee but is currently a PhD student in the cinema studies department at New York University. His forthcoming dissertation covers the production and exhibition of sports films intended for education and training in the interwar period. He is always looking for rare or unusual baseball movies that were shown outside of movie theaters. This is his second contribution to the SABR Biography Project, having written on Dave Campbell for the *Sock It to 'Em Tigers* book on the 1968 Detroit Tigers.

RUSSELL LAKE is a retired professor who was born in Belleville, Illinois, on the "other side of the river" from downtown St. Louis. The 1964 Cardinals remain his favorite team, and he was distressed to see Sportsman's Park (aka Busch Stadium I) demolished not long after he had attended the last game there on May 8, 1966. His wife, Carol, deserves an MVP Award for watching all of a fourteen-inning ballgame in Cincinnati with Russ in 1971—during their honeymoon. He joined SABR in 1994 and, later in that same year, was an editor for David Halberstam's *October 1964*.

JIM LEEFERS and his wife, Tina, live in Coffeen,

Illinois. They have two sons, Adam and Matt. Jim is a lifelong St. Louis Cardinals fan who has enjoyed the base running of Brock, the pitching of Gibby, the slick fielding of Ozzie, and the rise of Albert Pujols. He has been a member of SABR's Bob Broeg Chapter in St. Louis since 1994.

LEONARD LEVIN was deeply disappointed as a boy when the Cardinals defeated his beloved Red Sox in the 1946 World Series, but he has learned to admire the St. Louis team and its fans. A resident of Providence, Rhode Island, and a retired newspaper editor, he now spends much of his time editing for SABR-sponsored publications.

KRISTEN LOKEMOEN became a baseball fan as a young girl listening to the Milwaukee Braves games on the radio in her hometown of Merrill, Wisconsin. After a move to Missouri in 1976, Kris became a casual St. Louis Cardinals fan. It was Mark McGwire and the home run race of 1998 that brought her back seriously to the game she loved. Kris became involved in SABR in 2006 as the Bob Broeg St. Louis Chapter prepared for the convention in 2007. With a background in group tours, Kris created and escorted the sightseeing tours offered at that convention. Now a chapter board member, Kris is working on a book about baseball, as well as doing other freelance writing.

MEL MARMER is a baseball fan, and an artist with a degree in graphic design from the University of the Arts in Philadelphia. He currently works for Weavers Way, a local food cooperative, has a lovely girlfriend, Vickie, and four grandsons who are all active in sports. They provide encouragement to him as he edits a future SABR team book project about the 1964 Philadelphia Phillies.

KEVIN D. MCCANN has served as chairman of the SABR Minor League Committee and was a founder and president of the Grantland Rice–Fred Russell Tennessee Chapter. He is the author of *Jackson Diamonds: Professional Baseball in Jackson, Tennessee* and coauthor of *The Kitty League*. A third-generation St. Louis Cardinals fan, he is writing a biography of Ken Boyer.

ANDY MCCUE is a retired newspaper reporter in Southern California. He is a former president of SABR and the recipient of its highest honor, the Bob Davids Award. He is the author of *Baseball by the Books: A History and Complete Bibliography of Baseball Fiction* as well as numerous articles in baseball publications. He is currently working on a biography of Walter O'Malley to be published by the University of Nebraska Press. He is very married to Mary and is proud of Bernadette and Seanacchie.

JUSTIN MURPHY was born and raised in Rochester, New York. He has a bachelor's degree from the University of Chicago and a master's degree from the S. I. Newhouse School of Public Communications at Syracuse University. He has contributed to Seamheads.com and MLB.com and currently works as a newspaper reporter at the *Citizen* in Auburn, New York. A SABR member since 2007, Murphy received a Yoseloff grant for research on John Flynn of the 1885 Chicago White Stockings; a portion of that research was published in the fall 2010 *Baseball Research Journal*.

BILL NOWLIN is a lifelong Red Sox fan, and heard nothing but good things from friends about how gracious Cardinals fans were at Busch after the Red Sox won the final game of the 2004 World Series. He has been vice president of SABR for many years now and is the author of many books about the Red Sox. Bill is one of the founders of Rounder Records. In 2011 he returned to his professorial days, teaching an online course called "Baseball and Politics" at the University of Massachusetts.

JIM PRICE, who had a childhood addiction to Pacific Coast League baseball in Los Angeles and Hollywood, is a former play-by-play broadcaster, publicist, public address announcer, and official scorer for the Spokane Indians of the PCL. He also has served as a beat writer, scorer, and announcer for teams in the California League and the Northwest League and spent fourteen seasons as announcer and publicity director for several West Coast horse racing tracks. He won the 1996 MacMillan-SABR Award for an article marking the fiftieth anniversary of the bus accident that killed nine Indians players in 1946. In addition to working on an extensive history of Spokane baseball, he has contributed to several books, including *Rain Check*, the 2006 SABR convention publication, and a 2009 publication, *The Complete Lyrics of Johnny Mercer*. A recent chairman of the Spokane Historic Landmarks Commission, he has completed research for a biography of the once-famous jazz singer Mildred Bailey.

JOE SCHUSTER is the author of the novel *The Might Have Been* (Ballantine Books, 2012). The chair of the communications and journalism department at Webster University in St. Louis, Missouri, he has published articles in numerous magazines and newspapers, including the late, lamented *Sport* magazine, the *St. Louis Post-Dispatch*, and the St. Louis Cardinals' official team magazine, *Gameday*, among other periodicals. He is married and the father of five rabid Cardinals fans.

RICHARD L. SHOOK grew up in Michigan rooting for the National League after watching Willie Mays steal All-Star Games in the '50s and '60s. After graduation from Michigan State's journalism school, he began covering the Tigers and MLB for UPI out of Detroit in 1967, leaving the wire service in 1990 at a level that included postseason work and part-time national baseball columns. He currently freelances and self-publishes a Tigers newsletter.

MARK SIMON lives in Plymouth, Connecticut, and is the baseball research specialist for ESPN Stats & Information. He also is a regular contributor to ESPNNY.com and a cohost of the *Baseball Today* podcast on ESPN.com. He also contributed a biography to *The Miracle Has Landed*, which covered the fortieth anniversary of the 1969 Mets championship team.

TERRY W. SLOOPE lives in Cartersville, Georgia, and has been a SABR member since 1996, serving as chair of the Magnolia (Georgia) Chapter for more than ten years until recently "retiring." He was a contributor to Gary Land's *Growing Up with Baseball* (University of Nebraska Press, 2004) and David Porter's *Latino and African-American Athletes Today: A Biographical Dictionary* (Greenwood Press, 2004). He has been working on a biographical profile of former Tigers slugger Rudy York for far too long.

JOHN HARRY STAHL grew up in St. Louis rooting for Stan "the Man" Musial. He still has his Cardinal scorecard from the 1964 World Series. Later, he added the Red Sox, Orioles, and Nats to his baseball passions. He is a retired CPA and lives with his wife, Pamela, in suburban Maryland. They have two grown children and two young grandsons, whom they hope will be running the bases soon. As a member of SABR's Biography Project, he's researched and written a number of SABR biographies.

ADAM J. ULREY grew up being a fan of the Los Angeles Dodgers and the Cleveland Indians. He is a big fan of the history of the Montreal Expos. He has contributed to several SABR team baseball biographies, including *Go-Go Glory: 1959 Chicago White Sox*, *The Miracle Has Landed: 1969 New York Mets*, and *Deadball Stars of the American League*. He says, "I love to spend most of my time in the outdoors flyfishing and hiking with my dogs Behr and Suzie. Live in the most beautiful state of Oregon with my lovely wife, Jhody."

EDWARD W. VEIT saw his first Major League game in Shibe Park when the Philadelphia A's played the New York Yankees. Bob Savage bested Spud Chandler, and Joe DiMaggio hit a double in the first inning and was injured sliding into second base. Veit is a hardcore Phillies fan and grew up with the 1950 Whiz Kids. He presently lives in Maryland and belongs to the Bob Davids Chapter of SABR.

JOSEPH WANCHO lives in Westlake, Ohio, and is a lifelong Cleveland Indians fan. Working at AT&T since 1994 as a process/development manager, he has been a SABR member since 2005. He has made contributions to several bio book projects as well as the BioProject website. Currently, he serves as cochairman of the Minor League Research Committee.

DAVE WILLIAMS was six years old in 1969 when the Amazin' Mets embarked on their miracle ride and made him a fan for life. He has been a SABR member since 2001 and has contributed to other SABR biography projects, including bios of Yogi Berra, Tim McCarver, and Rube Walker. He lives in Glastonbury, Connecticut, with his wife, Julia, and their daughter, Clara.